The Broadview Anthology of

ROMANTIC DRAMA

The Broadview Anthology of

ROMANTIC DRAMA

Jeffrey N. Cox and Michael Gamer, Editors

broadview press

National Library of Canada Cataloguing in Publication

The Broadview anthology of Romantic drama / Jeffrey N. Cox, Michael Gamer, editors.

(Broadview anthologies of English literature)
ISBN 1-55111-298-1

1. English drama—19th century. 2. English drama—18th century.
I. Cox, Jeffrey N. II. Gamer, Michael III. Series.

PR1269.B76 2003   822'.708   C2002-905651-9

Broadview Press Ltd. is an independent, international publishing house, incorporated in 1985. Broadview believes in shared owner-ship, both with its employees and with the general public; since the year 2000 Broadview shares have traded publicly on the To-ronto Venture Exchange under the symbol BDP.

We welcome comments and suggestions regarding any aspect of our publications–please feel free to contact us at the addresses below or at broadview@broadviewpress.com.

North America
PO Box 1243, Peterborough, Ontario, Canada K9J 7H5
3576 California Road, Orchard Park, NY, USA 14127
Tel: (705) 743-8990; Fax: (705) 743-8353
email: customerservice@broadviewpress.com

UK, Ireland, and continental Europe
Thomas Lyster Ltd., Units 3 & 4a, Old Boundary Way
Burscough Road, Ormskirk
Lancashire, L39 2YW
Tel: (01695) 575112; Fax: (01695) 570120
email: books@tlyster.co.uk

Australia and New Zealand
UNIREPS, University of New South Wales
Sydney, NSW, 2052
Tel: 61 2 9664 0999; Fax: 61 2 9664 5420
email: info.press@unsw.edu.au

www.broadviewpress.com

Broadview Press Ltd. gratefully acknowledges the financial support of the Government of Canada through the Book Publishing Industry Development Program for our publishing activities.

PRINTED IN CANADA

CONTENTS

Acknowledgments

We are indebted to a long list of fine scholars of the drama of the romantic period upon whose work we have built, including Michael Booth, Catherine Burroughs, Frederick Burwick, Julie Carlson, Stuart Curran, Joseph Donohue, Jr., David Mayer III, Jane Moody, Marjean Purinton, Alan Richardson, and Michael Simpson. We owe a great deal to the hard work of a core of dedicated graduate students who have shown their knowledge of the drama of the period and their eye for detail: Scott Krawczyk, Myra Lotto, Dahlia Porter, Jared Richman, Juliet Shields, Brett Wilson, and Ksandra Wirick at the University of Pennsylvania; Terry Robinson, Dana Van Kooy, and Courtney Wennerstrom at the University of Colorado at Boulder; and Marco Roth at Yale University. For help with various matters, from decisions on play texts to particularly difficult annotations, we would like to thank: Toni Bowers, Christopher Braider, Catherine Burroughs, Fred Burwick, Thomas Crochunis, Stuart Curran, Frederick Denny, Michael Eberle-Sinatra, Margaret Ezell, Claire Farago, Kevin Gilmartin, Diane Hoeveler, Peter Knox, Greg Kucich, David Mayer III, Anne Mellor, Leonee Ormond, Dolores Pizarro, Ralph Rosen, Marlon Ross, Jennifer Snead, John Stevenson, John Stokes, and David Worrall. We also have had excellent help from the staff at Broadview; and, for advice and hard work, we want to thank Don LePan, Julia Gaunce, and Eileen Eckert.

This project was aided by generous financial support from the Huntington Library, the University of Pennsylvania, and the University of Colorado at Boulder. Special thanks go to Nancy Gamer for her timely assistance with the galley proofs, and to Elise Bruhl and Amy Cox for admirable patience and continuous support.

Note on the Text

We have sought to give the reader some sense of the dual life of these plays on the page and on the stage. We have—with the exception of *The Quadrupeds of Quedlinburgh* (which was never published) and *Harlequin and Humpo* (of which only a sketch was printed)—used the first edition as our text. We have then noted significant differences between this text and the Larpent licensing manuscript, since the latter reflects what the theater told the Examiner of Plays would be put on stage. In the case of *The Quadrupeds of Quedlinburgh*, there is only a Larpent text; in the case of *Harlequin and Humpo,* we have employed a combination of print and licensing texts to provide as full a sense as possible of the pantomime. We supply additional information on the texts at the end of each play's headnote.

The Appendix supplies reviews of the plays included along with some commentary on the theater of the period. The reviews follow the chronological order of the plays in the volume. Other material to be found includes objections to the licensing of theaters (325ff.), commentary on the size of the theaters (343ff. and 373ff); complaints about the decline of tragedy (356ff), Baillie's important prefaces to her first and third volumes of the *Plays on the Passions* (357ff.), and Leigh Hunt's account of pantomime (386ff.). The Glossary of Actors provides brief biographies for all those actors we could identify with their parts in these plays indicated at the opening of the entry.

Introduction

i. The Show of London

Imagine yourself heading on foot through the largely dark streets of London on January 25th, 1813.[1] Turning a corner, you see one of the few brightly lit buildings in the metropolis: the Theatre Royal at Drury Lane, where you hope to see the second night of a new tragedy, *Remorse*, which already has received positive reviews in the morning papers. As you consider yourself a lover of the great tradition of British drama and theatrical performance – of William Shakespeare, David Garrick, Richard Brinsley Sheridan, and Sarah Siddons – you are anxious to discover whether the sometimes brilliant, sometimes criticized poet Samuel Taylor Coleridge has indeed revived English tragedy. One thing is certain: no play has excited such anticipation since the debut of Joanna Baillie's *De Monfort* in 1800.

Throngs of people on foot work their way into the theater, as the more fashionable members of the audience – not as plentiful as they once were – arrive in sedan chairs and coaches. On inquiring about the availability of seats, you consider your options, which differ significantly from those of the twenty-first century. For one thing, there is not yet any so-called orchestra seating; the entire ground floor instead is given over to the pit – row after row of hard benches without backs. As you consider yourself a serious patron of the theater – rather than someone who comes merely wishing to be seen – you secure a slip admitting you to the pit where you will be able to see, to hear, and also to comment on what is occurring on stage. Those seeking cheaper seats, meanwhile, head for the doors that allow access to the "heavens," the two uppermost galleries of the theater. Others enter the door for the boxes that form the dress circle and the first two tiers

of balconies.[2] You note the convenience of these box entrances for the dress circle and above, which provide a path for women of fashion that does not require them to pass the lower or "basket" boxes, the haunt of prostitutes.

The hour is fairly early, the curtain a 6:30 one, and there are no assigned seats in the pit. Even while Wyatt's new Drury Lane – which opened on 10 October 1812 – has a central aisle not found in earlier theaters, you expect the inevitable rush down the three aisles and over the backless benches. Every night it is the same; people clamber to get the best seats in a race that would make a modern rock concert seem sedate. While you appreciate the lack of seat backs as you hurtle seventeen benches, you will miss them by the end of the evening. After all, you will remain in the theater until eleven o'clock or even midnight, and will see not a single play but an entire evening's entertainment.

Having seized a front seat, you find yourself in a very large theater. The great three-quarter-circle auditorium rises to a height of 48 feet above the pit. If anything, the stage itself seems even larger than the theater. At about 60 feet deep and 33 feet wide at the proscenium, it can accommodate dozens of actors at a time, and, faced with these large spaces, the managers of Drury

---

1 For a lively recreation of an evening in the theater of romanticism, see Ernest Bradlee Watson, *Sheridan to Robertson: A Study of the Nineteenth-Century London Stage* (Cambridge, MA: Harvard University Press, 1926), 80–6.

2 The architect of the theater, Benjamin Wyatt, described the seating as follows: the audience's portion of the theater formed "three-fourths of a circle" (to provide better sight lines) and contained "in four different heights, 80 boxes, holding 1,098 persons; with four Boxes (of larger size than the rest) next to the Stage, on each side of the Theatre, capable of containing 188 Spectators in addition to the 1,098 before mentioned; amounting in the aggregate to 1,286 persons. A Pit capable of containing 920 persons, a Two Shilling Gallery for 550 persons, a One Shilling Gallery of 350 persons, exclusive of four Private Boxes in the Proscenium, and 14 in the Basement of the Theatre, immediately under the Dress Boxes." See Benjamin Wyatt, *Observations on the Design of the Theatre Royal, Drury Lane* (London, 1813), quoted in Richard Leacroft, *The Development of the English Playhouse* (London: Methuen, 1973), 173.

Lane and Covent Garden since the 1790s have experimented with various kinds of processions, pitched battles, and spectacles. The new architect reportedly has tested how far the spoken word can carry and has decided that a circle with a diameter of 75 feet will allow everyone to hear. In other words, he has designed the theater so that those sitting at the back of a box are about 75 feet from center stage, with the boxes being about 54 feet from the front of the stage. While the architect has thought of the proscenium as a picture frame – imagining the interior stage as a room from which a "fourth wall" has been removed so that an audience might see in – the actors have continued to use the apron stage to deliver famous speeches. At such moments they seem to move out into the audience's space, attempting literally to upstage their colleagues.

The space, furthermore, is dazzling. Its gold, green, and crimson interior illuminated by what seems a thousand candles set in burners and chandeliers throughout the theater, Drury Lane seats over 3,100 people. Tonight it is quite full, both with those interested in Coleridge's play and those there to see the pantomime that will follow. Although some seats in the boxes are held by servants while their masters and mistresses continue dining, and other patrons will enter later in the evening when half-price tickets become available, you are pleased to see that so many have come to see tonight's tragedy. Hopeful for the new playwright and for a new golden age of legitimate drama, you purchase a playbill. Aside from listing the evening's plays and performers, it advertises that Mrs. Bland will perform an Invocation during Act III of *Remorse* accompanied by music composed by Mr. Kelly. Copies of Coleridge's play are for sale for those wishing to follow the text during the performance. You notice, however, that more patrons are buying the book sketching out the action of the second play of the evening, this year's Christmas pantomime, *Harlequin and Humpo*. With the cheap ink of the playbill coming off on your hands, you motion to one of the hawkers selling beer, cider, and fruit to fortify yourself for the evening's performance.

The orchestra begins playing, and continues performing for some time before the curtain opens and Mr. Carr steps out, dressed as a Spaniard, to speak the prologue written by Charles Lamb. It fulfills your expectations for the evening, speaking as it does with reverence about the greatness of English drama, especially the plays of Ben Jonson, Beaumont and Fletcher, and Shakespeare. Sitting in a theater boasting modern conveniences and great machines for creating illusions on stage, you consider how much better it is to see Shakespeare now than when his works were first performed. After a short piece of music following the prologue, the play begins, the theater remaining fully lit and the din of audience conversation never completely subsiding.

For this is no twenty-first century theater, where audiences respectfully attend to the action on stage while sitting in a darkened space. Roars of applause greet the popular Mr. Elliston as he takes the stage in the first scene, but attention waxes and wanes as more people enter the theater during the performance. For a moment a fine speech meets with such applause as to interrupt wholly the action; minutes later the majority of people find more of interest in the auditorium and in their fellow audience members than on the stage. In the third act, however, they are finally transfixed by the wonderful incantation scene, highlighted in the playbill, filled with eerie singing and music and ending in a climax of incense and fire that reveals an illumined painting of an assassination. Reviewers throughout the next week will uniformly praise this scene, with Thomas Barnes summarizing matters concisely in the January 31 issue of *The Examiner*:

> We never saw more interest excited in a theatre than was expressed at the sorcery-scene in the third act. The altar flaming in the distance, the solemn invocation, the pealing music of the mystic song, altogether produced a combination so awful, as nearly to overpower reality, and make one half believe the enchantment which delighted our senses. (73-4)

From this point to the closing curtain, and especially during Mrs. Glover's impassioned speeches as Alhadra, the audience is carried along by the power of the play. Even after a disappointing epilogue, "shouts from every corner of the theatre" greet the theater's announced decision that they will repeat the play again tomorrow.[3]

The evening is not over, however. There is another play to come, the ever-popular Christmas harlequinade. This almost ritualized form, in which an opening section, often based in fairy tale or myth, creates a problem for two lovers then resolved in the harlequinade proper, has been the most popular type of theater for decades. The financial success of Christmas pantomimes has been so great, in fact, that it essentially has underwritten the cost of performing the rest of the repertoire, including Shakespeare and other classic writers. The pantomime tonight, *Harlequin and Humpo*, is a variation on a familiar theme, that of Sleeping Beauty. It begins with a princess confined in a palace without windows. She has been cursed by Owletta, the evil Genius of the Night; if she sees the sun before her eighteenth birthday, she will become an owl. As the princess is about to perish, the good fairy, Aquila, helps her and her lover Arthur by transforming them into those archetypal lovers and rebellious spirits, Columbine and Harlequin. With this transformation, the two shed their papier-mâché "big heads" and with them, their previous identities. Their opponents, too, are relieved of their papier-mâché and revealed in their archetypal roles: the Dandy Lover, old Pantaloon, and the Clown. A wonderful series of scenes follows, filled with the food-fixated antics of Clown, the dancing of Columbine, and the magical tricks of Harlequin as he uses his sword to transform objects and to defeat their enemies. When the theater finally empties at midnight, the crowd is pleased with its evening's entertainment, with many vowing to return again to see Harlequin beat Humpo and his dwarves.

ii. The Theater of Romanticism

Such an evening's experience, were it possible to recreate rather than merely describe, would tell us much. It would provide us not only with a sense of what it was like to go to the theater around the turn of the nineteenth century, but also with a glimpse into the difficulties experienced by most scholars confronted with the legacy of Romantic period drama and theater. In trying to make sense of its cavernous theaters and impressive spectacles – what Walter Scott called its "drum and trumpet exhibitions"[4] – modern critics have seen the Romantic period as a time when literature and the stage experienced a near-complete divorce from one another.[5] They have felt that, while pantomime and spectacle might please the crowd, even a Coleridge had to stoop to the theatrical tricks of the incantation scene to win over the audience. Certainly critics and reviewers in Coleridge's time frequently blamed theater audiences and the theatrical managers who catered to them, but such an explanation does not get us very far when we place it next to the wealth of contemporary writing extolling the stage and its artists in the most glowing terms. Certainly Romantic theater audiences were mixed and frequently boisterous, but with the fashionable elite and intelligentsia accounting for the vast majority of receipts and paying between 3.5 and 10.5 times more per ticket than the "gods" of the one-shilling gallery, there is little question whose taste controlled the repertoire of London and provincial theaters. While the

---

3 *Universal Magazine* XIX (February 1813): 146.

4 Scott to George Ellis, 7–8 December 1801, *The Letters of Sir Walter Scott*, ed. H.J.C. Grierson, 12 vols. (London: Constable & Co. Ltd., 1932), 1:124.

5 We see this split being enforced in the criticism when, for example, William Jewett, *Fatal Autonomy: Romantic Drama and the Rhetoric of Agency* (Ithaca: Cornell University Press, 1997), eschews the theatrical world (p. 4), while Jane Moody, *Illegitimate Theatre in London, 1770–1840* (Cambridge: Cambridge University Press, 2000), turns away from the literary drama. We even find this split being replicated in anthologies with, for example, Gerald B. Kauvar and Gerald C. Sorenson's *Nineteenth-Century English Verse Drama* (Rutherford: Farleigh Dickinson University Press, 1973) offering only literary closet dramas and Michael C. Booth's *English Plays of the Nineteenth Century*, 2 vols. (Oxford: Clarendon Press, 1969) turning away from the plays of the poets. Even the most recent anthology, *Five Romantic Plays, 1768–1821*, ed. Paul Baines and Edward Burns (Oxford: Oxford University Press, 2000), notes that only one of the plays selected, Inchbald's *Lover's Vows*, was a theatrical success and goes on to say that this play is of interest today largely because of its role in Austen's *Mansfield Park* (vii).

astonishing variety of an evening at the theater likely stemmed from a need on the part of managers to appeal across barriers of sex and class, these same entertainments were eagerly attended by artist and artisan, reviewer and reveller. Rather than simply dismissing Romanticism's drama as the corrupted fare of vulgar tastes, then, we need to come to grips with its fundamental strangeness, its aims and ideals, and its ways and means. We need to join with critics like Jane Moody and Judith Pascoe in pursuing "a wide-ranging critique of theatre's position in the literary history of Romanticism," one that also can "examine the performative aspects of … romantic literary culture as a whole."[6] We need to do so, moreover, with ample historical sensitivity and sympathy.

While the drama of the Romantic period probably will never again appeal to such a wide audience, it has recently received significant and increasing interest from both academic and theatrical circles. We have seen a surge in scholarly essays and books, successful London productions of key German dramas from the period like Friedrich Schiller's *Maria Stuart* and *Don Carlos*, smaller productions of plays such as Wordsworth's *Borderers*, Shelley's *The Cenci*, and Byron's *Sardanapalus*, and even performances of such disparate pieces as *Prometheus Unbound* and *Obi; or Three Finger'd Jack*.[7] Yet many scholars and readers still retain the traditional, negative account of this same body of drama inherited from a previous generation of critics. Their account has remained so consistent over the years that it hardly needs to be repeated: overly large theaters suitable for spectacle but not for the spoken word;

celebrity actors who dominated the stage and cared more about star moments than the plays of which they were a part; and brilliant poets who, ambitious to write for the theater but with little sense of stage mechanics, penned unstageable closet dramas. Drama between Sheridan and Shaw is thus seen as a dismembered corpse, its poetic head in one place and its theatrical body residing in appropriately corrupted state elsewhere.

We find this negative view, moreover, within the period as well. In 1807, *The Satirist* issued an often-reproduced, untitled print that criticized what it saw as the divided, monstrous state of the British theater. Commonly dubbed "The Monster Melodrama" (Fig. 1), it depicts a many-headed beast that represents the theater of the day. With Drury Lane and Covent Garden in the background, the beast appears to be a transformed British lion, dressed in pantomime motley and sprouting multiple heads as well as teats from which a host of playwrights and shareholders suckle. The head of Sheridan, key playwright and proprietor of Drury Lane, laughs as the great actor Kemble cries out, having received a knife to the neck; Grimaldi, great pantomime clown, repeats one of his infrequent lines, "Nice Moon," while the head of Harlequin erupts from the back of the beast. The beast's tail is labeled "A Tail of Mystery," punning obviously on Thomas Holcroft's adaptation of Pixérécourt, *A Tale of Mystery* (Covent Garden, 1802), the first melodrama so called on the British stage. Holcroft stands beneath the beast along with other authors of "illegitimate" dramas such as Matthew "Monk" Lewis, in monk's robes and standing upon his play *The Wood Daemon* (Drury Lane, 1807), William Dimond, author of the melodramatic *Hunter of the Alps* (Haymarket, 1804), Frederic Reynolds, who rides Carlo the Wonder Dog, the star of his 1803 hit *Caravan*, Lumley Skeffington, who also came in for criticism by Byron in *English Bards and Scotch Reviewers* (l. 591), and Thomas Dibdin, author of *Harlequin and Humpo* and here identified as the author of *Harlequin and Mother Goose* (Covent Garden, 1806), also attacked by Byron (ll. 563, 591) and represented here by the Mother herself driving her geese. The beast, while suckling these authors of pantomimes and melo-

---

6 Moody, 2; Judith Pascoe, *Romantic Theatricality: Gender, Poetry, and Spectatorship* (Ithaca and London: Cornell University Press, 1997), 1.

7 Performance information is as follows: *Maria Stuart* (Royal National Theatre, London, 1996); *Don Carlos* (Pit Theatre, Barbican Centre, London, 2000); *The Borderers* (Willing Suspensions Theatre Co., Yale University and Boston University, 1997); *Sardanapalus* (Yale University, 1991); *Prometheus Unbound* (Rude Mechanicals, Austin, TX, 1998); *Obi* (Boston University and Arizona State University, 2000). Of course, German and French dramas of the period remain in the repertoire of those countries.

dramas, tramples upon the works of Shakespeare and a scroll bearing the names of the "legitimate" playwrights Congreve, Beaumont and Fletcher, and George Colman the Elder. Half human, half beast, half male, half female, the beast embodies the "illegitimate" assault upon the traditional drama that many felt was being launched by pantomimes and melodramas. Modern scholarship has tended merely to replicate this conservative attack upon theatrical innovation; even the best recent work on the theater of the period accepts while also inverting the opposition between "high" literary drama and "low" theatrical entertainment. What we must see instead is the dynamic relationship between the popular theater and the literary drama.

The continued neglect of the theater and drama of the Romantic period not only keeps from view wonderful individual plays but also limits our comprehension of the culture of the late eighteenth and early nineteenth centuries. It is hard to see how we will come to understand the period that gave birth to the Romantic moment if we fail to grasp its most popular and conspicuous art form.

With the four patent theaters in London (the two winter dramatic theaters of Covent Garden and Drury Lane, the summer theater at the Haymarket, and the King's Theatre given over to Italian opera) standing as central national institutions, with theaters found in every major city from Bath to Edinburgh, and with forms of staged entertainment present in every kind of venue from taverns to carnivals, the theater held the same place in the late eighteenth and early nineteenth centuries that television, film, and video hold in the twenty-first. The theater was a key meeting point between artists and the public, between aesthetic innovation and popular taste, between the worlds of art and letters and those of commerce and politics. Perhaps more important, it was both the home of spectacularly popular entertainments and the sanctum into which writers most wanted to win their way. All six of the so-called major male Romantic poets as well as the key women writers of the day wrote drama, and Keats at the height of his powers would say that all of his poetry, including the odes and his famous narrative poems, were mere apprentice work that might "nerve me up to the

Figure 1. "The Monster Melodrama." Reprinted with permission from U.C. Santa Barbara Davidson Library.

writing of a few fine Plays."[8] With such considerations in mind, this anthology seeks to provide a sense of the excitement of the period's theatrical entertainments and their enormous prestige in these years. We thus offer plays that were theatrical successes (such as *Blue-Beard* [Drury Lane, 1798] and *Timour the Tartar* [Covent Garden, 1811]) alongside dramas by major writers like Joanna Baillie, Percy Shelley, and Lord Byron. Part of our argument, consequently, will be that what we now see as disparate pieces – poetic tragedies, successful stage dramas, and staged spectacles – were part of a coherent, if complex, cultural configuration.

In approaching this body of dramatic writing, there is, of course, the problem of how best to wield the term "Romantic" within this cultural moment. As recent scholarship has made clear, many figures on the cultural scene in the late eighteenth and early nineteenth centuries espoused neither a Romantic style nor vision. Even the writers we now describe as synonymous with Romanticism were viewed by their contemporaries as members of differing and even opposed schools. We see such oppositions through the differing political and aesthetic visions of periodicals like the *Edinburgh* and *Quarterly* reviews, which in turn created and fostered the more well-known competitions between the "Lake School" of Wordsworth, Coleridge, and Southey, the "Satanic School" of Byron and the Shelleys, and the "Cockney School" of Hunt, Keats, Hazlitt, and their circle. As one might expect, then, it is difficult to label everything that was offered on stage in the late eighteenth and early nineteenth centuries as "Romantic" – not only because the repertoire remained dominated by plays from earlier eras but also because much of what was offered in the theater can be seen as arising from cultural movements preceding Romanticism, opposing Romanticism, or simply differing from Romanticism. Preserving the classics of earlier periods within the repertoire system, the theater was an essentially conservative institution; it also, however, strongly resembled our own modern entertainment industry by being open to the latest fads. Thus, when we consider that Romantic-period audiences in a given year would have attended both a revival of *Love for Love* and a production like *The Quadrupeds of Quedlinburgh* (Haymarket, 1811) – a send-up of German drama that also exploited the rage for seeing live horses on stage – we begin to wonder whether the drama of the period can be usefully labeled as "Romantic" in any way.

Still, there are, we believe, compelling reasons to reexamine the centrality both of Romantic drama and Romantic theater. First, we must dispel the notion that there is some opposition between Romanticism and the stage, as if the writers we identify as "Romantic" were somehow either violently antipathetic to or profoundly uninterested in the theater, or simply grossly incompetent in trying to write for it. Certainly the vast majority of Romantic writers, from Charles Lamb and William Wordsworth to Lord Byron and Joanna Baillie, wrote plays, and most of these plays were written with an eye to the stage. These writers, furthermore, were not without their successes. The most famous of these theatrical victories was that of Samuel Coleridge's *Remorse*, whose run of 20 nights in 1813 was the longest for tragedy in decades. It in turn was eclipsed by Charles Robert Maturin's 1816 smash hit at Drury Lane, *Bertram; or, The Castle of St. Aldobrand*, a tragedy with strong ties to both Romanticism and the Gothic, and especially to the works of Byron and Walter Scott. Scott himself began his career as a translator of German drama and poetry, twice attempting to get his own plays staged in London at the end of the eighteenth century. His sustained popularity as a poet and novelist not long after created a cottage industry for dramatists skilled enough to adapt his best-selling poems and novels to the stage.

Women writers we now link to Romanticism also had successes on the stage, most notably with comedy in the 1780s and 1790s. We can trace an active presence of more than ninety women writers in the theater of the long Romantic period, from Hannah More's admired and successful *Percy* (Covent Garden, 1777) to Felicia Hemans's *Vespers of Palermo* (Covent Garden, 1823). Furthermore,

8 Keats, letter to John Taylor, 17 November 1819, in *Letters of John Keats*, ed. Hyder Rollins (Cambridge: Harvard University Press, 1958), 2:234.

the intermittent successes by Cowley and Inchbald with tragedy set the stage for the dominance of Joanna Baillie in that genre after 1798. We now usually remember Baillie as the most critically acclaimed playwright of her age who nonetheless had difficulty getting her plays staged. We especially remember the moderately disappointing debut of *De Monfort* in 1800, which ran for a respectable eight nights with John Philip Kemble and Sarah Siddons in the lead roles. Even Baillie, however, had multiple stage successes. *De Monfort* was revived with far greater acclaim two decades later by Edmund Kean, while several of Baillie's other plays enjoyed considerable runs in the provinces. *The Family Legend* is the most notable of these, playing to packed houses and standing ovations in 1810 at the Theatre Royal in Edinburgh under the direction of Scott.

Other Romantic writers like Leigh Hunt had successes on stage either late in their careers or else posthumously. Hunt experienced one of his greatest cultural triumphs with *The Legend of Florence* in 1839, an event even Wordsworth wished he could attend so that he could "make his hands burn in welcoming the play."[9] And while only Byron's *Marino Faliero* (Drury Lane, 1821) would be staged in a moderately successful production during his lifetime, after his death his plays continued to be performed throughout the nineteenth century. *Sardanapalus*, included here, boasted an initial run of 23 nights before good houses in 1834, and even *Manfred* received a spectacular staging that same year, courtesy of those key theatrical technicians, the Grieve brothers. Shelley's *The Cenci* received similar interest, but only several decades after the poet's death. Initially rejected by London theaters and reviled by reviewers because of its content, the play has experienced success in subsequent productions, beginning with the famous performance in 1886 before the Shelley Society that involved George Bernard Shaw and including Artaud's key transformation of the drama for his "Theatre of Cruelty" in 1935. The continued theatrical appeal of the play has shown that Shelley was correct in seeing the play as "fitted for the stage."[10]

The involvement of Romantic writers in the theater was, in fact, deep and sustained: Byron sat on the governing board of Drury Lane; Baillie was regularly praised as the greatest playwright since Shakespeare; Hazlitt and Hunt were key reviewers of the period's drama; and Inchbald was one of its key actresses, critics, dramatists, and insiders. The idea that such an array of writers who cared deeply about the stage were able only to create antitheatrical "closet dramas," then, is at best a pervasive misconception and at worst a pernicious distortion shaping our response to Romanticism and its cultural contexts. This is not to say that these decades did not witness the production of several plays – including *Manfred* (1816) and *Prometheus Unbound* (1820) – designed to be read rather than performed. It is worth noting, however, that even these plays received later stage productions. In an age mad for theater, pieces as unlikely as Hunt's allegorical masque on the fall of Napoleon, *The Descent of Liberty*, were nonetheless written expressly for the London stage, while writers like Baillie imagined themselves to be writing both for the stage and with an eye to reforming it. Written with similar ideas in mind, *The Cenci* invokes still a different class of accidental closet drama, since Shelley's play failed to reach the stage for ideological rather than theatrical reasons: censorship prior to performance is one of the key features of the Romantic theater.

A considerable body of work intended for the stage thus came to be considered as closet drama only because it imagined a theater experience different from that found on the official stages of Drury Lane or Covent Garden. Here again Joanna Baillie's career provides an instructive example. Her preface to volume III of *Plays on the Passions*, excerpted in the appendix of this anthology, provided detailed criticisms of London theaters as physical spaces and systematic technical recommendations (especially

---

9 Wordsworth expressed his desire to Margaret Gilles; cited in Ann Baliney, *Immortal Boy: A Portrait of Leigh Hunt* (New York: St. Martin's, 1985), 172.

10 Letter to Charles Ollier, 13 March 1820, *Letters of Percy Bysshe Shelley*, ed. Frederick L. Jones (Oxford: Clarendon Press, 1964), 2:178.

about lighting) for their improvement.[11] Underlying her call for more theaters of smaller sizes is a critique of the patent system that limited the number of London theaters and in the process encouraged patent holders to build ever-larger auditoriums. While none of the plays within volume III of *Plays on the Passions* would be performed, nearly all of the recommendations of its preface would be enacted before Baillie's death. Our point is that even plays that strike us as turning from the stage still have to be understood in relation to it. Recent critical formulations – from Catherine Burroughs's and Michael Simpson's suggestion that the closet is an alternative stage to Julie Carlson's and Judith Pascoe's influential accounts of the inherent theatricality of Romantic culture – would appear to bear witness to the need for a fundamental reassessment of Romanticism and the stage.[12]

Such acts of re-evaluation inevitably must affect our sense of theater history as well. Along with seeing Romantic drama as either intended for the theater or as seeking to change it, we also need to understand how developments *within* the theater related to Romanticism. That is, reading plays like *Remorse* (Drury Lane, 1813), *The Cenci* (1819), *Orra* (1812), and *Sardanapalus* (1821) in relation to theatrical practice is necessary but not yet sufficient; we also must examine how theatrical successes, such as Colman's *Blue-Beard*, Lewis's *Timour the Tartar*, and even a harlequinade such as Dibdin's *Harlequin and Humpo* (Drury Lane, 1812) are successes in part because they draw

upon Romantic themes, images, ideas, and assumptions about cultural value. With these issues in mind, this anthology seeks to restage the fruitful interaction between Romantic writers and the contemporary stage, and between theatrical writers and the cultural movement we call Romanticism. For however we try to define it, we inevitably can find Romanticism's counterpart in the theater. If we focus on Romanticism's turn to nature, we can look to the increased naturalism of theatrical representations, including De Loutherberg's creation of sublime water and cloud effects. If we think of a Romantic embrace of the everyday, the popular, or the common, we can see the theater – perhaps especially in the domestic melodrama – taking up similar figures and locales. While a censored theater had more difficulty in dealing with the political upheavals we identify with the French Revolution and its aftermath than did the poetry of the period, we still find plays on the Fall of the Bastille, pieces (including *Harlequin and Humpo* and *Timour the Tartar*) that treat Napoleon, and many more plays (including *Remorse*, *The Cenci*, and *Sardanapalus*) that offer a more indirect vision of contemporary politics. And if we now are interested in Romanticism's relation to issues of gender, race, and empire, we find the theater offering more popular representations of these same issues than perhaps any other cultural arena. Even the exalted flights of the Romantic imagination find corresponding gestures in a theater devoted to allowing its audience to imagine a world transformed, whether by Shakespeare's poetry or Harlequin's bat.

iii. Material Stages, Performed Politics

Given the extent to which romantic drama is embedded in the theatrical, cultural, and social practices of the day, we have chosen to begin by stressing just how different late eighteenth- and early nineteenth-century London theaters and dramatic fare were from what we currently experience during a trip to Broadway or the West End. While we are used to moderately sized theaters, featuring most often a proscenium arch stage and a quiet and respectful audience, theater-goers around 1800 would have entered a huge theater, the stage of which still had features of the earlier apron stage, and would have found

---

11   In the Appendix, we have also included George Colman the Younger's essay, "[On the Size of the Theatres]," quoted in Richard Brinsley Peake, *Memoirs of the Colman Family, including their Correspondence with the most Distinguished Personages of their Time*, 2 vols. London: Richard Bentley, 1841. Volume 2, pages 224–7.

12   See Catherine Burroughs, *Closet Stages: Joanna Baillie and the Theater Theory of British Romantic Women Writers* (Philadelphia: University of Pennsylvania Press, 1997); Julie Carlson, *In the Theater of Romanticism: Coleridge, Nationalism, Women* (Cambridge and New York: Cambridge University Press, 1994); Pascoe, *Romantic Theatricality*; Michael Simpson, *Closet Performances: Political Exhibition and Prohibition in the Dramas of Byron and Shelley* (Stanford: Stanford University Press, 1998).

themselves in the midst of a diverse and often raucous crowd. We are used to attending the theater to see a single play; one went to the theater during the Romantic period to watch two or even three plays. Over the course of an evening, therefore, a company might put forth nearly the full range of genres, from five-act tragedies and comedies to comic operas, farces, re-enactments of current events, and musical romances. At Covent Garden on 1 June 1789, for example, one would have seen a triple bill that included *The Death of Captain Cook, Inkle and Yarico*, and *Don Juan; or, The Libertine Destroyed*. Audiences at Drury Lane on 2 March 1813, meanwhile, would have seen *Romeo and Juliet* followed by *An Irishman in London*. Between the acts and before and after performances, moreover, the stage was filled with other kinds of performers, from singers and rope-dancers to magicians and trained animals, including the infamous horses that would grace *Timour the Tartar* and Drury Lane's star performer, the dog Carlo.

These same audiences would have entered theaters experiencing incredible innovations, both artistic and technical. Perhaps the best known of these was the revolution in performance style that was brought about by a series of great actors, particularly Sarah Siddons and Edmund Kean, who can be seen as bringing a "Romantic" theory of acting to a stage that had been dominated by the "classical" approach of Siddons's brother, John Philip Kemble. Siddons forged a theatrical style of enormous power that inspired and overwhelmed; as her biographer James Boaden wrote of seeing her act, "I well remember (how is it possible I should ever forget?) the sobs, the shrieks…. We then, indeed, knew the luxury of grief; but the nerves of many a gentle being gave way before the intensity of such appeals, and fainting fits long and frequently alarmed the decorum of the house."[13] Kean's acting – famously described by Coleridge as "reading Shakespeare by flashes of lightning"[14] – was noted for its combination of art or artifice with nature, of his rapid movements from high emotion to colloquial and even coarse moments. It drew praise as well from Byron and William Hazlitt, and one notes additional, striking parallels between Kean's style and that of the so-called Cockney writers, Hazlitt himself along with Keats and Hunt, who also combined the high and the low, the natural and the artificial.

These decades also witnessed great advances in stage technique, as theater managers experimented with new devices for producing illusion and illumination. Most dramatic of these were the introduction of gas lighting and the vampire trap, so that, increasingly, theaters could boast of their ability to stage huge spectacles replete with a legion of special effects. Writing to actor Daniel Terry in 1817, Walter Scott aimed in a new gothic drama, *The Doom of Devorgoil* (composed 1817, published 1830), to exploit many of these technical advances, proposing an apocalyptic flood, a scene of divine judgement, and a specter feast:

> I will make the ghosts talk as never ghosts talked in the body or out of it; and the music may be as unearthly as you can get it. The rush of the shadows into the castle shall be seen through the window of the baron's apartment in the flat scene. The ghost's banquet, and many other circumstances, may give great exercise to the scene-painter and dresser.[15]

While Scott's play was never produced, we see its effects fully realized in the lavish procession crossing the mountains in Colman's *Blue-Beard* and the trickwork in *Harlequin and Humpo*, where a coach can be turned into a balloon and Owletta's cave can sink providentially into a chasm of flames. Such scenes remind us that special effects were as important to viewers of *Timour the Tartar* and Moncrieff's *The Cataract of the Ganges* (Drury Lane, 1824) as they are to modern audiences.

---

13 James Boaden, *Memoirs of Mrs. Siddons* (1827; rpt. Philadelphia: J.B. Kippincott, 1893), 435.
14 Coleridge, *Specimens of the Table Talk of the Late Samuel Taylor Coleridge*, 2 vols. (London: J. Murray 1835), 1:24.

15 Scott to Daniel Terry, 12 March 1817, *The Letters of Sir Walter Scott*, ed. H.J.C. Grierson, 12 vols. (London: Constable, 1932–7), 4:406.

Unlike our own movie houses and multiplexes, however, London's theaters were also sites for watching social change and engaging in various forms of contestation. This assertion at first may appear counterintuitive; its seating segregated clearly by price, the theater on first examination appears a model for a society broken into ranks or classes. Both contemporary commentators and modern theater historians, however, have amply documented the rebellious nature of London theater audiences, usually linking their increasingly politicized behavior to changing audience demographics.[16] By the end of the eighteenth century, the royal family generally stayed away from the theater, the aristocracy generally preferring the Italian opera unless a particularly fashionable piece was performed. As the nineteenth century turned, therefore, increasing numbers of audience members came from the "lower orders" who, in turn, made their presence felt and their concerns known.

Thus, while audiences were demanding and riotous throughout the eighteenth and early nineteenth centuries, the specifics of their demands and the nature of their riots changed as the century progressed. That the theater could become a battleground between various ranks within society was clearest during the famous Old Price (O.P.) Riots, which occurred when John Philip Kemble chose to combine the reopening of Covent Garden in 1809 with a rise in ticket prices. In many ways anticipating modern controversies over player salaries and stadium sky boxes, the Old Price Riots were sparked by a similar desire to increase the number of private boxes at the expense of gallery seating, and to offer the controversial Italian singer Angelica Catalani an enormous salary. For sixty-seven nights, O.P. protesters staged demonstrations inside the theater, essentially blocking the performance of plays until the Covent Garden management agreed to most of their terms. In the midst of the riots, Elizabeth Inchbald wrote, "If the public force the

managers to reduce their prices, a revolution in England is effected."[17]

This tradition of contentious demonstration begins to explain why the drama itself existed under vigilant government censorship. Becoming law in 1737, the Licensing Act had been an attempt by the government of Robert Walpole to stifle political opposition, which had found a powerful voice in the plays of Henry Fielding. While Walpole's government fell four years later, the act nonetheless remained a part of statutory law, requiring any new play, prior to being performed at one of the patent theaters royal, to be submitted for approval to the Examiner of Plays in the Lord Chamberlain's Office; the privileging of patent theaters royal would last until 1843, and prior censorship would be a fact of the British theater until 1968. Empowered to act autocratically and unencumbered by any appeals mechanism, the Examiner could reject the play or demand alterations. He also retained a copy of the play manuscript to facilitate enforcement. For most of the Romantic period, the Examiner was John Larpent, a close friend of Thomas and Harriet Bowdler and a man known for his unimaginative consistency and moral rectitude. One might expect Larpent's successor, George Colman the Younger, to have relaxed many of Larpent's longstanding strictures; Colman, after all, was himself a playwright and owner of the Haymarket Theatre, and had written on such controversial topics as slavery. Instead, Colman embraced his position with zeal and took Larpent's strictness to new levels. As Examiner he famously stated that he would ban from the stage "anything that may be so allusive to the times as to be applied to the existing moment, and which is likely to be inflammatory."[18] While the number of plays rejected by both Larpent and Colman was rela-

---

16 See Marc Baer, *Theatre and Disorder in Late Georgian London* (Oxford: Clarendon Press, 1992); Leo Hughes, *The Drama's Patrons* (Austin: University of Texas Press, 1971).

17 Quoted in James Boaden, *Memoirs of Mrs. Inchbald*, 2 vols. (London: R. Bentley, 1 833), 2:143.

18 Colman, testimony in *Report from the Select Committee Appointed to Inquire into the Laws Affecting Dramatic Literature* (1832), Irish University Press Series of British Parliamentary Papers, Stage and Theatre, vol. 1 (Shannon: Irish University Press, 1968), 66.

tively small, the very threat of censorship kept theaters from considering plays such as Shelley's *The Cenci*, since theatrical managers knew the Examiner would censor all references to political conflict, religious matters, or scandals involving the monarchy or the aristocracy. As one frustrated playwright put it, "politics is the forbidden fruit, lest the people's eyes should be opened and they become as gods knowing good and evil."[19] Thus, seventy years after Fielding was forced to move from writing plays to writing novels because of the 1737 Licensing Act, Elizabeth Inchbald would look back and lament the arbitrariness of stage censorship: "[The Novelist] lives in a land of liberty, whilst the Dramatic Writer exists but under a despotic government."[20]

While the drama thus received prior review by the government, it was also, of course, subject to review by the press after it was performed. Reviewing during the period underwent significant changes. At the beginning of the nineteenth century, there existed a general feeling that most reviews were "puffs" – paid advertisements parading as criticism – as reviewers were offered free seats and other perquisites by theatrical management. Leigh Hunt and William Hazlitt, however, changed the status of the theatrical reviewer by refusing to engage in any mutually beneficial relationship with the theaters. As a result, they provided some of the most perceptive criticism the theater has ever received.[21] The period's contemplation of the drama, furthermore, went beyond immediate reviews. With Inchbald's introductions to *The British Theatre*, Baillie's prefaces, James Boaden's theatrical memoirs, the *Dramatic Censors* of Thomas Dutton (1800–1) and John Williams (1811), and essays on Shakespeare by Coleridge, Lamb, and Hazlitt, a distinguished body of biographical,

historical, and theoretical reflections on the London stage emerged to accompany its productions. As Inchbald's and Baillie's work suggests, and as Catherine Burroughs has shown, an important portion of this critical work formed a body of women's theater theory.

Central to British culture in spite of internal limitations and external restrictions, the theater engaged key aesthetic, cultural, social, and political issues and experimented widely with literary forms. We discover in the drama, therefore, a version of the period's restless eclecticism, turning now to a classicizing tradition (as with Byron's *Sardanapalus*), now to domestic comedy (as with Cowley's *Bold Stroke for a Husband* [Covent Garden, 1783] and Inchbald's *Every Man Has His Fault* [Covent Garden, 1793]), now to the Gothic (as with Baillie's *Orra* and Shelley's *The Cenci*), and now to new popular forms like melodrama and spectacle (as with Colman's *Blue-Beard* and Lewis's *Timour the Tartar*). We discover plays tackling issues of empire and history across an array of genres and modes, and therefore find orientalist comedies (Lewis's *Timour the Tartar*) and tragedies (*Sardanapalus*), not to mention historically-minded plays set in Italy (*The Cenci*), Germany (*Orra*), and Spain (*Remorse*). Other plays resonate with the contemporary debate over the status of women, from Cowley's *Bold Stroke for a Husband* and Inchbald's *Every Man Has His Fault* to Baillie's *Orra* and Shelley's *The Cenci*. And while the government censor forbade direct references to the French Revolution, we still see its issues squarely taken up in *Remorse* and *The Cenci*, and find indirect references even in Gothic plays such as *Blue-Beard* and the pantomime *Harlequin and Humpo*. There existed, then, a Romantic theater very different from the "deserted stage" described by Terry Otten[22] – a theater that served a very large public, that concerned government officials enough to censor it rigorously, and that mattered to poets and critics enough to write with passion both for and about it.

---

19 Postscript to *Helvetic Liberty, An Opera in Three Acts by a Kentish Bowman* (London: Wayland, 1792), vi.

20 *The Artist* 14 (13 June 1807), 16.

21 See, for example, Hunt on the O.P. Riots (*Examiner*, 24 September 1809) and the pantomime (*Examiner* 5, 26 January 1817; included in Appendix), and Hazlitt on Kean's Shylock (*Morning Chronicle*, 27 January 1814) and Kemble's Coriolanus (*Examiner*, 15 December 1816).

22 See Terry Otten, *The Deserted Stage: The Search for Dramatic Form in Nineteenth-Century England* (Athens: Ohio University Press, 1972).

iv. A Proliferation of Forms

The turn of the nineteenth century has been famously represented as the era that saw the death of tragedy,[23] and readers of Romantic writing thus have often assumed a narrowing of dramatic forms in these years. Through our selections in this anthology and through the various reviews and essays contained in its appendix, we wish to dispel both of these notions. Romantic theater not only offered a reimagined and revitalized tragedy; it was also an exciting dramatic laboratory in which playwrights experimented with a wealth of new forms and technologies. If we wish to understand the drama of this especially rich period, we cannot limit ourselves to a consideration of tragedy and comedy of manners but must also explore the melodrama, the burletta, the harlequinade, the extravaganza, the comic pantomime, the dramatic romance, and the farce. Thus, we have included plays ranging from tragedies (such as *Orra* and *The Cenci*) and five-act comedies of manners (such as *Bold Stroke for a Husband*) to a "Dramatick Romance" (*Blue-Beard*), a Christmas pantomime or harlequinade (*Harlequin and Humpo*), a "Grand Dramatic Melo-Drama in Two Acts" (*Timour the Tartar*), and a burlesque satire of it (*The Quadrupeds of Quedlinburgh*). Our argument is that such formal theatrical experimentation bespeaks a dynamic dramatic scene whose innovation helped to revivify even older forms.

For far from revealing tragedy in its death throes, our texts show it thriving. The central figure in this flowering of new tragedy was Joanna Baillie, who without question revived tragedy as the nineteenth century turned, with Byron extolling her "dramatic power" as arguably the best living tragedian and Scott proclaiming her "the best dramatic writer since the days of Shakespeare and Massinger."[24] Appearing anonymously in the spring of 1798, the first volume of *Plays on the Passions* quickly became the talk of London literary circles, and famously led to breathless speculation over the identity of its author. Yet it also sparked intellectual and commercial interest in traditional dramatic forms, especially Elizabethan and Jacobean tragedy. Baillie's publication, moreover, was timely. Readers and critics anxious over potential military invasion by the French had found the English stage in 1798 overwhelmed by another European force: the German *drame* of Auguste von Kotzebue. Within such a climate, Baillie's championing of Shakespeare and other home-grown authors won her great praise from reviewers willing to overlook her persistent Gothicism. *De Monfort*'s respectable run of eight nights at Drury Lane in 1800 may have disappointed critics anticipating an immediate golden age of tragedy, but Baillie's continued production of excellent plays over the next decades ensured her position as the most respected dramatist of her day. The resounding success of *The Family Legend* at the Edinburgh National Theatre in 1810, furthermore, proved that her work had popular appeal. By the time she published *Orra* in 1812, Baillie was nourishing fresh hopes of another London production, and *Orra* shows her drawing upon the same German settings that had inspired her earlier plays *Rayner* (1804) and *De Monfort* to create her preferred form: tragedy hinging on the power of extreme emotions and irrational superstition. She thus wields the spectacular trappings of the Gothic – the looming castle, the legend of the ghostly huntsman, the band of noble robbers – to explore the inner workings of her heroine's mind as she struggles to find a place for herself in an oppressively patriarchal society. Put another way, Baillie finds in Gothic materials similar to those exploited by Colman in *Blue-Beard* the grounds for a new kind of tragedy.

Both Colman's and Baillie's plays center on an attempt to force a young woman to marry, and both plays present the male world as overwhelmingly destructive in its treatment of women. While Colman's pyrotechnic staging of the tale of a man who murders a succession of his wives for displaying the "female" trait of curiosity is hardly a feminist play, Baillie offers through this same foundational narrative a critique of the ways women can be trapped by

---

23 See George Steiner, *The Death of Tragedy* (New York: Knopf, 1961).

24 Lord Byron, Preface to *Marino Faliero*, in Volume 4 of *Byron: The Complete Poetical Works*, ed. Jerome J. McGann and Barry Weller, 7 vols. (Oxford: Oxford University Press, 1980–1992), 305; Sir Walter Scott, *Familiar Letters*, ed. David Douglas (Edinburgh: Douglas, 1894), 1:99.

economic, social, and political orders. An eligible young woman in possession of valuable lands, Orra is pursued by a veritable army of relentless suitors. Resisting a marriage that will end her freedom, she finds her only relief from the restrictions placed upon her through indulging her delight in terrifying stories, a pleasure she shares with her female companions. During the course of the play, however, Orra finds that even her imaginative life is made up of fantasies that derive from a male-dominated Gothic, fantasies that her suitors are able to manipulate in ways that finally drive her mad. Baillie draws upon the stage practices of the Gothic and the powerfully emotive acting style identified with Sarah Siddons to create what is finally a tragedy of the inner workings of fear and desire.

We sometimes forget that Baillie was not alone in this effort to create new tragedies at the century's turn. She was joined by the group we often call "first-generation" Romantics, many of whom wrote for the stage and, disappointed when their plays were rejected by London theater managers, did not publish their work until decades later. Thus Wordsworth's *The Borderers* (composed 1797–8; published 1842) and Scott's various dramas (composed 1797–9, 1817; published 1821, 1829–31) appeared in print long after they were written, while Southey's *Wat Tyler* (composed 1794; published 1817) famously appeared more than two decades after its composition, in a pirated edition designed to embarrass the poet laureate with his "Jacobin" past. Writing to George Ellis in December 1801, Scott diplomatically chose to blame Baillie's excellence rather than the bad taste of London managers for his retreat from the theater, claiming that the *Plays on the Passions* had put him "entirely out of conceit" with his own "Germanized" dramas.[25]

Yet the number of tragedies written by other authors appearing after Baillie's 1798 volume – a number of which received London performances – suggests she in fact initiated a vogue for tragedy both on stage and in print, one that accelerated in the second decade of the nineteenth century. Thus, having brought out *De Monfort* the previous spring, Drury Lane Theatre produced William Godwin's *Antonio* in the autumn of 1800. Covent Garden soon followed with William Sotheby's *Julian and Agnes* (1801), and in the next years both theaters regularly debuted an original tragedy as part of the theatrical season. Many of these were written by Matthew Lewis. Now mainly known for his Gothic extravaganzas, Lewis throughout his career was ambitious to be known as a legitimate dramatist, and devoted considerable time in writing and producing three tragedies: *Alfonso, King of Castille* (Covent Garden, 1803); *The Harper's Daughter*, an adaptation of Schiller's *Kabale und Liebe* (Covent Garden, 1803);[26] and *Adelgitha; or, The Fruits of a Single Error* (Drury Lane, 1807), which appeared in the same year as Godwin's second tragedy, *Faulkner* (Drury Lane, 1807).

Other dramatists took Baillie's cue of publishing their plays rather than submitting them to the managers of the theaters. Thus, of the tragedies produced by "first-generation" Romantics, we find Charles Lamb's *John Woodvil* (1802) and Walter Savage Landor's *Count Julian* (1812) appearing in print with success. And with the next generation of writers, we find something akin to a deluge, with plays by Lord Byron, Felicia Hemans, Charles Robert Maturin, Mary Russell Mitford, Richard Lalor Sheil, Percy Shelley, and John Wilson all appearing in print with at least moderate success.

Of course, Baillie's influence is seen most conspicuously in Coleridge's decision to revise his play *Osorio* under the title *Remorse*, the play whose success would help inspire the dramatic efforts of the younger generation. Like

---

25 Scott to George Ellis, *The Letters of Sir Walter Scott*, 1:124.

26 Other turns to Germany for tragic material at the time include: Georg Heinrich Noehden and J. Stoddart's translations of Schiller's *Fiesco* (London: J. Johnson, 1796) and *Don Carlos* (London: J. Miller, 1798); Sheridan's adaptation of Kotzebue, entitled *Pizarro* (Drury Lane, 1799); Scott's translation of Goethe's *Goetz of Berlichingen, With the Iron Hand* (London: John Bell, 1799); Coleridge's translation of Schiller, entitled *Wallenstein; a Drama in Two Parts* (London: T.N. Longman and O. Rees, 1800); Benjamin Thompson's ambitious *The German Theatre*, 6 vols. (London: Vernor and Hood, 1800–1), featuring translations of Goethe, Schiller, and Kotzebue; and the attempts to create tragedy out of Kotzebue's dramas by Lewis, Anne Plumptre, and the actor Alexander Pope.

Baillie's *Plays on the Passions*, the revised *Remorse* not only based itself in the exploration of a single emotion; it also freely invoked Shakespearean tragedy while wielding Gothic conventions to represent both the passions themselves and the psychological states of characters placed under great emotional strain. Certainly these are instances of "mental theatre" (to quote Byron's famous description of his dramatic practice);[27] but here what strikes us is the persistence with which Baillie and Coleridge seek to represent interior conflict as both dramatic and spectacular. Resembling the plot of *Orra* that hinges upon one of Orra's lovers pretending to be the ghost of a murdered kinsman, the action of *Remorse* revolves around a sham supernatural scene – in which Coleridge's audience witnesses one group of characters imposing on the belief of another – that nonetheless produces very real and permanent effects in the minds of central characters. Here, human emotion takes on an almost supernatural power, since it can, with the support of only the flimsiest of illusions, corrode otherwise rational minds.

The period's experimentation with tragedy is not, however, limited to finding a psychological ground for the tragic. Coleridge's *Remorse* itself has been read as a tragic exploration of politics in the days of revolution and Napoleon, while plays like Baillie's *Family Legend* and *Witchcraft* (1836) clearly engage issues of Scottish national identity. Matching this range of subject matter is an impressive formal experimentation. Just as the architecture of the day ranged through all available styles, so did dramatists explore the entire gamut of tragic prototypes. Shelley in *The Cenci* self-consciously turned to Elizabethan and Jacobean drama for inspiration; Byron in these same years wrote several plays and critical prefaces rejecting the early English drama in favor of a neoclassical tradition that included the heroic drama of Dryden and the classicizing plays of Alfieri. We can find Charles Robert Maturin forging his extremely successful Gothic tragedy in *Bertram* (Drury Lane, 1816), Henry Hart Milman turning to Italy in *Fazio* (Surrey, 1816; as *The Italian Wife*, Covent Garden, 1818), and Richard Lalor Sheil penning a series of successful tragedies[28] owing much to Beaumont and Fletcher and their contemporaries. While Hemans and Mitford would join Byron and Shelley in penning historical tragedies, Byron himself cultivated the Gothic in *Manfred* (1816) and Shelley sought to reimagine Greek tragedy in *Prometheus Unbound* (1820).

Of these later dramatists, Byron and Shelley without question have received the most scholarly attention and critical inquiry, with the interest accorded Byron being immediate and sustained. Of Byron's plays, *Sardanapalus* garnered at once the most praise and the lengthiest analyses. While much of this interest arose from Byron's immense popularity and mystique during the 1810s, a considerable portion also stemmed from his own longstanding involvement with the stage. Byron expended considerable effort not only as a dramatic writer but also as a reader, viewer, and reviewer, including serving on the committee overseeing Drury Lane. Perhaps as a result, his work demonstrates the same range we see in the drama of the period as a whole, including "mystery" plays such as *Cain* (1821) and *Heaven and Earth* (1822), history plays such as *Marino Faliero* and *The Two Foscari* (1821), and "German" dramas such as *Manfred* and *The Deformed Transformed* (1824). *Sardanapalus*, included here, combines a range of sources and styles – including Shakespeare's *Antony and Cleopatra*, the later seventeenth-century tradition of "eastern" heroic dramas (including Dryden's reworking of Shakespeare as *All for Love*), and Alfieri's *Myrrha* – to create a play that explores both the psychology of its central character and the nature of political leadership in a post-Napoleonic age. As one might expect, Byron's declarations that his plays were not intended for dramatic performance did not stop theater managers from producing them. Drury Lane staged *Marino Faliero* in 1821 and *Sardanapalus* in 1834 with great success, while Covent Garden produced *The Two Foscari*

---

27 Letter to John Murray, 23 August 1821, *Byron's Letters and Journals*, ed. Leslie Marchand, 13 vols. (London: John Murray, 1973–94), 8:186–87.

28 These included *The Apostate* (Covent Garden, 1817) and Sheil's adaptation of Shirley's *The Traitor* as *Evadne; or, The Statue* (Covent Garden, 1819).

in 1837; even *Werner* (1823) was staged successfully as a melodrama in the 1830s.

The cultural status of *The Cenci*, meanwhile, has undergone considerable transformation from that accorded to it during Shelley's lifetime. In the last decades it has received without question the most unreserved praise of any British Romantic play. Even its first reviews, surprising as they are in their viciousness and in their inability to cope with the play's focus on incest, nonetheless – grudgingly – acknowledge its immense beauties and dramatic power. As Shelley's reputation improved during the nineteenth century, so did the reputation of *The Cenci*, with the success of the Shelley Society's 1886 production giving rise to several twentieth-century stagings. Part of *The Cenci*'s power resides without question in the very aspects that Shelley's nineteenth-century critics noted: its elevated yet plain language; its masterful handling of horror and terror; and its powerfully subdued ending. These early reviews, moreover, also unknowingly provide a number of structural and thematic insights into the play. John Scott of the *London Magazine*, for example, complained of Shelley's determination to write a play focusing on "whatever 'is not to be named amongst men',"[29] while a reviewer for *The New Monthly Magazine* acknowledged that Shelley deserved praise for representing incest as truly horrific by understanding the degree to which it defied representation. Combining these two observations, we begin to see how the symbolic status of incest as a thing "not to be named" becomes a central theme of the play, so much so that in the play's second and third acts we find Beatrice at once unwilling and unable to name the thing that has happened to her. When Orsino urges her to go to the law to redress her wrongs, she responds:

> Oh, ice-hearted counsellor!
> If I could find a word that might make known
> The crime of my destroyer; and that done
> My tongue should like a knife tear out the secret
> Which cankers my heart's core; ay, lay all bare
> So that my unpolluted fame should be

With vilest gossips a stale-mouthed story;
A mock, a bye-word, an astonishment: –
If this were done, which never shall be done,
Think of the offender's gold, his dreaded hate,
And the strange horror of the accuser's tale,
Baffling belief, and overpowering speech;
Scarce whispered, unimaginable, wrapt
In hideous hints...
Oh, most assured redress! (III.i.152–65)

The problem, then, is less that Beatrice will become polluted in the public eye than that she must articulate the truth of the incest in order to make the accusation. Within the world of Shelley's Rome – not to mention that of the contemporary London stage – incest occupies such taboo status that Beatrice imagines her auditors either will not believe her story or will execrate her for it. Shelley thus transforms a familiar gothic convention into a structural motif; incest here takes on the epistemological status of something literally *unspeakable*, since Beatrice cannot speak the word "incest" without impeaching her credibility. In a more general sense, it also functions as an emblematic symbol for the play's treatment of patriarchal oppression, where the horrible secret sustaining papal power is that no "father" – whether parent, priest, or pope – will dare intrude on the prerogative of another father for fear of undermining his own authority.

While much ink has been spilt over the decline or death of tragedy, we believe that there was a vital Romantic tragic tradition that continued to bear fruit in Ibsen, whose work from *Brand* (1865) and *Peer Gynt* (1867) to *When We Dead Awaken* (1899) shows the influence of Romantic drama, through Strindberg, who loved Byron's plays, and beyond to Shaw, whose *Major Barbara* (1905) can be read as a rewrite of *The Cenci*, and Eliot, whose *Cocktail Party* (1949) appropriates an entire passage from *Prometheus Unbound*. In many ways our more pressing questions concern what happens to comedy, which Leigh Hunt and others by the second decade of the nineteenth century were calling a defunct dramatic form.[30] Looking

---

[29] See Appendix, page 394.

[30] See especially Hunt's essay "On Pantomime," included in the Appendix, page 386.

again to the 1807 *Satirist* cartoon, we see this death ar-restingly represented, with legitimate comedy and trag-edy in the process of being trampled by Mother Goose and by the Monster Melodrama.[31] Put another way, the print shows the traditional comedy of manners – which is seen to rely upon traditional aesthetic norms and so-cial hierarchies – falling before a newly democratized au-dience that preferred the fairy tale stories of the harlequinades and the stirring action of the melodramas. Yet London theater-goers a few decades earlier would have thought comedy in a state of rejuvenation. The mid-cen-tury comedies of Samuel Foote and of Garrick and Colman the Elder had been succeeded by those of Oliver Goldsmith and Richard Brinsley Sheridan, whose string of hits between 1775 and 1779 reconfirmed the profit-ability and prestige of legitimate comedy. With Sheridan's *School for Scandal* (1777) one of the most popular main-piece comedies of the last quarter of the eighteenth cen-tury, comedy became increasingly dominant among new dramatic productions, especially those of Hannah Cowley and Elizabeth Inchbald.

Our own texts, therefore, begin with Hannah Cowley's *A Bold Stroke for a Husband* (1783), exemplary of this revived comedy of manners. Most famous in re-cent histories of Romantic poetry for writing under the pseudonym "Anna Matilda" to Robert Merry's "Della Crusca,"[32] Cowley between 1779 and 1783 was arguably the London stage's premier practitioner of comedy and farce, her most successful plays paying homage to the ex-amples of earlier dramatists, particularly Aphra Behn (1640–89) and Susannah Centlivre (1667–1723). These same works, however, also anticipate the more flexible and far-reaching social comedies of Inchbald, Richard Cumberland, and Joanna Baillie. Set in Spain, *A Bold Stroke for a Husband* focuses on the efforts of two sisters to escape, through disguise and the practice of their own

wit, the ideological traps that accompany marriage. While Olivia must assume an array of personae and disguises to hold off a long line of suitors until she can gain a prom-ise of marriage from the man she prefers, Victoria must re-establish her existing marriage on more secure grounds by assuming both female and male disguises. Most inter-estingly, she assumes the role of a young cavalier in order to woo her husband's mistress (Donna Laura) away from him. The resulting plot not only celebrates female desire even as it interrogates and exposes male promiscuity; it also portrays marriage as inherently contractual and ideo-logical, since Don Carlos takes a mistress not because he has grown tired of his wife but because he considers it a marital entitlement and masculine duty. Cowley resolves in comedy some of the same issues faced in tragedy by Orra and Beatrice Cenci.

As with most contemporary critics of female drama-tists, those of *A Bold Stroke for a Husband* felt uneasiness over Cowley's departures from generic regularity and moral orthodoxy. While overwhelmingly positive, the play's first reviews expressed mild reservations because of its movement between broad comedy and tender senti-ment, a combination likened by the less positive *Monthly Review* to "the style of a Modern Novel."[33] Later assess-ments by Inchbald (1808) and James Boaden (1827) also called attention to these discordances, especially to Olivia's dialogue and to the stylistic discord between the charac-ters of Victoria and Olivia. In these latter cases, however, they tend to voice moral rather than aesthetic objections, with Boaden arguing such impurities to be typical of fe-male dramatists since Behn:

> They would inspire constancy, but they paint the rover: in their most perfect characters the heart al-ways pants for pleasure. But this I learn is the *creed*, as well as practice, among the dramatists of the fair sex … We have had four ladies eminent among our comic writers – Behn, Centlivre, Cowley, and Inchbald; and a not very rigid moralist would strike out much from the writings of each of them.[34]

---

31 See Sylvester Scrutiny, pseudonym of Samuel de Wilde, untitled print, published in *Satirist* 1 (1807).

32 See Jerome McGann, "The Literal World of the English Della Cruscans," in *Fins de Siecle: English Poetry in 1590, 1690, 1790, 1890, 1990*, ed. Elaine Scarry (Baltimore: Johns Hopkins University Press, 1995), 95–121; Pascoe, 68–94.

33 See Appendix, page 312.

34 See Appendix, pages 316–7.

Yet, as Jane Moody recently has argued, what is most striking about such reviews is not their tendency to censure female dramatists for moral and generic transgressions; rather, it is the ease with which such transgressions are conflated with one another.[35] Nowhere do we see this tendency more strongly than in the reception of Elizabeth Inchbald's *Every One Has His Fault* (1793), a play attacked on both aesthetic and ideological grounds. Angered over Inchbald's Jacobin sympathies and visibly shaken by the recent execution of Louis XVI in revolutionary France, periodicals like *The True Briton* attacked the play for its supposed democratic sentiments and alleged violations of probability and generic purity. Thus *The True Briton*'s assertions about Captain Irwin – that it was absolutely impossible for a military officer to contemplate suicide or highway robbery – are immediately followed by a condemnation of the play for its determination to confuse generic hierarchies: "We are at a loss what to term this new species of composition; 'tis neither Comedy, nor Tragi-Comedy, but something anomalous in which the two are jumbled together."[36] Such acts of innovative "jumbling," whether of social or of generic categories, always carry with them political, and often radical, significance.

This concern with "jumbling," seen in the "Monster Melodrama" cartoon and voiced repeatedly by early nineteenth-century critics like John Genest, was, of course, most pronounced in reviews of "illegitimate" forms – that plethora of new dramatic types that arose, at least in part, because the Licensing Act gave the patent theaters a legal monopoly on the spoken word. Responding to this effective ban on spoken drama outside of the patent theaters, other dramatic venues had to create forms that relied upon music, spectacle, and pantomime. "Legitimacy" thus functions as a key but slippery term in the period, at one moment organizing generic principle and at the next ideological category.[37] Within the tightly controlled world

of the London stage, legitimacy gestured towards patent or "major" theaters (as opposed to "minor" upstart ones), towards conventional tragedy and comedy (as opposed to innovative genres such as the melodrama and the burletta), and towards notions of traditional political authority (as opposed to the principles associated with revolutionary France and the "pretender" Napoleon). Members of the theatrical establishment in London, moreover, had reason to be uneasy. In the decades following the French Revolution, we find a slow erosion of the patent theaters' "legitimate" control over the London stage. Viewers could see "musical plays" at the Lyceum, enjoy burlettas, melodramas, and spectacular hippodramas at the Royal Circus or Astley's Royal Amphitheatre, and experience re-enactments of naval battles at Sadler's Wells. Even within the patent theaters, "illegitimate" forms such as melodrama and pantomime could frequently be found as the century turned, offered as afterpieces to mainpiece comedies, tragedies, or operatic dramas.

One key venue for the exploration of new forms was the Haymarket, licensed as a patent theater during the summer months when the other patent theaters were closed. Smaller in size than Drury Lane or Covent Garden, the Haymarket was able to experiment with new forms and showcase the talents of its actors more easily. In the decade before Thomas Holcroft introduced the term "melodrama" from France to describe his adaptation of Pixérécourt, *A Tale of Mystery*, Colman the Younger and Thomas Morton were inventing English melodrama at the Haymarket. Colman's string of hits at his own theater during the 1790s made his plays attractive to the larger winter theaters, and with *Blue-Beard; or, Female Curiosity!*, Colman transported the melodramatic tactics he had mastered at the Haymarket onto the stage of Drury Lane. The style of Colman's play, moreover, strongly resembled that of Drury Lane's biggest hit of that season, Matthew Lewis's *The Castle Spectre* (Drury Lane, 1797). Retelling the legend of the monstrous husband, Abomelique, who kills his wives if they dare enter his secret Blue Chamber, Colman provided his audience with fight scenes, sinking walls, a moving skeleton, and an incredible procession scene involving the use of perspective and mechanical

---

35 See Moody, 49.

36 See Appendix, page 319.

37 See Moody, 1–10; and Barry Sutcliffe, Introduction to *Plays by George Colman the Younger*, ed. Barry Sutcliffe (Cambridge: Cambridge University Press, 1983), 1–7.

elephants to give the impression of Abomelique's descent from the mountains. When the play was revived in 1811, the machines were replaced by live horses, much to the horror of the defenders of "legitimate" theater. Yet in this same year Lewis went even further in *Timour the Tartar* (Covent Garden, 1811), employing trained horses not only for scenic effect but also as an integral part of the action. As with the revived *Blue-Beard*, *Timour*'s opening act featured an impressive scene in which the Tartars entered on horseback. The subsequent scenes, however, exceeded their predecessors at every juncture. After a spectacular armed combat – in which the Tartar Kerim is saved by his horse, which leaps the barriers to retrieve his lost sword – Lewis culminated the play with a pitched siege of Timour's castle. Here, Agib's mother struggles with Timour and makes a daring leap into the water, where Agib on horseback leaps a cataract to save her from drowning. Calling his play "A Grand Dramatick Melodrama in Two Acts," Lewis was not only cashing in on the latest popular form but also signaling the importance of music to his play. As the manuscript sent by the theater to the Licenser of Plays indicates, Lewis deploys music throughout the drama as a way of enhancing and punctuating its moments of pantomimic action. These same tools, of course, are staples of pantomime and harlequinade, and figure centrally in the Christmas pantomime included here, *Harlequin and Humpo*.

As popular dramatic pieces, *Blue-Beard*, *Timour the Tartar*, and *Harlequin and Humpo* do more than reveal popular styles and changes in theater technology and dramatic technique. Like many pieces of popular culture, they engage with the topical issues, anxieties, and fascinations that held the attention of their respective publics. Thus the plays' ritualistic treatment of gender – *Blue-Beard*'s tale of violent misogyny, *Timour*'s "Amazonian" warrior queen, and *Harlequin and Humpo*'s celebration of liberated desire – all echo with key concerns in the age of Wollstonecraft and the subsequent backlash against her and other women writers and intellectuals. Even more striking are the "orientalist" motifs invoked in *Blue-Beard* and *Timour*, which show Colman, Lewis, and their wartime audiences constructing a collective fantasy of Asia.

Both plays direct their viewers to consider the importance of the "East" just as England comes to dominate India, as Napoleon moves into Egypt, and as diplomatic and military manoeuvring intensifies in the Balkans and around the Black Sea. It is no accident, then, that audiences of *Blue-Beard* drew parallels between Abomelique's minister Ibrahim and George III's prime minister William Pitt, or that viewers of *Timour* immediately recognized Lewis's portrait of the usurping tyrant Timour as a thinly veiled attack upon Napoleon. We even find such significances gleaned from Christmas pantomimes like *Harlequin and Humpo*, where audiences discerned a similar anti-Napoleon satire in the diminutive Humpo, King of the Dwarfs.

When we overcome the division between the "literary" and the "theatrical" that has dominated discussions of the Romantic period, we begin to see the rich dramatic scene that constitutes this theater of Romanticism. It is a theater that at once attracted and appalled Wordsworth and Shelley, that eventually gave Coleridge one of his major successes, that provided women writers like Inchbald and Cowley with the most powerful venue available for their work, and that had room for the contrasting styles of a Baillie, a Byron, a Colman, a Dibdin, and a Lewis. It is no wonder that the works of the major writers of the period resonate so acutely with the period's stage drama – most directly when we remember that a play such as *Remorse* shared the stage with a pantomime such as *Harlequin and Humpo*, but also indirectly when we think of Abomelique as a stage prototype for the equally vicious and misogynist Count Cenci, when we connect Orra with other Gothic stage heroines, or when we trace the orientalist gestures of *Sardanapalus* to the dramas of Colman and Lewis, as well as back to those of Dryden or Shakespeare. Perhaps no other physical space allots us so rich an arena to study cultural conflict and change. If the Romantic stage truly constituted such a meeting place – of high and low, legitimate and illegitimate, past and present, elite and popular – then we invite our readers, in this spirit of proliferating forms and generic hybrids, to engage with its full range of theatrical experience, whether tragedy or pantomime, comedy or extravaganza, melo- or hippodrama.

A Bold Stroke for a Husband

by Hannah Cowley

Hannah Cowley (1743–1809) was born Hannah Parkhouse, daughter of Philip Parkhouse, a bookseller in Tiverton. At age 25 she married Thomas Cowley, an officer in the East India Company. Part of Cowley's reputation as a dramatist, like that of Elizabeth Inchbald, rested on a well-circulated anecdote. On attending a play in London, she had remarked to her husband, "Why, I could write as well"; when he responded by laughing incredulously, she proceeded over the next two weeks to compose *The Runaway*, which was sent to David Garrick and produced at Drury Lane in February of 1776. Its success, running 17 nights before the end of the season, led her to write voluminously, producing some thirteen plays and four volumes of poetry over the next two decades.

Unlike Inchbald, however, Cowley neither was an actress nor had direct connections with the theater, and so Garrick's support and advice were important to *The Runaway*'s triumph. But Garrick's retirement in June of 1776 produced changes in management. In spite of *The Runaway*'s success, Cowley's next two plays, the comedy *Who's the Dupe* and the tragedy *Albina*, were allowed to languish until 1779, the former debuting as an afterpiece and so late in the season that it could not be assured of a proper run. Composed in 1776, *Albina* was passed from Richard Brinsley Sheridan at Drury Lane to Thomas Harris at Covent Garden; it finally premiered under the management of George Colman at the Haymarket in July. As Ellen Donkin has noted, the play's belated appearance and wide circulation in manuscript led Cowley to accuse Hannah More of plagiarism when she noted similarities between *Albina* and More's *The Fatal Falsehood* (Covent Garden, 1779). Aside from the newspaper war the accusation ignited, Cowley's play suffered from seriously miscasting and closed after

only seven nights; Colman's decision to schedule Cowley's third benefit night for the seventh instead of the ninth performance suggests an awareness of his own mismanagement.[2] These negative experiences at Drury Lane and Haymarket no doubt contributed to Cowley's decision to submit her next comedy, *The Belle's Strategem* (1780), to Covent Garden. Undeniably the hit of the 1779–80 season, it experienced an initial run of 28 performances. More importantly, it was the first of a string of hits for Cowley at Covent Garden that included *Which Is the Man?* (1782; 23 performances), *A Bold Stroke for a Husband* (1783; 18 performances), and *More Ways than One* (1783; 15 performances).

After the 1783–4 season Cowley became increasingly interested in writing poetry, and divided her dramatic output evenly between Drury Lane and Covent Garden. While not as popular as her earlier work, these plays also experienced considerable success. Both *A School for Grey-beards; or, The Mourning Bride* (Drury Lane, 1786) and *The Fate of Sparta; or, The Rival Kings* (Drury Lane, 1788) enjoyed runs of 9 performances, while *A Day in Turkey; or, The Russian Slaves* (Covent Garden, 1791) was performed 14 times in its opening run. Even with these continued successes, Cowley's prologue to her final play, *The Town before You* (Covent Garden, 1794), cited the changing tastes of London audiences as her primary reason for leaving off dramatic writing altogether.

With *The Belle's Strategem*, *A Bold Stroke for a Husband* became an established repertory piece and a mainstay of nineteenth-century anthologies of drama. While its title proclaims its kinship with

---

1 Ellen Donkin, *Getting into the Act: Women Playwrights in London, 1776-1829* (London and New York: Routledge, 1995), 65.

Susanna Centlivre's *A Bold Stroke for a Wife* (1718), Cowley's play also looks back to another successful female dramatist, Aphra Behn, for its liveliness, Spanish setting, and indulgence in disguise and masquerade. Part of its popularity no doubt stemmed from Cowley's ability to refashion, like Sheridan, the business of Restoration comedy to fit the moral demands of late eighteenth-century audiences. Dramatic historians usually describe Sheridan as dominating English comedy between 1775 and 1779; we might say the same of Cowley for the years 1780–3, particularly when we consider the degree to which Sheridan's advantageous position as proprietor of Drury Lane Theatre provided him unrivalled opportunity to stage his own works.

The copytext for the play is *A Bold Stroke for a Husband, a Comedy* (London: T. Evans, 1784). We have indicated in the notes some major variations found in the Larpent manuscript (Huntington Library LA 617). There are many later editions of the play, some of which provide additional information about staging choices.

PROLOGUE. Written by Two Gentlemen.[2]

Now, by my sanguine hopes, our author cries,
With expectation sparkling in her eyes,
There's nothing here should scare me that I see,
They all are saplings of the tough old tree:
Women, who wear Elysium[3] in their look,
And men, unconquer'd as their native oak.[4]
But yet a word or two I'll briefly say,
To prove we're right in naming of our play.

Of human conduct, in each varied scene,
Th' extreme succeeds beyond the patient mean; 10

If eminence in rank our bosoms fire,
If merit to preferment dare aspire,
Follow the active, not the formal part,
"And snatch a grace beyond the rules of art."[5]
Bold Strokes,[6] from bounding genius firmly struck,
Attract success, more than the turns of luck.
The bankrupt swindler, though to pay unable,
Oft mends his fortune by the E. O.[7] table;
Or, failing there, he acts a braver part,
And takes a purse,—*a Bold Stroke for the cart*.[8] 20
The gamester too forgets each tender tie,—
And ventures his last guinea on a die,
'Till ruin'd, and repenting of the evil,
He hangs himself—*a Bold Stroke for the Devil*.[9]

---

2 *Two Gentlemen*: unidentified.
3 *Elysium*: in Greek mythology, the supposed state or abode of the blessed after death; a place or state of ideal or perfect happiness.
4 *native oak*: The oak tree is often taken to be representative of English character because of its hardness and solidity. After this line the Larpent version adds the following:
   The God of tender joys whose genial Fire,
   Lights the gay Smile & kindles soft desire,
   Victorious waves his purple plumes in air,
   And sets his Standard up of beauty here.
   To shew his pow'r is our Author's aim.
   Suffer her each fair hand that Husbands claim.
   For what avails the products of her head,
   If Critic Judges say "She shan't have bread."

5 *"And snatch a grace beyond the rules of art"*: Alexander Pope, *An Essay on Criticism*, line 155.
6 *Bold Strokes*: vigorous attempts to attain some object; a measure, expedient, or device adopted for some purpose.
7 *E. O.*: a game of chance, in which the appropriation of the stakes is determined by the falling of a ball into one of several niches marked E or O respectively.
8 *cart*: i.e., prison; referring to the cart used to carry prisoners from prison either to criminal court or to the gallows, or used for the public exposure and chastisement of criminals.
9 *Devil*: referring here to the doctrine that suicides faced certain damnation.

The fortune hunter sports a suit of lace,
In this a Count, a Lord in t'other place,
Success at length, begins his married life
At Gretna Green[10]—*a Bold Stroke for a Wife.*

But are bold strokes to vicious men confin'd?
Does virtue lie inactive in the mind?   30
It cannot be, while England's genius breathes,
And many a brow is deck'd with laurel wreaths.
Bold strokes in war are England's greatest pride;
Think how a HOOD[11] has liv'd, a MANNERS[12] died!

Our play holds forth the conquest of a heart,
By one bold stroke of nature, not of art.
A female pen calls female virtue forth,
And fairly shews to man her sex's worth.
Could men but see what female sense can do,
How apt their wit, their constancy—how true;   40
In vain would rakes the married state revile,
Nor with the wanton, precious time beguile.

Such is our aim, to rectify the age,
By bringing rising follies on the stage;
Be then propitious, let our fears decrease,
While you, with plaudits,[13] ratify the peace!

DRAMATIS PERSONAE

MEN:

Don Julio	Mr. Lewis
Don Carlos	Mr. Wroughton
Don Caesar	Mr. Quick
Don Vincentio	Mr. Edwin
Don Garcia	Mr. Whitfield
Vasquez	Mr. Fearon
Gasper	Mr. Wilson
Pedro	Mr. Stevens

WOMEN:

Olivia	Mrs. Mattocks
Victoria	Mrs. Robinson
Laura	Mrs. Whitfield
Marcella	Miss Morris
Minette	Mrs. Wilson
Inis	Miss Platt
Sancha	Mrs. Davenett

Scene: *Spain*

Act I

Scene I: *A Street in Madrid. Enter Sancha from a House, she advances, then runs back, and beckons to Pedro within.*

Sancha. Hist![14] Pedro! Pedro!
(Enter Pedro).
There he is: do'st see him? just turning by St. Antony[15] in the corner. Now, do you tell him that your mistress is not at home; and if his jealous Donship should insist on searching the house, as he did yesterday, say that somebody is ill—the black has got a fever, or that——

---

10 *Gretna Green*: a Scottish village bordering England, famously a place where runaway couples from England could go to marry according to Scottish law, which did not require parental consent for those who had not attained the age of legal adulthood.

11 *HOOD*: Samuel Hood, First Viscount (1724–1816), British Admiral, who served in the Seven Years' War and in the American and French Revolutionary Wars. He was created first Viscount Hood of Whitley in 1796.

12 *MANNERS*: John Manners, Marquess of Granby (1721–70), British army officer and popular military hero of the Seven Years' War. He became Commander-in-chief of the British army in 1766.

13 *plaudits*: applause.

---

14 *Hist*: an onomatopoeic expression used to call upon someone to listen.

15 *St. Antony*: referring to a church named for Anthony of Egypt (ca. 251–356), the religious hermit considered the founder of organized Christian monasticism. During his retreat from 286 to 305, he engaged in a series of legendary combats with the devil, popularly represented in Christian iconography. He is the patron saint of swineherds.

Pedro. Pho, pho, get you in. Don't I know that the duty of a lacquey[16] in Madrid is to lie with a good grace? I have been studying it now for a whole week, and I'll defy Don or Devil to surprize me into a truth. Get you in, I say—here he comes. *(Exit Sancha).*

(Enter Carlos. Pedro struts up to him).

Donna Laura is not at home, Sir.

Carlos. Not at home!—come, Sir, what have you received for telling that lie?

Ped. Lie!—Lie!—Signor!—

Car. It must be a lie by your promptness in delivering it.——What a fool does your mistress trust!—A clever rascal would have waited my approach, and, delivering the message with easy coolness, deceived me——*thou* hast been on the watch, and runnest towards me with a face of stupid importance, bawling, that she may hear through the lattice[17] how well thou obeyest her,—"*Donna Laura is not at home, Sir.*"

Ped. Hear through the lettice[18]—hah! by'r lady she must have long ears, to reach from the grotto in the garden to the street.

Car. Hah! *(Seizes him).* Now, Sir, your ears shall be longer, if you do not tell me who is with her in the grotto.

Ped. In the grotto, Sir!——did I say any thing about the grotto? I——I only meant that—

Car. Fool!—dost thou trifle with me? who is with her? *(Pinching his ear).*

Ped. Oh!—why nobody, Sir—only the pretty young gentleman's valet, waiting for an answer to a letter he brought. There! I have saved my ears at the expence of my place. I have worn this fine coat but a week, and I shall be sent back to Segovia for not being able to lie, though I have been learning the art six days and nights.

Car. Well—come this way—if thou wilt promise to be faithful to me, I will not betray thee: nor at present enter the house.

Ped. Oh, Sir, blessings on you!

Car. How often does the pretty young gentleman visit her?

Ped. Every day, Sir—If he misses, madam's stark wild.

Car. Where does he live?

Ped. Truly, I know not, Sir.

Car. (Menacing). How!

Ped. By the honesty of my mother, I cannot tell, Sir. She calls him Florio;—that's his Christian name—his Heathen name[19] I never heard.

Car. You must acquaint me when they are next together.

Ped. Lord, Sir, if there should be any blood spilt!

Car. Promise,—or I'll lead thee by the ears to the grotto.

Ped. I promise, I promise.

Car. There, take that, *(Gives money)* and if thou art faithful I'll treble it. Now go in, and be a good lad—and, d'ye hear?—you may tell lies to every body else, but remember you must always speak truth to me.

Ped. I will, Sir,—I will. *(Exit, looking at the money).*

Car. 'Tis well my passion is extinguished, for I can now act with coolness; I'll wait patiently for the hour of their security, and take them in the softest moments of their love. But if ever I trust to woman more—may every——

(Enter two women, veiled, followed by Julio).

Julio. Fye, ladies! keep your curtains drawn so late! The sun is up—'tis time to look abroad—*(Tries to remove their veils)*—Nay, if you are determined on night and silence, I take my leave. A woman without prattle, is like Burgundy without spirit.—Bright eyes, to touch me, must belong to sweet tongues. *(Going).*

Car. Sure 'tis Julio. Hey!

Jul. (Returning). Don Carlos? Yes, by all the sober gods of matrimony!—Why, what business,

---

16 *lacquey*: i.e., lackey, a footman, especially a running footman or valet.

17 *lattice*: a structure made of wood or metal crossed together so as to form a screen, usually for a window.

18 *lettice*: a variant form of "lattice," punning on "lettuce," as the reference to the "garden" later in the sentence indicates.

19 *Heathen name*: family name or surname. Here the expression also plays on the play's interest in romantic love and disguise.

Goodman[20] Gravity, can'st thou have in Madrid—I understand you are *married*—quietly settled in your own pastures—father of a family, and the instructive companion of country vine dressers—ha! ha!

Car. 'Tis false, by heaven!—I have forsworn the country—left my family, and run away from my wife.

Jul. Really! then matrimony has not totally destroyed thy free will.

Car. 'Tis with difficulty I have preserv'd it though; for women, thou knowest, are most unreasonable beings! as soon as I had exhausted my stock of love tales, which, with management, lasted beyond the honey-moon, madam grew sullen,—I found home dull, and amused myself with the pretty peasants of the neighbourhood——Worse and worse!—we had nothing now but faintings, tears and hysterics for twenty-four honey-moons more.—So one morning I gave her in her sleep a farewell kiss, to comfort her when she should awake, and posted to Madrid; where, if it was not for the remembrance of the clog[21] at my heel, I should bound o'er the regions of pleasure, with more spirit than a young Arabian[22] on his mountains.

Jul. Do you find this clog no hindrance in affairs of gallantry?

Car. Not much.—In that house there—but, damn her, she's perfidious!—in that house is a woman of beauty, with pretensions to character and fortune, who devoted herself to my passion.

Jul. If she's perfidious, give her to the winds.

Car. Ah, but there *is* a rub, Julio, I have been a fool—a woman's fool!—In a state of intoxication, she wheedled me, or rather cheated me, out of a settlement.

Jul. Pho! is that——

Car. Oh! but you know not its nature. A settlement of lands that both honour and gratitude ought to

have preserved sacred from such base aliena-tion.[23]—In short, if I cannot recover them, I am a ruined man.

Jul. Nay, this seems a worse clog than t'other—Poor Carlos! so bewiv'd and be——

Car. Prithee have compassion.

(Enter a Servant with a letter to Julio, he reads it, and then nods to the Servant, who exits).

Car. An appointment, I'll be sworn, by that air of mystery and satisfaction—come, be friendly, and communicate.

Jul. (Putting up the letter). You are married, Carlos;—that's all I have to say—you are married.

Car. Pho, that's past long ago, and ought to be forgotten; but if a man does a foolish thing once, he'll hear of it all his life.

Jul. Aye, the time has been when thou might'st have been entrusted with such a dear secret,—when I might have opened the billet,[24] and feasted thee with the sweet meandring strokes at the bottom, which form her name, when——

Car. What, 'tis from a woman then?

Jul. It is.

Car. Handsome?

Jul. Hum—not absolutely handsome, but she'll pass, with one who has not had his taste spoilt by—*matrimony.*

Car. Malicious dog!—Is she young?

Jul. Under twenty—fair complexion, azure eyes, red lips, teeth of pearl, polished neck, fine turn'd shape, graceful——

Car. Hold, Julio, if thou lov'st me!—Is it possible she can be so bewitching a creature?

Jul. 'Tis possible—though, to deal plainly, I never saw her; but I love my own pleasure so well, that I could fancy all that, and ten times more.

Car. What star does she inhabit?

---

20 *Goodman*: a husband; also used as a vague title of dig-nity for a man of substance. The title is sometimes used ironically.

21 *clog*: a block or heavy piece of wood, attached to the leg or neck to prevent escape.

22 *Arabian*: an Arabian horse.

23 *alienation*: the action of estranging or of transferring ownership of anything from one person to another. Cowley here puns on both the psychological and ma-terial senses of the word, as she does on the word "base," since Don Carlos's action is at once base (lowly) and confers his wife's property upon a person of base (low) birth.

24 *billet*: letter.

Jul. **Irradiate** thou should'st have said, after such a description—but, faith, I know not; my orders are to be in waiting at seven, at the Prado.[25]   160

Car. Prado!—hey!—gad! can't you take me with you? for though I have forsworn the sex myself, and have done with them for ever, yet I may be of use to *you*, you know.

Jul. Faith, I can't see that—however, as you are a poor woe-begone *married* mortal, I'll have compassion, and suffer thee to come.

Car. Then I am a man again! Wife, avaunt![26]—mistress, farewell!—At seven you say?

Jul. Exactly.   170

Car. I'll meet thee at Philippi![27] *(Exit severally).*

Scene II: *A spacious Garden belonging to Don Caesar.*
Enter Minette and Inis.

Minette. There, will that do? My lady sent me to make her up a nosegay; these orange flowers are delicious, and this rose, how sweet!

Inis. Pho, what signifies wearing sweets in her bosom, unless they would sweeten her manners?—'tis amazing you can be so much at your ease; one might think your lady's tongue was a lute, and her morning scolds an agreeable serenade.

Min. So they are—Custom you know. I have been used to her music now these two years, and I don't   10 believe I could relish my breakfast without it.

Inis. I would rather never break my fast, than do it on such terms. What a difference between your mistress and mine; Donna Victoria is as much too gentle, as her cousin is too harsh.

Min. Aye, and you see what she gets by it; had she been more spirited, perhaps her husband would not have forsaken her;—men enlisted under the matrimonial banner, like those under the King's,

would be often tempted to run away from their   20 colours, if fear did not keep them in dread of desertion.

Inis. If making a husband *afraid* is the way to keep him faithful, I believe your lady will be the happiest wife in Spain.

Min. Ha, ha, ha! how people may be deceived!—nay, how people are deceived!—but time will discover all things.

Inis. What! what is there a secret in the business, Minette? if there is, hang time! let's have it directly.   30

Min. Now, if I dar'd but tell ye—lud! lud![28] how I could surprize ye!——*(Going).*

Inis (*Stopping her*). Don't go.

Min. I must go; I am on the very brink of betraying my mistress,—I must leave you—mercy upon me!—it rises like new bread.

Inis. I hope it will choak ye, if you stir 'till I know all.

Min. Will you never breathe a syllable?

Inis. Never.[29]   40

Min. Will you strive to forget it the moment you have heard it?

Inis. I'll swear to myself forty times a-day to forget it.

Min. You are sure you will not let me stir from this spot till you know the whole.

Inis. Not as far as a thrush hops.

Min. So! now, then, in one word,—here it goes. Though every body supposes my lady an errant scold, she's no more a—   50

Caesar (*Without*). Out upon't! e—h—h!

Min. Oh, St. Jerome![30]—here is her father, and his

---

25 *Prado*: the proper name for the public park of Madrid. More generally, a fashionable place to promenade, usually with flower beds and lawns.

26 *avaunt!*: an interjection meaning begone! away! onward! go on!, etc.

27 *I'll meet thee at Philippi!*: See William Shakespeare, *Julius Caesar* IV.iii.225 and IV.iii.282–6, and Abraham Cowley, *Brutus*, line 49.

28 *lud! lud!*: a contracted variation of "Lord."

29 The Larpent version handles this exchange somewhat differently; among other changes, it adds the following lines here:
    Min. Dear Inis, how thankful am I to your Curiosity! it is very violent is it not?
    Inis. Monstrous!

30 *St. Jerome*: also known in Latin as Eusebius Hieronymus, and by the pseudonym Sophronius (ca. 347–419/420), biblical translator and monastic leader, traditionally regarded as the most learned of the Latin Fathers. He is best known for his Latin translation of the Bible, the Vulgate.

privy counsellor, Gasper. I can never communicate a secret in quiet. Well! come to my chamber, for, now my hand's in, you shall have the whole.—I wou'd not keep it another day, to be confidant to an infanta.[31] *(Exeunt).*

(Enter Don Caesar and Gasper).

Gasper. Take comfort, Sir; take comfort.

Caes. Take it!—why where the devil shall I find it? You may say, take physic Sir, or, take poison, Sir— —they are to be had; but what signifies bidding me take comfort, when I can neither buy it, beg it, nor steal it?

Gasp. But patience will bring it, Sir.

Caes. 'Tis false, sirrah.[32] —Patience is a cheat, and the man that rank'd her with the cardinal virtues was a fool.—I have had patience at bed and board these three long years, but the comfort she promis'd, has never called in with a civil how d'ye.

Gasp. Aye, Sir, but you know the poets say that the twin sister and companion of comfort is good humour.—Now if you would but drop that agreeable acidity, which is so conspicuous——

Caes. Then let my daughter drop her perverse humour; 'tis a more certain bar to marriage than ugliness or folly; and will send me to my grave, at last, without male heirs. *(Crying).* How many have laid siege to her! But that humour of hers, like the works of Gibraltar,[33] no Spaniard can find pregnable.

Gasp. Aye, well—Troy held out but ten years[34]—— Let her once tell over her beads, *unmarried*, at five-

and-twenty, and, my life upon it, she ends the rosary, with a hearty prayer for a good husband.

Caes. What, d'ye expect me to wait till the horrors of old maidenism frighten her into civility? No, no;—I'll shut her up in a convent, marry myself, and have heirs in spite of her. There's my neighbour Don Vasquez's daughter, she is but nineteen——

Gasp. The very step I was going to recommend, Sir. You are but a young gentleman of sixty-three, I take it; and a husband of sixty-three, who marries a wife of nineteen, will never want heirs, take my word for it.

Caes. What! do you joke, sirrah?

Gasp. Oh no, Sir—not if you are serious. I think it would be one of the pleasantest things in the world—Madam would throw a new life into the family; and when you are above stairs in the gout, Sir, the music of her concerts, and the spirit of her converzationes[35] would reach your sick bed, and be a thousand times more comforting than flannels and panadas.[36]

Caes. Come, come, I understand ye.—But this daughter of mine—I shall give her but two chances more.——Don Garcia and Don Vincentio will both be here to-day, and if she plays over the old game, I'll marry to-morrow morning, if I hang myself the next.

Larpent version cuts this sentence on Troy and substitutes the following exchange:

Gasp. Then suppose you try her with a Frenchman: a Monsieur won't mind a few hard words, he'll smile at 'em as tho' they were spent Bullets.

Caes. Twou'd be one if she was to have a lover sent her by every Belligerent power in Europe. How the devil she continues to get rid of 'em all, I have never been able to find out, for tho' she is in general a Vixen, yet when she behaves with good humour 'tis the same thing, they all grow disaffected like Mercenaries when their Subsidy is Stopt.

---

31 *infanta*: a daughter of the king and queen of Spain or Portugal, especially the eldest daughter who is not heir to the throne.

32 *sirrah*: a term of address used to men or boys, often expressing reprimand or an assumption of authority on the part of the speaker.

33 *works of Gibraltar*: the military defenses around Gibraltar, a high point of land on the coast of southern Spain guarding the entrance to the Mediterranean Sea, held by the British since 1704 and unassailable as a military position.

34 *Troy held out but ten years*: referring to the war between Troy and Greece recorded most famously in Homer's *Iliad*. In Homer's account the war drags on ten years before the Greeks successfully conquer Troy. The

35 *converzationes*: social events in which people meet to confer, discuss, and debate; salons.

36 *panadas*: either referring to empanadas, a kind of traditional Spanish meat pie and comfort food, or else to "panada," a gruel of breadcrumbs soaked or boiled in milk.

Gasp. You decide right, Signor; at sixty-three the marriage noose and the hempen noose should always go together.

Caes. Why, you dog you, do you suppose—There's Don Garcia—there he is, coming through the portico. Run to my daughter, and bid her remember what I have said to her. *(Exit Gasper).* She has had her lesson—but another memento mayn't be amiss—a young slut!37—pretty, and witty, and rich—a match for a prince, and yet—   120
but hist!—Not a word to my young man, if I can but keep him in ignorance 'till he is married, he must make the best of his bargain afterwards, as other honest men have done before him.

(Enter Garcia).

Welcome, Don Garcia!—why you are rather before your time.

Garc. Gallantry forbid that I should not, when a fair lady is concern'd. Should Donna Olivia welcome me as frankly as you do, I shall think I have been tardy.

Caes. When you made your overtures, Signor, I   130
understood it was from inclination to be allied to my family, not from a particular passion to my daughter. Have you ever seen her?

Garc. But once—that transiently—yet sufficient to convince me that she is charming.

Caes. Why yes, tho' I say it, there are few prettier women in Madrid; and she has got enemies amongst her own sex accordingly. They pretend to say that——I say, Sir, they have reported that she is not bless'd with that kind of docility and   140
gentleness that a——now, tho' she may not be so very placid, and insipid, as some young women, yet, upon the whole——

Garc. Oh fye,38 Sir!—not a word—A beauty cannot be ill-temper'd; gratified vanity keeps her in good humour with herself, and every body about her.

Caes. Yes, as you say—vanity is a prodigious sweetener; and Olivia, considering how much she has been humoured, is as gentle and pliant as——

(Enter Minette).

Min. Oh, Sir! shield me from my mistress—She is   150
in one of her old tempers—the whole house is in an uproar.—I cannot support it!

Caes. Hush!

Min. No, Sir, I can't hush—A saint could not bear it. I am tired of her tyranny, and must quit her service.

Caes. Then quit it in a moment—go to my steward, and receive your wages—go—begone! 'Tis a cousin of my daughter's she is speaking of.

Min. A cousin, Sir!—No, 'tis Donna Olivia, your   160
daughter—my mistress. *(To Garcia).* Oh, Sir! you seem to be a sweet tender-hearted young gentleman—'twould move you to pity if——

Caes. I'll move you, hussey,39 to some purpose, if you don't move off.

Garc. I am really confounded——can the charming Olivia——

Caes. Spite, Sir—meer malice! My daughter has refus'd her some cast gown, or some——

Oliv. (Without). Where is she!—Where is Minette?   170

Caes. Oh 'tis all over!—the tempest is coming.

(Enter Olivia).

Oliv. Oh, you vile creature!—to speak to me!—to answer me!—am I made to be answer'd?

Caes. Daughter! Daughter! *(During the following conversation he shews the most anxious impatience).*

Oliv. Because I threw my work-bag at her, she had the insolence to complain; and, on my repeating it, said she would not bear it.—Servants chuse what they shall bear!   180

Min. When you are married, Ma'am, I hope your husband will bear your humour, less patiently than I have done.

Oliv. My husband!—dost think my husband shall contradict my will? Oh, I long to set a pattern to those milky wives, whose mean compliances degrade the sex.

Garc. (Aside). Opportune!

Oliv. The only husband on record who knew how to treat a wife was Socrates;40 and tho' his lady was   190

---

37 *slut*: a woman of bold and impudent behavior, or of low and loose character.

38 *fye*: obscure form of "fie," an exclamation expressing disgust or reproach.

39 *hussey*: a phonetic reduction of "housewife"; a rude or opprobrious mode of addressing a woman.

40 *The only husband ... was Socrates*: referring to the marriage of Socrates (470–399 BC) late in life to

a Grecian, I have some reason to believe her descendants match'd into our family; and never shall my tame submission disgrace my ancestry.

Garc. Heav'ns! why have you never curb'd this intemperate spirit, Don Caesar?

Oliv. (Starting). Curb'd, Sir! talk thus to your groom—curbs and bridles for a woman's tongue!

Garc. Not for yours, lady, truly! 'tis too late. But had the torrent, now so overbearing, been taken at its spring, it might have been stem'd, and turn'd in 200 gentle streamlets at the master's pleasure.

Oliv. A mistake, friend!—my spirit, at its spring, was too powerful for any master.

Garc. Indeed!—perhaps you may meet a Petruchio, gentle Catherine,[41] yet.

Oliv. But no gentle Catherine will he find me, believe it.——Catherine! why she had not the spirit of a roasted chestnut—a few big words, an empty oath, and a scanty dinner, made her as submissive as a spaniel. My fire will not be so soon extinguished— 210 it shall resist big words, oaths, and starving.

Min. I believe so indeed; help the poor gentleman, I say, to whose fate you fall.

Garc. Don Caesar, adieu! My commiseration for your fate subdues the resentment I should otherwise feel at your endeavouring to deceive me into such a marriage.

Oliv. (Apart to Caesar). Marriage! oh mercy!—Is this Don Garcia?

Caes. Yes, termagant![42] 220

Oliv. O, what a misfortune! Why did you not tell me it was the gentleman you design'd to marry me to? Oh, Sir! all that is past was in sport; a contrivance between my maid and me: I have no spirit at all—I am as patient as poverty.

Xanthippe. In his three-part justification of Socrates (*Apology*, *Symposium*, and *Memorabilia*), Xenophon (431–350 BC) presents Xanthippe as a woman of strong temper.

41 *Petruchio, gentle Catherine*: referring to William Shakespeare's *The Taming of the Shrew*, in which Petruchio subdues his wife Catherine by denying her food and sleep in the name of love.

42 *termagant*: a violent, overbearing, bullying, or quarrelsome person.

Garc. This mask sits too ill on your features, fair lady: I have seen you *without* disguise, and rejoice in your ignorance of my name, since, but for that, my peaceful home might have become the seat of perpetual discord. 230

Min. Aye, Sir, you would never have known what a quiet hour——

Oliv. (Strikes her). Impertinence! Indeed, Sir, I can be as gentle and forbearing as a pet lamb.

Garc. I cannot doubt it, Madam; the proofs of your placidity are very striking—But, adieu! though I shall pray for your conversion, rather than have the honour of it—I'd turn Dominican,[43] and condemn myself to perpetual celibacy. *(Exit).*

Caes. Now, hussey!—now, hussey!—what do you 240 expect?

Oliv. Dear me! how can you be so unreasonable! did ever daughter do more to oblige a father! I absolutely begg'd the man to have me.

Caes. Yes, vixen![44] after you had made him detest ye; what, I suppose, he did not hit your fancy, madam; tho' there is not in all Spain a man of prettier conversation.

Oliv. Yes, he has a very pretty kind of conversation; 'tis like a parenthesis. 250

Caes. Like a parenthesis!

Oliv. Yes, it might be all left out, and never miss'd. However, I thought him a modest kind of a well-meaning young man, and that he would make a pretty sort of a husband—for notwithstanding his blustering, had I been his wife, in three months he should have been as humble and complaisant as——

Caes. Aye, there it is—there it is!—that spirit of yours, hussey, you can neither conquer nor conceal; 260 but I'll find a way to tame it, I'll warrant me. *(Exit).*

(Olivia and Minette follow him with their eyes, and then burst into a laugh).

Min. Well, madam, I give you joy! had other ladies as much success in getting lovers, as you have in

---

43 *I'd turn Dominican*: i.e., I would become a Dominican monk.

44 *vixen*: literally, a female fox; here, an ill-tempered, quarrelsome woman.

getting rid of yours, what contented faces we should see.

Oliv. But to what purpose do I get rid of them, whilst they rise in succession like monthly pinks?[45] Was there ever any thing so provoking?—After some quiet, and believing the men had ceased to trouble themselves about me, no less than two proposals have been made to my inexorable father this very day—What will become of me?

Min. What shou'd become of you? You'll chuse one from the pair, I hope. Believe me, madam, the only way to get rid of the impertinence of lovers, is to take one, and make him a scare-crow to the rest.

Oliv. Oh, but I cannot!—Invention assist me this one day!

Min. Upon my word, madam, invention owes you nothing; and I am afraid you can draw on that bank no longer.—You must trust to your established character of vixen.

Oliv. But that won't frighten 'em all, you know, tho' it did its business with sober Don Garcia. The brave General Antonio would have made a property of me,[46] in spite of every thing, had I not luckily discovered his antipathy to cats, and so scar'd the hero, by pretending an immoderate passion for young kittens.

Min. Yes, but you was still harder push'd by the Castilian Count, and his engrav'd genealogy from Noah.[47]

Oliv. Oh, he would have kept his post as immovably as the griffins at his gate, had I not very seriously imparted to him, that my mother's great uncle sold oranges in Arragon. Ha! ha! ha! And my little delicate spark, who washes in rose-water, and has his bed strewed with violets, would never have dismissed himself, hadst thou not scented my mareschal[48] powder with assa foetida.[49]

Min. And pray, madam, if I may be so bold, who is the next gentleman?

Oliv. Oh, Don Vincentio, who distracts every body with his skill in music. He ought to be married to a Viol de Gamba.[50] I bless my stars I have never yet had a miser in my list—on such a character all art would be lost, and nothing but an earthquake, to swallow up my estate, could save me.

Min. Well, if some one did but know, how happy would some one be, that for his sake——

Oliv. Now, don't be impertinent, Minette. You have several times attempted to slide yourself into a secret, which I am resolv'd to keep to myself. Continue faithful, and suppress your curiosity. *(Exit).*

Min. Suppress my curiosity, madam!—why, I am a chambermaid, and a sorry one too, it should seem, to have been in your confidence two years, and never have got the master-secret yet.[51] I never was six weeks in a family before, but I knew every secret they had in it for three generations; aye, and I'll know this too, or I'll blow up all her plans, and declare to the world that she is no more a vixen than other fine ladies——they have most of 'em a touch on't. *(Exit).*

---

45 *pinks*: any of the several flowering plants of the genus *Dianthus* in the pink family (Caryophylaceae), grown widely in garden borders. They are found chiefly in the Mediterranean region, are usually perennial, and are characterized by their hardiness and tendency to spread once they take hold in the soil.

46 *made a property of me*: i.e., married me. Cowley's term, however, captures both the legal fate of married women (that both they and their property become the property of their husbands) and the entrepreneurial attitudes with which most men approached marriage.

47 *engrav'd genealogy from Noah*: i.e., a document showing a line of descent back to Noah.

48 *mareschal*: variant of "marechal," an aromatic powder used in the hair.

49 *assa foetida*: variant of asafoetida, a resinous gum with a strong odor similar to onions and garlic, often used as a spice in Central Asian cooking.

50 *Viol de Gamba*: a viol held between the legs of the player while being played, corresponding to the modern cello.

51 The Larpent version adds the following lines: "There must be a man in the Case but he may as well be in the Georgibus Sibus, for any Intelligence I can get. I wonder she has the Confidence to use me so Ungratefully!"

Act II

Scene I: *An Apartment at Donna Laura's.*
Enter Laura followed by Carlos.

Car. Nay, Madam, you may as well stop here, for I'll
follow you through every apartment, but I will be
heard. *(Seizing her hand).*

Laura. This insolence is not to be endured; within
my own walls to be thus——

Car. The time has been, when within your walls I
might be master.

Lau. Yes, you were then master of my heart, *that* gave
you a right which——

Car. You have now transferred to another. *(Flinging* 10
away her hand).

Lau. Well, Sir!

Car. "Well, Sir!"—Unblushing acknowledgment!
False, fickle woman!

Lau. Because I have luckily got the start of you; in a
few weeks I should have been the accuser, and *you*
the false and fickle.

Car. And to secure yourself from that disgrace, you
prudently looked out in time for another lover.

Lau. I can pardon your sneer, because you are 20
mortified.

Car. Mortified!

Lau. Yes, mortified to the soul. Carlos! I know your
sex: the vainest female, in the hour of her
exultation and power, is still out-done by man in
vanity.—'Tis more your ruling passion, than 'tis
ours; and 'tis wounded *vanity* that makes you thus
tremble with rage at being deserted.

Car. (Stamping). Madam! Madam!

Lau. This rage would have been all cool insolence, 30
had I waited for your change—the crime which
now appears so black in me. Then, whilst, with all
my sex's weakness, I had knelt at your feet, and
reproached you only with my tears; how *composed*
would have been your feelings.—Scarcely would
you have deigned to form a phrase of pity for me;
perhaps have bid me forget a man no longer
worthy my attachment, and recommended me to
hartshorn[52] and my women.

Car. Has any hour since I have first known you, given 40
you cause for such unjust——

Lau. Yes, every hour—Now, Carlos, I bring thee to
the test!—You saw, you lik'd, you lov'd me; was
there no fond trusting woman whom you deserted
to indulge the transient passion? Yes, one blest with
beauty, gentleness and youth; one, who more than
her own being lov'd thee, who made thee rich, and
whom thou mad'st thy wife.

Car. My wife!—here's a turn! So to revenge the
quarrels of my wife—— 50

Lau. No, do not mistake me—what I have done was
merely to indulge myself, without more regard to
your feelings, than you had to hers.

Car. And you dare avow to my face, that you have a
passion for another?

Lau. I do, and—for I am above disguise—I confess,
so tender is my love for Florio, it has scarcely left
a trace of that I once avow'd for Carlos.

Car. Well, Madam, if I hear this without some sudden
vengeance on the tongue which speaks it, thank the 60
annihilation of that passion, whose remembrance is
as dead in my bosom as in yours. Let us, however,
part friends, and with a mutual acquittal of every
obligation—so give up the settlement of that estate,
which left me almost a beggar.

Lau. Give it up!—ha, ha!——no, Carlos, you
consign'd me that estate as a proof of love; do not
imagine then, I'll give up the only part of our
connection, of which I am not ashamed.

Car. Base woman! you know 'twas not a voluntary 70
gift—after having in vain practis'd on my fondness,
whilst in a state of intoxication, you prevailed on
me to sign the deed, which you had artfully
prepar'd for the purpose—therefore, you must
restore it.

Lau. Never, never.

Car. Ruin is in the word!——Call it back, Madam,
or I'll be reveng'd on thee in thy heart's dearest
object—thy minion Florio!——*he* shall not riot on
my fortune. 80

Lau. Ha, ha, ha! Florio is safe—your lands are sold,
and in another country we shall enjoy the blessing

_____

[52] *hartshorn*: smelling salts. Literally, the substance obtained by rasping or slicing the horns of harts, formerly
the chief source of ammonia.

of thy fond passion, whilst that passion is indulging itself in hatred and execrations. *(Exit)*.

Car. (Following). My vengeance shall first fall on her. No, he shall be the first victim, or 'twill be incomplete.—Reduc'd to poverty, I cannot live;——Oh, folly! where are now all the gilded prospects of my youth? Had I——but 'tis too late to look back,—remorse attends the past, and ruin!—ruin waits me in the future! *(Exit)*. 90

Scene II: *Don Caesar's. Victoria enters perusing a letter; enter Olivia.*

Oliv. (Speaks as entering). To be sure—if my father should enquire for me, tell him I am in Donna Victoria's apartment.—Smiling, I protest! my dear gloomy cousin, where have you purchased that sun-shiny look?

Vict. It is but April sunshine, I fear; but who could resist *such* a temptation to smile? a letter from Donna Laura, my husband's mistress, stiling me her dearest Florio! her life! her soul! and complaining of a twelve hours absence, as the bitterest misfortune. 10

Oliv. Ha, ha, ha! most doughty Don! pray let us see you in your feather and doublet; as a Cavaleiro,[53] it seems, you are formidable. So suddenly to rob your husband of his charmer's heart! you must have us'd some witchery.

Vict. Yes, powerful witchery—the knowledge of my sex. Oh! did the men but know us, as well as we do ourselves;—but thank fate they do not, 'twould be dangerous. 20

Oliv. What, I suppose, you prais'd her understanding, was captivated by her wit, and absolutely struck dumb by the amazing beauties of——*her mind.*

Vict. Oh, no,—that's the mode prescribed by the *Essayists* on the female heart—ha, ha, ha!—Not a woman breathing, from fifteen to fifty, but would rather have a compliment to the tip of her ear, or the turn of her ancle, than a volume in praise of her intellects.

Oliv. So flattery then, is your boasted pill? 30

Vict. No, that's only the occasional gilding; but 'tis in vain to attempt a description of what changed its nature with every moment. I was now attentive—now gay—then tender—then careless. I strove rather to convince her that *I was charming*, than that I myself was charm'd; and when I saw love's arrow quivering in her heart, instead of falling at her feet, sung a triumphant air, and remember'd a sudden engagement.

Oliv. (Archly). Would you have done so, had you been a man? 40

Vict. Assuredly—knowing what I now do as a woman.

Oliv. But can all this be worth while, merely to rival a fickle husband with one woman, whilst he is setting his feather, perhaps, at half a score others?

Vict. To rival him was not my first motive. The Portuguese robbed me of his heart; I concluded she had fascinations which nature had denied to me; it was impossible to visit her as a woman;[54] I, therefore, assumed the Cavalier to study her, that I might, if possible, be to my Carlos, all he found in her. 50

Oliv. Pretty humble creature!

Vict. In this adventure I learnt more than I expected;—my (oh cruel!) my husband has given this woman an estate, almost all that his dissipations had left us.

Oliv. Indeed!

Vict. To make him more culpable, it was my estate, it was that fortune which my lavish love had made his, without securing it to my children.[55] 60

Oliv. How could you be so improvident?

Vict. Alas! I trusted him with my heart, with my happiness, *without* restriction. Should I have shewn a greater solicitude for any thing, than for these? *(Weeps).*

---

53 *Cavaleiro*: a form of "cavalier," i.e., a gentleman trained to arms; a military gallant.

54 *impossible to visit her as a woman*: Because of Laura's unrespectable reputation she is considered unfit company for respectable women, which means that no respectable woman can visit her without injuring her own reputation.

55 *without securing it to my children*: Victoria could have made it a condition of the marriage contract that her estate be entailed to her children, making Don Carlos holder of the property but unable to sell it.

Oliv. The event proves that you should; but how can you be thus passive in your sorrow? since I had assum'd the man, I'd make him feel a man's resentment for such injuries. 70

Vict. Oh, Olivia! what resentment can I shew to him I have vow'd to honour, and whom, both my duty and my heart compel me yet to love?

Oliv. Why, really now, I think—positively, there's no thinking about it; 'tis among the arcana[56] of the married life, I suppose.

Vict. You, who know me, can judge how I suffered in prosecuting my plan. I have thrown off the delicacy of sex; I have worn the mask of love to the destroyer of my peace—but the object is too 80 great to be abandoned—nothing less than to save my husband from ruin, and to restore him, again a lover, to my faithful bosom.

Oliv. Well, I confess, Victoria, I hardly know whether most to blame or praise you; but, with the rest of the world, I suppose, your success will determine me.

(Enter Gasper).

Gasp. *(To Olivia).* Pray, Madam, are your wedding shoes ready?

Oliv. Insolence!....*(Apart to Victoria)* I can scarcely 90 ever keep up the vixen to this fellow.

Gasp. You'll want them, Ma'am, to morrow morning, that's all—so I came to prepare ye.

Oliv. *I* want wedding shoes to-morrow! if you are kept on water gruel 'till I marry, that plump face of yours will be chap-fall'n,[57] I believe.

Gasp. Yes, truly, I believe so too. Lackaday,[58] did you suppose I came to bring you news of your own wedding? no such glad tidings for you, lady, believe me.—You married! I am sure the man who ties 100 himself to you, ought to be half a salamander,[59] and able to live in fire.

Oliv. What marriage then is it, you do me the honour to inform me of?

Gasp. Why, your father's marriage. You'll have a mother-in-law to-morrow, and having, like a dutiful daughter, danced at the wedding, be immur'd in a convent for life.

Oliv. Immur'd in a convent! then I'll raise sedition in the sisterhood, depose the abbess, and turn the 110 confessor's chair to a go-cart.

Gasp. So the threat of the mother-in-law, which I thought would be worse than that of the abbess, does not frighten ye?

Oliv. No, because my father dares not give me one.— Marry, without my consent! no, no, he'll never think of it, depend on't; however, lest the fit should grow strong upon him, I'll go and administer my volatiles[60] to keep it under. *(Exit).*

Gasp. Administer 'em cautiously then—too strong a 120 dose of your volatiles would make the fit stubborn. Who'd think that pretty arch look belong'd to a termagant? what a pity! 'twould be worth a thousand ducats to cure her.

Vict. Has Inis told you I wanted to converse with you in private, Gasper?

Gasp. Oh, yes, madam, and I took particular notice that it was to be in private.—Sure, says I, Mrs. Inis, Madam Victoria has not taken a fancy to me, and is going to break her mind. 130

Vict. Whimsical! ha, ha! suppose I should, Gasper?

Gasp. Why, then, madam, I should say fortune had used you dev'lish scurvily, to give me a grey beard in a livery.[61] I know well enough that some young ladies have given themselves to grey beards in a gilded coach, and others have run away with a handsome youth in worsted lace;[62] they each had

---

56 *arcana*: hidden things; mysteries; profound secrets of Nature.

57 *chap-fall'n*: with the chap or lower jaw hanging down, as an effect of extreme debility or exhaustion.

58 *Lackaday*: a form of "alack-a-day," originally meaning "shame or reproach to the day."

59 *salamander*: a lizard-like reptile supposed to live in, or to be able to endure, fire.

60 *volatiles*: substances characterized by their strong changeability or fickleness. In this case, likely referring to volatile salts, defined by their tendency to change from solid to gaseous form quickly, as with smelling salts.

61 *livery*: a distinctive uniform worn by a person's servants so that they might be recognized as members of a specific household.

62 *worsted lace*: lace made from thread that has been well-twisted.

their apology; but if you run away with me—pardon me, madam, I could not stand the ridicule.

Vict. Oh, very well; but if you refuse to run away with me, will you do me another favour? 140

Gasp. Any thing you'll order, madam, except dancing a fandango.[63]

Vict. You have seen my rich old uncle in the country?

Gasp. What, Don Sancho, who, with two-thirds of a century in his face, affects the misdemeanors of youth; hides his baldness with amber locks, and complains of the tooth-ache, to make you believe that the two rows of ivory he carries in his head, grew there. 150

Vict. Oh, you know him, I find; could you assume his character for an hour, and make love for him?[64] You know it must be in the stile of King Roderigo the First.[65]

Gasp. Hang it! I am rather too near his own age; to appear an old man with effect, one should not be above twenty; 'tis always so on the stage.

Vict. Pho! you might pass for Juan's grandson.[66]

Gasp. Nay, if your ladyship condescends to flatter me, you have me. 160

Vict. Then follow me, for Don Caesar, I hear, is approaching—in the garden I'll make you acquainted with my plan, and impress on your mind every trait of my uncle's character. If you can hit him off, the arts of Laura shall be foil'd, and Carlos be again Victoria's. *(Exeunt. Enter Don Caesar, followed by Olivia).*

---

63 *fandango*: a lively, showy dance in ¾ time popular in Spain and Spanish America.

64 For an idea of how large cuts in performance can be, note that in the Larpent version the rest of this scene is replaced by the following line: "Follow me into the Garden & I'll impress every trait of my uncle's Character on your Mind. *(Exeunt)*"

65 *King Roderigo the First*: probably referring to Roderigo Díaz de Vivar (ca. 1043–1099), the Castilian military leader and national hero usually known by the name "El Cid," who conquered Valencia in 1094. While nominally holding Valencia for Alfonso VI of Castile, he was in fact an independent ruler in all but name.

66 *Juan's grandson*: most likely meaning the grandson of Don Juan, the fictitious libertine usually represented as a mature man possessing extremely seductive and sexually predatory qualities.

Caes. No, no, 'tis too late—no coaxings; I am resolv'd, I say.

Oliv. But it is not too late, and you shan't be resolv'd, I say. Indeed, now, I'll be upon my guard with the next Don—what's his name? not a trace of the Xantippe[67] left.—I'll study to be charming. 170

Caes. Nay, you need not study it, you are always charming enough, if you would but hold your tongue.

Oliv. Do you think so? then to the next lover I won't open my lips; I'll answer every thing he says with a smile, and if he asks me to have him, drop a court'sey of thankfulness. 180

Caes. Pshaw! that's too much t'other way; you're always either above the mark or below it; you must talk, but talk with good humour. Can't you look gently and prettily, now, as I do? and say, "*yes, Sir, and no, Sir; and 'tis very fine weather, Sir; and pray, Sir, were you at the ball last night? and I caught a sad cold the other evening; and, bless me! I hear Lucinda has run away with her footman, and Don Philip has married his housemaid.*"——That's the way agreeable ladies talk, you never hear any thing else. 190

Oliv. Very true; and you shall see me as agreeable as the best of 'em, if you won't give me a mother-in-law to snub me, and set me tasks, and to take up all the fine apartments, and send up your poor little Livy to lodge next the stars.

Caes. Ha,——if thou wert but always thus soft and good-humour'd, no mother-in-law in Spain, though she brought the Castiles for her portion,[68] should have power to snub thee. But, Livy, the trial's at hand, for at this moment do I expect Don Vincentio to visit you. He is but just returned from England, and, probably, has yet heard only of your beauty and fortune; I hope it is not from you he will learn the other part of your character. 200

Oliv. This moment expect him! two new lovers in a day?

---

67 *Xantippe*: Xanthippe, wife of Socrates, represented in the writings of Xenophon as possessing a fierce temper.

68 *brought the Castiles for her portion*: i.e., brought the area of Castile as her dowry.

Caes. Beginning already, as I hope to live; aye, I see 'tis in vain; I'll send him an excuse, and marry Marcella before night. 210

Oliv. Oh, no! upon my obedience, I promise to be just the soft civil creature you have described.

(Enter Servant).

Servant. Don Vincentio is below, Sir.

Caes. I'll wait upon him——well, go and collect all your smiles and your simpers, and remember all I have said to you;——be gentle, and talk pretty little small talk, d'ye hear, and if you please him, you shall have the portion of a Dutch burgo-master's[69] daughter, and the pin-money of a princess, you jade[70] you. *(Aside)* I think at last I 220 have done it; the fear of this mother-in-law will keep down the fiend in her, if any thing can. *(Exit).*

Oliv. Hah! my poor father, your anxieties will never end 'till you bring Don Julio:——Command me to sacrifice my *petulence*, my *liberty* to him, and Iphigenia[71] herself, could not be more obedient. But what shall I do with this Vincentio?—I fear he is so perfectly harmoniz'd, that to put him in an ill temper will be impracticable.—I must try, however; if 'tis possible to find a discord in him, 230 I'll touch the string. *(Exit).*

Scene III: *Another Apartment.*
Enter Vincentio and Caesar.

Vincentio. Presto,[72] presto, Signor! where is the Olivia?—not a moment to spare. I left off in all the fury of composition; minums and crotchets have been battling it through my head the whole day, and trying a semibreve[73] in G sharp, has made me as flat as double F.

Caes. Sharp and flat!—trying a semibreve!—oh—gad, Sir! I had like not to have understood you; but a semibreve is something of a demi-culverin,[74] I take it; and you have been practising the art military. 10

Vin. Art military!—what, Sir! are you unacquainted with music?

Caes. Music! oh I ask pardon; then you are fond of music——*(Aside)* 'ware of discords.

Vin. Fond of it! devoted to it.—I compos'd a thing to-day in all the gusto of *Sachini*[75] and the sweetness of *Gluck*.[76] But this recreant finger fails me in composing a passage in E, octave: if it does not gain more elastic vigour in a week, I shall be tempted to have it amputated, and supply the 20 shake[77] with a spring.

Caes. Mercy! amputate a finger to supply a shake!

---

69 *burgomaster*: the chief magistrate of a Dutch or Flemish town.

70 *jade*: a term of reprobation applied to a woman; like "hussy" and "minx," it can be used ironically or affectionately.

71 *Iphigenia*: in Greek mythology, the eldest daughter of Agamemnon, king of Mycenae, and his wife Clytemnestra. Her father had to sacrifice her to the goddess Artemis in order to end the contrary winds that detained the Achaean fleet at Aulis and kept it from sailing to Troy. She is a key figure in the *Agamemnon* of Aeschylus, the *Electra* of Sophocles, and the two plays of Euripides that bear her name. She often figures as a symbol of sacrificed innocence.

72 *Presto*: quickly.

73 *minums and crotchets … a semibreve*: "Minums" are an obscure form of "minims," which are musical notes of a duration that is one-quarter the value of a breve, one-half the value of a semibreve, and double the value of a crotchet. Cowley plays upon the jargony nature of this word and the other technical terms used by Don Vincentio.

74 *demi-culverin*: a kind of cannon of about four and one-half inches bore.

75 *Sachini*: Antonio Maria Gaspare Sacchini (1734–86), Italian composer who produced several popular operas in Rome between 1762 and 1769 before receiving even greater acclaim in Venice. He came to London in 1772 and achieved brilliant success with four new operas: *Tamerlano*, *Lucio Vero*, *Nitetti e Perseo*, and *Il Gran Cid*. He later achieved a similar coup at Paris in 1783, where his *Rinaldo* was produced for Marie Antoinette. Sacchini's style is characterized by its liveliness rather than its elegance.

76 *Gluck*: Christoph Willibald Gluck (1714–87), German classical composer working in France best known for his operas, which include *Orfeo ed Euridyce* (1762), *Alceste* (1767), *Paride ed Elena* (1770), *Iphigénie en Aulide* (1774), and *Iphigénie en Tauride* (1779).

77 *shake*: a trill, a rapid alteration of two notes a degree apart.

Vin. Oh, that's a trifle in the road to reputation—to be talk'd of is the *summum bonum*[78] of this life.——A young man of rank shou'd not glide through the world without a distinguish'd rage,[79] or, as they call it in England——a hobby horse![80]

Caes. A hobby horse!

Vin. Yes; that is, every man of figure determines on setting out in life, in that land of liberty, in what line to ruin himself; and that choice is called his *hobby horse.* One, makes the turf[81] his scene of action—another drives about tall phaetons[82] to peep into their neighbour's garret windows; and a third rides his hobby horse in parliament, where it jerks him sometimes on one side, and sometimes on the other; sometimes in, and sometimes out, 'till at length he is jerk'd out of his honesty, and his constituents out of their freedom.

Caes. Aye!——Well, 'tis a wonder that with such sort of hobby horses as these they should still outride all the world to the goal of glory. I wish we had a few of 'em to jerk Spain into some consideration.

Vin. This is all *cantabile*;[83] nothing to do with the subject of the piece, which is Donna Olivia;—pray give me the key note to her heart.

Caes. Upon my word, Signor—to speak in your own phrase—I believe that note has never yet been sounded.—Ah! here she comes! look at her.——Isn't she a charming girl?

Vin. Touching! Musical I'll be sworn! her very air is harmonious!

Caes. (Aside). I wish thou may'st find her tongue so.

(Enter Olivia, court'seys profoundly to each).

Daughter, receive Don Vincentio——his rank, fortune and merit, entitle him to the heiress of a grandee;[84] but he is contented to become my son-in-law, if you can please him.

(Olivia court'seys again).

Vin. Please me! she entrances me! Her presence thrills me like a cadenza[85] of Pachierotti's,[86] and every nerve vibrates to the music of her looks.

> Her step *andante*[87] gently moves,
>   *Pianos*[88] glance from either eye;
> Oh how *largetto*[89] is the heart,
>   That charms so *forté*[90] can defy!

Donna Olivia, will you be contented to receive me as a lover?

Oliv. Yes, Sir——No, Sir.

Vin. Yes, Sir; no, Sir! bewitching timidity!

Caes. Yes, Sir, she's remarkably timid.——*(Aside)* She's in the right cue, I see.

Vin. 'Tis clear you have never travell'd——I shall be delighted to shew you England.—You will there see how entirely timidity is banish'd in the sex. You must affect a mark'd character, and maintain it at all hazards.

Oliv. 'Tis a very fine day, Sir.

Vin. Madam!

Oliv. I caught a sad cold the other evening.—Pray was you at the ball last night?

Vin. What ball, fair lady?

Oliv. Bless me! they say Lucinda has run away with her footman, and Don Philip has married his house-maid.——*(Apart to Caesar)* Now am I not very agreeable?

Caes. Oh, such perverse obedience!

---

78 *summum bonum*: the supreme good.

79 *rage*: an enthusiasm; an object for which one has a passion or enthusiasm.

80 *hobby horse*: a favorite pursuit or pastime, often taking on an obsessive quality.

81 *turf*: i.e., horseracing.

82 *phaetons*: a species of four-wheeled open carriage of light construction.

83 *cantabile*: a piece of music in a smooth flowing style.

84 *grandee*: a Spanish or Portuguese nobleman of high rank.

85 *cadenza*: a flourish of indefinite form given to a solo voice or instrument at the close of a movement or between two divisions of a movement.

86 *Pachierotti*: Gasparo Pachiarotti (1740–1821), Italian singer who, after an extremely successful career in the major cities of Italy, debuted in London in Metastasio's *Artaserse* in 1779 and who developed a warm relationship with Charles and Frances Burney. His last London performance was in *Idalide* at the Pantheon on 16 July 1791; he retired the following year and settled in Padua.

87 *andante*: in a musical movement, moderately slow and distinct.

88 *Pianos*: soft or quiet passages of music.

89 *largetto*: a variant of "larghetto"; in a musical movement, meaning fairly slow in time.

90 *forté*: in music, strong or robust.

Vin. Really, Madam, I have not the honour to know Don Philip and Lucinda——nor am I happy enough entirely to comprehend you.

Oliv. No! I only meant to be agreeable——but perhaps you have no taste for pretty little small talk? 90

Vin. Pretty little small talk!

Oliv. A *mark'd* character you admire; so do I; I doat on it.——I wou'd not resemble the rest of the world in any thing.

Vin. *My* taste to the fiftieth part of a crotchet!—— We shall agree admirably when we are married.

Oliv. And *that* will be unlike the rest of the world, and therefore charming.

Caes. (Aside). It will do! I have hit her humour at last——Why didn't this young dog offer himself before? 100

Oliv. I believe I have the honour to carry my taste that way farther than you, Don Vincentio. Pray now, what is your usual stile in living?

Vin. My winters I spend in Madrid, as other people do. My summers I drawl[91] through at my castle—

Oliv. As other people do!——and yet you pretend to taste and singularity, ha! ha! ha! Good Don Vincentio, never talk of a *mark'd* character again.—— 110 ——Go into the country in July to smell roses and woodbines, when *every body* regales on their fragrance! Now I wou'd rusticate only in winter, and my bleak castle shou'd be decorated with verdure and flowers, amidst the soft zephyrs[92] of December.

Caes. (Aside). Oh, she'll go too far!

Oliv. On the leafless trees I wou'd hang green branches—the labour of silk worms, and therefore *natural*; whilst my rose shrubs and myrtles shou'd be scented by the first perfumers in Italy—— 120 *Unnatural* indeed, but therefore singular and striking.

Vin. Oh, charming!—You beat me where I thought myself the strongest.——Wou'd they but establish newspapers here, to paragraph our singularities, we shou'd be the most envied couple in Spain.

Caes. (Aside). By St. Anthony, he is as mad as she is.

Vin. What say you, Don Caesar? Olivia and her winter garden, and I and my music. 130

Oliv. Music, did you say! Music! I am passionately fond of that!

Caes. (Aside). She has sav'd my life——I thought she was going to knock down his hobby horse.

Vin. You enchant me! I have the finest band in Madrid—My first violin draws a longer bow than Giardini;[93] my clarinets, my viol de gamba—— Oh you shall have such concerts!

Oliv. Concerts! Pardon me there——My passion is a single instrument. 140

Vin. That's carrying singularity very far indeed! I love a crash;[94] so does every body of taste.

Oliv. But my taste isn't like *every body's*—my nerves are so particularly fine, that more than one instrument overpowers them.

Vin. Pray tell me the name of that one: I am sure it must be the most elegant and captivating in the world.—I am impatient to know it.—We'll have no other instrument in Spain, and I will study to become its master, that I may woo you with its 150 music. Charming Olivia! tell me, is it a harpsichord?[95] a piano forte? a pentachord?[96] a harp?

---

91 *drawl*: move slowly or loiteringly.
92 *zephyrs*: usually a soft mild gentle wind or breeze; Olivia uses the word here with irony.
93 *Giardini*: Felice de Giardini (1716–96), Italian violinist, composer, and conductor, who established himself in London as a performer in 1751 and who held subscription concerts on Dean Street in Soho for over thirty years. He was painted by both Thomas Gainsborough and Joshua Reynolds and wrote several operas—among them *Rosmira* (1757), *Siroe* (1763), *Enea e Lavinia* (1764), and *Il re pastore* (1765)—as well as the music for William Mason's *Sappho* (1778) and *Elfrida* (1779).
94 *crash*: in music, the loud or sudden sound of violent percussion, usually united with other instruments.
95 *harpsichord*: a keyboard instrument resembling a grand piano especially popular from the sixteenth through the eighteenth centuries, in which the strings are plucked rather than struck by quills or leather jacks connected by levers to the keys.
96 *pentachord*: any musical instrument with five strings; various versions of the instrument were popular in mid-eighteenth-century London.

Oliv. You have it—you have it——a harp—yes, a Jew's harp,[97] is to me the only instrument.——Are you not charm'd with the delightful h—u—m of its base! running on the ear like the distant rumble of a state coach? It presents the idea of vastness and importance to the mind. The moment you are its master—I'll give you my hand.   160

Vin. Da capo, Madam, da capo![98] a *Jew's harp!!*

Oliv. Bless me, Sir, don't I tell you so? Violins chill me—clarinets by sympathy hurt my lungs; and, instead of maintaining a band under my roof, I wou'd not keep a servant who knew a bassoon from a flute, or could tell whether he heard a jigg[99] or a canzonetta.[100]

Caes. *(In great agitation).* Oh thou perverse one; you know you love concerts—you know you do!

Oliv. I detest 'em! It's vulgar custom that attaches   170 people to the sound of fifty different instruments at once; 'twould be as well to talk on the same subject in fifty different tongues. A band! 'tis a mere olio[101] of sound; I'd rather listen to a three-string'd guittar, serenading a sempstress in some neighbouring garret.

Caes. Oh you!——Don Vincentio, this is nothing but perverseness—wicked perverseness.—Hussey!—didn't you shake when you mention'd a garret? didn't bread and water and a step-mother   180 come into your head at the same time?

Vin. Piano,[102] piano, good Sir! Spare yourself all farther trouble. Should the Princess of Guzzarat,[103] and all her diamond mines, offer themselves, I wou'd not accept them in lieu of my band—a band that has half ruined me to collect.—I wou'd have allowed Donna Olivia a blooming garden in winter; I wou'd even have procur'd barrenness and snow for her in the dog-days;—but—to have my band insulted!—to have my knowledge in music   190 slighted!—to be rous'd from all the energies of composition by the drone of a Jew's harp! I cannot breathe under the idea.

Caes. Then—then you refuse her, Sir?

Vin. I cannot use so harsh a word—I *take my leave* of the lady—Adieu, Madam——I leave you to enjoy your solos, whilst I fly to the raptures of a crash. *(Exit).*

(Caesar goes up to her and looks her in the face; then goes off without speaking).

Oliv. Mercy! that silent anger is terrifying—I read a young mother-in-law, and an old lady abbess, in   200 every line of his face.

(Enter Victoria).

Oliv. Well, you heard the whole, I suppose—heard poor unhappy me scorn'd and rejected.

Vict. I heard you in imminent danger; and expected Signor Da Capo wou'd have snapp'd you up, in spite of caprice and extravagance.

Oliv. Oh they charm'd instead of scaring him.——I soon found that my only chance was to fall across *his* caprice.—Where is the philosopher who cou'd withstand that?   210

Vict. But what, my good cousin, does all this tend to?

Oliv. I dare say you can guess.—Penelope had never cheated her lovers with a never-ending web, had she not had an Ulysses.[104]

---

97 *Jew's harp*: a musical instrument of simple construction, consisting of an elastic steel tongue fixed at one end to a small lyre-shaped frame of brass or iron. It is played by holding the frame between the teeth and striking the free end of the tongue with the finger; variations in tone are produced by altering the size and shape of the cavity of the mouth.

98 *Da capo, Madam, da capo!*: literally, "from the beginning." Used often by the conductors of orchestras in rehearsals, the phrase here translates as "[Repeat yourself] from the beginning, Madam, from the beginning!"

99 *jigg*: usually "jig," referring to the music for a lively sprightly dance, or to the dance itself.

100 *canzonetta*: a little or short song of a light and airy character, usually with a vocal solo.

101 *olio*: hodgepodge; a mixture of heterogeneous things.

102 *Piano*: "softly" or "gently."

103 *Guzzarat*: referring to Gujarat, a northwest Indian state. English spellings of Indian words often substitute "zz" for the letter "j."

104 *Penelope had never...an Ulysses*: referring to Penelope, daughter of Icarius and Periboea and wife of Odysseus (here "Ulysses"). In Homer's *Odyssey*, Penelope is besieged by suitors during her husband's long absence after the Trojan war; she insists that they wait for her decision until she weaves a shroud for Laertes, father of Odysseus. For three years she undoes at night the work that she has woven by day in an effort to delay her decision.

Vict. An Ulysses! what are you then married?

Oliv. O, no, not yet!—but, believe me, my design is not to lead apes;[105] nor is my heart an icicle.——If you choose to know more, put on your veil, and slip with me through the garden to the Prado.

Vict. I can't indeed.—I am this moment going to dress *en homme*,[106] to visit the impatient Portuguese.

Oliv. Send an excuse—for positively you go with me. Heaven and earth! I am going to meet *a man!*—whom I have been fool enough to dream and think of these two years, and I don't know that ever he thought of me in his life.

Vict. Two years discovering that?

Oliv. He has been abroad. The only time I ever saw him was at the Duchess of Medina's—there were a thousand people; and he was so elegant, so careless, so handsome!—In a word, though he set off for France the next morning, by some witchcraft or other, he has been before my eyes ever since.

Vict. Was the impression mutual?

Oliv. He hardly notic'd me—I was then a bashful thing, just out of a convent, and shrunk from observation.

Vict. Why, I thought you were going to meet him?

Oliv. To be sure——I sent him a command this morning to be at the Prado. I am determined to find out if his heart is engaged, and if it is——

Vict. You'll cross your arms, and crown your brow with willows.[107]

Oliv. No, positively, not whilst we have myrtles.[108]—I wou'd prefer Julio, 'tis true, to all his sex; but if he is stupid enough to be insensible to me, I shan't

for that reason pine like a girl, on chalk and oatmeal.——No, no; in that case, I shall form a new plan, and treat my future lovers with more civility.

Vict. You are the only woman in love, I ever heard talk reasonably.

Oliv. Well, prepare for the Prado, and I'll give you a lesson against your days of widowhood. Don't you wish *this* the moment, Victoria? A pretty widow at four-and-twenty has more subjects and a wider empire than the first monarch upon earth.—I long to see you in your weeds.

Vict. Never may you see them! Oh, Olivia!—my happiness, my life, depend on my husband. The fond hope of still being united to him, gives me spirits in my affliction, and enables me to support even the period of his neglect, with patience. *(Exeunt).*

Act III

Scene I: *A long street. Julio enters from a Garden Gate with precipitation; a Servant within fastens the Gate.*

Jul. Yes, yes, bar the gate fast, Cerberus,[109] lest some other curious traveller should stumble on your confines.—If ever I am so caught again——*(Garcia enters, going hastily across, Julio seizes him).* Don Garcia, never make love to a woman in a veil.

Garc. Why so, prithee? Veils and secrecy are the chief ingredients in a Spanish amour; but in two years, Julio, thou art grown absolutely French.

Jul. That may be; but if ever I trust to a veil again, may no lovely, blooming beauty ever trust me.—Why dost know I have been an hour at the feet of a creature whose first birth-day must have been kept the latter end of the last century, and whose trembling, weak voice, I mistook for the timid cadence of bashful fifteen!

Garc. Ha, ha, ha!—What a happiness to have seen thee in thy raptures, petitioning for half a glance only, of the charms the envious veil conceal'd.

---

105 *to lead apes*: a contracted version of the phrase "lead apes into hell," a traditional punishment for dying unwed. See William Shakespeare, *Much Ado about Nothing* II.i.41.

106 *en homme*: in men's clothes.

107 *crown your brow with willows*: characterized by its drooping and pliant branches, the willow often functions as a symbol of grief for unrequited love or for the loss of a mate.

108 *myrtles*: a plant commonly found in Southern Europe, having shiny evergreen leaves and white sweet-scented flowers used in perfumery. The myrtle was held sacred to Venus and often is invoked as an emblem of love.

---

109 *Cerberus*: in Greek and Latin mythology, the name given to the watchdog guarding the entrance to the Underworld.

Jul. Yes; and when she unveil'd her Gothic[110] countenance, to render the thing compleatly ridiculous, she began moralizing; and positively would not let me out of the snare, 'till I had persuaded her she had work'd a conversion, and that I'd never make love—but in an *honest* way again.

Garc. Oh, that honest way of love-making is delightful, to be sure. I had a dose of it this morning; but happily the ladies have not yet learnt to veil their tempers, though they have their faces.

(Enter Vincentio).

Vin. Julio! Garcia! congratulate me!——Such an escape!

Jul. What have you escap'd?

Vin. Matrimony.

Garc. Nay, then our congratulations may be mutual.—I have had a matrimonial escape too, this very day. I was almost on the brink of the ceremony with the veriest Xantippe!

Vin. Oh, that was not my case—mine was a sweet creature, all elegance, all life.

Jul. Then where's the cause of congratulation?

Vin. Cause—why she's ignorant of music! prefers a jig to a canzonetta, and a Jew's harp to a pentachord.

Jul. Jew's harp!—Pho, prithee.

Garc. Had my nymph no other fault, I would pardon that, for she was lovely and rich.

Vin. Mine too was lovely and rich, and, I'll be sworn as ignorant of scolding as of the gama;[111]—but not to know music!—

Jul. Gentle, lovely, and rich—and ignorant *only* of music?

Garc. A venial crime indeed! if the sweet creature will marry me, she shall carry a Jew's harp always in her train, as a Scotch laird[112] does his bagpipes. I wish you'd give me your interest.

Vin. Oh, most willingly, if thou hast so gross an inclination;—I'll name thee as a dull-soul'd, *largo*[113] fellow, to her father, Don Caesar.

Garc. Caesar! what Don Caesar?

Vin. De Zuniga.

Garc. Impossible!

Vin. Oh, I'll answer for her mother. So much is De Zuniga her father, that he does not know a semibreve from a culverin.

Garc. The name of the lady?

Vin. Olivia.

Garc. Why you must be mad—that's my termagant.

Vin. Termagant!—ha! ha! ha! Thou hast certainly some vixen of a mistress, who infects thy ears towards the whole sex. Olivia is timid and elegant.

Garc. By Juno,[114] there never existed such a scold.

Vin. By Orpheus,[115] there never was a gayer temper'd creature—Spirit enough to be charming, that's all. If she lov'd harmony, I'd marry her to morrow.

Jul. Ha, ha! what a ridiculous jangle![116] 'Tis evident you speak of two different women.

Garc. I speak of Donna Olivia, heiress to Don Caesar de Zuniga.

Vin. I speak of the heiress of Don Caesar de Zuniga, who is called Donna Olivia.

Garc. Sir, I perceive you mean to insult me.

Vin. Your perceptions are very rapid, Sir—but if you chuse to think so, I'll settle that point with you immediately—But, for fear of consequences, I'll fly home, and add the last bar to my concerto, and then meet you where you please.

Jul. Pho! this is evidently misapprehension.—To clear the matter up, I'll visit the lady—if you'll introduce me, Vincentio;—but you shall both promise to be govern'd in this dispute by my decision.

Vin. I'll introduce you with joy, if you'll try to

---

110 *Gothic*: Usually meaning "medieval," "of the Goths," or describing a style of architecture, the word here playfully connotes the attributes of a Gothic ruin—i.e., weathered, crumbling, ancient, etc.

111 *gama*: in music, the gamut, i.e., the entire scale of recognized notes used by musicians.

112 *laird*: a landed proprietor; in ancient times limited to those who held land immediately from the king.

113 *largo*: in music, a term indicating that a passage is to be rendered in slow time and with a broad, dignified treatment.

114 *Juno*: in Latin mythology the wife of Jupiter; the goddess of marriage and childbirth.

115 *Orpheus*: in Greek mythology, the famous musician and singer of Thrace, who was said to move rocks and trees by the strains of his lyre.

116 *jangle*: discordant disagreement, contention, or bickering.

persuade her of the necessity of music, and the charms of harmony. 90

Garc. Yes, she needs that——You'll find her all jar and discord.

Jul. Come, no more Garcia—thou art but a sort of a male vixen thyself.—Melodious Vincentio, when shall I expect you?

Vin. This evening.

Jul. Not this evening; I have engag'd to meet a goldfinch in a grove, then *I* shall have music, you rogue! 100

Vin. It won't sing at night.

Jul. Then I'll talk to it till the morning, and hear it pour out its matins[117] to the rising sun.——Call on me to-morrow, I'll then attend you to Donna Olivia, and declare faithfully the impression her character makes on me.—Come, Garcia, I must not leave you together, lest his crotchets and your minums, should fall into a crash of discords. *(Exeunt opposite sides).*

Scene II: *The Prado. Enter Carlos.*

Car. All hail to the powers of Burgundy! Three flasks to my own share.—What sorrows can stand against three flasks of Burgundy? I was a damn'd melancholy fellow this morning, going to shoot myself to get rid of my troubles.—Where are my troubles now? Gone to the moon to look for my wits; and there, I hope, they'll remain together, if one cannot come back without t'other.—But where is this indolent dog, Julio? *He* fit to receive appointments from ladies! Sure I have not miss'd the hour——No—but 10 seven yet—*(Looking at his watch)*——Seven's the hour, by all the joys of Burgundy! The rogue must be here——let's reconnoitre.[118]

(Enter Victoria and Olivia, veil'd, from the top).

Oliv. Positively, mine's a pretty spark, to let me be first at the place of appointment. I have half resolv'd to go home again to punish him.

Vict. I'll answer for its being but *half* a resolution— to make it entire would be to punish yourself.— —There's a solitary man—Is not that he?

Oliv. I think not.——If he'd please to turn his face 20 this way—

Vict. That's impossible, while the loadstone[119] is the other way.——He is looking at the woman in the next walk. Can't you disturb him?

Oliv. (Screams) Oh! a frightful frog!

(Carlos turns).

Vict. Heav'ns, 'tis my husband.

Oliv. Your husband! Is that Don Carlos?

Vict. It is indeed.

Oliv. Why really, now I see the man, I don't wonder that you are in no hurry for your weeds.——He 30 is moving towards us.

Vict. I cannot speak to him, and yet my soul flies to meet him.

Car. Pray, lady, what occasioned that pretty scream? I shrewdly suspect it was a trap.

Oliv. A trap! Ha! ha! ha!—a trap *for you!*

Car. Why not, Madam?—Zounds, a man six feet high, and three flasks of Burgundy in his head, is worth laying a trap for.

Oliv. Yes, unless he happens to be trapp'd before.—'Tis 40 about two years since you was caught, I take it—— Do keep farther off!——Odious! a *married* man!

Car. The devil! Is it posted under every saint in the street, that I am a married man?

Oliv. No, you carry the marks about you; that rueful phiz[120] could never belong to a batchelor.—— Besides, there's an odd appearance on your temples—does your hat fit easily?

Car. By all the thorns of matrimony, if——

Oliv. Poor man! how natural to swear by what one 50 feels—but why were you in such haste to gather the thorns of matrimony? Bless us! had you but look'd about you a little, what a market might have been made of that fine, proper promising person of yours——

Car. Confound thee, confound thee! If thou art a wife, may thy husband plague thee with jealousies,

---

117 *matins*: morning songs, usually of a holy nature. In the Catholic religion, referring to the early morning service preceding the first mass on Sunday.

118 *reconnoitre*: to conduct a military-style inspection, survey, or reconnaissance.

119 *loadstone*: also "lodestone," a piece of iron oxide used as a magnet; something that attracts.

120 *phiz*: face; countenance.

and thou never be able to give him cause for them; and if thou art a maid, may'st thou be an *old* one! *(Going, meets Julio)*. Oh, Julio, look not that way; there's a tongue will stun thee. 60

Jul. Heav'n be prais'd! I love female prattle. A woman's tongue can never scare me.—Which of these two goldfinches makes the music?

Car. Oh, this is as silent as a turtle—*(Taking Victoria's hand)*—only coos now and then.—Perhaps *you* don't hate a married man, sweet one?

Vict. You guess right; *I* love a married man.

Car. Hah, say'st thou so! wilt thou love me?

Vict. Will you let me? 70

Car. Let thee, my charmer! how I'll cherish thee for't.—What would I not give for thy heart!

Vict. I demand a price that, perhaps, you cannot give—I ask unbounded love; but you have a wife.

Car. And, therefore, the readier to love every other woman;—'tis in your favour child.

Vict. Will you love me ever?

Car. Ever! yes ever, 'till we find each other dull company, and yawn, and talk of our neighbours for amusement. 80

Vict. Farewell! I suspected you to be a bad chapman,[121] and that you would not reach my terms. *(Going)*.

Car. Nay, I'll come to your terms if I can;—but move this way;—I am fearful of that wood-pecker at your elbow—should she begin again, her noise will scare all the pretty loves that are playing about my heart. Don't turn your head towards them; if you like to listen to love tales, you'll meet fond pairs enough in this walk. *(Forcing her gently off)*.

Jul. I really believe, though you deny it, that you are my destiny—that is, you *fated* me hither.—See, is not this your mandate? *(Taking a letter from his pocket)*. 90

Oliv. Oh, delightful! the scrawl of some chambermaid, or, perhaps, of your valet to give you an air—what is it signed? Marriatornes? Tomasa? Sancha?

Jul. Nay, now I am convinced the letter is yours, since you abuse it; so you may as well confess.

Oliv. Suppose I should, you can't be sure that I do not deceive you. 100

Jul. True; but there is one point in which I have made a vow not to be deceived; therefore, the preliminary is, that you throw off your veil.

Oliv. My veil!

Jul. Positively! if you reject this article, our negociation ends.

Oliv. You have no right to offer articles, unless you own yourself conquered.

Jul. I own myself willing to be conquer'd, and have, therefore, a right to make the best terms I can.— Do you accede to the demand? 110

Oliv. Certainly not.

Jul. You had better.

Oliv. I protest I will not.

Jul. (Aside). My life upon't I make you. Why, madam, how absurd this is—'tis reducing us to the situation of Pyramus and Thisbe,[122] talking through a wall;—yet 'tis of no consequence, for I know your features, as well as though I saw 'em.

Oliv. How can that be? 120

Jul. I judge of what you hide, by what I see—I could draw your picture.

Oliv. Charming! pray begin the portrait.

Jul. Imprimis,[123] a broad high forehead, rounded at the top, like an old-fashion'd gateway.

Oliv. Oh, horrid!

Jul. Little grey eyes, a sharp nose, and hair, the colour of rusty prunella.[124]

---

121 *chapman*: a person whose business is buying and selling; a trader, dealer or merchant.

122 *Pyramus and Thisbe*: the hero and heroine of a Babylonian love story related by Ovid in his *Metamorphosis*, in which the lovers, barred from marrying by their parents, converse through a chink in the wall separating their houses and resolve to meet under a mulberry tree and run away together. Thisbe, arriving there first, flees at the sound of a lioness, dropping her handkerchief, which the lioness proceeds to tear to shred with jaws recently stained by the blood of an ox. These fragments are in turn found by Pyramus, who stabs himself; Thisbe, returning moments later to find her lover mortally wounded, stabs herself as well.

123 *Imprimis*: in the first place; a word used to introduce a number of items.

124 *prunella*: either referring to the dark-colored material used in the seventeenth and eighteenth centuries for the gowns of graduates and clergymen, or else a variant of "prunello," the name for the finest variety of prune.

Oliv. Odious!

Jul. Pale cheeks, thin lips, and—— 130

Oliv. Hold, hold, thou villifier. *(Throws off her veil, he sinks on one knee).* There! yes, kneel in contrition for your malicious libel.

Jul. Say rather, in adoration.—What a charming creature!

Oliv. So, now for lies on the other side.

Jul. A forehead form'd by the Graces; hair, which Cupid would steal for his bow strings, were he not engag'd in shooting through those sparkling hazel circlets, which nature has given you for eyes; lips! 140 that 'twere a sin to call so—they are fresh gather'd rose leaves, with the fragrant morning dew, still hanging on their rounded surface.

Oliv. Is that extemporaneous, or ready cut, for every woman who takes off her veil to you?

Jul. I believe 'tis *not* extemporaneous, for nature, when she finish'd you, form'd the sentiment in my heart, and there it has been hid, till you, for *whom* it was form'd, called it into words.

Oliv. Suppose I should understand, from all this, that 150 you have a mind to be in love with me; wouldn't you be finely caught?

Jul. Charmingly caught! if you'll let me understand, at the same time, that you have a mind to be in love with me.

Oliv. In love with a man! heavens! I never lov'd any thing but a squirrel!

Jul. Make me your squirrel—I'll put on your chain, and gambol and play for ever at your side.

Oliv. But suppose you should have a mind to break 160 the chain?

Jul. Then loosen it; for, if once that humour seizes me, restraint won't cure it.—Let me spring and bound at liberty, and when I return to my lovely mistress, tired of all but her, fasten me again to your girdle, and kiss me while you chide.

Oliv. Your servant—to encourage you to leave me again.

Jul. No, to make *returning* to you, the strongest attraction of my life.—Why are you silent? 170

Oliv. I am debating whether to be pleased or displeased at what you have said.

Jul. Well?

Oliv. You shall know when I have determined. My friend and yours are approaching this way, and they must not be interrupted.

Jul. 'Twou'd be barbarous—we'll retire as far off as you please.

Oliv. But we retire separately, Sir,—that lady is a woman of honour, and this moment of the highest 180 importance to her. You may, however, conduct me to the gate, on condition that you leave me instantly.

Jul. Leave her instantly—oh, then I know my cue. *(Exit together at top).*

(Enter Carlos, followed by Victoria, unveiled).

Car. (Looking back on her). My wife!

Vict. Oh, heavens! I will veil myself again. I will hide my face for ever from you, if you will still feast my ears with those soft vows, which a moment since you poured forth so eagerly.

Car. My wife!—making love to my own wife! 190

Vict. Why should one of the dearest moments of my life, be to you so displeasing?

Car. So, I am caught in this snare, by way of *agreeable* surprize, I suppose.

Vict. Wou'd you cou'd think it so.

Car. No, madam! by heav'n 'tis a surprize fatal to every hope with which you may have flattered yourself.—What am I to be followed, haunted, watched?

Vict. Not to upbraid you.—I follow'd you, because 200 my castle without you seem'd a dreary desart.— Indeed, I will never upbraid you.

Car. Generous assurance!—never upbraid me—no by heavens, I'll take care you never shall.—*(Aside)* She has touch'd my soul, but I dare not yield to the impression.—Her softness is worse than death to me.

Vict. Would I could find words to please you!

Car. You cannot; therefore leave me, or suffer me to go without attempting to follow me. 210

Vict. Is it possible you can be so barbarous?

Car. Do not expostulate; your first vow'd duty is obedience—that word so grating to your sex.

Vict. To me it was never grating—to obey you has been my joy; even now I will not dispute your will, though I feel, for the first time, obedience hateful. *(Going, and then turning back).* Oh, Carlos! my dear Carlos! I go, but my soul remains with you. *(Exit).*

Car. Oh, horrible! had I not taken this harsh measure, 220
I must have kill'd myself, for how could I tell her
that I have made her a beggar? better she should
hate, detest me! than that my tenderness should
give her a prospect of felicity, which now she can
never taste.——Oh, wine-created spirit! Where art
thou now? Madness, return to me again; for reason
presents me nothing but despair.

(Enter Julio, from the top).

Jul. Carlos, who the devil can they be? my charming
little witch was inflexible.——I hope yours has
been more communicative. 230

Car. Folly!—Nonsense! *(Exit).*

Jul. Folly!—Nonsense! What, a pretty woman's smile!
ha, ha, ha! upon my soul it has more persuasion,
and, consequently, more reason, than a logical disquisition—but these married fellows have neither
taste nor joy.—Humph—suppose my fair one
should want to debase me into such an animal;—
she can't have so much villainy in her disposition:
and yet, if she should? pho! it won't bear thinking
about.—If I do so mad a thing, it must be as cow- 240
ards fight, without daring to reflect on the danger.

Scene III: *An apartment in the House of Don Vasquez,*
Marcella's Father. Enter Caesar and Vasquez.

Caes. Well, Don Vasquez, and a——you——then I
say, you have a mind that I should marry your
daughter?

Vasquez. It is sufficient, Signor, that you have signified
to us your intention—my daughter shall prove her
gratitude, in her attention to your felicity.

Caes. (Aside). Egad! now it comes to the push! hem,
hem!—but just nineteen, you say.

Vasq. Exactly, the eleventh of last month.

Caes. Pity it was not twenty. 10

Vasq. Why a year can make no difference, I should
think.

Caes. O, yes it does; a year's a great deal;—they are
so skittish at nineteen.

Vasq. Those who are skittish at nineteen, I fear, you
won't find much mended at twenty. Marcella is
very grave, and a pretty little, plump, fair——

Caes. Aye, fair, again! pity she isn't brown or olive—
I like your olives.

Vasq. Brown and olive! you are very whimsical, my 20
old friend.

Caes. Why these fair girls are so stared at by the men,
and the young fellows, now-a-days, have a damn'd
impudent stare with them,—'tis very abashing to
a woman—very distressing!

Vasq. Yes, so it is; but happily their distress is of that
nature that it generally goes off in a simper. But
come, I'll send Marcella to you, and she will——

Caes. (Gasping). No, no, stay my good friend. You
are in a violent hurry. 30

Vasq. Why, truly, Signor, at our time of life, when
we determine to marry, we have no time to lose.

Caes. Why, that's very true, and so—*(Aside)* oh! St.
Anthony, now it comes to the point—but there can
be no harm in looking at her—a look won't bind us
for better for worse. Well then—if you have a mind,
I say, you may let me see her. *(Exit Vasquez).*

Caes. (Puts on his spectacles). Aye, here she comes—I
hear her—trip, trip, trip! I don't like that step. A
woman should always tread steadily, with dignity, 40
it awes the men.

(Enter Vasquez, leading Marcella).

Vasq. There, Marcella, behold your future husband;
and remember that your kindness to him, will be
the standard of your duty to me. *(Exit).*

Marc. (Aside). Oh, heavens!

Caes. Somehow I am afraid to look round.

Marc. Surely he does not know that I am here!
(Coughs gently).

Caes. So——she knows how to give an item,[125] I find.

Marc. Pray, Signor, have you any commands for me? 50

Caes. Hum!—not non plus'd at all. *(Looks around).*
Oh! that eye, I don't like that eye.

Marc. My father commanded me——

Caes. (To her). Yes, I know—I know. *(Aside)* Why,
now I look again, there is a sort of a modest.—
Oh, that smile! that smile will never do.

Marc. I understand, Signor, that you have demanded
my hand in marriage.

Caes. (Aside). Upon my word, plump to the point!
Yes, I did a sort of—I can't say but that I did—— 60

Marc. I am not insensible of the honour you do me,
Sir, but—but——

---

125 *item*: an intimation or hint.

Caes. But!—What don't you like the thoughts of the match?

Marc. Oh, yes, Sir, yes—exceedingly. *(Aside)* I dare not say no.

Caes. (With ill humour). Oh, you do—*exceedingly!* What, I suppose, child, your head is full of jewels, and finery, and equipage?[126]

Marc. No indeed, Sir.

Caes. No, what then? what sort of a life do you expect to lead when you are my wife? what pleasures d'ye look forward to?

Marc. None!

Caes. Hey!

Marc. I shall obey my father, Sir; I shall marry you; but I shall be most wretched! *(Weeps).*

Caes. Indeed!

Marc. There is not a fate I would not prefer;—but pardon me!

Caes. Go on, go on, I never was better pleas'd.

Marc. Pleas'd at my reluctance!

Caes. Never, never better pleas'd in my life;—so you had really now, you young baggage, rather have me for a grandfather than a husband?

Marc. Forgive my frankness, Sir,—a thousand times!

Caes. My dear girl, let me kiss your hand.—Egad! you've let me off charmingly. I was frightened out of my wits lest *you* should have taken as violent an inclination to the match, as your father has.

Marc. Dear Sir, you charm me.

Caes. But hark ye;—you'll certainly incur your father's anger, if I don't take the refusal *entirely* on myself, which I will do, if you'll only assist me in a little business I have in hand.

Marc. Any thing to shew my gratitude.

Caes. You must know, I can't get my daughter to marry—there's nothing on earth will drive her to it, but the dread of a mother-in-law. Now, if you will let it appear to her, that you and I are driving to the goal of matrimony; I believe it will do—what say you? shall we be lovers in play?

Marc. If you are sure it will be *only* in play.

Caes. Oh, my life upon't—but we must be very fond, you know.

Marc. To be sure—exceedingly tender; ha, ha, ha!

Caes. You must smile upon me now and then roguishly; and slide your hand into mine, when you are sure she sees you, and let me pat your cheek, and—

Marc. Oh, no farther pray—that will be quite sufficient.

Caes. Gad, I begin to take a fancy to your rogue's face, now I'm in no danger—mayn't we—mayn't we salute[127] sometimes, it will seem infinitely more natural.

Marc. Never; such an attempt would make me fly off at once.

Caes. Well, you must be lady governess in this business.—I'll go home now, and fret madam, about her young mother-in-law—By'e sweeting!

Marc. By'e charmer!

Caes. Oh, bless its pretty eyes! *(Exit).*

Marc. Bless its pretty spectacles! ha, ha, ha! enter into a league with a cross old father against a daughter! why how could he suspect me capable of so much treachery? I cou'd not answer it to my conscience. No, no I'll acquaint Donna Olivia with the plot; and, as in duty bound, we'll turn our arms against Don Caesar. *(Exit).*

Act IV

Scene I: *Donna Laura's. Enter Laura and Pedro.*

Laura. Well, Pedro! hast thou seen Don Florio?

Ped. Yes, Donna.

Lau. How did he look when he read my letter?

Ped. Mortal well, I never see'd him look better—he'd got on a new cloak, and a——

Lau. Pho, blockhead! did he look pleas'd? did he kiss my name? did he press the billet to his bosom with all the warmth of love?

Ped. No, he didn't warm it that way; but he did another, for he put it into the fire.

Lau. How!

---

126 *equipage*: referring either to articles used to "outfit" or adorn a person (such as clothing and jewelry), or else to the articles required to maintain a domestic establishment (such as china, furniture, servants, or a carriage and horses).

127 *salute*: kiss, by way of salutation.

Ped. Yes, and when I spoke, he started, for, I think, he had forgot that I was by—so, says he, go home and tell Donna Laura, I fly to her presence. *(She waves her hand for him to go).*

Lau. Is it possible? so contemptuously destroy the letter in which my whole heart overflow'd with tenderness? in which my upbraidings were mingled with the most passionate love! But why do I question it? has he ever treated me but with the most mortifying coldness, even whilst he pretended to be sensible of my charms? I feel myself on the brink of hatred; and, by all the agonies I have felt, shou'd that passion be once rous'd.—Oh, how idly I talk! he is here; his very voice pierces my heart. I dare not meet his eye thus discomposed. *(Exit).*

(Enter Victoria, in Men's Cloaths, preceded by Sancha).

San. I will inform my mistress that you are here, Don Florio, I thought she had been in this apartment. *(Exit).*

Vict. Now must I, with a mind torn by anxieties, once more assume the lover of my husband's mistress—of the woman who has robb'd me of his heart, and his children of their fortune. Sure my task is hard.—Oh, love! Oh, *married* love assist me! If I can, by any art, obtain from her that fatal deed, I shall save my little ones from ruin—and then——But I hear her step—*(Agitated, pressing her hand on her bosom)*——There! I have hid my griefs within my heart, and now for all the impudence of an accomplished cavalier!

(Sings an air——sets her hat in the glass——dances a few steps, &c. then runs to Laura, and seizes her hand).

Vict. My lovely Laura!

Lau. That look speaks Laura *lov'd* as well as lovely.

Vict. To be sure! Petrarch immortaliz'd *his* Laura by his verses,[128] and mine shall be immortal in my passion.

Lau. I cannot conceive how you feed this immortal passion.

Vict. Oh, by thinking of you, and reading your letters, and——

Lau. My letters! how often do you read them?

Vict. A dozen times an hour; drink each dear line with my eyes, whilst my lips drink chocolate; place them every night under my pillow, and——

Lau. In the morning fling them into the fire.

Vict. Madam!

Lau. Oh, Florio, how deceitful! I know not what inchantment binds me to thee.

Vict. Me! my dear! is all this to me? *(Playing carelesly with the feather in her hat).*

Lau. Yes, ingrate, thee!

Vict. Positively, Laura, you have these extravagancies so often, I wonder my passion can stand them. To be plain, those violences in your temper may make a pretty relief in the flat of matrimony, child, but they do not suit that state of freedom which is necessary to *my* happiness.—It was by such destructive arts as these you cured Don Carlos of his love.

Lau. *Cured* Don Carlos! Oh, Florio! wer't thou but as he is!

Vict. *(Eagerly).* Why, you don't pretend he loves you still?

Lau. Yes, most ardently and truly.

Vict. Hah!

Lau. If thou would'st persuade me that thy passion is real, borrow *his* words, *his* looks;—be a hypocrite one dear moment, and speak to me in all the frenzy of that love, which warms the heart of Carlos.

Vict. The heart of Carlos!

Lau. *(Aside).* Hah, that seem'd a jealous pang—it gives my hopes new life. Yes, Florio, he, indeed, knows what it is to love.—For me he forsook a beauteous wife; nay, and with me he *wou'd* forsake his country.

Vict. Villain! Villain!

Lau. Nay, let not the thought distress you thus;—Carlos I despise—he is the weakest of mankind.

Vict. 'Tis false, madam, you cannot despise him—*Carlos* the weakest of mankind! heavens! what woman cou'd resist him? Persuasion sits on his tongue, and love, almighty love, triumphant in his eyes!

Lau. This is strange; you speak of your rival with the admiration of a mistress.

---

128 *Petrarch immortaliz'd ... by his verses*: referring to Francesco Petrarca (1304–74), Italian poet and scholar whose sonnets addressed to Laura, an idealized beloved, became a formative influence in sixteenth-century English poetry.

Vict. Laura! it is the fate of jealousy, as well as love, to see the charms of its object, increas'd and heighten'd.—*I* am jealous,—jealous to distraction, of Don Carlos, and cannot taste peace, unless you'll swear never to see him more.—*(Aside)* How nearly had I been betray'd!

Lau. I swear, joyfully swear, never to behold or speak 100 to him again. When, dear youth! shall we retire to Portugal? we are not safe here.

Vict. You know I am not rich.—*(Observing her with apprehension)* You must first sell the lands my rival gave you.

Lau. 'Tis done—I have found a purchaser, and tomorrow the transfer will be finished.

Vict. (Aside). Ah! I have now then nothing to trust to but the ingenuity of Gasper.—There is reason to fear Don Carlos had no right in that estate, with 110 which you supposed yourself endow'd.

Lau. No right! what can have given you those suspicions?

Vict. A conversation with Juan his steward—who assures me that his master never had an estate in Leon.

Lau. Never! what not by marriage?

Vict. Juan says so.

Lau. My blood runs cold—can I have taken pains to deceive myself? Cou'd I think so I should be mad. 120

Vict. These doubts may soon be annihilated; or confirm'd to certainty.—I have seen Don Sancho, the uncle of Victoria—he is now in Madrid—You have told me that he once profess'd a passion for you.

Lau. Oh, to excess; but at that time I had another object.

Vict. Have you convers'd with him much?

Lau. I never saw him nearer than from my Balcony, where he used to ogle me through a glass, suspended by a ribbon, like an order of knighthood; he is weak 130 enough to fancy it gives him an air of distinction, ha, ha! But where can I find him? I must see him.

Vict. Write him a billet, and I will send it to his lodgings.

Lau. Instantly.—Dear Florio, a new prospect opens to me—Don Sancho is rich and generous; and, by playing on his passions, without yielding to them, his fortune may be a constant fund to us.——I'll dip my pen in flattery. *(Exit)*.

Vict. Base woman! how can I pity thee, or regret the 140 steps which my duty obliges me to take? For myself, I wou'd not swerve from the nicest line of rectitude, nor wear the shadow of deceit——But for my children!——Is there a parental heart that will not pardon me? *(Exit)*.

Scene II: *Don Caesar's. Enter Olivia and Minette.*

Oliv. Well, here we are in private—what is this charming intelligence of which thou art so full this morning?

Min. Why, Ma'am, as I was in the balcony that overlooks Don Vasquez's garden—Donna Marcella told me, that Don Caesar had last night been to pay her a visit previous to their marriage, and——

Oliv. Their marriage! How can you give me the intelligence with such a look of joy? Their marriage!—what will become of me? 10

Min. Dear, Ma'am! if you'll but have patience.—— She says that Don Caesar and she are perfectly agreed.——

Oliv. Still with that smirking face——I can't have patience.

Min. Then, Madam, if you won't let me tell the story, please to read it——here's a letter from Donna Marcella.

Oliv. Why did you not give it me at first? *(Reads)*.

Min. Because I didn't like to be cut out of my story. If 20 orators were oblig'd to come to the point at once, mercy on us! what tropes and figures we shou'd lose!

Oliv. Oh, Minette! I give you leave to smirk again— listen—*(Reads)* "I am more terrified at the idea of becoming your father's wife, than you are in the expectation of a step-mother; and Don Caesar would be as loth as either of us.—He only means to frighten you into matrimony, and I have, on certain conditions, agreed to assist him; but whatever you 'may hear, or see, be assur'd that 30 nothing is so impossible, as that he shou'd become the husband of *Donna Marcella*."——Oh delightful girl! how I love her for this!

Min. Yes, Ma'am; and if you'd had patience, I shou'd have told you that she's now here with Don Caesar, in grave debate how to begin the attack, which must force you to take shelter in the arms of a husband.

Oliv. Ah, no matter how they begin it.—Let them amuse themselves in raising batteries;[129] my reserv'd fire shall tumble them about their ears, in the moment my poor father is singing his Io's[130] for victory.——But here come the lovers.—— Well, I protest now, sixteen and sixty is a very comely sight——'Tis contrast gives effect to every thing——Lud! how my father ogles! I had no idea he was such a sort of man.—I am really afraid he isn't quite so good as he shou'd be. 40

(Enter Don Caesar leading Marcella).

Caes. H—um—*(Apart)* Madam looks very placid; we shall discompose her, or I am mistaken. So, Olivia, here's Donna Marcella come to visit you—though, as matters are, that respect was due from you. 50

Oliv. I am sensible of the condescension—My dear Ma'am, how very good this is. *(Taking her hand).*

Caes. (Aside). Yes, you'll think yourself wonderfully oblig'd, when you know all. Pray, Donna Marcella, what do you think of these apartments? The furniture and decorations are my daughter's taste; wou'd you wish them to remain, or will you give orders to have them chang'd?

Marc. Chang'd, undoubtedly; I can have nobody's taste govern my apartments but my own. 60

Caes. (Apart). Ah, that touches—See how she looks. They shall receive your orders.——You understand, I suppose, from this, that every thing is fix'd on between Donna Marcella and me?

Oliv. Yes, Sir; I understand it perfectly, and it gives me infinite pleasure.

Caes. Eh! pleasure!

Oliv. Entirely, Sir——

Caes. Tol-de-rol! Ah that won't do—that won't do.— You can't hide it.—You are frighten'd out of your wits at the thought of a mother-in-law—especially a young, gay, handsome one. 70

Oliv. Pardon me, Sir; the thought of a mother-in-law was indeed disagreeable; but her being young and gay qualifies it.——I hope, Ma'am, you'll give us balls, and the most spirited parties——You can't think how stupid we have been.—My dear father

---

129 *batteries*: a platform or fortified work on which artillery is mounted.

130 *Io's*: a Greek or Latin exclamation of joy or triumph.

hates those things—but I hope now——

Caes. Hey, hey, hey! what's the meaning of all this? Why, hussey, don't you know you'll have no apartment but the garret? 80

Oliv. That will benefit my complexion, Sir, by mending my health. 'Tis charming to sleep in an elevated situation.

Caes. Here! here's an obstinate perverse slut!

Oliv. Bless me, Sir, are you angry that I look forwards to your marriage without murmuring?

Caes. Yes, I am—yes, I am—you ought to murmur, and you ought to—to—to—— 90

Oliv. Dear me! I find love taken up late in life, has a bad effect on the temper—I wish, my dear papa, you had felt the influence of Donna Marcella's charms somewhat sooner.

Caes. You do! you do! why this must be all put on.— This can't be real.

Oliv. Indeed, indeed it is; and I protest your engagement with this lady has given me more pleasure than I have tasted ever since you began to teaze me about a husband. You seem'd determin'd to have a marriage in the family; and I hope now I shall live in quiet, with my dear, sweet, young mother-in-law. 100

Caes. Oh—oh *(Walking about)*. Was there ever—— She doesn't care for a mother-in-law!——Can't frighten her!

Oliv. Sure, my fate is very peculiar; that being pleas'd with your choice, and submitting with humble duty to your will, shou'd be the cause of offence.

Caes. Hussey! I don't want you to be pleas'd with my choice—I don't want you to submit with humble duty to my will——Where I do want you to submit, you rebel—You are a—you are——But I'll mortify that wayward spirit yet. *(Exit Don Caesar and Marcella).* 110

Min. Well, really, my master is in a piteous passion— he seems more angry at your liking his marriage, than at your refusing to be married yourself.—— Wouldn't it have been better, Madam, to have affected discontent? 120

Oliv. To what purpose? but to lay myself open to fresh solicitations, in order to get rid of the evil I pretended to dread! Bless us! nothing can be more easy than for my father to be gratified, if he were but lucky in the choice of a lover.

Min. As much as to say, Madam, that there is——

Oliv. Why, yes, "as much as to say"—I see you are resolv'd to have my secret, Minette, and so——

(Enter Servant).

Serv. There is a gentleman at the door, Madam, call'd Don Julio de Melessina. He waits on you from Don Vincentio.

Oliv. Who? Don Julio! it cannot be—art thou sure of his name?

Serv. The servant repeated it twice—He is in a fine carriage, and seems to be a nobleman.

Oliv. Conduct him hither. *(Exit Servant). (Aside)* I am astonish'd, I cannot see him.—I wou'd not have him know the incognita to be Olivia for worlds!—There is but one way. Minette, ask no questions, but do as I order you—Receive Don Julio in my name; call yourself the heiress of Don Caesar, and on no account suffer him to believe that you are any thing else. *(Turning from her).* I am amaz'd and confus'd!——It is impossible that he can have discover'd me—Perhaps he comes with offers to my father—then my interview last night did not give him those impressions I hop'd.——I am jealous of myself.—If it is so, his *incognita* shall never pardon a passion for *the daughter of Don Caesar. (Exit).*

Min. So! then, this is some new lover whom she is determined to disgust; and fancies that making me pass for her, will compleat it. Perhaps her ladyship may be mistaken, though. *(Looking thro' the wing).* Upon my word, a sweet man! Oh, lud, my heart beats with the very idea of his making love to me, even though he takes me for another—Stay, I think he shan't find me here—Standing in the middle of a room gives one's appearance no effect.—I'll enter upon him with an easy swim, or an engaging trip, or a—something that shall strike—the first glance is every thing. *(Exit).*

(Enter Julio, preceded by Servant, who retires).

Jul. Not here! The ridiculous dispute between Garcia and Vincentio, gives me irresistable curiosity——though, if she is the character Garcia describes, I expect to be cuff'd for my impertinence——Here she comes!—A pretty, little, smiling girl, 'faith, for a vixen.

(Enter Minette, very affectedly).

Min. Sir, your most obedient humble servant. You are Don Julio de Melessina. I am extremely glad to see you, Sir.

Jul. (Aside). A very courteous reception!——You honour me infinitely, Madam—I must apologize for waiting on you without a better introduction—Don Vincentio promis'd to attend me, but a concert call'd him to another part of the town, at the moment I prepar'd to come hither.

Min. A concert——Yes, Sir, he is very fond of music.

Jul. He is, Madam:—You, I suppose, have a passion for that charming science?

Min. Oh, yes, I love it mightily.

Jul. (Aside). This is lucky! I think I have heard, Donna Olivia, that your taste that way is peculiar; you are fond of a—*(Aside)* faith I can hardly speak it.—of a——*(Smothering a laugh)* Jew's harp.

Min. A *Jew's harp!* Mercy! What do you think a person of my birth and figure, can have such fancies as that? No, Sir, I love fiddles, French horns, tabors,[131] and all the chearful, noisy instruments in the world.

Jul. (Aside). Vincentio must have been mad; and I as mad as him to mention it. Then you are fond of concerts, Madam?

Min. Doat on 'em! *(Aside)* I wish he'd offer me a ticket.

Jul. (Aside). Vincentio is clearly wrong.—Now to prove how far the other was right, in supposing her a vixen.

Min. There is a grand public concert, Sir, to be tomorrow. Pray do you go?

Jul. I believe I shall have that pleasure, Madam.

Min. My father, Don Caesar, won't let me purchase a ticket: I think it's very hard.

Jul. Pardon me, I think it's perfectly right.

Min. Right! what to refuse me a trifling expence, that would procure me a great pleasure?

Jul. Yes, doubtless——The ladies are too fond of pleasure.—I think Don Caesar is exemplary.

Min. Lord, Sir, you'd think it very hard if you were me, to be lock'd up all your life, and know nothing of the world but what you cou'd catch through the bars of your balcony.

---

131 *tabors*: small drums.

Jul. Perhaps I might; but as a man, I am convinc'd 'tis right. Daughters and wives should be equally excluded those destructive haunts of dissipation.— Let them keep to their embroidery, nor ever presume to shew their faces but at their own fire sides.——*(Aside)* This will bring out the Xantippe, surely.

Min. Well, Sir, I don't know—to be sure, home, as you say, is the fittest place for women.—For my part, I cou'd live for ever at home. *(Aside)* I am determin'd he shall have his way—who knows what may happen.

Jul. (Aside). By all the powers of caprice, Garcia is as wrong as the other!

Min. I delight in nothing so much as in sitting by my father, and hearing his tales of old times—and I fancy, when I have a husband, I shall be more happy to sit and listen to his stories of present times.

Jul. Perhaps your husband, fair lady, might not be inclined *so* to amuse you.—Men have a thousand delights that call them abroad; and probably your chief amusements wou'd be counting the hours of his absence, and giving a tear to each as it pass'd.

Min. Well, he shou'd never see 'em, however. I wou'd always smile when *he* enter'd, and if he found my eyes red, I'd say I had been weeping over the history of the unfortunate damsel, whose true love hung himself at sea, and appear'd to her afterwards in a wet jacket.—*(Aside)* Sure this will do.

Jul. I am every moment more astonish'd! Pray, Madam, permit me a question—Are you really—yet I cannot doubt it—are you really Donna Olivia, the daughter of Don Caesar, to whom Don Garcia and Don Vincentio, had lately the honour of paying their addresses?

Min. Am I Donna Olivia! ha, ha, ha! what a question! Pray, Sir, is this my father's house?—are you Don Julio?

Jul. I beg your pardon; but, to confess, I had heard you describ'd as a lady who had not quite so much sweetness, and——

Min. Oh, what you had heard that I was a termagant, I suppose—'Tis all slander, Sir—There is not in Madrid, though I say it, a sweeter temper than my own; and though I have refus'd a good many lovers, yet if one was to offer himself, that I cou'd like——

Jul. You wou'd take pity, and reward his passion. Lovely Donna Olivia, how charming is this frankness!——*(Aside)* 'tis a little odd, though!

Min. Why, I believe, I shou'd take pity, for it always seem'd to me to be very hard-hearted to be cruel to a lover that one likes, because in that case one shou'd——a——You know, Sir, the sooner the affair is over, the better for both parties.

Jul. What the deuce does she mean?—Is this Garcia's sour fruit?

Caes. (Without). Olivia!—Olivia!

Min. Bless me, I hear my father! Now, Sir, I have a particular fancy that you shou'd not tell him, in this first visit, your design.

Jul. Madam! my design!

Min. Yes, that you will not speak out, 'till we have had a little further conversation, which I'll take care to give you an opportunity for very soon.——He'll be here in a moment—Now, pray Don Julio, go—If he shou'd meet you, and ask who you are, you can say that you are—you may say that you came on a visit to my maid, you know.

Jul. (Aloud). I thank you, Madam—*(Aside)* for my dismission—I never was in such peril in my life.—I believe she has a license in her pocket, a priest in her closet, and the ceremony by heart. *(Exit).*

Act V

Scene I: *Don Carlos's. Carlos discover'd writing.*

Car. (Tearing paper, and rising). It is in vain! Language cannot furnish me with terms to soften to Victoria the horrid transaction. Cou'd she see the compunctions of my soul, her gentle heart wou'd pity me—But what then? *She's ruin'd!* My children are undone! Oh! the artifices of one base woman, and my villainy to another most amiable one, has made me unfit to live.—I am a wretch who ought to be blotted from society.

(Enter Pedro hastily).

Ped. Sir, Sir.

Car. Well!

Ped. Sir, I have just met Don Florio; he ask'd if my mistress was at home, so I guesses he is going to our house, and so I run to let you know—for I loves to keep my promises, though I am deadly afraid of some mischief.

Car. You have done well.—Go home, and wait for me at the door, and admit me without noise. *(Exit Pedro).* At least then, I shall have the pleasure of revenge; I'll punish that harlot by sacrificing her paramour in her arms—and then——Oh! *(Exit).*   20

Scene II: *Donna Laura's. Enter Laura with precipitation, followed by Victoria.*

Lau. 'Tis his carriage!—How successful was my letter! This, my Florio, is a most important moment.

Vict. It is indeed; and I will leave you to make every advantage of it. If I am present, I must witness condescensions from you, that I shall not be able to bear, though I know them to be but affected.———*(Aside)* Now, Gasper, play thy part well, and save Victoria! *(Exit).*

Lau. This tender jealousy is dear to me!—Keep in the saloon.[132] Here comes the dotard.   10

(Enter Gasper, dressed as an old Beau, two Servants follow him, and take off a rich cloak).

Gasp. Take my cloak; and, d'ye hear, Ricardo, go home and bring the eider-down cushions for the coach, and tell the fellow not to hurry me *post*[133] through the streets of Madrid. I have been jolted from side to side, like a pippin[134] in a mill stream.—Drive a man of my rank, as he wou'd a city vintner and his fat wife, going to a bull fight!———Hah, there she is! *(Looking through a glass, suspended by a red ribbon)*———there she is!   20 Charming Donna Laura, let me thus at the shrine of your beauty——*(Makes an effort to kneel, and falls on his face; Laura assists him to rise)* Fye, fye, those new shoes!—they have made me skate all day, like a Dutchman on a canal, and now—Well, you see how profound my adoration is, Madam.—Common lovers kneel; I was prostrate.

Lau. You do me infinite honour.——*(Aside)* Disgustful wretch!   30

Gasp. But how cou'd you be so barbarous, to leave me at Valencia, without granting me one interview nearer than your balcony?

Lau. I will be ingenuous—it was female artifice. I knew you wou'd follow me; and how cou'd I resist the *triumph* of shewing that I led in my chains the illustrious Don Sancho?

Gasp. Oh you dear charming——But stay *(Searching his pockets)*——Bless me, what a careless fellow I am! I had a casket, with some diamonds in it—a   40 necklace, and a few trifles, which I meant to have had the honour of placing on your toilette—— Left it at home——Oh, my giddy pate![135]

Lau. You are always elegant, Don Sancho. I'll send my servant.——*(Calling)* Pedro!

Gasp. No, no, to-morrow. It will be an excuse for me to come to morrow.——I shall often want excuses.

Lau. My wishes shall always be your excuse, but tomorrow be it then. You are thinner than you were, Don Sancho.—I protest, now I observe you,   50 you are much alter'd.

Gasp. Aye, Madam—Fretting. Your absence threw me into a fever, and that destroy'd my bloom:— —You see I look almost a middle-aged man, now.

Lau. No, really; far from it, I assure you.——*(Aside)* The fop is as wrinkled as a baboon.

Gasp. Then, jealousy, *that* gave me a jaundice. My niece's husband, I hear, Don Carlos, has been my happy rival—Oh, my blade will hardly keep in its scabbard, when I think of him.   60

Lau. Think no more of him—He has been long banish'd from my thoughts, be assured. I wonder you gave your niece to him, with such a fortune.

Gasp. Gave! She gave herself; and as to fortune, she had not a pistole[136] from me.

Lau. 'Twas indeed unnecessary, with so fine an estate as she had in Leon.

Gasp. My niece an estate in Leon! Not enough to give shelter to a field mouse; and if he has told you so, he is a braggart.   70

Lau. Told me so——I have the writings; he has made over the lands to me.

---

132 *saloon*: also "salon," a large and lofty room for the reception of guests.

133 *post*: i.e., at the speed of a post-coach; at high speed.

134 *pippin*: a pippiner; a small ship, usually engaged for its speed in transporting fresh fruit.

135 *pate*: head or skull.

136 *pistole*: synonymous with "pistolet," a Spanish gold coin worth between 16*s* 6*d* (16 shillings and 6 pence) and 18*s*.

A BOLD STROKE FOR A HUSBAND   31

Gasp. Made over the lands to you.—Oh a deceiver! I begin to suspect a plot. Pray let me see this extraordinary deed. *(She runs to a cabinet).* A plot, I'll be sworn.

Lau. Here is the deed which made that estate mine forever. No, Sir, I will intrust it in no hand but my own—Yet look over me, and read the description of the lands.

Gasp. (Reading through his glass). H—m—m—m—: "In the vicinage of Rosalva, bounded on the west by the river—h—m—m, on the east by the forest——" Oh, an artful dog! I need read no further; I see how the thing is.

Lau. How, Sir!——but hold——Stay a moment—I am breathless with fear.

Gasp. Nay, Madam, don't be afraid! 'Tis my estate—that's all—the very castle where I was born, and which I never did, nor ever will bestow on any Don in the two Castiles. Dissembling rogue! Bribe you with a fictitious title to my estate, ha, ha, ha!

Lau. (Aside). Curses follow him! The villain I employ'd, must have been *his* creature—His reluctance all art—and, whilst I believ'd myself undoing him, was duped myself!

Gasp. Cou'd you suppose I'd give Carlos such an estate for running away with my niece? No, no, the vineyards, and the corn-fields, and the woods of Rosalva, are not for him.—I've somebody else in my eye—in my eye, observe me—to give those to;—can't you guess who it is?

Lau. No, indeed!——*(Aside)* He gives me a glimmering that saves me from despair.

Gasp. I won't tell you, unless you'll bribe me.—I won't indeed——*(Kisses her cheek)* There, now I'll tell you—They are all for you.—Yes, this estate, to which you have taken such a fancy, shall be yours.—*I'll* give you the deeds, if you'll promise to love me, you little, cruel thing!

Lau. Can you be serious?

Gasp. I'll sign and seal to-morrow.

Lau. Noble Don Sancho! Thus then I annihilate the proof of his perfidy and my weakness. Thus I tear to atoms his detested name; and as I tread on these, so wou'd I on his heart.

(Enter Victoria).

Vict. (In transport). My children then are sav'd!

Lau. (Apart). Oh, Florio, 'tis as thou said'st—Carlos was a villain, and deceiv'd me.——Why this strange air? Ah, I see the cause—You think me ruin'd, and will abandon me.—Yes, I see it in thy averted face; thou dar'st not meet my eyes.—If I misjudge thee, speak!

Vict. Laura, I cannot speak.——You little guess the emotions of my heart.——Heav'n knows, I pity you!

Lau. Pity! Oh, villain! and has thy love already snatch'd the form of pity? Base, deceitful——

Car. (Without). Stand off, loose your weak hold; I'm come for vengeance!

(Enter Carlos).

Where is this youth? Where is the blooming rival, for whom I have been betray'd? Hold me not, base woman! In vain the stripling flies me; for, by Heav'n, my sword shall in his bosom write its master's wrongs!

(Victoria first goes towards the flat, then returns, takes off her hat, and drops on one knee).

Vict. Strike, strike it here! Plunge it deep into that bosom already wounded by a thousand stabs, keener and more painful than your sword can give.—Here lives all the gnawing anguish of love betray'd; here live the pangs of disappointed hopes, hopes sanctified by holiest vows, which have been written in the book of Heav'n.——Hah! he sinks.——*(She flies to him)*—Oh! my Carlos! My belov'd! my husband! forgive my too severe reproaches; thou art dear, yet dear as ever, to Victoria's heart!

Car. (Recovering). Oh, you know not what you do—you know not what you are.—Oh, Victoria, thou art a beggar!

Vict. No, we are rich, we are happy! See there, the fragments of that fatal deed, which had I not recover'd, we had been indeed *undone*; yet still not *wretched*, cou'd my Carlos think so!

Car. The fragments of the deed! the deed which that base woman——

Vict. Speak not so harshly.——To you, Madam, I fear, I seem reprehensible; yet when you consider my duties as wife and mother, you will forgive me.—Be not afraid of poverty—a woman has deceiv'd, but she will not desert you!

Lau. Is this real? Can I be awake?

Vict. Oh, may'st thou indeed awake to virtue!—You have talents that might grace the highest of our sex; be no longer unjust to such precious gifts, by burying them in dishonour.——Virtue is our first, most awful duty; bow, Laura! bow before her throne, and mourn in ceaseless tears, that ever you forgot her heav'nly precepts!

Lau. So, by a smooth speech about virtue, you think to cover the injuries I sustain. Vile, insinuating 170 monster!—but thou know'st me not.—Revenge is sweeter to my heart than love; and if there is a law in Spain to gratify that passion, your *virtue* shall have another field for exercise. *(Exit).*

Gasp. No, no; you'll find no help in the law, charmer! However, the long robes are rich—get amongst them; their gravities may administer to your avarice, though not to your revenge.

Car. (Turning towards Victoria). My hated rival, and my charming wife! How many sweet mysteries 180 have you to unfold!——Oh, Victoria! my soul thanks thee, but I dare not yet say I love thee, 'till ten thousand acts of watchful tenderness, have prov'd how deep the sentiment's engrav'd.

Vict. Can it be true that I have been unhappy?—— But the mysteries, my Carlos, are already explain'd to you—Gasper's resemblance to my uncle——

Gasp. Yes, Sir, I was always apt at resemblances—In our plays at home, I am always Queen Cleopatra[137]—You know she was but a gypsey 190 Queen, and I hits her off to a nicety.

Car. Come, my Victoria——Oh, there is a painful pleasure in my bosom—To gaze on thee, to listen to, and love thee, seems like the bliss of angels cheering whispers to repentant sinners! *(Exeunt Carlos and Victoria).*

Gasp. Lord help 'em! how easily the women are taken in!——Here's a wild rogue has plagu'd her heart these two years, and a whip syllabub[138] about angels and whispers clears scores.——'Tis pity but 200 they were a little——tho', now I think on't, the number of these *gentle* fair ones is so very small, that if it was lessen'd, the two sexes might be confounded together, and the whole world be suppos'd of the masculine gender. *(Exit).*

Scene III: *The Prado. Enter Minette.*

Min. Ah, here comes the man at last, after I have been sauntering in sight of his lodgings these two hours.—Now, if my scheme takes, what a happy person I shall be! and sure, as I was Donna Olivia to-day, to please my lady, I may be Donna Olivia to night, to please myself. I'll address him as the maid of a lady who has taken a fancy to him, then convey him to our house—then retire, and then come in again, and with a vast deal of confusion, confess I sent my maid for him. If he should dislike 10 my *forwardness*, the censure will fall on my lady; if he should be pleas'd with my *person*, the advantage will be mine. But perhaps he's come here on some wicked frolic or other.—I'll watch him at a distance before I speak. *(Exit).*

(Enter Julio).

Jul. Not here, 'faith; though she gave me last night but a faint refusal, and I had a right, by all the rules of gallantry, to construe that into an assent.—— Then she's a jilt—Hang her, I feel I am uneasy— The first woman that ever gave me pain.——I am 20 asham'd to perceive that this spot has attractions for me, only because it was here I convers'd with her. 'Twas here the little syren, conscious of her charms, unveil'd her fascinating face.—'Twas here——

(Enter Garcia and Vincentio).

Garc. '*Twas here* that Julio, leaving champaigne untasted, and songs of gallantry unsung, came to talk to the whistling branches.

Vin. '*Twas here* that Julio, flying from the young and

---

137 *Cleopatra*: Cleopatra VII (69 BC–30 BC), Egyptian queen famous in history and drama as the lover of Julius Caesar and as the wife of Mark Antony. She became queen in 51 BC and ruled successively with her two brothers Ptolemy XIII (51–47) and Ptolemy XIV (47–44) and with her son Ptolemy XV (44–30). After the Roman armies of Octavian defeated their combined forces, Cleopatra and Mark Antony committed suicide in 30 BC. In the next line Gaspar puns on "Egyptian" and "gypsey."

138 *whip syllabub*: a frothy and insubstantial whipped drink, here referring to Carlos's speech.

gay, was found in doleful meditation———*(Altering his tone)*—on a wench, for a hundred ducats! 30

Garc. Who is she?

Jul. Not Donna Olivia, Gentlemen; not Donna Olivia.

Garc. We have been seeking you, to ask the event of your visit to her.

Jul. The event has prov'd that *you* have been most grosly dup'd.

Vin. I knew that—Ha, ha, ha!

Jul. And you likewise, *I* know that—Ha, ha, ha!— 40 —The fair lady, so far from being a vixen, is the very essence of gentleness. To me, so much sweetness in a wife, wou'd be downright maukish[139]—I like the little acerbities which flow from quick spirits, and a consciousness of power.— One may as well marry a looking-glass as a woman who constantly reflects back one's own sentiments, and one's own whims.

Vin. Well, but she's fond of a Jew's harp.

Jul. Detests it; she would be as fond of *a Jew.* 50

Garc. Pho, pho, this is a game at cross purposes;— Let us all go to Don Caesar's together, and compare opinions on the spot.

Jul. I'll go most willingly—but it will be only to cover you both with confusion, for being the two men in Spain most easily impos'd on. *(All going).*

(Enter Minette).

Min. Gentlemen, my lady has sent me for one of you, pray which of you is it?

Jul. (Returning). Me, without doubt, child.

Vin. I don't know that. 60

Garc. Look at me, my dear, don't you think I am the man?

Min. Let me see—*(To Garcia)* a good air, and well made, you are the man for a dancer.—*(To Vincentio)* Well dress'd, and nicely put out of hands—you are the man for a bandbox. *(To Julio)* Handsome and bold—you are the man for my lady.

Jul. My dear little Iris, here's all the gold in my pocket.—*(Stalking by them with his arm round Minette)* Gentlemen, I wish you a good night—I 70 am your very obedient, humble—

Garc. Pho, prithee, don't be a fool. Are we not going to Donna Olivia?

Jul. Donna Olivia must wait, my dear boy; we can decide about her to-morrow. Come along, my little dove of Venus! *(Exit).*

Garc. What a rash fellow it is! ten to one but this is some common business, and he'll be robb'd and murder'd—they take him for a stranger.

Vin. Let's follow, and see where she leads him. 80

Garc. That's hardly fair; however, as I think there's danger, we will follow. *(Exit).*

Scene IV: *Don Caesar's. Enter Olivia and Servant.*

Oliv. Bring me my veil and follow me to the Prado. *(Exit Servant).* Julio will certainly be there—he has too much breeding not to translate my positive denial into assent—at least I must convince myself. If I see him compleatly vanquish'd, I can, by the most *unlucky chance in the world*, drop a card with my name, and then all the rest follows in course. *(Exit).*

(Enter Minette and Julio).

Min. There, Sir, please to sit down, 'till my lady is ready to wait on you—she won't be long..... *(Aside)* 10 I'm sure she's out, and I may do great things before she returns. *(Exit).*

Jul. Through fifty back lanes, a long garden, and a narrow stair-case, into a superb apartment—all that's in the regular way; as the Spanish women manage it, one intrigue is too much like another, whilst the sprightly dames of Paris have the art of giving the same intrigue every day a new air. Now, presently, in comes a stately dame with a veil on; she tells me, she fears I have but a slight opinion of her 20 virtue; I make her an answer about her beauty, and, after a dozen or two entreaties and denials, off comes her veil. A fat matron, perhaps of forty—I swear she's a Hebe[140]—she thinks me very obliging, and I find her very grateful; and this is the epitome of half the amours in Madrid. If it was not now and then

---

139 *maukish*: having a nauseating taste; having a faint, sickly flavor with little definite taste.

140 *Hebe*: in Greek mythology, the daughter of Zeus and Hera, goddess of youth, and wife of Heracles when he ascended into heaven. In Homer she appears as cupbearer to the gods.

for the little lively fillip[141] of a jealous husband or brother, which obliges one to leap from a window, or crawl, like a cat, along the gutters, there would be no bearing the *ennui. (Looking through the wing)*. Ah! ah! but this promises novelty; a young girl and an old man—wife or daughter? They are coming this way. My lovely incognita, by all that's propitious! Why did not some kind spirit whisper to me my happiness? but hold—she can't mean to treat the old gentleman with a sight of me. *(Goes behind the sopha)*.

(Enter Caesar and Olivia).

Caes. No, no, Madam, no going out—give me your veil; that will be useless 'till you put it on for life. There, madam, this is your *apartment*, your *house*, your *garden*, your *assembly*, 'till you go to your convent. Why, how impudent you are, to look thus unconcern'd!—Can hardly forbear laughing in my face!—Very well—very well! *(Exit, double locking the door)*.

Oliv. Ha, ha, ha! I'll be even with you, my dear father, if you treble lock it. I'll stay here two days, without once asking for my liberty, and you'll come the *third*, with tears in your eyes, to take me out.— He has forgot that door leading to the garden— *(Sitting down)* but I vow I'll stay, I can make the time pass pleasantly enough.

Jul. (Looking over the back of the sopha). I hope so.

Oliv. Heav'n and earth!

Jul. (Coming round). My dear creature, why are you so alarmed; am I here before you expected me?

Oliv. Expected you!

Jul. Oh, this pretty surprize! Come, let us sit down, I think your father was very obliging to lock us in together.

Oliv. (Calling at the door). Sir, Sir! my father!

Caes. (Without). Aye, 'tis all in vain—I won't come near you. There you are, and there you may stay.— I shan't return, make as much noise as you will.

Jul. Why are you not asham'd that your father has so much more consideration for your guest than you have?

Oliv. My guest! *(Aside)* how is it possible he can have discover'd me!

Jul. Pho, this is carrying the thing further than you need—if there was a third person here, it might be prudent.

Oliv. Why, this assurance, Don Julio, is really—

Jul. The thing in the world you are most ready to pardon.

Oliv. Upon my word I don't know how to treat you.

Jul. Consult your heart!

Oliv. I shall consult my honour.

Jul. Honour is a pretty thing to play with, but when spoken with that very grave face, after having sent your maid to bring me here, is really more than I expected. I shall be in an ill humour presently—I won't stay if you treat me thus.

Oliv. Well, this is superior to every thing! I have heard that men will slander women privately to each other, 'tis their common amusement, but to do it to one's face!—and you really pretend that I sent for you?

Jul. Ha, ha, ha! Well, if it obliges you, I will pretend that you did not send for me; that your maid did not conduct me hither, nay, that I have not now the supreme happiness——*(Catching her in his arms)*.

(Enter Minette, screams and runs out).

Jul. Donna Olivia de Zuniga! how the devil came she here?

Oliv. (Aside). That's lucky! Olivia, my dear friend, why do you run away? *(Apart to Minette)* Keep the character, I charge you. Be still Olivia!

Min. Oh! dear madam! I was——I was so frighten'd when I saw that gentleman.

Oliv. Oh, my dear, it's the merriest pretty kind of gentleman in the world; he pretends that I sent my maid for him into the streets, ha, ha!

Jul. That's right, always tell a thing yourself, which you wou'd not have believ'd.

Min. It is the readiest excuse for being found in a lady's apartment, however. *(Aside)*. Now will I swear I know nothing of the matter.

Oliv. Now, I think it a horrid poor excuse, he has certainly not had occasion to invent reasons for such impertinencies often. *(Apart)* Tell me that he has made love to you to day.

Min. I fancy that he *has* had occasion to excuse impertinencies often;——his impertinence to me today—

Jul. To you, madam?

---

141 *fillip*: a smart blow or stimulus; more generally, something that serves to rouse, excite, or animate.

Min. Making love to me, my dear, all the morning—
—could hardly get him away he was so desirous
to speak to my father. Nay, Sir, I don't care for your
impatience.

Jul. (Aside). Now wou'd I give a thousand pistoles if
she were a man! 120

Oliv. Nay, then, this accidental meeting is
fortunate—pray, Don Julio, don't let my presence
prevent your saying what you think proper to my
friend—shall I leave you together?

Jul. (Apart). To contradict a lady on such an assertion
wou'd be too gross; but, upon my honour, Donna
Olivia is the last woman upon earth who cou'd
inspire me with a tender idea. Find an excuse to
send her away, my angel, I entreat you. I have a
thousand things to say, and the moments are too 130
precious to be given to her.

Oliv. I think so too, but one can't be rude, you know.
(Seating herself) Come, my dear, sit down, have
you brought your work?

Jul. The devil! what can she mean? *(Pushing himself
between Minette and the sopha)* Donna Olivia, I am
sorry to inform you that my physician has just
been sent for to your father, Don Caesar.—The
poor gentleman was seized with a vertigo.[142]

Oliv. Vertigoes! *(To Minette)* Oh, he has 'em 140
frequently you know.

Min. Yes, and they always keep me from his sight.

Jul. Did ever one women prevent another from
leaving her at such a moment before? I really,
madam, cannot comprehend——

Caes. (Without). It is impossible—impossible,
gentlemen? Don Julio cannot be here.

Jul. Hah, who's that?

(Enter Caesar, Garcia, and Vincentio).

Garc. There! did we not tell you so? we saw him enter
the garden. 150

Caes. What can be the meaning of all this?
(Attempting to draw) A man in my daughter's
apartment!

Garc. Hold, Sir! Don Julio is of the first rank in
Spain, and will unquestionably be able to s a t i s f y
your honour, without troubling your sword.—

---

142 *vertigo*: a disordered condition in which the person affected has the sensation of whirling; giddiness or diz-
ziness.

(Apart) We have done mischief, Vincentio!

Jul. (To Olivia). They have been cursedly impertinent!
but I'll bring you off, never fear, by pretending a
passion for your busy friend, there. 160

Caes. Satisfy me then in a moment; speak, one of you.

Jul. I came here, Sir, by the merest accident.—The
garden door was open, curiosity led me to this
apartment.—You came in a moment after, and
very civilly lock'd me in with your daughter.

Caes. Lock'd you in! why then, did you not, like a
man of honour, cry out?

Jul. The lady cried out, Sir, and you told her you
would not return; but when Donna Olivia de
Zuniga entered, for whom I have conceived a most 170
violent passion——

Caes. A passion for her! Oh, let me hear no more
on't.—A passion for her! You may as well entertain
a passion for the untameable hyaena.

Garc. There, Vincentio, what think you now?
Xantippe or not!

Vin. I am afraid I must give up that—but pray
support me as to this point, Don Caesar; is not
the lady fond of a Jew's harp?

Caes. Fond! She's fond of nothing, but playing the 180
vixen; there is not such a fury upon earth.

Jul. These are odd liberties, with a person who does
not belong to him.

Caes. I'll play the hypocrite for her no more; the
world shall know her true character, they shall
know——but ask her maid there.

Jul. Her maid!

Min. Why, yes, Sir, to say truth, I am but Donna
Olivia's maid, after all.

Oliv. (Apart). Dear Minette! speak for me, or I am 190
now ruin'd.

Min. I will, ma'am.—*(Going up to Julio)* I must
confess, Sir, there never was so bitter a temper'd
creature, as my lady is. *(Olivia pulls her sleeve,
impatiently)* I have borne her humours for two
years; I have seen her by night and by day. *(To
Olivia)* I will, I will! and this I am sure, that if you
marry her, you'll rue the day every hour the first
month, and hang yourself the next. There, madam,
I have done it roundly now. 200

Oliv. (Aside). I am undone.—I am caught in my own
snare.

Caes. After this true character of my daughter, I suppose, Signor, we shall hear no more of your passion; so let us go down, and leave madam to begin her penance.

Jul. My ideas are totally confus'd.—You Donna Olivia de Zuniga, and the person I thought you, her maid! something too flattering darts across my mind.

Caes. If you have taken a fancy to her maid, I have 210 nothing farther to say, but as to that violent creature.—

Jul. Oh, do not prophane her.—Where is that spirit which you tell me of? Is it that which speaks in modest, conscious blushes on her cheeks? Is it that which bends her lovely eyes to earth?

Caes. Aye, she's only bending 'em to earth, considering how to afflict me with some new obstinacy—she'll break out like a tygress in a moment.

Jul. It cannot be—*are* you, charming woman! such 220 a creature?

Oliv. (Looking down). Yes, to all mankind—but one.

Jul. But one! Oh, might that excepted one, be me!

Oliv. Wou'd you not fear to trust your fate with her, you have cause to think so hateful?

Jul. No, I'd bless the hour that bound my fate to hers—permit me, Sir, to pay my vows to this fair vixen.

Caes. What are you such a bold man as that? Pho, but if you are, 'twill be only lost time—she'll 230 contrive some way or other, to return your vows upon your hands.

Oliv. If they have your authority, Sir, I will return them—only with my own.

Caes. What's that! what did she say? my head is giddy with surprize.

Jul. (Catching her hand). And mine with rapture.

Caes. Don't make a fool of me, Olivia.—Wil't marry him?

Oliv. When you command me, Sir. 240

Caes. My dear Don Julio, thou art my guardian angel—shall I have a son-in-law at last? Garcia, Vincentio, cou'd you have thought it?

Garc. No, Sir, if we had, we should have sav'd that lady much trouble; 'tis pretty clear now, *why* she was a vixen.

Vin. Yes, yes, 'tis clear enough, and I beg your pardon, madam, for the share of trouble *I* gave you—but pray have the goodness to tell me sincerely, what do you think of a crash? 250

Oliv. I love music, Don Vincentio, I admire your skill, and whenever you'll give me a concert, I shall be oblig'd.

Vin. You cou'd not have pleas'd me so well, if you had married me.

(Enter Carlos and Victoria).

Oliv. Hah, here comes Victoria and her Carlos. My friend, you are happy—'tis in your eyes, I need not ask the event.

Caes. What is this Don Carlos, whom Victoria gave 260 us for a cousin? Sir, you come in happy hour!

Car. I do indeed, for I am most happy.

Jul. My dear Carlos, what has new made thee thus, since morning?

Car. A wife! Marry, Julio, marry!

Jul. What! this advice from *you*?

Car. Yes; and when you have married an angel, when that angel has done for you such things, as makes your gratitude almost equal to your love, you may then guess something of what I feel, in calling *this* 270 angel mine.

Oliv. Now, I trust, Don Julio, after all this, that if I should do you the honour of my hand, you'll treat me cruelly, be a very bad man, that I, like my exemplary cousin——

Vict. Hold, Olivia! it is not necessary that a husband should be *faulty*, to make a wife's character *exemplary*.—Should he be tenderly watchful of your happiness, your gratitude will give a thousand graces to your conduct; whilst the purity of your 280 manners, and the nice honour of your life, will gain you the approbation of those, whose praise is fame.

Oliv. Pretty and matronly! thank you, my dear. We have each struck a bold stroke to-day;—yours has been to reclaim a husband, mine to get one; but the most important is yet to be obtain'd.—The approbation of our judges.

That meed with-held our labours have been vain;
Pointless *my* jests, and doubly keen your pain; 290
Might we their plaudits, and their praise provoke,
Our *bold* should then be term'd, a *happy* stroke.

THE END.

EPILOGUE. By a Gentleman.

Your servant, friends, from Spain, you see, I'm come,
A peace abroad,—but is it peace at home?
The sword is sheath'd, our heroes all are quiet,
A *gentle* woman I, and hate a riot.
To pick a lover from a croud of beaus,
A lady-stroke, though bold, you'll scarce oppose.
To night you've had a trial of our skill
In curing lethargy, that growing ill;
That lifeless inattention and neglect,
Which some deserve, some fear, and some expect;
Say, do you like our scheme? methinks I hear   10
A reverend sire, beyond his sixtieth year,
In grumbling accents, saying, "Stuff, sad stuff!
"Now there's a peace, you may have men enough:—
"They want a leg, perhaps, what's that to you?
"They're *Frenchmen* only, who make use of *two*.
"Then stay your whining, let your bold strokes cease,
"Each wound in war, is a bold stroke for peace."[143]

How weak your wit, ye lords of the creation,
When set to find a woman's inclination;
Her heart, though ice, the virgin fair and young,   20
Without an ear, with double share of tongue;
Let the fond youth she likes, but once appear,
His dulcet voice with rapture she can hear;
If she cou'd frown, by smiles her pride's disarm'd;
She *has* a heart, when *love* that heart has warm'd;
No tones discordant now, not even nay,
While sighs to sighs responsive seem to say,
In accents sweet,——"love, honour and obey."

Dear liberty, farewell! from babe to wife,
I've led a pretty, happy, checquer'd life;   30
I'll tell you how, the tale's not very long,
But, if you please, I'll give it you in song.

AIR.

When I was a little baby,
Plump and round as may be,
    For a lullaby
    I'd fret and cry,
When I was a little baby.

But at six years old, how froward,[144]
Naughty girl, untoward,
    To dress my doll,
    And prate like poll,[145]
A naughty girl untoward.

At twelve, what a blooming flower!   10
Around me every hour
    Butterflies gay,
    To sip and play,
Flew round this blooming flower.

At sweet sixteen, so pretty,
All I said was witty;
    A charming lass,
    So said my glass,
At dear sixteen so pretty.

Love's dart no more to parry,   20
At twenty-two to marry,
    To one dear youth
    I plight my truth,
And that's the youth I'll marry.

With him I'll toy and play so,
He'll wonder why I stay so;
    But your applause
    Must crown my cause,
So clap your hands and say so.

          30

FINIS.

---

[143] *bold stroke for peace*: likely referring to the Peace of Paris (1783), the collection of treaties concluding the U.S. War of Independence and signed by representatives of Great Britain on one side and the United States, France, and Spain on the other.

[144] *froward*: disposed to go counter to what is demanded or reasonable; perverse.

[145] *poll*: the conventional name for a parrot, and referring to the parrot's unintelligent repetition of words.

Every One Has His Fault: A Comedy, In Five Acts

Elizabeth Inchbald

Elizabeth Inchbald (1753–1821) was arguably the most successful author of the late eighteenth century, producing some 21 plays, two important and well-regarded novels, *A Simple Story* (1791) and *Nature and Art* (1796), and the groundbreaking *The British Theatre* (1808), a 25-volume collection of plays for which she provided critical prefaces to each play. Born Elizabeth Simpson, the daughter of Roman Catholic parents John and Mary Simpson, she left home at the age of eighteen to seek a career in acting, and two months later married actor John Inchbald, also a Roman Catholic, on 9 June 1772. The couple acted in the provinces, first in West Digges's and then in Tate Wilkinson's company, until John Inchbald's death in 1779, after which Elizabeth Inchbald secured a place with Thomas Harris's company at Covent Garden in London.

Inchbald's career as a dramatist is a testimony to her determination and resolve. It took her four years to convince George Colman to produce her first farce, *A Mogul Tale* (Haymarket, 1784), which capitalized on that summer's rage for ballooning as well as commenting on the dissolution of the Whig Fox-North government and, through its portrayal of the enlightened mogul, arguing for Indian self-rule.[1] The play's topicality and ironic portrayal of British chauvinism made it a hit with audiences, and an astounding run of stage successes followed, including *I'll Tell You What!* (Haymarket, 1785; 20 performances), *Such Things Are* (Covent Garden, 1787; 22 performances), and *The Child of Nature* (1788; 27 performances). Racking up nine hit plays in five years allowed Inchbald to give up acting altogether; after 1789 she devoted herself entirely to writing. No woman writer of the period more resolutely insisted on authorial and financial independ-

ence. Living frugally and investing shrewdly, she was able to maintain a brilliant social life, with wide acquaintance among both aristocracy and literati, while supporting herself and two sisters. After Harris infuriated her by cutting *The Child of Nature* to three acts after its fourth performance and playing it as an afterpiece—thus depriving her of the £500-£600 she could expect from her benefit nights—Inchbald became more exacting in her negotiating, eventually insisting on payment in advance for her work.

The popular and critical success of *Every One Has His Fault* is all the more remarkable when we consider the context in which it appeared. Opening less than a week after news of Louis XVI's execution in revolutionary France had reached England, the play was attacked for its supposed aesthetic and political transgressiveness. For a reviewer in *The True Briton* (included in the Appendix), the play's "exceptionable" mixing of comedy and sensibility were part and parcel of its "objectional" politics—not only Mr. Harmony's refrain "Provisions are so scarce!" but also Inchbald's representations of the vindictive father, Lord Norland, and the destitute officer, Captain Irvin.[2] When the play appeared in published form, Inchbald was instead accused of removing the offensive statements after the play's opening night. As the Larpent manuscript of the play makes clear, Inchbald justly denied such charges.[3]

The play's controversy, however, did not end there. As Gillian Russell has noted, the play's association with anti-war sentiment in turn spawned other attacks: its opening performance at the Brighton

---

[1] Betsy Bolton, *Women, Nationalism and the British Stage: Theatre and Politics in Britain, 1780–1800* (Cambridge: Cambridge University Press, 2001), 206.

[2] Jane Moody, *Illegitimate Theatre in London, 1770–1840* (Cambridge: Cambridge University Press, 2000), 49.

[3] James Boaden, *Memoirs of Mrs. Inchbald*, 2 vols. (R. Benley, 1833), 1:311.

Theatre in 1793 was interrupted by a group of military officers who succeeded in driving the Reverend Veccessimus Knox, a known opponent of the war with France, from the theater, while a performance at the Portsmouth Theatre in 1795 was the occasion of a riot by naval officers who "terminated the performance."[4] The increased publicity accorded Inchbald's drama may even have backfired; its initial run of 32 performances is the longest of any original Inchbald play, and was only exceeded in 1798 by her adaptation of August von Kotzebue's *Das Kind der Liebe, Lovers' Vows* (Covent Garden, 1798), which ran for 42 nights.

The copytext for the play is *Every One Has His Fault: A Comedy, in five acts, as it is performed at the Theatre Royal, Covent-Garden* (London: G. G. J. and J. Robinson, 1793). We have indicated some major variations found in the Larpent manuscript (Huntington Library LA 967) in the notes. There are many later editions of the play, some of which provide additional information about staging choices.

PROLOGUE. By the Rev. Mr. Nares.[6]
Spoken by Mr. Farren.

Our Author, who accuses great and small,
And says so boldly, there are faults in all;
Sends me with dismal voice, and lengthen'd phiz,[7]
Humbly to own one dreadful fault of his:
A fault, in modern Authors not uncommon,
It is,—now don't be angry—He's—*a woman*.

Can you forgive it? Nay, I'll tell you more,
One who has dar'd to venture here before;
Has seen your smiles, your frowns,—tremendous sight!
O, be not in a frowning mood to-night!   10
The Play, perhaps, has many things amiss;
Well, let us then reduce the point to this,
Let only those that have no failings, hiss.

The Rights of Women,[8] says a female pen,
Are, to do every thing as well as Men.
To think, to argue, to decide, to write,
To talk, undoubtedly—perhaps, to fight.
(For Females march to war, like brave Commanders,
Not in old Authors only—but in Flanders).[9]

I grant this matter may be strain'd too far,   20
And Maid 'gainst Man is most uncivil war:
I grant, as all my City friends will say,
That Men should rule, and Women should obey:
That nothing binds the marriage contract faster,
Than our—a "Zounds, Madam, I'm your Lord and
          Master."
I grant their nature, and their frailty such,
Women may make too free—and know too much.
But since the Sex at length has been inclin'd
To cultivate that useful part—the mind;—
Since they have learnt to read, to write, to spell;—   30
Since some of them have wit,—and use it well;—
Let us not force them back with brow severe,
Within the pale of ignorance and fear,

---

4 Gillian Russell, *The Theatres of War: Performance, Politics, and Society, 1793–1815* (Oxford: Clarendon Press, 1995), 11.

5 *Rev. Mr. Nares*: Edward Nares (1762–1841), miscellaneous writer, ordained in 1792 and appointed to the vicarage of St. Peter-in-the-East, Oxford. Between 1788 and 1797 he lived as the librarian at Bleinheim Palace, where he played in private theatricals with the daughters of the Duke of Marlborough, eloping with one of them and marrying her in 1797.

6 *phiz*: face or countenance.

7 *Rights of Women*: referring to Mary Wollstonecraft's *A Vindication of the Rights of Woman*, published in 1792.

8 *Not … but in Flanders*: presumably referring to the famous march of Parisian women on Versailles on 5 October 1789, in which parts of the Flanders Regiment appointed to guard Versailles went over to the side of the women.

Confin'd entirely to domestic arts,
Producing only children, pies, and tarts.
The fav'rite fable of the tuneful Nine,
Implies that female genius *is divine*.

Then, drive not, Critics, with tyrannic rage,
A supplicating Fair-one from the Stage;
The Comic Muse perhaps is growing old,   40
Her lovers, you well know, are few and cold.
'Tis time then freely to enlarge the plan,
And let all those write Comedies—that can.

DRAMATIS PERSONAE

MEN:

Lord Norland	Mr. Farren
Sir Robert Ramble	Mr. Lewis
Mr. Solus	Mr. Quick
Mr. Harmony	Mr. Munden
Mr. Placid	Mr. Fawcett
Mr. Irwin	Mr. Pope
Hammond	Mr. Powell
Porter	Mr. Thompson
Edward	Miss Grist

WOMEN:

Lady Eleanor Irwin	Mrs. Pope
Mrs. Placid	Mrs. Mattocks
Miss Spinster	Mrs. Webb
Miss Wooburn	Mrs. Esten
Servants, &c.	

Scene: *London*

Act I

Scene I: *An Apartment at Mr. Placid's.*
Enter Mr. Placid [9] *and Mr. Solus.*

Placid. You are to blame.

Solus. I say the same by you.

Plac. And yet your singularity pleases me; for you are the first elderly bachelor I ever knew, who did not hug himself in the reflection, that he was not in the trammels of wedlock.

Solus. No; I am only the first elderly bachelor who has truth and courage enough to confess his dissatisfaction.[11]

Plac. And you really wish you were married?   10

Solus. I do. I wish still more, that I had been married thirty years ago. Oh! I wish a wife and half-a-score children would now start up around me, and bring along with them all that affection, which we should have had for each other by being earlier acquainted. But as it is, in my present state, there is not a person in the world I care a straw for; and the world is pretty even with me, for I don't believe there is a creature in it who cares a straw for me.

Plac. Pshaw! You have in your time been a man of   20 gallantry; and, consequently, must have made many attachments.

Solus. Yes, such as men of gallantry usually make. I have been attached to women who have purloined my fortune, and to men who have partaken of the theft: I have been in as much fear of my mistress as you are of your wife.

Plac. Is that possible?

Solus. Yes; and without having one of those tender, delicate ties of a husband, an excuse for my   30 apprehension.—I have maintained children——

Plac. Then why do you complain for the want of a family?

Solus. I did not say I ever had any children; I said I had *maintained* them; but I never believed they were mine; for I could have no dependence upon the principles of their mother—and never did I take one of those tender infants in my arms, that the forehead of my Valet, the squint-eye of my Apothecary, or the double-chin of my Chaplain,   40 did not stare me in the face, and damp all the fine feelings of the parent, which I had just called up.

Plac. But those are accidents which may occur in the marriage state.

Solus. In that case, a man is pitied—in mine, he is only laughed at.

Plac. I wish to heaven I could exchange the pity which my friends bestow on me, for the merriment which your ill fate excites.

Solus. You want but courage to be envied.   50

Plac. Does any one doubt my courage?

---

9 *Mr. Placid*: In the Larpent version, Mr. Placid is referred to as "Colonel Placid."

10 *dissatisfaction*: In the Larpent version, "interior dissatisfaction."

Solus. No. If a Prince were to offend you, you would challenge him, I have no doubt.

Plac. But if my wife offend me, I am obliged to make an apology.—Was not that her voice? I hope she has not overheard our conversation.

Solus. If she have, she'll be in an ill humour.

Plac. That she will be, whether she have heard it or not.

Solus. Well, good-day. I don't like to be driven from my fixed plan of wedlock; and, therefore, I won't be a spectator of your mutual discontent. *(Going).* 60

Plac. But before you go, Mr. Solus, permit me to remind you of a certain concern, that, I think, would afford you much more delight, than all you can, at this time of life, propose to yourself in marriage. Make happy by your beneficence, a near relation whom the truest affection has drawn into that state, but who is denied the blessing of competency to make the state supportable.

Solus. You mean my nephew, Irwin? But do not you 70 acknowledge he has a wife and children? Did not he marry the woman he loved, and has he not, at this moment, a large family, by whom he is beloved? And is he not, therefore, with all his poverty, much happier than I? He has often told me, when I have reproached him with his indiscreet marriage, "that in his wife he possessed kingdoms!" Do you suppose I will give any part of my fortune to a man who enjoys such extensive domains? No:—let him preserve his territories, and 80 I will keep my little estate for my own use. *(Exit).*

Plac. John! John!—*(Enter Servant)* Has your mistress been enquiring for me?

John. Yes, Sir:—My Lady asked just now, if I knew who was with you?

Plac. Did she seem angry?

John. No, Sir;—pretty well.

Plac. You scoundrel, what do you mean by "pretty well?" *(In anger).*

John. Much as usual, Sir. 90

Plac. And do you call that "pretty well?" You scoundrel, I have a great mind——

(Enter Mrs. Placid, speaking very loud).

Mrs. Placid. What is the matter, Mr. Placid? What is all this noise about? You know I hate a noise. What is the matter?

Plac. My dear, I was only finding fault with that blockhead.

Mrs. P. Pray, Mr. Placid, do not find fault with any body in this house. But I have something which I must take *you* very severely to task about, Sir. 100

Plac. No, my dear, not just now, pray.

Mrs. P. Why not now?

Plac. (Looking at his watch). Because dinner will be ready in a few minutes. I am very hungry, and it will be cruel of you to spoil my appetite. John, is the dinner on table?

Mrs. P. No, John, don't let it be served yet—Mr. Placid, you *shall* first hear what I have to say. *(Sitting down).*

(Exit Servant).

Plac. But then I know I sha'n't be able to eat a morsel. 110

Mrs. P. Sit down. *(He sits)*—I believe, Mr. Placid, you are going to do a very silly thing. I am afraid you are going to lend some money?

Plac. Well, my dear, and suppose I am?

Mrs. P. Then, I don't approve of people lending their money.

Plac. But, my dear, I have known you approve of borrowing money: And, once in our lives, what should we have done, if every body had refused to lend? 120

Mrs. P. That is nothing to the purpose.—And now I desire you will hear what I say, without speaking a word yourself.

Plac. Well, my dear.

Mrs. P. Now mind you don't speak, till I have done.—Our old acquaintance, Captain Irwin, and Lady Eleanor, his wife (with whom we lived upon very intimate terms, to be sure, while we were in America), are returned to London; and I find you have visited them very frequently. 130

Plac. Not above two or three times, upon my word; for it hurts me to see them in distress, and I forbear to go.

Mrs. P. There! You own they are in distress; I expected as much. Now, own to me that they have asked you to lend them money.

Plac. I do own it—I do own it. Now, are you satisfied?

Mrs. P. No: for I have no doubt but you have promised they shall have it. 140

Plac. No, upon my word, I have not promised.

Mrs. P. Then promise me they shall not.

Plac. Nay, my dear, you have no idea of their distress!

Mrs. P. Yes, I have; and 'tis that which makes me suspicious.

Plac. His regiment is now broken; all her jewels and little bawbles are disposed of; he is in such dread of his old creditors, that, in the lodging they have taken, he passes by the name of Middleton[12]— They have three more children, my dear, than when we left them in New England; and they have in vain sent repeated supplications, both to his uncle, and her father, for the smallest bounty.

Mrs. P. And is not Lord Norland, her father, a remarkably wise man? and a good man? And ought you to do for them, what he has refused?

Plac. They have offended him, but they have never offended me.

Mrs. P. I think 'tis an offence to ask a friend for money, when there is no certainty of returning it.

Plac. By no means: for, if there *were* a certainty, even an enemy might lend.

Mrs. P. But I insist, Mr. Placid, that they shall not find a friend in you upon this occasion.—What do you say, Sir?

Plac. (*After a struggle*). No, my dear, they shall not.

Mrs. P. Positively shall not?

Plac. Positively shall not—since they have found an enemy in you.

(*Enter Servant*).

Servant. Dinner is on table.[13]

Plac. Ah! I am not hungry now.

Mrs. P. What do you mean by that, Mr. Placid? I insist on your being hungry.

Plac. Oh yes! I have a very excellent appetite. I shall eat prodigiously.

Mrs. P. You had best. (*Exeunt*).

Scene II: *An Apartment at Mr. Harmony's.*
Enter Mr. Harmony followed by Miss Spinster.

Miss Spinster. Cousin, cousin Harmony, I will not forgive you for thus continually speaking in the behalf of every servant whom you find me

offended with. Your philanthropy becomes insupportable; and, instead of being a virtue, degenerates into a vice.

Har. Dear Madam, do not upbraid me for a constitutional fault.

Miss S. Very true; you had it from your infancy. I have heard your mother say you were always foolishly tender-hearted, and never shewed one of those discriminating passions[14] of envy, hatred, or revenge, to which all her other children were liable.

Har. No: since I can remember, I have felt the most unbounded affection for all my fellow creatures. I even protest to you, dear Madam, that, as I walk along the streets of this large metropolis, so warm is my heart towards every person who passes me, that I long to say, "How do you do?" and "I am glad to see you," to them all. Some men, I should like even to stop and shake hands with;—and some women, I should like even to stop and kiss.

Miss S. How can you be so ridiculous!

Har. Nay, 'tis truth: and I sincerely lament that human beings should be such strangers to one another as we are. We live in the same street, without knowing one another's necessities; and oftentimes meet and part from each other at church, at coffee-houses, play-houses, and all public places, without ever speaking a single word, or nodding "Good bye!" though 'tis a hundred chances to ten we never see one another again.

Miss S. Let me tell you, kinsman, all this pretended philanthropy renders you ridiculous. There is not a fraud, a theft, or hardly any vice committed, that you do not take the criminal's part, shake your

---

11   *Middleton*: At this point in the speech, the Larpent version adds "for fear of being dunn'd."

12   *table*: The Larpent version, in a stage direction, indicates that the servant exits.

13   *passions*: strong and fundamental emotions of the mind, such as Love, Hatred, Anger, and Fear. In seventeenth-century Britain, the word possessed a technical and philosophical sense, as in Thomas Wright's *The Passions of the Minde in Generall* (London, 1601), Robert Burton's *Anatomy of Melancholy* (London, 1621), and Rene Descartes' *The Passions of the Soul* (first English translation: London, 1650). Most often associated with the literature of sensibility in the second half of the eighteenth century, the term receives its fullest treatment at the turn of the nineteenth century in Joanna Baillie's *A Series of Plays ... on the Passions*, 3 vols. (London, 1798–1812).

head, and cry, "Provisions are so scarce!" And no longer ago than last Lord-mayor's day,[15] when you were told that Mr. Alderman Ravenous was ill with an indigestion, you endeavoured to soften the matter, by exclaiming, "Provisions are so scarce!"—But, above all, I condemn that false humanity,[16] which induces you to say many things in conversation which deserve to stigmatize you with the character of deceit.

Har. This is a weakness I confess. But though my honour sometimes reproaches me with it as a fault, my conscience never does: for it is by this very failing that I have frequently made the bitterest enemies friends—Just by saying a few harmless sentences, which, though a species of falsehood and deceit, yet, being soothing and acceptable to the person offended, I have immediately inspired him with lenity and forgiveness; and then, by only repeating the self-same sentences to his opponent, I have known hearts cold and closed to each other, warmed and expanded, as every human creature's ought to be.

(Enter Servant).

Serv. Mr. Solus. *(Exit Servant).*

Miss S. I cannot think, Mr. Harmony, why you keep company with that old bachelor; he is a man, of all others on earth, I dislike; and so I am obliged to quit the room, though I have a thousand things to say. *(Exit angrily).*

(Enter Solus).

Har. Mr. Solus, how do you do?

Solus.[17] I am very lonely at home; will you come and dine with me?

Har. Now you are here, you had better stay with me: we have no company; only my cousin Miss Spinster and myself.

Solus. No, I must go home: do come to my house.

Har. Nay, pray stay: what objection can you have?

Solus. Why, to tell you the truth, your relation, Miss Spinster, is no great favourite of mine; and I don't like to dine with you, because I don't like her company.

Har. That is, to me, surprising!

Solus. Why, old bachelors and old maids never agree: we are too much alike in our habits: we know our own hearts so well, we are apt to discover every foible we would wish to forget, in the symptoms displayed by the other. Miss Spinster is peevish, fretful and tiresome, and I am always in a fidget when I am in her company.

Har. How different are her sentiments of you! for one of her greatest joys is to be in your company. *(Solus starts and smiles).* Poor woman! she has, to be sure, an uneven temper—

Solus. No, perhaps I am mistaken.

Har.—But I will assure you, I never see her in half such good humour as when you are here: for I believe you are the greatest favourite she has.

Solus. I am very much obliged to her, and I certainly *am* mistaken about her temper—Some people, if they look ever so cross, are good-natured in the main; and I dare say she is so. Besides, she never has had a husband[18] to soothe and soften her disposition; and there should be some allowance made for that.

Har. Will you dine with us?

Solus. I don't care if I do. Yes, I think I will. I must however step home first:—but I'll be back in a quarter of an hour.—My compliments to Miss Spinster, if you should see her before I return. *(Exit).*

(Enter Servant).

Serv. My lady begs to know, Sir, if you have invited Mr. Solus to dine? because if you have, she shall go out. *(Exit Servant).*

(Enter Miss Spinster).

Har. Yes, Madam, I could not help inviting him; for, poor man, his own house is in such a state for want of proper management, he cannot give a comfortable dinner himself.

---

14 *Lord-mayor's day*: November 9th, the day on which the Lord Mayor goes in procession with the Aldermen and other city dignitaries to and from Westminster, where he receives from the Lord Chancellor the assent of the Crown to his election.

15 *humanity*: disposition to treat human beings and animals with consideration and compassion, and to relieve their distresses; kindness, benevolence.

16 *Solus*: The Larpent version adds the stage direction, "Yawns."

---

17 *husband*: The Larpent version adds "poor thing."

Miss S. And so he must spoil the comfort of mine.

Har. Poor man! poor man! after all the praises he has been lavishing upon you.

Miss S. What praises?

Har. I won't tell you; for you won't believe them.

Miss S. Yes, I shall.—Oh no—now I recollect, this is some of your invention.

Har. Nay, I told him it was *his* invention: for he declared you looked better last night, than any other lady at the Opera.

Miss S. No, this sounds like truth:—and, depend upon it, though I never liked the manners of Mr. Solus much, yet—

Har. Nay, Solus has his faults.

Miss S.[19] So we have all.

Har. And will you leave him and me to dine by ourselves?

Miss S. Oh no, I cannot be guilty of such ill manners, though I talked of it. Besides, poor Mr. Solus does not come so often, and it would be wrong not to shew him all the civility we can. For my part, I have no dislike to the man; and, if taking a bit of dinner with us now and then can oblige either you or him, I should be to blame to make any objection. Come, let us go into the drawing-room to receive him.

Har. Ay! this is right: this is as it should be. *(Exeunt).*

Scene III: *A Room at the Lodgings of Mr. Irwin. Mr. Irwin and Lady Eleanor Irwin discovered.*

Lady Eleanor. My dear husband, my dear Irwin, I cannot bear to see you thus melancholy. Is this the joy of returning to our native country after a nine years banishment?

Irwin. Yes. For I could bear my misfortunes, my wretched poverty with patience, in a land where our sorrows were shared by those about us; but here, in London, where plenty and ease smile upon every face; where, by birth you claim distinction, and I by services:—here to be in want,—to be obliged to take another name in shame of our own,—to tremble at the voice of every stranger, for fear he should be a creditor,—to meet each old acquaintance with an averted eye, because we would not feel the pang of being shunned.—To have no reward for all this, even in a comfortable home; but there, to see our children looking up to me for that support I have not in my power to give—Can I,—can I love them and you, and not be miserable?

Lady E. And yet I am not so. And I am sure you will not doubt my love to you or them.

Irwin. I met my uncle this morning, and was mean enough to repeat my request to him;—he burst into a fit of laughter, and told me my distresses were the result of my ambition, in marrying the daughter of a nobleman, who himself was too ambitious ever to pardon us.

Lady E. Tell me no more of what he said.

Irwin. This was a day of trials:—I saw your father too.

Lady E. My father! Lord Norland! Oh Heavens!

Irwin. He passed me in his carriage.

Lady E. I envy you the blessing of seeing him! For, Oh!—Excuse my tears—he is my father still.—How did he look?

Irwin. As well as he did at the time I used to watch him from his house, to steal to you.—But I am sorry to acquaint you, that, to guard himself against all returning love for you, he has, I am informed, adopted a young lad, on whom he bestows every mark of that paternal affection, of which you lament the loss.

Lady E. May the young man deserve his tenderness better than I have done—May he never disobey him—May *he* be a comfort, and cherish his benefactor's declining years—And when his youthful passions teach him to love, may they not, like mine, teach him disobedience!

(Enter a Servant with a letter).

Irwin. What is that letter?

Serv. It comes from Mr. Placid, the servant who brought it, said, and requires no answer. *(Exit).*

Irwin (Aside).[20] It's strange how I tremble at every letter I see, as if I dreaded the contents. How

---

18 *Spinster.* The Larpent version adds the stage direction, "Good naturedly."

19 *(Aside):* The Larpent version does not mark this speech as an aside.

poverty has unmann'd me!—I must tell you, my dear, that finding myself left this morning without a guinea, I wrote to Mr. Placid to borrow a small sum. This is his answer: *(Reading the superscription)* "To Mr. Middleton"—That's right;—he remembers the caution I gave him. I had forgot whether I had, for my memory is not so good as it was. I did not even recollect this hand, though it is one I am so well acquainted with, and ought to give me joy rather than sorrow *(Opens the letter hastily, reads, and lets it drop)*. Now I have not a friend on earth.

Lady E. Yes, you have me. You forget me.

Irwin (In a transport of grief). I would forget you— you—and all your children.

Lady E. I would not lose the remembrance of you, or of them, for all my father's fortune.

Irwin. What am I to do? I must leave you! I must go, I know not where! I cannot stay to see you perish. *(Takes his hat, and is going)*.

Lady E. (Holding him). Where would you go? 'Tis evening—'tis dark—Whither would you go at this time?

Irwin (Distractedly). I must consider what's to be done—and in this room my thoughts are too confined to reflect.

Lady E. And are London streets calculated for reflection?

Irwin. No;—for action. To hurry the faint thought to resolution.[21]

Lady E. You are not well—Your health has been lately impaired.—Your temper has undergone a change too:—I tremble lest any accident—

Irwin. What accident? *(Wildly)*.

Lady E. I know your provocations from an ungrateful world: But despise it, as that despises you.

Irwin. But for your sake, I could.

Lady E. Then witness, Heaven! I am happy.—Though bred in all the delicacy, the luxury of wealth and splendour; yet I have never murmured at the change of fortune, while that change has made me wife to you, and mother of your children.

Irwin. We *will* be happy—if possible. But give me this evening to consider what plan to fix upon.— There is no time to lose; we are without friends— without money—without credit.—Farewell for an hour.—I will see Mr. Placid, if I can; and though he have not the money to lend, he may, perhaps, give me some advice.

Lady E. Suppose I call on *her?* Women are sometimes more considerate than men, and—

Irwin. Do you for the best, and so will I.—Heavens bless you! *(Exeunt separately)*.

Act II

Scene I: *A Coffee or Club-room at a Tavern. Enter Sir Robert Ramble—and Mr. Solus and Mr. Placid at the opposite Side.*

Solus. Sir Robert Ramble, how do you do?

Sir Robert. My dear Mr. Solus, I am glad to see you. I have been dining by myself, and now come into this public room to meet with some good company.

Solus. Ay, Sir Robert, you are now reduced to the same necessity which I frequently am—I frequently am obliged to dine at taverns and coffee-houses, for want of company at home.

Sir R. Nay, I protest I am never happier than in a house like this, where a man may meet his friend without the inconvenience of form, either as a host or a visitor.

Solus. Sir Robert, give me leave to introduce to you Mr. Placid: he has been many years abroad; but I believe he now means to remain in his own country for the rest of his life. This, Mr. Placid, is Sir Robert Ramble.

Sir R. (To Mr. Placid). Sir, I shall be happy in your acquaintance; and I assure you, if you will do me the honour to meet me now and then at this house, you will find every thing very pleasant. I verily believe, that since I lost my wife, which is now about five months ago, I verily believe I have dined here three days out of the seven.

Plac. Have you lost your wife, Sir? And so lately?

---

22 *resolution*: The Larpent version adds two speeches after this one:

> *Lady E.*: Oh! do not throw yourself into the way of such temptation as London Streets yield to the unfortunate.
>
> *Irwin*: What do you apprehend?

Sir R. (With great indifference). Yes, Sir; about five months ago—Is it not, Mr. Solus? You keep account of such things better than I do.

Solus. Oh! ask me no questions about your wife, Sir Robert; if she had been mine, I would have had her to this moment.

Plac. What, wrested her from the gripe of death?

Sir R. No, Sir; only from the gripe of the Scotch lawyers.

Solus. More shame for you. Shame! to wish to be divorced from a virtuous wife.

Plac. Was that the case? Divorced from a virtuous wife! I never heard of such a circumstance before. Pray, Sir Robert *(Very anxiously)*, will you indulge me, by letting me know in what manner you were able to bring about so great an event?

Sir R. It may appear strange to you, Sir; but my wife and I did not live happy together.

Plac. Not at all strange, Sir; I can conceive—I can conceive very well.

Solus. Yes; he can conceive that part to a nicety.

Sir R. And so, I was determined on a divorce.

Plac. But then her character could not be unimpeached.

Sir R. Yes, it was, Sir. You must know, we were married in Scotland,[22] and by the laws there, a wife can divorce her *husband* for breach of fidelity; and so, though my wife's character was unimpeached, mine was not, and she divorced me.

Plac. And is this the law in Scotland?

Sir R. It is. Blessed, blessed country! that will bind young people together before the years of discretion[23]—and, as soon as they have discretion to repent, will unbind them again!

Plac. I wish I had been married in Scotland.

Solus. But, Sir Robert, with all this boasting, you must own that your divorce has greatly diminished your fortune.

Sir R. (Taking Solus aside). Mr. Solus, you have frequently hinted at my fortune being impaired; but I do not approve of such notions being received abroad.

Solus. I beg your pardon; but every body knows that you have played very deep lately, and have been a great loser, and every body knows——

Sir R. No, Sir, every body does not know it, for I contradict the report wherever I go. A man of fashion does not like to be reckoned poor, no more than he likes to be reckoned unhappy. We none of us endeavour to *be* happy, Sir, but merely to be *thought* so; and for my part, I had rather be in a state of misery, and envied for my supposed happiness, than in a state of happiness, and pitied for my supposed misery.

Solus. But consider, these misfortunes which I have just hinted at, are not of any serious nature, only such as a few years economy——

Sir R. But were my wife and her guardian to become acquainted with these little misfortunes, they would triumph in my embarrassments.

Solus. Lady Ramble triumph! *(They join Mr. Placid).* She who was so firmly attached to you, that I believe nothing but a compliance with your repeated request to be separated, caused her to take the step she did.

Sir R. Yes, I believe she did it to oblige me, and I am very much obliged to her.

Solus. As good a woman, Mr. Placid——

Sir R. Very good—but very ugly.

Solus. She is beautiful.

Sir R. (To Solus). I tell you, Sir, she is hideous. And then she was grown so insufferably peevish.

Solus. I never saw her out of temper.

Sir R. Mr. Solus, it is very uncivil of you to praise her before my face. Lady Ramble, at the time I parted with her, had every possible fault both of mind and person, and so I made love to other women in her presence; told her bluntly that I was tired of her; that "I was very sorry to make her uneasy, but that I could not love her any longer."—And was not that frank and open?

---

21 *married in Scotland*: Scotland had less restrictive marriage laws than England, and the term "Scotch marriage" refers to a marriage according to the Scots law, effected by a mutal declaration before witnesses, without other formality; it is chiefly applied to the runaway marriages of couples who crossed from England into Scotland to escape the restrictions imposed by English law on the marriage of minors without the consent of their guardians.

22 *years of discretion*: the age at which one is considered legally mature and able to act without parental consent.

Solus. Oh! that I had but such a wife as she was!

Sir R. I must own I loved her myself when she was young.

Solus. Do you call her old?   110

Sir R. In years I am certainly older than she; but the difference of sex makes her a great deal older than I am. For instance, Mr. Solus, you have often lamented not being married in your youth; but if you had, what would you have now done with an old wife, a woman of your own age?

Solus. Loved and cherished her.

Sir R. What, in spite of her loss of beauty?

Solus. When she had lost her beauty, most likely I should have lost my eye-sight, and have been blind   120 to the wane of her charms.

Plac. (Anxiously). But, Sir Robert, you were explaining to me—Mr. Solus, give me leave to speak to Sir Robert—I feel myself particularly interested on this subject.—And, Sir, you were explaining to me——

Sir R. Very true: Where did I leave off? Oh! at my ill usage of my Lady Ramble. Yes, I did use her very ill, and yet she loved me. Many a time, when she has said to me, "Sir Robert, I detest your principles, your   130 manners, and even your person," often, at that very instant, I have seen a little sparkle of a wish peep out of the corner of one eye, that has called to me, "Oh! Sir Robert, how I long to make it up with you!"

Solus (To Mr. Placid). Do not you wish that your wife had such a little sparkle at the corner of one of her eyes?

Sir R. (To Mr. Placid). Sir, do you wish to be divorced?

Plac. I have no such prospect. Mrs. Placid is faithful,   140 and I was married in England.

Sir R. But if you have an unconquerable desire to part, a separate maintenance[24] will answer nearly the same end—for if your Lady and you will only lay down the plan of separation, and agree—

Plac. But, unfortunately, we never do agree!

Sir R. Then speak of parting as a thing you dread worse than death; and make it your daily prayer

to her, that she will never think of going from you—She will determine upon it directly.   150

Plac. I thank you; I'm very much obliged to you: I thank you a thousand times.

Sir R. Yes, I have studied the art of teasing a wife; and there is nothing vexes her so much as laughing at her. Can you laugh, Mr. Placid?

Plac. I don't know whether I can; I have not laughed since I married.—But I thank you, Sir, for your instructions—I sincerely thank you.

Solus. And now, Sir Robert, you have had the good nature to teach this Gentleman how to get rid of   160 his wife, will you have the kindness to teach me how to procure one?

(Enter Mr. Irwin).

Sir R. Hah! Sure I know that Gentleman's face?

Solus (Aside). My Nephew! Let me escape his solicitations—Here, waiter! *(Exit).*

Plac. Irwin! *(Starting, aside).* Having sent him a denial, I am ashamed to see him.—Here, Mr. Solus!—*(Exit, following Mr. Solus).*

Irwin (Aside). More cool faces! My necessitous countenance clears even a club-room.   170

Sir R. My dear Captain Irwin, is it you? Yes, 'faith it is—After a nine years' absence I most sincerely rejoice to see you.

Irwin. Sir Robert, you shake hands with a cordiality I have not experienced these many days, and I thank you.

Sir R. But what's the matter? You seem to droop—Where have you left your usual spirits? Has absence from your country changed your manners?

Irwin. No, Sir; but I find some of my countrymen   180 changed. I fancy them less warm, less friendly than they were; and it is that which, perhaps, has this effect upon me.

Sir R. Am I changed?

Irwin. You appear an exception.

Sir R. And I assure you, that instead of being grown more gloomy, I am even more gay than I was seven years ago; for then, I was upon the point of matrimony—but now, I am just relieved from its cares.   190

Irwin. I have heard as much. But I hope you have not taken so great an aversion to the marriage-state, as never to marry again.

---

23   *separate maintenance*: the action of providing a person with the requisites of life; in this case, support given by a husband to a wife when the parties are separated.

Sir R. Perhaps not: But then it must be to some rich heiress.

Irwin. You are right to pay respect to fortune. Money is a necessary article in the marriage contract.

Sir R. As to that—that would be no great object at present. No, thank Heaven, my estates are pretty large; I have no children; I have a rich Uncle, excellent health, admirable spirits;—and thus happy, it would be very strange if I did not meet my old friends with those smiles, which never for a moment quit my countenance.

Irwin. In the dispensation of the gifts of Providence, how few are found blest like you! *(Sighing).*

Sir R. And I assure you, my dear Mr. Irwin, it gives me the most serious reflections, and the most sincere concern, that they are not.

Irwin. I thank you, Sir, most heartily: I thank you for mankind in general, and for myself in particular. For after this generous, unaffected declaration (with less scruple than I should to any man in the world) I will own to you, that I am at this very time in the utmost want of an act of friendship.

Sir R. (Aside). And so am I—Now must I confess myself a poor man; or pass for an unfeeling one; and I will choose the latter. *(Bowing with great ceremony and coldness).* Any thing that I can command, is at your service.

Irwin (Confounded and hesitating). Why then, Sir Robert—I am almost ashamed to say it—but circumstances have been rather unfavourable.—My wife's father *(Affecting to smile)* is not reconciled to us yet—My regiment is broke—My Uncle will not part with a farthing.—Lady Eleanor, my wife, *(Wipes his eyes)* has been supported as yet, with some little degree of tenderness, elegance; and—in short, I owe a small sum which I am afraid of being troubled for; I want a trifle also for our immediate use, and if you would lend me a hundred pounds—though, upon my honour, I am not in a situation to fix the exact time when I can pay it.

Sir R. My dear Sir, never trouble yourself about the time of paying it, because it happens not to be in my power to lend it you.

Irwin. Not in your power? I beg your pardon; but have not you this moment been saying you are rich?

Sir R. And is it not very common to be rich without money? Are not half the town rich? And yet half the town has no money. I speak for this end of the town, the West end. The Squares, for instance, part of Piccadilly, down St. James's-street, and so home by Pall Mall. We have all, estates, bonds, drafts, and notes of hand without number; but as for money, we have no such thing belonging to us.

Irwin. I sincerely beg your pardon. And be assured, Sir, nothing should have induced me to have taken the liberty I have done, but the necessities of my unhappy family, and having understood by your own words, that you were in affluence.

Sir R. I *am* in affluence, I am, I am; but not in so much, perhaps, as my hasty, inconsiderate account may have given you reason to believe. I forgot to mention several heavy incumbrances, which you will perceive are great drawbacks on my fortune.—As my wife sued for the divorce, I have her fortune to return; I have also two sisters to portion off—a circumstance I totally forgot. But, my good friend, though I am not in circumstances to do what you require, I will do something that shall be better. I'll wait upon your father-in-law, (Lord Norland) and entreat him to forgive his daughter: and I am sure he will if I ask him.

Irwin. Impossible.

Sir R. And so it is, now I recollect: for he is no other than the guardian of my late wife, and a request from me, will be received worse than from any other person.—However, Mr. Irwin, depend upon it, that whenever I have an opportunity of serving you, I will. And whenever you shall do me the favour to call upon me, I shall be heartily glad to see you. If I am not at home, you can leave your card, which, you know, is all the same, and depend upon it, I shall be extremely glad to see you or that, at any time. *(Exit).*

Irwin. Is this my native country? Is this the hospitable land which we describe to strangers? No—We are savages to each other; nay worse—The savage[25]

---

24 *savage*: a primitive, uncivilized person. In the mid-eighteenth century, the figure of the savage was reha-bilitated most famously in the writings of Jean-Jacques Rousseau (1712–78), French philosopher, novelist, and

makes his fellow-savage welcome; divides with him his homely fare; gives him the best apartment his hut affords, and tries to hush those griefs that are confided in his bosom—While in this civilized city, among my own countrymen, even among my brother officers in the army, and many of my nearest relations, so very civilized they are, I could not take the liberty to enter under one roof, without a ceremonious invitation, and that they will not give me. I may leave my card at their door, but as for me, or any one of mine, they would not give us a dinner; unless, indeed, it was in such a style, that we might behold with admiration their grandeur, and return still more depressed, to our own poverty.—Can I bear this treatment longer? No, not even for you, my Eleanor. And this *(Takes out a pistol)* shall now be the only friend to whom I will apply—And yet I want the courage to be a villain.

(Enter Mr. Harmony, speaking as he enters. Irwin conceals the pistol instantly).

Har. Let me see half a dozen newspapers—Every paper of the day.

(Enter Waiter).

Waiter. That is about three dozen, Sir.

Har. Get a couple of porters, and bring them all.

(He sits down; they bring him papers, and he reads—Irwin starts, sits down, leans his head on one of the tables, and shews various signs of uneasiness; then comes forward).

Irwin. Am I a man, a soldier?—And a coward? Yes, I run away, I turn my back on life—I forsake the post, which my commander, Providence, has allotted me, and fly before a banditti[26] of rude misfortunes. Rally me, love, connubial[27] and

---

political theorist whose writings are often invoked as foundational texts of the French Revolution. Rousseau's figure of the "noble savage" is most famously portrayed in *Discours sur l'origine de l'inegalité* (*Discourse on the Origin of Inequality*, 1755) and *Du Contrat social* (*The Social Contract*, 1762).

25 *banditti*: literally, a plural form of "bandit," used most often to refer to an organized band of robbers or outlaws.

26 *connubial*: married; of or pertaining to marriage.

parental love, rally me back to the charge! No, those very affections sound the retreat. *(Sits down with the same emotions of distraction as before).*

Har. (Aside). That gentleman does not seem happy. I wish I had an opportunity of speaking to him.

Irwin (Comes forward and speaks again). But Oh! my wife, what will be your sufferings when I am brought home to your wretched habitation!—And by my own hand!

Har. I am afraid, Sir, I engross all the news here. *(Holding up the papers).*

Irwin (Still apart). Poor soul, how her heart will be torn!

Har. (After looking steadfastly on him). Captain Irwin, till this moment I had not the pleasure of recollecting you! It is Mr. Irwin, is it not?

Irwin (His mind deranged by his misfortunes). Yes, Sir: But what have you to say to him more than to a stranger?

Har. Nothing more, Sir, than to apologize to you, for having addressed you just now in so familiar a manner, before I knew who you were; and to assure you, that although I have no other knowledge of you, than from report, and having been once, I believe, in your company at this very house before you left England; yet, any services of mine, as far as my abilities can reach, you may freely command.

Irwin. Pray, Sir, do you live at the West end of the town?

Har. I do.

Irwin. Then, Sir, your services can be of no use to me.

Har. Here is the place where I live, here is my card. *(Gives it to him).*

Irwin. And here is mine. And now I presume we have exchanged every act of friendship, which the strict forms of etiquette, in this town, will admit of.

Har. By no means, Sir. I assure you my professions never go beyond my intentions; and if there is any thing that I can serve you in—

Irwin. Have you no sisters to portion off? no lady's fortune to return? Or, perhaps, you will speak to my wife's father, and entreat him to forgive his child.

Har. On that subject you may command me; for I have the honour to be intimately acquainted with Lord Norland.

Irwin. But is there no reason you may recollect, "why you would be the most unfit person in the world to apply to him?"

Har. None. I have been honoured with marks of his friendship for many years past; and I do not know any one who could, with less hazard of his resentment, venture to name his daughter to him. 360

Irwin. Well, Sir, if you should see him two or three days hence, when I am set out on a journey I am going, if you will then say a kind word to him for my wife and children, I'll thank you.

Har. I will go to him instantly. *(Going).*

Irwin. No, do not see him yet; stay till I am gone. He will do nothing till I am gone.

Har. May I ask where you are going?

Irwin. No very tedious journey; but it is a country, 370 to those who go without a proper passport, always fatal.

Har. I'll see Lord Norland to-night: perhaps I may persuade him to prevent your journey. I'll see him to-night, or early in the morning, depend upon it.—I am a man of my word, Sir; though I must own I do live at the West end of the town. *(Exit).*

Irwin. 'Sdeath,[27] am I become the ridicule of my fellow-creatures? or am I not in my senses?—I know this is London—this house a tavern—I 380 know I have a wife. Oh! 'twere better to be mad than to remember her! She has a father—he is rich and proud—that I will not forget. But I will pass his house, and send a malediction as I pass it— *(Furiously).* No; breathe out my last sigh at his inhospitable door, and that sigh shall breathe— forgiveness. *(Exit).*

Scene II: *The Lodgings of Mr. Irwin. Enter Mrs. Placid, followed by Lady Eleanor Irwin.*

Lady E. I am ashamed of the trouble I have given you, Mrs. Placid. It had been sufficient to have sent me home in your carriage; to attend me yourself was ceremonious.

Mrs. P. My dear Lady Eleanor, I was resolved to come home with you, as soon as Mr. Placid desired I would not.

Lady E. Was that the cause of your politeness? I am sorry it should.

Mrs. P. Why sorry? It is not proper he should have 10 his way in every thing.

Lady E. But I am afraid you seldom let him have it at all.

Mrs. P. Yes, I do.—But where, my dear, is Mr. Irwin?[28]

Lady E. (Weeping). I cannot hear the name of Mr. Irwin without shedding tears: his health has been so much impaired of late, and his spirits so bad— sometimes I even fear for a failure in his mind. *(Weeps again).* 20

Mrs. P. Is not he at home?

Lady E. I hope he is. *(Goes to the side of the scenes).* Tell your master, Mrs. Placid is here.

(Enter Servant).

Serv. My master is not come in yet, Madam.

Lady E. Not yet? I am very sorry for it;—very sorry indeed.

Mrs. P. Bless me, my dear, don't look thus pale. Come sit down, and I'll stay with you till he returns. *(Sits down herself).*

Lady E. My dear, you forget that Mr. Placid is in the 30 carriage at the door all this time.

Mrs. P. No, I don't. Come, let us sit and have half an hour's conversation.

Lady E. Nay, I insist upon your going to him, or desiring him to walk in.

Mrs. P. Now I think of it, they may as well drive him home, and come back for me.

(Enter Mr. Placid).

Why surely, Mr. Placid, you were very impatient! I think you might have waited a few minutes longer. 40

Plac. I would have waited, my dear, but the evening is so damp.

Lady E. Ah! 'tis the evening, which makes me alarmed for Mr. Irwin.

Plac. Lady Eleanor, you are one of the most tender, anxious, and affectionate wives I ever knew.

Mrs. P. There! Now he wishes he was your husband— He admires the conduct of every wife but his own,

---

27 *'Sdeath*: a contraction for "God's death."

28 *But where, my dear, is Mr. Irwin?*: The Larpent cuts this sentence, and adds in its place "There are times, when his will is a law to me." Lady Eleanor then begins the subsequent speech with "Where is Mr. Irwin?"

and envies every married man of his acquaintance. But it is very ungenerous of you. 50

Plac. So it is, my dear; and not at all consistent with the law of retaliation; for I am sure there is not one of my acquaintance who envies me.

Mrs. P. Mr. Placid, your behaviour throughout this whole day has been so totally different to what it ever was before, that I am half resolved to live no longer with you.

Plac. (Aside). It will do—It will do.

Lady E. Oh, my dear friends, do not talk of parting: how can you, while every blessing smiles on your 60 union? Even I, who have reason to regret mine, yet, while that load of grief, a separation from Mr. Irwin, is but averted, I will think every other affliction supportable. *(A loud rapping at the door).* That is he.

Mrs. P. Why, you seem in raptures at his return.

Lady E. I know no greater rapture.

(Enter Irwin pale, trembling, and disordered).

Lady E. My dear, you are not well, I see.

Irwin. Yes.—*(Aside to her in anger).*—Why do you speak of it? 70

Plac. How do you do, Irwin?

Irwin. I am glad to see you. *(Bows).*

Mrs. P. But I am sorry to see you look so ill.

Irwin. I have only been taking a glass too much.

(Lady Eleanor weeps).

Plac. Pshaw! Don't I know you never drink?

Irwin. You are mistaken: I do when my wife is not by. I am afraid of her.

Plac. Impossible.

Irwin. What! To be afraid of one's wife?

Plac. No; I think that very possible. 80

Mrs. P. But it does not look well when it is so; it makes a man appear contemptible, and a woman a termagant. Come, Mr. Placid, I cannot stay another moment. Good night. Heaven bless you! *(To Lady Eleanor)*—Good night, my dear Mr. Irwin; and now, pray take my advice and keep up your spirits.

Irwin. I will, Madam. *(Shaking hands with Placid).* And do you keep up your spirits.

(Exeunt Mr. and Mrs. Placid. Irwin shuts the door with care after them, and looks round the room as if he feared to be seen or overheard).

I am glad they are gone. I spoke unkindly to you 90 just now, did I not? My temper is altered lately; and yet I love you.

Lady E. I never doubted it, nor ever will.

Irwin. If you did, you would wrong me; for there is not a danger I would not risk for your sake; there is not an infamy I would not be branded with to make you happy, nor a punishment I would not undergo, with joy, for your welfare.—But there is a bar to this; we are unfortunately so entwined together, so linked, so rivetted, so cruelly, painfully 100 fettered to each other, you could not be happy unless I shared the self same happiness with you.— But you will learn better—now you are in London, and amongst fashionable wives; you must learn better. *(Walks about and smiles, with a ghastly countenance).*

Lady E. Do not talk, do not look thus wildly— Indeed, indeed, you make me very uneasy.

Irwin. What! uneasy when I come to bring you comfort; and such comfort as you have not 110 experienced for many a day? *(He pulls out a pocket-book).* Here is a friend in our necessity,—a friend that brings a thousand friends; plenty and—no, not always—peace. *(He takes several papers from the book, and puts them into her hands—She looks at them, then screams).*

Lady E. Ah! 'Tis money. *(Trembling).* These are Bank notes.

Irwin. Hush! For heaven's sake, hush! We shall be discovered. *(Trembling and in great perturbation).* 120 What alarms you thus?

Lady E. What alarms you?

Irwin. Do you say I am frightened?

Lady E. A sight so new has frightened me.

Irwin. Nay, they are your own: by heaven, they are! No one on earth has a better, or a fairer right than you have. It was a laudable act by which I obtained them.—The parent-bird had forsook its young, and I but forced it back to perform the rites of nature.

Lady E. You are insane, I fear. No, no, I do not *fear*— 130 *hope* you are.

(A loud rapping at the street-door—He starts, takes the notes from her, and puts them hastily into his pocket).

Irwin. Go to the door yourself; and if 'tis any one who asks for me, say I am not come home yet.

(She goes out, then returns).

Lady E. It is the person belonging to the house: no one to us.

Irwin. My dear Eleanor, are you willing to quit London with me in about two hours time?

Lady E. Instantly.

Irwin. Nay, not only London, but England.

Lady E. This world, if you desire it. To go in company with you, will make the journey pleasant; and all I loved on earth would still be with me. 140

Irwin. You can, then, leave your father without regret, *never, never* to see him more?

Lady E. Why should I think on him, who will not think of me? *(Weeps).*

Irwin. But our children—

Lady E. We are not to leave them behind?

Irwin. One of them we must: but do not let that give you uneasiness. You know he has never lived with us since his infancy, and cannot pine for the loss of parents whom he has never known. 150

Lady E. But I have *known him.* He was my first; and, sometimes, I think more closely wound around my heart, than all the rest. The grief I felt on being forced to leave him when we went abroad, and the constant anxiety I have since experienced lest he should not be kindly treated, have augmented, I think, my tenderness.

Irwin. All my endeavours to-day, as well as every other day, have been in vain to find into what part of the country his nurse has taken him.—Nay, be not thus overcome with tears; we will (in spite of all my haste to be gone) stay one more miserable day here, in hopes to procure intelligence, so as to take him with us; and then smile with contempt on all we leave behind. *(Exeunt).* 160

Act III

Scene I: *A Library at Lord Norland's.*
Enter Lord Norland, followed by Mr. Harmony.

Lord Norland (In anger). I tell you, Mr. Harmony, that if an indifferent person, one on whom I had never bestowed a favour in my life, were to offend me, it is in my nature never to forgive. Can I then forgive my own daughter, my only child, on whom I heaped continually marks of the most affectionate fondness? Shall she dare to offend me in the tenderest point, and you dare to suppose I will pardon her?

Har. Your child, consider. 10

Lord N. The weakest argument you can use. As my child, was not she most bound to obey me? As my child, ought she not to have sacrificed her own happiness to mine? Instead of which, mine has been yielded up for a whim, a fancy, a fancy to marry a beggar; and as such is her choice, let her beg with him.

Har. She does by me;—pleads hard for your forgiveness.

Lord N. If I thought she dared to send a message to me, though dictated on her knees, she should find that she had not yet felt the full force of my resentment. 20

Har. What could you do more?

Lord N. I have done nothing yet. At present, I have only abandoned her;—but I can persecute.

Har. I have no doubt of it: and, that I may not be the means of aggravating your displeasure, I assure you, that what I have now said has been entirely from myself, without any desire of hers; and, at the same time, I give you my promise, I will never presume to intrude the subject again. 30

Lord N. On this condition (but on no other) I forgive you now.

Har. And now then, my Lord, let us pass from those who have forfeited your love, to those who possess it.—I heard some time ago, but I never presumed to mention it to you, that you had adopted a young man as your son?

Lord N. "A young man!" Pshaw!—No; a boy—a mere child, who fell in my way by accident. 40

Har. A chance child! Ho! ho!—I understand you.

Lord N. Do not jest with me, Sir. Do I look——

Har. Yes,[29] you look as if you would be ashamed to own it, if you had one.

Lord N. But this boy I am not ashamed of:—he is a favourite—rather a favourite.—I did not like him so well at first;—but custom,—and having a poor

---

29 *Yes*: The Larpent version deletes this word and adds "I can't say you do, but."

creature entirely at one's mercy, one begins to love it merely from the idea of—What would be its fate 50 if one did not?

Har. Is he an orphan then?

Lord N. No.

Har. You have a friendship for his parents?

Lord N. I never saw the father: his mother I had a friendship for once. *(Sighing).*

Har. Ay, while the husband was away?

Lord N. (Violently). I tell you, no.—But ask no more questions. Who his parents are, is a secret, which neither he, nor any one (that is now living) knows, 60 except myself; nor ever shall.

Har. Well, my Lord, since 'tis your pleasure to consider him as your child, I sincerely wish you may experience more duty from him than you have done from your daughter.

Lord N. Thank Heaven, his disposition is not in the least like hers.—No: *(Very much impassioned)* I have the joy to say, that never child was so unlike its mother.

Har. (Starting). How! His mother! 70

Lord N. Confusion!—what have I said?—I am ashamed——

Har. No,—be proud.

Lord N. Of what?

Har. That you have a lawful heir to all your riches; proud that you have a grandson.

Lord N. I would have concealed it from all the world; I wished it even unknown to myself. And let me tell you, Sir, (as not by my design, but through my inadvertency, you are become acquainted with this 80 secret) that, if ever you breathe it to a single creature, the boy shall answer for it; for, were he known to be hers, though he were dearer to me than ever *she* was, I would turn him from my house, and cast him from my heart, as I have done her.

Har. I believe you;—and in compassion to the child, give you my *solemn promise* never to reveal who he is. I have heard that those unfortunate parents left an infant behind when they went abroad, and that they now lament him as lost. Will you satisfy my 90 curiosity, in what manner you sought and found him out?

Lord N. Do you suppose I searched for him? No;—he was forced upon me. A woman followed me, about eight years ago, in the fields adjoining to my country seat, with a half-starved boy in her hand, and asked my charity for my grand-child: the impression of the word, made me turn round involuntarily; and casting my eyes upon him, I was rejoiced, not to find a feature of his mother's in all his face; and I began 100 to feel something like pity for him. In short, he caught such fast hold by one of my fingers, that I asked him carelessly "if he would go home and live with me?" On which, he answered me so willingly "Yes," I took him at his word.

Har. And did never your regard for him, plead in his mother's behalf?

Lord N. Never. For, by Heaven, I would as soon forgive the robber who met me last night at my own door, and, holding a pistol to my breast, took 110 from me a sum to a considerable amount, as I would pardon her.

Har. Did such an accident happen to you?

Lord N. Have you not heard of it?

Har. No.

Lord N. It is amazing we cannot put a stop to such depredations.[30]

Har. Provisions are so scarce![31]

(Enter Servant).

Serv. Miss Wooburn, my Lord, if you are not engaged, will come and sit an hour with you. 120

Lord N. I have no company but what she is perfectly acquainted with, and shall be glad of her visit. *(Exit Servant).*

Har. You forget I am a stranger, and my presence may not be welcome.

Lord N. A stranger! What, to my ward? to Lady Ramble? for that is the name which custom would authorise her to keep; but such courtesy she disdains, in contempt of the unworthy giver of the title. 130

---

30 *depredations*: acts of robbery or pillaging.

31 *Provisions are so scarce!*: After this speech, the Larpent version adds the following exchange:

Lord N. How! Do you take the part of public ruffians.

Har. No. I wish them still extirpated—But if there are persons who, by their oppression provoke those outrages, I wish them punished first.

Har. I am intimate with Sir Robert,[32] my Lord; and though I acknowledge that both you and his lady have cause for complaint, yet Sir Robert has still many virtues.

Lord N. Not one. He is the most vile, the most detestable of characters. He not only contradicted my will in the whole of his conduct, but he seldom met me that he did not give me some personal affront.

Har. It is, however, generally held better to be uncivil in a person's presence, than in his absence. 140

Lord N. He was uncivil to me in every respect.

Har. That I will deny; for I have heard Sir Robert, in your absence, say such things in your praise!—

Lord N. Indeed!

Har. Most assuredly.

Lord N. I wish he had sometimes done me the honour to have spoken politely to my face.

Har. That is not Sir Robert's way;—he is no flatterer. But then, no sooner has your back been turned, than I have heard him lavish in your praise. 150

Lord N. I must own, Mr. Harmony, that I never looked upon Sir Robert as incorrigible. I could always discern a ray of understanding, and a beam of virtue through all his foibles; nor would I have urged the divorce, but that I found his wife's sensibility could not bear his neglect; and even now, notwithstanding her endeavour to conceal it, she pines in secret, and laments her hard fortune. All my hopes of restoring her health rest on one prospect—that of finding a 160 man worthy my recommendation for her second husband, and, by creating a second passion, expel the first.—Mr. Harmony, you and I have been long acquainted—I have known your disposition from your infancy—Now, if such a man as you were to offer—

Har. You flatter me.

Lord N. I do not.—Would you venture to become her husband?

Har. I cannot say I have any particular desire; but if 170 it will oblige either you or her,—for my part, I think the short time we live in this world, we should do all we can to oblige each other.

Lord N. I should rejoice at such an union myself, and I think I can answer for her.—You permit me then to make overtures to her in your name?

Har. (Considering). This is rather a serious piece of business——However, I never did make a difficulty when I wished to oblige a friend.—But there is one proviso,[33] my Lord; I must first 180 mention it to Sir Robert.

Lord N. Why so?

Har. Because he and I have always been very intimate friends; and to marry his wife, without even telling him of it, will appear very uncivil!

Lord N. Do you mean then to ask his consent?

Har. Not absolutely his consent; but I will insinuate the subject to him, and obtain his approbation in a manner suitable to my own satisfaction.

Lord N. You will oblige me then if you will see him as 190 early as possible; for it is reported he is going abroad.

Har. I will go to him immediately;—and, my Lord, I will do all in my power to oblige you, Sir Robert and the Lady; *(Aside)*—but as to obliging myself, that was never one of my considerations. *(Exit).*

(Enter Miss Wooburn).

Lord N. I am sorry to see you thus; you have been weeping? Will you still[34] lament your separation from a cruel husband, as if you had followed a kind one to the grave?

Miss Wooburn. By no means, my Lord. Tears from 200 our sex are not always the result of grief; they are frequently no more than little sympathetic tributes which we pay to our fellow-beings, while the mind and the heart are steeled against the weakness which our eyes indicate.

Lord N. Can you say, your mind and heart are so steeled?

Miss W. I can: My mind is as firmly fixed against Sir Robert Ramble, as at our first acquaintance it was fixed upon him. And I solemnly protest—— 210

---

32 *Sir Robert*: The Larpent version here calls Sir Robert "Sir Ralph."

33 *proviso*: a clause inserted in a legal or formal document, making some condition, stipulation, exception, or limitation.

34 *weeping? Will you still*: After "weeping," the Larpent version adds, "Surely your pride should teach you to overcome this continual sorrow." It then replaces "Will you still" with "You appear to."

Lord N. To a man of my age and observation, protestations are vain.—Give me a proof that you have rooted him from your heart.

Miss W. Any proof you require, I will give without a moment's hesitation.

Lord N. I take you at your word; and desire you to accept a Gentleman, whom I shall recommend for your second husband. *(Miss Wooburn starts).*—You said you would not hesitate a moment.

Miss W. I thought I should not;—but this is 220 something so unexpected——

Lord N. You break your word then, and still give cause for this ungrateful man, to ridicule your fondness for him.

Miss W. No, I will put an end to that humiliation; and whoever the Gentleman is whom you mean to propose—Yet, do not name him at present—but give me the satisfaction of keeping the promise I have made to you (at least for a little time) without exactly knowing how far it extends; for, 230 in return, I have a promise to ask from you, before I acquaint you with the nature of your engagement.

Lord N. I give my promise. Now name your request.

Miss W. Then, my Lord, *(Hesitating and confused)*—the law gave me back, upon my divorce from Sir Robert, the very large fortune which I brought to him.—I am afraid, that in his present circumstances, to enforce the strict payment of this debt, would very much embarrass him. 240

Lord N. What if it did?

Miss W. It is my entreaty to you (in whose hands is invested the power to demand this right of law) to lay my claim aside for the present. *(Lord Norland offers to speak)* I know, my Lord, what you are going to say; I know Sir Robert is not *now*, but I can never forget that he *has been* my husband.

Lord N. To shew my gratitude for your compliance with the request I have just made you,[35] *(Goes to a table in the library)* here is the bond by which I 250 am impowered to seize on the greatest part of his estates in right of you: take the bond into your own possession till your next husband demands it

of you;[36] and by the time you have called him husband for a few weeks, this tenderness, or delicacy to Sir Robert, will be worn away.

(Enter Harmony, hastily).

Har. My Lord, I beg pardon; but I forgot to mention——

Miss W. Oh, Mr. Harmony, I have not seen you before I know not when: I am particularly happy 260 at your calling just now, for I have—*(Hesitating)* a little favour to ask of you.

Har. If it were a great favour, Madam, you might command me.

Miss W. But—my Lord, I beg your pardon—but the favour I have to ask of Mr. Harmony must be told to him in private.

Lord N. Oh! I am sure I have not the least objection to you and Mr. Harmony having a private conference. I'll leave you together. *(Harmony* 270 *appears embarrassed).* You do not derange my business—I'll be back in a short time. *(Exit).*

Miss W. Mr. Harmony, you are the very man on earth I most wanted to see. *(Harmony bows).* I know the kindness of your heart, the liberality of your sentiments, and I wish to repose a charge to your trust, very near to me indeed—but you must be secret.

Har. When a Lady reposes a trust in me, I should not be a man if I were not. 280

Miss W. I must first inform you, that Lord Norland has just drawn from me a promise, that I will once more enter into the marriage-state; and without knowing to whom he intends to give me, I will keep my promise—But it is in vain to say, that, though I mean all duty and fidelity to my second husband, I shall not experience moments when my thoughts—will wander on my first.

Har. (Starting). Hem!—Hem!—*(To her)*—Indeed?

Miss W. I must always rejoice in Sir Robert's successes, 290 and lament over his misfortunes.

Har. If that is all—

Miss W. No, I would go one step further: *(Harmony starts again)* I would secure him from those

---

35 *I have just made you*: Here, the Larpent version adds, "I will go as far as possible in granting yours."

36 *till your next husband demands it of you*: Here, the Larpent version adds, "He will be the properest person to enforce it."

misfortunes, which to hear of, will disturb my peace of mind. I know his fortune has suffered very much, and I cannot, *will not*, place it in the power of the man, whom my Lord Norland may point out for my next marriage, to distress him farther.— This is the writing, by which that Gentleman may claim the part of my fortune from Sir Robert Ramble, which is in landed property; carry it, my dear Mr. Harmony, to Sir Robert instantly; and tell him, that in separating from him, I meant only to give him liberty; not make him the debtor, perhaps the prisoner of my future husband.

Har. Madam, I will most undoubtedly take this bond to my friend; but will you give me leave to suggest to you, that the person on whom you bestow your hand, may be a little surprised to find, that while he is in possession of you, Sir Robert is in the possession of your fortune?

Miss W. Do not imagine, Sir, that I shall marry any man, without first declaring what I have done—I only wish at present it should be concealed from Lord Norland—When this paper is given, as I have required, it cannot be recalled; and when that is past, I shall divulge my conduct to whom I please; and first of all, to him, who shall offer me his addresses.

Har. And if he is a man of my feelings, his addresses will be doubly importunate for this proof of liberality to your former husband.—But are you sure, that in the return of this bond, there is no secret affection, no latent spark of love?

Miss W. None. I know my heart; and if there was, I could not ask you, Mr. Harmony (nor any one like you), to be the messenger of an imprudent passion. Sir Robert's vanity, I know, may cause him to judge otherwise; but undeceive him; let him know this is a sacrifice to the golden principles of duty, and not an offering to the tinselled shrine of love.

(Enter Lord Norland).

Put up the bond.—*(Harmony conceals it).*

Lord N. Well, my dear, have you made your request?

Miss W. Yes, my Lord.

Lord N. And has he granted it?

Har. Yes, my Lord. I am going to grant it.

Lord N. I sincerely wish you both joy of this good understanding between you. But, Mr. Harmony, *(In a whisper)* are not you going to Sir Robert?

Har. Yes, my Lord, I am going this moment.

Lord N. Make haste then, and do not forget your errand.

Har. No, my Lord, I sha'n't forget my errand; it won't slip my memory—Good morning, my Lord— good morning, Madam. *(Exit).*

Lord N. Now, my dear, as you and Mr. Harmony seem to be on such excellent terms, I think I may venture to tell you (if he has not yet told you himself), that he is the man, who is to be your husband.

Miss W. He! Mr. Harmony!—No, my Lord, he has not told me; and I am confident he never will.

Lord N. What makes you think so?

Miss W. Because—because—he must be sensible he would not be the man I should choose.

Lord N. And where is the woman who marries the man she would choose? You are reversing the order of society; men, only, have the right of choice in marriage. Were women permitted theirs, we should have handsome beggars allied to our noblest families, and no such object in our whole island as an old maid.

Miss W. But being denied that choice, why forbid to remain as I am?

Lord N. What are you now? Neither a widow, a maid, nor a wife. If I could fix a term to your present state, I should not be thus anxious to place you in another.

Miss W. I am perfectly acquainted with your friendly motives, and feel the full force of your advice.—I therefore renew my promise—and although Mr. Harmony (in respect to the marriage state) is as little to my wishes as any man on earth, I will nevertheless endeavour—whatever struggles it may cost me—to be to him, if he prefers his suit, a dutiful, an obedient—but, for a loving wife, that I can never be again. *(Exeunt severally).*

Scene II: *An Apartment at Sir Robert Ramble's. Enter Sir Robert and Mr. Harmony.*

Sir R. I thank you for this visit. I was undetermined what to do with myself. Your company has determined me to stay at home.

Har. I was with a Gentleman just now, Sir Robert, and you were the subject of our conversation.

Sir R. Had it been a Lady, I should be anxious to know what she said.

Har. I have been with a Lady likewise; and she made you the subject of her discourse.

Sir R. But was she handsome? 10

Har. Very handsome.

Sir R. My dear fellow, what is her name? What did she say, and where may I meet with her?

Har. Her name is Wooburn.

Sir R. That is the name of my late wife.

Har. It is her I mean.

Sir R. Zounds, you had just put my spirits into a flame, and now you throw cold water all over me.

Har. I am sorry to hear you say so, for I came from her this moment; and what do you think is the 20 present she has given me to deliver to you?

Sir R. Pshaw! I want no presents. Some of my old love-letters returned, I suppose, to remind me of my inconstancy?

Har. Do not undervalue her generosity: this is her present;—this bond, which has power to take from you three thousand a year, her right.

Sir R. Ah! this is a present indeed. Are you sure you speak truth? Let me look at it:—Sure my eyes deceive me!—No, by Heaven it is true! *(Reads*[37]*)* 30 The very thing I wanted, and will make me perfectly happy. Now I'll be generous again: my bills shall be paid, my gaming debts cancelled, poor Irwin shall find a friend; and I'll send her as pretty a copy of verses as ever I wrote in my life.

Har. Take care how you treat with levity a woman of her elevated mind. She charged me to assure you, "that love had no share whatever in this act, but merely compassion to the embarrassed state of your affairs." 40

Sir R. Sir, I would have you to know, I am no object of compassion. However, a Lady's favour one cannot return; and so, I'll keep this thing. *(Puts it in his pocket).*

Har. Nay, if your circumstances are different from what she imagines, give it me back, and I will return it to her.

Sir R. No, poor thing! it would break her heart to

send it back—No, I'll keep it—She would never forgive me, were I to send it back. I'll keep it. And 50 she is welcome to attribute her concern for me to what she pleases. But surely you can see—you can understand—But Heaven bless her for her love! and I would love her in return—if I could.

Har. You would not talk thus, if you had seen the firm dignity with which she gave me that paper—"Assure him," said she, "no remaining affection comes along with it, but merely a duty which I owe him, to protect him from the humiliation of being a debtor to the man whom I am going to marry." 60

Sir R. (With the utmost emotion). Why, she is not going to be married again!

Har. I believe so.

Sir R. But are you sure of it, Sir? Are you sure of it?

Har. Both she and her guardian told me so.

Sir R. That guardian, my Lord Norland, is one of the basest, vilest of men.—I tell you what, Sir, I'll resent this usage.

Har. Wherefore?—As to his being the means of bringing about your separation, in that he obliged 70 you.

Sir R. Yes, Sir, he did, he certainly did;—but though I am not the least offended with him on that head (for at that I rejoice), yet I will resent his disposing of her a second time.

Har. And why?

Sir R. Because, little regard as I have for her myself, yet no other man shall dare to treat her so ill, as I have done.

Har. Do not fear it—Her next husband will be a 80 man, who, I can safely say, will never insult, or even offend her; but soothe, indulge, and make her happy.

Sir R. And do you dare to tell me, that her next husband shall make her happy? Now, that is worse than the other—No, Sir, no man shall ever have it to say "he has made her either happy or miserable," but myself.

Har. I know of but one way to prevent it.

Sir R. And what is that? 90

Har. Pay your addresses to her, and marry her again yourself.

Sir R. And I would, rather than she should be happy with any body else. The devil take me if I would not.

---

37 *Reads*: To this stage direction, the Larpent version adds "Estate Entail."

Har. To shew that I am wholly disinterested in this affair, I will carry her a letter from you if you like, and say all I can in your behalf.

Sir R. Ha, ha, ha! Now, my dear Harmony, you carry your good-natured simplicity too far. However, I thank you, I sincerely thank you—But do you imagine I should be such a blockhead, as to make love to the same woman I made love to seven years ago, and who for the last six years I totally neglected?

Har. Yes: for if you neglected her six years, she will now be a novelty.

Sir R. Egad, and so she will. You are right.

Har. But being in possession of her fortune, you can be very happy without her.

Sir R. Take her fortune back, Sir. *(Taking the bond from his pocket and offering it to Harmony).* I would starve, I would perish, die in poverty and infamy, rather than owe an obligation to a vile, perfidious, inconstant woman.

Har. Consider, Sir Robert, if you insist on my taking this bond back, it may fall into the husband's hands.

Sir R. Take it back—I insist upon it. *(Gives it him, and Harmony puts it up).* But, Mr. Harmony, depend on it, Lord Norland shall hear from me, in the most serious manner, for his interference— I repeat, he is the vilest, the most villanous of men.

Har. How can you speak with such rancour of a nobleman, who speaks of *you* in the highest terms?

Sir R. Does he, 'faith?

Har. He owns you have some faults.

Sir R. I know I have.

Har. But he thinks your good qualities are numberless.

Sir R. Now dam'me, if ever I thought so ill of *him*, as I have appeared to do!—But who is the intended husband, my dear friend? Tell me, that I may laugh at him, and make you laugh at him.

Har. No, I am not inclined to laugh at him.

Sir R. Is it old Solus?

Har. No.

Sir R. But I will bet you a wager it is somebody equally ridiculous.

Har. I never bet.

Sir R. Solus is mad for a wife, and has been praising mine up to the heavens; you need say no more; I know it is he.

Har. Upon my honour, it is not. However, I cannot disclose to you at present the person's name; I must first obtain Lord Norland's permission.

Sir R. I shall ask you no more. I'll write to her—she will tell me;—or, I'll pay her a visit, and ask her boldly myself.—Do you think *(Anxiously)*—do you think she would see me?

Har. You can but try.

(Enter Servant).

Serv. Mr. Solus.

Sir R. Now I will find out the secret immediately.— I'll charge him with being the intended husband.

Har. I will not stay to hear you.

(Enter Solus).

Mr. Solus, how do you do? I am extremely sorry that my engagements take me away as soon as you enter. *(Exit Harmony running, to avoid an explanation).*

Solus. Sir Robert, what is the matter? Has any thing ruffled you? Why, I never saw you look more out of temper, even while you were married.

Sir R. Ah! that I had never married! never known what marriage was! for, even at this moment, I feel its torments in my heart.

Solus. I have often heard of the torments of matrimony; but I conceive, that at the worst, they are nothing more than a kind of violent tickling, which will force the tears into your eyes, though at the same time you are bursting your sides with laughter.

Sir R. You have defined marriage too favourably; there is no laughter in the state: all is melancholy, all gloom.

Solus. Now I think marriage is an excellent remedy for the spleen. I have known a Gentleman at a feast receive an affront, disguise his rage, step home, vent it all upon his wife, return to his companions, and be as good company as if nothing had happened.

Sir R. But even the necessary expences of a wife should alarm you.

Solus. I can then retrench some of my own. Oh! my dear Sir, a married man has so many delightful privileges to what a bachelor has!—An old Lady will introduce her daughters to you in a dishabille[38]—"It does not signify, my dears, it's a

---

38 *dishabille*: a garment worn in a state of undress; a dress or costume in a negligent or informal style.

married man"—One Lady will suffer you to draw on her glove—"Never mind, it's a married man"—Another will permit you to pull on her slipper; a third will even take you into her bed-chamber—"Pshaw, it's *nothing* but a married man."

Sir R. But the weight of your fetters will overbalance all these joys.

Solus. And I cannot say, notwithstanding you are relieved from the bond, that I see much joy or brightness here.

Sir R. I am not very well at present; I have the headache; and, if ever a wife can be of comfort to her husband, it must be when he is indisposed. A wife, then, binds up your head, mixes your powders, bathes your temples, and hovers about, in a way that is most endearing.

Solus. Don't speak of it; I long to have one hover about me. But I will—I am determined I will, before I am a week older. Don't speak, don't attempt to persuade me not. Your description has renewed my eagerness—*I* will be married.

Sir R. And without pretending not to know who you mean to make your wife, I tell you plainly, it is, Miss Wooburn, it is my late wife.—I know you made overtures to my Lord Norland, and that he has given his consent.

Solus. You tell me a great piece of news—I'll go ask my Lord if it be true; and if he says it is, I shall be very glad to find it so.

Sir R. That is right, Sir; marry her, marry her;—I give you joy,—that's all.—Ha, ha, ha! I think I should know her temper.—But if you will venture to marry her, I sincerely wish you happy.

Solus. And if we are not, you know we can be divorced.

Sir R. Not always. Take my advice, and live as you are.

Solus. You almost stagger my resolution.—I had painted such bright prospects in marriage:—Good day to you. *(Going, returns)*—You think I had better not marry?

Sir R. You are undone if you do.

Solus (Sighing). You ought to know from experience.

Sir R. From that I speak.

Solus (Going to the door, and returning once or twice, as unstable in his resolution). But then, what a poor disconsolate object shall I live, without a wife to hover about me; to bind up my head, and bathe my temples! Oh! I am impatient for all the chartered rights, privileges, and immunities of a married man. *(Exit).*

Sir R. Furies, racks, torments—I cannot bear what I feel, and yet I am ashamed to own I feel any thing!

(Enter Mr. Placid).

Plac. My dear Sir Robert, give me joy. Mrs. Placid and I are come to the very point you advised; matters are in the fairest way for a separation.

Sir R. I do give you joy, and most sincerely.—You are right; you'll soon be as happy as I am. *(Sighing).* But would you suppose it? that deluded woman, my wife, is going to be married again! I thought she had had enough of me!

Plac. You are hurt, I see, lest the world should say she has forgot you.

Sir R. She cannot forget me; I defy her to forget me.

Plac. Who is her intended husband?

Sir R. Solus, Solus. An old man—an ugly man.[39] He left me this moment, and owned it—owned it! Go after him, will you, and persuade him not to have her.

Plac. My advice will have no effect, for you know he is bent upon matrimony.

Sir R. Then could not you, my dear Sir (as you are going to be separated), could not you recommend him to marry your wife?—It will be all the same to him, I dare say, and I shall like it much better.

Plac. Ours will not be a divorce, consider, but merely a separate maintenance. But were it otherwise, I wish no man so ill, as to wish him married to Mrs. Placid.

Sir R. That is my case exactly. I wish no man so ill, as to wish him married to my Lady Ramble; and poor old Solus in particular, poor old man! a very good sort of man—I have a great friendship for Solus.—I can't stay a moment in the house—I must go somewhere—I'll go to Solus.—No, I'll go to Lord Norland—No, I will go to Harmony; and then I'll call on you, and we'll take a bottle

---

39 *man*: At this point in the Larpent version, Sir Robert then asks, "What do you think of him?", to which Placid responds, "Are you sure 'tis him?" Sir Robert then continues his speech as in the text.

together; and when we are both free *(Takes his hand)* we'll join, from that moment we'll join, to laugh at, to contemn, to despise all those who boast of the joys of conjugal love. *(Exeunt)*. 270

Act IV

Scene I: *An Apartment at Mr. Harmony's.*
Enter Mr. Harmony.

Har. And now, for one of the most painful tasks that brotherly love ever draws upon me; to tell another, the suit, of which I gave him hope, has failed.— Yet, if I can but overcome Captain Irwin's delicacy so far, as to prevail on him to accept one proof more of my good wishes towards him;—but to a man of his nice sense of obligations, the offer must be made with caution.

(Enter Lord Norland).

Lord N. Mr. Harmony, I beg your pardon: I come in thus abruptly, from the anxiety I feel concerning 10 what passed between us this morning in respect to Miss Wooburn. You have not changed your mind, I hope?

Har. Indeed, my Lord, I am very sorry that it will not be in my power to oblige you.

Lord N. (In anger). How, Sir? Did not you give me your word?

Har. Only conditionally, my Lord.

Lord N. And what were the conditions?

Har. Have you forgot them? Her former husband. 20

(Enter Servant).

Serv. Sir Robert Ramble is in his carriage at the door, and, if you are at leisure, will come in.

Har. Desire him to walk up. I have your leave, I suppose, my Lord?

(Exit Servant).

Lord N. Yes; but let me get out of the house without meeting him. *(Going to the opposite door)*. Can I go this way?

Har. Why should you shun him?

Lord N. Because he used his wife ill.

Har. He did. But I believe he is very sorry for it.— 30 And as for you, he said to me only a few hours ago—but no matter.

Lord N. What did he say? I insist upon knowing.

Har. Why then he said, "that if he had a sacred trust to repose in any one, *you* should be the man on earth, to whom he would confide it."

Lord N. Well, I am in no hurry; I can stay a few minutes.

(Enter Sir Robert Ramble).

Sir R. Oh! Harmony! I am in such a distracted state of mind—*(Seeing Lord Norland, he starts, and bows* 40 *with the most humble respect)*.

Lord N. Sir Robert, how do you do?

Sir R. My Lord, I am pretty well.—I hope I have the happiness of seeing your Lordship in perfect health.

Lord N. Very well, Sir, I thank you.

Sir R. Indeed, my Lord, I think I never saw you look better.

Lord N. Mr. Harmony, you and Sir Robert may have some business—I'll wish you a good morning.

Har. No, my Lord, I fancy Sir Robert has nothing 50 particular.

Sir R. Nothing, nothing, I assure you, my Lord.

Lord N. However, I have business myself in another place, and so you will excuse me. *(Going)*.

Sir R. (Following him). My Lord—Lord Norland,— I trust you will excuse my enquiries.—I hope, my Lord, all your family are well?

Lord N. All very well.

Sir R. Your little Elevè,—Master Edward,—the young Gentleman you have adopted—I hope he 60 is well—*(Hesitating and confused)* And—your Ward, Sir—Miss Wooburn—I hope, my Lord, she is well?

Lord N. Yes, Sir Robert, Miss Wooburn is tolerably well.

Sir R. Only tolerably, my Lord? I am sorry for that.

Har. I hope, my Lord, you will excuse my mentioning the subject; but I was telling Sir Robert just now, of your intentions respecting a second marriage for that Lady; but Sir Robert does 70 not appear to approve of the design.

Lord N. What objection can *he* have?

Sir R. My Lord, there are such a number of bad husbands; there are such a number of dissipated, unthinking, unprincipled men!—And—I should be extremely sorry to see any Lady with whom I have had the honour of being so closely allied, united to one who would undervalue her worth.

Lord N. Pray, Sir Robert, were you not then extremely sorry for her, while she was united to you? 80

Sir R. Very sorry for her indeed, my Lord. But, at that time, my mind was so taken up with other cares, I own I did not feel the compassion which was her due; but, now that I am single, I shall have leisure to pay her more attention; and should I find her unhappy, it must, inevitably, make me so.

Lord N.[40] Depend upon it, that on the present occasion, I shall take infinite care in the choice of her husband. 90

Sir R. If your Lordship would permit me to have an interview with Miss Wooburn, I think I should be able at least—

Lord N. You would not sure insult her by your presence?

Sir R. I think I should be able at least to point out an object worthy of her taste—I know what she will like better than any body in the world.

Lord N. Her request has been, that I may point her out a husband the reverse of you. 100

Sir R. Then, upon my honour, my Lord, she won't like him.

Lord N. Have not you liked women the reverse of her?

Sir R. Yes, my Lord, perhaps I have, and perhaps I still do. I do not pretend to love *her*; I did not say I did; nay, I positively protest I do not; but this indifference I acknowledge as one of my faults; and, notwithstanding all my faults, give me leave to acknowledge my gratitude that your Lordship 110 has nevertheless been pleased to declare you think my virtues are numberless. *(Lord Norland shews surprise).*

Har. (Aside to Sir Robert). Hush, hush!—Don't talk of your virtues now.

Lord N. Sir Robert, to all this incoherent language, this is my answer, this is my will: The Lady, to whom I have had the honour to be guardian, shall never (while she calls me friend) see you more.

(Sir Robert, at this sentence, stands silent for some time, then, suddenly recollecting himself).

Sir R. Lord Norland, I am too well acquainted with 120 the truth of your word, and the firmness of your temper, to press my suit one sentence farther.

Lord N. I commend your discernment.

Sir R. My Lord, I feel myself a little embarrassed.— I am afraid I have made myself a little ridiculous upon this occasion—Will your Lordship do me the favour to forget it?

---

40 *Lord N*: From this speech until the speech of Lord Norland's that ends with the stage direction, *"(Lord Norland shews suprise),"* the Larpent version handles the scene differently:

Lord N. Sir Robert, depend upon it, that on the present occasion, I shall take infinite care in the choice of her husband.

Sir R. Might I, my Lord, presume to recommend any one sort of man, it should be a reformed rake.

Har. I have a notion Sir Robert could point out the exact person.

Sir R. If your Lordship would permit me to have an interview with Miss Wooburn, I think I should be able at least——

Lord N. You would not sure insult her by your presence.

Sir R. Never, if you will promise me not to dispose of her without my consent.

Lord N. Why your consent?

Sir R. Because I know her taste, I know what she will like better than anybody in the world.

Lord N. Her request has been, that I may point her out a husband the reverse of you.

Sir R. Then, upon my honour, my Lord, she won't like him.

Lord N. Have not you liked women the reverse of her?

Sir R. But I don't think I ever shall again—For oh! let me confess to you, my lord (tho' it goes damnably against me to do so *[Aside]*) Let me declare to you, that from the moment our marriage has been dissolved, from that very moment, I have been languishing in the most torturing, tho' concealed desire, to become her husband again—I know I have neglected her for others; but I now find I cou'd neglect all the world for her—I have treated you, my Lord, oftentimes, with an unwarrantable liberty, but I am at present ready to implore your pardon, and to acknowledge my gratitude in the highest degree, that with all my vices, you have nevertheless allowed, my virtues are numberless.

Lord N. I will forget whatever you please.[41]

Har. (Following him, whispers). I am sorry to see you going away in despair. 130

Sir R. I never did despair in my life, Sir; and while a woman is the object of my wishes, I never will. *(Exit).*

Lord N. What did he say?

Har. That he thought your conduct that of a just and an upright man.

Lord N. To say the truth, he has gone away with better manners than I could have imagined, considering his jealousy is provoked.

Har. Ah! I always knew he loved his wife, 140 notwithstanding his behaviour to her; for, if you remember, he always spoke well of her behind her back.

Lord N. No, I do not remember it.

Har. Yes, he did; and that is the only criterion of a man's love, or of his friendship.

(Enter Servant).

Serv. A young gentleman is at the door, Sir, enquiring for Lord Norland.

Lord N. Who can it be?

Har. Your young gentleman from home, I dare say. 150 Desire him to walk in. Bring him here. *(Exit Servant).*

Lord N. What business can he have to follow me?

(Enter Edward).

Edward. Oh, my Lord, I beg your pardon for coming hither; but I come to tell you something you will be glad to hear.

Har. Good Heaven! how like his mother!

Lord N. (Taking him by the hand). I begin to think he is—but he was not so when I first took him. No, no, if he had, he would not have been thus 160 near me now;—but to turn him away because his countenance is a little changed, I think would not be right.

Edw. (To Harmony). Pray, Sir, did you know my mother?

Har. I have seen her.

Edw. Did *you* ever see her, my Lord?

Lord N. I thought you had orders never to enquire about your parents? Have you forgot those orders?

Edw. No, my Lord; but when this gentleman said I 170 was like my mother—it put me in mind of her.

Har. You do not remember your mother, do you?

Edw. Sometimes I think I do. I think sometimes I remember her kissing me, when she and my father went on board of a ship; and so hard she pressed me—I think I feel it now.

Har. Perhaps she was the only Lady that ever saluted you?

Edw. No, Sir; not by many.

Lord N. But pray, young man (to have done with this 180 subject), what brought you here? You seem to have forgot your errand?

Edw. And so I had, upon my word. Speaking of my mother, put it quite out of my head.—But, my Lord, I came to let you know, the robber who stopped you last night is taken.

Lord N. I am glad to hear it.

Edw. I knew you would; and therefore I begged to be the first to tell you.

Har. (To Lord Norland). Should you know the person 190 again?

Lord N. I cannot say I should, his face seemed so much distorted.

Har. Ay, wretched man! I suppose with terror.

Lord N. No; it appeared a different passion from fear.

Edw. Perhaps, my Lord, it was *your* fear that made you think so.

Lord N. No, Sir, I was not frightened.

Edw. Then why did you give him your money?

Lord N. It was surprise caused me to do that. 200

Edw. I wondered what it was! You said it was not fear, and I was sure it could not be love.

Har. How has he been taken?

Edw. A person came to our steward, and informed against him;—and, Oh! my Lord, his poor wife told the officers who took him, they had met with misfortunes, which she feared had caused a fever in her husband's head; and, indeed, they found him too ill to be removed; and so, she hoped, she said, "that as a man, not in his perfect mind, you 210 would be merciful to him."

Lord N. I will be just.

Edw. And that is being merciful, is it not, my Lord?

---

41 *please:* After this speech, the Larpent version adds the following:
   Sir R. Lord, I take my leave.

Lord N. Not always.

Edw. I thought it had been.—It is not *just* to be unmerciful, is it?

Lord N. Certainly not.

Edw. Then it must be *just*, to have mercy.

Lord N. You draw a false conclusion. Great as is the virtue of *mercy, justice* is greater still. *Justice* holds its place among those cardinal virtues which include all the lesser.—Come, Mr. Harmony, will you go home with me? And before I attend to this business, let me persuade you to forget there is such a person in the world as Sir Robert, and suffer me to introduce you to Miss Wooburn, as the man who—

Har. I beg to be excused—Besides the consideration of Sir Robert, I have another reason why I cannot go with you. The melancholy tale which this young gentleman has been telling, has cast a gloom on my spirits which renders me unfit for the society of a Lady.

Lord N. Now I should not be surprised were you to go in search of this culprit and his family, and come to me to intreat me to forego the prosecution; but, before you ask me, I tell you it is in vain—I will not.

Har. Lord Norland, I have lately been so unsuccessful in my petitions to you, I shall never presume to interpose between your rigour and a weak sufferer more.

Lord N. Plead the cause of the good, and I will listen; but you find none but the wicked for your compassion.

Har. The good in all states, even in the very jaws of death, are objects of envy; it is the bad who are the only real sufferers: There, where no internal consolation cheers, who can refuse a little external comfort?—And let me tell you, my Lord, that amidst all your authority, your state, your grandeur, I often pity you. *(Speaking with unaffected compassion).*

Lord N. Good-day, Mr. Harmony; and when you have apologised for what you have said, we may be friends again. *(Exit, leading off Edward).*

Har. Nay, hear my apology now. I cannot—no, it is not in my nature to live in resentment, nor under the resentment of any creature in the world. *(Exit, following Lord Norland).*

Scene II: *An Apartment at Lord Norland's.*
Enter Sir Robert Ramble, followed by a Servant.

Sir R. Do not say who it is—but say a Gentleman who has some very particular business with her.

Serv. Yes, Sir. *(Going).*

Sir R. Pray, *(Servant returns)* you are but lately come into this service, I believe?

Serv. Only a few days, Sir.

Sir R. You don't know me, then?

Serv. No, Sir.

Sir R. I am very glad of it. So much the better. Go to Miss Wooburn, with a Stranger's compliments who is waiting, and who begs to speak with her upon an affair of importance.

Serv. Yes, Sir. *(Exit).*

Sir R. I wish I may die if I don't feel very unaccountably! How different are our sensations towards our wives, and all other women! This is the very first time she has given me a palpitation since the honey-moon.

(Enter Miss Wooburn, who starts on seeing Sir Robert; —he bows in great confusion).

Miss W. Support me, Heaven! *(Aside).*

Sir R. *(Bows repeatedly, and does not speak till after many efforts. Aside).* Was ever man in such confusion before his wife!

Miss W. Sir Robert, having recovered in some measure, from the surprise into which this intrusion first threw me, I have only to say, that whatever pretence may have induced you to offer me this insult, there are none to oblige me to bear with it. *(Going).*

Sir R. Lady Ramb—*(Recalling himself)* Miss Woo— *(She turns)* Lady Ramble—*(Recalling himself again)* Miss Wooburn—Madam—You wrong me—There was a time when I insulted you, I confess; but it is impossible that time should ever return.

Miss W. While I stay with you, I incur the danger. *(Going).*

Sir R. *(Holding her).* Nay, listen to me as a friend, whom you have so often heard as an enemy.—You offered me a favour by the hands of Mr. Harmony—

Miss W. And is this the motive of your visit—this the return—

Sir R. No, Madam, that obligation was not the motive which drew me hither—The real cause of this seeming intrusion is—you are going to be married once more, and I come to warn you of your danger.

Miss W. That you did sufficiently in the marriage-state.

Sir R. But now I come to offer you advice that may be of the most material consequence, should you really be determined to yield yourself again into the power of a husband. 50

Miss W. Which I most assuredly am.

Sir R. Happy, happy man! How much is he the object of my envy! None so well as I, know how to envy him, because none so well as I, know how to value you. *(She offers to go).* Nay, by Heaven you shall not go till you have heard all that I came to say!

Miss W. Speak it then instantly.

Sir R. No, it would take whole ages to speak; and should we live together, as long as we *have* lived together, still I should not find time to tell you— how much I love you. 60

(A loud rapping at the street-door).

Miss W. That, I hope, is Lord Norland.

Sir R. And what has Lord Norland to do with souls free as ours? Let us go to Scotland again; and again bid defiance to his stern commands.

Miss W. Be assured, that through him only, will I ever listen to a syllable you have to utter.

Sir R. One syllable only, and I am gone that instant.

Miss W. Well, Sir? 70

(He hesitates, trembles, seems to struggle with himself; then approaching her slowly, timidly, and as if ashamed of his humiliation, kneels to her—She turns away).

Sir R. (Kneeling). Maria, Maria, look at me!—Look at me in this humble state—Could you have suspected this, Maria?

Miss W. No: nor can I conceive what this mockery means.

Sir R. It means, that now you are no longer my wife, you are my Goddess; and thus I offer you my supplication, that (if you are resolved not to live single) amongst the numerous train who present their suit, you will once more select me. 80

Miss W. You!—You who have treated me with cruelty; who made no secret of your love for others—but gloried, boasted of your gallantries?

Sir R. I did, I did—But here I swear, only trust me again—do but once more trust me, and I swear by all I hold most sacred, that I will for the future carefully conceal all my gallantries from your knowledge—though they were ten times more frequent than before.

(Enter Edward).

Edw. Oh, my dear Miss Wooburn—What! Sir 90 Robert here too! *(Goes to Sir Robert and shakes hands).* How do you do, Sir Robert? Who would have thought of seeing you here? I am glad to see you though, with all my heart; and so I dare say is Miss Wooburn, though she may not like to say so.

Miss W. You are impertinent, Sir.

Edw. What, for coming in? I will go away then.

Sir R. Do, do—There's a good boy—do.

Edw. (Going, returns). I cannot help laughing, 100 though, to see you two together!—For you know you never were together when you lived in the same house.

Sir R. Leave the room instantly, Sir, or I shall call Lord Norland.

Edw. Oh, don't take that trouble, I will call him myself. *(Runs to the door)*—My Lord, my Lord, pray come here this moment—As I am alive, here is Sir Robert Ramble along with Lady Ramble!

(Enter Lord Norland. Sir Robert looks confounded, Lord Norland points to Edward to leave the room. Exit Edward).

Lord N. Sir Robert, on what pretence do you come 110 hither?

Sir R. On the same pretence, as when I was for the first time admitted into your house; to solicit this Lady's hand. And, after having had it once, no force shall compel me to take a refusal.

Lord N. I will try however—Madam, quit the room instantly.

Sir R. My Lord, she shall not quit it.

Lord N. I command her to go.

Sir R. And I command her to stay. 120

Lord N. Which of us will you obey?

Miss W. My inclination, my Lord, disposes me to obey you;—but I have so lately been accustomed to obey him, that *custom* inclines me to obey him still.

Sir R. There! There! There, my Lord! Now I hope you will understand better for the future, and not attempt to interfere between a man and his wife.

Lord N. (To her). Be explicit in your answer to this question—Will you consent to be his wife? 130

Miss W. No, never.

Sir R. Zounds, my Lord, now you are hurrying matters.—You should do it by gentle means;—let me ask her gently. *(With a most soft voice).* Maria, Maria, will you be my wife once again?

Miss W. Never.

Sir R. So you said seven years ago when I asked you, and yet you consented.

Lord N. And now, Sir Robert, you have had your answer; leave my house. *(Going up to him).* 140

Sir R. Yes, Sir; but not without my other half.

Lord N. "Your other half?"

Sir R. Yes; the wife of my bosom—the wife, whom I swore at the altar "to love and to cherish, and, forsaking all others, cleave only to her as long as we both should live."

Lord N. You broke your oath, and made the contract void.

Sir R. But I am ready to take another oath; and another after that, and another after that—And, 150 Oh, my dear Maria, be propitious to my vows, and give me hopes you will again be mine. *(He goes to her, and kneels in the most supplicating attitude).*

(Enter Edward, shewing in Mr. Solus and Mr. Placid; Edward points to Sir Robert [who has his back to them] and goes off).

Sir R. (Still on his knees, and not perceiving their entrance). I cannot live without you.—Receive your penitent husband, thus humbly acknowledging his faults, and imploring you to accept him once again.

Solus (Going up to Sir Robert). Now, is it wonderful that I should want a wife?

Plac. And is it to be wondered at, if I should hesitate 160 about parting with mine?

Sir R. (Starts up in great confusion). Mr. Solus, Mr. Placid, I am highly displeased that my private actions should be thus inspected.

Solus. No one shall persuade me now, to live a day without a wife.

Plac. And no one shall persuade me now, not to be content with my own.

Solus. I will procure a special licence, and marry the first woman I meet. 170

Sir R. Mr. Solus, you are, I believe, interested in a peculiar manner, about the marriage of this Lady.

Solus. And, poor man, you are sick, and want somebody to "bathe your temples," and to "hover about you."

Miss W. You come in most opportunely, my dear Mr. Solus, to be a witness—

Sir R. "My dear Mr. Solus!"

Solus. To be a witness, Madam, that a man is miserable without a wife. I have been a fatal 180 instance of that, for some time.

Miss W. Come to me then, and receive a lesson.

Sir R. No, Madam, he shall not come to you; nor shall he receive a lesson. No one shall receive a lesson from you, but me.

Lord N. Sir Robert, one would suppose by this extraordinary behaviour, you were jealous.

Sir R. And so I am, my Lord; I have cause to be so.

Lord N. No cause to be jealous of Mr. Solus—He is not Miss Wooburn's lover, I assure you. 190

Sir R. Then, my Lord, I verily believe it is yourself. Yes, I can see it is; I can see it by her eyes, and by every feature in your face.

Miss W. Oh! my good friend, Mr. Placid, only listen to him.

Sir R. And why "my good friend, Mr. Placid?" *(To Placid).* By Heavens, Sir, I believe that you only wished to get rid of your own wife, in order to marry mine.

Plac. I do not wish to part with my own wife, Sir 200 Robert, since what I have just seen.

Sir R. (Going up to Solus and Lord Norland). Then, pray, gentlemen, be so good as to tell me, which of you two is the happy man, that I may know how to conduct myself towards him?

Miss W. Ha, ha, ha!

Sir R. Do you insult me, Maria?—Oh! have pity on my sufferings.

Solus. If you have a mind to kneel down again, we will go out of the room. 210

Plac. Just as I was comforting myself with the prospect of a divorce, I find my instructor and director pleading on his knees to be remarried.

(Enter Mrs. Placid).

Mrs. P. What were you saying about a divorce?

Sir R. Now, down on your knees, and beg pardon.

Miss W. My dear Mrs. Placid, if this visit is to me, I take it very kind.

Mrs. P. Not absolutely to you, my dear. I saw Mr. Placid's carriage at the door, and so I stepped in to desire him to go home. Go home directly. 220

Plac. Presently, my dear; I will go presently.

Mrs. P. Presently won't do; I say directly. There is a lady at my house in the greatest possible distress *(Whispers to him).*—Lady Eleanor—I never saw a creature in such distraction; *(Raising her voice)*— therefore go home this moment; you sha'n't stay an instant longer.

Solus. Egad, I don't know whether I will marry or no.

Mrs. P. Why don't you go, Mr. Placid, when I bid you? 230

Solus. No;—I think I won't marry.

Plac. But, my dear, will not you go home with me?

Mrs. P. Did not I tell you to go by yourself?

(Placid bows, and goes off).

Solus. No;—I am sure I won't marry.

Lord N. And now, Mr. Solus and Sir Robert, these ladies may have some private conversation. Do me the favour to leave them alone.

Miss W. My Lord, with your leave *we* will retire. *(Turns when she gets to the door).* Sir Robert, I have remained in your company, and compelled myself 240 to the painful task of hearing all you have had to say, merely for the satisfaction of exposing your love, and then enjoying the triumph of bidding you farewell for ever. *(Exit with Mrs. Placid).*

Solus (Looking steadfastly at Sir Robert). He turns pale at the thoughts of losing her. Yes, I think I'll marry.

Lord N. Come, Sir Robert, it is in vain to loiter; your doom is fixed.

Sir R. (In a melancholy musing tone). Shall I then never again know what it is to have a heart like 250 hers, to repose my troubles on?

Solus. Yes, I am pretty sure I'll marry.

Sir R. —A friend in all my anxieties, a companion in all my pleasures, a physician in all my sicknesses—

Solus. Yes, I *will* marry.

Lord N. Come, come, Sir Robert, do not let you and I have any dispute. *(Leading him towards the door).*

Sir R. Senseless man, not to value those blessings— Not to know how to estimate them, till they were 260 lost. *(Lord Norland leads him off).*

Solus (Following). Yes,—I am determined;—nothing shall prevent me—I will be married. *(Exit).*

Act V

Scene I: *An Apartment at Lord Norland's.* *Enter Hammond, followed by Lady Eleanor.*

Hammond. My Lord is busily engaged, Madam; I do not suppose he would see any one, much less a stranger.

Lady E. I am no stranger.

Ham. Your name then, Madam?

Lady E. That, I cannot send in. But tell him, Sir, I am the afflicted wife of a man, who for some weeks past has given many fatal proofs of a disordered mind. In one of those fits of phrensy, he held an instrument of death, meant for his own destruction, to the 10 breast of your Lord (who by accident that moment passed), and took from him, what he vainly hoped might preserve his own life, and relieve the wants of his family. But his paroxysm over, he shrunk from what he had done, and gave the whole he had thus unwarrantably taken, into a servant's hands to be returned to its lawful owner. The man, admitted to this confidence, betrayed his trust, and instead of giving up what was so sacredly delivered to him, secreted it; and, to obtain the promised reward, 20 came to this house, but to inform against the wretched offender; who now, only resting on your Lord's clemency, can escape the direful fate he has incurred.

Ham. Madam, the account you give, makes me interested in your behalf, and you may depend, I will repeat it all with the greatest exactness. *(Exit Hammond).*

Lady E. (Looking around her). This is my father's house! It is only through two rooms and one short 30 passage, and there he is sitting in his study. Oh! in that study, where I (even in the midst of all his business) have been so often welcome; where I have urged the suit of many an unhappy person, nor ever urged in vain. Now I am not permitted to speak for myself, nor have one friendly voice to do that office for me, which I have so often undertaken for others.

(Re-enter Hammond, Edward following).

Ham. My Lord says, that any petition concerning the person you come about, is in vain. His respect for the laws of his country demands an example such as he means to make.[42]   40

Lady E. Am I, am I to despair then? *(To Hammond)* Dear Sir, would you go once more to him, and humbly represent—

Ham. I should be happy to oblige you, but I dare not take any more messages to my Lord; he has given me my answer.—If you will give me leave, Madam, I'll see you to the door.[43] *(Crosses to the other side, and Exit).*   50

Lady E. Misery—Distraction!—Oh, Mr. Placid! Oh, Mr. Harmony! Are these the hopes you gave me, could I have the boldness to enter this house? But you would neither of you undertake to bring me here!—neither of you undertake to speak for me! *(She is following the Servant; Edward walks softly after her, till she gets near the door; he then takes hold of her gown, and gently pulls it; she turns and looks at him).*

Edw. Shall I speak for you, Madam?

Lady E. Who are you, pray, young Gentleman? Is it you, whom Lord Norland has adopted for his son?   60

Edw. I believe he has, Madam; but he has never told me so yet.

Lady E. I am obliged to you for your offer; but my suit is of too much consequence for *you* to undertake.

Edw. I know what your suit is, Madam, because I was with my Lord when Hammond brought in your message; and I was so sorry for you, I came out on purpose to see you—and, without speaking to my Lord, I could do you a great kindness—if I durst.   70

---

[42] *make*: After this speech, the Larpent version adds the following:

    Lady E. Did he say this with a voice and look determined?

    Ham. He did.

[43] *door*: At the end of this speech, the Larpent version adds, "Go Hammond, I will show the lady out. *(Exit Hammond)*"

Lady E. What kindness?

Edw. But I durst not—No, do not ask me.

Lady E. I do not. But you have raised my curiosity; and in a mind so distracted as mine, it is cruel to excite one additional pain.

Edw. I am sure I would not add to your grief for the world.—But then, pray do not speak of what I am going to say.—I heard my Lord's lawyer tell him just now, "that as he said he should not know the person again, who committed the offence about which you came, and as the man who informed against him was gone off, there could be no evidence that he did the action, but from a book, a particular pocket-book of my Lord's, which he forgot to deliver to his servant with the notes and money to return, and which was found upon him at your house: and this, Lord Norland will affirm to be his."—Now, if I did not think I was doing wrong, this is the very book—*(Takes a pocket-book from his pocket)* I took it from my Lord's table;—but it would be doing wrong, or I am sure I wish you had it. *(Looking wishfully at her).*   80 ... 90

Lady E. It will save my life, my husband's and my children's.

Edw. (Trembling). But what is to become of me?

Lady E. That Providence, who never punishes the deed, unless the *will* be an accomplice, shall protect you for saving one, who has only erred in a moment of distraction.   100

Edw. I never did any thing to offend my Lord in my life;—and I am in such fear of him, I did not think I ever should.—Yet, I cannot refuse *you*;—take it.—*(Gives her the book).* But pity me, when my Lord shall know of it.

Lady E. Oh! should he discard you for what you have done, it will embitter every moment of my remaining life.

Edw. Do not frighten yourself about that.—I think he loves me too well to discard me quite.   110

Lady E. Does he indeed?

Edw. I think he does;—for often, when we are alone, he presses me to his bosom so fondly, you would not suppose.—And, when my poor nurse died, she called me to her bed-side, and told me (but pray keep it a secret)—she told me I was—his grandchild.

Lady E. You are—you are his grand-child—I see,—
I feel you are;—for I feel that I am your mother.
(Embraces him). Oh! take this evidence back 120
(Returning the book)—I cannot receive it from thee,
my child;—no, let us all perish, rather than my
boy, my only boy, should do an act to stain his
conscience, or to lose his grand-father's love.

Edw. What do you mean?

Lady E. The name of the person with whom you
lived in your infancy, was Heyland?

Edw. It was.

Lady E. I am your mother; Lord Norland's only child,
(Edward kneels) who, for one act of disobedience, 130
have been driven to another part of the globe in
poverty, and forced to leave you, my life, behind.
(She embraces and raises him). Your father, in his
struggles to support us all, has fallen a victim;—
but Heaven, which has preserved my child, will
save my husband, restore his sense, and once
more—

Edw. (Starting). I hear my Lord's step,—he is coming
this way:—Begone, mother, or we are all undone.

Lady E. No, let him come—for though his frown 140
should kill me, yet must I thank him for his care
of thee.

*(She advances towards the door to meet him. Enter
Lord Norland. Falling on her knees).* You love me,—
'tis in vain to say you do not: You love my child;
and with whatever hardships you have dealt, or still
mean to deal by me, I will never cease to think you
love me, nor ever cease my gratitude for your
goodness.

Lord N. Where are my servants? Who let this woman 150
in?

(She rises, and retreats from him alarmed and confused).

Edw. Oh, my Lord, pity her.—Do not let me see her
hardly treated—Indeed I cannot bear it.

(Enter Hammond).

Lord N. (To Lady Eleanor). What was your errand
here? If to see your child, take him along with you.

Lady E. I came to see my father;—I have a house too
full of such as he already.

Lord N. How did she gain admittance?

Ham. With a petition, which I repeated to your
Lordship. *(Exit Hammond).* 160

Lord N. Her husband then it was, who—*(To Lady
Eleanor)* But let him know, for this boy's sake, I
will no longer pursue him.

Lady E. For that boy's sake you will not pursue his
father; but for whose sake are you so tender of that
boy? 'Tis for mine, for my sake; and by that I
conjure you—*(Offers to kneel).*

Lord N. Your prayers are vain—*(To Edward).* Go,
take leave of your mother *for ever,* and instantly
follow me; or shake hands with me for the last 170
time, and instantly begone with her.

*(Edward stands between them in doubt for some little
time: looks alternately at each with emotions of
affection; at last goes to his grandfather, and takes
hold of his hand).*

Edw. Farewell, my Lord,—it almost breaks my heart
to part from you;—but, if I have my choice, I must
go with my mother. *(Exit Lord Norland instantly.
Lady Eleanor and her Son go off on the opposite side).*

Scene II: *Another Apartment at Lord Norland's.
Enter Miss Wooburn and Mrs. Placid.*

Mrs. P. Well, my dear, farewell.—I have staid a great
while longer than I intended—I certainly forgot
to tell Mr. Placid to come back after he had spoken
with Lady Eleanor, or he would not have taken the
liberty not to have come.

Miss W. How often have I lamented the fate of Lord
Norland's daughter! But, luckily, I have no personal
acquaintance with her, or I should probably feel a
great deal more on her account than I do at
present.—She had quitted her father's house before 10
I came to it.

(Enter Mr. Harmony).

Har. My whole life is passed in endeavouring to make
people happy, and yet they won't let me.—I
flattered myself, that after I had resigned all
pretensions to you, Miss Wooburn, in order to
accommodate Sir Robert—that, after I had told
both my Lord and him, in what high estimation
they stood in each other's opinion, they would of
course be friends; or, at least, not have come to any
desperate quarrel:—instead of which, what have 20
they done, but, within this hour, had a duel!—and
poor Sir Robert—

Miss W. For Heaven's sake, tell me of Sir Robert—

Har. You were the only person he mentioned after he received his wound; and such encomiums as he uttered—

Miss W. Good Heaven! If he is in danger, it will be vain to endeavour to conceal what I shall suffer. *(Retires a few paces to conceal her emotions).*

Mrs. P. Was my husband there? 30

Har. He was one of the seconds.

Mrs. P. Then he shall not stir out of his house this month, for it.

Har. He is not likely; for he is hurt too.

Mrs. P. A great deal hurt?

Har. Don't alarm yourself.

Mrs. P. I don't.

Har. Nay, if you had heard what he said!

Mrs. P. What did he say?

Har. How tenderly he spoke of you to all his 40 friends—

Mrs. P. But what did he say?

Har. He said you had imperfections.

Mrs. P. Then he told a falsehood.

Har. But he acknowledged they were such as only evinced a superior understanding to the rest of your sex;—and that your heart—

Mrs. P. (Bursting into tears). I am sure I am very sorry that any misfortune has happened to him, poor, silly man! But I do not suppose *(Drying up her tears* 50 *at once)* he will die.

Har. If you will behave kind to him, I should suppose not.

Mrs. P. Mr. Harmony, if Mr. Placid is either dying or dead, I shall behave with very great tenderness; but if I find him alive and likely to live, I will lead him such a life as he has not led a long time.

Har. Then you mean to be kind? But, my dear Miss Wooburn, *(Going to her)* why this seeming grief? Sir Robert is still living; and should he die of his 60 wounds, you may at least console yourself, that it was not your cruelty which killed him.

Miss W. Rather than have such a weight on my conscience, I would comply with the most extravagant of his desires, and suffer *his* cruelty to be the death of me.

Har. If those are your sentiments, it is my advice that you pay him a visit in his affliction.

Miss W. Oh no, Mr. Harmony, I would not for the universe. Mrs. Placid, do you think it would be 70 proper?

Mrs. P. No, I think it would not—Consider, my dear, you are no longer a wife, but a single Lady, and would you run into the clutches of a man?

Har. He has no clutches, Madam; he is ill in bed, and totally helpless.—But, upon recollection, it would, perhaps, be needless to go; for he may be too ill to admit you.

Miss W. If that is the case, all respect to my situation, my character, sinks before the strong desire of 80 seeing him once more. Oh! were I even married to another, I feel, that in spite of all my private declarations, or public vows, I should fly from him, to pay my duty where it was first plighted.

Har. My coach is at the door; shall I take you to his house? Come, Mrs. Placid, wave all ceremonious motives on the present melancholy occasion, and go along with Miss Wooburn and me.

Miss W. But, Mrs. Placid, perhaps poor Mr. Placid is in want of your attendance at home. 90

Har. No, they were both carried in the same carriage to Sir Robert's.

Miss W. (As Harmony leads her to the door). Oh! how I long to see my dear husband, that I may console him!

Mrs. P. Oh! how I long to see my dear husband, that I may quarrel with him! *(Exeunt).*

Scene III: *The Hall at Sir Robert Ramble's. The Porter discovered asleep. Enter a Footman.*

Footman. Porter, porter, how can you sleep at this time of the day?—It is only eight o'clock.

Porter. What did you want, Mr. William?

Footman. To tell you my master must not be disturbed, and so you must not let in a single creature.

Por. Mr. William, this is no less than the third time I have received those orders within this half hour:—First, from the butler, then from the valet, and now from the footman.—Do you all suppose 10 I am stupid?

Footman. I was bid to tell you. I have only done what I was desired; and mind you do the same. *(Exit).*

Por. I'll do my duty, I warrant you. I'll do my duty.

(A loud rapping at the door). And there's a rap to put my duty to the trial.

(Opens the door. Enter Harmony, Miss Wooburn, and Mrs. Placid).

Har. These ladies come on a visit to Sir Robert. Desire one of the servants to conduct them to him instantly.

Por. Indeed, Sir, that is impossible—My master is 20 not—

Har. We know he is at home, and therefore we can take no denial.

Por. I own he is at home, Sir; but indeed he is not in a situation—44

Miss W. We know his situation.

Por. Then, Madam, you must suppose he is not to be disturbed. I have strict orders not to let in a single soul.

Har. This Lady, you must be certain, is an exception. 30

Por. No Lady can be an exception in my master's present state; for I believe, Sir, but perhaps I should not speak of it, I believe my master is nearly gone.

Miss W. Oh! support me, Heaven!

Mrs. P. But has he his senses?

Por. Not very clearly, I believe.

Miss W. Oh! Mr. Harmony, let me see him before they are quite lost.

*Por.*45 It is as much as my place is worth, to let a creature farther than this hall; for my master is but 40 in the next room.

Mrs. P. That is a dining-room. Is not he in bed?

Har. (Aside to the Ladies). In cases of wounds, the patient is oftentimes propped up in his chair.

Miss W. Does he talk at all?

Por. Yes, Madam, I heard him just now very loud.

Miss W. (Listening). I think I hear him rave.

Har. No, that murmuring is the voice of other persons.

Mrs. P. The Doctors in consultation, I apprehend.— 50 Has he taken any thing?

---

44 *in a situation*—: For this phrase, the Larpent version substitutes "to be seen." It then adds the following:
   Mrs. P. But let him know who we are.
   Por. Indeed, Madam, my master is not in a situation.

45 *Por.*: The Larpent version opens this speech with "I cannot let you go to him indeed, madam—He must not be disturbed—."

Por. A great deal, I believe, Madam.

Mrs. P. No amputation, I hope?

Por. What, Madam?

Har. He does not understand you. *(To Miss Wooburn).*—Come, will you go back?

Por. Do, my Lady, and call in the morning.

Miss W. By that time he may be totally insensible, and die without knowing how much I am attached to him. 60

Mrs. P. And my husband may die without knowing how much I am enraged with him!—Mr. Harmony, never mind this foolish man, but force your way into the next room.

Por. Indeed, Sir, you must not. Pray, Mr. Harmony, pray, Ladies, go away.

Miss W. Yes, I must go from my husband's house for ever; never to see that, or him again. *(Faints on Mr. Harmony).*

Mrs. P. She is fainting—open the windows—give her 70 air.

Por. Pray go away:—There is plenty of air in the streets, Ma'am.

Har. Scoundrel! Your impertinence is insupportable. Open these doors; I insist on their being opened. *(He thrusts at a door in the centre of the stage; it opens, and discovers Sir Robert and Mr. Placid at a table surrounded by a company of Gentlemen).*

Sir R. A song—a song—another song—

(Miss Wooburn, all astonishment, is supported by Mr. Harmony and Mrs. Placid—the Porter runs off).

Oh! what do I see!—Women! Ladies! Celestial 80 beings we were talking of.—Can this be real? *(Sir Robert and Mr. Placid come forward—Sir Robert perceiving it is Miss Wooburn, turns himself to the company).* Gentlemen, Gentlemen, married men and single men, hear me thus publicly renounce every woman on earth but this; and swear henceforward to be devoted to none but my own wife. *(Goes to her in raptures).*

Plac. (Looking at Mrs. Placid, then turning to the Company). Gentlemen, Gentlemen, married men 90 and single men, hear me thus publicly declare, I will henceforth be master;—and from this time forward, will be obeyed by my wife. *(Sir Robert waves his hand, and the door is closed on the company of Gentlemen).*

Mrs. P. Mr. Placid—Mr. Placid, are not you afraid?

Plac. No, Madam;—I have consulted my friends, I have drank two bottles of wine, and I never intend to be afraid again.

Miss W. (To Sir Robert). Can it be, that I see you without a wound?   100

Sir R. No, my life, that you do not; for I have a wound through my heart, which none but you can cure. But in despair of your aid, I have flown to wine, to give me a temporary relief by the loss of reflection.

Mrs. P. Mr. Placid, you will be sober in the morning.

Plac. Yes, my dear; and I will take care that you shall be dutiful in the morning.

Har. For shame! How can you treat Mrs. Placid thus?   110
You would not, if you knew what kind things she has been saying of you; and how anxious she was when I told her you were wounded in a duel.

Mrs. P. Was not I, Mr. Harmony? *(Bursting into tears).*

Plac. (Aside to Harmony and Sir Robert). I did not know she could cry;—I never saw it before, and it has made me sober in an instant.[46]

Miss W. Mr. Placid, I rely on you to conduct me immediately from this house.

Sir R. That I protest against; and will use even violent   120
measures to prevent it.

(Enter Servant).

Serv. Lord Norland.[47]

(Enter Lord Norland).

Miss W. He will protect me.

Sir R. Who shall protect you in my house but I? My Lord, she is under my protection; and if you offer to take her from me, I'll exert the authority of a husband, and lock her up.

Lord N. (To Miss Wooburn). Have you been deluded hither, and wish to leave the place with me? Tell me instantly, that I may know how to act.   130

Miss W. My Lord, I am ready to go with you, but—

Har.—But you find she is inclined to stay; and do have some compassion upon two people that are so fond of you.

(Enter Mr. Solus, drest in a suit of white clothes).

Solus. I am married!—I am married!—Wish me joy! I am married!

Sir R. I cannot give you joy, for envy.

Solus. Nay, I do not know whether you will envy me much when you see my spouse—I cannot say she was exactly my choice. However, she is my wife now;   140
and that is a name so endearing, I think I love her better since the ceremony has been performed.

Mrs. P. And pray, when did it take place?

Solus. This moment. We are now returning from a friend's house, where we have been joined; and I felt myself so happy, I could not pass Sir Robert's door, without calling to tell him of my good fortune.—And, as I see your Lady here, Sir Robert, I guess you are just married too; and so I'll hand my wife out of the carriage, and introduce the two   150
Brides to each other. *(Exit Solus).*

Sir R. You see, my Lord, what construction Mr. Solus has put on this Lady's visit to me. And by Heaven, if you take her away, it will be said, that she came and offered herself, and that I rejected her!

Miss W. Such a report would kill me.

(Enter Solus, leading on Miss Spinster).

Solus. Mistress Solus. *(Introducing her).*

Har. (Starting). My Relation! Dear Madam, by what strange turn of fortune do I see you become a wife?

Mrs. Solus. Mr. Harmony, it is a weakness I   160
acknowledge; but you can never want an excuse for me, when you call to mind "the scarcity of provisions."

Solus. Mr. Harmony, I have loved her ever since you told me she spoke so well of me behind my back.

(Enter Servant, And whispers Mr. Harmony, who follows him off).

Lord N. I agree with you, Mr. Solus, that this is a most excellent proof of a person's disposition; and in consideration, Sir Robert, that, throughout all our many disagreements, you have still preserved a respect for my character in my absence, I do at   170

---

46 *instant*: At the end of this speech, the Larpent version adds, "Sir Robert, come hither, and see me laugh at her, ha, ha, ha!" Sir Robert then replies, "I have been perfectly myself, from the moment I saw my beloved Lady Ramble."

47 *Norland*: Here, the Larpent version instead has the Servant say, "Lord Norland is in his carriage at the door, and desires to speak with Miss Wooburn." Norland does not enter until the end of Sir Robert's next speech.

last say to that Lady, she has my consent to trust you again.

Sir R. And she will trust me; I see it in her smiles. Oh! unexpected ecstasy!

(Enter Mr. Harmony).

Har. (Holding a letter in his hand). Amidst those bright prospects of joy which this company are contemplating, I come to announce an event that ought to cloud the splendour of the horizon.—A worthy, but an ill-fated man, whom ye were all acquainted with, has just breathed his last. 180

Lord N. Do you mean the husband of my daughter?

Solus. Do you mean my nephew?

Plac. Is it my friend?

Sir R. And my old acquaintance?

Har. Did Mr. Irwin possess all those titles you have given him, Gentlemen? Was he your son? *(To Lord Norland).* Your nephew? *(To Solus).* Your friend? *(To Mr. Placid).* And your old acquaintance? *(To Sir Robert)*—How strange he did not know it!

Plac. He did know it. 190

Har. Still more strange that he should die for want, and not apply to any of you!

Solus. What! Die for want in London! Starve in the midst of plenty!

Har. No; but he seized that plenty, where law, where honour, where every social and religious tie forbad the trespass; and in punishment of the guilt, has become his own executioner.

Lord N. Then my daughter is wretched, and her boy involved in his father's infamy. 200

Solus. The fear of his ghost haunting me, will disturb the joys of my married life.

Plac. Mrs. Placid, Mrs. Placid, my complying with your injunctions in respect of Mr. Irwin, will make me miserable for ever.

Miss W. I wish he had applied to me.

Sir R. And as I refused him his request, I would give half my estate he had *not* applied to me.

Har. And a man who always spoke so well of you all behind your backs!—I dare say, that, in his dying 210 moments, there was not one of you whom he did not praise for some virtue.

Solus. No, no—when he was dying he would be more careful of what he said.

Lord N. Sir Robert, good-day. Settle your marriage as

you and your Lady shall approve; you have my good wishes. But my spirits have received too great a shock to be capable of any other impression at present.

Miss W. (Holding him). Nay, stay, my Lord. 220

Solus. And, Mrs. Solus, let me hand you into your carriage to your company; but excuse my going home with you. *My* spirits have received too great a shock, for me to be capable of any other impression at present.

Har. (Stopping Solus). Now, so loth am I to see any of you, only for a moment, in grief, while I have the power to relieve you, that I cannot help—Yes, my philanthropy will get the better of my justice. *(Goes to the door, and leads on Lady Eleanor, Irwin,* 230 *and Edward).*

Lord N. (Runs to Irwin, and embraces him). My son! *(Irwin falls on his knees).* I take a share in all your offences—The worst of accomplices, while I impelled you to them.

Irwin (On his knees). I come to offer my returning reason; to offer my vows, that, while *that* reason continue, so long will I be penitent for the phrensy which put your life in danger.

Lady E. (Moving timidly to her Father, leading Edward 240 *by the hand).* I come to offer you this child, this affectionate child; who, in the midst of our caresses, droops his head and pines for your forgiveness.

Lord N. Ah! there is a corner of my heart left to receive him. *(Embraces him).*

Edward. Then, pray, my Lord, suffer the corner to be large enough to hold my mother.

Lord N. My heart is softened, and receives you all. *(Embraces Lady Eleanor, who falls on her knees; he then turns to Harmony)*—Mr. Harmony, I thank 250 you, I most sincerely thank you for this, the joyfullest moment of my life. I not only experience release from misery, but return to happiness.

Har. (Goes hastily to Solus, and leads him to Irwin; then turns to Mr. and Mrs. Placid). And now, that I see you all reconciled, I can say, there are not two enemies in the whole circle of my acquaintance, that I have not within these three days made friends.

Sir R. Very true, Harmony; for we should never have known half how well we all love one another, if 260 you had not told us.

Har. And yet, my good friends, notwithstanding the merit you may attribute to me, I have one most tremendous fault; and it weighs so heavy on my conscience, I would confess what it is, but that you might hereafter call my veracity in question.

Sir R. My dear Harmony, without a fault, you would not be a proper companion for any of us.

Lord N. And while a man like you, may have (among so many virtues) some faults; let us hope there may   270
be found in each of us, (among all our faults) some virtues.

Har. Yes, my Lord,—and notwithstanding all our faults, it is my sincere wish, that the world may speak well of us—behind our backs.

THE END.

EPILOGUE. By Miles Peter Andrews, Esq.
Spoken by Mrs. Mattocks.

"Each has his fault," we readily allow,
To this Decree, our dearest friends must bow;
One is too careless, one is too correct,
All, save our own sweet self, has some defect:
And characters to ev'ry virtue dear,
Sink from a hint, or suffer by a sneer.
"Sir Harry Blink! Oh, he's a worthy man,
"Still anxious to do all the good he can;
"To aid distress, wou'd share his last poor guinea,
"Delights in kindness—but then, what a ninny!"   10
Lady Doll Primrose says to Lady Sly,
"You know Miss Tidlikins? Yes—looks awry—
"She's going to be married,—that won't mend it;—
"They say she'll have a fortune,—and she'll spend it.
"I hope your La'aship visits Lady Hearty,
"We meet to-night—a most delightful party.
"I don't like Dowagers, who *would* be young,
"And 'twixt ourselves they say—She has a tongue."
If such the general blame that all await,
Say, can our Author 'scape the general fate?   20
Some will dislike the saucy truths she teaches,
Fond bachelors, and wives who wear the breeches.
"Let me be wedded to a handsome youth,"
Cries old Miss Mumblelove, without a tooth.
"These worn-out Beaux, because they've heavy purses,
"Expect us, spinsters, to become their nurses.

"To love, and be beloved's the happy wife,
"A mutual passion is the charm of life."
"Marriage is Heaven's best gift, we must believe it,
"Yet some with weak ideas can't conceive it.—   30
"Poor Lady Sobwell's grief the town wou'd stun;
"Oh, Tiffany! Your mistress is undone.
"Dear Ma'am—I hope my Lord is well—don't cry—
"Hav'n't I cause?—The monster will not die—
"The reason why I married him, is clear,
"I fondly thought he cou'd not live a year:
"But now his dropsy's[48] better, and his cough—
"Not the least chance for that to take him off.
"I, that cou'd have young husbands now in plenty,
"Sha'n't be a widow till I'm one-and-twenty—   40
"No lovely weeds—No sweet dishevelled hair—
"Oh! I cou'd cry my eyes out in despair."
(Sobbing and crying).
Sir Tristram Testy, worn with age and gout;
Within, all spleen, and flannel all without;
Roars from his elbow-chair, "Reach me my crutches,
"Oh! if Death had my wife within his clutches,
"With what delight her funeral meats I'd gobble,
"And tho', not dance upon her grave, I'd hobble;
"No longer then, my peace she could unhinge,   50
"I shou'd cut capers soon, *(Tries to jump, and
        stumbles)* Zounds! What a twinge!"—
These playful pictures of discordant life.
We bring to combat discontent and strife,
And, by the force of contrast, sweetly prove
The charm that waits on fond and faithful love.
When suited years, and pliant tempers join,
And the heart glows with energy divine,
As the lov'd offspring of the happy pair
Oft climb the knee, the envied kiss to share.   60
Such joys this happy country long has known,
Rear'd in the Cot, reflected from the Throne;
Oh! may the glorious zeal, the loyal stand
Which nobly animate this envied land,
Secure to every breast, with glad increase,
The heartfelt blessings of domestic peace!

---

48 *dropsy*: a morbid condition characterized by the accumulation of watery fluid in the serous cavities or the connective tissue of the body.

Blue-Beard; or, Female Curiosity!

George Colman the Younger

George Colman the Younger (1762–1836) came from an intensely theatrical family, being the son of the actress Sarah Ford (Mrs. Colman after young George was born) and George Colman the Elder, important playwright, manager of the Haymarket Theatre, and friend to David Garrick, Richard Brinsley Sheridan, Samuel Johnson, and Joshua Reynolds. Young George's parents, however, did not want him to enter the theater but instead to practice law, and so had him educated at Marylebone Seminary and at Westminster. He was to attend Christ Church College, Oxford in 1780, but his penchant for London's actresses resulted in his being sent further afield to King's College, Aberdeen in 1781. In Scotland, he began to write plays, first a lost satire on Charles Fox and then *The Female Dramatist*, which his father premiered anonymously at the Haymarket on 26 August 1782. This piece failed, but working with the composer Samuel Arnold, Colman the Younger next produced a hit in *Two to One*, which opened 19 June 1784 with a prologue by Colman the Elder introducing his son to the public. It ran for 18 evenings. Young Colman was then allowed to leave Scotland, but he was sent to Europe to try to separate him from the actress Catherine Morris, whom he married anyway, first clandestinely at Gretna Green on 3 October 1784 and then publicly on 10 November 1788.

· Colman was now supposed to pursue the law at Lincoln's Inn, but his real love remained the theater. On 4 August 1787, he had his first major hit with *Inkle and Yarico*, taking up an incident on the slave trade from Richard Steele. By July 1789, he was managing the Haymarket after a Commission of Lunacy pronounced his father insane; when the elder Colman died in 1794, the son took over the theater in his own name. From 1805 until 1818, when he relinquished control of it, the Haymarket's financial difficulties and his own extravagant spending habits would weigh heavily upon Colman despite his successes as a playwright. Upon giving up the theater, he was appointed by his friend the Prince Regent, soon to be George IV, first to the honorary post of Lieutenant of Yeomen of the Guard in 1820 and then replacing John Larpent as Examiner of Plays in 1824. In this latter office he became quite controversial for his censoring of the same bawdy humor, religious language, and political references that he himself had used in his own plays. He fell ill in February 1830 from complications arising from gout, and, though he recovered, finally succumbed on 17 October 1836.

As playwright and manager of the Haymarket, and later as the government's Examiner of Plays, Colman was one of the key men of the theater for the later eighteenth and early nineteenth centuries. Arguably the most important British playwright at the end of the eighteenth century, he was a master of comedy and farce and a creator of the new theatrical hybrid that would come to be known as melodrama. He wrote some of the most popular pieces of the age, including *Blue-Beard* and *John Bull; or, The Englishman's Fireside* (Covent Garden, 1803), as well as penning some of its more interesting dramas. Among these are *The Iron Chest* (Drury Lane, 1796), his adaptation of Godwin's *Caleb Williams* (1794), and *The Africans; or, War, Love and Duty* (Haymarket, 1808), which attempted to portray life in Africa in the year of the abolition of the slave trade. Other key plays include *The Battle of Hexham* (Haymarket, 1789), performed 20 times in its first season, *The Surrender of Calais* (Haymarket, 1791), staged 28 nights its first year, and *New Hay at the Old Market* (Haymarket, 1795), which ran 32 times as a prelude and then long into the next century as the afterpiece *Sylvester Daggerwood*.

Blue-Beard; or, Female Curiosity! premiered at Drury Lane on 16 January 1798. Within three seasons, it had been performed more than nearly any afterpiece of the eighteenth century. Part of its success can be traced to its place in the theater's programming: it took the place of the usual Christmas harlequinade, the holiday entertainment that brought in most of the theater's profits each year (see *Harlequin and Humpo* in this volume). Featuring music by Michael Kelly, *Blue-Beard* provided stirring action, easily digested humor, and the spectacular sets of pantomime. Over £2,000 was expended on the sets, including the huge animated panorama that showed the advance of Abomelique's party and the "Blue Chamber," complete with moving skeleton and bleeding walls, which drew upon the same Gothic tactics also in evidence in the other smash hit of the season, Matthew Lewis's *The Castle Spectre* (Drury Lane, 1797). In moving the story of Blue-Beard from its European roots to Turkey, Colman also gave his play an orientalist cast in a period where events in India and Napoleon's actions drew public attention eastward. The play also challenges us to think about the ramifications of staging this fairy tale of misogyny—where a tyrannical husband kills his wives when they inevitably display an essentialized "female curiosity"—in the era of Mary Wollstonecraft and the backlash against her. Colman's play could be seen either as re-enacting masculinist stereotypes or as using conventional orientalist imagery to decry the subjugation of women to oppressive men.

The copytext for the play is *Blue-Beard! Or Female Curiosity* (London: Cadell and Davies, 1798). We have indicated some major variations found in the Larpent manuscript (Huntington Library LA 1191) in the notes. There are many later editions of the play, some of which provide additional information about staging choices. A survey of editions in the Harvard Theatre Collection also reveals many copies cut down for local and (as difficult as it is to believe) even private performances. There was a famous revival of *Blue-Beard* at Covent Garden on 18 February 1811 when the great machinist Johnston's mechanical animals were replaced by real horses, resulting not only in outcries that the legitimate theater was dead but also in Covent Garden's managers, Henry Harris[1] and John Philip Kemble, commissioning and producing a second "hippodrama," Matthew Lewis's *Timour the Tartar* (included here).

---

1   *Henry Harris*: Son of Thomas Harris, the long-standing manager-proprietor of Covent Garden Theatre. Very little is known about him beyond his being stage-manager at Covent Garden for a short time during these years.

EPIGRAPH:
Sacrae / Panduntur Portae. —Virgil.[2]

INTRODUCTION:

The following Trifle is not a Translation from the French,[3] nor any other Language:—I have an exclusive right to all its imperfections.

I am far from endeavouring to vitiate the taste of the Town, and over-run the Stage with Romance, and Legends:—but English Children, both old and young, are disappointed without a Pantomime, at Christmas;[4]—and, a Pantomime not being forth-coming, in Drury-Lane, I was prevail'd upon to make out the subsequent Sketch, 10

expressly for that season, to supply the place of Harlequinade:—Accidents, however, retarded its representation, a fortnight beyond its intended appearance.

I feel nothing upon my conscience in having substituted a Blue Beard for a Black Face.[5]—I have not attempted to make Magick usurp that space of the Evening's Entertainment much better occupied by Dramas of instruction, and probability. I have kept my Enchantment within 20 the limits where rational minds, without pedantry, have not only long tolerated it, but have found pleasure in unbending with it, after they have been more solidly engaged. In short my Syllabub[6] does not make its appearance until the substantial part of the repast is over.—I am careless, therefore, of those sapient Gentlemen, who, in the words of Gresset,[7]

> "Portent leur petite sentence
> "Sur la rime, & sur les Auteurs, 30
> "Avec autant de connoissance
> "Qu'un aveugle en a des couleurs."[8]

But, I could tell such Gentlemen that I have done some good.—I have given an opportunity to Mr. Kelly of fully establishing his reputation, as a Musical Composer, with a Publick, whose favour he has long, and deservedly experienced as a Singer.

---

2 *Sacrae / Panduntur Portae. Virgil*: "having opened the sacred door." Publius Vergilius Maro (70–19 BCE) was the great Roman poet, author of the *Eclogues*, *Georgics*, and the *Aeneid*.

3 *not a Translation from the French*: Colman refers to the fact that there was an earlier French opera based on the story, *Barbe Bleu* by A. M. E. Grétry, which Michael Kelly saw in Paris in 1790. Kelly brought back a "programme" of the opera which he asked Colman to convert into a play. Here, Colman asserts the independence of his drama.

4 *without a Pantomime, at Christmas*: It had become customary to open a pantomime or harlequinade (see *Harlequin and Humpo* in this volume) as an afterpiece at Christmas time, often on Boxing Day; these popular spectacles often made the most profit of any piece during the season. This year, however, Drury Lane offered no pantomime, and *Blue-Beard* was clearly conceived as a replacement piece, though it did not open until January. The reasons for the decision not to offer a pantomime during this season are not clear, but it must have had something to do with the spectacular success of Lewis's *The Castle Spectre*, which had opened on 14 December 1797: Lewis's play simply did not need the help of a pantomime to draw an audience. It is interesting that *Blue-Beard* never appears during the season as an afterpiece for *The Castle Spectre*, though it is paired with *Hamlet* and *The Tempest*. It is also interesting that the rival theater at Covent Garden, which did offer a Christmas pantomime, opened a second pantomime on 9 April 1798 in what appears to be an attempt to compete with the incredible popularity of Colman's afterpiece.

5 *Black Face*: a reference to the fact that Harlequin, the main figure in the Christmas pantomime, wore a black mask.

6 *Syllabub*: a drink made of milk mixed with wine, cider, rum, etc. and often sweetened, spiced, and served warm. Later, a cold dessert made of milk or cream (usually mixed with white wine), flavored, sweetened, and whipped to a thick but light consistency.

7 *Gresset*: Jean Baptiste Gresset (1709–77), French author, was a teacher in a Jesuit college until his epicurean poem "La Chartreuse" (1735) caused his dismissal from the Society of Jesus. He then turned to the stage, writing *Edouard III*, a tragedy (1740), *Sidney*, a drama (1745), and *Le Méchant*, a comedy (1747), considered one of the best of the century.

8 *Portent … couleurs*: Gresset is commenting on critics who "carry out their little judgments on poetry and its authors with as much knowledge as a blindman has of colors."

Crowded audiences have testified the most strong, and decided approbation of his original Musick, in *Blue-Beard*; and amply applauded his taste, and judgment, in Selection. 40

Dully as the matter of fact may be stated, I feel gratified in relating this Truism of a worthy and industrious man.

Add to this, I have brought forward *Young Greenwood* (a Scene-Painter of Nineteen!) to shew Design, and Execution of uncommon promise:—

And *Johnstone*, a *classical* Machinist, (a *rara avis*,[9] alas! in Theatres) has added another wreath to his well-earn'd laurels. 50

I have made the Dialogue and Songs (such as they are) subservient to the above-mention'd Artists:—and, no men, surely, ever made better use of a vehicle.

I have only, now, to say that I heartily thank the Performers for the kind, and zealous exertions, of their well-known talents:—and that it would be as ungrateful as impudent to deny that I took the outline of my Story from the works of the celebrated Mrs. Goose:[10]—at whose feet with all 60 due deference I beg to lay my present weighty labour;—and I do hereby inscribe to her the Grand Dramatick Romance of *Blue-Beard*.

George Colman, the Younger.
Piccadilly, Feb. 2, 1798.

---

9 *rara avis*: a rare bird, an unusual find.
10 *Mrs. Goose*: Mother Goose. Charles Perrault (1628–1703) first published a volume of tales by Mother Goose, including "Barbe-Bleu," the ultimate source for *Blue-Beard*, in 1697. *Tales of Past Times. By Mother Goose* was translated from the French as early as 1729. Playwrights were often accused (as in Byron's *English Bards and Scotch Reviewers*, line 591) of drawing their plots from such children's stories; *Harlequin and Humpo*'s author, Thomas Dibdin, for example, offered *Harlequin and Mother Goose* in 1806.

DRAMATIS PERSONAE

MEN:

Abomelique, *(Blue Beard)*	Mr. Palmer
Ibrahim,	Mr. Suett
Selim,	Mr. Kelly
Shacabac,	Mr. Bannister, Jun.
1st. Spahi,	Mr. Dignum
2d. Spahi,	Mr. Sedgwick
3d. Spahi,	Mr. Wathen
4th. Spahi,	Mr. Bannister
5th. Spahi,	Mr. Trueman
Hassan,	Mr. Hollingsworth
1st. Slave,	Mr. Webb
2d. Slave,	Mr. Maddocks

WOMEN:

Fatima,	Mrs. Crouch
Irene,	Miss De Camp
Beda,	Mrs. Bland

SCENE: *Turkey.*

ACT I.

Scene I: *A Turkish Village—A Romantick, Mountainous Country beyond it. Selim is discovered under Fatima's Window, to which a Ladder of Silken Ropes is fastened. Dawn.*

DUET: *Selim and Fatima.*
Selim. Twilight glimmers o'er the Steep:
    Fatima! Fatima! wakest thou, dear?
Grey-eyed Morn begins to peep:
    Fatima! Fatima! Selim's here!
Here are true-love's cords attaching
    To your window.—List! List![11]
(Fatima opens the Window).
Fatima. Dearest Selim! I've been watching;
    Yes, I see the silken twist.
Sel. Down, Down, Down, Down, Down!
Down the Ladder gently trip; 10
Pit a pat, pit a pat,—haste thee, dear!
Fati. O! I'm sure my foot will slip!

---

11 *List*: for listen.

(With one foot out of the Window).

Sel. Fatima!—

Fati.   Well Selim?—

Sel.   Do not fear!

(She gets upon the Ladder—they keep time in singing to her steps as she descends, towards the end of the last line she reaches the ground and they embrace).

Both. Pit a pat, pit a pat, Pit a pat,

Pit a pat, pit a pat—Pat, Pat, Pat.

(As they embrace, Ibrahim puts his head out, from the door of the House).

Ibrahim. Ah, Traitress!—Have I caught you! *(Comes forward)* Attempt to run away with a Man?—and, not only with a man, but a Trooper!—One of the Spahis.[12]—Wicked Fatima!—Much as Mahomet's brood must have increased, there isn't one turtle[13] in all our Prophet's pigeon-house, that wouldn't be ready to pick at you. *(Pushes her into the house).* In,—in, and repent! 20

Sel. Hear me Ibrahim!

Ibra. I won't hear you, as I'm a Mussulman![14]

Sel. Credit me to suppose that——

Ibra. I won't credit any thing, as I'm a True Believer!

Sel. Did not you promise her to me in marriage? 30

Ibra. Um?—Why, I did say something like getting a Licence from the Cadi.[15]

Sel. And, what has made you break your word?

Ibra. A better Bridegroom for my daughter.

Sel. Why better than I?

Ibra. He's richer.—You have your merits—but he's a Bashaw,[16] with Three Tails.[17]

Sel. Does that make him more deserving?

Ibra. To be sure it does, all the world over. Throw Riches and Power into the scale, and simple Merit soon kicks the beam.[18]—Now to cut the matter short. You're a very pretty Trooper; so troop off:—for Abomelique—the great Abomelique,[19] comes, this day, to carry my daughter to his magnificent Castle, and espouse her. 40

Sel. Abomelique!—The pest of all the neighbouring country.

Ibra. Yes—he's by far the best of all the neighbouring country.

Sel. Who deals, as all around declare, in spells and magick. 50

Ibra. Aye—You can't say of him, as they do of many great folks, that he's no Conjuror.

Sel. And you think this man calculated to make a good husband to Fatima?

Ibra. Positively.

Sel. Better than I?

Ibra. Um—Comparatively.

Sel. And you now look upon me with contempt?

Ibra. Superlatively—I do, by the Temple of Mecca![20] 60

Sel. Now, by my injuries old man!—but I curb my just resentment:—You are the Father of my Fatima;—but for my Rival——

Ibra. He is able enough to maintain his own cause.

Sel. Oh! he shall rue the day when, serpent-like he stung me. Yes, Abomelique!—Spite of thy wealth and power,—thy mystick spells, and hellish incantations,—a Soldier's vengeance shall persue thee.

---

12 *Spahis*: corruption of the Turkish word "sipahi." A member of a cavalry corps within the Ottoman Turkish army; the Larpent version calls them Boslangees.

13 *turtle*: i.e. turtle-dove, an emblem of marital fidelity.

14 *Mussulman*: from Persian "musulman" or Muslim. A follower of Muhammad, here Mohamet.

15 *Cadi*: a civil judge in a Muslim country.

16 *Bashaw*: a grandee, or a haughty imperious man; variant of pasha, the title of a Turkish officer of high rank, as for example a military commander, provincial governor, etc.

17 *Tails*: the tail of a horse, of which one, two, or three were borne before a bashaw as insignia of rank.

18 *kicks the beam*: to be greatly outweighed, so that one side of a balance rises up and strikes the beam.

19 *Abomelique*: The "Barbe-Bleu" of Perrault's tale had been linked with both the infamous Gilles De Rais and Comorre the Cursed, a Breton chief of the sixth century. Colman, drawing upon the current orientalist fad, makes his villain a Turk.

20 *Temple of Mecca*: Mecca, the birthplace of Muhammad, is also the site of the Kaaba, the shrine Muslims face when they pray. The Kaaba, containing the Black Stone which Muslims believe was sent by Allah, is a cube-shaped building located in the center of the Great Mosque, the center of worship for all Muslims.

Quartetto: Selim.—Ibrahim.—Fatima and Irene.

Sel. Ruthless Tyrant! dread my force!   70
    A Soldier's Sabre hangs o'er thee!
Thou soon shalt fall a headless corse,
    Who now would'st tear my love from me.
Ibra. How prettily, now, he rails!
    But 'tisn't so easily done as said
To smite a Bashaw, and cut off the Head
    Of a Man who has got three Tails.
*(Fatima and Irene come from the House, and kneel
to Ibrahim).*
Fati. & Irene. Turn, turn, my Father! turn thee hither!
    A Daughter would thy pity move!
Ire. Why doom the opening Rose to wither?   80
Both. Why blight the early bud of Love?
Ibra., Sel., Fati. O! how teizing!
O! how trying! O! how vexing
Are the fears which Fathers/Lovers/Daughters[21]
    prove
How distressing! How perplexing
Are the cares that wait on Love!
Ire. & Fati. Hear me! Hear me!
Ibra. I'll not hear thee!
Ire. & Fati. Can you now our suit refuse?
Cheer me! You alone can cheer me—   90
'Tis a wretched daughter sues.
Ibra. 'Tis a silly daughter sues.
All. O! how trying! Oh! how vexing! &c.

Ire. Dear! how can you think of marrying my Sister
to this Bashaw?
Ibra. And pray, good mistress Irene, with all the
submission of a dutiful Father, may I crave to
know your objections?
Ire. Why in the first place, then, Father, he has a Blue
Beard.   100
Ibra. And who, in the name of all the Devils, made
you a judge of Beards?
Ire. Well, I do think it was sent as a punishment to
him, on account of all his unfortunate wives.
Ibra. Ha! now, under favour, I do think that a man's
wives are punishment enough, in themselves.

---

21 *Fathers/Lovers/Daughters*: The slashes indicate those
    points where each character, respectively, says a differ-
    ent word at the same time.

Praised be the wholesome Law of Mahomet that
stinted a Turk to only four at a time![22]
Ire. The Bashaw had never more than one at a
time;—and 'tis whispered that he beheaded the   110
poor souls one after another:—for in spite of his
power there's no preventing talking.
Ibra. That's true, indeed;—and, if cutting off
women's heads won't prevent talking, I know of no
method likely to prosper!—But, I'll make You
silent, Mistress, depend on't.—No more of this
prate!
Ire. I have done, Father!
Ibra. Prepare to take up your abode with your Sister,
at the Castle.   120
Ire. O, I am very, very glad I am to be with her! Are
not you, Fatima?
Fati. I am indeed, Irene. A loved Sister's presence will
be a consolation to me, in my miseries.
Ibra. Perhaps I may contrive to go with you, too.—
If I could bring it about, I should dwell there in
all the respect due to a relation of the mighty
Abomelique. Let me once get footing in Old
Three-Tails Castle, and I'll tickle up the Slaves for
a great man's Father-in-Law, I'll warrant me!—   130
Hark!—I hear him on the march over the
mountain:—and here are all our neighbours,
pouring out of their houses, to see the
procession.[23]
*(The Sun rises gradually.—A March is heard at a great
distance.—Abomelique, and a magnificent train, appear,
at the top of the Mountain.—They descend through a*

---

22 *stinted a Turk to only four at a time*: reference to the
    existence of polygamy under Islamic law, with the hus-
    band being limited to four wives.
23 *procession*: Kelly in his *Reminiscences* (London: H.
    Colborn, 1826), 2:131–3, tells us that the "horses were
    admirably made of pasteboard, and answered every
    purpose for which they were wanted"; he also notes
    that the "Blue Beard, who rode the elephant in per-
    spective over the mountains, was little Edmund Kean."
    With perspective painting, with a child playing
    Abomelique at a distance, and with pasteboard horses
    operated by the machinists, the theater could provide
    the illusion of watching the procession from a distance,
    which is then lost from view in a turn in the road, al-
    lowing the real procession then to come on stage.

winding path:—Sometimes they are lost to the sight, to mark the irregularities of the road. The Musick grows stronger as they approach.—At length, Abomelique's train range themselves on each side of the Stage, and sing the Chorus, as he marches down through their ranks.—The Villagers come from their Houses).

GRAND CHORUS.

Mark his approach with Thunder! Strike on the
    trembling Spheres!
      With martial crash,
      The Cymbals clash;
    'Tis the Bashaw appears.
War in his eye-ball glistens! Slave of his lip is
    Law;[24]
      Our Life, and Death   140
      Hang on his breath:—
    Hail to the great Bashaw!

Abomelique. Now, Ibrahim;—I come to claim my Bride,—the lovely Fatima. To take this village rose from the obscure and lowly shade, and place her in a warmer soil; where the full Sun of Wealth shall shine upon her, and add a richer glow to the sweet blush of beauty.

Ibra. Most puissant[25] Bashaw!—I am proud that any twig of mine is thought worthy of a place in your 150 Shrubbery.—Irene, as you desired, shall go with Fatima, as companion. For myself, mighty Sir, I am a tough Stick, somewhat dry, and a little too old, perhaps, to be moved:—but, to say the truth, since you are going to take off my suckers,[26] if I were to be transplanted along with them, I think I should thrive.

Abom. It shall be order'd so.

Ibra. Shall it!—Then, if I don't make shift to flourish, cut me down, and make fire-wood of me. 160

Abom. Be satisfied—you shall along with us. There shall not be one countenance on which my power, and this day's festival, does not impress a smile.

Sel. That's false, by Mahomet!

Abom. How now!—Who dares utter that?

Ibra. (Stopping Selim's mouth). Hush!—He's nobody—Only a poor mad Trooper.—You may know he's a Trooper by his swearing.—Beneath your mighty notice.

Abom. What prompts him to this boldness? 170

Sel. Injury—You have basely wronged me.

Abom. Rash fool!—know my power and respect it.

Sel. When Power is respected, its basis must be Justice. 'Tis then an edifice that gives the humble shelter and they reverence it:—But, 'tis a hated shallow fabrick, that rears itself upon oppression:—the breath of the discontented swells into a gale around it, 'till it totters.

Abom. Speak—how are you aggrieved?

Fati. Let me inform him. 180

Ibra. O, plague!—Hold your tongue!—A woman always makes bad worse.

Abom. Proceed, sweet Fatima!

Fati. I was poor, and happy;—for my wishes were lowly as my state.—Content and Peace dwelt in our Cottage;—nor were these smiling inmates ruffled, when Love stole in, and found a shelter in my bosom. My Father placed my hand in this young Soldier's, and taught me that our fortunes soon should be united.—Poor Selim's soul spoke 190 in his eyes, and mine replied, (for true love's eyes are eloquent) that, through my life, I wished no other protector than a brave youth, whose lot, being humble like my own, the more endeared him to me. Our hopes and joys were ripening daily: You came, and all are blighted! *(Falls in Selim's arms).*

Abom. Tear them asunder.—Insulted! and by a Slave that——*(Selim offers to draw, and is restrained by Abomelique's Attendants).* Thou art beneath my 200 notice.—You, Fatima, must to the Castle.—*(To the Attendants)* Prepare the Palanquin![27] We are advanced too far, Lady—we cannot now recede.

---

24 *Slave of his lip is Law*: "Slave" for "slaver" or saliva; the sense is that one obeys everything that comes from his mouth, even his spit.

25 *puissant*: powerful.

26 *suckers*: shoots sent out from the base of a plant or tree.

---

27 *Palanquin*: a covered conveyance for one person, consisting of a large box carried on two horizontal poles by four or six bearers, used in the Indian subcontinent and other Eastern countries.

(A Magnificent Palanquin is brought in, drawn by Black Slaves).

GRAND CHORUS.[28]

 Advance!
 See us the Bride attending!
  Echo shall now the chaunt prolong,
  Torn with a lusty Turkish Song,
 While the Star of the World is ascending.
(Abomelique leads Fatima towards the Palanquin).
  Hark to the Drum!
  Come, Comrades, Come!   210
 Time will not brook delaying.—
(Abomelique forces Fatima into the Palanquin, who struggles).
  See she resists—her Struggles note!
Sel. & Fati. O give me her/him on whom I dote!
(Abomelique draws his sabre—all the Slaves draw).
 Sabres are gleaming round the throat
  Of Beauty disobeying.
(Exeunt, hurrying off Fatima. Irene is seated with her in the Palanquin).

Scene II: *A Hall in Abomelique's Castle.*
Enter Beda, (with a Guittar).

Beda. Where can he be loitering so long!—Why, Shacabac!—Poor melancholy fool! he's in some dark corner of the Castle, now,—moping, and sighing as usual—This is the hour he should come to take his daily lesson with me on the Guittar. Musick is the only thing that makes him merry.— Why, Shacabac!
(Enter Shacabac, with a Guittar).
Shacabac. Here I am, Beda!
Beda. Why, where have you been, all this time, Shacabac?   10
Shac. Getting all in readiness for the Bashaw's return, with his intended Bride.—They say she's very handsome.—*(Half aside)* Poor soul!—I pity her.
Beda. Pity a woman because she is handsome!—Pray, then, keep out of my way, for I don't like to be pitied.

Shac. Did I say, Pity?—Oh no—I didn't intend that—Heigho!—
Beda. Now what can you be sighing for?—
Shac. That wasn't sighing.—I'm like our old blind 20 camel,—a little short winded, that's all.
Beda. I'm sure, Shacabac, you ought to be the happiest creature in the Castle.—The Bashaw loads you with his favours.
Shac. O, very heavily, indeed!—I don't dispute that.
Beda. You are his chief attendant; and he honours you with more employment than all the other slaves put together.
Shac. Works me like a mule;—it would be ungrateful to deny it.   30
Beda. And every body thinks that he trusts you with all his secrets.
Shac. *(Alarmed).* No!—Do they think that?
Beda. Yes; and, to say truth, you keep them lock'd up as close——
Shac. *(Starting).* Lock'd up!—how!—why, you— where should I keep them lock'd up?
Beda. In your breast, to be sure.
Shac. Oh!—Yes—yes:—That is if he trusts me with any:—but to think that a Bashaw would tell his 40 secrets to a slave!—nonsense!
Beda. Nay, it isn't for nothing he takes you to talk with him, in private, in the Blue Chamber.
Shac. *(Very earnestly).* Don't mention that, Beda!— Never mention the Blue Chamber again!
Beda. Why, what harm is there in the Blue Chamber?
Shac. None in the world:—but you know I'm full of melancholy fancies:—and I never go into that Blue Chamber that I don't feel as if I were tormented with Devils.   50
Beda. Mercy!—What Devils, Shacabac?
Shac. *(Recovering himself, & smiling).* Only Blue Devils,[29] Beda!—Nothing more. Come—Hang Sorrow!—Let's strike up a tune, on the Guittar.
Beda. Aye, that makes you merry, at the worst of times.
Shac. That it does, Beda.

---

28 *GRAND CHORUS*: In the Larpent version, the villagers pour out and sing the lines that follow.

29 *Blue Devils*: depression, "the blues."

DUET: *Shacabac and Beda.*

Shac. Yes, Beda,—This, Beda, when I melancholy
grow,
  This tinking heart-sinking soon can drive away.
Beda. When hearing sounds cheering, then we   60
blythe and jolly grow;
  How do you, while to you, Shacabac, I play?
  Tink, tinka, tinka, tink—the sweet Guittar
shall cheer you.
  Clink, clinka, clinka, clink—So gaily let us
sing!
Shac. Tink, tinka, tinka, tink—A pleasure 'tis to
hear you,
  While, neatly, you sweetly, sweetly touch the
string!
Both. Tink, tinka, &c.
Shac. Once sighing, sick, dying, Sorrow hanging
over me,
  Faint, weary, sad, dreary, on the ground I lay;
  There moaning, deep groaning, Beda did
discover me—
Beda. Strains soothing, Care smoothing, I began   70
to play.
  Tink, tinka, tinka, tink,—the sweet Guittar
could cheer you:
  Clink, clinka, clinka, clink, so gaily did I sing!
Shac. Tink, tinka, tinka, tink,—A pleasure 'twas
to hear you,
  While, neatly, You sweetly, sweetly touch'd the
string!
Both. Tink, tinka, &c.

(A Horn is sounded without).
Shac. Hark!—the Horn sounds at the Castle Gate.—
The Bashaw is return'd.
Beda. And brings his Bride with him. I long to see
her! I must join the rest of the slaves presently. You
know, Shacabac, we are all to kneel, and cry "May   80
she live long and happy!"
Shac. Heaven send she may!—Hush! The Bashaw!
(Enter Abomelique).
Abom. Oh, you are here.
Shac. To obey your pleasure. Your Slave humbly trusts
that, in preparing for our new Mistress, nothing
has been neglected.

Abom. I commend your care;—and, while the lovely
Fatima is inspecting her apartments, I have
employment for you. You must attend me.
Shac. Whither, mighty Sir?   90
Abom. To the Blue Chamber.
Shac. The Blue Cha——*(drops the Guittar).*
Abom. What ails the driveller?—
Shac. No——Nothing—nothing.—*(Half aside)* That
terrible sound sets me a shivering!
Abom. What say you?
Shac. I say the Guittar fell to the ground, and I was
afraid of its shivering.[30]
Abom. Attend me.
Shac. I follow.   100
(Exit Abomelique, followed by Shacabac).
Beda. Poor Shacabac! what can be the matter with
him!—Perhaps he has been crossed in Love—and,
now I think of it, he must have a mistress some
where—or he never would be so often alone with
me without saying one tender thing to me—Ah,
Love, Love!—I never shall forget my poor, dear,
lost Cassib.

SONG: *Beda.*

His sparkling eyes were dark as jet;
Chica, Chica, Chica, Cho.
Can I my comely Turk forget?—   110
Oh! never, never, never, no!
Did he not watch 'till Night did fall,
And sail in silence on the Sea;
Did he not climb our sea-girt wall,
To talk so lovingly to me?—
O! his sparkling eyes, &c.
His Lips were of the coral hue,
His Teeth of ivory so white;
But he was hurried from my view,
Who gave to me so much delight!   120
And, why should tender Lovers part!
And why should Fathers cruel be!
Why bid me banish from my heart
A heart so full of Love for me!
O! his sparkling eyes, &c. *(Exit).*

---

30 *shivering*: Shacabac puns on the word's two meanings:
"trembling with fear" and "breaking into pieces."

Scene III: *A Blue Apartment.*[31] *A winding Stair-case on one side.—A Large door in the middle of the Flat.—Over the door, a Picture of Abomelique, kneeling in amorous supplication to a beautiful woman.—Other Pictures, and Devices, on Subjects of Love, decorate the Apartment. Abomelique and Shacabac descend the Stair. Shacabac in apparent terror.*

Abom. You know my purpose.

Shac. I guess it.

Abom. Why do you tremble?

Shac. The air of this Apartment chills me:—and the business we are going upon isn't the best to inspire courage.

Abom. Fool!—When this mysterious Portal shall be open'd, what hast thou to dread?

Shac. Oh, nothing at all. The inhabitants of the inner apartment might terrify a man of tender nerves;— but what are they to me?—Only a few flying Phantoms, sheeted Spectres, skipping Skeletons, and grinning Ghosts at their gambols:—and as to those who had once the honour to be your wives,—poor souls!—they are harmless enough, now, whatever they might have been formerly.

Abom. 'Twas to prevent the harm with which their conduct threaten'd me, that they have suffer'd. Their crimes were on their heads.

Shac. Then their Crimes were as cleanly taken off their shoulders as Scymetar[32] could carry them.— That Curiosity should cost so much!—If all women were to forfeit their heads for being inquisitive, what a number of sweet, pretty, female faces we should lose in the world!

Abom. Such punishment might outrun even Turkish Justice—but in me, 'tis prudence; Self preserva- tion.—You are not ignorant of the prediction.

Shac. That it is your fate to marry, and your Life will be endangered by the Curiosity of the woman whom you espouse.

Abom. Thou hast the secret. Dare not to breathe it, or——

Shac. Don't look so terrible then,—for, if you scare away my senses, who knows but the secret may pop out along with them.

Abom. Well, I know thou darest not utter it. The mystick ceremonies, in which, from mere necessity, I have employ'd thee—thou weak and unapt agent—bear in them a supernatural force, fettering thy tongue in silence. *(Gives him a Key decorated with Jewels)* Take the Key: apply it to the door.

Shac. Yes, I—but I was always from a boy, the merest bungler at a Lock that——

Abom. Dastard![33]—Thou know'st how readily 'twill open.

Shac. But must I once more open it to——

Abom. Be speedy! This Talisman[34] must, ere my marriage rites are solemnized, be placed within the Tomb of those whose rashness has laid them cold beneath the icy hand of Death.

Shac. Mercy on us!—I know not for the icy hand of Death:—But if Fear would do me the favour to keep his chilly paws off me, I should be much warmer than I am at present.

Abom. No dallying.

Shac. I obey.—

(Shacabac puts the Key into the Lock; the Door instantly sinks, with a tremendous crash: and the Blue Chamber appears streaked with vivid streams of Blood. The figures in the Picture, over the door, change their position, and Abomelique is represented in the action of beheading the Beauty he was, before, supplicating.—The Pictures, and Devices, of Love, change to subjects of Horror and Death. The interior apartment (which the sinking of the door discovers), exhibits various Tombs, in a sepulchral building;—in the midst of which ghastly and supernatural forms are seen;—some in motion, some fix'd—In the centre, is a large Skeleton seated on a

---

31 Colman's Note: "The Dialogue of this Scene has un- dergone some alteration, since it was first represented: by which means the Blue Apartment is not shewn 'till the Second Act. The Author, however, prefers print- ing it as it was originally written."

32 *Scymetar*: for scimitar, a short, curved, single-edged sword identified particularly with the Turks and Per- sians.

33 *Dastard*: someone who basely shrinks from danger.

34 *Talisman*: a charm, such as a stone or gem engraved with figures or characters possessing occult powers, used to protect from evil or harm.

tomb,[35] *(with a Dart in his hand) and, over his head, in characters of Blood, is written "THE PUNISHMENT OF CURIOSITY."*[36]*)*

Abom. (Pointing to the Skeleton). Thou seest yon fleshless form.

Shac. (Giving Abomelique the Key). O, yes!—and my own flesh crawls whenever I look upon him. 60

Abom. Henceforward he must be my destiny. *(Addressing the Skeleton)* Daemon of Blood!— Death's Courier!—whose sport it is to sound War's Clarion;[37]—to whet the knife of Suicide!—to lead the hired Murderer to the Sleeping Babe; and, with a ghastly smile of triumph, to register the Slaughter'd, who prematurely drop in Nature's Charnel-house;[38]—here, here have I pent thee!— A prisoner to my Art,—here—to circumscribe thy 70 general purposes, for my particular good—twelve winters have I kept thee!

Shac. Have you!—Allah preserve us!—but I must say that, considering the time, he looks so lean that he does his keeper no credit.

Abom. Approach him with respect.

Shac. Who, I?—I'd rather keep at a respectful distance.

Abom. Take this Talisman.

Shac. 'Tis a Dagger.

Abom. 'Tis a charmed one. While it remains beneath 80 the foot of that same ghastly form, I am free from mortal power. Another hand than mine must place it there. Thou must perform the office. *(Gives him the Talisman).*

Shac. Must I!—well—I—*(Approaching the figure)* O, Mahomet!—If ever I get away safe from this gentleman who has jumped out of his Skin, I shall jump out of my own, for joy!—

---

35 *Skeleton seated on a tomb*: The Larpent version adds that the skeleton is smiling.

36 *Shacabac...CURIOSITY*: Flats could be made to sink beneath the stage through the use of traps, openings in the stage floor covered by hinged doors called "flaps" that could be opened at a moment's notice. Here they drop to reveal the interior of the Blue Chamber. The changes in the pictures could be done through the kind of trick-work found in pantomimes.

37 *Clarion*: horn.

38 *Charnel-house*: a house or vault for dead bodies.

(Shacabac lays the Dagger at the foot of the Skeleton.—It Thunders and Lightens violently. The inscription, over the Skeleton's head, changes to the following—"THIS SEPULCHRE SHALL INCLOSE HER WHO MAY ENDANGER THE LIFE OF ABOMELIQUE"—— The Skeleton raises his arm which holds the Dart; then lets his arm fall again. Shacabac staggers from the Sepulchre, into the Blue Chamber, and falls on his face; when the Door, instantly rising, closes the interior building.—The streaks of blood vanish from the walls of the Blue Chamber, and Abomelique's Picture, with the other Pictures, and Devices, resume their original appearance).

Abom. It omens prosperously! This Sepulchre shall inclose Her who may endanger the Life of 90 Abomelique.—Her death then is the penalty of her rashness. May Fatima be prudent, and avoid it.— Rouse thee, dull fool!—Thy Task is ended: arise, and follow me hence.

Shac. (Getting up). That I will, if my Legs have power to carry me.

Abom. Hark!—I hear a foot in yonder gallery:— Ascend the Stairs with me, in silence. Chattering will cost thy Life.

Shac. Then I am sure you must pull out my teeth, 100 for they chatter in spite of me. *(Abomelique makes a sign to him to follow)* I attend!—*(They ascend the Stair-case, and the Scene closes).*

Scene IV: *An Apartment in the Castle.*
—Enter Fatima and Irene.

Ire. Prythee, dearest sister, take comfort.

Fati. Where shall I find it? Torn from the man I love, and forced into the arms of one whom I, and all around, detest, where should I look for comfort! My waking thoughts are torments; and, since this marriage was proposed, my very dreams have foreboded misery.

SONG: *Fatima.*[39]

While, pensive, I thought on my Love,
The Moon, on the Mountain, was bright;

---

39 *SONG: Fatima*: This song is moved to the end of the scene in the Larpent version.

And Philomel,[40] down in the grove,　　　　10
Broke, sweetly, the silence of Night.

O, I wish'd that the tear-drop would flow!
But I felt too much anguish to weep;
'Till, worn with the weight of my woe,
I sunk on my pillow, to sleep.

Methought that my Love, as I lay,
His ringlets all clotted with gore,
In the paleness of Death, seem'd to say,
"Alas! we must never meet more!"

"Yes, yes, my beloved! we must part;　　　　20
"The Steel of my Rival was true;—
"The Assassin has struck on that heart,
"Which beat with such fervour for you."

Ire. Why, to be sure, 'tis a sad thing to lose Selim.—
He is a good youth.—And we women have,
somehow, such a pleasure in looking at a good
young man, when he happens to be very
handsome! Yet the Bashaw, bating[41] his Beard, isn't
so very ugly neither. Then, you know, he rolls in
riches.　　　　30
Fati. He abuses them, Irene. Wealth, when its
purpose is perverted, makes the possessor odious.
When virtuous men have gold they purchase their
own happiness, by making others happy:—Heap
treasure on the vicious, they strengthen their
injustice with the sweet means of Charity, and turn
the poor man's blessing to a curse.
Ire. Well now it's a great pity you happen'd to love
Selim first. Who knows but the Bashaw may turn

out good to us, after all. See what fine cloaths he　　40
has given us already.
Fati. Alas, my sister! these gay trappings
communicate no pleasure to an aching heart.
Ire. I wish they could see us in them, in our village,
for all that. Then we are to have a fine feast,
tonight, in honour of your nuptials, which are to
take place to-morrow.
(Enter Shacabac).[42]
Shac. Madam, the Bashaw waits, to attend you, to
the illuminated Garden.
Ire. There—the illuminated Garden! I told you so.　　50
Fati. I attend him. Come, Sister. *(Exeunt Fatima and
Irene).*
Shac. Poor soul! must she be sacrificed, too, to the
Bashaw's cruelty! His savage spirit settles all family
disputes with the edge of the Scymetar.

SONG: *Shacabac.*

A Fond Husband, will, after a conjugal Strife,
Kiss, forgive, weep, and fall on the neck of his Wife.
But Abomelique's wife other conduct may dread—
When he falls on her Neck, 'tis to cut off her head.

How many there are, when a Wife plays the fool,　　60
Will argue the point with her, calmly, and cool;
The Bashaw, who don't relish debates of this sort,
Cuts the Woman, as well as the Argument, short.

But, whatever her errors, 'tis mighty unfair
To cut off her Head, just as if 'twere all Hair;—
For, this truth is maintain'd by Philosophers still,—
That the Hair grows again, but the Head never will.

40　*Philomel*: In Greek myth, Philomel is raped by her sister Procne's husband, Tereus, who then cuts out her
tongue to prevent her from accusing him; she man-
ages to embroider her story on a piece of fabric sent
to her sister, who in revenge serves her husband his
own child disguised in a meal. When he discovers what
has happened, he pursues the two women, but the
gods turn them into a nightingale and a swallow, with
Philomel now usually being identified as the nightin-
gale.
41　*bating*: excepting.

42　*Enter Shacabac*: The Larpent version handles the close
of this scene differently. A slave, not Shacabac, enters
and joins the conversation. Irene's speech is longer:
"There!—The illuminated Garden!—I told you they
were getting ready. Come, now, look cheerily!—and,
who knows what may happen yet. Perhaps Selim may
find some means to rescue you. There is hope, Sister."
To which Fatima responds: "None, I fear for me, Irene.
My waking thoughts are torments; and since this marriage was proposed, my very dreams have forboded
misery." The song dropped from the beginning of the
scene is then sung by Fatima.

And, among all the basest, sure he is most base,
Who can view, then demolish, a Woman's sweet face!   70
Her smiles might the malice of Devils disarm;
And the Devil take Him who would offer her
    harm! *(Exit).*

Scene V: *A Garden—brilliantly and fancifully*
    illuminated—A Fountain playing in the middle
    of it—An elevated Sofa on one side, under a rich
    Canopy. A Large Company of Slaves discovered—some
    Dancers—others with Musical instruments—They
    all appear as preparing for an entertainment.
    Beda is foremost among them. Enter Ibrahim.

Ibra. That's right! You poor abominable Devils, who
    have the happiness to be Slaves to my Son-in-Law,
    that's right! Thrum your guittars, puff your
    trumpets, and blow your flutes, in honour of your
    new Mistress, my daughter. *(To a slave with a*
    trumpet) Come here you long winded dog!—Tell
    me who I am.
Slave. You are old Ibrahim.
Ibra. Old Ibrahim!—These Slaves are remarkably
    free!—I am the Father of the Lady who is to be   10
    Wife of the Man, who is the Master of you.—
    What a fine thing it is to be Father-in-Law to
    Three Tails!—*(Sees Beda)* O, dear! there's a pretty
    black-eyed girl!—Come here, and tell me your
    name.
Beda. My name is Beda, so please you!
Ibra. Beda, is it?—Why you little Devil, you're an
    Angel.
Beda. Oh no, Sir,—I'm only one of the family.
Ibra. Then give me a family kiss.—   20
Beda. Dear! if the Bashaw should see you!
Ibra. Then he'd say you have a good taste.—Cheer
    up, little one!—I rule the roast[43] here.—It shan't
    go worse with you that I have power, and you have
    charms. It's amazing, when Beauty pleads with a
    Great Man, how much quicker it rises to
    promotion than ugly-faced merit.—*(A Flourish of*
    Musick without) Silence! Here comes the great

Abomelique!—Son-in-Law to me, who am the
Father to the Lady, who is to marry the man, that   30
is master to you.—Stand aside!—be ready—Strain
your throats, kick your heels, and shew obedience.
(Abomelique enters with Fatima, Irene accompanying
them. Abomelique and Fatima seat themselves under the
Canopy).

A GRAND DANCE. CHORUS.[44]
Lowly we bend in Duty.
    Queen of the peaceful Bowers!
We bow to the foot-steps of beauty:
    And strew her path with flowers.
The mellow flute is blowing,
    Bounce goes the Tambourin;
Sweet harmony is flowing,
    To welcome Beauty's Queen.   40

ACT II.

Scene I: *A Wood. A Company of Spahis (or Turkish*
    Soldiers) discovered in ambush.

GLEE.
Stand close!—Our Comrade is not come:
    Ere this, he must be hovering near;—
    Give him a Signal we are here,
By gently tapping on the Drum.
        Rub, Dub, Dub.

A Comrade's wrong'd: Revenge shall work:
Thus, till our project's ripe, we lurk;—
    And still, to mark that we are here,
    Yet not alarm the distant ear,

---

43 *rule the roast*: for "rule the roost," to be in charge, with
    a possible pun suggesting what he really rules is the
    food.

44 *A GRAND DANCE. CHORUS*: The Larpent version
    offers a different song:
        Rosy are the hours of Love;
            The Pleasures revel in his way;
        And on downy Pinions move
            To cheer the night and glad the day.
        Wanton God!—in Conquest finding,
            Bless the Hero, now your Slave;
        And guard the Beauty, here presiding,
            When in her Chamber she leads the Brave.
    (A Grand Dance).

With caution, ever and anon,   10
  The Drum we gently tap upon.
    Rub, Dub, Dub.

1st Spahi. Selim tarries long.

2nd Spahi. Disappointed Love is a heavy luggage;—
and he who travels with it generally proceeds
slowly.

3rd Spahi. Not when the hope of redress is pack'd
up with his disappointments: and Revenge has
long spurs to quicken a dull motion.—*(To a sullen
rough looking companion)* Were you ever in love, 20
Comrade?

4th Spahi (Very gruffly). I once knew the tender
passion.

3rd Spahi. Were you successful when you adored?

4th Spahi. Um!—Why the chances were against me.

3rd Spahi. How so?

4th Spahi. I adored eleven, and obtained but five,—
'Twas hard, for a man who was so constant to'em.

1st Spahi. Well, we are all Soldiers. War is the mistress
I pursue.   30

2nd Spahi. You must take pains to keep sight of her,
for you have lost one eye in her service already.

1st Spahi. Wounds of honour, brother, form the
Warrior's proudest Epitaph. My loss perhaps may
live in story.

4th Spahi. It must live in a blind story,[45] then, if it
live at all, brother.

3rd Spahi. Come, no more of this.

1st Spahi. Nay, let them proceed. They are only in
sport. My Comrades know that the breath of a few 40
ribald jesters can never wither the laurels a Soldier
gains in protecting his Country.—Look out!—
Here comes Selim!—

(Enter Selim).

2nd Spahi. Well met.—We have been a full hour at
our post, here.

Sel. Your pardon. The entanglements of the Wood
retarded my progress.

3rd Spahi. Now, Comrade:—The time's at hand
when we will redress you.

---

45 *blind story*: a pun, with "blind story" being both a story
    without a point and a story in a building without win-
    dows or other openings for light.

Sel. I know your zeal. A Spahi never permits a 50
brother's injuries to remain unrevenged.

4th Spahi. We'll seize upon Blue-Beard, and dry-shave
him with a two-edged Scymetar.

Sel. If it be expedient to attack the Castle, be
cautious, friends, in the procedure. My Fatima,
else, may fall in the confusion.

2nd Spahi. Fear not that.—We'll crack the walls like
a nut-shell, and extract your mistress, safe and
sound, like the kernel.

4th Spahi. Our Horses stand a few paces hence. Let 60
us mount, and away!

Sel. We will, my Comrades!—We have some distance
yet to ride, ere we reach the domain of
Abomelique. Prepare,—I'll follow, instantly.—
Thanks for your aid.

1st Spahi. Nay, we want no thanks. Men are
unworthy of succour in their own time of need,
who will not be active to relieve the sufferings of
their fellows.—March, Comrades! *(Exeunt Spahis).*

Sel. Now, Fortune! Smile upon a Soldier's honest love, 70
struggling to rescue injured virtue from oppression.

SONG: Selim.

Hear me, O Fortune, hear me!
  Thy aid, O let me prove!
Now in this struggle cheer me,
  And crown the hopes of Love!

Then Vice no more shall revel;—
  Yes, Tyrant, we shall meet:
A Soldier's Sword shall level
  Oppression at my feet. *(Exit).*

Scene II: *An Apartment in Abomelique's Castle. Enter
Abomelique, Fatima, and Shacabac.*

Abom. Yes, Fatima; business of import calls me.—for
a few hours I leave you. Soon as the Sun slopes
through the azure vault of Heaven, to kiss the
mountain's top, and Evening's lengthen'd shadows
forerun the dew drops of the night, then look for
my return. Then shall our marriage be
accomplished.

Fati. Alas!—if ever pity——

Abom. No more of this—Off with this maiden

coyness:—And, in my absence, be gay and jocund. 10
This Castle can afford diversion, Lady. Rove freely
through it.—Here are the keys——

Shac. (Involuntarily interrupting). What *all* the keys?

Abom. Peace, Slave! Inspect the rich Apartments.
These open every door:—This Slave, here, shall
conduct you—But, with them, take this caution.

Fati. A Caution!

Abom. Yes: this Key, sparkling with diamonds, opens
a door within the blue apartment.

Shac. (Sighing). Oh! 20

Abom. That Door, and that alone—is sacred. Dare
to open it, and the most dreadful punishment that
tongue can utter will await you. *(Here Shacabac
gives Abomelique a look of supplication for Fatima,
and is repelled by a ferocious frown from his Master).*
It is the sole restraint I ever shall impose. In all else
you have ample scope.—Merit my indulgence, and
tremble to abuse it. *(Gives the Keys).*

Fati. I tremble now, to hear your words, and mark
your manner. 30

Shac. (Aside). So do I, I'm sure!

Fati. If this Key be of such import, 'twere best not
trust it to my keeping.

Shac. Oh, much the best.—Pray take it again!—Pray
do! *(Anxiously).*

Abom. Be dumb!—No, Fatima.—A Wife were
unworthy of my love, could I not confide in her
discretion.—Prove I may trust in yours
implicitly.—Follow me, Slave, to the Castle gate;—
then hasten back to attend your mistress. 40

Shac. Yes, I——Pray then don't stir from here till I
come, Lady!—*(Aside)* If the poor soul should get
to the Blue Chamber before I return, and——

Abom. Farewell, Fatima!—Come on. *(Exit).*

Shac. I come——Oh!—*(First looks at Fatima, then
at his Master, between anxiety for the one and terror
of the other:—Then Exit, after Abomelique).*

Fati. What can this mean?—His ferocious look, as
he pronounced the solemn charge, struck horror
through me!—The countenance, too, of the 50
trembling Slave was mark'd with mystery!

(Enter Irene).

Ire. So, Sister!—The Bashaw is going, I hear, 'till the
evening.—What are those keys in your hand?

Fati. They open every door within the walls.—

Abomelique has left them with me, that we may
wander through the Castle.

Ire. Well, now, that is very kind of him.

Fati. I have no joy, now, Irene, in observing the idle
glitter, and luxury of wealth.

Ire. Haven't you?—but I have. We'll have a rare 60
rummage!—I won't leave a single nook, nor corner,
unexamined.

Fati. That must not be. There is one room we are
forbidden to enter.

Ire. A forbidden Room!—Dear, now, I had rather see
that room than any other in the Castle! Did the
Bashaw forbid us?

Fati. He did;—and with an emphasis so earnest, a
manner so impressive, that he has taught me a fatal
consequence would wait on disobedience. 70

Ire. Mercy!—How I do long to see that room!—Do
let me just look at the key.

Fati. (Shewing her the key). Beware, Irene!

Ire. Dear, there can be no harm in looking at a key.—
What, is this it?—Well, it is a monstrous fine one,
I declare! Dear Fatima! how pretty it would be just
to take one peep!

Fati. Tempt me not to a breach of faith, Irene. When
we betray the confidence reposed in us, to gratify
our curiosity, a crime is coupled to a failing, and 80
we employ a vice to feed a weakness.—The door
within the blue apartment must remain untouch'd.

Ire. Well, I have done:—but we may see the rest of
the rooms, I suppose?

Fati. If that can please you, Sister, I will accompany
you.

Ire. That's my good, kind Fatima!—*(Aside)* If I could
but get her by degrees to this Blue Apartment!
Come;—we'll go, and look over the Castle.—I saw
some rich dresses, in a wardrobe, at the end of the 90
gallery, that would have suited me, nicely, in the
dance last night.

SONG: Irene.
Moving to the melody of musick's note,
   Observe the Turkish fair advance,
Lightly as the Gossamer she seems to float,
   Thro' mazes of the Dance.
     Sportive is the measure,
     Thrilling is the pleasure,
   While in merry glee, the Sexes join;

      Deeper-blushing roses,   100
        Ev'ry cheek discloses,
          Eyes with Lustre shine.
  Moving to the melody, &c.

When the lover takes her glowing hand,
    With manly grace and ease,
Can the dancing female, then, withstand
      His gentle squeeze?
No—She gives him then so languishing a glance,
Grown tender, soft, and melting with the dance.
    Cupid, Cupid—God of hearts,   110
      Dancing sharpens all your darts!
  Moving to the melody, &c. *(Exeunt).*

Scene III: *Another Apartment in Abomelique's Castle.*
Enter Ibrahim, running after Beda.

Ibra. Come here you little skipping jade,[46] and let
  me look at you!—*(Takes hold of her).* Tell me
  now—Don't you think you are very pretty?

Beda. I am such as Nature made me, Sir.

Ibra. Nature has been very kind to you, hussey! She
  has given you two black eyes.

Beda. That wasn't so very kind of her, Sir.

Ibra. Don't you know I am made *Major Domo*?[47]

Beda. Yes.—The Bashaw has given you the
  command, it seems, over the slaves.   10

Ibra. Then obey me.

Beda. How, Sir?

Ibra. How?—Why—Shew me your teeth.

Beda. My teeth?

Ibra. Yes.—Giggle.—*(Beda laughs)* O, Mahomet!—
  There's ivory!—She has a handsomer mouth than
  an elephant!—Where were you born, child?

Beda. In Constantinople,[48] Sir. My poor mother was
  carried off with a plague, there. My father had it
  at the same time.   20

Ibra. Did it kill him, then?

Beda. No, Sir:—he was very bad with it:—but when
  my mother died—

Ibra. Then your Father got rid of his Plague.

Beda. Yes, Sir.

Ibra. I don't doubt it. And, how came you a slave?

Beda. O, that's a very long story.

Ibra. Don't tell it, then. We've no need of long stories,
  while there's opium in Turkey:—But I'll lighten the
  load of your bondage.   30

Beda. Will you, indeed, Sir?

Ibra. Yes.—I am a true Turkish lover.—And know
  all the amorous phraseology of our Country.—You
  shall be the Nutmeg of my affections, my All-spice
  of delight. When I meet you in the grove of
  Nightingales, let not your eyes be disdainful as the
  Stag's.—There!—Now, go and tell Mustapha to
  mend the hole the rat gnaw'd in my slipper last
  night!—in that damn'd cock-loft[49] my Son-in-Law
  crams me into, by way of a bed-chamber.   40

Beda. Am I to go now, Sir?

Ibra. Aye.—Stay!—Give me a kiss first.—What you
  are loth to take it?

Beda. O, Sir, we slaves must take any thing. *(He kisses
  her).*

Ibra. Adieu!—Crown of my head!

Beda. Good bye, Sir!—*(Aside).* An old dotard! *(Exit
  Beda).*

Ibra. My fortune's made! Abomelique marries my
  daughter to-night, and puts me into power,   50
  because he can't help it.[50]

        SONG: Ibrahim.
  I.

    Major Domo am I
    Of this grand Family;
  My word through the Castle prevails:
    I'm appointed the Head
    That must keep up the dread,
  And the pomp, of my Son-in-Law's Tails.
    I strut as fine as any Macaw,[51]

---

46 *jade*: a hussy, minx, or flirt.

47 *Major Domo*: the head servant of a wealthy household.

48 *Constantinople*: now Istanbul; named for Constantine
    as the capital of the Eastern Roman empire.

49 *cock-loft*: a small upper loft; a small apartment under
    the ridge of the roof reached by a ladder.

50 *puts me into power, because he can't help it*: The Larpent
    version adds: "What a fine thing it is to be a great man
    in office, when nobody dares turn him out."

51 *Macaw*: a tropical and subtropical bird known for
    gaudy plumage.

I'll change for down my bed of straw,
On perquisites I lay my paw, 60
I pour wine, slily, down my maw,
I stuff good victuals in my craw.
'Tis a very fine thing to be Father-in-Law
To a very magnificent three tail'd Bashaw!

II.

The Slaves, black and white,
Of each Sex own my might;
I command full three hundred and ten.
The Females I'll kiss,
But it won't be amiss
To fright them, with thumping the Men. 70
I strut as fine &c.

III.

At the Head of Affairs,
Turn me out, then who dares.—
Let them prove the Head pilfers and steals:
No three tail'd Bashaw
Kicks his Father-in-Law,
And makes his Head take to his Heels.
I strut as fine &c. *(Exit Ibrahim).*

Scene IV: *The Blue Apartment. Fatima and Irene
are discovered on the Top of the Stair-case.*

Fati. I am tired, already, with the search we have
made, Irene.

Ire. O, I could never be tired with such fine things
as we have seen!—Do, now, just come down the
stair, and walk through this wing of the building.

Fati. Well, I——

Ire. Aye, now, that's a sweet, good-natured sister!—
(They descend the stair).—Now here's a pretty
room!—All furnish'd with Blue, I see.

Fati. With Blue!—'tis the very chamber we were 10
caution'd to avoid. Imprudent girl!—Whither have
you led me? Haste, haste, Irene, and let us leave it
instantly.

Ire. Dear! where's the hurry?—I'm sure 'tis a very
pretty room:—Besides, 'tis only the *door* in this
room, which leads to another, you know, that you
were bid not to touch.

Fati. No matter: 'Tis rash to tarry. Our being here
may excite suspicion.

Ire. Suspicion!—Why, we have no bad purpose:— 20
And, even, if we were to open the door—and there
it stands, as if it seemed to invite the very key in
your hand to come and unlock it—Why I see no
such great crime in the action.

Fati. The Bashaw's charge, Irene——

Ire. Is a very ill-natured one. And should you disobey
him, we could keep our own counsel.—Then if
nobody knows we have found out his secret, what
have we to fear, while we continue mute as death?

A Voice within. Death!—*(The women look at each* 30
other, and tremble).

Fati. Did you hear nothing, Irene?

Ire. Yes.—I—I——I thought I heard something
that—Stay——O, it must be an echo.—These
large old buildings are full of them.

Fati. It had an aweful sound!—A tone like that, they
say, will sail upon the flagged wing of midnight,
crossing the fear struck traveller upon the desart,
to give him token of a foul murder.

(A deep groan is heard from the interior apartment).

Fati. O, Heaven have mercy!—What can this mean? 40

Ire. I know not!—It seems the accent of distress.—
If so, it were humanity to succour the wretched
soul who breathes it.

Fati. Humanity alone, my sister, could induce me to
penetrate the mystery this Portal, here, incloses.

Ire. No eye can see us!

DUET. Fatima and Irene.
All is hush'd! No footstep falls!
And Silence reigns within the Walls!
The Place invites; the Door is near;
The Time is apt—The Key is here. 50
Say shall we? Yes. Say shall we? No!
What is it makes us tremble so!
Mischief is not our intent;
Then wherefore fear we should repent?
Say shall we? Yes. The Door is near.
Say shall we? Yes. The Key is here.

*(At the end of the Duet, Fatima puts the Key in the Door,
which sinks, and discovers the interior Apartment,
as at first represented——The inscription over the*

Skeleton's head, is, now, "THE PUNISHMENT OF CURIOSITY." The Blue Chamber undergoes the same change, as in the first instance. The Women shriek, and run to each other, and hide their heads in each other's bosoms.—At this moment Shacabac appears at the top of the Stair-case:—then runs down hastily. As he descends, the Door rises, and the Chamber resumes its original appearance).

Shac. (Speaking as descending) O, 'tis as I fear'd! This comes of her not waiting for me.—She knows the secret, and she dies!—O, Lady! what have you done?— 60

Fati. Begone!—You knew of this. Your look, when late Abomelique left me, now is explained.—You are an accomplice in this bloody business.

Shac. I!

Fati. My Death, no doubt, is certain;—and, in you, perhaps, I see my executioner.

Shac. How a man's looks may belye[52] him! This comes now, of my being such an ugly dog!—I wouldn't hurt a hair of your head to be made a Sultan.[53]

Fati. Prove it, then, by saving us. 70

Shac. How?

Ire. Conduct us from the Castle.

Shac. Impossible. The outward Gates are closely guarded.

Fati. Nay, nay, you do not pity us.

Shac. Not pity you!—Oh! he must have a hard heart to see a lovely woman in extremity and not try to soften her distress.—Stay!—Perhaps we may conceal the—Where's the Key?—

Ire. It fell upon the ground and—— 80

Shac. The ground!—Aye—Here—Perhaps we may be able to—*(Taking it up)* Nay, then, every hope is lost!—The Key is broke!

Fati. All is discover'd then!

Ire. Certain. O, Fatima! would the Bashaw had any humanity within his breast, and that fatal Key could unlock it!—

Shac. O, would he had! I'd stuff the Key down his throat, as soon as he came home, to get at it——
(The Horn of the Castle Gate is sounded) There!— 90

The Bashaw return'd!—full six hours before his time!

Ire. O Heaven! what are we to do?

Fati. I am wreckless[54] of the future. Perhaps 'twere better I should die!—'Twill end a Life, which promised nought but misery.

Ire. Die!—Oh, Sister! *(Embracing her).*

Shac. Do not weep! do not weep!—I'm almost distracted—Hurry hence—come, Lady!—meet him as if nothing had happen'd—Collect your 100 spirits,—Smooth your looks.—This way, now!— O! if choaking can save your Life, my sorrow for you bids fair to preserve it. Come, Lady, come! *(Exeunt, up Stair-case).*

Scene V:[55] *Another Apartment in the Castle. Enter Shacabac.—looking behind him as he enters.*

Shac. I have left them on the top of the Stair, that I may avoid observation.—If they get far enough from the Blue Chamber before inquiry is made for them, they may conceal the——

(Enter Hassan. Shacabac runs against him).

Shac. Umph!—Who's that?

Hassan. Hassan—The black Eunuch.[56]

Shac. Whither are you going?

Has. To seek the Lady Fatima by the Bashaw's order.

Shac. Are you?—*(Aside).* If he meets them so near the fatal Chamber, and mentions it to the Bashaw, 10 they are lost.—I must detain him.——I—— Hassan!——I say, Hassan—How d'ye do, Hassan?—

Has. I'm well, I thank you, Shacabac.

Shac. Well, are you?—Are you sure you are well?

Has. Very well.

Shac. Very well?—Very well, I'm glad of it.—So am I, thank you, Hassan. That is I'm tolerable as the time goes.—But you had never the kindness to ask me;—Me, your fellow Slave!—Pray, now, do ask 20 me:—*(Aside)* Do,—for that will take up a little time.

---

52 *belye*: for belie; betray.

53 *Sultan*: the sovereign of an Islamic nation, especially Turkey.

54 *wreckless*: for reckless: careless, heedless.

55 *Scene V*: This scene is dropped in the Larpent version.

56 *Eunuch*: a castrated male usually serving in a harem.

Has. Why then, how dy'e do Shacabac?

Shac. Very ill indeed, Hassan!—Only feel my pulse.—Count it 'till it beats just one hundred and twenty.—*(Aside)* Twice sixty seconds will delay him about two minutes.

Has. I don't know how to count Shacabac.

Shac. Don't you?—Why not?

Has. I can't read. 30

Shac. That's a good reason.—*(Aside)* I should think, ere this, they are far enough from the Blue Chamber to——A little longer to make all sure. I have been thinking Hassan, why you and I should be of different colours.

Has. Fortune has disposed it so—She has made me black, and you white;—but don't let that mortify you.

Shac. It shan't. But as you say, Hassan, Fortune will make men of different shades.—Fortune's 40 checquer'd:—and she checquers men alternately—black and white—like the Squares in the Bashaw's Chess-Board.—When I think how much Fortune is checquer'd, I think—I think that—*(Aside)* I think I have almost kept you long enough for my purpose. What are the Bashaw's orders to the Lady Fatima?

Has. That he must attend her, instantly, in the Garden.

Shac. In the Garden?—Was that the command, 50 Hassan?

Has. It was, Shacabac.

Shac. Then I'll tell you what, Hassan—if ever the Master of the Slaves gave you a sound drubbing, for staying so long on a message, you'll get one now.

Has. Why have you delay'd me, then?

Shac. I!—You have delay'd me. You have a brain for business, Hassan;—but, whenever you meet any one in your way, you will stop, and gabble.— 60 That's your fault—Away!

Has. I'll go find her. *(Exit Hassan).*

Sha. And I'll to the Garden, to watch her interview with the Bashaw: And weak as my means are, I'll catch at every straw to preserve her! *(Exit Shacabac).*

Scene VI: *A Garden.—In the back of which is a part of Abomelique's Castle—and a Draw-bridge leading to the Castle Gate.—A Corridor before the Apartments on the first story.—A Door beneath it.—A Turret on the top of the Building overlooking the Country. Enter Abomelique, and a Slave.*

Abom. Is Fatima inform'd I wait her presence here?

Slave. Hassan by your command——She comes. *(Enter Fatima).*

Abom. Leave us. *(Exit Slave).*

Fati. (In apparent confusion). This speedy return I— I look'd not for.

Abom. I had accounts to settle,—with Traders,—Merchants from Gallipoli: But when worldly business draws men abroad who leave their hearts at home, then, Fatima, Love's wings give swiftness to the leaden hours of dull negotiation; and the 10 mercurial spirit of an enamour'd mind consolidates a volume, ere Commerce, dozing o'er his Day-book,[57] can plod a page. How have your hours pass'd in my absence? Have you view'd the Castle?

Fati. I have, Sir.

Abom. Well, saw you aught worthy your inspection?

Fati. Worthy, Sir?

Abom. Aye worthy—There are sights here, perhaps, that common eyes ne'er look'd upon.

Fati. There are indeed! 20

Abom. Now, please you, give me back the Keys.

Fati. They are here, *(Delivers them in great agitation).*

Abom. How now?—You tremble!

Fati. Tremble, Sir!—Why should I?

Abom. You best can answer that.—Sometimes, Lady, 'twill betray Guilt.

Fati. And know You, then, no instance where the Guilty do *not* betray themselves by trembling?

Abom. Umph!—I comprehend not that. One Key is wanting! *(Sternly)* where is it? 30

Fati. I have it.

Abom. Give it me.

Fati. Be not impatient.—'Tis in my pocket.

Abom. Produce it.

---

57 *Day-book*: a book into which the day's events are recorded; a journal or diary.

Fati. I shall——*(Gives it)* but, by mere accident, you
    see 'tis broken.

Abom. Damnation!—Lady, this Key is Charm-
    fraught; forged in a sulphurous Cave, within whose
    blood-besprinkled mouth nothing but Witchcraft
    enters, to celebrate her frantick revels. This speaks   40
    a damning proof against you, and you die! *(Draws*
    his Scymetar and holds it over her head.—She falls
    on her Knees).

Fati. Oh, Spare me! Spare me!—If ever I approach'd
    the door but to——

Abom. (Going to strike). No protestations!

Fati. Beseech you, hold!—Alas! if I must die, grant
    me some little time, for preparation.

Abom. (After a short pause).—Well,—be it so.
    (Pointing to an Apartment within the Corridor)   50
    Yonder's your chamber. Thither instantly: soon
    expect me there—then to expiate your crime by
    Death.—Before me to the Castle!

(Exit Fatima through the Door under the Corridor,
Abomelique following her with his drawn Scymetar.
Enter Shacabac, on the opposite side).

Shac. Allah, preserve her poor soul! But I fear she goes
    to certain Death! O that I were able to save her!
    Are there no means to——This hellish
    Abomelique whips off women's heads as if they
    were a parcel of buttons.—Let me listen. *(Fatima*
    comes from her Apartment, upon the Corridor). Hist!   60
    Lady! Lady Fatima!

Fati. O get you hence, good fellow! Your anxiety may
    make you a sharer with me, in the Bashaw's
    resentment.

Shac. Where is he?

Fati. I expect him instantly to ascend the Stair, and
    execute his dreadful purpose.

Shac. O, Mahomet, holy Prophet! if ever you break
    a Bashaw's neck over a Stair-case, now's your time!

Fati. Hark!—I hear him!—No.

(Irene appears on the Top of the Turret).

Ire. Sister! Sister Fatima!   70

Fati. Irene! Is it you?—O, Sister, fare you well! I die
    a cruel death!—

Ire. My heart bleeds for you!

Shac. So does mine, I'm sure!

Ire. Should Travellers appear, I'll call to them to
    succour us.

Abom. (Calling from Fatima's Apartment). Fatima!

Fati. O, Heaven! he has enter'd the Apartment!

Abom. (Without). Why Fatima!

Shac. (Retires under the Corridor). 'Tis he!   80

Fati. One moment, I beseech you! I have but one
    poor prayer to offer up to Heaven, and then I
    come.—Is there no help!

QUARTETTO. *Abomelique, Fatima, Irene, Shacabac.*

Fati. Look from the Turret, Sister dear!
And see if succour be not near.—
O tell me what do you descry?
Ire. Nothing but dreary Land and Sky.
Fati., Ire., Shac. Alas! Alas! then I/You/She, must
    die!
Abom. Prepare.—
Fati. He calls! Look out, again!   90
Look out, look out across the plain!
Ah me! does nothing meet your eyes?
Ire. I see a Cloud of Dust arise.
Fati., Ire., Shac. That Cloud of Dust a hope
    supplies!
    Abom. No more delay.
    Fati. A moment stay!
Fati. O, watch the Travellers, my Sister dear!
Ire. I'll wave my handkerchief, 'twill draw them
    near.
Shac. They'll see it speedily, and hurry here.
    Abom. Prepare!   100
Ire., Shac. I see them galloping, they're spurring
    on amain!
Now, faster galloping, they skim along the plain!
    Abom. No more delay.
    Fati. A moment stay!
Fati., Ire., Shac. They come.
    Abom. Prepare!
Fati., Ire., Shac. They'll be too late!
Now they dismount!—They're at the Gate!—
    Abom. Prepare!

(Abomelique, as they finish the Quartetto, rushes from
the Apartment upon the Corridor, seizes Fatima, and is
upon the point of beheading her, when Selim and his
Companions having cross'd the Drawbridge, sound the
Horn loudly at the Gate.—Abomelique, alarm'd at the
Noise, retires hastily, dragging Fatima into the

Apartment. Shacabac comes from under the Corridor).

Shac. (*To Selim, who is on the Drawbridge).* You'll get 110
no entrance there.

Sel. Say, where is Fatima!

Shac. Trembling under the Bashaw's clutches.

Sel. We force the Gate, then.

Shac. 'Tis impossible. Get round to the Eastern
Battlement; we are weakest there.—Away! and
success attend you!

Sel. To judge you from your conduct, you should be
a friend. What are you?

Shac. What every man should be—a Friend to Virtue 120
in distress wherever I meet it. Away, or you will
be too late.

Sel. Come, Comrades!—be firm! fight lustily. Quick
March!—(*They hurry from the Bridge, to quick
Martial Musick. Exit Shacabac).*

Scene VII: *An Apartment in the Castle. Alarums,
Shouts, &c. Enter A Body of Slaves.*

1st Slave. We are attack'd.—Up to the Ramparts.—
Where is Ibrahim, our Leader?

2nd Slave. He's no where to be found.

1st Slave. We must begin without him, then. It is the
Bashaw's order.—Follow!—

(Exeunt Slaves. Shouts without. Enter Ibrahim).

Ibra. Mercy on me!—I quake in my cloaths like a cold
jelly in a bag![58] They are battering the Castle to
pieces. I am the unluckiest Mussulman in all Turkey!
Here's a Building that has stood wind and weather
this age, and, the moment I pop my nose into it, it 10
begins tumbling about my ears.—(*Shouts. A cry of
TO ARMS! TO ARMS!).* To Arms! O, dear!—I had
much rather to Legs, if I knew which way to escape.
Now shall I be expected to put myself in the front of
the ranks, because I am *Major-Domo*;—but, if I do,
I'll give them leave to mince the *Major-Domo* for his
Son-in-Law's supper.

(ALARUM. Enter 1st Slave).
O Mahomet! what's that?

1st Slave. An Enemy is on the Walls.

Ibra. Then, you cowardly rascal, do you go and knock 20
him into the ditch.

---

[58] *cold jelly in a bag*: A jelly bag is used for straining jelly.

1st Slave. We wait for you. You are appointed our
Leader—There is no discipline without you.—We
want a Head.

Ibra. Do you?—So shall I, if I go with you.—Get
on before—Tell 'em to fight like fury;—and I'll be
with them, to reward their valour, when it's all
over.—Run that way, that leads into the action.

1st Slave. I will. (*Exit Slave).*

Ibra. And I'll run this way, that leads out of it. (*Exit.* 30
Shouts Alarum, &c).

Scene Last: *The inside of the Sepulchre.*
The Inscription, over the Skeleton's head, is now,—
*"THIS SEPULCHRE SHALL INCLOSE HER
WHO MAY ENDANGER THE LIFE OF
ABOMELIQUE"——The Shouts and Alarums
continue. Enter Abomelique with his Scymetar
drawn—dragging in Fatima.*

Abom. On every side it rages: The Slaves give way.
You still are in my power. You Sorceress, have led
me to the toil! Your Death will extricate me—Meet
it then here:—Here, in the Sepulchre, which you
have violated.

Fati. Nay take me hence.—Let me not perish in this
abode of horror!

Abom. Thy prayers are vain.——

*(As he raises his Scymetar to strike, a near Attack is
heard, and a violent crash in the Building:—Part of the
wall, in the back of the Sepulchre, towards the roof, is
beat down, and Selim appears in the Aperture).*

Sel. Hold, Ruffian! hold thy arm!

Fati. Oh Selim! 10

Abom. Rash fool! I know thee, and thy purpose. Thy
presence, now, swells the full tide of my resentment,
and gives a higher zest to vengeance. Know the
decrees of Destiny, and curse thy weakness which
would counteract it.—"This Sepulchre shall inclose
Her who shall endanger the Life of Abomelique."
This wretch, here, has endanger'd it—This
Sepulchre incloses her, and——

Sel. But not in Death: Tyrant, thy hell-born Spells
promise not that. 20

Abom. Does my Fate juggle with me, then!—Hold—
No, (*Pointing to the Talisman*) yon dagger is my
safe guard 'till mortal hands can reach it. Weak
boy! Despair, and see her die.

Fati. While Selim lives—So near me too,—my life is precious, and I struggle to preserve it.

(She struggles with Abomelique, who attempts to kill her;—and, in the struggle, snatches the Dagger from the pedestal of the Skeleton.—The Skeleton rises on his feet—lifts his arm which holds the Dart, and keeps it suspended. At that instant the entire wall of the Sepulchre falls to pieces, and admits Selim to the ground.—Behind—among fragments of the building, a body of Spahis is discovered, on foot, with Abomelique's Slaves under their Sabres, in postures of submission, and farther back is seen a large Troop of Horse—The neighbouring Country terminates the view. Selim advances towards Abomelique).

Sel. Now, turn thee hither!

Abom. Baffled!—I still have mortal means, and thus I use them.

(Selim and Abomelique fight with Scymetars—During the Combat, Enter Irene and Shacabac.—After a hard contest, Selim overthrows Abomelique at the foot of the Skeleton.—The Skeleton instantly plunges the Dart, which he has held suspended, into the breast of Abomelique, and sinks with him beneath the earth. A volume of Flame arises, and the earth closes.[59] Selim and Fatima embrace).[60]

Shac. Huzza!—If ever the Bashaw was in fit company,   30 he has got into it now.

Fati. Oh Selim!

Sel. Thus safe, at last, I clasp thee!

Ire. Joy, joy, my Sister! we have conquer'd.

Fati. Where is my Father?—

Shac. Hid in the dust-hole.[61]—When the noise is over, we may chance to get sight of him.

Sel. All shall be explain'd: Our Marriage now, my Fatima, may meet his sanction—*(To Shacabac)* And you my honest fellow must not go unrewarded.—   40 Thanks my brave Comrades!—*(Spahis and Slaves come forward).* We are victors—and in the countenance, here, of every Slave I see a smile imprest, which betokens joy, in having lost a Tyrant.

Slaves. Thanks to our Deliverer!

Sel. Come, Fatima.—Let us away from this rude Scene of horror:—and bless the Providence which nerves the arm of Virtue to humble Vice, and Oppression.

CHORUS.

Monsters of Hell, and Noxious Night,
Howl your Songs of wild delight!   50
To your gloomy Caves descending,
His career of Murder ending,
Now the Tyrant's Spirit flies:
   Bathed in a flood
   Of guilty Blood,
   He dies! He dies!

How great is the transport, the joy how complete,
When, raised from Despair, thus Love's votaries meet!
   Sweet the Delight that Lovers prove!
   Sweet, when Fortune, tired of frowning,   60
   Hymen[62] comes, with pleasure crowning
     Happy Love!

THE END.

---

59 *sinks...closes*: An actor could sink beneath the stage via one of the traps, which could be made to rise or sink by means of counterweights attached by ropes running over pulleys to the trap. Here, Abomelique sinks into one of the two large traps in the center of the Drury Lane stage, with the one closest to the audience being a rectangular opening used for the grave in *Hamlet* and the second a square opening used for the witches' scene in *Macbeth*. The flames would be created by igniting pans of "red fire," a compound of strontium, sulphur, potash, and antimony.

60 *Selim and Fatima embrace*: The Larpent version indicates the entire cast enters after Abomelique's death.

61 *dust-hole*: a pit toilet.

62 *Hymen*: the god of marriage, usually the child of Apollo and a Muse.

Timour the Tartar; A Grand Romantic Melo-drama in Two Acts

Matthew Lewis

With Ann Radcliffe, Matthew Lewis (1775–1818) was the best-known Gothic writer of his age and the most popularly successful British dramatist during the thirteen years (1798–1811) in which he produced plays for the London stage. The eldest son of Matthew and Frances Lewis, he was groomed for a political career. After attending Marylebone Seminary, Westminster School, and Christ Church, Oxford, Lewis served from 1794 to 1796 on the embassy staff at the Hague. On his return he was elected to the House of Commons as the member from Hindon, Wiltshire, serving from 1796 to 1802. His parents separated while he was still at school, and he gradually became estranged from his father over the issue of his father's mistress, Sophia Ricketts. As D. L. Macdonald's recent biography documents, Lewis's conflicted relationships with both parents repeatedly surface in his writing.

The defining event of Lewis's literary career occurred in September of 1796 when, on the publication of its second edition, he claimed authorship for his Gothic romance, *The Monk*, allowing himself full vanity of social rank as "M. G. Lewis, Esq., M. P." The small flourish of these two final letters cost him dearly; reviewers, satirists, clergy, and politicians immediately joined in calling for the book's suppression for its alleged obscenity and blasphemy. With the controversy still raging over a year later, Lewis's drama *The Castle Spectre* opened in December of 1797 at Drury Lane and ran for an unrivalled three months to popular acclaim and critical attacks of plagiarism, German-centeredness, improbability, fatalism, and violent Jacobin sympathies. Because of the ensuing controversies surrounding him, Lewis proceeded to take the unorthodox step of publishing the play not as performed but as originally written, defending it as apolitical and himself as persecuted.

While he was able to neutralize any threat of formal prosecution by publishing a bowdlerized fourth edition of *The Monk* in February of 1798, the notoriety of his romance defined the remainder of his literary career. "Monk" Lewis was, without question, a man of considerable celebrity, whose penchant for supernatural spectacle commanded considerable audiences and enabled him to travel in the highest society. The considerable success of *The Castle Spectre* and the publication of his anthology, *Tales of Wonder* (1801), only confirmed his position in London literary circles. Lewis's reputation for Gothic sensationalism, however, also interfered with the reception of his more serious dramas. Thus, when Lewis offered Drury Lane his tragedy, *Alfonso, King of Castille*, Richard Brinsley Sheridan instead chose Lewis's earlier melodrama, *Adelmorn the Outlaw* (Drury Lane, 1801), leaving Lewis to take *Alfonso* to Covent Garden, where it opened successfully in 1802. Thereafter Lewis alternated between serious works like *The Captive* (Covent Garden, 1803) and *Adelgitha; or the Fruits of a Single Error* (Drury Lane, 1807), and spectacular dramas like *Rugantino; or, The Bravo of Venice* (Covent Garden, 1805), *The Wood Daemon* (Covent Garden, 1806), and *Venoni* (Drury Lane, 1808). In 1812 he inherited his father's large plantations in Jamaica, and in 1818 died of yellow fever returning from his second voyage there. His efforts to improve the working conditions of his slaves are described in his *Journal of a West India Proprietor*, published posthumously in 1834.

Timour the Tartar (Covent Garden, 1811) was Lewis's last dramatic work. Beckoning Lewis from retirement, Covent Garden manager Henry Harris presented him with a challenge difficult to refuse: to write a spectacular afterpiece to succeed Covent Garden's recent revival of *Blue-Beard*, which for the first time had featured live horses on the stage of a legitimate theater. With *Timour*, Lewis responded with characteristic verve, providing an elaborate equestrian procession, a mounted single combat, and a final pitched battle with full cavalry to conclude the play. While audiences met the drama with enthusiasm, reviewers and satirists complained with characteristic energy. Performed forty-four times and condemned as a degradation of legitimate theater, *Timour the Tartar* inspired multiple stage burlesques in its first season. These included George Colman the Younger's "Tragico-Comico-Anglo-Germanico-Hippodramatico Romance," *The Quadrupeds of Quedlinburgh; or, The Rovers of Weimar* (Haymarket, 1811; included in this anthology); Samuel James Arnold's "New Heroic, Tragic, Operatic Drama," *Quadrupeds; or The Manager's Last Kick!* (Lyceum, 1811); and G. Male's "New and Splendid Equestrian and Pedestrian Romantic Melodrama," *One Foot by Land and One Foot by Sea; Or, The Tartars Tartared!* (Astley's Pavilion, 1811). The opening of the "New Grand Oriental Melo-Dramatic Burlesque Extravaganza" *Timour, the Cream of All the Tartars* (Princess Theatre, 1845) over three decades later is testimony to the play's longevity and centrality within British popular culture.

The copytext for the play is *Timour the Tartar; A Grand Romantic Melo-Drama in Two Acts* (London: Lowndes & Hobbs, 1811). We have indicated some major variations found in the Larpent manuscript (Huntington Library LA 1670) in the notes. Among other things, the Larpent manuscript indicates in its stage directions where and when music was played during the performance. This occurs during important scenes, particularly the longer pantomimic ones, which suggests that Lewis deployed music strategically to punctuate and heighten key moments of action rather than continuously behind the action (as became usual with strict melodrama). Some later editions of the play provide additional information about staging choices.

EPIGRAPH:

"I see them galloping! I see them galloping!"[1]
BLUE-BEARD

ADVERTISEMENT.

The idea of Zorilda's disguise was suggested by an incident in a French Drama called "La Fausse Iseulte";[2] in which to effect her Husband's release a Wife assumes the character of his Bride; but in every other respect the two Pieces are totally different.

This trifle was written merely to oblige Mr. Harris, who prest me very earnestly to give him a Spectacle, in which Horses might be introduced; But having myself great doubts of the success of these New Performers, I constructed the Drama in such a manner, that by substituting a combat on foot for one on horse-back, the Cavalry might be omitted without injury to the Plot; and I understand, that the Piece has been acted in the Country with the above alteration, and still with some applause.—For that which it obtained in London, it was clearly indebted to the magnificence of the Scenery and Dresses, to the exertions of the Performers, and above all to the favour with which the Horses were received by the Public. 10 ... 20

M. G. Lewis.

---

1 *"I see them galloping! I see them galloping!"*: Lewis's epigraph shows his characteristic generosity in noting sources, here paying overt homage to Colman the Younger's *Blue-Beard*. See the text of Colman's play, page 94, line 101.

2 *"La Fausse Iseulte"*: unidentified; perhaps Louis Ponet, *La fausse Isaure; ou Le chateau des Alpes; drame, en trois actes, en prose et a spectacle* (Paris: Fages, 1803).

DRAMATIS PERSONAE[3]

Timour,[4] Khan[5] of
 the Afghan Tartars[6]   Mr. Farley
Agib, Prince of
 Mingrelia   Master Chapman
Bermeddin   Mr. Treby
Abdalec   Mr. King
Octar   Mr. Jeffries
Kerim   Mr. Crossman
Sanballat   Mr. Makeen
Orasmin   Mr. Field
Oglou   Mr. Fawcett
Zorilda   Mrs. H. Johnston
Selima   Miss Bolton
Liska   Mrs. Liston, Miss Feron
Georgians, Tartars, Africans.

---

3   *DRAMATIS PERSONAE*: The Larpent version adds "Captain of the Escort" to the *dramatis personae*.

4   *Timour*: Timour (1336–1405), also spelled Timur, also known as Timur Lenk ("Timur the lame"), and thus in English as Tamerlane or Tamberlaine; Turkish conqueror of Islamic faith, chiefly remembered for the barbarity of his conquests from India and Russia to the Mediterranean Sea and for his dynasty's cultural achievements, including the Timurid architectural monuments of Samarkand. He inspired Christopher Marlowe's *Tamberlaine the Great* (1590) and Nicholas Rowe's *Tamerlane* (1701), which nearly always was performed either on November 4th, the anniversary of William III's birth, or November 5th, the anniversary of William III's 1688 landing in England to claim the British crown.

5   *Khan*: the ruler or monarch of a Mongol tribe. At the time of Genghis Khan (early thirteenth century) a distinction was made between the title of *kan* and that of *khákan*, which was the title Genghis assumed as *Great Khan*, or supreme ruler of the Mongols. Thereafter the term *khan* was deployed by many Muslim societies.

6   *Tartars*: members of a Turkish-speaking people living primarily east of the Ural Mountains along the Volga and Kama rivers. The ancient name Tartar (or Tatar) was sometimes given to single tribes or to all nomads of the Asian steppes and deserts, including Mongols and Turks generally, and was applied to peoples and

SCENE: *Lies near the Caspian Sea.*

Act I .

Scene I: *The interior of a Fortress, with a Bridge in the back ground.—On one side appears a Tower supposed to serve as a State Prison.—Day break.—Oglou enters from a low gate in the Wall, looks round cautiously, advances to the Tower, and claps his hands thrice.*[7]

Oglou. Hist! Agib!—Prince Agib!—He answers not!—Can he be sleeping,—Or are his Guards awake? shall I repeat the signal?—I'm half afraid!—Oh! that I were but still a Shepherd, and subject only to a Shepherd's fears!—Yet once again I'll venture; If that fails——*(He claps his hands again—Agib appears on the battlements of the Tower).*

Agib. Oh! my kind Gaoler! Are you then come at last?—May I descend?

Oglou. Are your Guards secure?   10

Agib. Fear not; they sleep soundly.

Oglou. Then for a few moments come down, and come quickly—Softly! Softly!—*(Agib disappears, Oglou unlocks the Tower grating).*—There, pretty Bird; the door of your Cage is open—Ha! Daybreak?—Then it's but for a few moments indeed, that my princely Captive must enjoy his liberty. Now shame on my old drowzy pate[8] for sleeping away those hours, which I might have employed in lightening a heavy heart.[9]   20

(Agib enters and embraces Oglou, who kneels and kisses his hand).

Agib. Oh! good, good Oglou, why did you tarry so long?—If you knew, how mournful it is to sit and

---

states of the Mongol Empire (thirteenth and fourteenth centuries) such as Crimean Tartars, Siberian Tartars, Kazan Tartars, and Kasimov Tartars.

7   The Larpent version differs here: "*The court yard of a Tartarian Fortress. On one side appears a Tower, with a grated door. Daybreak—Musick. Oglou enters from a low gate in the wall, looks around cautiously, advances to the Tower, and claps his hands thrice. Musick ceases.*"

8   *pate*: head or skull.

9   *heavy heart*: The Larpent version indicates "musick" here.

watch the pale expiring Lamp——To hear no sounds but the murmurs of my dreaming Guards——To see no object but dungeon-walls, and the faces of iron-hearted men——and still to turn and turn the sand-glass——and still to wait and to wait for one, who comes not!——

Oglou. Alack, pretty Prince! I can well believe it!

Agib. 'Tis to *you*, that I owe my every little comfort! If ever my fevered lips drink one breath of pure sweet air,——If ever my fettered limbs enjoy one wholesome hour of exercise——If I have health——If I have life itself——all is *your* gift! Since I became your Son's captive, no eye has looked on me with mercy—save *yours*: No voice has spoken to me with kindness——save yours, yours only! 30

Oglou (*Interrupting him, and dashing away a tear*). No more! No more!

Agib. Now then, when *you* too seemed to forget the poor Prisoner——Oglou, from the moment I heard that my Father was slain by Timour, that I was myself a Captive, and should never see my Mother more——From that moment, Oglou, never did I shed one tear[10]—But to night, when still you came not,——and when I began to think, that you would come no more——Oh! then my heart felt so sad, so hollow, and so painful; and my courage failed me, Oglou, and I wept——Oh! bitterly, bitterly!—Good Friend, have mercy for the future; Never make me suffer again, what I have this night suffered! 40 50

Oglou. I suffer as much to hear you say so!—Trust me, sweet lad, my very heart bleeds for you; and you know well, I only consented to act as Governor of this Fortress, that I might be enabled to lighten the weight of your chains—But the fact is, that last night my dear terrible Son held a grand carousal[11] in honor of his approaching nuptials: I dared not absent my-self, and He detained us so late— 60

Agib. Dare not?—Oglou, is he not your Son?

Oglou. Um! For a Man who prides himself on his veracity, that's rather a ticklish question to answer—to be sure, his Mother told me so—— Ah! and my own heart tells it me still more loudly!

Agib. And what then can a Father fear?

Oglou. Why, you see, *my* Son——isn't like other people's Sons—Oh! Prince, if you knew, what a terrible Mortal it is! His very speaking to me gives me a fit of the ague;[12] and I never leave his presence without shaking my head to be certain, that it still sits tight between my shoulders. 70

Agib. Indeed? then he loves you not?

Oglou. Yes; yes! he loves me well enough—Only it's after a fashion of his own: He'd kill me first, and be very sorry for it afterwards. Now to be sure, that would be mighty amiable in *Him*; But if my head were once fairly off, I doubt much whether all his regrets would be able to make it stick on again— nay, at this moment I'm not at my ease, I promise you. Were Timour to know that while your Guards sleep, I suffer you to leave your dungeon, I warrant, in the next half hour it would be all so,— (*Making the motion of cutting his throat*)—or so with me!—(*Making the motion of strangling*). 80

Agib. Horrible! what! his Father?

Oglou. Why, the truth is,[13] that in the first impulse of his fury, my dear terrible Son spares neither Friend nor Foe, neither Men, Women, nor Children; and unluckily He's so used to those little colloquial phrases of—"String me up those Miscreants!"—"Strike me off those heads!"— and—"Squeeze me together those wind-pipes!"— that they pop upon his lips on all occasions, and come so trippingly off his tongue, that it's a perfect wonder to hear him. 90

Agib. The Monster!

Oglou. And yet in spite of all his vices, I dote upon him still! Nay, 'tis this affection alone, which prevents my flying with you this moment to your widowed Mother. But I cannot abandon my son; and should 100

---

10 *tear.* The Larpent version differs slightly here: "I swear to you, from that moment, Oglou, never had I shed one tear."

11 *carousal:* a drinking feast.

12 *ague:* a malarial fever with hot, cold, and sweating stages; more generally, any fit of shaking or shivering.

13 *and be very sorry ... Why, the truth is:* The Larpent version cuts these lines.

I suffer you to escape without me, his vengeance——
—No, no! I dare not!—Yet all that I dare do, I will.
Time flies; let us to the business, which brought me
hither. The Letter for your Mother——

Agib (Giving it). 'Tis here—You will convey it?

Oglou. For my success I'll not answer; But depend
on my zeal—Yet tell me; this Letter may be
intercepted; should it contain...... 110

Agib. Oh! no! indeed, I have been cautious! I've only
told my Mother, that I am well, but not that I am
wretched! I've only said that I think of Her all day,
that I dream of Her all night, that She is the only
Being in the world, whom I love——except *One*—
But fear not, good Oglou; I've not mentioned,
who that One is!

(The Sun appears).

Oglou. Good! Good!—But see! the Sun rises! Your
Guards may wake: You may be seen from the
Battlements. Dear Agib, You must return to your 120
Tower.

Agib. To my melancholy Tower!

Oglou. Now plagues upon me for waking so late! But
To-morrow——Hark!—Footsteps!—Away! Away!

Agib. So soon?—Nay, chide not! I obey!—Farewell
then, pleasant Air! and glorious Sunshine! and thou
too, gay lovely happy World farewell!—Now then
I go, dear Oglou! Go once more to my dungeon's
darkness! Go to form day-dreams of liberty, and
pray for *You!*—Farewell, till night, Farewell!—*(He* 130
re-enters the Tower).

Oglou *(Locking the grate).* The little Rogue!—He'll
certainly tempt me some day to release him; and
if once I open his prison-doors, I'm persuaded, the
next thing opened, will be my own wind-pipe.—
Surely, I heard footsteps?

Liska (Singing without).
　Then showed the King a costly Ring,
　　Set with a precious Jewell.
　The Maid, she blush'd; her fears were hush'd;
　　Quoth she,—"I can't be cruel."——14 140

Oglou. Oh! it's only my Daughter.

Liska (Continuing her Song).
　And golden store, and jewells, more,
　　Than I can tell, he bought her:
　So now She's seen to shine a Queen,
　　Though born a Shepherd's Daughter.

*(Enter Liska).*15

Oglou. Now, Liska! what brings you abroad so early?

Liska. Truly, Father, I could not sleep for thinking
of all those fine plans that his Highness, my
Brother, was laying down last night. Such
conquests, and such changes! Such pulling down 150
Kingdoms in *this* quarter, and building up others
in *that!*—Well! Lucky was the day when the Tartars
came to our Cottage, and showed us in their Chief
the Son of the Shepherd, Oglou.

Oglou. A lucky day?—Girl, 'twas the saddest of my
life, for it showed me in my long-lost Darling my
sovereign's Murderer, and the Oppressor of my
Country. The virtuous Prince of Mingrelia16 fell
by Timour's sword; His Widow is a Fugitive; His
Son languishes in prison, and only owes his life to 160
the consciousness, that his Mother and her Friends
must remain inactive, while the Child is in the
Usurper's power. 'Twere better to have lost my Son
for ever, than have found him such; 'Twere better
never to hear him named, than only hear him
named with curses.

Liska. Well, Father; at least you'll not deny, that his
Highness, my Brother, is a mighty Conquerer, and
a very great Man!

Oglou. True, Child, True; But I'd rather have had him 170
a good One.

Liska (Affectedly). Lord, Father, you've no soul for
Heroism! Now for my part, I dote upon a Hero;
and therefore I'm quite dying for the arrival of my
Brother's intended Bride, of this "Warrior

---

14 *Quoth she,—"I can't be cruel."—*: The Larpent version
indicates at the end of this verse that she sings "Fal de
ral &—."

15 *(Enter Liska)*: The Larpent version handles this a bit
differently: "*(Entering)* Fal de ral &."

16 *Mingrelia*: lowland region in western Georgia, bordering the Black Sea. This is the Colchis of the ancients.
It was a vassal principality under the Ottoman Empire but was annexed by Russia in 1803 as part of the
maneuvers in the region that lie behind, for example,
the War Cantos of Lord Byron's *Don Juan.*

Princess," as they call her. They say, She's an absolute Amazon;[17] Heads her Father's armies, Rides the Great Horse, Fights Battles, Swims rivers, and shoots flying. Now who knows but under her direction, Father, who knows but I may turn out   180
a Heroine Myself?

Oglou. And you'll swim and shoot flying too, will you?—The Girl's distracted!

Liska. I'm certain, we shall be congenial souls; and to tell you a secret, Father, I always thought that Destiny designed me to be a Great Woman!

Oglou. Indeed?—then Destiny and Nature must have had very different intentions.

Liska. Even when I was a Cottager, you know, I always carried my head high.   190

Oglou. That you did: Three feet from the ground at the very lowest.

Liska. And moreover his Highness my Brother has already announced that He means to marry me to the very first King He can catch! though indeed I don't mean to take the first that offers: No! I'll wait till I see Princes, Emperors, and Sultans bowing down by dozens to my Highness's footstool.

Oglou. Then pray take care, that your Highness's footstool is a very lofty one, or the poor Princes   200
will have so far to stoop, they'll infallibly disclocate some of their illustrious back-bones.

Liska. La! Father, how can you snub one so! I wonder, living at Court hasn't taught you how rude it is to talk of one's *figure* to one's *face*. Besides I'd have you to know, that Beauty don't consist in immensity of size, but in exquisite proportion; and without being seven feet high, a woman may display a vast deal of grace and dignity.—But to hear you talk, because I happen not to be   210
absolutely a Giantess (for which Heaven be thanked!) one would really think that I were actually under-sized! *(Walking about conceitedly).*

Oglou. Mad! Vanity-mad!—Liska, Liska! You once had a heart, kind, grateful, humane!

Liska. It's unchanged, Father; but still——

Oglou. Then how can you forget, that the Throne, which your Brother has usurped, belongs to the Son of Her, to whom we both owe our existence? we were in sickness, in poverty, without help,   220
without hope, when chance led to my hut the Mother of yon little Captive. Though we were but peasants, and she was Mingrelia's Princess, she disdained not to fulfill the humblest duties of humanity—yet now, ungrateful Girl——

(Trumpets and Cymbals.[18] Enter Bermeddin).

Bermeddin. His Highness approaches.

Oglou. Does his Highness?—then my lowliness shall get out of his way as fast as possible.

Liska. And trust me, Father, I'll not stay behind; for though his Highness is my own Brother, I'm always   230
so frightened in his presence——*(Trumpets again)* —Here He comes!—then here I go. *(Exit running).*

Oglou. Away, Girl; I'll not be long after you!—mercy on me! Of what materials must that Man be framed, whose nearest and dearest Relations are compelled to fly in terror from his presence. *(Exit).*

(Timour, holding papers, enters hastily, with Tartars).

Timour. What? Is't possible?—Dare then the Slaves but whisper[19] a wish for freedom?—Holds Mingrelia still a wretch so desperate, that when I trample him, the worm dares turn? Look! Look, Bermeddin! a   240
Plot! a Plot against my life! with the blood of their Chiefs have I deluged my Scaffolds; with the blaze of their burning Towns have I crimsoned the Heavens; and have I still left them spirit enough to groan?[20] Go! Bear my orders for instant vengeance: To death with the Assassins; and from henceforth, whoever mention Agib's name though but in prayers, 'tis sufficient; wait for no orders;—Off with their heads!—Begone!—*(A Tartar goes off).* Now, Bermeddin—Wait the Two Rival Chiefs?   250

Berm. They attend your summons.

---

17 *Amazon*: originally, a race of female warriors alleged by Herodotus and others to exist in Scythia; more generally, a female warrior or a very tall, masculine woman.

18 *Trumpets and Cymbals*: The Larpent version indicates "musick" here, and places Bermeddin "*(On the Portal steps).*"

19 *Dare then the Slaves but whisper*: The Larpent version differs here: "Dare then the Slaves even whisper."

20 *with the blood … enough to groan?*: The Larpent version cuts this passage and indicates that the next lines are spoken "*(To a Tartar).*"

Tim. Let them approach.

(Kerim and Sanballat enter,[21] *each holding a hand of Selima who is veiled—they pay their homage).*

Tim. Now, gallant Chieftains; your feuds distract my Court and Army, and my service demands, that your strife should cease. Is that the Circassian Captive, whose possession you so ardently dispute?—*(Selima, unveiling, kneels, and implores his protection).*—Both have rendered me good service; Gladly would I preserve the lives of both. Let one then resign the Maid, and be himself the awarder of her ransom: My treasure shall defray it—*(Both express their love for Selima, who seems terrified at their violence—they demand the Combat).*[22]—Then be it so; the Combat must decide your claims. In Twelve hours meet on this spot; Hither will I conduct the Captive, and let the best sword win her.—*Guards,* lead her to the Fortress!—Chieftains, withdraw!—*(They express joy, exchange pledges, threaten each other, and depart after taking leave of Selima, who is led into the Fortress).*— No news yet of my Georgian Bride?—This tardy Octar!—How must he loiter with his illustrious Charge!

Berm. How would he wonder at the impatience which that delay creates! Has then at length the heart of Timour learnt to love?

Tim. To love?—away!—It's true, Report speaks this Warrior-Princess fair beyond the race of Women: But the choicest flowers of Asia have bloomed within my Haram, yet never charmed me beyond an idle hour—they pleased my senses; I gathered, and I threw away!

Berm. This eagerness then....

Tim. Regards not the Woman, but Georgia's Heiress. *Her* daring mind, *Her* martial talents can alone obstruct my progress; and her Father's power, if employed in Agib's cause, might yet wrest Mingrelia

from my grasp—But she once mine, what glorious, what boundless visions blaze on my enraptured eye?

Berm. It's true—Possessing the Diadems both of Georgia and Mingrelia....

Tim. Of Georgia and Mingrelia? of Asia! of the world!—Tartary, China, India—These are but steps, on which I'll raise the towering Column of my greatness! No single Kingdom exists, which I would *deign* to rule: A hundred Thrones must be dashed in pieces, and I'll form with their Ruins one Throne that's worthy of Me!—

(The Bugle sounds).

Berm. The Sentinel gives the appointed signal—and see! 'Tis Abdalec.

(Abdalec enters, and Kneels).

Abdalec. Illustrious Lord!....

Tim. Speak!—the Warrior-Princess....

Abd. From hence you may discern her Escort.

Tim. 'Tis well—But wherefore came not Octar forward?

Abd. Illness, which detains him at the Georgian Court forbad——

(March at a distance).

Berm. I hear the trampling of Horses.

Tim. 'Tis the Princess!—Chiefs, to your stations, and receive her with all honours.

(The Tartars arrive on horse-back, conducting Zorilda, drest as an Amazon, holding an arrow, and wearing a quiver. She is mounted on a Courser[23] *richly caparisoned,*[24] *and attended by four African Boys in golden Chains, and holding fans of painted feathers—Two of them prostrate themselves; the others throw a tapestry over them; the Courser kneels, and She steps on the Slaves to dismount, Abdalec giving her his hand—The Horses withdraw, after paying their homage*[25] *to Timour).*

Tim. (In the greatest surprise and admiration). 'Tis sure some vision——some Enchantment!—Princess— —My Bride——My Sovereign!—*(Kneeling).*

---

21 *Kerim and Sanballat enter:* The Larpent version indicates "musick" beginning before their entrance and ceasing after it.

22 *(Both express ... the Combat):* The Larpent version indicates that "musick" accompanies the pantomimic action.

23 *Courser:* a large powerful horse, usually ridden in battle or in a tournament.

24 *caparisoned:* appareled with trappings; decked, harnessed.

25 *homage:* a formal acknowledgement of superiority; reverence; an expression of dutiful respect.

Zorilda. Nay, rise, Prince, rise! An union formed like ours, admits no flattery!—You have sought *me* unseen, unknown, for I am Georgia's Heiress; I seek in *you* the Conqueror of Mingrelia, for I fain would see the Victor vanquished by Me.—Timour, by my Father's commands I come to be your Bride.... 320

Tim. And could the Universe....

Zor. Hold!—your Bride on one condition—You term yourself Mingrelia's Sovereign ....

Tim. Term myself? and such I am!

Zor. Are *not*——while Agib lives.

Tim. Indeed? then Agib dies ere sunset.

Zor. And in that instant will his Mother's Friends rush to arms, and all Mingrelia burst into rebellion—No, Prince: *your* interest requires that 330 the Boy should live, but mine that He should lose all hopes of escaping.

Tim. All hopes *are* lost to him—Safe in yon Tower....

Zor. (With interest). That Tower?—and is it there then?——*that* Tower?—It may be scaled; His Gaolers may be bribed——

Tim. My Father has the Keys: who can keep him safer?

Zor. That can Mine!—Teflis has dungeons no strength can force, no art discover; and in their 340 depths must the Boy be buried! then indeed may you call Mingrelia's Diadem your own, and claim as a Sovereign the hand of Georgia's Heiress!—How?—you doubt?—I have declared my pleasure, and you hesitate to obey?—Then mark me, Timour! Agib must be the Prince of Georgia's Captive, or never shalt thou be the Prince of Georgia's Son! with To-morrow's dawn the Boy departs for Teflis——or I do!

Tim. So peremptory?—Haughty Lady——yet even 350 in scorn how beauteous!—Hear me; and ere you answer, reflect, where you are, and who *I* am!—You will depart? First ask my pleasure! This Fortress is mine! These Guards are mine!—You are in my power....

Zor. Your power?—Oh! no!—who wears a dagger and dares use it, can never be in the power of Man!—*I* in your power, *I*?—Ha! do I live to hear that menace!—Speak it but again, Timour! Speak but those words again, and that instant I'll sheathe this 360 javelin in your heart, or, failing to reach that, in my own!

Tim. Amazement! Am I really Timour? Where is his pride, his storm of fury, his sense of insult? I rage, yet I adore! She tramples on my heart, and I kiss the foot which spurns me!—Princess——Proud charming Princess——Say what thou wilt, do what thou wilt; Dispose of the Boy, of my Subjects, of myself! Never till now did I dread the frown of Mortal; never till now did I know, what Beauty 370 was!

Zor. Ha![26] the Boy then——

Tim. Sets forth To-morrow.

Zor. Abdalec is wary; under his guard——

Tim. Be it so—Hoa! Abdalec!——

(Abdalec advances, and while Timour and Zorilda give their orders, Oglou enters).

Oglou. I couldn't come here more unwillingly, if instead of coming to see my Daughter-in-law, I were coming to see my Wife!—I never saw a fighting Princess in all my life, and what to say——Faith, there She is!—I have a great mind to run 380 away again—But if I don't welcome his Bride, my dear terrible Son may fly into one of his tantrams, and any thing's better than that.—Hist! Bermeddin!—this Princess——Is she civil? Good-natured?

Berm. Civil?—You've heard of the pride of Lucifer?[27]

Oglou. What?—By the head of my Fathers, then I'm gone!

Berm. (Detaining him). No, no! the Prince sees you! He beckons you. 390

Oglou. Then I'm in for it—What shall I say?—How shall I begin?—Your Highness——I hope——I rejoice——

Tim. Princess——'Tis my Father.

Zor. (Turning round haughtily). Your Father?—Where?—Ha!—*(Starting).*

---

26 *Ha!*: The Larpent version indicates this to be an aside.

27 *Lucifer*: in Greek mythology, the morning star (i.e., the planet Venus at dawn); in Christianity, the name of Satan before his fall, employed most famously in John Milton's *Paradise Lost* (1667). The phrase "as proud as Lucifer" is proverbial.

(The next two speeches are spoken together).

Oglou. Yes—who comes, your High——Ha!—Can I believe my eyes?—Is it possible?

Zor. Oglou here?—Oglou his Father? undone! Betrayed!   400

Oglou. Why, do I really see the Princess of....

Zor. (Interrupting him eagerly). Of Georgia!—

Oglou. (Bewildered). Of Georgia?

Zor. Yes, good Oglou! Yes, 'tis even so!—'Tis the Princess of Georgia——'Tis she *who saved your life!*—Remember that, Oh! remember it.

Tim. His life?

Zor. Yes, Prince; a service, which it now is in his power to repay.

Oglou. (Eagerly). How? By what?   410

Zor. (Imploringly). Silence!—*(Then haughtily)*—Silence, I say!

Oglou. (Aside). By silence?

Zor. When *I* deign to speak, silence may well become the best and proudest.

Oglou. I see——I guess——Lady, you shall be obeyed—Lady——*(Expressively).*—I *will be silent.*——

(Zorilda, unseen by Timour, expresses her gratitude).

Tim. Princess, You saved his life? How? When?

Zor. The tale were tedious.—He fell among Robbers——I heard his cries——I flew with my warriors to his rescue——I saved his life——*(To Oglou)*—You forget it not?   420

Oglou. When I do, Lady, may Heaven forget me!

Tim. You have explained his obligations; But "repay them,"——How can He repay them?

Zor. (Graciously). By shewing kindness to *your* Wife,——who then will be *his* Daughter—*(Timour seems delighted with her answer).*—But said you not, Prince, that your Father was Agib's Guardian?   430

Oglou. And he said truly, Lady.

Zor. (To Oglou). Look to the Boy well!—Should He escape——

Oglou. I warrant you! I have kept him safe hitherto, and shall take double care of him, since I know that He interests *You.*

Zor. Be not too secure; Freedom is sweet, and Bondage is ingenious. Pines He not much for liberty?   440

Oglou. He pines for his Mother more.

Zor. Indeed?—Speaks He of her often?

Oglou. Of little else! Her virtues, her affection are for ever on his lips. Nay; 'twas but yesterday, that He prest me so earnestly to convey to her a letter——

Zor. A letter?

Oglou. That at last I even took it, and promised——

Tim. (Angrily). To transmit it?

Oglou. Yes, I *promised*; but promise is one thing, and performance is another.   450

Tim. You took it?—Produce it!

Oglou. You'd like to see it?

Tim. This instant!

Oglou. Bless me, how unlucky! I've destroyed it.—*(Timour looks angry).*

Zor. 'Twas wisely done—your Charge will soon expire; To-morrow, this dangerous Boy departs for Teflis. Till then, keep upon him still a watchful eye, and to requite your care, good Oglou, wear for my sake this jewelled rosary—Should more letters be offered—   460

Oglou *(Kneeling, that she may throw the chain round his neck).* Oh! depend on my vigilance, Lady: His Mother's no more likely to get any of his letters through *Me*—than you are yourself, Lady—*(He gives her the letter; when Timour suddenly turns from Bermeddin, who had addrest him).*

Zor. (Concealing the letter hastily). Ha!—did he observe....

Tim. Princess—How? You tremble? You change colour?   470

Zor. Fatigue——the Heat——a sudden faintness——

Tim. Let us to the Fortress!—Bermeddin!—

(Her Courser is brought forward).

Zor. Willingly—Farewell, good Oglou—*(Expressively).*—Let us soon meet again!—and for that Boy——Guard him well!

Oglou *(Pressing his hand on his heart).* Lady, in *my custody*, He's safe as in your own.

Zor. (Gratefully). 'Tis enough—*(Assuming her dignity).*—Prince, I attend you!—   480

(She mounts her Courser, Timour holding the rein, and departs. Oglou goes off expressing, that his ideas are still bewildered.—the Scene shuts).

Scene II: *The Castle-Battlements.*
Enter Selima and Liska.

Liska. Nay, pr'ythee, dear Selima, take comfort! I
protest, were I in your place, and were two mighty
Chiefs on the point of cutting each other's throats
in honor of my bright eyes, instead of
complaining, I should think it uncommonly polite
in them. Come! come! be composed.

Sel. Impossible.—Liska, on the issue of this Combat
depends my happiness, my life!

Liska. *Your* life? Bless me, no, Child; you quite
mistake the matter. Why, it's not with *You*, that the   10
Chieftains are going to fight?

Sel. And yet on this combat involves my life, for mine
depends on Kerim's.

Liska. And for your sake, sweet Selima, Kerim shall
have all my good wishes. Yet let the worst happen,
to marry the valiant Sanballat would be no such
great misfortune, for——[28]

Sel. Ah! Liska, *you* have never loved!

Liska. Oh! fie, to be sure not:—Love would be quite
beneath my dignity! None but the Vulgar are   20
allowed to marry for love; But we, who happen to
be distinguished for rank or beauty, must espouse
the first King or Mogul[29] who comes in our way—
But isn't that Kerim yonder?

Sel. It is,—at this hour He promised to meet me
here—Oh! let me fly to bid him farewell, and
swear, that the sword, which ends *his* life, shall
sever the thread of Selima's! Farewell, kind Liska.
Oh! pray for Kerim, and for Me! *(Exit).*

Liska. Alas, poor Girl! To be sure, they've the strangest   30
notions about weddings in this Fortress!——There's
Selima going to be married, but must stop to see a
man killed by the way; and as to my Brother and his
Bride, they tell me, She held a knife to his throat at
their very first meeting—Well! for my part, I'm
resolved to have a little civility at least, *before* mar-

riage, for fear I shouldn't be able to meet with any
after; and I'm quite prepared to fall desperately in
love with the first young Prince, that offers, provided
his breath is sweet, and his legs are not bandy.   40

SONG.[30]

Fancy now shows me the Phoenix of Creatures
    Vowing—"My hand will his happiness make!"
His pleading eyes, they are fixed on my features,
    Mine on the carpet for Modesty's sake.
Lud! how he sighs, while his wishes relating!
    Mercy! what passion his glances display!—
But why don't he come then? I'm weary of
    waiting!
    Ah! why does my Monarch so long delay!

—"Fairest!" says He, "at your feet see me lying!"—
—"Rise, Sir! Oh! fie, Sir!"[31] must be my reply.   50
—"Oh! but," says He, "for your beauty I'm
    dying!"—
—"Oh! but," says I, "I shall faint, if you die!"—
—"Hear me!"—"I must not!"—"Nay, show me
    my fate in
    Those speaking eyes!"—"Oh! I fear they'd
    betray——"

---

28 *Come! Come! be composed … great misfortune, for——:*
    The Larpent version cuts these lines.

29 *Mogul:* originally referring to a descendent of
    Tamerlaine, who founded the Mongol empire of
    Hindustan in 1526; more generally, a great personage
    or autocratic ruler from central Asia.

30 *SONG:* The Larpent version offers a different song:
    Oh Lud! Oh Lud! what joy 'twill be
    Some King to see on his bended knee,
        And hear him cry,
        "For you I die,
    Oh, Lovely Liska, pity me!" oh! yo, yo, yo, yo, you.

    He'll give me jewells rich and rare,
    And then, whenever I take the air,
        My Palanquin
        (As suits a queen)
    I'll have twelve black slaves in state to bear. Oh! yo, &c.

    Then when I've reach'd this high degree
    Perhaps some day so kind I'll be
        As to bring
        The King
    A little Ba-bye
    Or, if he pleases, two or three. Oh! you! &c. *(Exit)*

31 *fie, Sir!:* an exclamation expressing disgust or reproach.

But why don't He come then? I'm weary of waiting! Ah! why does my Monarch so long delay. *(Exit)*.

(Enter Oglou).

Oglou. She must have observed my signs!—Yes; for she moves this way—She dismisses her attendants—and now She hastens hither—Lady——

(Enter Zorilda).

Zor. Oh! worthy Oglou, but a few moments are my own: Let me use them to thank you for your secrecy, to implore your protection and your aid!

Oglou. Nay, in truth my secrecy had but a narrow escape! I was on the point of blabbing out every thing; for how could I expect in the person of Timour's Bride to see Zorilda, the Princess of Mingrelia?

Zor. Or I to find in the Usurper's Father the kind, the grateful Oglou?

Oglou. But now for Heaven's love, Princess, what brings you here?

Zor. You know, that I am a Mother; and yet you ask that question?

Oglou. You come then——

Zor. To save my Agib, or perish in the attempt! Mingrelia burns to throw aside her chains: Indignation, Terror, Vengeance have united the neighbouring Princes against this Usurper: But fears for Agib's life still kept our arms inactive, when Timour's Ambassadors arrived at Teflis. The proud and generous Almeyda would instantly have spurned his insolent addresses; But I saw the advantage to be drawn from their acceptance, resolved to personate the Princess, and under this disguise——

Oglou. But the Ambassadors—Your Tartar Guards ——

Zor. None had ever seen Almeyda or myself save Abdalec, and Octar: the first is in my interests; the Second, a Prisoner in the dungeons of Teflis.

Oglou. And your hopes——

Zor. Keep but my secret, and those hopes are certainties: Timour consents to delay our nuptials, till I shall be assured, that Agib has been delivered to the Prince of Georgia. Now mark! this Fortress is old and weak, and therefore was it named as the spot, where Timour should receive his Bride: The Usurper is off his guard; His Troops are few, and a numerous band of chosen Warriors near at hand

wait but my summons to attack him. My Boy once safe, easily can I escape to join them, and then falling on the Tyrant by surprize—

Oglou (Shaking his head). Aye! aye! aye!

Zor. You, good Oglou, shall be the partner of my flight, and every reward which gratitude——

Oglou. Flight? Reward?—Lady, what price would tempt you to forsake your Son?

Zor. Not Thrones! Not Worlds!

Oglou. Then what price, think you, can bribe me to abandon mine?

Zor. Oglou! a Tyrant——a Regicide[32]——

Oglou. True, Princess, True!—But still my Son!

Zor. But *such* a Son——and can you then still love him?

Oglou. Still?—Ah! when can a Father *cease* to love, and what guilt can exceed the measure of paternal patience? this Tyrant, this Regicide is still dear to me, dear as the air I breathe: His very vices chain me to him closer, and I feel that I love him the more, because being what He is, no one but myself *can* love him—Then observe me, Lady—I will be secret, I will even aid your escape; But in return you must allow my Son's: your Georgians must retire without drawing a single arrow—Fly with your Child; Collect your Troops; If you can, regain your empire:—and then if Timour should fall into your power, I'll kneel before your Throne, and say—"Timour slew your Husband, but his Father's silence saved your Son: Spare Mine!"—

Zor. And I *will* spare him, good old Man: I swear it!

Oglou. I receive your oath; I thank, and bless you!— *(Trumpets)*.—Hark! you are summoned to the Lists! and see! Bermeddin approaches.

(Bermeddin enters, and informs Zorilda, that she is waited for. She follows him, but returns to express her gratitude to Oglou, and then goes off).[33]

Oglou (Alone). Well! Friend Oglou, thou'rt getting into a rare hobble,[34] that's the truth on't! If ever

---

32 *Regicide*: one who has killed a king, especially one's own king; also, the act of killing a king.

33 *(Bermeddin enters … goes off)*: The Larpent version indicates "musick" here.

34 *hobble*: an awkward or perplexing situation from which extrication is difficult.

my dear terrible Son should learn, that I had a hand in this business!——The very thought gives me a creak in my neck. By this time, I suppose, I've the Fortress to myself: Every soul will have gone to see the combat, and——Ha! Mercy on me!—that Horseman in such haste——He looks like——'Tis He! we're undone! all's over—Is there no device——no loop-hole——By my head I must venture!—It's desperate—But it must be risqued. Thus at least I may save myself, and perhaps——Oh Lord! Oh! Lord! How loose my head feels! Oh! what a terrible thing it is to be the Father of a mighty Hero! (Exit). 140

Scene III: *The Lists,*[35]*—the Circle is formed by Balconies filled with Spectators—On each side is a decorated Throne.—Zorilda, Timour and Selima arrive in a Car of triumph, followed by Bermeddin, Abdalec, and Tartars:*[36] *They descend; Timour and Zorilda occupy one Throne, and Selima the other.— Agib's Tower appears as in the First Scene.—A Trumpet sounds, and is answered; the Barriers are thrown open, and Kerim and Sanballat enter on Horseback, from opposite sides. They charge with lances: at length Kerim's Horse takes part in the Combat, seizes Sanballat, and drags him to the ground—Sanballat rises, and attributes the victory solely to the Horse. Kerim proposes to renew the Combat on foot; the Horses are led away, and the fight begins: Kerim falls, and loses his sword. His Rival rushes to dispatch him, when Kerim's Horse leaps the Barrier, prevents Sanballat from advancing, picks up the sword, and carries it to his Master. Sanballat in fury stabs the Horse, who falls, and expires.*

Zor. Hold! Hold!—Oh! Coward!
(*Kerim's desire to avenge the faithful Animal increases his strength. He disarms his Rival, drags him to the Horse, and sacrifices him on the Body: During which all descend. Selima embraces Kerim: Zorilda crowns him: But He takes off the wreath, breaks it, strews the flowers*

on the Horse, and falls upon Him weeping—Selima hangs over them greatly affected).
Oglou (Without). Give me way there!—make way this instant![37]
Zor. Oglou's voice?
(*Enter Oglou, hastily*).
Oglou. Oh! my Son!—Oh! Timour!—I was right! I've found it all out!
Tim. Found out....
Zor. (*Anxiously*).—What means....
Oglou (To Timour). This Bride——This Georgian Heiress.... 10
Zor. Oglou! Oglou!
Oglou. When I first saw her, You remarked, that I started?
Tim. I did!
Oglou. I thought I recollected her—So I watched her——I examined——I sifted——I got it all out of her!—In short, 'tis your mortal Foe! 'Tis the Princess of Mingrelia! 'Tis Zorilda!
Zor. Ungrateful! Perfidious!
Tim. Zorilda?—Can it be? 20
Zor. No, no! Believe him not....
Oglou. Not believe me?—What? Haven't you gained the Georgian Prince to your cause? Haven't you plann'd Agib's escape? Isn't poor Octar shut up in a dungeon at Teflis?—Not believe me?—Oh! if Octar were but here, he'd soon make it clear, whether....
Octar. (Without). Where is the Prince?
Oglou. Why, that's his voice, as I live! was ever any thing so lucky! (*Octar enters hastily*). 30
Tim. Speak, Octar, speak!—the Warrior-Princess....
Oct. Prince, you are betrayed—Even now I have escaped from a Georgian Dungeon to tell you....
Tim. One word, and I know all—Know you this face?
Oct. For an Impostor's! For Zorilda's!
Tim. Scarce can I believe my senses!—Bewildered ——Confused——Rage, Love, Disappointment, all at once contend within my bosom!—Her charms———Yet to resign all hopes of Georgia's Heiress——I must to solitude, and consult—— 40 Bermeddin! Guards! Bear her to the Fortress! Away!

---

35 *The Lists*: The Larpent version indicates music throughout the pantomimic opening of this scene.
36 *and Tartars*: The Larpent version adds "four African boys" to this list.

---

37 *make way this instant!*: The Larpent version notes "(*musick ceases abruptly*)."

Zor. (Kneeling). Oh! hear me, Timour! Show but one
  spark of mercy! Listen to the sobs of a breaking
  heart, of a distracted desperate Mother! Yon Tower
  confines my Boy: Send me to a dungeon, send me
  to death; But till I die, let me share the prison of
  my Child.

Tim. Slaves obey me!—

(They drag her towards the Fortress).

Zor. Barbarian! Tyrant!—My Boy!—My Darling!—
  Let my shrieks rend your dungeon-walls! Let my   50
  anguish, my despair....

Agib (Within). My Mother! 'Tis my Mother!—

Guards. (Within). Detain him! Seize him!—

(Agib appears on the Tower, pursued by two Guards).

*Zor. (Breaking from Octar and Bermeddin, and rushing
  forwards).* 'Tis *He!* 'Tis *He* himself!

Agib (Struggling, and holding by the Battlements). Bless
  me, my Mother! Bless me, ere you go!

Zor. (Kneeling, and extending her arms towards Agib).
  My Child! My Child!

Tim. Force her away!   60

Oglou (Protecting her from Octar and Bermeddin).
  Hurt her not! Touch her not!—Oh! no! no! no!—
  (a Groupe—the Curtain falls).[38]

Act II.

Scene I: *A Splendid Chamber, with large folding doors
  in the centre. On one side is an Alcove with curtains
  drawn up in drapery by golden Cords. On the other is
  a large Window and Balcony, to which the ascent is by
  a double flight of steps with a gilt balustrade—the
  window is open, and the Moon is seen through it—
  Numerous Lamps are burning. Vases with flowers, &c,
  are dispersed about the apartment. Zorilda (with her
  hair dishevelled) is discovered on a pile of cushions,
  Selima stands near her.*

Sel. Dear Lady, do not thus give way to grief. Heaven
  knows, if I could give you comfort——

Zor. There exists none for Me! No comfort! No hope!
  Agib, Agib! shall I then never see thee more!—His
  release seemed so near——Success appeared so

certain——Oh! Disappointment too bitter to be
  endured!—Yet deep as the arrow has pierced, 'tis
  Oglou's ingratitude which has poured most venom
  in the wound.

Sel. I cannot excuse him, Lady; and yet his conduct   10
  appears so strange——He seemed to feel so much
  for you——for your Son——

Zor. Seemed? Away with the Traitor's seeming!

Sel. In short, Lady, it's a vile wicked World, and
  there's no knowing whom to trust; that's the truth
  on't. But do not take on so piteously, for Hope may
  still....

Zor. Alas! kind Selima, you would fain give me
  comfort, but dangers like mine, mock the attempt.
  A Captive to my Husband's Murderer—to my   20
  deadly Enemy——

Sel. Nay, there you wrong him, Lady; He's not *your*
  Enemy at least; for when Timour sent me hither
  to soothe you, He bade me tell you to be of good
  chear, and said, there was happiness in store for
  you, of which you little dreamt.

Zor. Ha!—Indeed?—Oh! thou hast raised a fear more
  dreadful than all others.—When Timour first
  beheld me, I marked his flashing eyes——his
  burning cheeks——and now alone—defenceless   30
  ——Away with that thought!—'Tis Horror!—'Tis
  distraction!

Sel. Don't I hear——Yes——Hark, Lady, some one
  is unlocking the door.[39]

Zor. By all my fears, Timour! It must be He!—
  Selima, dear dear Selima!—Leave me not, Oh!
  leave me not!

Sel. Not if I can help it, Lady; but perhaps——Ha!
  I protest, it's Oglou.

---

[38] *(a Groupe—the Curtain falls):* The Larpent version indicates "musick" here.

[39] *There exists … unlocking the door.* For this long passage, the Larpent version substitutes a shorter one:
    Zor. There exists none for Me! No comfort! No hope!
    Yet, deep as the arrow has pierced, 'tis Oglou's in-
    gratitude, which makes the wound most painful.
    Sel. Nay, 'tis but too certain, Lady; of Oglou's assist-
    ance there is now no hope; yet, do not thus give
    way to despair, I implore you; for when the prince
    sent me hither to soothe you, he bade me tell you
    that——Hark! don't I hear——Yes——Hark, Lady,
    some one is unlocking the door.

(Oglou enters, closing the doors again cautiously).

Zor. Oh! calm thee, my heart; thy fears were idle— 40
Now then perfidious Man; can you then endure
to look upon....

Oglou. Hush, Princess, hush! Reserve your reproaches
for a fitter time, since the present moments are
precious—At the hazard of my life I come to save
you!

Zor. You?

Oglou. To save you——and to save your Child.

Zor. Blessed are those sounds, and blessed be the lips,
that breathe them!—Yet can I believe——You, 50
Oglou? you, who betrayed my secret....

Oglou. And do you think, that Octar would have kept
it better? I knew He was at hand; knew, that all must
out; and hastened to make a merit with my Son of
a discovery, which else would have been made
without me. Thus did I preserve my own neck, my
Son's confidence, and the Keys of the Fortress; and
thus am I now enabled to unlock your prison-doors.

Zor. Oh! worthy, faithful Oglou, how could I ever
doubt your truth! 60

Oglou. Nay, I was obliged to make up my mind
quickly!—Even now I parted from my Son—He
loves you....

Zor. He? the Insolent!

Oglou. He has resigned all views on the Georgian
Princess, has ordered the Nuptial preparations to
go on, and has sworn, that ere four-and-twenty
hours elapse, you either shall become his Bride, or
see Agib's blood bedew the scaffold.

Zor. Horror chills me! 70

Oglou. I heard him, and was decided. My danger is
great in suffering you to go, but yours would be
greater in staying; and after all, I know that my
Son loves me in his heart, and all that I have to
dread is the first burst of his fury—however, come
what, come may, Princess, you shall away this very
night.

Zor. This night? this instant!

Oglou. Hold! not so fast!—Your flight might be
discovered———you might be pursued—— 80
overtaken——

Zor. But what resource....

Oglou. I have found one. Even now Abdalec by my
instructions summons your Georgian Warriors to

this Tower's foot: their Escort will secure your
retreat unmolested, and at midnight your Boy and
yourself shall be delivered into their protection.

Zor. At midnight? Oh! how tedious will the hours
seem till then!

Oglou. Why truly, I was afraid of that; and therefore 90
to beguile the time, I brought with me——

(He leads in Agib, muffled in a cloak).[40]

Agib (Throwing off the cloak). Mother!

Zor. My Child! My Blessing; *(Embracing him).*

Oglou. Now then to business—Fair Selima, might we
but count upon your assistance....

Sel. Oh! task my services to the utmost.

Oglou. Then pr'ythee, away, and watch the chamber,
where Timour sits carousing with Octar and
Bermeddin.

Sel. Willingly; and I go this instant. *(Exit).* 100

Oglou. And I'll away, to see, that all's safe below—
But forget not your promise, Princess: Your
Georgians must respect this Fortress; and the life
of Timour....

Zor. Shall be sacred as my own—as my Agib's.

Oglou. I'm satisfied—Now then I'll leave you; But
when the great Bell announces midnight, expect
my return, and be ready! *(Exit).*

Zor. Thou best of Friends, farewell!—My comfort!
My delight! and do I then fold you to my heart 110
once more? Oh! Heaven! a Mother's pains are
exquisite, but still more exquisite are a Mother's
pleasures!

Agib. And now shall I remain with you always,
Mother? Will not the Barbarians separate us again!
Oh! I have suffered so, since we parted....

Zor. And I! and I, my dear one;—Alas! that wasted
form——that hollow eye——Oh! how has the
blight of sorrow faded my lovely Rose!—and yet
——Oh! Heaven! and yet his Father's living Image! 120

Agib. Aye, Mother, and it would have fared with me
much worse, had not that kind Oglou——

Zor. Was he so Kind?—Reward him, Angels!

Agib. He comforted, He soothed me, He talked to me
of *You*, Mother. Nightly, while my Guards slept, He
unlocked my prison——and that too at the hazard

---

40 *(He leads in Agib, muffled in a cloak)*: The Larpent version
indicates "musick" here.

of his life, for if Timour had known it——and yet Timour is his Son; only think of that, Mother!—Ah! surely if *my* Father had asked me for my life, I would have bared my breast, and kissed even in dying the 130 hand with which He pierced it.

Zor. My joy! My Treasure!

(Enter Selima).

Sel. Oh! Lady, Lady!—Timour—He's coming hither, Lady!

Zor. Hither? Now?

Sel. This instant!—He seems frantic with wine, and———Hark! Quick! Quick! away with the Prince!

Zor. But where?

Sel. Yonder closet—*(The closet is near the Couch, and* 140 *on the side opposite to the Alcove, Selima, and Agib hasten to it).*—Alas! It's locked.

Zor. Distraction!—Fly, fly, my Child; In yon Alcove———*(The doors are thrown open)*—Stop, you'll be seen———

Sel. Here! here! beneath these cushions—that cloak— *(They cover him with the cushions and cloak).*—He's here!—To the Couch and pretend to sleep, Lady—

(Zorilda leans on the cushions as if asleep, while Selima sits at her feet, and fans away the flies. Timour enters, followed by Bermeddin with a Torch).[41]

Tim. How's this? the doors unlocked——— unguarded——— 150

Berm. Mighty Lord, no orders———

Tim. Careless slave, were orders needful? Hence! Summon the proper Guards, and straight return with them. *(Bermeddin retires).* Princess———

Sel. Hush! She sleeps! Exhausted with weeping—

Tim. I must disturb her slumbers—Princess, awake! Arise!

Zor. How now?—Whose daring voice———

Tim. His, who in this Fortress dares do all! 'Tis good you know it. 160

Zor. Timour! this ill-timed visit———this wild demeanour.———

Tim. I heed no hours; I laugh at forms; for Here my will is law. Now learn that will, Zorilda; on your decision hangs my fate, and my nature brooks not

delay. Zorilda, you came hither as my Bride; For my Bride was this chamber prepared; My Bride you must become, or perish—Nay, start not! The Tartar Timour cannot stoop to court your love, and if He *could* so stoop, He could not hope to gain it. I know 170 well, that you abhor me; know well too, that you have cause: But you have kindled a frantic passion in my breast, that will, and *shall* be satisfied. Frown on me still then; Still wear that look of horror; Hate me, if you will, But mine you *shall* be!

Zor. Oh! Monster!

Tim. I love you! Love you with that madness——— that desperation———Love you, as Timour *ought* to love! You are my Captive; I offer you my hand—

Zor. Your hand?—a hand stained with my Husband's 180 blood!

Tim. A hand, which your refusal will crimson yet deeper with your Son's.

Zor. Barbarian! that to a Mother?

Tim. If the mere sound thus shocks you, how will you bear the sight? Nay, 'tis decreed: the Altars blaze; the Priest is waiting; this night makes you mine, or—

Zor. This night? Oh! show some mercy, some compassion! Grant me but till To-morrow— 190

Tim. This night! this night!

Zor. But a few hours! But time for reflection!

Tim. For reflection?—Well then for once I'll yield;— *(The Bell strikes Twelve).*[42]—and, Hark! the Fortress Bell! It announces Midnight.

Sel. (Aside). The signal!

Zor. Should Oglou———

(During the previous speeches Selima has assisted Agib to steal away from the Couch, and conceal himself in the Alcove, unobserved by Timour and Zorilda).

Tim. Now mark me! One hour shall be your own— *(Zorilda expresses great joy, aside).*—See that you use it wisely; Bend your stubborn mind to obey my 200 will, and learn to value justly the glory of having vanquished Timour!—Now then I leave you to your thoughts; and while they employ you, I'll throw me on yon Couch, and by gazing on your charms—

---

[41] *(Zorilda … Torch):* The Larpent version indicates "musick" here, ceasing before Timour speaks.

[42] *(The Bell strikes Twelve):* The Larpent version indicates "musick" here.

Zor. (*Shrieking*). Oh! hold!—Not there! not there!—
(*Detaining him*).—

Tim. What means this alarm? Release me!

Zor. You must not——shall not——I know not
what I say! Terror distracts me! 210

Tim. Ha!—then yon Couch conceals some mystery!
Some Spy, Some Traitor lurks there!

Zor. Oh! no, no, no! No Spy! no Traitor!

Tim. If thou say'st true, it's well for Him and for thee!
If false——Thus I'm revenged?—(*Strikes his dagger
through the Cloak*).

Zor. (*With a cry of horror, and staggering back*). Oh!
Monster!

Sel. (*Running to support her, and whispering*). In the
Alcove! (*Agib, from the Alcove, Kisses his hand to her*). 220

Zor. (*In rapture*). Ha! then I live again!

Tim. What can this mean? there's no one!—yet her
Alarm—Answer, Princess! that shriek—that
terror—(*A tap at the door*).—By Heaven, Some
one is at the door!

Zor. (*Aside*). 'Tis Oglou!

Oglou (*Without*).—Come! Come!—'Tis I!

Tim. A Man's voice!

Oglou (*Without*).—All's ready!

Tim. Indeed?—I'll see—— 230

Sel. (*Going towards the door*). Could I warn him—
(*Aside*).

Tim. (*Seizing her; She shrinks back trembling*).—Stir
not or by Heaven!——

(*Oglou enters hastily*).

Oglou. Come Princess, come!—Come, Little Dear—
—(*He turns full upon Timour*).—I'm a dead Man!

Tim. Oglou? My Father?—Speak! Father! What
brings you here?

Oglou. I come—I come—

Tim. (*Impatiently*). For what? 240

Oglou. To look for——

Tim. For whom?

Oglou. For——For——For——Why, For *You*; whom
should I look for?

Tim. For Me? You sought for Me? and what is ready?

Oglou. Ready?

Tim. You said, "All was ready." Ready for what?

Oglou. For what?—Why, for——for your Nuptials,
to be sure; and that was precisely, what I came here
to tell you. 250

Tim. You *came* in search of Me—But you *called* the
Princess!

Oglou. Yes, to be sure, I did: Why, you couldn't be
married by yourself, could you?

Tim. You called also "Your little Dear": Whom meant
you by "Little Dear?"

Oglou. I meant——I didn't mean *You* by that.

Tim. (*Stamping his foot*). Whom did you mean?

Oglou. By "Little Dear?"—I meant——I meant by
Little Dear——I meant Selima—I always call her 260
"my little Dear"!—(*To Selima*)—Little Dear, don't I?

Tim. And if you *did* mean Selima——If you *really*
came to announce my Nuptials——If you really
were in search of Me——Why did you start and
tremble at the sight of Me?

Oglou. Why, because I always *do* start and tremble
at the sight of you!—When you look at me, my
Knees knock together; When you speak to me, my
blood runs cold; and I never think of you without
wondering, how I could ever have courage enough 270
to beget such a Firebrand.

Tim. (*Aside*). My mind misgives me——His
midnight visit—Zorilda's alarm——For a moment,
Father, your pardon; but we must speak further ere
we part.

Oglou. Oh! At your leisure. I know what's fitting; and
you've always found me a very dutiful Father, I'm
sure.—(*Aside*)—what's become of the Boy?

Tim. Now, Princess—(*To Selima who is drawing near
to Oglou*).—Girl, keep your place! No whispering. 280

Oglou (*Aside*). He must be still in the room?

Tim. Now to my question, Princess. Yon
Couch....Some mystery...

Zor. Timour, I will be frank; there *was* a mystery, but
it exists no longer. When you approached yon
cushions, I feared for the life of an humble but
faithful Favourite. It was a Dove, a Carrier-Dove,
which I had given my Son long ago; which had
been the Partner of his prison; which had found
his way to me, even here, and beneath whose wing 290
was suspended a letter from my Agib. Judge how
that gift endeared the Bird; Judge, when you drew
near the Couch, on which He had perched, how
I trembled, lest suddenly your weight should crush
Him.—I grasped your arm, and my terrified Dove
took refuge in yon Alcove.

Oglou (Aside). The Alcove! 'Tis there then——
(Agib shows himself for a moment in an attitude of supplication).

Tim. (Aside). A Dove?—this may be true——Yet hold!—Princess, confirm your story; If the Dove did really bring a letter——Produce it! 300

Zor. (Eagerly). That Letter?—Timour, 'tis here!—*(She gives the Letter, which she received from Oglou in the First Act).*

Oglou (Aside). The door is unguarded!—No one observes us!—Come! Come!—*(Softly to Agib, who steals from the Alcove, and with Oglou approaches the door, while Timour opens the letter. At the moment they reach the doors, they are thrown open; Agib retreats to the Alcove, and Oglou regains his former station).*[43] 310

(Bermeddin enters with Tartars, bearing Torches).

Berm. Prince, the Guard——

Tim. 'Tis well. Station them near yon doors, and let no one pass without my orders. Retire!

(Exeunt Bermeddin and Tartars).

Oglou (Aside). Nay then all's over with us!

Tim. (Examining the letter). 'Tis his signet: Her story then was true.—Yet if this was all the mystery, wherefore, Princess, not at first reveal it?—you had obtained the letter; the Dove had done his duty—

Zor. Had done it but in part, Timour. His wing was still burthened with my answer; I feared, lest it 320 should fall into your hands, and I was silent, that he might have time to escape—through yon window.

Oglou (Aside). The window?—Ha! Perhaps the Georgians beneath it might——*(He makes signs to Selima; She picks up the dagger, which Timour had thrown away in rage, and she cuts off a part of the Cords, which support the drapery of the Alcove. She gives it to Agib; He steals softly across with it to Oglou, who has mounted the Staircase, and is now waving 330 his scarf from the window).*

Zor. While you spoke, marked you not my uneasiness? Saw you not how anxiously I watched the entrance of the Alcove?—and when at length my little Favorite appeared—when he approached the Staircase——Oh! how my heart beat! How I trembled, lest you should turn your head!—and once, Prince, you were on the very point of turning it, as now——But I interpos'd myself, as it might be *thus*——and drawing you round *in this manner,* 340 I diverted your attention—I fixed it on myself, while *thus* I watched my Favourite. He had past the Balustrade——He entered the Balcony—— He rested on the Ledge——He paused for a moment——Oh! that moment was dreadful.— But when I saw him pass through the Window— When at length He quite disappeared—Oh! then I sank on my knees in an agony of rapture, and burst into a flood of grateful tears.—*(During this speech, Oglou fastens the cord to Agib's girdle, and* 350 *lowers him from the window).*

Tim. (Amazed). Princess!—Zorilda! This strange agitation——this excess of joy....

(Agib, without, gives a loud shriek).

Oglou. Heaven forgive me!

Zor. (Rising in terror). Speak!

Oglou. The Cord has broken!—*(Wringing his hands).*—

Zor. Horror!—and my Child——I die!—*(Attempting in vain to reach the window, She sinks on the Couch).*— 360

(Loud and joyful shout from without).

Oglou. Hark!—a shout!—*(Looking from the window).*—Huzza! Huzza! Huzza![44] the Georgians have caught him! they raise him in their arms! He's safe! He's safe! He's safe!—

Zor. (Starting from the Couch). Safe? Safe?—All merciful!—*(She folds her hands on her bosom, and remains motionless with her eyes raised to Heaven).*

Tim. (Looking from the window). The Georgians?— Rage! Distraction! Vengeance!—Bermeddin! Octar!—*(Descending).*—I must myself give 370 orders.—*(Bermeddin and Tartars enter with Torches, Timour grasps Oglou by the arm, and says in a tone of reproach).*—Father, I loved you—I trusted you— You have betrayed me—Remember that *(To Bermeddin).* Away!—

---

43 *(Softly … station)*: The Larpent version indicates "musick" here, ceasing with Bermeddin's entrance.

44 *Huzza! Huzza! Huzza!*: an exclamation meaning "hooray." Lewis employs a similar escape scene in *The Castle Spectre* (Drury Lane, 1797), Act II, scene iii.

(Exit with Bermeddin and Tartars).

Oglou. Remember it? You need not tell me to do that!—How terrible He looked! alas! alas! I hoped that Nature——that Duty——that the love He ever bore me——Oh! what have I done! wretched old Man! Oh! would to Heaven that the Boy had not escaped! 380

Zor. *(As if awakening from a dream).* Where am I?— Ha!—*(Seeing Oglou, she hastens to him, falls prostrate before him, and kisses his feet).*—Preserver of my Child!

Oglou. Princess!—Zorilda!—that voice——those tears—Now praised be Heaven, that the Boy *has* escaped; suffer as I may, this moment overpays me!—

(The Scene shuts).[45]

Scene II:[46] *A Gallery. Night. Alarum—Kerim enters, marshalling the Tartars, who having received his orders, go off severally to man the walls. Selima enters, and detains Kerim, intreating him not to leave her. He represents that Duty calls him away, takes an affectionate leave of her, and on Octar's entering to chide his delay, He breaks from her arms, and goes off with Octar.*

(Enter Liska).

Liska. Oh! Selima, Selima! What shall we do? What will become of us? the Georgians threaten to sack the Fortress, and my frantic Brother declares, that rather than yield the Princess, He'll fire the Place with his own hands.

(Enter Bermeddin).

Sel. Oh! say, Bermeddin, what hopes....

Berm. We are caught in a snare. Trusting for security to his Georgian Alliance, and to the possession of Agib, Timour has lost himself. The Fortress is weak and ill-manned; the Enemy's numbers treble ours; 10 If the Prince continues obstinate, ruin must overwhelm us.

Liska. But Zorilda's promise....My Father's services....

Berm. All are remembered; and the Georgian Chief proffers to withdraw his Troops if Zorilda be set at liberty. At first Timour rejected the terms with scorn; But perhaps Reflection has since made him judge more wisely. At this moment He summons the hostile Chiefs to the Southern Tower, whither by his orders I must instantly conduct Zorilda— 20 your pardon, Lady. *(Exit).*

(Alarum).

Liska. Oh! mercy on me; those Trumpets will be the death of Me!—I find, I've no talent for playing the Heroine; and if once the Siege begins, I shall certainly die of fright in the very first onset.

Sel. Oh! Kerim, Kerim! Wert thou but safe!—— Wretched is the Maid, who loves a Warrior.

(Enter Oglou).

Oglou *(Speaking as He enters).* Then be it so; Ungrateful, Cruel Boy, I'll spare you the sight of a Father's tears, and myself the sight of your 30 vices!—Come, Liska, come! We must away, Girl. Your Brother spares our lives, but commands us from his presence: Nay, He offers us wealth, but I'll none of his ill-gotten treasures. Come then, My only Child: the gates are open to us; the Georgians will not impede our passage; we'll kiss Zorilda's hand once more, and then....

Liska. E'en now Bermeddin leads her to the Southern Tower.

Oglou. How? and what purpose.... 40

Liska.[47] The Georgian Chiefs are summoned thither: Perhaps Timour will accept their terms.

Oglou. No, no, Liska; Timour is desperate; He meditates some dreadful act, which——Oh! let me hasten myself to the Tower; Perhaps I may spare his soul the weight of another crime.—Liska, bid your Friend farewell: the rising Sun must light us back to our Cottage. *(Exit).*

Liska. Indeed?—So there's an end of all my visions of greatness! 50

Sel. And can the loss of those visions cost you, Liska, one sigh of regret? Ah! believe me, 'tis only in the Cottage, that real Happiness resides. Desolate with snow, or terrible with fire, on the haughty

---

45 *(The Scene shuts)*: The Larpent version has "*(Musick— A groupe—The Scene closes).*"

46 *Scene II*: The Larpent version indicates "musick," which ceases before Liska enters.

47 *Liska*: The Larpent version gives this speech to Selima and has Oglou reply, "No, no, Selima."

Mountain's Summit never yet did flowret bloom: the Rose and the Violet are only found in the lowly verdant valley!

DUO.—*Selima and Liska.*
Eagle Wings the clouds impelling,
    All with wonder see them move!
But the Bird, who shares our Dwelling,   60
    Is the fond and gentle Dove.

Suns, while pouring floods of splendor,
    Blind us with oppressive light;
But the Moonshine, mild and tender,
    Long detains the Lover's sight. *(Exeunt).*

Scene the Last: *The Fortress by Moonlight. The whole of it is entirely surrounded by water, except a lofty Tower on one side, with a Terrace beneath, of which only one Angle is visible: a variety of smaller Towers, and hanging Terraces appear beyond.*[48]

(Trumpet. Abdalec. Orasmin, and Georgians, are discovered).

Orasmin. That Trumpet demands a parley.

Abd. And see! Timour himself appears.

Tim. (On the side Tower). Georgians, I summon you—But where is Agib? what I would say, requires that He should hear it.

Abd. (To a Georgian). Inform the Prince, and conduct him hither.—Timour you already know.... *(Exit Georgian).*

Tim. Traitor! Renegado! with a wretch like Thee never will Timour deign to exchange one word!—   10 Georgian Chief, to you I speak. Your Sovereign has deceived me;[49] Yet for once vengeance shall yield to Policy.—Withdraw your Troops; Restore young Agib, and your Prince shall still be suffered to reign: Timour will pardon him.

Ora. Oh! pride unequalled! Surrounded on all sides by our Troops, or by the Caspian waves; Compleatly in our toils, all hopes of flight debarred you....

Tim. Flight? Timour fly?—Within there!   20

(Bermeddin leads Zorilda on the Tower, and retires).

Tim. Georgians, look on this Captive.

Abd. Unmanly Tyrant; If your own life be dear to you, dare not....

Tim. Life? Learn how that Bauble rates with Him, who sees in it no worth but glory:—*(He claps his hands: the Fortress is illuminated, and the Towers, Terraces, &c. are filled with Tartars bearing Torches).*—Look on yon Torches; Let me but strike my hands again, and the Fortress shall be wrapt in flames; In flames, my Grave, and Zorilda's—   30 *(The Georgians seem horror-struck, and in doubt what to do).*—The Boy, the Boy! Why comes He not? He must resume my chains, or hear the dying groan of his Mother: He must submit to my mercy, or Zorilda shall find none.

Zor. No, Georgians, no; Fear not for Me! Wait not for my Son's arrival; Suffer not the Tyrant to work upon his noble nature!

Tim. Ha! Zorilda, dare you?....

Zor. All! All! For my Child is in safety. Then forward   40 brave Georgians!—Mount o'er the Walls! Down with the Gates! Rescue me, if living; If dead, avenge Me!

Tim. Insolent Woman! Provoke not my rage or I swear....

Zor. I scorn thy rage, defy it! No choice is left me but Death's arms, or *thine,* and doubt you which I prefer? No, Tyrant, no! Here is my heart! Pierce it, Usurper!

Tim. Rage! Fury!....   50

Zor. Pierce it, and hear my last groan cry to Heaven for vengeance! vengeance on *Thee,* Murderer of my Husband! *Thee,* Despoiler of my dear native Land!

Tim. I can endure no more![50]—Die, Sorceress! Die!

(Oglou rushes in, and arrests Timour's arm).

---

[48] *Terraces appear beyond*: The Larpent version adds to this description as follows: "The extremity of the Fortress is formed by a Bastion, advancing far into the water, which is completely separated from the land by a parapet, with a Cheveaux de Frise. *(Musick while the Scene appears)."* A *Cheveaux de Frise* is a defensive appliance of war, employed chiefly to check cavalry charges and stop breaches.

[49] *deceived me*: The Larpent version adds "betrayed me."

[50] *I can endure no more!*: The Larpent version adds *"(Drawing his dagger)."*

Oglou. Hold, Hold, my Son! what would you do?

Tim. Old Man, away, or my resentment....

Oglou. A Woman! a helpless Woman!

Tim. (Struggling). You plead in vain!

Zor. (Disengaging herself from Timour's grasp). This moment's mine! Oh! let me fly—*(She springs from the Tower upon the Terrace beneath, and disappears).* 60

Tim. (Shaking off Oglou). Release me, or I swear....Fled!—Escaped!—Ha!—Traitress!—*(He springs after her).*—

Oglou. Oh! lend her your speed, ye Lightnings!

(The Georgian re-enters).

Georgian. Room there, Room for the Prince!

Tim. (Within). Vainly you fly!

Zor. (Within). Help, help me Heaven!

Oglou. Alack! Alack! He gains upon her....and now....and now.... 70

Zor. (Rushing upon the furthest Terrace through the Portal). He comes! He comes!

Tim. (Pursuing her, and seizing her veil). Thou'rt mine!

Zor. I'm lost!

Tim. And thus....*(Raising his dagger).*—

Zor. (Plunging from the Terrace into the Sea). My Son! Farewell for ever!

Tim. Ha! She sinks!—There let her perish.

Agib (Entering on Horseback, followed by Georgians).[51]—Not while I live to save her—*(He* 80

seizes a banner, leaps his Horse over the Parapet, and disappears. The Georgians give a shout of admiration, and all rush towards the Water).*

Oglou. Oh, gallant Youth! Oh! generous Daring!—and see! She rises....She struggles!—He's near her—He extends the banner....She has missed it! she has missed it! Now....now again—Huzza! Huzza! Huzza! She has it! She grasps it! and See, See, See! Her arms are round the neck of her Son![52]

(The Horse rises out of the Water, bearing Agib and Zorilda. The Tartars sally[53] from the Fortress, and endeavour to re-take the Princess; the Georgians come to her assistance; a general Engagement takes place, in which Timour is overthrown; but Zorilda spares his life, at the intercession of Agib and Oglou. The Georgians form a groupe round their Sovereign, while Oglou expresses his joy, and Timour his desperation).

CHORUS of GEORGIANS.

Praise to high Heaven!—Each heart with rapture burns!
  That life the Mother gave, the Son returns.
    Praise to high Heaven!

FINIS.

---

51 *(Entering on Horseback, followed by Georgians)*: The Larpent version indicates "musick" here, which ceases before Oglou's speech.

52 *Son!*: The Larpent version indicates "musick" after the end of Oglou's speech, continuing until the curtain drops.

53 *sally*: to issue suddenly from a place of defence in order to make an attack.

The Quadrupeds of Quedlinburgh; Or, The Rovers of Weimar

George Colman the Younger

(We supply a sketch of George Colman the Younger's life and career in the introductory note to *Blue-Beard*.)

The Quadrupeds of Quedlinburgh opened at Colman's Haymarket Theatre on 26 July 1811, less than three months after the debut of Matthew Lewis's *Timour the Tartar* (Covent Garden, 29 April 1811) and less than six months after the revival of Colman's own *Blue-Beard* (Covent Garden, 18 February 1811). It was without question the most successful of the parodies of Lewis's hippodrama, playing 39 times during its first season. Given the fanfare accorded to the revived *Blue-Beard* at Covent Garden, Colman's response to the revival and his subsequent decision to parody *Timour* could be read as mean-spirited or at least as opportunistic. Standing behind the excuse that he had never intended *Blue-Beard* to include horses, Colman had publicly disapproved of the Covent Garden revival while simultaneously bringing out a new edition containing stage directions for the equestrian version. For Covent Garden's managers Henry Harris and John Philip Kemble, however, no such excuse had existed, particularly after they commissioned *Timour* as *Blue-Beard*'s successor. Reviewers and rival theater managers were quick to respond with satirical attack, mocking Harris's and Kemble's attempts to clothe *Timour* and *Blue-Beard* in the legitimacy of Shakespeare by pairing each on opening night with *The Comedy of Errors*. At least one contemporary parody exploited this implied association of *Blue-Beard* and *Timour*: *One Foot by Land and One Foot by Sea; Or, The Tartars Tartared!* (Astley's Pavilion, November 1811). Here, Baghwan Ho leads four other nobles in vanquishing Timour and Blue-Beard (named, as in Colman's play, Abomelique) at Timour's castle. Like *The Quadrupeds of Quedlinburgh*, *One Foot by Land* ends with a full-scale siege of the castle that is half parody and half spectacle.

The Quadrupeds of Quedlinburgh adds to this rich performance history an equally rich textual history. Scrambling to exploit the popular rage for hippodrama and the critical rage against it, Colman followed the example of the Lyceum Theatre's Samuel James Arnold. Arnold had created a viable parody of *Timour* by refitting an older play, *The Tailors; or, A Tragedy for Warm Weather* (Haymarket, 1805), adding new text to it, and renaming it *Quadrupeds: or, The Manager's Last Kick* (Lyceum, 18 July 1811). *The Quadrupeds of Quedlinburgh* follows a similar textual pattern, with Colman having recourse to *The Rovers; or, The Double Arrangement*, perhaps the most famous of the parodies to have appeared at the end of the previous century in the *Anti-Jacobin; or Weekly Examiner* (1797-8).[1] Besides renaming his source play, Colman added a prologue and epilogue and rewrote the play's dramatic frame to render it fit for the stage. *The Rovers* had been strictly a closet drama, its text framed as a submission to the *Anti-Jacobin* by the fictitious radical Mr. Higgins, who had explained in a prefatory letter the nefarious and revolutionary aims of his play. *The Quadrupeds of Quedlinburgh* substitutes for this letter the device of the staged dress rehearsal, where Higgins's substitute, the playwright and veterinary student Mr. Bathos, is free to explain to the harried theater manager the aesthetic and political aims of his drama. While *The Rovers* had directed its satire almost entirely at German drama—presenting it as part of a larger foreign conspiracy to debauch British political, moral, and aesthetic rectitude—*The Quadrupeds of Quedlinburgh* tones down the political attacks of its source. Instead, it presents a British theater besieged

---

[1] The original installments of *The Rovers* appeared in *The Anti-Jacobin: or Weekly Examiner* 30-1 (4-11 June 1798), pages 235-9, 242-6.

by debilitating economic pressures into accepting the substandard productions of illegitimate authors hawking popular spectacle.

The timing of *The Quadrupeds of Quedlinburgh*'s debut shows it ironically to be a product of the very forces it parodies. Arnold's *Quadrupeds* had debuted 18 July 1811, Arnold having made application to the Licenser on 12 July. Colman's own application to the Licenser was made in a hurried and piecemeal fashion on 15 July (the date of submission of the letter of application by the Haymarket's James Winston), 18 July (the date of submission of the play MS), and 24 July (the date of submission of the prologue). Advertisements for *The Quadrupeds of Quedlinburgh*, moreover, began to appear in *The Times* and other newspapers on 18 July next to announcements for Arnold's *Quadrupeds*. These advertisements, and the timing and the manner of Colman's application to the Licenser, suggest that Colman learned of Arnold's plans to produce *Quadrupeds* while that play was still in dress rehearsal, and scrambled immediately to fit up a rival production by cobbling a new play out of *The Rovers* and his own previous parody of a dress rehearsal, *New Hay at the Old Market* (Haymarket, 1795).

The copytext for the play is *A Grand Dress'd Rehearsal of a Tragico-Comico-Anglo-Germanico-Hippodramatico Romance, call'd The Quadrupeds of Quedlinburgh; or The Rovers of Weimar* (Huntington Library LA 1685). There is no print text.

CASTLIST.[2]

Characters of a vehicular description, but on foot:

Mr. Bartholomew Bathos (*An English Dramatist on the German Model; and Student in the Veterinary College*)	Mr. Elliston
Manager of the Hay-Market Theatre (*a very "Poor Gentleman"*)	Mr. Eyre
Call Boy (*a Go-Between*)	Mr. Smith

Characters in the Romance:

Duke of Saxe Weimar (*A Sanguinary Tyrant with red hair, and an amorous complexion*)	Mr. Noble
Rogero (*A Prisoner in the Abbey of Quedlinburgh; in love with Matilda Pottingen, and Husband to Cecilia Muckenfield*)	Mr. Liston
Casimere (*A Polish Emigrant, in Dembrowsky's Legion, married to Cecilia, and having several Children by Matilda*)	Mr. Munden
Beefington and Puddingfield (*English Noblemen, exiled by the tyranny of King John, previously to the signature of Magna Charta*[3])	Mr. Mallinson and Mr. Grove
Doctor Pottingen (*L. L. D.*)	Mr. Martin
Young Pottingen (*Son of Doctor Pottingen and Brother to Matilda*)	Mr. Payne
Waiter at Weimar (*A Knight Templar*[4] *in disguise*)	Mr. Finn

---

2 *CASTLIST*: The Castlist in the Larpent MS of *The Quadrupeds of Quedlinburgh* is less complete in its descriptions of the characters, and does not list the actors. We therefore have substituted the castlist from the opening night playbill of the performance.

3 *King John … Magna Charta*: John was King of England from 1199 to 1216. Because of conflicts with clergy and nobles, he eventually was forced in 1215 to sign the great charter, or Magna Carta, which established the constitutional principle that the king must govern according to law.

4 *Knight Templar*: a knight who is a member of the religious order, founded in 1118 chiefly for the protection of Christian pilgrims visiting the Holy Land; named from their occupation of a building on or near the site of the Temple of Solomon at Jerusalem.

Monk, with a Firelock (*A Military Ecclesiastick*)	Mr. Lewes
Matilda Pottingen (*in love with Rogero, Mother to Casimere's Children*)	Mrs. Glover
Cecilia Muckenfield (*A Passenger in the Dilly,*[5] *and Wife to Casimere*)	Mrs. Gibbs
Dame Shüttenbrüch (*Widow and Landlady of the Inn at Weimar*)	Mrs. Grove

Dumbies:[6]

Neddycrantz (*Jack Ass to the Wheel of the Well in the Abbey of Quedlinburgh*)	A New Performer
Female Captive (*A Corpulent Virgin*)	Miss Leserve

Pantalowski, and Britchinda
 (*Children of Matilda by Rogero*)
Children of Casimere and Cecilia, with
 their respective Nurses
Several Children, Fathers and Mothers unknown
Officers, Soldiers of the Light and Heavy Horse[7]
Grenadiers, Troubadours, Monks, Donkeys, &c.
 &c. &c.

Act I.

Scene I: *The Stage. Enter Manager & Call-Boy.*

Manager. Every thing ready for the Dress'd Rehearsal you say?

Call-Boy. Yes, Sir. The Performers have been waiting in the Green Room[8] these ten minutes.

Man. Strange the Author isn't come!—Poets for the most part, are sensitively punctual in attending to

their own Pieces.—Look out at the Stage Door; and see whether Mr. Bartholomew Bathos is coming up Suffolk Street. (*Exit Call-Boy*). I scarcely know what to make of this Play. Twenty to one, like many others long in Preparation, it will be damn'd.—Yet 'tis constructed according to the present rage, for throughout the performance, probability——

Bathos without. Eh? What the Manager waiting for me, on the Stage?—I'll be with him in a——

(*Enter Bathos*).

Bath. My dear Mr. Manager, I beg you ten thousand pardons;—The first time I have been impunctual since my name was Bartholomew Bathos.—An Author making a Manager dance attendance is rather reversing the custom, I take it.

Man. You are only ten minutes after the hour, Sir. We are used to a little law, here.

Bath. Not a little I'm told, lately (*Aside*). Why I live a long way off:—in Southwark;[9] for the Benefit of the Surry Air; being a little asthmatick my self;—while poor dear lively Mrs. Bathos wheezes like a sick turtle toss'd into a Tavern Passage. Miss Hylonome Bathos has mighty delicate nerves, like most young Ladies who are humpy;[10] and Master Centaur Bathos—(a precious prodigy of genius) is terribly tormented with the rickets in his hind quarters:—So we all lodge together; (a little family of Love and Literature) in a small rural room up three pair of Stairs, in Horsemonger Lane;—facing the Parish pump, which they tell me will have excellent water, when mended. With a Gold-beater on one side of me, and a melting Tallow-Chandler on the other——

Man. Your abode, Sir, is doubtless, quite as convenient as it is Salubrious,—besides Horsemonger Lane is a very appropriate residence for an equestrian Writer, Mr. Bathos.

Bath. Come, that's not amiss!

Man. The very appellations of your children, too are expressive of your hippodramatick propensity. *Master Centaur* Bathos;—Miss *Hylonome*: —the

---

5 *Dilly*: i.e., a diligence; a public stage-coach.

6 *Dumbies*: denoting non-speaking parts and parts literally played by mannequins and pasteboard cutout figures.

7 The playbill for *The Quadrupeds of Quedlinburgh* here notes "Pedigrees of the Horses, *when published*, will be distributed in the Theatre."

8 *Green Room*: a room in a theater provided for the accommodation of actors and actresses when not required on the stage, probably so called because it was originally painted green.

9 *Southwark*: the area of London on the south bank of the Thames, now marked by Southwark Bridge.

10 *humpy*: prone to fits of ill-humor or sulkiness.

name of the four footed Lady in Ovid's Metamorphoses,—wife to Cyllanis,[11] half man and half horse. 50

Bath. Egad, you have hit it.

Man. Yet I presume you must have baptized your family before the present fashion:—You had a presentiment, surely, in christening them.

Bath. No;—but you shall hear. When I first took a turn for the Stage, I wriggled myself into three Eighths of a Booth at Smithfield;[12]—and was pronounced, by some paragraphs, popt into the papers by myself, to be a much respected Gentleman, as the Treasurer—Thence annually, 60 after the three days Fair, by Charter, I skirr'd[13] the country; & having bought some nags I taught them to Curvet,[14] Kick & Whinny in the Provincial Towns. The Horses are always licensed by the Mayor—This fill'd my pockets, and in allusion to my success I christened my children accordingly, whenever poor dear lively wheezing Mrs. Bathos brought me a babe.

Man. A happy mode of recording your good fortune.

Bath. Little did I think, then, Mr. Manager, how my 70 avocation would rise—But modern Taste and Genius have, at last, naturalized neighing foreignness;—the Circenses[15] have trotted into Town, over the Bridges; and the hoof and the postern have distanced the Sock and the Buskin.[16]

Man. And by such Taste and Genius, you hope, speedily, to profit.

Bath. Directly;—in a hard canter. I must make hay while the sun shines; for the present harvest mayn't be of long continuance. It puts me in mind of— 80 —Did you ever hear the ridiculous riddle about the Dog, and a man sitting on a tripod, with a leg of mutton in his hand?

Man. Why then I was a boy——

Bath. I'll give you a very loose kind of paraphrase upon it.—Performers first went upon two legs—Managers got on their last legs, so in came four legs, and kick'd out two legs;—now, soon, Sir, up will start the Town upon two legs, drive away four legs, and Dramas, which have lately been on their 90 left legs, will fall on their right legs again. But equestrian pieces, Sir, are the only things to go down, now.

Man. I beg your pardon, Sir; Theatres that can't well afford to give equestrian Pieces are going down quite as fast.

Bath. Come, come take all in good humour. Remember among all the downs, there is laughing down.

Man. That will never do Mr. Bathos.—We must not 100 adopt the arrogant fancy of having the power to laugh down rival amusements, which our Patrons, the Publick, have sanctioned by their approbation.

Bath. Then try to laugh yourself up.

Man. Up?

Bath. Yes;—into crowded houses;—by some harmless, good temper'd raillery towards the costly magnificence which your limited concern does not enable you to emmulate.—A playful Extrava-ganza;—in which (though allusive to recent 110 exhibitions) no disrespect to publick opinion, and no ill nature to any party being intended, no offence, it is to be hoped, will be discover'd.

Man. Then really and truly, Mr. Bathos, there may be some hope that your present Piece may just answer the purpose.

Bath. How!—my pie——The Devil!—I can tell you, Sir, that I meant to be very serious when I wrote it.

Man. So did I when I read it;—but upon my soul, I 120 couldn't.

Bath. I shall be quite in earnest, though, with the performers, at rehearsal.—But come, to be

---

11 *Miss Hylonome … wife to Cyllanis* i.e., the centaur lovers Hylonome and Cyllarus, whose story is told in Book XII of the *Metamorphoses* of Ovid.

12 *Smithfield*: Smithfield Market, the central meat market of London.

13 *skirr'd*: moved with great rapidity, passed rapidly over.

14 *Curvet*: to leap with the fore-legs raised together and equally advanced, and with the hind-legs raised with a spring before the fore-legs reach the ground.

15 *Circenses*: Latin for circuses.

16 *Sock and the Buskin*: symbols for the theater. A sock is a light shoe worn by comic actors on the Greek and Roman stage; a buskin is a half-boot, high and thick-soled, often worn in Greek tragedy.

candid:—no room for me at present in the Winter Theatres[17]—In doubt which way my piece wou'd be received, I have for the sake of experiment, put up with your small house, Osier Tits, and basket-work Chargers,[18] instead of a grand stage, and real horseflesh.

Man. Sir, this small house must be highly gratified 130 by such a compliment.

Bath. I believe the only animal quadruped expence with which I shall saddle you, will be one live Donkey. If the piece shou'd succeed as a grave representation, in that case, you gain; if it shou'd be well-taken as a Burlesque, why, in that case, you gain also. In short, Mr. Manager, I am a poet whose principle is "*ad captandum*,"[19] and so they *take* me, I don't care how.—And *that* I believe, (in spite of Aristotle[20]), has been the principle of most 140 English Poets past; is the principle of most English Poets present, & will be the principle of most English Poets to come.

Man. But, Mr. Bathos, isn't the vehicle to which you have harness'd your horses—I mean are not the style and plan of your piece very germanick?

Bath. Sir—I have composed, in immitation of the most popular pieces of Germany, which have met with such general admiration and reception in this country,—the present drama, which according as 150 it is taken, gravely or ludicrously,[21] will I think

either add much to unhinging the present notions in regard to Nature, and probability, or else bring men to their senses.

Man. Pray, Sir, how?

Bath. The German Theatre, Sir, teaches the most lofty truths in the most humble style, and deduces them from the most ordinary occurrences. It proportions the infraction of law, religion or morality, which it recommends, to the capacity of 160 a reader or spectator. If you tell an apprentice of the virtues of some celebrated conspirator you may excite his *desire* to be equally conspicuous, but how is he to set about it? Now, Sir, paint the beauties of *forgery* to him, in glowing colours, and he, presently, understands you.—These *haberdasher's heroics* come home to the business & bosoms of men; and you may readily make ten *footpads*, where you would not have materials, nor opportunity, for one Traitor. 170

Man. A Play of German construction, with horses grafted upon it, must be a sweet exhibition.——

Bath. Sweet?—quite luscious—& fit for grown Children. My molasses of immorality, beat up with the treacle of nonsense.—And such a Play is mine. It will make your fortune.

(Enter Call-Boy).

C. Boy. (To the Manager). The Performers, Sir, are very impatient to begin. 'Tis much after the time the rehearsal was call'd.

Man. Then let down the drop Cloth, and set the first 180 Scene.—In the mean time, I'll go into the Green room and look at their dresses. Mr. Bathos, I shall return to you in three minutes. *(Exeunt Manager & Call-Boy).*

(Bathos comes to the front of the Stage and the Painted drop Curtain to the Proscenium is let down).

Bath. And in the mean time, I'll have a touch at the Prologue, which I intend for somebody else to

---

17 *Winter Theatres*: i.e., the two legitimate theaters, Drury Lane and Covent Garden, open during the regular winter season from October to June.

18 *Osier Tits, and basket-work Chargers*: Osier is a species of willow (*Salix viminalis*) much used in basket-work. A tit is a small horse, sometimes used as a depreciatory word to describe a horse wanting in size or stature. Thus, an "Osier Tit" is a small horse made from willow. A charger is a large warhorse.

19 "*ad captandum*": for the purpose of taking or capturing; in order to take or to capture.

20 *in spite of Aristotle*: likely referring to Aristotle's notion that objects are best used when used for the purpose for which they were made.

21 *gravely or ludicrously*: referring to the reputation of German drama in England for combining tragic and comic elements in unaccustomed ways. See Henry Mackenzie, "Account of the German Theatre," *Trans-*

---

actions of the Royal Society of Edinburgh 2 (1790), 160, where he refers to German "*drames*, a species of performance for which we have not yet got in English a very definite term … holds a sort of middle place between tragedy and comedy, borrowing from the first its passions and sentiments, from the last the rank of its persons, and the fortunate nature of its conclusion."

speak.—Gad it must be very nervous to speak a
Prologue, on the first night;—I'll suppose the
audience to be all there.—Band all scraping
away—tum te tum & then Prompter's Bell—   190
tingle-ting-ting—Band stops—On comes the
Actor—then—"down, down, Silence! hats off!"—
"Hush!"—A dead solemn silence—Actor bows
(Bows). Come—not so bad a bow, by the bye.—
And now for it:

Prologue.[22]

To lull the soul by spurious strokes of art,
To warp the genius, and mislead the heart;
To make mankind revere wives gone astray,
Love pious sons who rob on the highway;
For this the foreign Muses trod our Stage,   200
Commanding *German Schools* to be *the rage.*
Hail to such Schools!—Oh, fine False-Feeling,
  hail!

---

22 *Prologue*: In the MS, the space is left blank, the pro-
logue appearing on another page (v), submitted sepa-
rately to the Licenser 24 July 1811. The original
prologue of *The Rovers* is quite different:
Too long the triumphs of our early times,
With civil discord, and with regal crimes,
Have stain'd these boards; while Shakspeare's pen has
  shewn
Thoughts, manners, men, to modern days unknown.
Too long have Rome and Athens been *the rage*; *(Ap-
  plause).*
And classic buskins soil'd a British stage.

To-night our bard, who scorns pedantic rules,
His plot has borrow'd from the German schools;
—The German schools—where no dull maxims bind
The bold expansion of th' electric mind.
Fix'd to no period, circled by no space,
He leaps the flaming bounds of time and place.
Round the dark confines of the forest raves,
With *gentle* Robbers stocks his gloomy caves;
Tells how prime Ministers are shocking things,
And *reigning Dukes* as bad as tyrant Kings;
How to *two* swains, *one* nymph her vows may give,
And how *two* damsels with *one* lover live!
Delicious scenes!—such scenes *our* Bard displays,
Which, crowned with German, sue for British, praise.

Thou bade'st non-natural Nature to prevail;
Through Thee, soft Super-Sentiment arose,—
Musk to the mind, like Avit[23] to the nose,—
'Till fainting Taste (as invalids do wrong),
Snuff'd the sick perfume, and grew weakly
  strong.—

Dear Johnny Bull![24] you boast much resolution,
With, thanks to Heaven! a glorious
  constitution:[25]

Slow are the steeds, that thro' Germania's roads
With hempen rein the slumb'ring post-boy goads.
Slow is the slumb'ring post-boy, who proceeds
Thro' deep sands floundering, on these tardy steeds;
More slow, more tedious, from his husky throat
Twangs through the twisted horn the struggling note.

These truths confess'd—Oh! yet, ye TRAVELL'D
  FEW,
Germania's *plays* with eyes unjaundiced view!
View and approve!—though in each passage fine
The faint translation mock the genuine line,
Tho' the nice ear the erring sight belie,
For *U dotted* is pronounced like *I. (Applause).*
Yet oft the scene shall Nature's fire impart,
Warm *from* the breast, and glowing *to* the heart?

Ye TRAVELL'D FEW, attend!—On *you* our Bard
Builds his fond hope! Do you his genius guard! *(Applause).*

Nor let succeeding generations say
—A British Audience *damn'd* a German Play! *(Loud
  and continued applauses).*

*(Flash of lightning.—The ghost of Prologue's Grand-
mother, by the Father's side, appears to soft music, in a
white tiffany riding-hood. Prologue kneels to receive her
blessing, which she gives in a solemn and affecting manner, the audience clapping and crying all the while.—
Prologue and his Grandmother sink through the trap
door).*

23 *Avit*: presumably short for "aqua-vitae," meaning dis-
tilled spirits like brandy.
24 *Johnny Bull!*: a personification of the English nation;
or the typical Englishman.
25 *glorious constitution*: punning on both senses of the
word constitution, and also referring to the event of

Your taste, recover'd half, from foreign quacks,　210
Takes airings, now, on English Horses' backs;
While every Bard may now erect his name,
If not on lasting praise, on Stable Fame.
Think that to Germans you have given no check,
Think how each Actor horsed has risk'd his
　　neck;—
You've shewn them favour:—Oh! then once more
　　shew it!
To this night's Anglo-German, Horse-Play Poet!

(Enter Manager).

Man. Now, Mr. Bathos, we are ready;—and, if you
　please, we'll up with the Curtain.

Bath. Here we go then.　220

*(The Painted Curtain rises. Roderick, the Duke of Saxe
Weimar, is discover'd seated on a high Chair something
like a Throne).*

Bath. Very well; very well indeed!—a fine drop for
　the Duke of Saxe Weimar—You'll see this is one
　of the most artful Scenes of my whole piece, by
　letting the Spectators into my Plot at once.—Now
　for the Tap at the door.—*(A tap at the door).*

Duke. Come in. *(Enter Doctor Pottingen).* Good
　morning, Doctor Pottingen.

Doctor. Good morning to my Prince. You sent for
　me, from the University and——

Duke. Doctor, sit down. *(Doctor bows & draws a*　230
　Chair).

Bath. Hey, the Devil!—a Chair before the Sovereign
　of a German Dutchy!—Take a stool, Doctor.

*(The Doctor takes a very low footstool & seats himself
at the feet of the Duke).*

Doct. Thus to be seated in your presence, is an
　honour that——

Duke. Wave compliments;——

Bath. Put your hand on his mouth; then you'll be
　sure of him.

Duke. Wave compliments;—Life, like yourself, is
　short;—and words of ceremony are Locusts, that　240
　eat up our shrivelling leaves of time.

---

the Glorious Revolution, which inaugurated constitutional monarchy in England and which was seen, with
Magna Carta, as a key event in forming England's constitution.

Man. That figure, of the Locusts, Mr. Bathos, is truly
　German.

Bath. And very like a man of business, who has no
　time to spare.

Duke. Rogero was the Son of my late Prime Minister.

Doct. I was his Tutor.

Duke. You know him then?

Doct. Too well. While at College, he grew enamour'd
　of my paternal bosom's darling, my daughter, Miss　250
　Matilda Pottingen.

Duke. You prevented ill consequences?—

Doct. I sent her to her aunt's in Wetteravia.

Duke. Lynx-eyed Parent! Proceed.

Doct. She became acquainted with Captain Casimere
　the Pole.

Duke. A Pole!

Doct. Yes;—quarter'd near her aunt's:—and——

Bath. Now begin to be affected.

Doct. And——　260

Duke. Go on.

Doct. My Cherub Matilda;—sweet as the blushing
　rose——

Duke. Well?

Bath. Now be agonized.

Doct. *(Almost convulsed).* Had several rosebuds by
　him.

Duke. Do not weep—Get up.—*(Rises and brings him
　forward)* Man! Man! Professor of Civil Law, be
　firm!—Graduate of a College, learn Philosophy!　270

Doct. My story is short.

Duke. So much the better.

Doct. Your present prime Minister——

Duke. Yes;—Gaspar.——

Doct. The same.

Bath. You must know this Gaspar is a crafty villain,
　who has risen to his post by first ruining, & then
　putting to death, Rogero's father; and dreads the
　power and popularity young Rogero may enjoy—
　if he returns to Court.　280

Man. Thank you, Sir, for giving me some light into
　a part of the story, where the audience may be in
　the dark.

Doct. He;—Gaspar,—hearing of the loves of my
　Pupil & my Daughter.

Duke. Did you inform him of it?—

Doct. By an official letter.

Bath. Observe now, how closely, like a deep Politician, the Duke questions the Doctor.

Doct. Gaspar sent an order to recall Rogero from college; committing him by a *lettre de cachet*[26] to the custody of the Prior of an Abbey. 290

Duke. What Prior?

Doct. The Revd Doct Quashingthump of Quedlinburgh. In a dungeon of that Abbey, Rogero, many years, has languished. His daily sustenance—

Duke. Aye—what is that?

Doct. As I am credibly informed, Pea-soup.

Duke. And how provided?

Doct. Gaspar contracts for his board, in your name, illustrious Prince, with the Landlady of the Golden Eagle. 300

Duke. What is become of Casimere, the Polish Captain?

Doct. Call'd away from my Matilda's neighbourhood to other quarters, one evening the Officers gave a Ball; they wore half-boots with tassels;—Casimere singled out Cecilia Muckinfield—They waltz'd and married.

Duke. Half booted perjurer! Have they children? 310

Doct. Happily but seven.

Man. This Casimere is a devil of a fellow for rosebuds, Mr. Bathos.

Bath. Don't interest the interest.

Doct. Then tired of matrimony, after eight years he, likewise, left Cecilia; under pretence of business that call'd him to Kamschatka.

Duke. And is this all?

Doct. My story's done.

Duke. Doctor Pottingen,—good bye. *(Exit).* 320

Bath. That *exit*, I dare say, is a fine stroke of Character.

Man. I don't exactly perceive it.

Bath. Then, Sir, you must be blind. Don't you observe after he has civilly worried out all he wanted to learn, from the Doctor, he directly turns his back upon him? Now, if that isn't like a great man, I don't know what is.—But listen to Doctor Pottingen's soliloquy.

Doct. I am eight & seventy—Let me, before my death, collecting Children & my grand Children around me. I will send in search of thee, my Matilda:—My son young Pottingen shall go, with the heart-fluttering injunctions of a father not to return without thee.—He shall bring thee back to me, with thy Casimere:—hold!—I am too Sanguine:—that may be impossible;—why then, Matilda, thy first love, if we can rescue him from Quedlinburgh, will do as well. *(Exit).* 330

Man. That's a mighty tender-hearted, forgiving old gentleman. 340

Bath. And if the audience are not prepared for what's to come, after this artful development, that's none of my fault.

Man. Then the next Scene is—

Bath. The next Scene, Sir, is the unexpected meeting of Matilda Pottingen, & Cecilia Muckenfield, both unknown to each other, at the Golden Eagle, in Weimar—Then arrives Captain Casimere, husband to one and lover to the other;—and then—But change the Scene, Carpenters, and on with the Table. 350

(Scene changes to a Room in the Golden Eagle at Weimar—Table is brought on).

Bath. I hope the Property man has been particular in all the articles—Let us see—Jellies—lemons in Nets—part of a cold fowl in the bar—Table with a clean Huckabuck cloth—Plates. Buckhorn handled knives and forks &c. &c. &c. Come— pretty correct. Now Enter Matilda Pottingen in a great coat, and a travelling Habit follow'd by the Golden Eagle. 360

(Enter Matilda Pottingen and Landlady).

Matilda. Is it impossible for me, Mrs. Schüttenbrück, to have dinner[27] sooner?

Man. Seeming to be just arrived. How does she know the Landlady's name?

Bath. Written over the door, to be sure. Zooks![28] one would think you had never gone beyond a turnpike.

---

26 *lettre de cachet*: a letter under the private seal of the French king, containing an order, often for exile or imprisonment.

27 *dinner*: the chief meal of the day, originally eaten around midday.

28 *Zooks!*: an exclamation expressing vexation, surprise, or other emotion.

Landlady. Madam, the Brunswick post-waggon isn't yet come in; and the ordinary[29] is never before two o'clock.

Bath. (To Matilda). Now, Madam, seat yourself pensively, if you please. Your elbow on the Huckabuck tablecloth;—with a look of disappointment, but immediately recomposing yourself.

Mat. Well then I must have patience.

Bath. Exit Mrs. Schüttenbrück. *(Landlady goes out).*

Mat. Oh Casimere! How often have the thoughts of thee served to amuse these moments of expectation!—Alas! what a difference!—*(Here the Manager goes to sleep).* Dinner;—it is taken away as soon as over—and we regret it not!—It returns again, with the return of appetite. The beef of to-morrow will succeed the mutton of to-day, as the mutton of to-day succeeded to the veal of yesterday.

Bath. Very well spoken indeed, Madam!

Mat. Love only, dear delusive, delightful love, restrains our wandering appetites & confines them to a particular gratification.

Bath. Now blow the post horn. *(Post-horn blows).* That has a devilish good effect, at rehearsal at least—for it has waked the Manager.

Man. Eh!—faith, I beg pardon.

Bath. Oh, Sir, the loss is your own.

(Re-enter Landlady).

Land. Madam; the post-waggon has come in, with only a single gentlewoman.

Man. Single?—an unmarried gentlewoman I presume.

Bath. Damn it, Sir; if you'd condescend to keep your eyes open, and listen to the plot, you needn't ask unnecessary questions—No, Sir; she is a married gentlewoman—no less than Cecilia Muckenfield, Wife to Casimere, who has deserted both her and Matilda Pottingen:—Here, they meet, perfect strangers to each other, and that, I think, is an incident.

Mat. Shew up the Lady;—and let us have dinner instantly *(Landlady going)*; and remember—remember the toasted cheese. *(Exit Landlady).*

Bath. Not quite so energetick there, Madam, for fear the audience should mistake you for a Welch-woman[30]—Enter Cecilia in a brown cloth riding Dress, as if just alighted from the post Waggon.

(Enter Cecilia Muckenfield).

Mat. Madam, you seem to have had an unpleasant journey, if I may judge from the dust on your riding-habit.

Cecilia. The way was dusty, Madam, but the weather was delightful. It recalled to me those blissful moments when the rays of desire first vibrated thro' my soul.

Mat. (Aside). Thank heaven! I have at last found a heart which is in unison with my own—*(To Cecilia)*—Yes I understand you—the first pulsation of sentiment—the silver tones upon the yet unsounded harp.—

Cec. The dawn of life—when this blossom—*(Her hand to her heart)* first expanded its petals to the penetrating dart of Love!

Mat. Yes the time—the golden time, when the first beams of the morning meet and embrace one another! The blooming blue upon the yet unpluck'd plum!—A sudden thought strikes me—Let us swear an eternal friendship.

Cec. Let us agree to live together!

Mat. Willingly.

Cec. Let us embrace. *(They embrace).*

Mat. Yes; I too have loved!—you, too, like me, have been forsaken!

Cec. Too true!

Both. Ah these men! these men.

Bath. Now, enter the Landlady, & places a leg of mutton on the table with sour krout, pruin sauce, & a small dish of black puddings.[31]

(Landlady Enters and does all this. Matilda & Cecilia do not notice her).

Mat. Oh! Casimere.

Cec. (Aside). Casimere! That name!—Oh my heart!—how it is distracted with anxiety.

Mat. Heavens! madam, you turn pale.

Cec. Nothing;—a slight megrim.[32]—I left my

---

29 *ordinary*: a courier conveying dispatches or letters at regular intervals.

30 *Welch-woman*: i.e., a Welsh woman.

31 *black puddings*: sausages made of blood and suet.

32 *megrim*: a migraine headache.

smelling bottle in the Dilly—with your leave, I will
retire.   450

Mat. I will attend you.—Lean on your new and ever
faithful friend—This—way—come.

Cec. Oh!

Mat. Come, come, come. *(They Exit).*

Bath. Charmingly acted—now mark the waiter: he'll
turn out a great character in the catastrophe.

(Enter Waiter).

Land. Have you carried the dinner to the prisoner
in the vaults of the abbey?

Waiter. Yes.—Pea soup as usual—with the scrag
end[33] of a neck of mutton.—The emissary of the   460
Prime Minister was here again this morning, and
offer'd me a large sum if I wou'd poison him.

Land. Which you refused? *(With anxiety).*

Wait. Can you doubt it?

Bath. A little more indignation.—Can you doubt it?

Wait. (Imitating). Can you doubt it?

Bath. Now Landlady:—great expression of dignity
here.

Land. The conscience of a poor man is as valuable
to him, as that the sworn attorney.   470

Wait. It ought to be still more so, in proportion as it
is generally more pure.

Land. Thou say'st truly.

Bath. Waiter, with more enthusiasm.

Wait. He who can spurn at wealth when proffered
as the price of crime, is greater than an Emperor.

Bath. That sentiment is quite in the modern taste.

Man. Yes;—and, coming from a waiter it gives an air
of novelty to what has been said an hundred times
over.   480

Bath. Blow the post horn again, to announce the
arrival of Captain Casimere—now for him.

(Enter Casimere).

Casimere. Waiter, pull off my boots & bring me a
pair of slippers. And hark ye, my lad, a bason of
water,—and a bit of soap;—I haven't wash'd since
I began my journey.

Wait. (Aside). "My Lad"—Down swelling bosom.
(Exit).

Bath. 'Tis easy to see that waiter will turn out a great
man.   490

---

33 *scrag end*: the lean or inferior end.

Cas. Well, Landlady, what company are we to have?

Land. Only two gentlewomen, Sir.—They are just
stept into the next room—they will be back again
in a minute. *(Waiter Enters with a Bason of water,
Slippers & Soap for Casimere).* There is one of them,
I think, comes from Nuremburgh.

Cas. From Nuremburgh!—Her name?

Land. Matilda.

Cas. (Aside). How does this idiot Landlady torment
me!—What else?   500

Land. I can't recollect.

Cas. Oh, agony!

Bath. That, Sir, if you please, in a paroxysm of
agitation.—"Oh agony!"

Cas. Oh! agony!

Wait. Behold her name upon the travelling trunk:—
Matilda Pottingen.

Cas. Ecstasy! Ecstasy!

Bath. Zounds! Sir!—you have forgot to embrace the
Waiter.   510

Cas. (Embracing the Waiter). Ecstasy! Ecstasy!

Wait. You seem to be acquainted with the Lady.—
Shall I call her?

Cas. Instantly—Instantly:—tell her—her loved, her
long lost, tell her.——

Land. Shall I tell her dinner is on the table?

Cas. Do so—in the mean while I will look after my
portmanteau.[34]

(Exeunt severally).

Bath. That Scene, Mr. Manager, I flatter myself will
excite a sensation. But come, Sir, draw off, and   520
discover Rogero in his dungeon at Quedlin-
burgh—which ends the first Act.

Man. Stay a moment, Sir.—Here is something in
Rogero's Song, to which Mr. Liston[35] objects.

Bath. Obje——Very pretty, upon my soul!—and
pray, Sir, what is it?—

Man. Merely a marginal direction. *(Reading it)*
"During the last stanza Rogero dashes his head
repeatedly against the walls of his prison; &
produces a visible contusion."   530

---

34 *portmanteau*: a case or bag for carrying clothing and
other necessities.

35 *Mr. Liston*: i.e., John Liston; see Glossary of Actors and
Actresses.

Bath. And he objects to *that*?

Man. Says he won't do it.

Bath. Then, curse me, if actors aren't the most exceptious,[36] disobliging people, I ever met with! Well, then, he must throw himself on the floor in agony, and the Curtain will drop to slow Musick.—Draw off the Scene.

(Scene changes to a subterraneous vault in the abbey of Quedlinburgh. Rogero appears in Chains, in a suit of rusty Armour, with his beard grown, and a Cap of grotesque form upon his head.—Beside him a Crock, or Pitcher, supposed to contain his daily allowance of sustenance. He rises and comes slowly forward, with his arms folded).

Rogero. Eleven years! it is now eleven years since I was first immured in this living sepulchre—the cruelty of a minister—the perfidy of a monk—yes, 540
Matilda! for thy sake—alive amidst the dead, chained, coffined, confined *(Stumbles over a bundle of sticks).* The register of my captivity *(Takes up a stick, and turns it over with a melancholy air; then stands silent for a few moments, as if absorbed in calculation).*

Bath. Now count the Notches.

Rog. Eleven years and fifteen days;—Hah! the twenty-eighth of August! It was on this day that I took my last leave of my Matilda. It was a summer 550
evening. Matilda departed in the Dilly—The tears were petrified under my eye-lids.—My heart was crystallized with agony. Anon—I looked along the road. The Dilly seemed to diminish every instant.—Here in the depths of an eternal dungeon—in a nest of demons, where despair in vain sits brooding over the putrid eggs of hope; where patience beside the bottomless pool of despondency, sits angling for impossibilities. Yet even here, to behold her, to embrace her.—Soft, 560
what air was that? It seemed a sound of more than human warblings—again—*(Listens attentively for some minutes).*—Only the Wind—It is well, however—it reminds me of that melancholy air, which has so often solaced the Hours of my captivity. Let me see whether the Damps of this Dungeon have not yet injured my guitar. *(Takes*

his guitar and sings the following air; with full accompaniment by the Orchestra).

Song.

Whene'er with haggard eyes I view
  This Dungeon, that I'm rotting in,
I think of those Companions true 570
  Who studied with me at the U—
    —niversity of Gottingen—
    —niversity of Gottingen.

Bath. Now, pull out the blue check'd handkerchief spotted with cockchafers[37] and gaze at it, tenderly.

Sweet kerchief, check'd with heavenly blue,
  Which once my love sat knotting[38] in—
Alas! Matilda *then* was true!—
  At least I thought so at the U—
    —niversity of Gottingen— 580
    —niversity of Gottingen.
(Clanks his chains in cadence).

There first for thee my passion flew,
  Sweet! sweet Matilda Pottingen!
Thou wast the daughter of my Tu—
  —tor, Law Professor at the U—
    —niversity of Gottingen—
    —niversity of Gottingen.—

Sun, moon, and thou vain world, adieu,
  That kings and priests are plotting in:
Here doom'd to starve on water-gru— 590
  —el[39] never shall I see the U—
    —niversity of Gottingen!—
    —niversity of Gottingen!—

(The Musick continues to play till the Curtain is Down).

---

36 *exceptious*: disposed to make objections; contrary; caviling.

37 *cockchafers*: a beetle (*Melolontha vulgaris*) that emerges from its chrysalis in May and flies with a whirring sound; a Maybug.

38 *knotting*: knitting knots for fringes.

39 *Anti-Jacobin*'s note: "A manifest error—since it appears from the Waiter's conversation that Rogero was not doomed to starve on water-gruel, but on peas-soup;

Act II.

Scene I: *A Room in an ordinary Lodging-house at Weimar. Barons Puddingfield and Beefington, two English Noblemen, discovered at a small deal Table[40] playing at All-Fours.[41] Young Pottingen, with a Pipe in his Mouth, and an empty Mug in his hand, fast asleep.*

Puddingfield. Lord Beefington, I deal.—Cursed be the Cards—they stick—*(Wets his thumb & deals on)*. Lord Beefington, are you satisfied?—

Beefington. Lord Puddingfield, enough. What have you?

Pudd. High, Low, & Game.

Beef. Perdition! 'tis my deal *(Deals & turns up a knave[42])* bless'd change! One for his heels, my Lord.

Pudd. Is King highest?   10

Beef. The game is mine—*(They rise)*.

Pudd. Still the same proud spirit, my Lord Beefington, which caused King John to exile you from England.

Beef. What are *All-Fours*?—Can they soothe banishment? Oh my Lord Puddingfield, thy limber and lightsome Spirit bounds up against affliction; but mine. Oh mine!

Young Pottingen. *(Waking & starting up)*. What is the matter?   20

Beef. Peace, greenhorn traveller, & fresh acquaintance. Son as thou sayst of Doctor Pottingen, peace, peace!

Y. Pot. Nay, tell me, have you lost or won?

Beef. Lost?—He has lost my Country.

Y. Pot. And I my sister, & my saddle bags.—

Beef. Oh, England!

Y. Pot. Oh, Matilda!

Beef. Exiled by the Tyranny of King John, I seek revenge and restoration to my Country.   30

Y. Pot. Oppress'd by a Prime Minister, and a Prior, the betroth'd husband of my sister languishes in a prison—Her lover fled—no one knows whither & I her brother Trismagistus Pottingen, torn from my paternal roof, & my studies in chirurgery.[43]—To seek Casimere, I know not where—to rescue Rogero, I know not how. In yonder abbey—there lies Rogero—there Matilda's heart—

(Enter Waiter).

Wait. *(Giving letter to Beefington)*. Letters from England—Three & tuppence halfpenny.   40

Beef. Still I have tick.[44]—Borrow the money at the Bar.—*(Exit Waiter. Opens the letter)*. Hah, my friend, what joy!—an English Newspaper.

Pudd. Its name?

Beef. The Daily Advertiser—[45]

Pudd. Rapture!

Beef. *(With a dignified severity)*. Lord Puddingfield, repress your ecstasies—Remember, though you are fat—you are a man.

Pudd. I will be calm;—yet tell me, Beefington, what   50
is the news?

Beef. King John has been defeated.—Magna Charta was signed last Friday three weeks, the third of July Old Style.[46]

Pudd. Show me the Paragraph.

Beef. Here.

---

which is a much better thing. Possibly the length of Rogero's imprisonment had impaired his memory; or he might wish to make things appear worse than they really were; which is very natural, I think, in such a case as this poor unfortunate gentleman's.

                    PRINTER'S DEVIL."

40 *deal Table*: a card table.

41 *All-Fours*: a game of cards, played by two; called after the four points, *high, low, jack,* and *the game,* which make all-fours.

42 *knave*: a jack.

43 *chirurgery*: surgery.

44 *tick*: credit; a reputation for solvency.

45 *The Daily Advertiser*: a London daily newspaper that began publication in 1730. Its assumption that readers would find advertisements interesting in and of themselves made it one of the most successful and influential newspapers of the eighteenth century.

46 *Old Style*: referring to the unreformed Julian calendar, used in England until 1752, when the Gregorian calendar was adopted. On 2 September 1752, Britain reformed its calendar to New Style, the one used now. In order to correct the discrepancies between Old Style and New Style, the day after 2 September 1752 was 14 September 1752.

Pudd. (Reading). "The great demand for Packwood's razor strops"—

Beef. (Snatching the Paper). Pshaw!—let me read. "The Charter of our Liberties received 60
"The Royal Signature at five o'clock,
"When messengers were instantly dispatched
"To Cardinal Pandulfo; and King John,
"After partaking of a cold collation,[47]
"Returned to Windsor."—I am satisfied.

Beef. Yet here again,—here are more particulars—
"Extract of a letter from Egham"—

Pudd. No matter;—I have here a letter from our friend, the immortal Bacon,[48] who is appointed Chancellor.—Our outlawry is reversed.——What 70 says, my friend —shall we return by the next packet?

Pudd. How get a Packet;—being inland?

Beef. That ne'er occur'd.—The Coast can't travel up to us;—I've hit on't.—We'll travel to the Coast.

Pudd. By the next coach that starts from Weimar.

Beef. Agreed.—Oh glorious news!—Before we take our places, cry Huzza.[49]—Join with us, ingenuous youth!—Issue, as thou informest us, of the loins of Doctor Pottingen.

Y. Pot. I am scarce conscious of the meaning of what 80 has made you glad.

Beef. What can that signify?—When there are *rows*[50] in England—the Multitude, still cries Huzza, and seldom knows for what.

Y. Pot. Why then Huzza!—*(Exeunt).*

Bath. The next Scene, Mr. Manager, I think will produce a prodigious effect!—The outside of the Abbey;—A Summer's Evening—Moon light— Companies of Austrian and Prussian Grenadiers march across the Stage, as if returning from the 90 seven years war.[51]—Shouts and martial Musick.

Man. That is all very fine, Sir.

Bath. Hear me out.—The abbey gates are opened.— The Monks pass in procession with the Prior at their head.—The choir is heard chaunting Vespers:—after which a Pause.—Then the Vesper bell rings for supper.—Soon after, a noise of singing & jollity.—Eh! whatd'ye think of that?

Man. Charmingly design'd:—but I have taken the Liberty to cut it all out, Mr. Bathos. 100

Bath. Zounds! I've heard of a Manager's hatchet— —but, pray, Sir, why have you mangled me, so confoundedly?

Man. Because, Sir, we cannot afford, here, the splendour of dulness;—and the trick is so stale that managers have been oblig'd to fly from Processions to the Stable, to produce any attraction.—We'll omit that Scene if you please, Sir.

Bath. It must be as you chuse, Sir:—but if I wrote a Pantomime, I suppose you would cut out 110 Harlequin, Columbine, the Clown, & all the Machinery?—We must suppose the night over, then, and go to the morning.—Change to the Inn door, Carpenters.

Scene II: *The inn door at Weimar. Casimere appears superintending the Package of his Portmanteau. Enter Beefington and Puddingfield and Coachmen.*

Pudd. Well, Coachy, have you got two places?

Coachman. Only outside.

Pudd. (Aside). Lord Beefington!

Beef. Let us conceal our rank, Lord Puddingfield, & ride upon the roof.—We'll go with thee. *(Exit Coachman).*

---

47 *collation*: a light repast taken after a gathering.

48 *Bacon*: Sir Francis Bacon (1561–1626), statesman, philosopher, and Lord Chancellor of England, 1618– 21.

49 *Huzza*: a shout of exultation or applause; a hurrah.

50 *rows*: violent disturbances or quarrels; civil disturbances.

51 *seven years war*: The Seven Years' War (1756–63) was the last major conflict before the French Revolution to involve all the great powers of Europe. Generally, France, Austria, Saxony, Sweden, and Russia were aligned on one side against Prussia, Hanover, and Great Britain on the other. The war arose out of the attempt of the Austrian Habsburgs to win back the rich province of Silesia, which had been wrested from them by Frederick II (the Great) of Prussia during the War of the Austrian Succession (1740–48). But the Seven Years' War also involved overseas colonial struggles between Great Britain and France, the main points of contention between these two traditional rivals being the struggle for control of North America and India.

Pudd. (Turning round & observing Casimere).
Casimere!

Cas. (Perceiving Puddingfield). My Puddingfield!

Pudd. My Casimere! My Pole!

Cas. What Beefington too! *(Discovering him)*—then
is my joy complete.

Beef. Our fellow-traveller, as it seems.

Cas. Yes, my Lord Beefington:—but, wherefore to
Hamburgh?

Beef. To fly—to fly—England—our Country—

Cas. You fly to Liberty, and home:—I, driven from
my home, am exposed to domestic Slavery, in a
foreign country.

Beef. Domestic *Slavery*?

Cas. Too true: Two wives!—Besides, just now, I miss
one Shirt from my Portmanteau.—You knew my
Cecilia?

Pudd. Yes;—five years ago.

Cas. Before that period I was quarter'd at
Wetteravia:—I visited the Baroness of Hunchin-
brunck's;—My Matilda was under her
protection:—alighting at a peasant's Cabin, I saw
her on a charitable visit, spreading bread & butter
for the children, in a light blue riding habit.

Beef. Touching!—proceed.

Cas. Her simple appearance—the fineness of the
weather,—all appear'd to interest me—By a
magnetick Sympathy, we wept, embraced, went
home together,—She became the mother of my
Pantalowsky.

Pudd. I'm moved—forgive these tears—they fall in
spite of me.—

Cas. Five years of enjoyment have not still'd the
reproaches of my conscience. Her Rogero
languishes in captivity:—Could I but restore her
to *him*!

Beef. Wherefore?

Cas. I've met two Ladies at the Inn.—Matilda, &
Cecilia—I have my Charms—they both have
sworn eternal love to me:—but I would fain get
rid of one of them.

Beef. Delicate sensibility! Rogero must be rescued.

Cas. Poh, poh!—Will without power is a
consumptive running footman.

(Waiter enters listening).

Pudd. Ten brave men might defy all Quedlinburgh.

Beef. Ten! but where to find them?

Cas. I will tell you:—marked you the Waiter?

Beef. The Waiter?—*(The Waiter rushes forward).*

Wait. (Opening his Waistcoat). No waiter, but a
Knight Templar in disguise. Returning from the
crusade, my order was dissolved, my person
proscribed——

Cas. Paying my bill, I remember'd him & gain'd his
confidence.—He has dissembled his rank, and
embraced the profession of a Waiter.—With the
troops return'd from the Holy War he has a large
connection—& can pour them in by hundreds—
I will to the Abbey in disguise, and apprize Rogero
of our intentions.

Wait. I have troops in Ambush.—Come hither
friends—*(Enter a large party of Lodgers).*

Beef. Ha!—Soon then for the execution!

Wait. Soft!—Let us, for fear we should be
overheard—all join in Chorus.

RECITATIVE & CHORUS.

Cas. (Recitative). Let prudence, upon tiptoe, now go
out,
And whisper, cautiously, a secret shout.

Full Chorus. Hush! Hush! Hush! *(Very loud).*
Lest, noisily, we make a dash! *(Pianissimo)*[52]
Bid the secret cymbals clash! *(Fortissimo)*[53]
Be still my friends *(Soft)*—let no one know *(Loud)*
The enemy is near;—
Zephyr[54] a Trumpet's blast must blow *(Fortissimo)*
Which nobody must hear.
Be dumb! be dumb!
Thump the gentle Kettle Drum! *(Loud)*
Through the streets so soft, & strong *(Piano)*
Puff the delicate Trombone *(Forte)*
Prudence on tiptoe, now, goes out,
Whispering a secret shout! *(Exeunt).*

---

52 *Pianissimo*: As the word *piano* is a musical expression
meaning "soft," *pianissimo* would mean "very soft."

53 *Fortissimo*: Where *forte* means "strong" or "loud," *fortissimo* would mean "very strong" or "very loud."

54 *Zephyr*: the west wind personified; the god of the west
wind.

Scene III: *A Subterraneous Passage in the Abbey of Quedlinburgh. A Strong grated Door in the wall, leading to Rogero's Dungeon. Enter Rogero, follow'd by a Monk with a gun upon his Shoulder.*

Rog. For the last time, this fortnight, from my cleft dungeon's roof I have walk'd forth into the Cloister, with permission to be shav'd. *(Enter Waiter thro' grated Doorway).* What bear you there?

Wait. A dish—behold 'tis rivetted—'twas fill'd with Soup which I was order'd, yesterday, to bring into your Dungeon.

Rog. By whom order'd?

Wait. By Mrs. Schüttenbrüch, the Lady of the Golden Eagle. 10

Rog. Bear back to her my humblest thanks—I have eat the Soup:—Take thou the Dish, friend;—I need it not.

Wait. Pardon my saying, I wish you out of Quad. *(Exit).*

Rog. In the Abbey of Quedlinburgh, to wish Rogero out of Quad, no doubt, demands forgiveness.— Surely, even now, the glimmering light steals on the darkness of the east, like lean in streaky bacon.—I had three Children, by Matilda ere I left 20 the University—Grant me, ye Gods! they ne'er may cost me any thing—all else is worthless. *(Enters the Cavern).*

Monk. Who's there? Answer, or I'll cock my Gun.

Cas. (Without). An Apothecary, come to visit your prisoner.

(Enter Casimere, disguis'd as an Apothecary).

Cas. Inform me, Monk;—Is not Rogero, the Snub-nosed prisoner, confined in this Dungeon?

Monk. He is.

Cas. I must speak with him. 30

Monk. You must not.

Cas. He is my patient.

Monk. Back! Back! It is impossible.

Cas. Look on this massive Seven shilling piece.

Man. Had Germans seven shilling pieces in those times, Mr. Bathos?

Bath. I can't tell, Sir;—But German pieces, now, have plenty of anachronisms, & that's enough for me.— Proceed!

Monk. Away!—would'st thou corrupt me?—Me!— 40

an old Monk!—with such a trifle too.—I know my interest better.

Cas. Have you a wife?

Monk. I must not.

Cas. Hast thou Children?

Monk. Four and Twenty;—jolly girls & boys.—

Cas. Where did'st thou leave them?

Monk. In their native parishes,—e'en in the cots where they themselves were born.

Cas. Pray take *two* seven shilling. 50

Monk. Go in. *(Exit).*

Cas. Oh, sacred money!—thou dost seldom plead in vain!—There is not of our earth, a creature bearing form adult around whose bosom Interest has not *some* cord entwined, of power to tie them.—On wooden Hustings[55] borne, the noisy Patriot cleaves our ears;—yet is the feeling, closest to his heart, a soft St. Stephen's seal —and o'er his unchang'd gold, the murmuring Miser broods not more anxiously.—Rogero!—Rogero!—ha—he snores.— 60 Rogero,—rise!

Rog. How!—has a fortnight elapsed?—Is the Barber come again?—Well.—I am ready.

Cas. Rogero, know me.—

Rog. What voice is that?

Cas. 'Tis Captain Casimere's.

Rog. Casimere! my slight acquaintance, How do you do? *(Embracing).* Heavens! how could you pass the Monk?—this Coat and Periwig—[56]

Cas. There is not a moment to be lost in words— 70 This disguise I tore from the living body of an Apothecary, as I pass'd his shop—it has gain'd me entrance to thy Dungeon—Now take it thou, & fly.

Rog. And Captain Casimere——

Cas. Will remain here in thy place.

Rog. And eat pea-soup for me?—No!—rather let tortures rack me.

Cas. The being of Miss Pottingen hangs upon thy presence—Go, go, Rogero!—the state I left her in 80 forbids all hope, but from thy quick return.

---

55 *Hustings*: a temporary platform on which candidates for Parliament formerly stood for nomination, and while addressing the electors.

56 *Periwig*: an artificial head of hair; a wig.

Rog. Oh lawk!⁵⁷

Cas. Fear not for me—I shall gain time—while thou with a chosen band whom thou wilt find, may batter down my dungeon's wall which frowns above the moat.

Rog. But how wilt thou o'er leap it?

Cas. There is a favourite Donkey in the Abbey that turns the wheel which raises water from the well.—

Rog. He is call'd Neddycrantz.   90

Cas. I'll bribe the Monk again to bring him to my dungon—Make but a break, and on his faithful back, I'll jump across the water. But hasten, dear Rogero!—Haste! haste! haste!

Rog. Oh, my preserver!

Cas. Go! There! *(Putting the Coat & Wig upon Rogero).* Conceal thy face; for it is most particular—And that they may not clank, hold up thy Darbies.⁵⁸

Rog. I return to save—or perish with thee. *(Exit).*   100

Cas. There's a fat Virgin also here imprison'd—She waved a towel to me from the walls—I'll rescue her or die. *(Exit into Dungeon).*

Scene Last: *The outside of the Abbey. Grand Battle with the Soldiers &c. on basket Horses, against the Monks—The Wall batter'd down. Casimere discovered in Rogero's Dungeon upon a Donkey—leaps the Moat. Fat Virgin discover'd on the Drawbridge. She is rescued—and ultimately brought down the Stage in a Car, drawn by Donkies—decorated with Dove.——*

Finis.

---

⁵⁷ *Oh lawk!*: a vulgarization of "Oh Lord!"

⁵⁸ *Darbies*: handcuffs; fetters.

Orra

Joanna Baillie

Joanna Baillie (1762–1851) was the most respected playwright of her day, ranked by writers like Walter Scott and Lord Byron as the best writer of English tragedy since the Renaissance. Born the third child of Dorothea Hunter Baillie and the Reverend James Baillie, she spent her childhood in Scotland in the towns of Bothwell and Hamilton before being sent to boarding school in Glasgow, where she developed her interest in reading books and composing dramas. With the premature death of their father, Joanna, Agnes, and Matthew Baillie were forced to depend on the benevolence of an uncle, John Hunter, who provided support to the two sisters and to Matthew's medical studies. When Matthew inherited Hunter's medical practice and London home in 1783, Joanna and Agnes Baillie moved to London to manage his household. Joanna also began to write, publishing an anonymous collection of *Poems* in 1790. On Matthew's marriage in 1791, she and Agnes moved to Hampstead, where they were able to establish a stable household and settle permanently.

Hampstead's literary scene afforded Baillie ample opportunity to socialize with authors such as Anna Laetitia Barbauld, Henry Mackenzie, Samuel Rogers, and William Sotheby. It also likely strengthened her resolve to write. Disappointed by the all but silent reception to her *Poems*, she began writing plays, eventually publishing two tragedies and a comedy under the title *A Series of Plays: in which it is attempted to delineate the stronger passions of the mind—each passion being the subject of a tragedy and a comedy* (1798). The volume also included a lengthy "Introductory Discourse," which theorized not only the psychological workings of stage representations upon audiences but also the theater's social function. Quickly rechristened *Plays on the Passions*, the anonymous volume was an immediate success and produced energetic

speculation regarding the identity of the author, with likely candidates ranging from William Cowper and Matthew Lewis to Ann Radcliffe and Anne Hunter. It would be nearly two years—and only then on the eve of the opening of her tragedy *De Monfort* (Drury Lane, 1800), with Sarah Siddons and John Philip Kemble in the starring roles—before Baillie would finally identify herself. We gain a sense of her unassuming demeanor and remarkable self-control when we realize that even her close friends Samuel Rogers and Mary Berry were shocked at the revelation.

The lukewarm success of *De Monfort* onstage led London theater managers to shy away from producing Baillie's plays in the first decade of the nineteenth century in spite of their receiving critical encomiums and going through multiple editions. She therefore had little choice but to continue publishing her work: two more volumes of *Plays on the Passions* appeared to laudatory reviews in 1802 and 1812, as well as a volume of *Miscellaneous Plays* in 1804. Still, Baillie did not experience a real stage hit until Walter Scott, a trustee of the Edinburgh theater, helped to arrange for the production of her *The Family Legend* (Edinburgh, 1810), which played to full houses and enthusiastic applause; in 1815 it was staged at Drury Lane. It is probable that the success of this play contributed to her decision to publish no new plays and to hope for further stage productions. With some productions in the provinces and a successful revival of *De Monfort* in 1820, she stuck by her decision not to publish until her four-volume *Dramas* (1836), which contained a final volume of *Plays on the Passions* and three other volumes of plays, including *Witchcraft*.

Published in the third volume of *Plays on the Passions*, *Orra* was the first of Baillie's tragedies to feature a female lead character. The volume's prefatory essay (included in the Appendix) shows Baillie keenly aware of issues of gender, particularly of the association of femininity with fear (the passion featured in *Orra*). To combat such stereotypes, Baillie not only made Orra "a lively, cheerful, buoyant character, when not immediately under its [fear's] influence"[1] but also included as a companion piece to *Orra* another tragedy on fear (*The Dream*) with a male lead character as a way of balancing between the sexes the derogatory associations of fear. Like her earlier plays *Rayner* and *De Monfort*, *Orra* is set in Germany and strongly partakes of the Gothic of Matthew Lewis, whose novel *The Monk* (1796) had helped to establish the earlier

vogue for German horror among British reading audiences. Unlike *The Monk*, *Orra* is strongly feminist, celebrating Orra's resistance to the tyranny of her guardian Count Hughobert and, even at the play's ending, maintaining her dignity as a heroine. Even with its Gothic trappings and its strong Shakespearean allegiances, *Orra* is surprisingly restrained in its sensationalism, its catastrophe taking place offstage in the classical manner.

The copytext for the play is volume three of *A Series of Plays* (London: Cadell and Davies, 1812), pages 1–100.

DRAMATIS PERSONAE

MEN:

Hughobert, Count of Aldenberg

Glottenbal, his son

Theobald of Falkenstein, a Nobleman of reduced Fortune, and Co-burgher of Basle

Rudigere, a Knight, and Commander of one of the Free Companies returned from the Wars, and Bastard of a Branch of the Family of Aldenberg

Hartman, Friend of Theobald, and Banneret of Basle

Urston, a Confessor

Franko, Chief of a Band of Outlaws

Maurice, an Agent of Rudigere's

Soldiers, Vassals, Outlaws, &c.

WOMEN:

Orra, Heiress of another Branch of the Family of Aldenberg, and Ward to Hughobert

Eleanora, Wife to Hughobert

Cathrina, Lady attending on Orra

Alice, Lady attending on Orra

Scene: *Switzerland, in the Canton of Basle, and afterwards on the Borders of the Black Forest in Suabia.*

Time: *Towards the end of the 14th century.*

Act I

Scene I: *An open Space before the Walls of a Castle, with wild Mountains beyond it; enter Glottenbal, armed as from the Lists, but bare-headed and in Disorder, and his Arms soiled with Earth or Sand, which an Attendant is now and then brushing off, whilst another follows bearing his Helmet; with him enters Maurice, followed by Rudigere, who is also armed, and keeps by himself, pacing to and fro at the bottom of the Stage, whilst the others come forward.*

Glottenbal. (Speaking as he enters, loud and boastingly).
  Aye, let him triumph in his paltry honours,
  Won by mere trick and accident. Good faith!
  It were a shame to call it strength or skill.
  Were it not, Rudigere? *(Calling to Rudigere, who answers not).*
Maurice. His brow is dark, his tongue is lock'd, my Lord;

---

1   *"a lively ... influence"*: See the Preface to volume three of *Plays on the Passions*, included in the Appendix, page 371.

There come no words from him; he bears it not
So manfully as thou dost, noble Glottenbal.
Glot. Fy on't!² I mind it not.
Maur. And wherefore should'st thou? This same
    Theobald,
Count and co-burgher³—mixture most unseemly   10
Of base and noble,—know we not right well
What powers assist him? Mark'd you not, my Lord,
How he did turn him to the witchy north,
When first he mounted; making his fierce steed,
That paw'd and rear'd and shook its harness'd neck
In generous pride, bend meekly to the earth
Its maned crest, like one who made obeisance?⁴
Glot. Ha! did'st thou really see it?
Maur.   Yes, brave Glottenbal,
I did right truly; and besides myself,
Many observ'd it.
Glot.   Then 'tis manifest   20
How all this foil hath been. Who e'er before
Saw one with such advantage of the field,
Lose it so shamefully? By my good fay!⁵
Barring foul play and other dev'lish turns,
I'd keep my courser's⁶ back with any lord,
Or Knight, or Squire that e'er bestrode a steed.
Think'st thou not, honest Maurice, that I could?
Maur. Who doubts it, good my Lord? This Falkenstein
Is but a clown to you.

2 *Fy on't!*: a variant of "fie on it!", i.e., an exclamation expressing disgust or indignant reproach.
3 *co-burgher*: "Burgher" usually denotes a citizen of a municipality, but the prefix "co-" here suggests Baillie means "burgomaster," a governing member of a town. "Co-burgher" here would mean that Theobald shares the rights of a single town council member with one other individual. In many ways, Theobald's rank of "co-burgher" indicates his status as poor noble—i.e., as a count with a ruined castle, but also suggests that he is at once noble and bourgeois.
4 *obeisance*: a bodily act or gesture expressing submission or respect, such as bowing, kneeling, or curtsying.
5 *fay*: i.e., faith; in this case meaning credit, authority, promise, or assurance.
6 *courser*: originally, a large and powerful horse used for tournaments and battle; since the seventeenth century, a swift horse used for racing.

Glot.   Well let him boast.   30
Boasting I scorn; but I will shortly shew him
What these good arms, with no foul play against
    them,
Can honestly atchieve.
Maur. Yes, good my Lord; but chuse you well your day:
A moonless Friday luck did never bring
To honest combatant.
Glot. Ha! blessing on thee! I ne'er thought of this:
Now it is clear how our mischance befell.
Be sure thou tell to every one thou meet'st,
Friday and a dark moon suit Theobald.
Ho! Rudigere! hear'st thou not this?   40
Rudigere. (As he goes off, aside to Maurice).
Flatter the fool awhile and let me go,
I cannot join thee now. *(Exit).*
Glot. (Looking after Rudigere). Is he so crest-fallen?
Maur. He lacks your noble spirit.
Glot.   Fy upon't!
I heed it not. Yet, by my sword and spurs!
'Twas a foul turn, that for my rival earn'd
A branch of victory from Orra's hand.
Maur. Aye, foul indeed! My blood boil'd high to see it.
Look where he proudly comes.
(Enter Theobald arm'd, with Attendants, having a green sprig stuck in his helmet).
Glot. (Going up to Theobald). Comest thou to face
    me so? Audacious Burgher!
The Lady Orra's favour suits thee not,   50
Though for a time thou hast upon me gain'd
A seeming 'vantage.
Theobald. A seeming 'vantage!—Then it is not true,
That thou, unhors'd, layd'st rolling in the dust,
Asking for quarter?—Let me crave thy pardon!
Some strange delusion hung upon our sight
That we believed it so.
Glot.   Off with thy taunts!
And pull that sprig from its audacious perch:
The favour of a Dame too high for thee.
Theo. Too high indeed; and had'st thou also added,   60
Too good, too fair, I had assented to it.
Yet, be it known unto your courteous worth,
That were this sprig a Queen's gift, or received
From the brown hand of some poor mountain maid;
Yea, or bestow'd upon my rambling head,
As in the hairy sides of brouzing kid

The wild rose sticks a spray, unprized, unbidden,
I would not give it thee.
Glot. Dost thou so face me out? Then I will have it.
   (Snatching at it with rage).
(Enter Hartman).
Hartman. (Separating them). What! Malice after   70
   fighting in the lists
As noble courteous knights!
Glot. (To Hartman). Go, paltry Banneret![7] Such
   friends as thou
Become such Lords as he, whose ruined state
Seeks the base fellowship of restless burghers;
Thinking to humble still, with envious spite,
The great and noble houses of the land.
I know ye well, and I defy you both,
With all your damned witchery to-boot. *(Exit*
   grumbling, followed by Maurice, &c.).
(Manent Theobald and Hartman).
Theo. How fierce the creature is, and full of folly!
Like a shent[8] cur to his own door retired,   80
That bristles up his furious back, and there
Each passenger annoys.—And this is he,
Whom sordid and ambitious Hughobert,
The guardian in the selfish father sunk,
Destines for Orra's husband.—O foul shame!
The carrion-crow and royal eagle join'd,
Make not so cross a match.—But think'st thou,
   Hartman,
She will submit to it?
Hart. That may be as thou pleasest, Falkenstein.
Theo. Away with mockery!
Hart.   I mock thee not.   90
Theo. Nay, Banneret, thou dost. Saving this favour,
Which every victor in these listed combats
From Ladies' hands receives, nor then regards
As more than due and stated courtesy,
She ne'er hath honour'd me with word or look
Such hope to warrant.

---

7 *Banneret*: originally, a knight entitled to bring a company of vassals into the field under his own banner, and who ranked next to a baron and above other knights; subsequently, the rank was conferred upon knights doing valiant deeds in battle.

8 *shent*: an archaic term meaning disgraced, lost, ruined, or stupified.

Hart.   Wait not thou for looks.
Theo. Thou would'st not have me to a Dame like this,
With rich domains and titled rights encompass'd,
These simple limbs, girt in their soldier's geer,
My barren hills and ruin'd tower present,   100
And say, "Accept—these will I nobly give
In fair exchange for thee and all thy wealth."
No, Rudolph Hartman, woo the maid thyself,
If thou hast courage for it.
Hart. Yes, Theobald of Falkenstein, I will,
And win her too; but all for thy behoof.[9]
And when I do present, as thou hast said,
Those simple limbs, girt in their soldier's geer,
Adding thy barren hills and ruin'd tower,
With some few items more of gen'rous worth   110
And native sense and manly fortitude;
I'll give her in return for all that she
Or any maid can in such barter yield,
Its fair and ample worth.
Theo.   So dost thou reckon.
Hart. And so will Orra. Do not shake thy head.
I know the maid: for still she has received me
As one who knew her noble father well,
And in the bloody field in which he died
Fought by his side, with kind familiarity:
And her stern guardian, viewing these grey hairs   120
And this rough visage with no jealous eye,
Hath still admitted it.——I'll woo her for thee.
Theo. I do in truth believe thou mean'st me well.
Hart. And this is all thou say'st? Cold frozen words!
What has bewitch'd thee, man? Is she not fair?
Theo. O fair indeed as woman need be form'd
To please and be belov'd! Tho', to speak honestly,
I've fairer seen; yet such a form as Orra's
For ever in my busy fancy dwells,
Whene'er I think of wiving my lone state.   130
It is not this; she has too many lures;
Why wilt thou urge me on to meet her scorn?
I am not worthy of her.
Hart. (Pushing him away with gentle anger).
Go to! I praised thy modesty short-while,
And now with dull and senseless perseverance,
Thou would'st o'erlay me with it. Go thy ways!
If thro' thy fault, thus shrinking from the onset,

---

9 *behoof*: use, benefit, or advantage.

She should with that furious cub be match'd, 'twill
   rest
Upon thy conscience like a damning sin,
And may it gnaw thee shrewdly! *(Exeunt).*   140

       Scene II: *A small Apartment in the Castle,*
enter Rudigere musing gloomily, and muttering
to himself some time before he speaks aloud.

Rud. No no; it is to formless air dissolved,
   This cherish'd hope, this vision of my brain!
(Pacing to and fro, and then stopping and musing as
before).
   I daily stood contrasted in her sight
   With an ungainly fool; and when she smiled,
   Methought——But wherefore still upon this
      thought,
   Which was perhaps but a delusion then,
   Brood I with ceaseless torment? Never, never!
   O never more on me, from Orra's eye,
   Approving glance shall light, or gentle look!
   This day's disgrace mars all my goodly dreams.   10
   My path to greatness is at once shut up.
   Still in the dust my grovling fortune lies.
(Striking his breast in despair).
   Tame thine aspiring spirit, luckless wretch!
   There is no hope for thee!
   And shall I tame it? No, by saints and devils!
   The laws have cast me off from every claim
   Of house and kindred, and within my veins
   Turn'd noble blood to baseness and reproach:
   I'll cast them off: why should they be to me
   A bar, and no protection?   20
(Pacing again to and fro, and muttering low for some
time before he speaks aloud).
   Aye; this may still within my toils enthral her:
   This is the secret weakness of her mind,
   On which I'll clutch my hold.
(Enter Cathrina behind him, laying her hand upon him).
Cathrina. Ha! speak'st thou to thyself?
Rud. (Starting).   I did not speak.
Cath. Thou did'st; thy busy mind gave sound to
      thoughts
   Which thou did'st utter with a thick harsh voice,
   Like one who speaks in sleep. Tell me their meaning.
Rud. And dost thou so presume? Be wise; be humble.

(After a pause). Has Orra oft of late requested thee
To tell her stories of the restless dead?   30
Of spectres rising at the midnight watch
By the lone trav'ller's bed?
Cath. Wherefore of late dost thou so oft inquire
   Of what she says and does?
Rud. Be wise, and answer what I ask of thee;
   This is thy duty now.
Cath. Alas, alas! I know that one false step
   Has o'er me set a stern and ruthless master.
Rud. No, madam; 'tis thy grave and virtuous seeming;
   Thy saint-like carriage, rigid and demure,   40
   On which thy high repute so long has stood,
   Endowing thee with right of censorship
   O'er every simple maid, whose cheerful youth
   Wears not so thick a mask, that o'er thee sets
   This ruthless master. Hereon rests my power:
   I might expose, and therefore I command thee.
Cath. Hush, hush! approaching steps! They'll find
      me here!
   I'll do whate'er thou wilt.
Rud. It is but Maurice: hie thee to thy closet,
   Where I will shortly come to thee. Be thou   50
   My faithful agent in a weighty matter,
   On which I now am bent, and I will prove
   Thy stay and shelter from the world's contempt.
Cath. Maurice to find me here! Where shall I hide me?
Rud. Nowhere, but boldly pass him as he enters.
   I'll find some good excuse; he will be silent:
   He is my agent also.
Cath.   Dost thou trust him?
Rud. Avarice his master is, as shame is thine:
   Therefore I trust to deal with both.—Away!
(Enter Maurice, passing Cathrina as she goes out).
Maur. What, doth the grave and virtuous Cathrina,   60
   Vouchsafe to give thee of her company?
Rud. Yes, rigid saint! she has bestowed upon me
   Some grave advice to bear with pious meekness
   My late discomfiture.[10]
Maur.   Ay, and she call'd it,
   I could be sworn! heaven's judgment on thy pride.
Rud. E'en so: thou'st guessed it.—Shall we to the
      ramparts
   And meet the western breeze? *(Exeunt).*

---

10   *discomfiture*: utter defeat in battle or complete over-
    throw of plans.

Scene III: *A spacious Apartment.*
Enter Hughobert and Urston.

Hughobert. (Speaking with angry gesticulation as he
enters).
    I feed and clothe these drones, and in return
    They cheat, deceive, abuse me; nay, belike,
    Laugh in their sleeve the while. By their advice,
    This cursed tourney I proclaim'd; for still
    They puffed me up with praises of my son—
    His grace, his skill in arms, his horsemanship—
    Count Falkenstein to him was but a clown—
    And so, in Orra's eyes to give him honour,
    Full surely did I think—I'll hang them all!
    I'll starve them in a dungeon shut from light: 10
    I'll heap my boards no more with dainty fare
    To feed false flatterers.
Urston.   That indeed were wise:
    But art thou sure, when men shall speak the truth,
    That thou wilt feed them for it? I but hinted
    In gentle words to thee, that Glottenbal
    Was praised with partial or affected zeal,
    And thou receiv'dst it angrily.
Hugh. Aye, true indeed: but thou did'st speak of him
    As one bereft of all capacity.
    Now though, God wot![11] I look on his defects   20
    With no blind love, and even in my ire
    Will sometimes call him fool; yet, ne'ertheless,
    He still has parts and talents, tho' obscur'd
    By some untoward failings.—Heaven be praised!
    He wants not strength at least and well turn'd limbs,
    Had they but taught him how to use them. Knaves!
    They have neglected him.
(Enter Glottenbal, who draws back on seeing his Father).
    Advance, young Sir: art thou afraid of me?
    That thus thou shrinkest like a skulking thief
    To make disgrace the more apparent on thee?   30
Glot. Yes, call it then disgrace, or what you please;
    Had not my lance's point somewhat awry
    Glanced on his shield——
Hugh.   E'en so; I doubt it not;
    Thy lance's point, and every thing about thee
    Hath glanced awry. Go, rid my house, I say,
    Of all those feasting flatterers that deceive thee;

    They harbour here no more: dismiss them quickly.
Glot. Do it yourself, my Lord; you are, I trow,
    Angry enough to do it sharply.
Hugh. (Turning to Urston).   Faith!
    He gibes[12] me fairly here; there's reason in't;   40
    Fools speak not thus. *(To Glottenbal).* Go to! if I
      am angry,
    Thou art a graceless son to tell me so.
Glot. Have you not bid me still to speak the truth?
Hugh. (To Urston). Again thou hear'st he makes an
      apt reply.
Urst. He wants not words.
Hugh.   Nor meaning neither, Father.
(Enter Eleanora).
    Well Dame; where hast thou been?
El.   I came from Orra.
Hugh. Hast thou been pleading in our son's excuse?
    And how did she receive it?
El. I tried to do it, but her present humour
    Is jest and merriment. She is behind me,   50
    Stopping to stroke a hound, that in the corridor
    Came to her fawningly to be carest.
Glot. (Listening). Aye she is coming; light and quick
      her steps;
    So sound they, when her spirits are unruly.
    But I am bold; she shall not mock me now.
(Enter Orra, tripping gaily, and playing with the folds
of her scarf).
    Methinks you trip it briskly, gentle Dame.
Orra. Does it offend you, noble Knight?
Glot.   Go to!
    I know your meaning. Wherefore smile you so?
Orra. Because, good sooth! with tired and aching sides
    I have not power to laugh.   60
Glot. Full well I know why thou so merry art.
    Thou think'st of him to whom thou gav'st that sprig
    Of hopeful green, his rusty casque[13] to grace,
    Whilst at thy feet his honour'd glave[14] he laid.
Orra. Nay, rather say, of him, who at my feet,
    From his proud courser's back, more gallantly
    Laid his most precious self: then stole away,
    Thro' modesty, unthank'd, nor left behind

---

11   *wot:* know or knows.

12 *gibes:* to speak sneeringly; to scoff or taunt.
13 *casque:* a piece of armor to cover the head; a helmet.
14 *glave:* lance or spear.

Of all his geer that flutter'd in the dust,
Or glove or band, or fragment of torn hose,   70
For dear remembrance-sake, that in my sleeve
I might have stuck it. O! thou wrong'st me much
To think my merriment a ref'rence hath
To any one but him. *(Laughing).*

El. Nay, Orra; these wild fits of uncurb'd laughter,
Athwart the gloomy tenor of your mind,
As it has low'r'd of late, so keenly cast,
Unsuited seem and strange.

Orra. O nothing strange, my gentle Eleanora!
Did'st thou ne'er see the swallow's veering breast,   80
Winging the air beneath some murky cloud
In the sunn'd glimpses of a stormy day,
Shiver in silv'ry brightness?
Or boatman's oar, as vivid lightning flash
In the faint gleam, that like a spirit's path
Tracks the still waters of some sullen lake?
Or lonely Tower, from its brown mass of woods,
Give to the parting of a wintry sun
One hasty glance in mockery of the night
Closing in darkness round it?—Gentle Friend!   90
Chide not her mirth, who was sad yesterday,
And may be so to-morrow.

Glot. And wherefore art thou sad, unless it is
From thine own way-ward humour? Other Dames
Were they so courted, would be gay and happy.

Orra. Way-ward it needs must be, since I am sad
When such perfection woos me.
                                        Pray, good Glottenbal,
How did'st thou learn with such a wond'rous grace
To toss thy armed heels up in the air,
And clutch with outspread hands the slipp'ry sand?   100
I was the more amaz'd at thy dexterity,
As this, of all the feats which thou, before-hand,
Did'st promise to perform, most modestly,
Thou did'st forbear to mention.

Glot.   Gibe away!
I care not for thy gibing. With fair lists,
And no black arts against me——

*Hugh. (Advancing angrily from the bottom of the stage
    to Glottenbal).*
                                        Hold thy peace!
(To Orra). And, madam, be at least somewhat
    restrained
In your unruly humour.

Orra. Pardon, my Lord: I knew not you were near me.
My humour is unruly: with your leave,   110
I will retire till I have curb'd it better.
(To Eleanora). I would not lose your company,
    sweet Countess.

El. We'll go together then.

*(Exeunt Orra and Eleanora. Manet Hughobert; who
paces angrily about the stage, while Glottenbal stands on
the front, thumping his legs with his sheath'd rapier).*

Hugh. There is no striving with a forward girl,
Nor pushing on a fool. My harassed life,
Day after day, more irksome grows.—Curs'd bane!
I'll toil no more for this untoward match.

(Enter Rudigere, stealing behind and listening).

Rud. You are disturb'd, my Lord.

Hugh. What, is it thou? I am disturbed in-sooth.

Rud. Aye, Orra has been here, and some light words   120
Of girlish levity have mov'd you. How!
Toil for this match no more! What else remains,
If this should be abandon'd, noble Aldenberg!
That can be worth your toil?

Hugh. I'll match the cub elsewhere.

Rud. What call ye matching?

Hugh. Surely for him some other virtuous maid
Of high descent, tho' not so richly dowried,
May be obtain'd.

Rud.   Within your walls, perhaps,
Some waiting gentle-woman, who perchance   130
May be some fifty generations back
Descended from a king, he will himself,
Ere long obtain, without your aid, my Lord.

Hugh. Thou mak'st me mad! the dolt! the senseless dolt!
What can I do for him? I cannot force
A noble maid entrusted to my care.
I, the sole guardian of her helpless youth.

Rud. That were indeed unfit: but there are means
To make her yield consent.

Hugh. Then by my faith, good friend, I'll call thee   140
    wizard,
If thou can'st find them out. What means already,
Short of compulsion, have we left untried?
And now the term of my authority
Wears to its close.

Rud. I know it well; and therefore powerful means,
And of quick operation, must be sought.

Hugh. Speak plainly to me?

Rud. I've watch'd her long.
I've seen her cheek flush'd with the rosy glow
Of jocund spirits, deadly pale become
At tale of nightly sprite or apparition,   150
Such as all hear, 'tis true, with greedy ears,
Saying, "Saints save us!" but forget as quickly.
I've mark'd her long: she has, with all her shrewdness
And playful merriment, a gloomy fancy,
That broods within itself on fearful things.

Hugh. And what doth this avail us?

Rud. Hear me out.
Your ancient castle in the Suabian forest
Hath, as too well you know, belonging to it,
Or false or true, frightful reports. There hold her
Strictly confined in sombre banishment;   160
And doubt not but she will, ere long, full gladly
Her freedom purchase at the price you name.

Hugh. On what pretence can I confine her there?
It were most odious.

Rud. Can pretence be wanting?
Has she not favour shewn to Theobald,
Who in your neighbourhood, with his sworn friend
The Banneret of Basle, suspiciously
Prolongs his stay? A poor and paltry Count,
Unmeet to match with her. And want ye then
A reason for removing her with speed   170
To some remoter quarter? Out upon it!
You are too scrupulous.

Hugh. Thy scheme is good, but cruel.

Glot. (*Who has been drawing nearer to them, and
    attending to the last part of their discourse*).
O much I like it, dearly wicked Rudigere!
She then will turn her mind to other thoughts
Than scornful gibes at me.

Hugh. I to her father swore I would protect her:
I would fulfill his will.

Rud. And, in that will, her father did desire
She might be match'd with this your only son;
Therefore you're firmly bound all means to use   180
That may the end attain.

Hugh. Walk forth with me, we'll talk of this at large.
(*Exeunt Hughobert and Rudigere. Manet Glottenbal,
who comes forward from the bottom of the stage with
the action of a knight advancing to the charge*).

Glot. Yes, thus it is; I have the slight o't now:
And were the combat yet to come, I'd shew them

I'm not a whit behind the bravest knight,
Cross luck excepted.

(*Enter Maurice*).

Maur. My Lord, indulge us of your courtesy.

Glot. In what I pray?

Maur. Did not Fernando tell you?
We are all met within our social bower;
And I have wager'd on your head, that none   190
But you alone, within the Count's domains,
Can to the bottom drain the chased horn.
Come; do not linger here when glory calls you.

Glot. Think'st thou that Theobald could drink so
    stoutly?

Maur. He, paltry chief! he herds with sober burghers;
A goblet, half its size, would conquer him.
    (*Exeunt*).

Act II

Scene I: *A Garden with Trees, and Shrubs, &c. Orra,
Theobald, and Hartman, are discovered in a shaded
Walk at the bottom of the Stage, speaking in dumb
Show, which they cross, disappearing behind the Trees;
and are presently followed by Cathrina and Alice, who
continue walking there. Orra, Theobald, and Hartman
then appear again, entering near the front of the Stage.*

Orra (*Talking to Hartman as she enters*).
And so, since fate has made me, woe the day!
That poor and good-for-nothing, helpless being.
Woman yclept,[15] I must consign myself
With all my lands and rights into the hands
Of some proud man, and say, "Take all, I pray,
And do me in return the grace and favour
To be my master."

Hart. Nay, gentle Lady! you constrain my words
And load them with a meaning harsh and foreign
To what they truly bear.—A master! No: 10
A valiant gentle mate, who in the field
Or in the council will maintain your right:
A noble, equal partner.

Orra (*Shaking her head*). Well I know
In such a partnership, the share of power
Allotted to the wife. See; noble Falkenstein

---

15 *yclept*: called, named, or styled.

Hath silent been the while, nor spoke one word
In aid of all your specious arguments.
(To Theobald). What's your advice, my Lord?
Theo.   Ah, noble Orra!
'Twere like self-murder to give honest counsel,
Then urge me not.—I frankly do confess   20
I should be more heroic than I am.
Orra. Right well I see thy head approves my plan,
And by and by, so will thy gen'rous heart.
In short, I would, without another's leave,
Improve the low condition of my peasants,
And cherish them in peace. Ev'n now methinks
Each little cottage of my native vale
Swells out its earthen sides, up-heaves its roof,
Like to a hillock mov'd by lab'ring mole,
And with green trail-weeds clamb'ring up its walls,   30
Roses and ev'ry gay and fragrant plant,
Before my fancy stands, a fairy bower.
Aye, and within it too do fairies dwell.
(Looking playfully thro' her fingers like a shew-glass).
Peep thro' its wreathed window, if indeed
The flowers grow not too close; and there within
Thou'lt see some half a dozen rosy brats,
Eating from wooden bowls their dainty milk;—
Those are my mountain elves. See'st thou not
Their very forms distinctly?
Theo. O most distinctly! And most beautiful   40
The sight! Which sweetly stirreth in the heart
Feelings that gladden and ennoble it,
Dancing like sun-beams on the rippled sea:
A blessed picture! Foul befall the man
Whose narrow selfish soul would shade or mar it!
Hart. To this right heartily I say Amen!
But if there be a man, whose gen'rous soul
(Turning to Orra) Like ardour fills; who would
    with thee pursue
Thy gen'rous plan; who would his harness don—
Orra (Putting her hand on him in gentle interruption).
Nay, valiant Banneret, who would, an' please you,   50
His harness doff: all feuds, all strife forbear,
All military rivalship, all lust
Of added power, and live in steady quietness
A mild and fost'ring Lord. Know you of one
That would so share my task?—You answer not.
And your brave friend methinks casts on the ground
A thoughtful look; *(To Theobald)* wots he of such
    a Lord?

Theo. Wot I of such a Lord!—No, noble Orra,
I do not, nor does Hartman, tho' perhaps
His friendship may betray his judgment. No;   60
None such exist; we are all fierce, contentious,
Restless and proud, and prone to vengeful feuds;
The very distant sound of war excites us,
Like coursers list'ning to the chase, who paw
And fret and bite the curbing rein. Trust none
To cross thy gentle, but most princely purpose,
Who hath on head a circling helmet wore,
Or ever grasp'd a glave.—But ne'ertheless
There is—I know a man.— Might I be bold?
Orra. Being so honest, boldness is your right.   70
Theo. Permitted then, I'll say, I know a man,
Tho' most unworthy Orra's Lord to be,
Who, as her champion, friend, devoted soldier,
Might yet commend himself; and, so received,
Who would at her command, for her defence
His sword right proudly draw. An honour'd sword,
Like that which at the gate of Paradise
From steps profane the blessed region guarded.
Orra. Thanks to the gen'rous knight! I also know
The man thou would'st commend; and when my   80
    state
Such service needeth, to no sword but his
Will I that service owe.
Theo. Most noble Orra! greatly is he honour'd;
And will not murmur that a higher wish,
Too high, and too presumptuous, is represt.
(Kissing her hand with great respect).
Orra. Nay, Rudolph Hartman, clear that cloudy brow,
And look on Falkenstein and on myself,
As two co-burghers of thy native city,
(For such I mean ere long to be), and claiming
From thee, as cadets from an elder born,   90
Thy cheering equal kindness.
(Enter a Servant).
Servant. The count is now at leisure to receive
The Lord of Falkenstein, and Rudolph Hartman.
Hart. We shall attend him shortly. *(Exit Servant).*
(Aside to Theobald).   Must we now
Our purpos'd suit, to some pretended matter
Of slighter import change?
Theo. (To Hartman aside).   Assuredly.—
Madam, I take my leave with all devotion.
Hart. I with all friendly wishes.

(Exeunt Theobald and Hartman. Cathrina and Alice now advance through the shrubs, &c. at the bottom of the stage, while Orra remains, wrapped in thought, on the front).

Cath. Madam, you're thoughtful; something occupies
    Your busy mind.   100
Orra. What was't we talk'd of, when the worthy
    Banneret
    With Falkenstein upon our converse broke?
Cath. How we should spend our time, when in your
    castle
    You shall maintain your state in ancient splendour,
    With all your vassals round you.
Orra. Aye, so it was.
Alice.   And you did say, my Lady,
    It should not be a cold unsocial grandeur:
    That you would keep, the while, a merry house.
Orra. O doubt it not! I'll gather round my board
    All that heav'n sends to me of way-worn folks,   110
    And noble travellers, and neighb'ring friends,
    Both young and old. Within my ample hall,
    The worn-out man of arms, (of whom too many,
    Nobly descended, rove like reckless vagrants
    From one proud chieftain's castle to another,
    Half chid, half honour'd) shall o' tiptoe tread,
    Tossing his grey locks from his wrinkled brow
    With cheerful freedom, as he boasts his feats
    Of days gone by.—Music we'll have; and oft
    The bick'ring dance upon our oaken floors   120
    Shall, thund'ring loud, strike on the distant ear
    Of 'nighted trav'llers, who shall gladly bend
    Their doubtful footsteps tow'rds the cheering din.
    Solemn, and grave, and cloister'd, and demure
    We shall not be. Will this content ye, damsels?
Alice. O passing well! 'twill be a pleasant life;
    Free from all stern subjection; blithe and fanciful;
    We'll do whate'er we list.
Cath. That right and prudent is, I hope thou meanest.
Alice. Why ever so suspicious and so strict?   130
    How could'st thou think I had another meaning?
    (To Orra). And shall we ramble in the woods full oft
    With hound and horn?—that is my dearest joy.
Orra. Thou runn'st me fast, good Alice. Do not doubt
    This shall be wanting to us. Ev'ry season
    Shall have its suited pastime: even Winter
    In its deep noon, when mountains piled with snow,

And chok'd up valleys from our mansion bar
    All entrance, and nor guest nor traveller
    Sounds at our gate; the empty hall forsaking,   140
    In some warm chamber, by the crackling fire,
    We'll hold our little, snug, domestic court,
    Plying our work with song and tale between.
Cath. And stories too, I ween,[16] of ghosts and spirits,
    And things unearthly, that on Michael's eve[17]
    Rise from the yawning tombs.
Orra. Thou thinkest then one night o' th' year is truly
    More horrid than the rest.
Cath. Perhaps 'tis only silly superstition:
    But yet it is well known the Count's brave father   150
    Would rather on a glacier's point have lain,
    By angry tempests rock'd, than on that night
    Sunk in a downy couch in Brunier's castle.
Orra. How pray? What fearful thing did scare him so?
Cath. Hast thou ne'er heard the story of Count Hugo,
    His ancestor, who slew the hunter-knight?
Orra (Eagerly). Tell it I pray thee.
Alice. Cathrina, tell it not: it is not right:
    Such stories ever change her cheerful spirits
    To gloomy pensiveness; her rosy bloom   160
    To the wan colour of a shrouded corse.
    (To Orra). What pleasure is there, Lady, when thy
    hand,
    Cold as the valley's ice, with hasty grasp
    Seizes on her who speaks, while thy shrunk form
    Cow'ring and shiv'ring stands with keen turn'd ear
    To catch what follows of the pausing tale?
Orra. And let me cow'ring stand, and be my touch
    The valley's ice: there is a pleasure in it.
Alice. Say'st thou indeed there is a pleasure in it?
Orra. Yea, when the cold blood shoots through   170
    every vein:
    When every hair's-pit on my shrunken skin
    A knotted knoll becomes, and to mine ears
    Strange inward sounds awake, and to mine eyes
    Rush stranger tears, there is a joy in fear.
(Catching hold of Cathrina).
    Tell it, Cathrina, for the life within me
    Beats thick, and stirs to hear it.
    He slew the hunter-knight?

---

16 *ween:* think, surmise, or suppose.
17 *Michael's eve:* September 28; the evening before the
    feast of St. Michael, or Michaelmas.

Cath. Since I must tell it, then, the story goes
  That grim Count Aldenberg, the ancestor
  Of Hughobert and also of yourself,   180
  From hatred or from envy, did decoy
  A noble knight, who hunted in the forest,
  Well the Black Forest named, into his castle,
  And there, within his chamber, murder'd him—
Orra. Merciful Heaven! and in my veins there runs
  A murderer's blood. Said'st thou not, *murder'd him?*
Cath. Aye; as he lay asleep, at dead of night.
Orra. A deed most horrible!
Cath. It was on Michael's eve; and since that time,
  The neighb'ring hinds[18] oft hear the midnight yell   190
  Of spectre-hounds, and see the spectre shapes
  Of huntsmen on their sable steeds, with still
  A nobler hunter riding in their van
  To cheer the desp'rate chase, by moonlight shewn,
  When wanes its horn, in long October nights.
Orra. This hath been often seen?
Cath.   Aye, so they say.
  But, as the story goes, on Michael's eve,
  And on that night alone of all the year,
  The hunter-knight himself, having a horn
  Thrice sounded at the gate, the castle enters;   200
  And, in the very chamber where he died,
  Calls on his murd'rer, or in his default
  Some true descendant of his house, to loose
  His spirit from its torment; for his body
  Is laid i' the earth unbless'd, and none can tell
  The spot of its interment.
Orra. Call on some true descendant of his race!
  It were to such a fearful interview.
  But in that chamber, on that night alone——
  Hath he elsewhere to any of the race   210
  Appear'd? or hath he power——
Alice.   Nay, nay, forbear:
  See how she looks. *(To Orra)* I fear thou art not well.
Orra. There is a sickly faintness come upon me.
Alice. And did'st thou say there is a joy in fear?
Orra. My mind of late has strange impressions ta'en.
  I know not how it is.
Alice.   A few nights since,
  Stealing o'tiptoe, softly thro' your chamber,
  Towards my own——

Orra. O heaven defend us! did'st thou see aught there?
Alice. Only your sleeping self. But you appear'd   220
  Distress'd and troubled in your dreams; and once
  I thought to wake you ere I left the chamber,
  But I forbore.
Orra.   And glad I am thou did'st.
  It is not dreams I fear; for still with me
  There is an indistinctness o'er them cast,
  Like the dull gloom of misty twilight, where
  Before mine eyes pass all incongruous things,
  Huge, horrible and strange, on which I stare
  As idiots do upon this changeful world
  With nor surprise nor speculation. No;   230
  Dreams I fear not: it is the dreadful waking,
  When in deep midnight stillness, the roused fancy
  Takes up th' imperfect shadows of its sleep,
  Like a marr'd speech snatch'd from a bungler's[19]
    mouth,
  Shaping their forms distinctively and vivid
  To visions horrible:—this is my bane;—
  It is the dreadful waking that I fear.
Alice. Well, speak of other things. There in good time
  Your ghostly father comes with quicken'd steps,
  Like one who bears some tidings good or ill.   240
  Heaven grant they may be good!
(Enter Urston).
Orra. Father, you seem disturb'd.
Urst. Daughter, I am in truth disturb'd. The Count
  Has o' the sudden, being much enraged
  That Falkenstein still lingers near these walls,
  Resolves to send thee hence, to be awhile
  In banishment detained, till on his son
  Thou look'st with better favour.
Orra.   Aye, indeed!
  That is to say perpetual banishment:
  A sentence light or heavy, as the place   250
  Is sweet or irksome he would send me to.
Urst. He will contrive to make it, doubt him not,
  Irksome enough. Therefore I would advise thee
  To feign at least, but for a little time,
  A disposition to obey his wishes.
  He's stern, but not relentless; and his Dame,
  The gentle Eleanor, will still befriend you,
  When fit occasion serves.

---

18 *hinds*: agricultural laborers or servants; rustics.

19 *bungler*: a clumsy or unskilled worker.

Orra. What said'st thou, Father?
To feign a disposition to obey!
I did mistake thy words.
Urst. No, gentle daughter; 260
So press'd, thou mayest feign and yet be blameless.[20]
A trusty guardian's faith with thee he holds not,
And therefore thou art free to meet his wrongs
With what defence thou hast.
Orra (Proudly). Nay, pardon me; I, with an unshorn
crown,
Must hold the truth in plain simplicity,
And am in nice distinctions most unskilful.
Urst. Lady, have I deserv'd this sharpness? oft
Thine infant hand has strok'd this shaven crown:
Thou'st ne'er till now reproach'd it. 270
Orra (Bursting into tears). Pardon, O pardon me, my
gentle Urston!
Pardon a wayward child, whose eager temper
Doth sometimes mar the kindness of her heart.
Father, am I forgiven? *(Hanging on him).*
Urst. Thou art, thou art:
Thou art forgiven; more than forgiven, my child.
Orra. Then lead me to the Count, I will myself
Learn his stern purpose.
Urst. In the hall he is,
Seated in state, and waiting to receive you.
(Exeunt).

Scene II: *A spacious Apartment, or Baron's Hall, with
a Chair of State, Hughobert, Eleanora, and Glottenbal
enter near the Front, speaking as they enter; and
afterwards enter Vassals and Attendants, who range
themselves at the bottom of the Stage.*

Hugh. Cease, Dame! I will not hear; thou striv'st in vain
With thy weak pleadings. Orra hence must go
Within the hour, unless she will engage
Her plighted word to marry Glottenbal.
Glot. Aye, and a mighty hardship, by the mass!
Hugh. I've summon'd her in solemn form before me,
That these my vassals should my act approve,

Knowing my right of guardianship; and also
That her late father, in his dying moments,
Did will she should be married to my son; 10
Which will, she now must promise to obey,
Or take the consequence.
El. But why so hasty?
Hugh. Why, say'st thou! Falkenstein still in these parts
Lingers with sly intent. Even now he left me,
After an interview of small importance,
Which he and Hartman, as a blind pretence
For seeing Orra, formally requested.
I say again she must forthwith obey me,
Or take the consequence of wayward will.
El. Nay, not for Orra do I now entreat 20
So much as for thyself. Bethink thee well
What honour thou shalt have, when it is known
Thy ward from thy protecting roof was sent;
Thou who should'st be to her a friend, a father.
Hugh. But do I send her unprotected? No!
Brave Rudigere conducts her with a band
Of trusty spearmen. In her new abode
She will be safe as here.
El. Ha! Rudigere!
Put'st thou such trust in him? Alas, my Lord!
His heart is full of cunning and deceit. 30
Wilt thou to him the flower of all thy race
Rashly intrust? O be advised, my Lord!
Hugh. Thy ghostly father tells thee so, I doubt not.
Another priest confesses Rudigere,
And Urston likes him not. But can'st thou think,
With aught but honest purpose, he would chuse
From all her women the severe Cathrina,
So strictly virtuous, for her companion?
This puts all doubt to silence. Say no more,
Else I shall think thou plead'st against my son, 40
More with a step-dame's than a mother's feelings.
Glot. Aye, marry does she father! And forsooth!
Regards me as a fool. No marvel then
That Orra scorns me; being taught by her,—
How should she else?—So to consider me.
Hugh. (To Glottenbal). Tut! hold thy tongue.
El. He wrongs me much, my Lord.
Hugh. No more, for here she comes.
*(Enter Orra, attended by Urston, Alice and Cathrina,
and Hughobert seats himself in his chair of state, the
Vassals, &c. ranging themselves on each side).*

---

20 *So press'd ... yet be blameless:* Baillie here echoes volume 1, chapter 8 of Ann Radcliffe's *The Italian* (1797),
 in which Olivia instructs Ellena that she should feign
 submission in order to escape "unnecessary torments."

Hugh. (To Orra). Madam and ward, placed under
    mine authority,
  And to my charge committed by my kinsman,
  Ulric of Aldenberg, thy noble father;   50
  Having all gentle means essay'd to win thee
  To the fulfilment of his dying will,
  That did decree his heiress should be married
  With Glottenbal my heir; I solemnly
  Now call upon thee, ere that rougher means
  Be used for this good end, to promise truly
  Thou wilt, within a short and stated time,
  Before the altar give thy plighted faith
  To this my only son. I wait thine answer.
  Orra of Aldenberg, wilt thou do this?   60
Orra. Count of the same, my Lord and guardian,
  I will not.
Hugh.   Have a care thou froward[21] maid!
  'Tis thy last opportunity: ere long
  Thou shalt, within a dreary dwelling pent,
  Count thy dull hours, told by the dead man's watch,
  And wish thou had'st not been so proudly wilful.
Orra. And let my dull hours by the dead man's watch
  Be told; yea, make me too the dead man's mate,
  My dwelling place the nailed coffin; still
  I would prefer it to the living Lord   70
  Your goodness offers me.
Hugh.   Art thou bewitch'd?
  Is he not young, well featured and well form'd?
  And dost thou put him in thy estimation
  With bones and sheeted clay?[22]
  Beyond endurance is thy stubborn spirit.
  Right well thy father knew that all thy sex
  Stubborn and headstrong are; therefore, in wisdom,
  He vested me with power that might compel thee
  To what he will'd should be.
Orra.   O not in wisdom!
  Say rather in that weak, but gen'rous faith,   80
  Which said to him, the cope[23] of heaven would fall
  And smother in its cradle his swath'd babe,
  Rather than thou, his mate in arms, his kinsman,

---

21 *froward*: disposed to go counter to what is demanded
    or reasonable; perverse.
22 *sheeted clay*: i.e., skin.
23 *cope*: usually, a long, dark cloak or cape worn by ec-
    clesiastics; here, the over-arching canopy of heaven.

Who by his side in many a field had fought,
Should'st take advantage of his confidence
For sordid ends.—
           My brave and noble father!
A voice comes from thy grave and cries against it,
And bids me to be bold. Thine awful form
Rises before me,—and that look of anguish
On thy dark brow!—O no! I blame thee not.   90
Hugh. Thou seem'st beside thyself with such wild
    gestures
  And strangely-flashing eyes. Repress these fancies,
  And to plain reason listen. Thou hast said,
  For sordid ends I have advantage ta'en.
  Since thy brave father's death, by war and compact,
  Thou of thy lands hast lost a third; whilst I,
  By happy fortune, in my heir's behalf,
  Have doubled my domains to what they were
  When Ulric chose him as a match for thee.
Orra. O, and what speaketh this, but that my father   100
  Domains regarded not; and thought a man
  Such as the son should be of such a man
  As thou to him appear'dst, a match more honourable
  Than one of ampler state. Take thou from Glottenbal
  The largely added lands of which thou boastest,
  And put, in lieu thereof, into his stores
  Some weight of manly sense and gen'rous worth,
  And I will say thou keep'st faith with thy friend:
  But as it is, did'st thou unto thy wealth
  A kingdom add, thou poorly would'st deceive him.   110
Hugh. (Rising from his chair in anger).
  Now, madam, be all counsel on this matter
  Between us closed. Prepare thee for thy journey.
El. Nay, good my Lord! consider.
Hugh. (To Eleanora).   What, again!
  Have I not said thou hast an alien's heart
  From me and mine. Learn to respect my will
  In silence, as becomes a youthful Dame.
Urst. For a few days may she not still remain?
Hugh. No, priest; not for an hour. It is my pleasure
  That she for Brunier's castle do set forth
  Without delay.
Orra (With a faint starting movement).
        In Brunier's castle!
Hugh.   Aye;   120
  And doth this change the colour of thy cheek,
  And give thy alter'd voice a feebler sound?

(Aside to Glottenbal). She shrinks, now to her, boy;
    this is thy time.
Glot. (To Orra). Unless thou wilt, thou need'st not
    go at all.
There is full many a maiden would right gladly
Accept the terms we offer, and remain.
(A pause). Wilt thou not answer me?
Orra.   I did not hear thee speak.—
I heard thy voice, but not thy words: What said'st
    thou?
Glot. I say, there's many a maiden would right gladly
Accept the terms we offer, and remain.   130
The daughter of a King hath match'd ere now
With mine inferior. We are link'd together
As 'twere by right and natural property.
And as I've said before I say again,
I love thee too: What more could'st thou desire?
Orra. I thank thee for thy courtship, tho' uncouth;
For it confirms my purpose; and my strength
Grows as thou speak'st, firm like the deep-bas'd rock.
(To Hughobert). Now for my journey when you
    will, my Lord;
I'm ready.
Hugh.   Be it so! on thine own head   140
Rest all the blame. *(Going from her).* Perverse past
    all belief!
(Turning round to her sternly). Orra of Aldenberg,
    wilt thou obey me?
Orra. Count of that noble house, with all respect,
    Again I say I will not.
*(Exit Hughobert in anger, followed by Glottenbal,
Urston, &c. Manent only Eleanora, Cathrina, Alice, and
Orra, who keeps up with stately pride till Hughobert and
all Attendants are gone out, and then throwing herself
into the arms of Eleanora, gives vent to her feelings).*
El. Sweet Orra! be not so depress'd; thou goest
For a short term, soon to return again;
The banishment is mine who stays behind.
But I will beg of heaven with ceaseless prayers
To have thee soon restored: and, when I dare,
Will plead with Hughobert in thy behalf;   150
He is not always stern.
Orra. Thanks, gentle friend! Thy voice to me doth
    sound
Like the last sounds of kindly nature; dearly
In my remembrance shall they rest.—What sounds,

What sights, what horrid intercourse I may,
Ere we shall meet again, be doom'd to prove,
High heaven alone doth know.—If that indeed
We e'er shall meet again! *(Falls on her neck and weeps).*
El. Nay, nay! come to my chamber. There awhile
Compose your spirits. Be not so deprest.   160
*(Exeunt. Rudigere, who has appear'd, during the last
part of the above scene, at the bottom of the stage, half
concealed, as if upon the watch, now comes forward.
Speaking as he advances).*
Rud. Hold firm her pride till fairly from these walls
Our journey is begun; then fortune hail!
Thy favours are secured. *(Looking off the stage).*
                Ho, Maurice there!
(Enter Maurice).
My faithful Maurice, I would speak with thee.
I leave thee here behind me; to thy care,
My int'rests I commit; be it thy charge
To counteract thy Lady's influence,
Who will entreat her Lord the term to shorten
Of Orra's absence, maiming thus my plan,
Which must, belike, have time to be effected.   170
Be vigilant, be artful; and be sure
Thy services I amply will repay.
Maur. Aye, thou hast said so, and I have believed thee.
Rud. And dost thou doubt?
Maur.   No; yet meantime, good sooth!
If somewhat of thy bounty I might finger,
'Twere well: I like to have some actual proof.
Did'st thou not promise it?
Rud.   'Tis true I did,
But other pressing calls have drain'd my means.
Maur. And other pressing calls within my mind,
May make my faith to falter.   180
Rud. Go to! I know thou art a greedy leech,
Tho' ne'ertheless thou lov'st me.
(Taking a small case from his pocket, which he opens).
                  See'st thou here?
I have no coin; but look upon these jewels:
I took them from a knight I slew in battle.
When I am Orra's lord, thou shalt receive,
Were it ten thousand crowns, whate'er their worth
Shall by a skilful lapidary[24] be
In honesty esteem'd. *(Gives him the jewels).*

---

[24] *lapidary*: one concerned with stones; a cutter or pol-
isher of precious stones.

Maur. I thank thee, but methinks their lustre's dim.
  I've seen the stones before upon thy breast   190
  In gala days, but never heard thee boast
  They were of so much value.
Rud. I was too prudent: I had lost them else.
  To no one but thyself would I entrust
  The secret of their value.
(Enter Servant).
Serv. Sir Rudigere, the spearmen are without,
  Waiting your further orders, for the journey.
Rud. (To Servant). I'll come to them anon. *(Exit*
  Servant).
  Before I go, I'll speak to thee again. *(Exeunt severally).*

Act III

Scene I: *A Forest with a half-ruined Castle in the*
Back-Ground, seen through the Trees by Moon-light.
Franko and several Outlaws are discovered sitting
on the Ground, round a Fire, with Flaggons, &c.
by them, as if they had been drinking.

Song of Several Voices:

The chough[25] and crow to roost are gone,
  The owl sits on the tree,
The hush'd wind wails with feeble moan,
  Like infant charity.
The wild-fire dances on the fen,
  The red star sheds its ray,
Up-rouse ye, then, my merry men!
  It is our op'ning day.

Both child and nurse are fast asleep,
  And clos'd is every flower,   10
And winking tapers faintly peep
  High from my Lady's bower;
Bewilder'd hinds with shorten'd ken[26]
  Shrink on their murky way,
Uprouse, ye, then, my merry men!
  It is our op'ning day.

Nor board nor garner own we now,
  Nor roof nor latched door,
Nor kind mate, bound by holy vow
  To bless a good man's store;   20
Noon lulls us in a gloomy den,
  And night is grown our day,
Uprouse ye, then, my merry men!
  And use it as ye may.

Franko (To 1st Outlaw). How lik'st thou this, Fernando?
1st Outlaw. Well sung i'faith![27] but serving ill our turn,
  Who would all trav'llers and benighted[28] folks
  Scare from our precincts. Such sweet harmony
  Will rather tempt invasion.
Franko. Fear not, for mingled voices, heard afar,   30
  Thro' glade and glen and thicket, stealing on
  To distant list'ners, seem wild-goblin-sounds;
  At which the lonely trav'ller checks his steed,
  Pausing with long-drawn breath and keen-turn'd ear;
  And twilight pilferers cast down in haste
  Their ill-got burthens, while the homeward hind
  Turns from his path, full many a mile about,
  Thro' bog and mire to grope his blund'ring way.
  Such, to the startled ear of superstition,
  Were seraph's song, could we like seraphs[29] sing.   40
(Enter 2nd Outlaw, hastily).
2nd Outlaw. Disperse ye diff'rent ways: we are undone.
Franko. How say'st thou, shrinking poltroon?[30] we
    undone!
  Outlaw'd and ruin'd men, who live by daring!
2nd Out. A train of armed men, some noble Dame
  Escorting, (so their scatter'd words discover'd
  As unperceiv'd I hung upon their rear),
  Are close at hand, and mean to pass the night
  Within the castle.
Franko.   Some benighted travellers,
  Bold from their numbers, or who ne'er have heard
  The ghostly legend of this dreaded place.   50
1st Out. Let us keep close within our vaulted haunts;
  The way to which is tangled and perplex'd,

---

25 *chough*: a bird of the crow family, formerly applied to
    the common jackdaw.
26 *ken*: range of sight or vision.

27 *i'faith*: i.e., in faith, here meaning "to be sure."
28 *benighted*: overtaken by the darkness of the night;
    unenlightened.
29 *seraph*: one of the seraphim; an angel.
30 *poltroon*: a spiritless coward.

And cannot be discover'd: with the morn
   They will depart.
Franko. Nay, by the holy mass! within those walls
   Not for a night must trav'llers quietly rest,
   Or few or many. Would we live securely,
   We must uphold the terrors of the place:
   Therefore, let us prepare our midnight rouse.
(Lights seen from the castle).
   See, from the windows of the castle gleam   60
   Quick passing lights, as tho' they moved within
(Bell heard).
   In hurried preparation; and that bell,
   Which from yon turret its shrill 'larum sends,
   Betokens some unwonted[31] stir. Come, hearts!
   Be all prepared, before the midnight watch,
   The fiend-like din of our infernal chace
   Around the walls to raise.—Come; night
     advances. *(Exeunt).*

Scene II: *A Gothic Room in the Castle,*
with the Stage darkened. Enter Cathrina,
bearing a Light, followed by Orra.

Orra (Catching her by the robe and pulling her back).
   Advance no further: turn, I pray! This room
   More dismal and more ghastly seems than that
   Which we have left behind. Thy taper's light,
   As thus aloft thou wav'st it to and fro,
   The fretted ceiling gilds with feeble brightness,
   While over-head its carved ribs glide past
   Like edgy waves of a dark sea, returning
   To an eclipsed moon its sullen sheen.
Cath. To me it seems less dismal than the other.
   See, here are chairs around the table set,   10
   As if its last inhabitants had left it
   Scarcely an hour ago.
(Setting the light upon the table).
Orra. Alas! how many hours and years have past
   Since human forms around this table sat,
   Or lamp or taper on its surface gleam'd!
   Methinks I hear the sound of time long past
   Still murm'ring o'er us in the lofty void
   Of those dark arches, like the ling'ring voices
   Of those who long within their graves have slept.

---

[31] *unwonted*: not habitual; strange or unusual.

It was their gloomy home; now it is mine.   20
(Sits down, resting her arm upon the table, and
covering her eyes with her hand. Enter Rudigere,
beckoning Cathrina to come to him; and speaks to her
in a low voice at the corner of the stage).
Rud. Go and prepare thy lady's chamber; why
   Dost thou for ever closely near her keep?
Cath. She charged me so to do.
Rud.   I charge thee also
   With paramount authority, to leave her:
   I for awhile will take thy station here.
   Thou art not mad? Thou dost not hesitate?
(Fixing his eyes on her with a fierce threatening look,
from which she shrinks. Exit Cathrina).
Orra. This was the home of bloody lawless power.
   The very air rests thick and heavily
   Where murder hath been done.
(Sighing heavily).
   There is a strange oppression in my breast: 30
   Dost thou not feel a close unwholesome vapour?
Rud. No; ev'ry air to me is light and healthful,
   That with thy sweet and heavenly breath is mix'd.
Orra (Starting up). Thou here! *(Looking round).*
     Cathrina gone?
Rud. Does Orra fear to be alone with one,
   Whose weal, whose being on her favour hangs?
Orra. Retire, Sir Knight. I chuse to be alone.
Rud. And dost thou chuse it, wearing now so near
   The midnight hour, in such a place?—Alas!
   How loath'd and irksome must my presence be!   40
Orra. Dost thou deride my weakness?
Rud.   I deride it!
   No, noble Maid! say rather that from thee
   I have a kindred weakness caught. In battle
   My courage never shrunk, as my arm'd heel
   And crested helm do fairly testify:
   But now when midnight comes, I feel by sympathy,
   With thinking upon thee, fears rise within me
   I never knew before.
Orra (In a softened kindlier voice). Ha! dost thou too
   Such human weakness own?
Rud.   I plainly feel
   We are all creatures, in the wakeful hour   50
   Of ghastly midnight, form'd to cower together,
   Forgetting all distinctions of the day,
   Beneath its awful and mysterious power.

(Stealing closer to her as he speaks, and putting his arms round her).

Orra (Breaking from him). I pray thee hold thy
    parley[32] further off:
  Why dost thou press so near me?

Rud. And art thou so offended, lovely Orra?
  Ah! wherefore am I thus presumptuous deem'd?
  The blood that fills thy veins enriches mine;
  From the same stock we spring; tho' by that glance
  Of thy disdainful eye, too well I see   60
  My birth erroneously thou countest base.

Orra. Erroneously!

Rud.   Yes, I will prove it so.
  Longer I'll not endure a galling wrong
  Which makes each word of tenderness that bursts
  From a full heart, bold and presumptuous seem,
  And severs us so far.

Orra.   No, subtile snake!
  It is the baseness of thy selfish mind,
  Full of all guile, and cunning, and deceit,
  That severs us so far, and shall do ever.

Rud. Thou prov'st how far my passion will endure   70
  Unjust reproaches from a mouth so dear.

Orra. Out on hypocrisy! who but thyself
  Did Hughobert advise to send me hither?
  And who the jailor's hateful office holds
  To make my thraldom[33] sure?

Rud. Upbraid me not for this: had I refused,
  One less thy friend had ta'en th' ungracious task.
  And, gentle Orra! dost thou know a man,
  Who might in ward all that his soul holds dear
  From danger keep, yet would the charge refuse,   80
  For that strict right such wardship[34] doth condemn?
  O! still to be with thee; to look upon thee;
  To hear thy voice, makes ev'n this place of horrors,—
  Where, as 'tis said, the spectre of a chief,
  Slain by our common grandsire, haunts the night,
  A paradise—a place where I could live
  In penury and gloom, and be most bless'd.
  Ah! Orra! if there's misery in thraldom,

---

32 *parley*: speech, talk, or conversation.
33 *thraldom*: the state of being in captivity, bondage, or
   servitude.
34 *wardship*: the office or position of guardian, usually of
   a minor.

Pity a wretch who breathes but in thy favour:
  Who till he look'd upon that beauteous face,   90
  Was free and happy.—Pity me or kill me!

(Kneeling and catching hold of her hand).

Orra. Off, fiend! let snakes and vipers cling to me,
  So thou dost keep aloof.

Rud. (Rising indignantly). And is my love with so
    much hatred met?
  Madam, beware lest scorn like this should change me
  Ev'n to the baleful thing your fears have fancied.

Orra. Dar'st thou to threaten me?

Rud. He, who is mad with love and gall'd with scorn,
  Dares any thing.—But O! forgive such words
  From one who rather, humbled at your feet,   100
  Would of that gentleness, that gen'rous pity,
  The native inmate of each female breast,
  Receive the grace on which his life depends.
  There was a time when thou did'st look on me
  With other eyes.

Orra.   Thou dost amaze me much.
  Whilst I believ'd thou wert an honest man,
  Being no fool, and an adventurous soldier,
  I look'd upon thee with good-will; if more
  Thou did'st discover in my looks than this,
  Thy wisdom with thine honesty, in truth,   110
  Was fairly match'd.

Rud. Madam, the proud derision of that smile
  Deceives me not. It is the Lord of Falkenstein,
  Who better skill'd than I in tournay-war,
  Tho' not i' th' actual field more valiant found,
  Engrosses now your partial thoughts. And yet
  What may he boast which, in a lover's suit,
  I may not urge? He's brave, and so am I.
  In birth I am his equal; for my mother,
  As I shall prove, was married to Count Albert,   120
  My noble father, tho' for reasons tedious
  Here to be stated, still their secret nuptials
  Were unacknowledged, and on me hath fallen
  A cruel stigma which degrades my fortunes.
  But were I—O forgive th' aspiring thought!—
  But were I Orra's Lord, I should break forth
  Like the unclouded sun, by all acknowledged
  As ranking with the highest in the land.

Orra. Do what thou wilt when thou art Orra's Lord;
  But being as thou art, retire and leave me: 130
  I chuse to be alone. *(Very proudly).*

Rud.   Then be it so.
  Thy pleasure, mighty Dame, I will not balk.
  This night, to-morrow's night, and every night,
  Shalt thou in solitude be left; if absence
  Of human beings can secure it for thee.
(Pauses and looks on her, while she seems struck and disturbed).
  It wears already on the midnight hour;
  Good night!
(Pauses again, she still more disturbed).
           Perhaps I understood too hastily
  Commands you may retract.
Orra (Recovering her state). Leave me, I say; that part
    of my commands
  I never can retract.
Rud.   You are obey'd. *(Exit).*   140
*Orra. (Paces up and down hastily for some time, then
    stops short, and after remaining a little while in a
    thoughtful posture).*

  Can spirit from the tomb, or fiend from hell,
  More hateful, more malignant be than man—
  Than villainous man? Altho' to look on such,
  Yea, even the very thought of looking on them,
  Makes natural blood to curdle in the veins
  And loosen'd limbs to shake.
  There are who have endured the visitation
  Of supernatural Beings.—O forfend[35] it!
  I would close couch[36] me to my deadliest foe
  Rather than for a moment bear alone   150
  The horrors of the sight.
  (Looking round).   Who's there? who's there?
  Heard I not voices near? That door ajar
  Sends forth a cheerful light. Perhaps, Cathrina,
  Who now prepares my chamber. Grant it be!
  *(Exit, running hastily to a door from which a light is
    seen).*

Scene III: *A chamber, with a small bed or couch in it.
  Enter Rudigere and Cathrina, wrangling together.*

Rud. I say begone, and occupy the chamber
  I have appointed for thee: here I'm fix'd,
  To pass the night.

---

35 *forfend*: prevent, keep away, or avert.
36 *couch*: lie down.

Cath.   Did'st thou not say my chamber
  Should be adjoining that which Orra holds?
  I know thy wicked thoughts: they meditate
  Some dev'lish scheme; but think not I'll abet it.
Rud. Thou wilt not!—angry, restive, simple fool!
  Dost thou stop short and say, "I'll go no further?"
  Thou, whom concealed shame hath bound so fast,—
  My tool,—my instrument?—Fulfil thy charge   10
  To the full bent of thy commission, else
  Thee, and thy bantling too, I'll from me cast
  To want and infamy.
Cath.   O, shameless man!
  Thou art the son of a degraded mother
  As low as I am, yet thou hast no pity.
Rud. Aye, and dost thou reproach my bastardy
  To make more base the man who conquer'd thee,
  With all thy virtue, rigid and demure?
  Who would have thought less than a sov'reign prince
  Could e'er have compass'd such achievement? Mean   20
  As he may be, thou'st given thyself a master,
  And must obey him.—Dost thou yet resist?
  Thou know'st my meaning. *(Tearing open his vest
    in vehemence of action).*
Cath. Under thy vest a dagger!—Ah! too well,
  I know thy meaning, cruel, ruthless man!
Rud. Have I discovered it?—I thought not of it:
  The vehemence of gesture hath betray'd me.
  I keep it not for thee, but for myself;
  A refuge from disgrace. Here is another:
  He who with high, but dangerous fortune grapples,   30
  Should he be foil'd, looks but to friends like these.
  (Pulling out two daggers from his vest).
  This steel is strong to give a vig'rous thrust;
  The other on its venom'd point hath that
  Which, in the feeblest hand, gives death as certain,
  As tho' a giant smote the destin'd prey.
Cath. Thou desp'rate man! so arm'd against thyself!
Rud. Aye; and against myself with such resolves,
  Consider well how I shall deal with those
  Who may withstand my will or mar my purpose.
  Think'st thou I'll feebly——
Cath.   O be pacified.   40
  I will begone: I am a humbled wretch
  On whom thou tramplest with a tyrant's cruelty.
    (Exit).
(Rudigere looks after her with a malignant laugh, and

*then goes to the door of an adjoining chamber, to the
lock of which he applies his ear).*
Rud. All still within—I'm tired and heavy grown:
  I'll lay me down to rest. She is secure:
  No one can pass me here to gain her chamber.
  If she hold parley now with any thing,
  It must in truth be ghost or sprite.—Heigh ho!
  I'm tired, and will to bed.
*(Lays himself on the couch and falls asleep. The cry
of hounds is then heard without at a distance, with
the sound of a horn; and presently Orra enters,
bursting from the door of the adjoining chamber, in
great alarm).*
Orra. Cathrina! sleepest thou? Awake! awake!
*(Running up to the couch and starting back on seeing
Rudigere).*
  That hateful viper here!   50
  Is this my nightly guard? Detested wretch!
  I will steal back again.
*(Walks softly on tiptoe to the door of her chamber,
when the cry of hounds, &c. is again heard without,
nearer than before).*
          O no! I dare not.
  Tho' sleeping, and most hateful when awake,
  Still he is natural life and may be 'waked.
(Listening again).
  'Tis nearer now: that dismal thrilling blast!
  I must awake him.
(Approaching the couch and shrinking back again).
        O no! no, no!
  Upon his face he wears a horrid smile
  That speaks bad thoughts.
(Rudigere speaks in his sleep).
      He mutters too my name.—
  I dare not do it. *(Listening again).*
  The dreadful sound is now upon the wind, 60
  Sullen and low, as if it wound its way
  Into the cavern'd earth that swallow'd it.
  I will abide in patient silence here;
  Though hateful and asleep, I feel me still
  Near something of my kind.
*(Crosses her arms, and leans in a cowering posture over
the back of a chair at a distance from the couch; when
presently the horn is heard without, louder than before,
and she starts up).*
  O it returns! as tho' the yawning earth

Had given it up again, near to the walls.
  The horribly mingled din! 'tis nearer still:
  'Tis close at hand: 'tis at the very gate!
(Running up to the couch).
  Were he a murd'rer, clenching in his hands 70
  The bloody knife, I must awake him.—No!
  That face of dark and subtile wickedness!
  I dare not do it. *(Listening again).* Aye; 'tis at the
    gate—
  Within the gate.—
          What rushing blast is that
  Shaking the doors? Some awful visitation
  Dread entrance makes! O mighty God of Heaven!
  A sound ascends the stairs.
          Ho, Rudigere!
  Awake, awake! Ho! Wake thee, Rudigere!
Rud. (Waking). What cry is that so terribly
    strong?—Ha Orra!
  What is the matter?   80
Orra. It is within the walls. Did'st thou not hear it?
Rud. What? The loud voice that called me?
Orra. No, it was mine.
Rud.   It sounded in my ears
  With more than human strength.
Orra.   Did it so sound?
  There is around us, in this midnight air,
  A power surpassing nature. List, I pray:
  Altho' more distant now, dost thou not hear
  The yell of hounds; the spectre-huntsman's horn?
Rud. I hear, indeed, a strangely mingled sound:
  The wind is howling round the battlements. 90
  But rest secure where safety is, sweet Orra!
  Within these arms, nor man nor fiend shall harm
    thee.
*(Approaching her with a softened winning voice, while
she pushes him off with abhorrence).*
Orra. Vile reptile! touch me not.
Rud. Ah! Orra! thou art warp'd by prejudice,
  And taught to think me base; but in my veins
  Lives noble blood, which I will justify.
Orra. But in thy heart, false traitor! what lives there?
Rud. Alas! thy angel-faultlessness conceives not
  The strong temptations of a soul impassion'd
  Beyond controul of reason.——At thy feet— 100
    (Kneeling).
  O spurn me not!

(Enter several Servants, alarmed).

Rud. What, all these fools upon us! Staring knaves,
   What brings ye here at this untimely hour?

1st Servant. We have all heard it—'twas the yell of
      hounds
   And clatt'ring steeds, and the shrill horn between.

Rud. Out on such folly!

2nd Servant. In very truth it pass'd close to the walls;
   Did not your Honour hear it?

Rud. Ha! say'st thou so? thou art not wont to join
   In idle tales.—I'll to the battlements   110
   And watch it there: it may return again.

(Exeunt severally, Rudigere followed by servants, and
Orra into her own chamber).

         Scene IV: *The Outlaws' cave. Enter Theobald.*

Theo. (Looking round). Here is a place in which
      some traces are
   Of late inhabitants. In yonder nook
   The embers faintly gleam, and on the walls
   Hang spears and ancient arms: I must be right.
   A figure thro' the gloom moves towards me.
   Ho there! Whoe'er you are: Holla, good friend!

(Enter an Outlaw).

Out. A stranger! Who art thou, who art thus bold,
   To hail us here unbidden?

Theo. That thou shalt shortly know. Thou art, I guess,
   One of the Outlaws, who this forest haunt.   10

Out. Be thy conjecture right or wrong, no more
   Shalt thou return to tell where thou hast found us.
   Now for thy life! *(Drawing his sword).*

Theo.   Hear me, I do entreat thee.

Out. Nay, nay! no foolish pleadings; for thy life
   Is forfeit now; have at thee!

(Falls fiercely upon Theobald, Who also draws and
defends himself bravely, when another Outlaw enters
and falls likewise upon him. Theobald then recedes,
fighting, till he gets his back to the wall of the cavern,
and there defends himself stoutly. Enter Franko).

Franko. Desist, I charge you! Fighting with a stranger,
   Two swords to one—a solitary stranger!

1st Out. We are discover'd; had he master'd me,
   He had return'd to tell his mates above
   What neighbours in these nether caves they have.   20
   Let us dispatch him.

Franko.   No, thou hateful butcher!
   Dispatch a man alone and in our power!
   Who art thou, stranger, who dost use thy sword
   With no mean skill; and in this perilous case
   So bold an air and countenance maintainest?
   What brought thee hither?

Theo. My name is Theobald of Falkenstein;
   To find the valiant Captain of these bands,
   And crave assistance of his gen'rous arm:
   This is my business here.   30

Franko (Struck and agitated, to his men).
   Go, join your comrades in the further cave.
      (Exeunt outlaws).
   And thou art Falkenstein? In truth thou art.
   And who think'st thou am I?

Theo. Franko, the gen'rous leader of those Outlaws.

Franko. So am I call'd, and by that name alone
   They know me. Sporting on the mountain's side,
   Where Garva's wood waves green, in other days,
   Some fifteen years ago, they call'd me Albert.

Theo. (Rushing into his arms). Albert; my playmate
      Albert! Woe the day!
   What cruel fortune drove thee to this state?   40

Franko. I'll tell thee all; but tell thou first to me
   What is the aid thou camest here to ask.

Theo. Aye, thou wert ever thus: still forward bent
   To serve, not to be serv'd.
                     But wave we this.
   Last night a Lady to the castle came,
   In thraldom by a villain kept, whom I
   Would give my life to rescue. Of arm'd force
   Being at present destitute, I crave
   Assistance of you in counsel and your arms.

Franko. When did'st thou learn that Outlaws   50
      harbour here,
   For 'tis but lately we have held these haunts?

Theo. Not till within the precincts of the forest,
   Following the traces of that villain's course,
   One of your band I met, and recogniz'd
   As an old soldier, who, some few years back,
   Had under my command right bravely serv'd.
   Seeing himself discover'd, and encouraged
   By what I told him of my story, freely
   He offer'd to conduct me to his captain.
   But in a tangled path some space before me,   60
   Alarm'd at sight of spearmen thro' the brake,

He started from his way, and so I missed him,
Making, to gain your cave, my way alone.
Franko. Thou'rt welcome here: and gladly I'll assist thee,
Tho' not by arms, the force within the castle
So far out-numbering mine. But other means
May serve thy purpose better.
Theo. What other means, I pray?
Franko. From these low caves, a passage under-ground
Leads to the castle—to the very tower   70
Where, as I guess, the Lady is confined.
When sleep has still'd the house, we'll make our way.
Theo. Aye, by my faith it is a noble plan!
Guarded or not we well may overcome
The few that may compose her midnight guard.
Franko. We shall not shrink from that.——But by
    my fay!
To-morrow is St. Michael's Eve: 'twere well
To be the spectre-huntsman for a night,
And bear her off, without pursuit or hindrance.
Theo. I comprehend thee not.
Franko.   Thou shalt ere long.   80
But stand not here; an inner room I have
Where thou shalt rest and some refreshment take,
And then we will more fully talk of this,
Which, slightly mention'd, seems chimerical.
Follow me. *(Turning to him as they go out).*
                    Hast thou still upon thine arm
That mark which from mine arrow thou receiv'dst
When sportively we shot? The wound was deep,
And gall'd thee much, but thou mad'st light of it.
Theo. Yes, here it is. *(Pulling up his sleeve as they go
    out, and Exeunt).*

Act IV

Scene I: *The Ramparts of the Castle.
Enter Orra and Cathrina.*

*Cath. (After a pause in which Orra walks once or
    twice across the stage, thoughtfully).*
Go in, I pray; thou wand'rest here too long.
(A pause again).
The air is cold; behind those further mountains
The sun is set. I pray thee now go in.
Orra. Ha! sets the sun already? Is the day
Indeed drawn to its close?

Cath.   Yes, night approaches.
See, many a gather'd flock of cawing rooks
Are to their nests returning.
Orra (Solemnly).   Night approaches!—
This awful night which living beings shrink from.
All now of every kind scour to their haunts,
While darkness, peopled with its hosts unknown,   10
Awful dominion holds. Mysterious night!
What things unutterable thy dark hours
May lap!—What from thy teeming darkness burst
Of horrid visitations, ere that sun
Again shall rise on the enlighten'd earth!
(A pause).
Cath. Why dost thou gaze intently on the sky?
See'st thou aught wonderful?
Orra. Look there; behold that strange gigantic form
Which yon grim cloud assumes; rearing aloft
The semblance of a warrior's plumed head,   20
While from its half-shaped arm a streamy dart
Shoots angrily? Behind him too, far stretch'd,
Seems there not, verily, a seried[37] line
Of fainter misty forms?
Cath.   I see, indeed,
A vasty cloud, of many clouds composed,
Towering above the rest; and that behind
In misty faintness seen, which hath some likeness
To a long line of rocks with pine-wood crown'd:
Or, if indeed the fancy so incline,
A file of spearmen, seen thro' drifted smoke.   30
Orra. Nay, look how perfect now the form becomes:
Dost thou not see?—Aye, and more perfect still.
O thou gigantic Lord, whose robed limbs
Beneath their stride span half the heavens! art thou
Of lifeless vapour form'd? Art thou not rather
Some air-clad spirit—some portentous thing—
Some mission'd[38] Being?——Such a sky as this
Ne'er usher'd in a night of nature's rest.
Cath. Nay, many such I've seen; regard it not.
That form, already changing, will ere long   40
Dissolve to nothing. Tarry here no longer.
Go in I pray.

---

37 *seried*: i.e., serried, pertaining to files or ranks of armed
    men, and meaning pressed close together, shoulder to
    shoulder, in close order.
38 *mission'd*: having a mission.

Orra.　　　　　No; while one gleam remains
　Of the sun's blessed light, I will not go.
Cath. Then let me fetch a cloak to keep thee warm,
　For chilly blows the breeze.
Orra.　　　　　　　　Do as thou wilt.
*(Exit Cathrina. Enter an Outlaw, stealing softly
behind her).*
Out. (In a low voice). Lady!—the Lady Orra!
Orra (Starting). Merciful heaven! Sounds it beneath
　　my feet
　In earth or air? *(He comes forward).*
　　　　　　　　Ha, a man!
　Welcome is aught that wears a human face.
　Did'st thou not hear a sound?
Out.　　　　　　　What sound, an' please you? 50
Orra. A voice which call'd upon me now: it spoke
　In a low hollow tone, suppress'd and low,
　Unlike a human voice.
Out.　　　　　　　　It was my own.
Orra. What would'st thou have?
Out.　　　　　　　　Here is a letter, Lady.
Orra. Who sent thee hither?
Out.　　　　　　　　It will tell thee all.
　(Gives a letter). I must begone, your chieftain is at
　　hand. *(Exit).*
Orra. Comes it from Falkenstein? It is his seal.
　I may not read it here. I'll to my chamber. *(Exit
　　hastily, not perceiving Rudigere, who enters by the
　　opposite side, before she has time to go off).*
Rud. A letter in her hand, and in such haste!　60
　Some secret agent here from Falkenstein?
　It must be so. *(Hastening after her, Exit).*

Scene II: *The Outlaws' Cave;
enter Theobald and Franko by opposite sides.*

Theo. How now, good Captain; draws it near the time?
　Are those the keys?
Franko.　　　　　They are: this doth unlock
　The entrance to the staircase, known alone
　To Gomez, ancient keeper of the castle,
　Who is my friend in secret, and deters
　The neighb'ring peasantry with dreadful tales
　From visiting by night our wide domains.
　The other doth unlock a secret door,
　That leads us to the chamber where she sleeps.

Theo. Thanks, gen'rous friend! thou art my better 10
　　genius.
　Did'st thou not say, until the midnight horn
　Hath sounded thrice, we must remain conceal'd?
Franko. Even so. And now I hear my men without
　Telling the second watch.
Theo.　　　　　　　　How looks the night?
Franko. As we could wish: the stars do faintly twinkle
　Thro' sever'd clouds, and shed but light sufficient
　To shew each nearer object closing on you
　In dim unshapely blackness. Aught that moves
　Across your path, or sheep or straggling goat,
　Is now a pawing steed or grizzly bull,　20
　Large and terrific; every air-mov'd bush
　Or jutting crag, some strange gigantic thing.
Theo. Is all still in the castle?
Franko. There is an owl sits hooting on the tower,
　That answer from a distant mate receives,
　Like the faint echo of his dismal cry;
　While a poor houseless dog by dreary fits
　Sits howling at the gate. All else is still.
Theo. Each petty circumstance is in our favour,
　That makes the night more dismal.　30
Franko. Aye, all goes well: as I approach'd the walls,
　I heard two sentinels—for now I ween,
　The boldest spearman will not watch alone—
　Together talk in the deep hollow voice
　Of those who speak at midnight, under awe
　Of the dead stillness round them.
Theo. Then let us put ourselves in readiness,
　And heaven's good favour guide us! *(Exeunt).*

Scene III: *A gloomy Apartment;
enter Orra and Rudigere.*

Orra (Aside). The room is darken'd: yesternight a lamp
　Threw light around on roof and walls, and made
　Its dreary space less dismal.
Rud. (Overhearing her, and calling to a Servant without).
　Ho! more lights here! *(Servant enters with a light
　　and Exit).*
　　　　　　　　Thou art obey'd.
　　　　　　　　　　　In aught,
　But in the company of human kind,
　Thou shalt be gratified. Thy lofty mind
　For higher super-human fellowship,
　If such there be, may now prepare its strength.

Orra. Thou ruthless tyrant! They who have in battle
 Fought valiantly, shrink like a helpless child   10
 From any intercourse with things unearthly.
 Art thou a man? And bear'st thou in thy breast
 The feelings of a man? It cannot be!
Rud. Yes, madam; in my breast I bear too keenly
 The feelings of a man—a man most wretched:
 A scorn'd, rejected man.—Make me less miserable;
 Nay rather should I say, make me most blest;
 And then——
*(Attempting to take her hand, while she steps back
from him, drawing herself up with an air stately and
determined, and looking steadfastly in his face).*
         Thou know'st my firm determination:
 Give me thy solemn promise to be mine.
 This is the price, thou haughty, scornful maid,   20
 That will redeem thee from the hour of terror!
 This is the price——
Orra.   Which never shall be paid.
(Walks from him to the further end of the apartment).
Rud. (After a pause). Thou art determin'd then. Be
   not so rash:
 Bethink thee well what flesh and blood can bear:
 The hour is near at hand.
*(She, turning round, waves him with her hand to leave
her).*
         Thou deign'st no answer.
 Well; reap the fruits of thine unconquer'd pride.
    (Exit).
(Manet Orra).
Orra. I am alone: That closing door divides me
 From every being owning nature's life.—
 And shall I be constrain'd to hold communion
 With that which owns it not?
(After pacing to and fro for a little while).
         O that my mind   30
 Could raise its thoughts in strong and steady fervour
 To him, the Lord of all existing things,
 Who lives and is where'er existence is;
 Grasping its hold upon his skirted robe,
 Beneath whose mighty rule Angels and Spirits,
 Demons and nether powers, all living things,
 Hosts of the earth, with the departed dead
 In their dark state of mystery, alike
 Subjected are!—And I will strongly do it.—
 Ah! Would I could! Some hidden powerful hindrance   40

 Doth hold me back, and mars all thought.—
*(After a pause, in which she stands fixed with her arms
crossed on her breast).*
         Dread intercourse!
 O, if it look on me with its dead eyes!
 If it should move its lock'd and earthy lips
 And utt'rance give to the grave's hollow sounds!
 If it stretch forth its cold and bony grasp——
 O horror, horror!
*(Sinking lower at every successive idea, as she repeats
these four last lines, till she is quite upon her knees on
the ground).*
 Would that beneath these planks of senseless matter
 I could, until the dreadful hour is past,
 As senseless be! *(Striking the floor with her hands).*
         O open and receive me,
 Ye happy things of still and lifeless being,   50
 That to the awful steps which tread upon ye
 Unconscious are!
(Enter Cathrina behind her).
         Who's there? Is't any thing?
Cath. 'Tis I, my dearest Lady; 'tis Cathrina.
Orra (Embracing her). How kind! such blessed
   kindness! keep thee by me;
 I'll hold thee fast: an angel brought thee hither.
 I needs must weep to think thou art so kind
 In mine extremity.—Where wert thou hid?
Cath. In that small closet, since the supper hour,
 I've been conceal'd. For searching round the
   chamber,
 I found its door and enter'd. Fear not now: 60
 I will not leave thee till the break of day.
Orra. Heaven bless thee for it! Till the break of day!
 The very thought of daybreak gives me life.
 If but this night were past, I have good hope
 That noble Theobald will soon be here
 For my deliv'rance.
Cath.   Wherefore think'st thou so?
Orra. A stranger, when thou left'st me on the ramparts,
 Gave me a letter, which I quickly open'd,
 As soon as I, methought, had gain'd my room
 In privacy; but close behind me came   70
 That Daemon Rudigere, and, snatching at it,
 Forced me to cast it to the flames, from which,
 I struggling with him still, he could not save it.
Cath. You have not read it then.

Orra.   No; but the seal
Was Theobald's, and I could swear ere long
He will be here to free me from this thraldom.
Cath. God grant he may!
Orra. If but this night were past! How goes the time?
Has it not enter'd on the midnight watch?
Cath. (Pointing to a small slab at the corner of the
        stage on which is placed a sand-glass).
That glass I've set to measure it. As soon   80
As all the sand is run, you are secure;
The midnight watch is past.
Orra (Running to the glass and looking at it eagerly).
There is not much to run: O an't were finish'd!
But it so slowly runs!
Cath.   Yes; watching it,
It seemeth slow. But heed it not; the while,
I'll tell thee some old tale, and ere I've finish'd,
The midnight watch is gone. Sit down I pray!
(They sit, Orra drawing her chair close to Cathrina).
What story shall I tell thee?
Orra. Something, my friend, which thou thyself hast
        known   90
Touching the awful intercourse which spirits
With mortal men have held at this dread hour.
Did'st thou thyself e'er meet with one whose eyes
Had look'd upon the spectred dead—had seen
Forms from another world?
Cath.   Never but once.
Orra (Eagerly). Once then thou did'st! O tell it! Tell
        it me!
Cath. Well; since I needs must tell it, once I knew
A melancholy man, who did aver,
That, journeying on a time, o'er a wild waste,
By a fell storm o'erta'en, he was compell'd
To pass the night in a deserted tower,   100
Where a poor hind, the sole inhabitant
Of the sad place, prepared for him a bed.
And, as he told his tale, at dead of night,
By the pale lamp that in his chamber burn'd,
As it might be an arm's-length from his bed—
Orra. So close upon him?
Cath.   Yes.
Orra.   Go on; what saw he?
Cath. An upright form, wound in a clotted shroud—
Clotted and stiff, like one swath'd up in haste
After a bloody death.

Orra.   O horrible!
Cath. He started from his bed and gaz'd upon it.   110
Orra. And did he speak to it?
Cath.   He could not speak.
Its visage was uncover'd, and at first
Seem'd fix'd and shrunk, like one in coffin'd sleep:
But, as he gaz'd, there came, he wist[39] not how,
Into its beamless eyes a horrid glare,
And turning towards him, for it did move,——
Why dost thou grasp me thus?
Orra.   Go on, go on!
Cath. Nay, heaven forfend! Thy shrunk and
        sharpen'd features
Are of the corse's colour, and thine eyes
Are full of tears. How's this?
Orra.   I know not how.   120
A horrid sympathy jarr'd on my heart,
And forced into mine eyes these icy tears.
A fearful kindredship there is between
The living and the dead: an awful bond:
Wo's me! that we do shudder at ourselves—
At that which we must be!——A dismal thought!
(Seeing Cathrina go towards the sand-glass).
Where dost thou run? thy story is not told.
Cath. (Shewing the glass). A better story I will tell
        thee now;
The midnight watch is past.
Orra.   Ha! let me see.
Cath. There's not one sand to run.   130
Orra. But it is barely past.
Cath.   'Tis more than past.
For I did set it later than the hour,
To be assur'dly sure.
Orra. Then it is gone indeed: O heaven be praised!
The fearful gloom gone by!
(Holding up her hands in gratitude to heaven, and
then looking round her with cheerful animation).
                                In truth, already
I feel as if I breath'd the morning air:
I'm marvellously lighten'd.
Cath.   Ne'ertheless,
Thou art forspent; I'll run to my apartment,
And fetch some cordial drops that will revive thee.

---

39 *wist*: knew.

Orra. Thou need'st not go: I've ta'en thy drops already: 140
  I'm bold and buoyant grown. *(Bounding lightly*
    from the floor).
Cath.   I'll soon return:
  Thou art not fearful now?
Orra.   No; I breathe lightly;
  Valour within me grows most powerfully,
  Would'st thou but stay to see it, gentle Cathrine.
Cath. I will return to see it, ere thou can'st
  Three times repeat the letters of thy name. *(Exit*
    hastily by the concealed door).
Orra (Alone). This burst of courage shrinks most
    shamefully.
  I'll follow her.—*(Striving to open the door).* 'Tis
    fast: it will not open.
  I'll count my footsteps as I pace the floor
  Till she return again.   150
(Paces up and down, muttering to herself, when a horn
is heard without, pausing and sounding three times, each
time louder than before. Orra runs again to the door).
  Despair will give me strength: where is the door?
  Mine eyes are dark, I cannot find it now.
  O God! protect me in this awful pass!
(After a pause, in which she stands with her body bent
in a cowering posture, with her hands locked together,
and trembling violently, she starts up and looks wildly
round her).
  There's nothing, yet I felt a chilly hand
  Upon my shoulder press'd. With open'd eyes
  And ears intent I'll stand. Better it is
  Thus to abide the awful visitation,
  Than cower in blinded horror, strain'd intensely
  With ev'ry beating of my goaded heart.
(Looking round her with a steady sternness, but
shrinking again almost immediately).
  I cannot do it: on this spot I'll hold me   160
  In awful stillness.
(Bending her body as before; then, after a momentary
pause, pressing both her hands upon her head).
  The icy scalp of fear is on my head,—
  The life stirs in my hair: it is a sense
  That tells the nearing of unearthly steps,
  Albeit my ringing ears no sounds distinguish.
(Looking round, as if by irresistible impulse, to a great
door at the bottom of the stage, which bursts open, and
the form of a huntsman, clothed in black with a horn
in his hand, enters and advances towards her. She
utters a loud shriek, and falls senseless on the ground).
Theo. (Running up to her, and raising her from the
    ground).
  No semblance but real agony of fear.
  Orra, oh Orra! Know'st thou not my voice?
  Thy knight, thy champion, the devoted Theobald?
  Open thine eyes and look upon my face:
    (Unmasking).
  I am no fearful waker from the grave: 170
  Dost thou not feel? 'Tis the warm touch of life.
  Look up, and fear will vanish.—Words are vain!
  What a pale countenance of ghastly strength
  By horror changed! O ideot that I was
  To hazard this!—The villain hath deceiv'd me!
  My letter she has ne'er received. Oh Fool!
  That I should trust to this! *(Beating his head*
    distractedly).
(Enter Franko, by the same door).
Franko. What is the matter? What strange turn is this?
Theo. O cursed sanguine fool! could I not think——
  She moves—she moves! rouse thee, my gentle Orra! 180
  'Tis no strange voice that calls thee: 'tis thy friend.
Franko. She opens now her eyes.
Theo.   But oh that look!
Franko. She knows thee not, but gives a stifled groan,
  And sinks again in stupor.
  Make no more fruitless lamentation here,
  But bear her hence: the cool and open air
  May soon restore her. Let us, while we may,
  Occasion seize, lest we should be surprised.
(Exeunt: Orra borne off in a state of insensibility).

Act V

Scene I: *The great Hall of the Castle: Enter Rudigere,*
    Cathrina, and Attendants, by different Doors.

Rud. (To Attendant). Return'd again! Is any thing
    discover'd?
  Or door or passage? garment dropt in haste?
  Or footstep's track, or any mark of flight?
1st Attendant. No, by my faith! tho' from its highest
    turrets
  To its deep vaults, the castle we have search'd.
Cath. 'Tis vain to trace the marks of trackless feet.

If that in truth it hath convey'd her hence,
The yawning earth has yielded them a passage,
Or else, thro' rifted roofs, the buoyant air.
Rud. Fools! search again. I'll raze the very walls   10
From their foundations but I will discover
If door or pass there be, to us unknown.
(Calling off the stage). Ho! Gomez there! He keeps
    himself aloof:
Nor aids the search with true and hearty will.
I am betray'd.—Ho! Gomez there, I say!
He shrinks away: go drag the villain hither,
And let the torture wring confession from him.
(A loud knocking heard at the gate).
    Ha! who seeks entrance at this early hour
In such a desert place?
Cath.   Some hind, perhaps,
Who brings intelligence. Heaven grant it be!   20
(Enter an armed Vassal).
Rud. Ha! One from Aldenberg! What brings thee
    hither:
Vassal. (Seizing Rudigere). Thou art my prisoner. *(To*
    Attendants). Upon your peril,
Assist me to secure him.
Rud. Audacious hind! by what authority
Speak'st thou such bold commands? Produce thy
    warrant.
Vass. 'Tis at the gate, and such as thou must yield to:
Count Hughobert himself, with armed men,
A goodly band, his pleasure to enforce. *(Secures him).*
Rud. What sudden freak[40] is this? am I suspected
Of aught but true and honourable faith?   30
Vass. Aye, by our holy Saints! more than suspected.
Thy creature Maurice, whom thou thought'st to bribe
With things of seeming value, hath discover'd
The cunning fraud; on which his tender conscience,
Good soul! did o' the sudden so upbraid him,
That to his Lord forthwith he made confession
Of all the plots against the Lady Orra,
In which thy wicked arts had tempted him
To take a wicked part. All is discover'd.
Cath. (Aside). All is discover'd! Where then shall I   40
    hide me?
(Aloud to Vassal). What is discover'd?

---

40 *freak*: a sudden causeless change of mind; a capricious
    humor, notion, or whim.

Vass.   Ha! most virtuous Lady!
Art thou alarmed? Fear not: the world well knows
How good thou art; and to the Countess shortly,
Who with her Lord is near, thou wilt no doubt
Give good account of all that thou hast done.
Cath. (Aside, as she retires in agitation).
    O heaven forbid! What hole o' th' earth will hide
    me! *(Exit).*
(Enter by the opposite side, Hughobert, Eleanora, Alice,
Glottenbal, Urston, Maurice, and Attendants).
Hugh. (Speaking as he enters). Is he secured?
Vass. (Pointing to Rudigere).   He is, my Lord; behold!
Hugh. (To Rudigere). Black artful traitor! Of a sacred
    trust,
Blindly reposed in thee, the base betrayer
For wicked ends; full well upon the ground   50
May'st thou decline those darkly frowning eyes,
And gnaw thy lip in shame.
Rud. And rests no shame with him, whose easy faith
Entrusts a man unproved; or, having proved him,
Lets a poor hireling's unsupported testimony
Shake the firm confidence of many years?
Hugh. Here the accuser stands; confront him boldly,
And spare him not. *(Bringing forward Maurice).*
Maur. (To Rudigere). Deny it if thou can'st. Thy
    brazen[41] front,
All brazen as it is, denies it not.   60
Rud. (To Maurice). Fool! that of prying curiosity
And av'rice art compounded! I in truth
Did give to thee a counterfeited treasure
To bribe thee to a counterfeited trust;
Meet recompense! Ha, ha! Maintain thy tale,
For I deny it not. *(With careless derision).*
Maur.   O, subtile traitor!
Dost thou so varnish it with seeming mirth?
Hugh. Sir Rudigere, thou dost, I must confess,
Out-face him well. But call the Lady Orra;
If towards her thou hast thyself comported   70
In honesty, she will declare it freely.
(To Attendant). Bring Orra hither.
1st Att. Would that we could; last night i' the
    midnight watch
She disappear'd; but whether man or devil
Hath borne her hence, in truth we cannot tell.

---

41 *brazen*: hardened in effrontery; shameless.

Hugh. O both! Both man and devil together join'd.
  (To Rudigere furiously). Fiend, villain, murderer!
    Produce her instantly.
  Dead or alive, produce thy hapless charge.
Rud. Restrain your rage, my Lord; I would right
    gladly
  Obey you, were it possible: the place,   80
  And the mysterious means of her retreat,
  Are both to me unknown.
Hugh.   Thou liest! thou liest!
Glot. (Coming forward). Thou liest, beast, villain,
    traitor! think'st thou still
  To fool us thus? Thou shalt be forced to speak.
  (To Hughobert). Why lose we time in words when
    other means
  Will quickly work? Straight to those pillars bind him,
  And let each sturdy varlet of your train
  Inflict correction on him.
Maur. Aye, this alone will move him.
Hugh.   Thou say'st well:
  By heaven it shall be done!   90
Rud. And will Count Hughobert degrade in me
  The blood of Aldenberg to shame himself?
Hugh. That plea avails thee not; thy spurious birth
  Gives us full warrant, as thy conduct varies,
  To reckon thee or noble or debas'd.
  (To Attendant). Straight bind the traitor to the
    place of shame.
*(As they are struggling to bind Rudigere he gets one of
his hands free, and, pulling out a dagger from under
his clothes, stabs himself).*
Rud. Now, take your will of me, and drag my corse
  Thro' mire and dust; your shameless fury now
  Can do me no disgrace.
Urst. (Advancing). Rash, daring, thoughtless wretch!   100
    dost thou so close
  A wicked life in hardy desperation?
Rud. Priest, spare thy words: I add not to my sins
  That of presumption, in pretending now
  To offer up to heaven the forced repentance
  Of some short moments for a life of crimes.
Urst. My son, thou dost mistake me: let thy heart
  Confession make——
Glot. (Interrupting Urston). Yes, dog! Confession make
  Of what thou'st done with Orra; else I'll spurn
    thee,

And cast thy hateful carcase to the kites.[42]
*Hugh. (Pulling back Glottenbal as he is going to spurn
    Rudigere with his foot, who is now fallen upon the
    ground).* Nay, nay, forbear; such outrage is   110
  unmanly.
*(Eleanora, who with Alice had retired from the
shocking sight of Rudigere, now comes forward to him).*
El. Oh, Rudigere! thou art a dying man,
  And we will speak to thee without upbraiding.
  Confess, I do entreat thee, ere thou goest
  To thy most awful change, and leave us not
  In this our horrible uncertainty.
  Is Orra here conceal'd?
Alice.   Thou hast not slain her?
  Confession make, and heaven have mercy on thee!
Rud. Yes, Ladies; with these words of gentle meekness
  My heart is changed; and that you may perceive
  How greatly changed, let Glottenbal approach me;   120
  Spent am I now, and can but faintly speak—
  Ev'n unto him, in token of forgiveness
  I'll tell what ye desire.
El. Thank heaven, thou art so changed!
Hugh. (To Glottenbal).   Go to him, boy.
*(Glottenbal goes to Rudigere, and stooping over him to
hear what he has to say, Rudigere, taking a small
dagger from his bosom, strikes Glottenbal on the neck).*
Glot. Oh, he has wounded me!—Detested traitor!
  Take that and that; would thou hadst still a life
  For every thrust. *(Killing him).*
Hugh. (Alarmed). Ha! Has he wounded thee, my son?
Glot.   A scratch;
  'Tis nothing more. He aim'd it at my throat,
  But had not strength to thrust.
Hugh.   Thank God, he had not!   130
(A trumpet sounds without).
  Hark! martial notice of some high approach!
  (To attendants). Go to the gate. *(Exeunt attendants).*
El. Who may it be? This castle is remote
  From every route which armed leaders take.
(Enter a Servant).
Serv. The Banneret of Basle is at the gate.
Hugh. Is he in force?

---

42 *kites*: a bird of prey of the family *Falconidae* and sub-
    family *Milvinae*, having long wings, forked tail, and
    no tooth in the bill.

Serv. Yes, thro' the trees his distant bands are seen
  Some hundreds strong, I guess; tho' with himself
  Two followers only come.
(Enter Hartman attended).
Hugh. Forgive me, Banneret, if I receive thee   140
  With more surprise than courtesy. How is it?
  Com'st thou in peace?
Hart. To you, my Lord, I frankly will declare
  The purpose of my coming: having heard it,
  It is for you to say if I am come,
  As much I wish, in peace.
    (To Eleanora). Countess, your presence much
      emboldens me
  To think it so shall be.
Hugh. (Impatiently).   Proceed, I beg.
  When burghers gentle courtesy affect,
  It chafes me more than all their sturdy boasting.   150
Hart. Then with a burgher's plainness, Hughobert,
  I'll try my tale to tell,—nice task I fear!
  So that it may not gall a baron's pride.
  Brave Theobald, the Lord of Falkenstein,
  Co-burgher also of our ancient city,
  Whose cause of course is ours, declares himself
  The suitor of thy ward, the Lady Orra;
  And learning that within these walls she is,
  By thine authority, in durance kept,
  In his behalf I come to set her free;   160
  As an Oppressed Dame, such service claiming
  From every gen'rous knight. What is thy answer?
  Say, am I come in peace? Wilt thou release her?
Hugh. Ah, would I could! In faith thou gall'st me
      shrewdly.
Hart. I've been inform'd of all that now disturbs
      you,
  By one who held me waiting at the gate.
  Until the maid be found, if 'tis your pleasure,
  Cease enmity.
Hugh. Then let it cease. A traitor has deceiv'd me,
  And there he lies. *(Pointing to the body of Rudigere).*   170
Hart. (Looking at the body). A ghastly smile of fell
      malignity
  On his distorted face death has arrested.
    (Turning again to Hughobert). And has he died,
      and no confession made?
  All means that may discover Orra's fate
  Shut from us?

Hugh.   Ah! the fiend hath utter'd nothing
  That could betray his secret. If she lives——
El. Alas, alas! think you he murder'd her?
Alice. Merciful heaven forfend!
(Enter a Soldier in haste).
Soldier. O, I have heard a voice, a dismal voice!
Omnes. What hast thou heard?
El.   What voice?
Sold.   The Lady Orra's.   180
El. Where? Lead us to the place.
Hugh. Where did'st thou hear it, Soldier?
Sold. In a deep-tangled thicket of the wood,
  Close to a ruin'd wall, o'ergrown with ivy,
  That marks the ancient outworks of the castle.
Hugh. Haste; lead the way.
*(Exeunt all eagerly, without order, following the soldier,
Glottenbal and one attendant excepted).*
Att.   You do not go, my Lord?
Glot. I'm sick, and strangely dizzy grows my head,
  And pains shoot from my wound. It is a scratch,
  But from a devil's fang.—There's mischief in it.
  Give me thine arm, and lead me to a couch: 190
  I'm very faint.
Att. This way, my Lord; there is a chamber near.
    (Exit Glottenbal, supported by the attendant).

Scene II: *The Forest near the Castle; in Front a rocky
Bank crowned with a ruined Wall o'ergrown with Ivy,
and the Mouth of a Cavern shaded with Bushes. Enter
Franko, conducting Hughobert, Hartman, Eleanora,
Alice, and Urston, the Soldier following them.*

Franko (to Hughobert). This is the entry to our secret
      haunts.
  And now, my Lord, having inform'd you truly
  Of the device, well meant, but most unhappy,
  By which the Lady Orra from her prison
  By Falkenstein was ta'en; myself, my outlaws,
  Unhappy men that better days have seen,
  Drove to this lawless life by hard necessity,
  Are on your mercy cast.
Hugh. Which shall not fail you, valiant Franko. Much
  Am I indebted to thee: hadst thou not   10
  Of thine own free good will become our guide,
  As wand'ring here thou found'st us, we had ne'er
  The spot discover'd; for this honest Soldier,

A stranger to the forest, sought in vain
To thread the tangled path.
El. (To Franko). She is not well, thou say'st, and
  from her swoon
Imperfectly recover'd.
Franko.   When I left her,
She so appear'd.—But enter not, I pray,
Till I give notice.—Holla, you within!
Come forth and fear no ill.   20
(A shriek heard from the cave).
Omnes. What dismal shriek is that?
Alice.   'Tis Orra's voice.
El. No, no! it cannot be! It is some wretch,
In maniac's fetters bound.
Hart. The horrid thought that bursts into my mind!
  Forbid it, righteous Heaven!
*(Running into the cave, he is prevented by Theobald,
who rushes out upon him).*
Theo. Hold, hold! no entry here but o'er my corse,
When ye have master'd me.
Hart.   My Theobald,
Dost thou not know thy friends?
Theo. Ha! thou, my Hartman! Art thou come to me?
Hart. Yes, I am come. What means that look of 30
  anguish?
  She is not dead!
Theo.   Oh, no! it is not death!
Hart. What meanst thou? Is she well?
Theo.   Her body is.
Hart. And not her mind?——Oh direst wreck of all!
  That noble mind!——But 'tis some passing seizure,
  Some powerful movement of a transient nature;
  It is not madness?
Theo. (Shrinking from him, and bursting into tears).
  'Tis heaven's infliction; let us call it so;
  Give it no other name. *(Covering his face).*
El. (To Theobald). Nay, do not thus despair: when
  she beholds us,
  She'll know her friends, and, by our kindly soothing, 40
  Be gradually restored.
Alice. Let me go to her.
Theo.   Nay, forbear, I pray thee;
  I will myself with thee, my worthy Hartman,
  Go in and lead her forth.
*(Theobald and Hartman go into the cavern, while
those without wait in deep silence, which is only*
broken once or twice by a scream from the cavern and
the sound of Theobald's voice speaking soothingly, till
they return, leading forth Orra, with her hair and dress
disordered, and the appearance of wild distraction in
her gait and countenance).*
*Orra (Shrinking back as she comes from under the
  shade of the trees, &c. and dragging Theobald and
  Hartman back with her).*
  Come back, come back! The fierce and fiery light!
Theo. Shrink not, dear love! it is the light of day.
Orra. Have cocks crow'd yet?
Theo.   Yes; twice I've heard already
  Their mattin[43] sound. Look up to the blue sky;
  Is it not daylight there? And these green boughs
  Are fresh and fragrant round thee: every sense 50
  Tells thee it is the cheerful early day.
Orra. Aye, so it is; day takes his daily turn,
  Rising between the gulphy dells of night
  Like whiten'd billows on a gloomy sea.
  Till glow-worms gleam, and stars peep thro' the dark,
  And will-o'-the-wisp[44] his dancing taper light,
  They will not come again. *(Bending her ear to the
  ground).*
       Hark, hark! Aye, hark:
  They are all there: I hear their hollow sound
  Full many a fathom down.
Theo. Be still, poor troubled soul! they'll ne'er return: 60
  They are for ever gone. Be well assured
  Thou shalt from henceforth have a cheerful home
  With crackling faggots on thy midnight fire,
  Blazing like day around thee; and thy friends—
  Thy living, loving friends still by thy side,
  To speak to thee and cheer thee.—See my Orra!
  They are beside thee now; dost thou not know
  them? *(Pointing to Eleanora and Alice).*
*Orra (Gazing at them with her hand held up to shade
  her eyes).*
  No, no! athwart the wav'ring garish light,
  Things move and seem to be, and yet are nothing.

---

43 *mattin*: belonging to, or appropriate to, the morning.
44 *will-o'-the-wisp*: an *ignis fatuus* or phosphorescent light
  seen hovering or flitting over marshy ground, and supposed to be due to the spontaneous combustion of in-
  flammable gas derived from decaying vegetable matter.
  More generally, a thing (rarely a person) that deludes
  or misleads by means of fugitive appearances.

El. (Going near her). My gentle Orra! hast thou then 70
    forgot me?
  Dost thou not know my voice?
Orra. 'Tis like an old tune to my ear return'd.
  For there be those, who sit in cheerful halls,
  And breathe sweet air, and speak with pleasant
    sounds;
  And once I liv'd with such; some years gone by;
  I wot not now how long.
Hugh. Keen words that rend my heart!—Thou
  had'st a home,
  And one whose faith was pledged for thy protection.
Urst. Be more composed, my Lord, some faint
  remembrance
  Returns upon her with the well-known sound 80
  Of voices once familiar to her ear.
  Let Alice sing to her some fav'rite tune,
  That may lost thoughts recall.
*(Alice sings an old tune, and Orra, who listens eagerly
and gazes on her while she sings, afterwards bursts into
a wild laugh).*
Orra. Ha, ha! the witched air sings for thee bravely.
  Hoot owls thro' mantling fog for mattin birds?
  It lures not me.—I know thee well enough:
  The bones of murder'd men thy measure beat,
  And fleshless heads nod to thee.—Off, I say!
  Why are ye here?—That is the blessed sun.
El. Ah, Orra! do not look upon us thus! 90
  These are the voices of thy loving friends
  That speak to thee: this is a friendly hand
  That presses thine so kindly. *(Putting her hand
    upon Orra's, who gives a loud shriek, and shrinks
    from her with horror).*
Hart. O grievous state. *(Going up to her).* What
  terror seizes thee?
Orra. Take it away! It was the swathed dead:
  I know its clammy, chill, and bony touch.
(Fixing her eyes fiercely on Eleanora).
  Come not again; I'm strong and terrible now:
  Mine eyes have look'd upon all dreadful things;
  And when the earth yawns, and the hell-blast 100
    sounds,
  I'll 'bide the trooping of unearthly steps
  With stiff-clench'd, terrible strength.
*(Holding her clenched hands over her head with an air
of grandeur and defiance).*

Hugh. (Beating his breast). A murd'rer is a guiltless
  wretch to me.
Hart. Be patient; 'tis a momentary pitch;
  Let me encounter it.
*(Goes up to Orra, and fixes his eyes upon her, which
she, after a moment, shrinks from and seeks to avoid,
yet still, as if involuntarily, looks at him again).*
Orra. Take off from me thy strangely-fasten'd eye:
  I may not look upon thee, yet I must.
*(Still turning from him, and still snatching a hasty
look at him as before).*
  Unfix thy baleful glance: Art thou a snake?
  Something of horrid power within thee dwells.
  Still, still that powerful eye doth suck me in 110
  Like a dark eddy to its wheeling core.
  Spare me! O spare me, Being of strange power,
  And at thy feet my subject head I'll lay.
*(Kneeling to Hartman and bending her head
submissively).*
El. Alas the piteous sight! to see her thus;
  The noble, generous, playful, stately Orra!
*Theo. (Running to Hartman, and pushing him away
    with indignation).*
  Out on thy hateful and ungenerous guile!
  Think'st thou I'll suffer o'er her wretched state
  The slightest shadow of a base controul?
(Raising Orra from the ground).
  No, rise thou stately flower with rude blasts rent;
  As honour'd art thou with thy broken stem, 120
  And leaflets strew'd, as in thy summer's pride.
  I've seen thee worshipp'd like a regal Dame
  With every studied form of mark'd devotion,
  Whilst I in distant silence, scarcely proffer'd
  Ev'n a plain soldier's courtesy; but now,
  No liege-man[45] to his crowned mistress sworn,
  Bound and devoted is as I to thee;
  And he who offers to thy alter'd state
  The slightest seeming of diminish'd rev'rence,
  Must in my blood——*(To Hartman).* O pardon 130
  me, my friend!
  Thou'st wrung my heart.

---

45 *liege-man:* in feudal law, a vassal sworn to the service
    and support of his superior lord, who in return was
    obliged to afford him protection.

Hart. Nay, do thou pardon me: I am to blame:
　　Thy nobler heart shall not again be wrung.
　　But what can now be done? O'er such wild ravings
　　There must be some controul.
Theo. O none! none, none! but gentle sympathy
　　And watchfulness of love.
　　　　　　　　　　My noble Orra!
　　Wander where'er thou wilt; thy vagrant steps
　　Shall follow'd be by one, who shall not weary,
　　Nor e'er detach him from his hopeless task;　　140
　　Bound to thee now as fairest, gentlest beauty
　　Could ne'er have bound him.
Alice. See how she gazes on him with a look,
　　Subsiding gradually to softer sadness.
　　Half saying that she knows him.
El. There is a kindness in her changing eye.
　　Yes, Orra, 'tis the valiant Theobald,
　　Thy knight and champion, whom thou gazest on.
Orra. The brave are like the brave; so should it be.
　　He was a goodly man—a noble knight.　　150
　　(To Theobald). What is thy name, young
　　　　soldier?—Woe is me!
　　For prayers of grace are said o'er dying men,
　　Yet they have laid thy clay in unblest earth—
　　Shame! shame! not with the still'd and holy dead.
　　This shall be rectified; I'll find it out;
　　And masses shall be said for thy repose;
　　Thou shalt not troop with these.
El. 'Tis not the dead, 'tis Theobald himself,
　　Alive and well, who standeth by thy side.
Orra (Looking wildly round).
　　Where, where? All dreadful things are near me,　　160
　　　　round me,
　　Beneath my feet and in the loaded air.
　　Let him begone! The place is horrible!
　　Baneful to flesh and blood.——The dreadful blast!
　　Their hounds now yell below i' the centre gulph;
　　They may not rise again till solemn bells
　　Have given the stroke that severs night from morn.
El. O rave not thus! Dost thou not know us, Orra?
Orra (Hastily). Aye, well enough I know ye.
Urst. Ha! think ye that she does?
El. It is a terrible smile of recognition,　　170
　　If such it be.
Hart. Nay, do not thus your restless eye-balls move,
　　But look upon us steadily, sweet Orra.

Orra. Away! your faces waver to and fro;
　　I'll know you better in your winding-sheets,
　　When the moon shines upon ye.
Theo. Give o'er, my Friends; you see it is in vain;
　　Her mind within itself holds a dark world
　　Of dismal phantasies and horrid forms!
　　Contend with her no more.　　180
(Enter an Attendant in an abrupt disturbed manner).
Att. (To Eleanora, aside). Lady, I bring to you most
　　　　dismal news:
　　Too grievous for my Lord, so suddenly
　　And unprepar'd to hear.
El. (Aside).　　　　　　　What is it? Speak.
Att. (Aside to Eleanora). His son is dead, all swell'd
　　　　and rack'd with pain;
　　And on the dagger's point, which the sly traitor
　　Still in his stiffen'd grasp retains, foul stains,
　　Like those of limed[46] poison, shew full well
　　The wicked cause of his untimely death.
Hugh. (Overhearing them). Who speaks of death?
　　　　What did'st thou whisper there?
　　How is my son?——What look is that thou wear'st?　　190
　　He is not dead?——Thou dost not speak! O God!
　　I have no son. *(After a pause).* I am bereft!——
　　　　But this!
　　But only him!—Heaven's vengeance deals the stroke.
Urst. Heaven oft in mercy smites, ev'n when the blow
　　Severest is.
Hugh.　　　　I had no other hope.
　　Fell is the stroke, if mercy in it be!
　　Could this—could this alone atone my crime?
Urst. Submit thy soul to Heaven's all-wise decree.
　　Perhaps his life had blasted more thy hopes
　　Than ev'n his grievous end.　　200
Hugh. He was not all a father's heart could wish;
　　But, oh! he was my son!—my only son:
　　My child—the thing that from his cradle grew,
　　And was before me still.—Oh, oh! Oh, oh!
(Beating his breast and groaning deeply).
Orra (Running up to him). Ha! dost thou groan, old
　　　　man? Art thou in trouble?
　　Out on it! tho' they lay him in the mould,

46　*limed*: containing lime or quicklime, the alkaline earth
　　which is the chief constituent of mortar and which is
　　powerfully caustic; calcium oxide (CaO).

He's near thee still.—I'll tell thee how it is:
A hideous burst hath been: the damn'd and holy,
The living and the dead, together are
In horrid neighbourship.—'Tis but thin vapour, 210
Floating around thee, makes the wav'ring bound.
Poh! blow it off, and see th' uncurtain'd reach.
See! from all points they come; earth casts them
    up!
In grave-clothes swath'd are those but new in death;
And there be some half bone, half cased in shreds

Of that which flesh hath been; and there be some
With wicker'd ribs, thro' which the darkness scowls.
Back, back!—They close upon us.—Oh! the void
Of hollow unball'd sockets staring grimly,
And lipless jaws that move and clatter round us 220
In mockery of speech!—Back, back, I say!
Back, back!
*(Catching hold of Hughobert and Theobald, and
dragging them back with her in all the wild strength of
frantic horror, whilst the curtain drops).*

Remorse: A Tragedy in Five Acts

Samuel Taylor Coleridge

Samuel Taylor Coleridge (1772–1834) was born into the large family of an impoverished clergyman. A gifted child, he was sent to Christ's Hospital, a fine London school for the poor that would also boast Charles Lamb and Leigh Hunt as its pupils. He attended Cambridge but left without a degree, partially for financial reasons and partially to pursue his dreams of a radically transformed society. Together with Robert Southey, Coleridge had hoped to create an ideal "Pantisocracy" along the banks of the Susquehanna River in Pennsylvania. As a result, Coleridge left Cambridge and joined Southey in Bristol. Still pursuing the plan, the two married a pair of sisters (Edith and Sarah Fricker), Coleridge going through with the marriage as a matter of honor and obligation even as the Pantisocratic plan was falling through. The marriage was to cause him great unhappiness in future years.

The mid-1790s found Coleridge concerned about his vocation but also energized by his encounter and growing friendship with William Wordsworth, with whom he co-authored *Lyrical Ballads* in 1798. We sometimes forget, however, that the collaboration that produced several of Wordsworth's and Coleridge's best-known poems began as a dramatic one. The two spent the first half of their celebrated *annus mirabilis*—from June 1797 to January 1798—working on two tragedies, *The Borderers* and *Osorio*, both of which were submitted to Drury Lane for consideration. It was only after the rejection of both plays that plans for a volume of poetry began to emerge, Coleridge pillaging *Osorio* for two of his contributions to *Lyrical Ballads*: "The Foster-Mother's Tale" and "The Dungeon."

Given an annuity of £150 by the Wedgwood brothers, Coleridge, to the detriment of his marriage, decided to travel to Germany with the Wordsworths

in October of 1798. Wintering in the cultural center of Gottingen while the Wordsworths were forced to find cheaper lodgings in the remote town of Goslar, Coleridge studied German literature and metaphysics before returning to England in 1799. He hoped to revive the vital connection with Wordsworth of earlier years, but connubial disquiet, a sense of his poetic inferiority in relation to his fellow poet, and a hopeless love for Sara Hutchinson, the sister of Wordworth's future wife Mary Hutchinson, all contributed to an increasing sense of inadequacy. Coleridge finally withdrew to Malta in 1804, returning in 1806 thoroughly addicted to opium, which he had been taking for his ailments since at least 1796. Upon his return, he separated from his wife and eventually quarreled with Wordsworth, moving to London in 1810. His opium addiction finally led him in 1814 to place himself under the care of Highgate physician James Gillman, who succeeded in stabilizing and then curbing Coleridge's opium usage.

Although containing some of his finest prose, Coleridge's periodical *The Friend* (1809–10) largely failed in gaining a sustained readership. The courses of lectures he offered in 1811–12, however, attracted large audiences. In the next years Coleridge became a major London lecturer on literature and philosophy and an increasingly conservative commentator on the political scene. His *Biographia Literaria* (1817) offered one of the period's most profound explorations of aesthetics and provided an ideological argument that would be opposed by Lord Byron, Percy Shelley, Hunt, and John Keats. Among these younger poets, there was a mixed response: deep admiration for his wonderfully allusive poetry and dismay at his increasingly strident conservative politics.

Coleridge's *Remorse* opened on 23 January 1813. The play proved to be both a critical and popular success, receiving largely positive reviews and running for twenty nights, the longest run for a new tragedy in decades, and the greatest stage success for verse drama of the nineteenth century. While many modern critics have preferred the earlier *Osorio* to the revised *Remorse*, the staged version realized the dream of many writers of the day of finding a way to bring the poetic drama successfully into the theater. The play combined strong poetry with spectacular stage effects; reviewers were especially taken with the incantation scene that forms the play's center. Partaking of the Gothic dramas of James Boaden and Matthew Lewis but also looking to the examples of Joanna Baillie,

Friedrich Schiller, and William Shakespeare, *Remorse*, like Baillie's *Orra*, explores a strong internal emotional state. It also offers a commentary on contemporary politics, with the character of Ordonio functioning both as a prototype of the revolutionary usurper and as commentary on the political career of Napoleon.

The copytext is the British Library's copy of Samuel Taylor Coleridge, *Remorse: A Tragedy in Five Acts* (London: W. Pople, 1813), shelfmark Ashley 2847, which contains corrections and additions in Coleridge's hand. We also have indicated in the notes some major variations found in the Larpent manuscript (Huntington Library LA 1753).

Epigraph Printed on Title Page:

Remorse is as the heart, in which it grows:
If that be gentle, it drops balmy dews
Of true repentance; but if proud and gloomy,
It is a poison-tree, that pierced to the inmost
Weeps only tears of poison!

Act I. Scene I.

PREFACE

This Tragedy was written in the summer and autumn of the year 1797; at Nether Stowey, in the county of Somerset. By whose recommendation,[1] and of the manner in which both the Play and the Author were treated by the Recommender, let me be permitted to relate: that I knew of its having been received only by a third person; that I could procure neither answer nor the manuscript; and that but for an accident I should have had no copy of the Work itself. That such

treatment would damp a young man's exertions may be easily conceived: there was no need of after-misrepresentation and calumny, as an additional sedative.

As an amusing anecdote, and in the wish to prepare future Authors, as young as I then was and as ignorant of the world, for the treatment they may meet with, I will add, that the Person who by a twice conveyed recommendation (in the year 1797) had urged me to write a Tragedy: who on my own objection that I was utterly ignorant of all Stage-tactics had promised that *he* would himself make the necessary alterations, if the Piece should be at all representable; who together with the copy of the Play (hastened by his means so as to prevent the full developement[2] of the characters) received a letter from the Author to this purport, "*that conscious of his inexperience, he had cherished no expectations, and should therefore feel no disappointment from the rejection of the Play; but that if beyond his hopes Mr. ——— found in it any capability of being adapted to the Stage, it was delivered to him as if it had been his own Manuscript, to add, omit, or alter, as he saw occasion; and that (if it were rejected) the Author would*

---

1 *whose recommendation*: Richard Brinsley Sheridan (1751–1816), Whig politician and statesman, playwright, and proprietor of Drury Lane Theatre, best known for his plays *The Rivals* (Covent Garden, 1775), *The School for Scandal* (Drury Lane, 1777), *The Critic* (Drury Lane, 1779), and *Pizarro* (Drury Lane, 1798).

---

2 Coleridge's note: "I need not say to Authors, that as to the *essentials* of a Poem, little can be superinduced without dissonance, after the first warmth of conception and composition."

deem himself amply remunerated by the addition to his Experience, which he should receive, if Mr. ——— would but condescend to point out to him the nature of its unfitness for public Representation";—that this very Person not only returned me no answer, and, spite of repeated applications, retained my Manuscript when I was not conscious of any other Copy being in existence (my duplicate having been destroyed by an accident); not only suffered this Manuscript to wander about the Town from his house, so that but ten days ago I saw for the first time the song in the third Act *printed* and set to music, without my name, by Mr. Carnaby,[3] in the year 1802; not only asserted (as I have been assured) that the Play was rejected, because I would not submit to the alteration of one ludicrous line; and finally in the year 1806 amused and delighted (as who was ever in his society, if I may trust the universal report, without being amused and delighted?) a large company at the house of a highly respectable Member of Parliament,[4] with the ridicule of the Tragedy, as "*a fair specimen,*" of the *whole* of which he adduced a line:

"*Drip! drip! drip! there's nothing here but dripping.*"
In the original copy of the Play, in the first Scene of the fourth Act, Isidore *had* commenced his Soliloquy in the Cavern with the words:

"*Drip! drip! a ceaseless sound of water-drops,*"
as far as I can at present recollect: for on the possible ludicrous association being pointed out to me, I instantly and thankfully struck out the line. And as to my obstinate *tenacity*, not only my old acquaintance, but (I dare boldly aver) both the Managers of Drury Lane Theatre, and every Actor and Actress, whom I have recently met in the Green Room, will repel the accusation: perhaps not without surprise.[5]

I thought it right to record these circumstances; but I turn gladly and with sincere gratitude to the converse. In the close of last year I was advised to present the Tragedy once more to the Theatre. Accordingly having altered the names, I ventured to address a letter to Mr. Whitbread,[6] requesting information as to whom I was to present my Tragedy. My Letter was instantly and most kindly answered, and I have now nothing to tell but a Tale of Thanks. I should scarce know where to begin, if the goodness of the Manager, Mr. Arnold,[7] had not called for my first acknowledgements. Not merely as an *acting Play*, but as a dramatic *Poem*, the "Remorse" has been importantly and manifoldly benefited by his suggestions. I can with severest truth say, that every hint he gave me was the ground of some improvement. In the next place it is my duty to mention Mr. Raymond, the Stage Manager. Had the "Remorse" been his own Play—nay, that is saying too little—had I been his brother, or his dearest friend, he could not have felt or exerted himself more zealously.

---

3 *Mr. Carnaby*: William Carnaby (1772–1839), composer, who set Coleridge's song to music in 1802 as *Invocation to a Spirit: Serious Glee, for Soprano, Counter Tenor, Tenor and Bass.*

4 *Member of Parliament*: Richard Brinsley Sheridan.

5 This paragraph was cut from the second edition of *Remorse*, but retained in Coleridge's corrected first edition. Presumably Coleridge, gratified by the success of the play, decided it was diplomatic to remove the paragraph.

6 *Mr. Whitbread*: Samuel Whitbread (1758–1815), a wealthy Whig politician, friend of Fox, supporter of Charles Grey, and sometime ally of Francis Burdett on the radical left. After Drury Lane burned down on 24 February 1809, he became a member and soon after chairman of the committee for rebuilding the theater. He became a defender of Drury Lane's interests in Parliament and an important figure in determining its future. Suffering from depression, he committed suicide three weeks after the defeat of his admired Napoleon at Waterloo.

7 *Mr. Arnold*: Samuel James Arnold (1774–1852), son of the composer Samuel Arnold, was a dramatist and theater manager. In 1794, he saw his first play, *Auld Robin Gray,* staged at the Haymarket. Perhaps his most successful play was *Man and Wife, or More Secrets than One,* which had more than thirty performances at Drury Lane in 1809. In that same year, he received a license to open an English opera house, the Lyceum in the Strand, but the Drury Lane company moved in after the fire for the next three years. In 1812, he was invited to manage Drury Lane; he resigned when Whitbread killed himself in 1815, and in 1816 he reopened the English Opera House which, among other things, was the site of the first performance of a play based on *Frankenstein* in 1823.

As the Piece is now acting, it may be thought presumptuous in me to speak of the Actors: yet how can I abstain, feeling, as I do, Mrs. Glover's powerful assistance, and knowing the circumstances under which she consented to act Alhadra? A time will come, when without painfully oppressing her feelings, I may speak of this more fully. To Miss Smith I have an equal, though different acknowledgement to make, namely, for her acceptance of a character not fully developed, and quite inadequate to her extraordinary powers. She enlivened and supported many passages, which (though not perhaps wholly uninteresting in the closet) would but for her have hung heavy on the ears of a Theatrical Audience. And in speaking the Epilogue, a composition which (I fear) my hurry will hardly excuse, and which, as unworthy of her name, is here omitted, she made a sacrifice, which only her established character with all judges of Tragic action, could have rendered compatible with her duty to herself. To Mr. De Camp's judgement and full conception of Isidore; to Mr. Pope's accurate representation of the partial, yet honourable Father; to Mr. Elliston's energy in the character of Alvar, and who in more than one instance *gave* it beauties and striking points, which not only delighted but surprized me; and to Mr. Rae, to whose zeal, and unwearied study of his part I am not less indebted as a *Man*, than to his impassioned realization of Ordonio, as an *Author*;——to these, and to all concerned with the bringing out of the Play, I can address but one word—THANKS!—but that word is uttered sincerely! and to persons constantly before the eye of the Public, a public acknowledgement becomes appropriate, and a duty.

I defer all answers to the different criticisms on the Piece to an Essay, which I am about to publish immediately, on Dramatic Poetry, relatively to the present State of the Metropolitan Theatres.[8]

From the necessity of hastening the Publication I was obliged to send the Manuscript intended for the Stage: which is the sole cause of the number of directions printed in italics.

S. T. Coleridge.

PROLOGUE. By C. Lamb[9]
(Spoken by Mr. Carr)

There are, I am told, who sharply criticise
Our modern theatres' unwieldy size.[10]
We players shall scarce plead guilty to that charge,
Who think a house can never be too large:
Griev'd when a rant, that's worth a nation's ear,
Shakes some prescrib'd Lyceum's petty sphere;[11]
And pleased to mark the grin from space to space
Spread epidemic o'er a town's broad face.—
O might old Betterton or Booth return
To view our structures from their silent urn,   10

Works of Samuel Taylor Coleridge (Princeton University Press, 1987), 1: 132–136, 479–597.

9 *C. LAMB*: Charles Lamb (1775–1834), best known as an essayist (his "Elia" essays appeared in the *London Magazine* in the 1820s). Lamb had met Coleridge at school at Christ's Hospital, where he also met Hunt. He was thus a friend of both the Lake Poets and Hunt's Cockney School. He had written his own tragedy, *John Woodvil*, in 1802, and a farce, *Mr. H—*, which had failed at Drury Lane in 1806. His prologue was originally written for the opening of the new Drury Lane Theatre in 1813 but was rejected; a piece by Byron was finally adopted.

10 *unwieldy size*: The size of the two major theaters in London was often criticized, with the playwright Richard Cumberland, for example, claiming that they had become "theaters for spectators rather than playhouses for hearers." Benjamin Wyatt's Drury Lane of 1812 held about 3,100 people, while the 1809 Covent Garden designed by Robert Smirke held about 3,000 not counting standing room.

11 *Lyceum's petty sphere*: From 1809, when Drury Lane burned to the ground, until 1812 when the new theater was opened, the Drury Lane troupe acted at the smaller Lyceum Theatre on the Strand (later the English Opera House).

---

8 *Essay … on Dramatic Poetry … State of the Metropolitan Theatres*: Coleridge evidently did not publish such an essay, but he did make it part of a lecture given around the time of *Remorse*'s staging. See Coleridge's "Desultory Remarks on the Stage, & the present state of the Higher Drama," part of his 1808 *Lectures on Principles of Poetry*, his *Lectures on Belle Lettres* of 1812–13, and his *Lectures on Shakespeare & Education* of 1813, all in Samuel Taylor Coleridge, *Lectures 1808–1819 On Literature*, ed. R.A. Foakes, 2 vols., No. 5 in *The Collected*

Could Quin[12] come stalking from Elysian glades,[13]
Or Garrick[14] get a day-rule[15] from the shades—
Where now, perhaps, in mirth which Spirits approve,
He imitates the ways of men above,
And apes the actions of our upper coast,
As in his days of flesh he play'd the ghost:—[16]
How might they bless our ampler scope to please,
And hate their own old shrunk up audiences.—
Their houses yet were palaces to those,

Which Ben[17] and Fletcher[18] for their triumphs chose.   20
Shakspeare, who wish'd a kingdom for a stage,
Like giant pent in disproportion'd cage,
Mourn'd his contracted strengths and crippled rage.
He who could tame his vast ambition down
To please some scatter'd gleanings of a town,
And, if some hundred auditors supplied
Their meagre meed of claps, was satisfied,
How had he felt, when that dread curse of Lear's
Had burst tremendous on a thousand ears,
While deep-struck wonder from applauding bands   30
Return'd the tribute of as many hands!
Rude were his guests; he never made his bow
To such an audience as salutes us now.
He lack'd the balm of labor, female praise.
Few Ladies in his time frequented plays,[19]
Or came to see a youth with aukward art
And shrill sharp pipe burlesque the woman's part.
The very use, since so essential grown,
Of painted scenes, was to his stage unknown.[20]

---

[12] *Betterton or Booth ... Quin*: Along with Garrick, mentioned below, these were the great actors of the Restoration and eighteenth-century stage. Thomas Betterton (1635?–1710) joined Davenant's company (the Duke's men) in 1661 and rose to become its leading actor. Praised by Addison, Cibber, Dryden, and Pepys, he was the key actor of the Restoration. Barton Booth (1681–1733) was first rejected by Betterton when he applied for a job, but after a stint in Ireland, he joined Betterton's company at Lincoln Inn Fields in 1700. His performance in 1713 as Cato in Addison's tragedy of the same name was perhaps the highpoint in his career. James Quin (1693–1766) began his acting career in Dublin, moving to Drury Lane in 1714 or 1715. He played at the various major theaters, including at the opening night of the Covent Garden Theatre 7 December 1732. He was considered the greatest actor of his day, until Garrick arrived on the stage.

[13] *Elysian glades*: Elysium is the paradise to which heroes in classical myth are admitted after their death.

[14] *Garrick*: David Garrick (1717–1779), considered the greatest actor of the eighteenth century, was also a playwright (*The Clandestine Marriage*, written with George Colman the Elder in 1766, was his most successful piece) and the manager of Drury Lane Theatre (1747–76). He was the key figure defining the stage of the middle part of the eighteenth century, arguing, among other things, for Shakespeare over popular entertainments such as pantomimes.

[15] *day-rule*: a court order allowing a prisoner to leave his prison for a day.

[16] *play'd the ghost*: The reference here is unclear, since none of Garrick's major roles was a ghostly one. Perhaps his most famous role, however, was as Hamlet, and there is a portrait of him by Zoffany as Hamlet with his father's ghost.

[17] *Ben*: Ben Jonson (1572/3–1637), author of such great comedies as *Volpone* (1605–6) and *The Alchemist* (1610) as well as a large number of court masques, and John Fletcher (1579–1625), author of such plays as *The Faithful Shepherdess* (1610), sometime collaborator with Shakespeare and best known for his collaborations with Francis Beaumont, together with Shakespeare formed the triumvirate of great Renaissance playwrights who defined the English dramatic repertoire into the nineteenth century.

[18] *Fletcher*: John Fletcher (1579–1625), who with Francis Beaumont (1585?–1616) collaboratively produced *The Woman Hater* (1606); *Philaster* (1608–10); *The Coxcombe* (1608–10); *The Maide's Tragedy* (1608–11); *The Captaine* (1609–12); *A King and No King* (1611); *Cupid's Revenge* (1611); *The Scornful Ladie* (1613–17); *Love's Pilgrimage* (1616?); and *The Noble Gentleman* (1625?).

[19] *Few Ladies ... frequented plays*: a reference to the notion that few women attended the Renaissance theater where, for example, women were not allowed to act on stage (as the next lines indicate); women had become an increasingly important part of the theater audience in the eighteenth century.

[20] *painted scenes ... unknown*: a reference to the fact that Shakespeare's Globe Theatre did not use moveable

The air-blest castle, round whose wholesome crest,   40
The martlet,[21] guest of summer, chose her nest—
The forest walks of Arden's fair domain,
Where Jaques fed his solitary vein—[22]
No pencil's aid as yet had dared supply,
Seen only by the intellectual eye.[23]
Those scenic helps, denied to Shakspeare's page,
Our Author owes to a more liberal age.
Nor pomp nor circumstance are wanting here;
'Tis for himself alone that he must fear.
Yet shall remembrance cherish the just pride,   50
That (be the laurel[24] granted or denied)
He first essay'd in this distinguish'd fane,[25]
Severer muses and a tragic strain.

DRAMATIS PERSONAE

Marquis Valdez, Father to the two brothers, and Donna Teresa's Guardian	Mr. Pope
Don Alvar, The eldest son	Mr. Elliston
Don Ordonio, The youngest son	Mr. Rae
Monviedro, A Dominican and Inquisitor	Mr. Powell
Zulimez, The faithful attendant on Alvar	Mr. Crooke
Isidore, A Moresco Captain, ostensibly a Christian	Mr. De Camp
Familiars of the Inquisition	
Naomi	Mr. Wallack
Moors and Servants, &c.	
Donna Teresa, An Orphan Heiress	Miss Smith
Alhadra, Wife to Isidore	Mrs. Glover

Time: *The reign of Philip II, just, at the close of the civil wars against the Moors, and during the heat of the persecution which raged against them, shortly after the edict which forbade the wearing of Moresco apparel under pain of Death.*[26]

---

21 *martlet*: a swift. These lines allude to William Shakespeare, *Macbeth* I.iv.1–10.

22 *Arden ... Jaques*: allusions to Shakespeare's *As You Like It*.

23 *Seen only by the intellectual eye*: In his "On the Tragedies of Shakspeare, Considered with Reference to their Fitness for Stage Representation," Lamb famously argued that Shakespeare's plays could be better appreciated by the reader than by a theatergoer. Here, however, he offers a more ambivalent evaluation of stage scenery and effect.

24 *laurel*: Classical poets of distinction were crowned with laurel; thus, the title "poet laureate."

25 *fane*: a temple.

painted sets such as were used increasingly in London's theaters after the Restoration.

26 *The reign of Philip II ... Moors ... forbade the wearing of Moresco apparel under pain of Death*: The play is set during the reign (1556–98) of Philip II, son of Charles V and at the time of his ascension the most powerful ruler in Europe, controlling not only Spain but also parts of Italy and France, colonies in Mexico and Peru, and, most importantly for the play, the Low Countries; students of English literature most likely know him as the husband of Mary Tudor (his second wife) and as the king who sent the Spanish Armada against England after Elizabeth refused to marry him upon Mary's death. The Moors against whom Philip is fighting were descendants of the followers of Islam who had begun a conquest of the Spanish peninsula in 711. The last Islamic kingdom, Granada, was not captured by Ferdinand and Isabella until 1492. While Coleridge uses Moor and Moresco interchangeably to refer to the remaining descendants of the Islamic invaders, the Morescos or Moriscos (earlier known as the Mudejars) were, more precisely, one of several Islamic minorities on the peninsula. The conversion of the Morescos had begun with the fall of Granada, but Philip was not satisfied with its pace. In 1567, it was decreed that the Morescos could not use their Muslim names, speak the Arabic language, or wear Muslim dress. In 1568, there was a Moresco uprising that was put down brutally over the next two years, so the play—"*at the close of the civil wars against the Moors*"—most likely takes place in 1569.

Philip II was also engaged in putting down dissent in the Low Countries (the "Belgic states" below), where he attempted to maintain Spanish control and Catholicism against demands for autonomy and the growth of Protestantism. His attempt to repress dissent through the brutal tactics of the Duke de Alba, who went to the Netherlands in 1567, led to open revolt and an Eighty Years War (1568–1648) that would

Act I

Scene I: *The Sea Shore on the Coast of Granada.*
Don Alvar, wrapt in a Boat Cloak, and Zulimez
(a Moresco), both as just landed.

Zulimez. No sound, no face of joy to welcome us!
Alvar. My faithful Zulimez, for one brief moment
  Let me forget my anguish and their crimes.
  If aught on earth demand an unmix'd feeling,
  'Tis surely this—after long years of exile,
  To step forth on firm land, and gazing round us,
  To hail at once our country, and our birth place.
  Hail, Spain! Granada, hail! once more I press
  Thy sands with filial awe, land of my fathers!
Zul. Then claim your rights in it! O, revered Don Alvar, 10
  Yet, yet give up your all too gentle purpose.
  It is too hazardous! reveal yourself,
  And let the guilty meet the doom of guilt!
Alv. Remember, Zulimez! I am his brother,
  Injur'd indeed! O deeply injur'd! yet
  Ordonio's brother.
Zul.   Nobly minded Alvar!
  This sure but gives his guilt a blacker die.
Alv. The more behoves it, I should rouse within him
  REMORSE! that I should save him from himself.
Zul. REMORSE is as the heart in which it grows: 20
  If that be gentle, it drops balmy dews
  Of true repentance; but if proud and gloomy,
  It is a poison-tree, that pierced to the inmost
  Weeps only tears of poison!
Alv.   And of a brother,
  Dare I hold this, unprov'd? nor make one effort
  To save him?—Hear me, friend! I have yet to tell
    thee,
  That this same life, which he conspir'd to take,
  Himself once rescued from the angry flood,
  And at the imminent hazard of his own.
  Add too my oath—
Zul.   You have thrice told already 30

seriously weaken the Spanish empire. These events also
form the background for two plays Coleridge would
have known: Schiller's *Don Carlos* (Don Carlos was
Philip's son) and Goethe's *Egmont*, which depicts the
beginnings of the revolt in the Low Countries.

The year of absence and of secrecy,
To which a forced oath bound you; if in truth
A suborn'd murderer have the power to dictate
A binding oath.
Alv.   My long captivity
Left me no choice: the very *Wish* too languish'd
With the fond *Hope*, that nurs'd it; the sick babe
Droop'd at the bosom of its famish'd mother.
But (more than all) Teresa's perfidy;[27]
The assassin's strong assurance, when no interest,
No motive could have tempted him to falsehood; 40
In the first pangs of his awaken'd conscience,
When with abhorrence of his own black purpose
The murderous weapon, pointed at my breast,
Fell from his palsied hand—
Zul.   Heavy presumption!
Alv. It weigh'd not with me—Hark! I will tell thee all.
  As we pass'd by, I bade thee mark the base
  Of yonder Cliff—
Zul.   That rocky seat you mean,
  Shaped by the billows?—
Alv.   There Teresa met me
  The morning of the day of my departure.
  We were alone: the purple hue of dawn, 50
  Fell from the kindling east aslant upon us,
  And blending with the blushes on her cheek
  Suffus'd the tear-drops there with rosy light.
  There seem'd a glory round us, and Teresa
  The angel of the vision!
  (Then with agitation). Had'st thou seen
  How in each motion her most innocent soul
  Beam'd forth and brighten'd, thou thyself would'st
    tell me,
  Guilt is a thing impossible in her!
  She must be innocent!
Zul. (With a sigh).   Proceed, my Lord!
Alv. A portrait which she had procur'd by stealth, 60
  (For even then it seems her heart foreboded
  Or knew Ordonio's moody rivalry)
  A portrait of herself with thrilling hand
  She tied around my neck, conjuring me
  With earnest prayers, that I would keep it sacred
  To my own knowledge: nor did she desist,

27 *Teresa's perfidy*: The Larpent version cuts this suggestion of Alvar's suspicions of Teresa.

Till she had won a solemn promise from me,
That (save my own) no eye should e'er behold it
Till my return. Yet this the assassin knew,
Knew that which none but she could have disclos'd. 70
Zul. A damning proof!
Alv.   My own life wearied me!
And but for the imperative Voice within
With mine own hand I had thrown off the burthen.
That Voice, which quell'd me, calm'd me: and I sought
The Belgic states:[28] there join'd the better cause;
And there too fought as one that courted death!
Wounded, I fell among the dead and dying,
In death-like trance: a long imprisonment follow'd.
The fulness of my anguish by degrees
Waned to a meditative melancholy;   80
And still the more I mus'd, my soul became
More doubtful, more perplex'd: and still *Teresa*—
Night after night, she visited my sleep,
Now as a saintly sufferer, wan and tearful,
Now as a saint in glory beckoning to me!
Yes, still as in contempt of proof and reason,
I cherish the fond faith that she is guiltless!
Hear then my fix'd resolve: I'll linger here
In the disguise of a Moresco chieftain.—
The Moorish robes?—
Zul.   All, all are in the sea-cave, 90
Some furlong[29] hence. I bade our mariners
Secrete the boat there.
Alv.   Above all, the picture
Of the assassination—
Zul.   Be assur'd
That it remains uninjur'd.
Alv.   Thus disguised
I will first seek to meet Ordonio's—*wife!*
If possible, alone too. This was her wonted walk,
And this the hour; her words, her very looks
Will acquit her or convict.
Zul. Will they not know you?
Alv. With your aid, friend, I shall unfearingly   100
Trust the disguise; and as to my complexion,
My long imprisonment, the scanty food,
This scar,—and toil beneath a burning sun,

Have done already half the business for us.
Add too my youth, when last we saw each other.
Manhood has swoln my chest, and taught my voice
A hoarser note—Besides, they think me dead:
And what the mind believes impossible,
The bodily sense is slow to recognize.
Zul. 'Tis yours, sir, to command, mine to obey.   110
Now to the cave beneath the vaulted rock,
Where having shap'd you to a Moorish chieftain,
I'll seek our mariners; and in the dusk
Transport whate'er we need to the small dell
In the Alpuxarras[30]—there where Zagri liv'd.
Alv. I know it well: it is the obscurest haunt
Of all the mountains— *(Both stand listening).*
                              Voices at a distance!
Let us away! *(Exeunt).*

Scene II: *The Sea-Shore, but within view of the Castle.*
Enter Teresa and Valdez.

Teresa. I hold Ordonio dear; he is your son
And Alvar's brother.
Valdez.   Love him for himself,
Nor make the living wretched for the dead.
Ter. I mourn that you should plead in vain, Lord
    Valdez,
But heaven hath heard my vow, and I remain
Faithful to Alvar, be he dead or living.
Val. Heaven knows with what delight I saw your loves,
And could my heart's blood give him back to thee,
I would die smiling. But these are idle thoughts!
Thy dying father comes upon my soul   10
With that same look, with which he gave thee to me;
I held thee in my arms a powerless babe,
While thy poor mother with a mute entreaty
Fixed her faint eyes on mine. Ah not for this,
That I should let thee feed thy soul with gloom,
And with slow anguish wear away thy life,
The victim of a useless constancy.
I must not see thee wretched.
Ter.   There are woes
Ill bartered for the garishness of joy!   20

---

28 *Belgic states*: See note 27.
29 *furlong*: a length of 220 yards, or one eighth of a stat-
    ute mile.

30 *Alpuxarras*: Las Alpujarras is a mountainous region in
    southern Spain. After the fall of the Moslem kingdom
    of Granada in 1492, it was a refuge for the Morescos.

If it be wretched with an untired eye
To watch those skiey tints, and this green ocean;
Or in the sultry hour beneath some rock,
My hair dishevell'd by the pleasant sea breeze,
To shape sweet visions, and live o'er again
All past hours of delight! If it be wretched
To watch some bark, and fancy Alvar there,
To go through each minutest circumstance
Of the blest meeting; and to frame adventures
Most terrible and strange, and hear *him* tell them;[31] 30
(As once I knew a crazy Moorish maid,
Who drest her in her buried lover's cloaths,
And o'er the smooth spring in the mountain cleft
Hung with her lute, and play'd the self same tune
He used to play, and listened to the shadow
Herself had made)—if this be wretchedness,
And if indeed it be a wretched thing
To trick out mine own death bed, and imagine
That I had died, died just ere his return!
Then see him listening to my constancy, 40
Or hover round, as he at midnight oft
Sits on my grave and gazes at the moon;
Or haply in some more fantastic mood,
To be in Paradise, and with choice flowers
Build up a bower where he and I might dwell,
And there to wait his coming! O my sire!
My Alvar's sire! if this be wretchedness
That eats away the life, what were it, think you,
If in a most assured reality
He should return, and see a brother's infant 50
Smile at him from *my* arms?
  (*Clasping her forehead*).   Oh what a thought!
Val. A thought? even so! mere thought! an empty
    thought.
The very week he promised his return——
Ter. (Abruptly). Was it not then a busy joy? to see him,
After those three years travels! we had no fears—
The frequent tidings, the ne'er failing letter,
Almost endear'd his absence! Yet the gladness,
The tumult of our joy! What then if now——

Val. O power of youth to feed on pleasant thoughts,
    Spite of conviction! I am old and heartless! 60
    Yes, I am old—I have no pleasant fancies,
    Hectic and unrefresh'd with rest—
Ter. (With great tenderness).   My father!
Val. The sober truth is all too much for me!
    I see no sail which brings not to my mind
    The home-bound bark[32] in which my son was
        captur'd
    By the Algerine[33]—to perish with his captors!
Ter. Oh no! he did not!
Val.   Captur'd in sight of land!
    From yon hill point, nay, from our castle watch tower
    We might have seen——
Ter.   His capture, not his death.
Val. Alas! how aptly thou forgett'st a tale 70
    Thou ne'er didst wish to learn! my brave Ordonio
    Saw both the pirate and his prize go down,
    In the same storm that baffled his own valor,
    And thus twice snatch'd a brother from his hopes:
    Gallant Ordonio! *(Pauses, then tenderly).* O
        beloved Teresa,
    Would'st thou best prove thy faith to generous Alvar,
    And most delight his spirit, go thou, make
    His brother happy, make his aged father
    Sink to the grave in joy.
Ter.   For mercy's sake
    Press me no more. I have no power to love him. 80
    His proud forbidding eye, and his dark brow,
    Chill me like dew damps of the unwholesome night:
    My love, a timorous and tender flower,
    Closes beneath his touch.
Val.   You wrong him, maiden!
    You wrong him, by my soul! Nor was it well
    To character by such unkindly phrases
    The stir and workings of that love for you
    Which he has toil'd to smother. 'Twas not well,
    Nor is it grateful in you to forget
    His wounds and perilous voyages, and how 90
    With an heroic fearlessness of danger
    He roam'd the coast of Afric for your Alvar.
    It was not well—You have moved me even to tears.

---

31 Coleridge's note: "Here Valdez bends back, and smiles
    at her wildness: which Teresa noticing checks her en-
    thusiasm, and in a soothing half-playful tone and man-
    ner apologizes for her fancy by the little tale in the
    parenthesis."

---

32 *bark*: a ship.
33 *Algerine*: a ship from Algeria, hostile to Spain and
    known for piracy.

Ter. Oh pardon me, Lord Valdez! pardon me!
　It was a foolish and ungrateful speech,
　A most ungrateful speech! But I am hurried
　Beyond myself, if I but hear of one
　Who aims to rival Alvar. Were we not
　Born in one day, like twins of the same parent?
　Nursed in one cradle? Pardon me, my father!　　100
　A six years' absence is a heavy thing,
　Yet still the hope survives——
Val. (Looking forwards).　　Hush! 'tis Monviedro.
Ter. The Inquisitor![34] on what new scent of blood?
(Enter Monviedro with Alhadra).
Monviedro (Having first made his obeisance to Valdez
　and Teresa).
　Peace and the truth be with you! Good my Lord,
　My present need is with your son. *(Looking forward).*
　We have hit the time. Here comes he! Yes, 'tis he.
(Enter from the opposite side Don Ordonio).
　My Lord Ordonio, this Moresco woman
　(Alhadra is her name) asks audience of you.
Ordonio. Hail, reverend father! what may be the
　　business?
Mon. My lord, on strong suspicion of relapse　　110
　To his false creed, so recently abjured,
　The secret servants of the inquisition
　Have seized her husband, and at my command
　To the supreme tribunal would have led him,
　But that he made appeal to you, my lord,
　As surety for his soundness in the faith.
　Tho' lessen'd by experience what small trust
　The asseverations of these Moors deserve,
　Yet still the deference to Ordonio's name,
　Nor less the wish to prove, with what high honor　　120
　The Holy Church regards her faithful soldiers,
　Thus far prevailed with me that——
Ord.　　　　　　　　Reverend father,
　I am much beholden to your high opinion,
　Which so o'erprizes my light services. *(Then to*
　　Alhadra).
　I would that I could serve you; but in truth
　Your face is new to me.
Mon.　　　　　　My mind foretold me,

That such would be the event. In truth, Lord Valdez,
　'Twas little probable, that Don Ordonio,
　That your illustrious son, who fought so bravely
　Some four years since to quell these rebel Moors,　　130
　Should prove the patron of this infidel!
　The guarantee of a Moresco's faith!
　Now I return.
Alhadra.　　　　My Lord, my husband's name
　Is Isidore. *(Ordonio starts).*—You may remember it:
　Three years ago, three years this very week,
　You left him at Almeria.[35]
Mon.　　　　　　　　Palpably false!
　This very week, three years ago, my lord,
　(You needs must recollect it by your wound)
　You were at sea, and there engaged the pirates,
　The murderers doubtless of your brother Alvar![36]　　140
(Teresa looks at Monviedro with disgust and horror.
Ordonio's appearance to be collected from what follows).
Mon. (To Valdez and pointing at Ordonio).
　What is he ill, my Lord? how strange he looks!
Val. (Angrily). You started on him too abruptly, father!
　The fate of one, on whom, you know, he doted.
Ord. (Starting as in sudden agitation).
　O Heavens! *I?—I doted? (Then recovering himself).*
　　　　　　　　　　　Yes! I *doted* on him.
(Ordonio walks to the end of the stage, Valdez follows,
soothing him).
Ter. (Her eye following Ordonio).
　I do not, can not, love him. Is my heart hard?
　Is my heart hard? that even now the thought
　Should force itself upon me?—Yet I feel it!
Mon. The drops did start and stand upon his forehead!
　I will return. In very truth, I grieve
　To have been the occasion. Ho! attend me, woman!　　150
Alh. (To Teresa). O gentle lady! make the father stay,
　Until my lord recover. I am sure,
　That he will say, he is my husband's friend.

34　*Inquisitor*: an officer of the Inquisition or the Holy
　Office, a religious tribunal charged with the suppres-
　sion of heresy and the punishment of heretics.

35　*Almeria*: a mountainous province in southeast Spain
　contiguous to Granada.
36　*Alvar*: Following line 140, the Larpent version has the
　following lines:
　　For that they had destroy'd him ere the encounter
　　Heaven gave a proof in the swift retribution
　　Which met the assassins, when tho' from yr. vengeance
　　Snatch'd by the Storm, they founder'd in yr. sight.

Ter. Stay, father! stay! my lord will soon recover.
Ord. (As they return, to Valdez). Strange, that this Monviedro
  Should have the power so to distemper me!
Val. Nay, 'twas an amiable weakness, son!
Mon. My lord, I truly grieve——
Ord.   Tut! name it not.
  A sudden seizure, father! think not of it.
  As to this woman's husband, I *do* know him.   160
  I know him well, and that he *is* a christian.
Mon. I hope, my lord, your merely human pity
  Doth not prevail——
Ord. 'Tis certain that he *was* a catholic;
  What changes may have happen'd in three years,
  I can not say; but grant me this, good father:
  Myself I'll sift him: if I find him sound,
  You'll grant me your authority and name
  To liberate his house.
Mon.   Your zeal, my lord,
  And your late merits in this holy warfare   170
  Would authorize an ampler trust—you have it.
Ord. I will attend you home within an hour.[37]
Val. Meantime return with us and take refreshment.[38]
Alh. Not till my husband's free! I may not do it.
  I will stay here.
Ter. (Aside).   Who is this Isidore?
Val.   Daughter![39]
Ter. With your permission, my dear lord,
  I'll loiter yet awhile t'enjoy the sea breeze.
(Exeunt Valdez, Monviedro and Ordonio).
Alh. Hah! there he goes! a bitter curse go with him,
  A scathing curse!
(Then as if recollecting herself, and with a timid look)
             You hate him, don't you, lady?
Ter. (Perceiving that Alhadra is conscious she has spoken imprudently).
  Oh fear not me! *my* heart is sad for you.   180
Alh. These fell inquisitors! these sons of blood!
  As I came on, his face so madden'd me,

That ever and anon I clutch'd my dagger
And half unsheath'd it——
Ter.   Be more calm, I pray you.
Alh. And as he walk'd along the narrow path
  Close by the mountain's edge, my soul grew eager;
  'Twas with hard toil I made myself remember
  That his Familiars[40] held my babes and husband.
  To have leapt upon him with a tyger's plunge,
  And hurl'd him down the rugged precipice,   190
  O, it had been most sweet!
Ter.   Hush! hush for shame!
  Where is your woman's heart?
Alh.   O gentle lady!
  You have no skill to guess my many wrongs,
  Many and strange. Besides, *(Ironically)* I am a christian,
  And christians never pardon—'tis their faith!
Ter. Shame fall on those who so have shewn it to thee.
Alh. I know that man; 'tis well he knows not me.
  Five years ago (and he was the prime agent)
  Five years ago the holy brethren seized me.
Ter. What might your crime be?
Alh.   I was a Moresco!   200
  They cast me, then a young and nursing mother,
  Into a dungeon of their prison house,
  Where was no bed, no fire, no ray of light,
  No touch, no sound of comfort! The black air,
  It was a toil to breathe it! when the door,
  Slow opening at the appointed hour, disclosed
  One human countenance, the lamp's red flame
  Cower'd as it enter'd and at once sunk down.
  Oh miserable! by that lamp to see
  My infant quarrelling with the coarse hard bread   210
  Brought daily: for the little wretch was sickly—
  My rage had dried away its natural food.[41]
  In darkness I remain'd, the dull Bell counting,
  Which haply told me, that the all-cheering sun
  Was rising on my garden. When I dozed,
  My infant's moanings mingled with my slumbers
  And waked me.—If you were a mother, lady,
  I should scarce dare to tell you, that its noises

---

37 *I … hour*: The Larpent version adds a stage direction: "*to Alhadra.*"

38 *Meantime … refreshment*: The Larpent version gives this speech to Ordonio.

39 *Daughter*: The Larpent version adds a stage direction: "*offering to lead her out.*"

40 *Familiars*: officers of the Inquisition employed in arresting and imprisoning the accused.

41 *Brought … food*: Lines 211–12 are cut in the Larpent version. "Natural food" refers to mother's milk.

And peevish cries so fretted on my brain
That I have struck the innocent babe in anger.   220
Ter. O Heaven! it is too horrible to hear.
Alh. What was it then to suffer? 'Tis most right
That such as you should hear it.—Know you not,
What nature makes you mourn, she bids you heal?
Great Evils ask great Passions to redress them,
And Whirlwinds fitliest scatter Pestilence.
Ter. You were at length released?
Alh.   Yes, at length
I saw the blessed arch of the whole heaven!
'Twas the first time my infant smiled. No more—
For if I dwell upon that moment, Lady,   230
A trance comes on which makes me o'er again
All I then was—my knees hang loose and drag,
And my lip falls with such an idiot laugh,
That you would start and shudder!
Ter.   But your husband——
Alh. A month's imprisonment would kill him, Lady.
Ter. Alas, poor man!
Alh.   He hath a lion's courage,
Fearless in act, but feeble in endurance;
Unfit for boisterous times, with gentle heart
He worships nature in the hill and valley,
Not knowing what he loves, but loves it all—   240
(Enter Alvar disguised as a Moresco, and in Moorish garments).
Ter.[42] Know you that stately Moor?
Alh.   I know him not:
But doubt not he is some Moresco chieftain,
Who hides himself among the Alpuxarras.
Ter. The Alpuxarras? Does he know his danger,
So near this seat?
Alh.   He wears the Moorish robes too,
As in defiance of the royal edict.
(Alhadra advances to Alvar, who has walked to the back of the stage near the rocks. Teresa drops her veil).
Alh. Gallant Moresco! An inquisitor,
Monviedro, of known hatred to our race——
Alv. (Interrupting her).[43] You have mistaken me. I
am a christian.

Alh.[44] He deems, that we are plotting to ensnare him: 250
Speak to him, Lady—none can hear *you* speak,
And not believe you innocent of guile.[45]
Ter. If ought enforce you to concealment, Sir—
Alh. He trembles strangely.
(Alvar sinks down and hides his face in his robe).
Ter.   See, we have disturbed him.
(Approaches nearer to him).
I pray you, think us friends—uncowl your face,
For you seem faint, and the night-breeze blows
     healing.
I pray you, think us friends!
Alv. (Raising his head).   Calm, very calm!
'Tis all too tranquil for reality!
And she spoke to me with her innocent voice,
That voice, that innocent voice! She is no traitress![46]   260
Ter. (Haughtily to Alhadra). Let us retire.
(They advance to the front of the Stage).[47]
Alh. (With scorn).   He is indeed a Christian.
Alv. (Aside). She deems me dead, yet wears no
     mourning garment.
Why should my brother's—wife—wear mourning
     garments?[48]
(To Teresa). Your pardon, noble dame! that I
     disturb'd you:
I had just started from a frightful dream.
Ter. Dreams tell but of the past, and yet, 'tis said,
They prophesy—
Alv.   The Past lives o'er again
In its effects, and to the guilty spirit
The ever frowning Present is its image.
Ter. Traitress! *(Then aside).* What sudden spell   270
     o'ermasters me?
Why seeks he me, shunning the Moorish woman.

---

42 *Ter.*: The Larpent version adds a stage direction: "*Observing him.*"
43 *Interrupting her.* The Larpent version replaces this with "*advancing as if to pass them.*"
44 *Alh.*: The Larpent version adds a stage direction: "*To Teresa.*"
45 *guile*: The Larpent version adds a stage direction: "*Alvar on hearing this turns around.*"
46 *traitress*: The Larpent version adds the following lines after line 260:
     It was a dream, a Phantom of my sleep!
     A lying dream! *(Starts up & abruptly addresses her).*
     Teresa are you not wedded?
47 *They … Stage*: The Larpent version substitutes "*They advance, as if to retire.*"
48 *Why … garments*: The Larpent version cuts this line.

(Teresa looks round uneasily, but gradually becomes attentive as Alvar proceeds in the next speech).

Alv. I dreamt I had a friend, on whom I leant
    With blindest trust, and a betrothed maid,
    Whom I was wont to call not mine, but me:
    For mine own self seem'd nothing, lacking her.
    This maid so idolized that trusted friend
    Dishonour'd in my absence, soul and body!
    Fear, following guilt, tempted to blacker guilt,
    And murderers were suborned against my life.
    But by my looks, and most impassion'd words,   280
    I roused the virtues that are dead in no man,
    Even in the assassins' hearts! they made their terms,
    And thank'd me for redeeming them from murder.
Alh. You are lost in thought: hear him no more,
    sweet Lady!
Ter. From morn to night I am myself a dreamer,
    And slight things bring on me the idle mood!
    Well sir, what happen'd then?
Alv.   On a rude rock,
    A rock, methought, fast by a grove of firs,
    Whose threaddy[49] leaves to the low-breathing gale
    Made a soft sound most like the distant ocean,   290
    I stay'd, as though the hour of death were pass'd,
    And I were sitting in the world of spirits—
    For all things seem'd unreal! There I sate—
    The dews fell clammy, and the night descended,
    Black, sultry, close! and ere the midnight hour
    A storm came on, mingling all sounds of fear,
    That woods, and sky, and mountains, seem'd one
      havock.
    The second flash of lightning shew'd a tree
    Hard by me, newly scath'd. I rose tumultuous:
    My soul work'd high, I bar'd my head to the storm,   300
    And with loud voice and clamorous agony
    Kneeling I pray'd to the great spirit, that made me,
    Prayed, that REMORSE might fasten on their
      hearts,
    And cling with poisonous tooth, inextricable
    As the gor'd lion's *bite!*
Ter. (Shuddering).   A fearful curse!
Alh. (Fiercely). But dreamt you not that you return'd
    and kill'd them?
    Dreamt you of no revenge?

---

49 *threaddy*: for thready; bearing thread-like fibres.

Alv. (His voice trembling, and in tones of deep distress).
                         She would have died,
    Died in her guilt—perchance by her own hands!
    And bending o'er her self-inflicted wounds,
    I might have met the evil glance of frenzy,   310
    And leapt myself into an unblest grave!
    I pray'd for the punishment, that cleanses hearts:
    For still I lov'd her!
Alh.   And you dreamt all this?
Ter. My soul is full of visions all as wild!
Alh. There is no room in this heart for puling love tales.
Ter. (Lifts up her veil, and advances to Alvar).
    Stranger, farewell! I guess not, who you are,
    Nor why you so address'd your tale to me.
    Your mien is noble, and I own, perplex'd me
    With obscure memory of something past,
    Which still escaped my efforts, or presented   320
    Tricks of a fancy pampered with long wishing.
    If, as it sometimes happens, our rude startling,
    Whilst your full heart was shaping out its dream,
    Drove you to this, your not ungentle wildness,
    You have my sympathy, and so farewell!
    But if some undiscover'd wrongs oppress you,
    And you need strength to drag them into light,
    The generous Valdez, and my Lord Ordonio,
    Have arm and will to aid a noble sufferer:—
    Nor shall you want my favourable pleading.   330
(Exeunt Teresa and Alhadra).
Alv. (Alone). 'Tis strange! It can not be! *my* Lord
    Ordonio!
    Her Lord Ordonio! Nay, I will not do it![50]
    I curs'd him once—and one curse is enough!
    How sad she look'd, and pale! but not like guilt—
    And her calm tones—sweet as a song of mercy!
    If the bad spirit retain'd his angel's voice,
    Hell scarce were Hell. And why not innocent?
    Who meant to murder me, might well cheat her?
    But ere she married him, he had stained her honor—
    Ah! there I am hamper'd.[51] What if this were a lie   340
    Fram'd by the assassin? Who should tell it *him*,

---

50 *'Tis ... it*: The Larpent version cuts these lines.
51 *hamper'd*: The Larpent version has "perplex'd" for "hamper'd" and cuts the rest of this line and lines 341–343.

If it were truth? Ordonio would not tell him.
Yet why one lie? all else, I *know*, was truth.

No start, no jealousy of stirring conscience!
And she referr'd to *me*—fondly, methought!
Could she walk here, if she had been a traitress?
Here where we play'd together in our childhood?
Here where we plighted vows? where her cold cheek
Received my last kiss, when with suppress'd feelings
She had fainted in my arms? It can not be,   350
'Tis not in nature! I will die believing,
That I shall meet her where no evil is,
No treachery, no cup dash'd from the lips.
I'll haunt this scene no more! live she in peace!
Her husband—aye her *husband!* May this angel
New mould his canker'd heart! Assist me, heaven!
That I may pray for my poor guilty brother. *(Exit).*

Act II

Scene I: *A wild and mountainous Country.*
Ordonio and Isidore are discovered, supposed
at a little distance from Isidore's house.[52]

Ord. Here we may stop: your house distinct in view,
    Yet we secured from listeners.
Isidore.   Now indeed
    My house! and it looks cheerful as the clusters
    Basking in sunshine on yon vine-clad rock,
    That over brows it! Patron! Friend! Preserver!
    Thrice have you saved my life. Once in the battle
    You gave it me: next rescued me from suicide,
    When for my follies I was made to wander,
    With mouths to feed, and not a morsel for them:
    Now but for you, a dungeon's slimy stones   10
    Had been my bed and pillow.
Ord.   Good Isidore!
    Why this to me? It is enough, you know it.
Isi. A common trick of Gratitude, my lord,
    Seeking to ease her own full heart—
Ord.   Enough!—
    A debt repaid ceases to be a debt.

You have it in your power to serve me greatly.
Isi. And how, my lord? I pray you to name the thing.
    I would climb up an ice-glazed precipice
    To pluck a weed you fancied!
Ord. (With embarrassment and hesitation). Why—
        that—Lady—
Isi. 'Tis now three years, my lord, since last I saw you: 20
    Have you a son, my lord?
Ord.   O miserable— *(Aside).*
    Isidore! you are a man, and know mankind.
    I told you what I wish'd—now for the truth—
    She loved the man, you kill'd.
Isi. (Looking as suddenly alarmed). You jest, my lord?
Ord. And till his death is proved she will not wed me.
Isi. You sport with me, my lord?
Ord.   Come, come! this foolery
    Lives only in thy looks, thy heart disowns it!
Isi. I can bear this, and any thing more grievous
    From you, my lord—but how can I serve you here?
Ord. Why you can utter with a solemn gesture   30
    Oracular sentences of deep no-meaning,
    Wear a quaint garment, make mysterious antics—
Isi. I am dull, my lord! I do not comprehend you.
Ord. In blunt terms, you can play the sorcerer.
    She has no faith in Holy Church, 'tis true,
    Her lover school'd her in some newer nonsense.[53]
    Yet still a tale of spirits works upon her.
    She is a lone enthusiast, sensitive,
    Shivers, and can not keep the tears in her eye:
    And such do love the marvellous too well   40
    Not to believe it. We will wind up her fancy
    With a strange music, that she knows not of—
    With fumes of frankincense,[54] and mummery![55]
    Then leave, as one sure token of his death,
    That portrait, which from off the dead man's neck
    I bade thee take, the trophy of thy conquest.

---

52 *house:* The Larpent version adds that the house *"stands*
    under the brow of a rock cover'd with vines." It also cuts
    lines 1–5.

53 *She … nonsense:* a reference to the fact that Alvar, who
    has gone to fight on the Protestant side in the Neth-
    erlands, has taught Teresa his religious beliefs. These
    lines were cut in the Larpent version, perhaps because
    the theater would know that Larpent would not like
    any reference to religious controversy.

54 *frankincense:* an aromatic gum resin burned as incense.

55 *mummery:* a dumbshow, usually with a ridiculous show
    of ceremony.

Isi. Will that be a sure sign?

Ord.   Beyond suspicion.
  Fondly caressing him, her favour'd lover,
  (By some base spell he had bewitch'd her senses)
  She whisper'd such dark fears of me forsooth,
  As made this heart pour gall into my veins.   50
  And as she coyly bound it round his neck
  She made him promise silence; and now holds
  The secret of the existence of this portrait
  Known only to her lover and herself.
  But I had traced her, stoln unnotic'd on them,
  And unsuspected saw and heard the whole.

Isi. But now I should have cursed the man who told me
  You could ask ought, my lord, and I refuse—
  But this I can not do.

Ord.   Where lies your scruple?   60

Isi. (With stammering). Why—why, my lord!
  You know you told me that the lady loved you,
  Had loved you with *incautious* tenderness;—
  That if the young man, her betrothed husband,
  Returned, yourself, and she, and the honour of both,
  Must perish. Now, tho' with no tenderer scruples
  Than those which being *native* to the heart—
  Than those, my lord, which merely being a man—[56]

*Ord. (Aloud, though to express his contempt he speaks
    in the third person).*
  This Fellow is a *Man!*—he kill'd for Hire
  One whom he knew not, yet has tender scruples!   70

(Then turning to Isidore).
  These doubts, these fears, thy whine, thy
      stammering—
  Pish, fool! thou blunder'st thro' the book of guilt,
  Spelling thy villainy——

Isi.   My lord—my lord—
  I can bear much—yes, very much from you!
  But there's a point, where sufferance is meanness;
  I am no villain—never kill'd for hire—
  My gratitude——

Ord.   O aye—your gratitude!
  'Twas a well sounding word—what have you done
    with it?

Isi. Who proffers his past favours for my virtue—

Ord. (With bitter scorn).   Virtue——

Isi. Tries to o'erreach me—is a very sharper,[57]   80
  And should not speak of gratitude, my lord.
  I knew not 'twas your brother!

Ord. (Alarmed).   And who told you?

Isi. He himself told me.

Ord.   Ha! you talk'd with him?
  And those, the two Morescoes who were with you?

Isi. Both fell in a night brawl at Malaga.[58]

Ord. (In a low voice). My brother—

Isi.   Yes, my lord, I could not tell you!
  I thrust away the thought—it drove me wild.
  But listen to me now—I pray you listen——

Ord. Villain! no more. I'll hear no more of it.

Isi. My lord, it much imports your future safety   90
  That you should hear it.

Ord. (Turning off from Isidore). Am not *I* a Man?
  'Tis as it should be! tut—the deed itself
  Was idle, and these after-pangs still idler!

Isi. We met him in the very place you mentioned,
  Hard by a grove of firs——

Ord.   Enough—enough—

Isi. He fought us valiantly, and wounded all;
  In fine, compell'd a parley—[59]

Ord. (Sighing as if lost in thought). Alvar! brother!

Isi. He offer'd me his purse—

Ord. (With eager suspicion). Yes?

Isi. (Indignantly).   Yes—I spurn'd it.
  He promised us I know not what—in vain!
  Then with a look and voice that overawed me,   100
  He said, What mean you, friends? My life is dear:
  I have a brother and a promised wife,
  Who make life dear to me—and if I fall,
  That brother will roam earth and hell for vengeance.
  There was a likeness in his face to yours—
  I ask'd his brother's name: he said—Ordonio,
  Son of lord Valdez! I had well nigh fainted.
  At length I said (if that indeed *I* said it,
  And that no Spirit made my tongue its organ),
  That woman is dishonor'd by that brother,   110
  And he the man who sent us to destroy you.

---

56 *Now ... man*: For these lines, the Larpent version substitutes: "—now my lord—to be a *man*."

57 *sharper*: a cheat or swindler.

58 *Malaga*: the capital of a province in southern Spain, west of Granada; it was taken by Ferdinand and Isabella in 1487.

59 *parley*: a truce, usually to discuss terms.

He drove a thrust at me in rage. I told him
He wore her portrait round his neck.—He look'd
As he had been made of the rock that propt his
 back—
Aye, just as you look now—only less ghastly!
At length recovering from his trance, he threw
His sword away, and bade us take his life—
It was not worth his keeping.
Ord.   And you kill'd him?
Oh blood hounds! may eternal wrath flame round
 you!
He was the image of the Deity—[60]   120
(A pause).[61]
It seizes me—by Hell I will go on!
What—would'st thou stop, man? thy pale looks
 won't save thee!
(A pause).
Oh cold—cold—cold! shot through with icy cold!
Isi. (Aside). Were he alive he had return'd ere now—
The consequence the same—dead thro' his plotting!
Ord. O this unutterable dying away—here—
This sickness of the heart!
(A pause).
       What if I went
And liv'd in a hollow tomb, and fed on weeds?
Aye! that's the road to Heaven! O fool! fool! fool!
(A pause).
What have I done but that which nature destin'd,   130
Or the blind elements stirr'd up within me?
If good were meant, why were we made these beings?
And if not meant—
Isi.   You are disturb'd, my lord![62]
*Ord. (Starts, looks at him wildly; then, after a pause
 during which his features are forced into a smile).*
A gust of the soul! i'faith, it overset me.
O 'twas all folly—all! idle as laughter!
Now, Isidore! I swear that thou shalt aid me.

---

60   *He was the image of the Deity*—: In the second edition of *Remorse*, Coleridge changes this line to "He was
  his Maker's Image undefac'd!"
61   *A pause*: The Larpent stage direction substitutes "*then
  suddenly pressing his forehead.*"
62   *You … lord*: The Larpent version substitutes "How feel
  you now, my Lord?"

Isi. (In a low voice). I'll perish first!
Ord.   What dost thou mutter of?
Isi. Some of your servants know me, I am certain.
Ord. There's some sense in that scruple; but we'll
 mask you.
Isi. They'll know my gait: but stay! last night I watch'd   140
A stranger near the ruin in the wood,
Who as it seem'd was gathering herbs and wild
 flowers.
I had follow'd him at distance, seen him scale
Its western wall, and by an easier entrance
Stoln after him unnoticed. There I marked,
That mid the chequer work of light and shade
With curious choice he pluck'd no other flowers,
But those on which the moonlight fell: and once
I heard him muttering o'er the plant. A wizard—
Some gaunt slave prowling here for dark   150
 employment.
Ord. Doubtless you question'd him?
Isi.   'Twas my intention,
Having first traced him homeward to his haunt.
But lo! the stern Dominican, whose spies
Lurk every where, already (as it seem'd)
Had given commission to his apt Familiar
To seek and sound the Moor; who now returning
Was by this trusty agent stopp'd midway.
I, dreading fresh suspicion if found near him
In that lone place, again conceal'd myself:
Yet within hearing. So the Moor was question'd,   160
And in *your* name, as lord of this domain.
Proudly he answer'd, Say to the Lord Ordonio,
"He that can bring the dead to life again!"
Ord. A strange reply!
Isi.   Aye, all of him is strange.
He call'd himself a christian, yet he wears
The Moorish robes, as if he courted death.
Ord. Where does this wizard live?
Isi. (Pointing to the distance).   You see that brooklet?
Trace its course backward: thro' a narrow opening
It leads you to the place.
Ord.   How shall I know it?
Isi. You cannot err. It is a small green dell   170
Built all around with high off-sloping hills,
And from its shape our peasants aptly call it
The Giant's Cradle. There's a lake in the midst,
And round its banks tall wood that branches over,

And makes a kind of faery[63] forest grow
Down in the water. At the further end
A puny cataract falls on the lake:
And there, a curious sight! you see its shadow
For ever curling, like a wreath of smoke,
Up thro' the foliage of those faery trees.   180
His cot[64] stands opposite. You cannot miss it.
(Ordonio is retiring: when Isidore calls after him, he turns round to listen).

Some three yards up the hill a mountain ash
Stretches its lower boughs and scarlet clusters
O'er the old thatch.
Ord.   I shall not fail to find it.
(Exeunt Ordonio and Isidore).[65]

Scene II: *The inside of a Cottage, around which*
flowers and plants of various kinds are seen.
Discovers Alvar, Zulimez[66] *and Alhadra,*
as on the point of leaving.

Alh. (Addressing Alvar).
Farewell then! and tho' many thoughts perplex me,

---

63   *faery*: belonging to fairyland.
64   *cot*: a cottage.
65   In the second edition of *Remorse*, Coleridge replaces lines 182–4 with the following:
     Ord. (In retiring stops suddenly at the edge of the scene, and then turning round to Isidore).
          Ha!—Who lurks there! Have we been overheard?
          There where the smooth high wall of slate-rock
               glitters—
     Isi. 'Neath those tall stones, which propping each the
               other,
          Form a mock portal with their pointed arch?—
          Pardon my smiles! 'Tis a poor Ideot Boy,
          Who sits in the Sun, and twirls a Bough about,
          His weak eyes seeth'd in most unmeaning tears.
          And so he sits, swaying his cone-like Head,
          And staring at his Bough from Morn to Sun-set
          See-saws his Voice in inarticulate Noises.
     Ord. 'Tis well! and now for this same Wizard's Lair.
     Isi. Some three strides up the hill, a mountain ash
          Stretches its lower boughs and scarlet clusters
          O'er the old thatch.
     Ord. I shall not fail to find it.
     (Exeunt Ordonio and Isidore).
66   *Alvar, Zulimez*: The Larpent version indicates that they are "*in Moorish habits.*"

Aught evil or ignoble never can I
Suspect of Thee! If what thou seem'st thou art,
The oppressed brethren of thy blood have need
Of such a leader.
Alv.   Nobly-minded woman!
Long time against oppression have I fought,
And for the native liberty of faith
Have bled and suffer'd bonds. Of this be certain,
Time, as he courses onward, still unrolls
The volume of Concealment. In the FUTURE,   10
As in the optician's glassy cylinder,[67]
The indistinguishable blots and colors
Of the dim PAST collect and shape themselves,
Upstarting in their own completed image,
To scare or to reward.[68]
                    I sought the guilty,
And what I sought I found: but ere the spear
Flew from my hand, there rose an angel form
Betwixt me and my aim. With baffled purpose
To the Avenger I leave Vengeance, and depart!
Whate'er betide, if aught my arm may aid,   20
Or power protect, my word is pledged to thee:
For many are thy wrongs, and thy soul noble.[69]
Once more farewell. *(Exit Alhadra).*
                    Yes, to the Belgic states
We will return. These robes, this stain'd complexion,
Akin to falsehood, weigh upon my spirit.
Whate'er befall us, the heroic Maurice[70]
Will grant us an asylum, in remembrance
Of our past services.
Zul. And all the wealth, power, influence which is
          yours,
     You let a murderer hold?
Alv.   O faithful Zulimez!   30
That my return involved Ordonio's death,
I trust, would give me an unmingled pang,

---

67   *glassy cylinder*: a telescope.
68   *Of this … to reward*: The Larpent version cuts lines 8–15 from "Of this…" through "…to reward."
69   *Whate'er … noble*: The Larpent version cuts lines 20–22.
70   *Maurice*: Maurice of Nassau (1567–1625), Prince of Orange and Count of Nassau, was a brilliant general for the Seven United Provinces who repeatedly defeated Spanish forces in the Low Countries.

Yet bearable:—but when I see my father
Strewing his scant grey hairs, e'en on the ground,
Which soon must be his grave, and my TERESA—
Her husband proved a murderer, and *Her* infants
His infants—poor TERESA!—all would perish,
All perish—all! and I (nay bear with me)
Could not survive the complicated ruin!
Zul. (Much affected). Nay now! I have distress'd   40
    you—you well know,
I ne'er will quit your fortunes. True, 'tis tiresome!
You are a painter,[71] one of many fancies!

---

71   *You are a painter*: In the second edition of *Remorse*,
    Coleridge included the following note:

    The following lines I have preserved in this place,
not so much as explanatory of the picture of the assassination, as (if I may say so without disrespect to
the Public) to gratify my own feelings, the passage being no mere *fancy* portrait; but a slight, yet not un-
faithful, profile of one [Sir George Beaumont
(1753–1827), painter and patron of the arts who
helped shaped Coleridge's attitudes towards the visual
arts], who still lives, nobilitate felix, arte clarior, vita
colendissimus [happy in his nobility, more distinguished in his art, and most worthy of honor by virtue of his life].

    Zul. (Speaking of Alvar in the third person).
    Such was the noble Spaniard's own relation.
    He told me, too, how in his early youth,
    And his first travels, 'twas his choice or chance
    To make long sojourn in sea-wedded Venice;
    There won the love of that divine old man,
    Courted by mightiest kings, the famous TITIAN!
    Who, like a second and more loved Nature,
    By the sweet mystery of lines and colors
    Changed the blank canvass to a magic mirror,
    That made the Absent present; and to Shadows   10
    Gave light, depth, substance, bloom, yea,
      thought and motion.
    He lov'd the old man, and rever'd his art:
    And though of noblest birth and ample fortune,
    The young enthusiast thought it no scorn
    But his inalienable ornament,
    To be his pupil, and with filial zeal
    By practice to appropriate the sage lessons,
    Which the gay, smiling old man gladly gave.
    The Art, he honour'd thus, requited him:
    And in the following and calamitous years   20
    Beguil'd the hours of his captivity.

You can call up past deeds, and make them live
On the blank canvas; and each little herb,
That grows on mountain bleak, or tangled forest,
You have learnt to name———[72]

           Hark! heard you not some footsteps?
Alv. What if it were my brother coming onwards?
    I sent a most mysterious message to him.
(Enter Ordonio).
Alv.[73] It is he!
Ord. (To himself as he enters).
    If I distinguish'd right her gait, and stature,   50
    It was the Moorish woman, Isidore's wife,
    That pass'd me as I enter'd. A lit taper,
    In the night air, doth not more naturally
    Attract the night flies round it, than a conjuror
    Draws round him the whole female
      neighbourhood.[74]
(Addressing Alvar).
    You know my name, I guess, if not my person.
    I am Ordonio, son of the Lord Valdez.
Alv. (With deep emotion).[75] The Son of Valdez!
*(Ordonio walks leisurely round the room, and looks
attentively at the plants).*
Zul. (To Alvar).   Why what ails you now?
    How your hand trembles! Alvar, speak! what wish
    you?
Alv. To fall upon his neck and weep forgiveness!   60
Ord. (Returning, and aloud).
    Pluck'd in the moonlight from a ruin'd abbey—
    Those only, which the pale rays visited!
    O the unintelligible power of weeds,

    Alh. And then he fram'd this picture? and unaided
      By arts unlawful, spell, or talisman?
    Alv. A potent spell, a mighty talisman!
      The imperishable memory of the deed,
      Sustain'd by love, and grief, and indignation!
      So vivid were the forms within his brain,
      His very eyes, when shut, made pictures of them!

72   *True ... name*: The Larpent version cuts lines 41–46
    from "True, 'tis ..." through "...to name."

73   *Alv.*: The Larpent version has Alvar "*Starting*."

74   *A lit ... neighbourhood*: The Larpent version cuts lines
    52–5 from "A lit ..." through "...neighbourhood."

75   *(With deep emotion)*: The Larpent version substitutes
    "*(Groaning aloud)*."

When a few odd prayers have been mutter'd o'er
  them:
Then they work miracles! I warrant you,
There's not a leaf, but underneath it lurks
Some serviceable imp.—[76]
            There's one of you
Hath sent me a strange message.
Alv.   I am he.
Ord. With you, then, I am to speak:
(Haughtily waving his hand to Zulimez).
            And mark you, alone.
(Exit Zulimez).
  "He that can bring the dead to life again!"—   70
Such was your message, Sir! You are no dullard,
But one that strips the outward rind of things!
Alv. 'Tis fabled there are fruits with tempting rinds,
That are all dust and rottenness within.
Would'st thou I should strip such?
Ord.   Thou quibbling fool,
What dost thou mean? Think'st thou I journey'd
  hither
To sport with thee?
Alv.   O no, my lord! to sport
Best suits the gaiety of innocence.
Ord. (Aside). O what a thing is man![77] the wisest
  heart
A Fool! a Fool that laughs at its own folly,   80
Yet still a Fool! *(Looks round the cottage).*
           You are poor!
Alv. What follows thence?
Ord.   That you would fain be richer.
The inquisition, too—You comprehend me?
You are poor, in peril. I have wealth and power,
Can quench the flames, and cure your poverty:
And for the boon I ask of you but this,
That you should serve me—once—for a few hours.
Alv. (Solemnly). Thou art the son of Valdez! would
  to Heaven
That I could truly and for ever serve thee.
Ord. (Aside). The Slave begins to soften!—
          You are my Friend, 90

"He that can bring the dead to life again"—
Nay, no defence to me. The holy brethren
Believe these calumnies—I know thee better.
(Then with great bitterness).
  Thou art a man, and as a man I'll trust thee!
Alv. Alas! this hollow mirth[78]—Declare your
  business.
Ord. I love a lady, and she would love me
But for an idle and fantastic scruple.
Have you no servants here, no listeners?
(Ordonio steps to the door).
Alv.[79] What, faithless too? False to his angel wife?
To such a wife? Well might'st thou look so wan,   100
Ill-starr'd Teresa!——Wretch! my softer soul
Is pass'd away! and I will probe his conscience!
Ord. In truth this lady lov'd another man,
But he has perish'd.
Alv.   What! you kill'd him? hey?
Ord. I'll dash thee to the earth, if thou but think'st it!
Insolent slave! how dar'dst thou—
(Turns abruptly from Alvar, and then to himself).
           Why! what's this?
'Twas idiotcy! I'll tie myself to an aspen,
And wear a fool's cap—
Alv. (Watching his agitation). Fare thee well—
I pity thee, Ordonio, even to anguish. *(Alvar is
  retiring).*
Ord. (Having recovered himself). Ho! *(Calling to Alvar).*
Alv.   Be brief, what wish you? 110
Ord. You are deep at bartering—You charge yourself
At a round sum. Come, come, I spake unwisely.
Alv. I listen to you.
Ord.   In a sudden tempest
Did Alvar perish—he, I mean—the lover—
The fellow.
Alv.   Nay, speak out, 'twill ease your heart
To call him villain!—Why stand'st thou aghast?
Men think it natural to hate their rivals.
Ord. (Hesitating). Now, till she knows him dead, she
  will not wed me.

---

76 *Those only … imp*: For lines 63–67, the Larpent version substitutes "Such Plants must needs have power."

77 *O what a thing is man!*: See *Hamlet* 2.2.293ff: "What
a piece of work is a man!"

---

78 *Alas! this hollow mirth*: All published editions of *Remorse* mark this phrase as an aside; but Coleridge's corrected first edition deletes "aside," indicating that these
words are spoken to Ordonio.

79 *Alv.*: The Larpent version marks this speech as an aside.

Alv. (With eager vehemence). Are you not wedded,
    then? Merciful Heaven!
  Not wedded to TERESA?
Ord.   Why, what ails thee?   120
  What, art thou mad? why look'st thou upward so?
  Dost pray to Lucifer, Prince of the Air?
Alv. (Recollecting himself). Proceed. I shall be silent.
(Alvar sits, and leaning on the table, hides his face).
Ord.   To Teresa?
  Politic wizard! ere you sent that message,
  You had conn'd your lesson, made yourself proficient
  In all my fortunes. Hah! you prophesied,
  A golden crop! Well, you have not mistaken—
  Be faithful to me and I'll pay thee nobly.
Alv. (Lifting up his head). Well! and this lady!
Ord. If we could make her certain of his death,   130
  She needs must wed me. Ere her lover left her,
  She tied a little portrait round his neck,
  Entreating him to wear it.
Alv. (Sighing).   Yes! he did so!
Ord. Why no: he was afraid of accidents,
  Of robberies, and shipwrecks, and the like.
  In secrecy he gave it me to keep,
  Till his return.
Alv.   What! he was your friend then?
Ord. (Wounded and embarrassed).
  I was his friend.—
              Now that he gave it me,
  This lady knows not. You are a mighty wizard—
  Can call the dead man up—he will not come.—   140
  He is in Heaven then—there you have no influence.
  Still there are tokens—and your imps may bring you
  Something he wore about him when he died.
  And when the smoke of the incense on the altar
  Is pass'd, your spirits will have left this picture.
  What say you now?[80]

---

[80] *Still … now*: The Larpent version handles lines 142–
  46 differently:
    Still there are tokens!—and your imps may bring
      you
    That which he grasp'd in death—
  Alv. (Aside). My very words!
    He must—'tis plain—he must have overheard us!
  Ord. Nay, mutter *me* no charms 'till I have need of
    them.

Alv. (After a pause). Ordonio, I will do it.
Ord. We'll hazard no delay. Be it to-night,
  In the early evening. Ask for the Lord Valdez.
  I will prepare him. Music too, and incense,
  (For I have arranged it—Music, Altar, Incense)   150
  All shall be ready. Here is this same picture,
  And here, what you will value more, a purse.
  Come early for your magic ceremonies.
Alv. I will not fail to meet you.
Ord. Till next we meet, farewell! *(Exit Ordonio).*
Alv. (Alone, indignantly flings the purse away and
  gazes passionately at the portrait).
                   And I did curse thee?
  At midnight? on my knees? and I believed
  Thee perjur'd, *thee* a traitress! *thee* dishonor'd?
  O blind and credulous fool! O guilt of folly!
  Should not thy inarticulate Fondnesses,
  Thy *Infant* loves—should not thy *Maiden* Vows   160
  Have come upon my heart? And this sweet Image
  Tied round my neck with many a chaste endearment,
  And thrilling hands, that made me weep and
    tremble!
  Ah, coward dupe! to yield it to the miscreant,
  Who spake pollution of thee![81]

  I am unworthy of thy love, Teresa,
  Of that unearthly smile upon those lips,
  Which ever smil'd on me! Yet do not scorn me—
  I lisp'd thy name, ere I had learnt my mother's.

  Dear Portrait! rescued from a traitor's keeping,   170
  I will not now profane thee, holy Image,
  To a dark trick. That worst bad man shall find
  A picture, which will wake the hell within him,
  And rouse a fiery whirlwind in his conscience. *(Exit).*

    When the Smoke is pass'd of the Incense on the
      altar
    (For we will have an Altar, Incense, Musick)
    Your aery servants will have left this *Portrait*.
    What say you now?
[81] In the second edition of *Remorse*, Coleridge adds the
  following lines:
                  barter for Life
    This farewell Pledge, which with impassion'd Vow
    I had sworn, that I would grasp—ev'n in my
    Death-pang!

Act III

Scene I:[82] *A Hall of Armory, with an Altar at the back of the Stage. Soft Music from an Instrument of Glass or Steel. Valdez, Ordonio, and Alvar in a Sorcerer's robe, are discovered.*

Ord. This was too melancholy, Father.
Val.   Nay,
  My Alvar lov'd sad music from a child.
  Once he was lost; and after weary search
  We found him in an open place in the wood,
  To which spot he had followed a blind boy,
  Who breath'd into a pipe of sycamore
  Some strangely moving notes, and these, he said,
  Were taught him in a dream. Him we first saw
  Stretch'd on the broad top of a sunny heath-bank:
  And lower down poor ALVAR, fast asleep,   10
  His head upon the blind boy's dog. It pleas'd me
  To mark how he had fasten'd round the pipe
  A silver toy his grandam had late given him.
  Methinks I see him now as he then look'd—
  Even so!—He had outgrown his infant dress,
  Yet still he wore it.[83]
Alv. (Aside).   My tears must not flow!
  I must not clasp his knees, and cry, My father!

---

82 *Scene I*: The Larpent version inserts a different open-
    ing scene; the current scene becomes Larpent's Scene
    II. Here is the Larpent Scene I:
    Scene I: *The court before Lord Valdez' Castle.*
    (Enter Monviedro & a Spy).
    Monv. Fear not the name of Spy—This disclosure is
       most meritorious.—
    Spy. Had it been any ordinary crime, your reverence!
       I had remained silent but sorcery,—
    Monv. It is most foul—yea inexpiable!
    Spy. Don Ordonio's trustiest servants have been placed
       at the Sorcerer's bidding—their preparations are just
       finished and I can place your reverence where un-
       observed you may be a witness of the whole.
    Monv. 'Tis well—collect the other servants of the
       household—Two of our Familiars are waiting: when
       the proof is compleated, I will give thee the signal
       and let them follow me.
    Spy. This way, may it please your reverence. *(Exit).*
83 *Once … wore it*: The Larpent version cuts these lines,
    3–16.

(Enter Teresa, and Attendants).
Ter. Lord Valdez, you have asked my presence here,
  And I submit; but (Heaven bear witness for me)
  My heart approves it not! 'tis mockery.   20
Ord. Believe you then no preternatural influence?
  Believe you not that spirits throng around us?
Ter. Say rather that I have imagin'd it
  A possible thing: and it has sooth'd my soul
  As other fancies have; but ne'er seduced me
  To traffick with the black and frenzied hope
  That the dead hear the voice of witch or wizard.
  (To Alvar). Stranger, I mourn and blush to see you here,
  On such employment! With far other thoughts
  I left you.
Ord. (Aside). Ha! he has been tampering with her?   30
Alv. O high-soul'd Maiden! and more dear to me
  Than suits the *Stranger's* name!—
                               I swear to thee
  I will uncover all concealed Guilt.
  Doubt, but decide not! Stand from off the altar.
(Here a strain of music is heard from behind the scene).
Alv. With no irreverent voice or uncouth charm
  I call up the Departed!
                        Soul of Alvar!
  Hear our soft suit, and heed my milder spell:
  So may the Gates of Paradise, unbarr'd,
  Cease thy swift toils! Since haply thou art one
  Of that innumerable company   40
  Who in broad circle, lovelier than the rainbow,
  Girdle this round earth in a dizzy motion,
  With noise too vast and constant to be heard:[84]
  Fitliest unheard! For oh, ye numberless,
  And rapid Travellers! what ear unstunn'd,
  What sense unmadden'd, might bear up against
  The rushing of your congregated wings?
(Music).
  Even now your living wheel turns o'er my head!
(Music expressive of the movements and images that follow).
  Ye, as ye pass, toss high the desert Sands,

---

84 *Since … to be heard*: An image of angelic spirits cir-
    cling the earth making something like the music of the
    sphere; see the angelic spirits who descend in Part V
    of Coleridge's "The Rime of the Ancient Mariner."

That roar and whiten, like a burst of waters,   50
A sweet appearance, but a dread illusion
To the parch'd caravan that roams by night!
And ye build up on the becalmed waves
That whirling pillar, which from Earth to Heaven
Stands vast, and moves in blackness! Ye too split
The ice mount! and with fragments many and huge
Tempest the new-thaw'd sea, whose sudden gulphs
Suck in, perchance, some Lapland wizard's skiff![85]
Then round and round the whirlpool's marge[86]
    ye dance,
Till from the blue swoln Corse[87] the Soul toils out,   60
And joins your mighty Army.[88]
(Here a voice behind the scenes sings "Hear, sweet spirit").
                   Soul of Alvar!
Hear the mild spell, and tempt no blacker Charm!
By sighs unquiet, and the sickly pang
Of a half-dead, yet still undying Hope,
Pass visible before our mortal sense!
So shall the Church's cleansing rites be thine,
Her knells and masses, that redeem the Dead!

SONG.

(Behind the Scenes, accompanied by the same Instrument as before).
Hear, sweet spirit, hear the spell,
Lest a blacker charm compel!
So shall the midnight breezes swell   70
With thy deep long-lingering knell.

And at evening evermore,
In a Chapel on the shore,
Shall the Chaunters[89] sad and saintly,
Yellow tapers burning faintly,
Doleful Masses chaunt for thee,
Miserere Domine![90]

Hark! the cadence dies away
   On the quiet moonlight sea:
The boatmen rest their oars and say,   80
   Miserere Domine!

(A long pause).
Ord. The innocent obey nor charm nor spell!
My brother is in heaven. Thou sainted spirit,
Burst on our sight, a passing visitant!
Once more to hear thy voice, once more to see thee,
O 'twere a joy to me!
Alv.   A joy to thee!
What if thou heard'st him now? What if his spirit
Re-enter'd its cold corse, and came upon thee
With many a stab from many a murderer's
    poniard?[91]
What if (his stedfast Eye still beaming Pity   90
And Brother's love) he turn'd his head aside,
Lest he should look at thee, and with one look
Hurl thee beyond all power of Penitence?
Val. These are unholy fancies!
Ord. (Struggling with his feelings). Yes, my father,
He is in Heaven!
Alv. (Still to Ordonio). But what if he had a brother,
Who had liv'd even so, that at his dying hour,
The name of heaven would have convuls'd his face,
More than the death-pang?
Val.   Idly prating man!
Thou hast guess'd ill: Don Alvar's only brother
Stands here before thee—a father's blessing on him!   100
He is most virtuous.
Alv. (Still to Ordonio). What, if his very virtues
Had pamper'd his swoln heart and made him proud?
And what if Pride had dup'd him into guilt?
Yet still he stalk'd a self-created God,
Not very bold, but exquisitely cunning;

---

85   *Lapland wizard's skiff*: Lapland was reputed to be the home of wizards and witches; a skiff is a boat.
86   *marge*: margin, edge.
87   *Corse*: corpse.
88   *Ye as ye … mighty Army*: In lines 49–61, the spirits are imagined creating mirages, waterspouts, icebergs, and whirlpools.
89   *Chaunters*: chanters.
90   *Miserere Domine*: "Have mercy, Lord." "Miserere mei Deus" ("have mercy on me, o God") is the Latin open-

ing of the fifty-first Psalm, a penitential psalm often set to music. Michael Kelly in his *Reminiscences* (2:277) indicates that Coleridge found Kelly's music "every thing he could have wished" and that "when he was in Sicily, and other parts of Italy, he had this '*Miserere Domine*' set to music by different Italian composers, none of whom satisfied him by giving his poetry the musical expression which he desired."
91   *poniard*: a dagger.

And one that at his Mother's looking glass
Would force his features to a frowning sternness?[92]
Young Lord! I tell thee, that there are such Beings—
Yea, and it gives fierce merriment to the damn'd,
To see these most proud men, that loath mankind,   110
At every stir and buz of coward conscience,
Trick, cant,[93] and lie, most whining hypocrites!
Away, away! Now let me hear more music.
(Music again).
Ter. 'Tis strange, I tremble at my own conjectures!
   But whatsoe'er it mean, I dare no longer
   Be present at these lawless mysteries,
   This dark Provoking of the Hidden Powers!
   Already I affront—if not high Heaven—
   Yet Alvar's Memory!—Hark! I make appeal
   Against th' unholy rite, and hasten hence   120
   To bend before a lawful Shrine, and seek
   That voice which whispers, when the still Heart
      listens,
   Comfort and faithful Hope! Let us retire.[94]
Alv. (To Teresa anxiously).
   O full of faith and guileless love, thy Spirit
   Still prompts thee wisely. Let the pangs of guilt
   Surprise the guilty: thou art innocent!
(Exeunt Teresa and Attendant. Music as before).
   The spell is mutter'd—Come, thou wandering
      Shape,
   Who own'st no master in a human eye,
   Whate'er be this man's doom, fair be it, or foul,
   If he be dead, O come![95] and bring with thee   130
   That which he grasp'd in death! But if he live,
   Some token of his obscure perilous life.
(The whole Music clashes into a Chorus).

---

92 The Larpent version cuts lines 106–107.
93 *cant*: to affect religious phraseology; to speak in a hypo-
   critically pious way.
94 *But whatsoe'er … retire*: For lines 116–23, the Larpent
   version substitutes:
      Be present at these dark, and lawless mysteries.
      I seem to offend against the memory
      Of my betrothed lord! Let us retire. *(To attendants).*
95 *fair be it … O come*: The Larpent version cuts this passage.

CHORUS.
   Wandering Demons! hear the spell!
   Lest a blacker charm compel—
*(The incense on the altar takes fire suddenly, and an
illuminated picture[96] of Alvar's assassination is
discovered, and having remained a few seconds is then
hidden by ascending flames).*
Ord. (Starting in great agitation). Duped! duped!
      duped!—the traitor Isidore!
*(At this instant the doors are forced open, Monviedro
and the familiars of the inquisition, servants, &c. enter
and fill the stage).*
Mon. First seize the sorcerer! suffer him not to speak!
   The holy judges of the Inquisition
   Shall hear his first words.—Look you pale, Lord
      Valdez?
   Plain evidence have we here of most foul sorcery.   140
   There is a dungeon underneath this castle:
   And as you hope for mild interpretation,
   Surrender instantly the keys and charge of it.
Ord. (Recovering himself as from stupor, to the servants).
   Why haste you not? Off with him to the dungeon!
(All rush out in tumult).[97]

---

96 *picture*: The Larpent version indicates that it is "*at a
   Signal*" that the picture is illuminated.
97 *All rush out in tumult*: In the Larpent version, there is
   no scene break here, and the rest of the scene is han-
   dled differently, as indicated in various places below.
   Here is the bridge between the scenes:
   (All rush out in Tumult).
   Ord. "He that can bring the dead to life again"—
   Mon. You heard it likewise?
   Ord.   Yes—and plann'd this Scheme
      To work a full conviction. Ha! A wizard!
      Thought I—But where's the proof? I plann'd this
         Scheme,
      The scheme has answer'd—We have proof enough.
   Mon. My Lord! Your pious Policy astounds me—
      I trust my honest zeal—
   Ord.   Nay, reverend father!
      It has but rais'd my veneration for you.
      'Twere well we should prevent all intertalk
      Between our servants, of this chief of darkness.
      Myself—
   Mon.   I re-deliver you the keys
      And leave him wholly to your charge.

Scene II: *Interior of a Chapel, with painted Windows.*
Enter Teresa.

Ter. When first I enter'd this pure spot, forebodings
Press'd heavy on my heart: but as I knelt,
Such calm unwonted bliss possess'd my spirit,
A trance so cloudless, that those sounds, hard by,
Of trampling uproar, fell upon mine ear
As alien and unnoticed as the rain-storm
Beats on the roof of some fair banquet-room,
While sweetest melodies are warbling——
(Enter Valdez).
Val. Ye pitying saints, forgive a father's blindness,
And extricate us from this net of peril!   10
Ter. Who wakes anew my fears, and speaks of peril?
Val. O best Teresa, wisely wert thou prompted!
This was no feat of mortal agency!
That picture—Oh, that picture tells me all!
With a flash of light it came, in flames it vanish'd,
Self-kindled, self-consum'd: bright as thy Life,
Sudden and unexpected as thy Fate,
Alvar! My Son! My Son!—The Inquisitor—
Ter. Torture me not! But Alvar—Oh of Alvar?
Val. How often would thou[98] plead for these   20
Morescoes!
The brood accurst! remorseless, coward murderers!
Ter. (Wildly). So? so?—I comprehend you—He is——
Val.   He is no more!
Ter. O sorrow! that a Father's Voice should say this,
A Father's Heart believe it!
Val.   A worse sorrow
Are Fancy's wild Hopes to a heart despairing!
Ter. These rays that slant in thro' those gorgeous
windows,
From yon bright orb—tho' color'd as they pass,

Ord.   Believe me
Some plot lurkes here, & of not trivial moment—
I doubt some fresh rebellion of the Moors.
This is no ordinary man.
Mon.   Tomorrow
I will return! We'll force it into light. *(Exit).*
[At this point, the Larpent version joins the printed
text at III.ii.71]

98 *thou*: Later editions of *Remorse* change "thou" to "he"
in order to make clear "thou" is Alvar.

Are they not Light?—Even so that voice, Lord
Valdez!
Which whispers to my soul, tho' haply varied
By many a Fancy, many a wishful Hope,   30
Speaks yet the Truth: and Alvar lives for me!
Val. Yes, for three wasting years, thus and no other,
He has liv'd for thee—a spirit for thy spirit!
My child, we must not give religious faith
To every voice which makes the heart a listener
To its own wish.
Ter.   I breath'd to the Unerring
Permitted prayers. Must those remain unanswer'd,
Yet impious Sorcery, that holds no commune
Save with the lying spirit, claim belief?
Val. O not to-day, not now for the first time   40
Was Alvar lost to thee—
(Turning off, aloud, but yet as to himself).
                              Accurst assassins!
Disarm'd, o'erpower'd, despairing of defence,
At his bared breast he seem'd to grasp some relict[99]
More dear than was his life——
Ter. (With a faint shriek).   O Heavens! *my* portrait!
And he *did* grasp it in his death pang!
                              Off, false Demon,
That beat'st thy black wings close above my head!
*(Ordonio enters with the keys of the dungeon in his
hand).*
Hush! who comes here? The wizard Moor's
employer!
Moors were his murderers, you say? Saints shield us
From wicked thoughts—
*(Valdez moves towards the back of the stage to meet
Ordonio, and during the concluding lines of Teresa's
speech appears as eagerly conversing with him).*
                              Is Alvar dead? what then?
The nuptial rites and funeral shall be one.   50
Here's no abiding-place[100] for thee, Teresa.—
Away! they see me not—*Thou* seest me, Alvar!
To thee I bend my course.—But first one question,
One question to Ordonio.—My limbs tremble—
There I may sit unmark'd—a moment will restore
me. *(Retires out of sight).*

---

99 *relict*: relic, something kept as a remembrance.
100 *abiding-place*: resting place.

Ord. (As he advances with Valdez).
    Those are the dungeon keys. Monviedro knew not,
    That I too had received the wizard's message,
    "He that can bring the dead to life again."
    But now he is satisfied, I plann'd this scheme
    To work a full conviction on the culprit,   60
    And he entrusts him wholly to my keeping.
Val. 'Tis well, my son! But have you yet discover'd
    (Where is Teresa?) what those speeches meant—
    Pride, and Hypocrisy, and Guilt, and Cunning?
    Then when the wizard fix'd his eye on you,
    And you, I know not why, look'd pale and
        trembled—
    Why—why, what ails you now?—
Ord. (Confused).   Me? what ails me?
    A pricking[101] of the blood—It might have happen'd
    At any other time.—Why scan you me?
Val. His speech about the corse, and stabs and   70
        murderers,
    Bore reference to the assassins——
Ord.   Dup'd! dup'd! dup'd!
    The traitor, Isidore! *(A pause, then wildly).*[102]
                I tell thee, my dear father!
    I am most glad of this.
Val. (Confused).   True—Sorcery
    Merits its doom; and this perchance may guide us
    To the discovery of the murderers.
    I have their statures and their several faces
    So present to me, that but once to meet them
    Would be to recognize.
Ord.   Yes! yes! we recognize them!
    I was benumb'd, and stagger'd up and down
    Thro' darkness without light—dark—dark—dark! 80
    My flesh crept chill, my limbs felt manacled,
    As had a snake coil'd round them!—Now 'tis sun
        shine,
    And the blood dances freely through its channels!
(Turns off abruptly: then to himself).
    This is my virtuous, *grateful* Isidore!
(Then mimicking Isidore's manner and voice).

   "A common trick of gratitude, my lord!"
   Old Gratitude! a dagger would dissect
   His "own full heart"—'twere good to see its color.
Val. These magic sights! O that I ne'er had yielded
   To your entreaties! Neither had I yielded,
   But that in spite of your own seeming faith   90
   I held it for some innocent stratagem,
   Which Love had prompted, to remove the doubts
   Of wild Teresa—by fancies quelling fancies!
Ord. (In a slow voice, as reasoning to himself).
   Love! Love! and then we hate! and what? and
       wherefore?[103]
   Hatred and Love! Fancies oppos'd by fancies!
   What? if one reptile sting another reptile?
   Where is the crime? The goodly face of nature
   Hath one disfeaturing stain the less upon it.
   Are we not all predestin'd Transiency,[104]
   And cold Dishonor?[105] Grant it, that this hand   100
   Had given a morsel to the hungry worms
   Somewhat too early—Where's the crime of this?
   That this must needs bring on the idiocy
   Of moist-eyed Penitence—'tis like a dream!
Val. Wild talk, my son! But thy excess of feeling——
   (Averting himself). Almost I fear, it hath unhinged
      his brain.[106]
Ord. (Now in soliloquy, and now addressing his father:
   and just after the speech has commenced, Teresa
   reappears and advances slowly).
   Say, I had lay'd a body in the sun!
   Well! in a month there swarm forth from the corse
   A thousand, nay, ten thousand sentient beings
   In place of that one man.—Say, I had *kill'd* him! 110
(Teresa starts, and stops listening).
   Yet who shall tell me, that each one and all
   Of these ten thousand lives is not as happy,
   As that one life, which being push'd aside,

---

101 *pricking*: spurring.

102 *Dup'd ... Isidore*: This is where the Larpent and the
    published versions once again come together, though
    the Larpent version has Ordonio "*looking eagerly at the
    Picture*" and then cuts through line 78.

103 *These magic ... wherefore*: The Larpent version cuts
    lines 88–94.

104 *Transiency*: transitoriness, brevity of existence.

105 *Fancies ... Dishonor*: For lines 95–100, the Larpent
    version substitutes:
        Hatred & love! Strange things! Both strange alike.
        What if one reptile sting another reptile?
        Where is the crime—

106 *Wild ... brain*: The Larpent version cuts lines 105–6.

Made room for these unnumbered——107
Val.   O mere madness!
(Teresa moves hastily forwards, and places herself
directly before Ordonio).

—————

107 *Unnumbered*: From this point, the Larpent version of-
    fers a different end to the scene:
    Ord. A rim of the Sun lies yet upon the Sea
       And now 'tis gone.—All shall be done this night.
    [186–7 in print version]
       Hollo! Who waits there! *(Enter Servant)*.
       Know'st thou a man, once a Moresco Chieftain
       Call'd Isidore?
    Serv.   He lives in the Alpuscarras
       Beneath a Slate rock.
    Ord. The Cavern, aye the cavern. *(Muttering to himself)*.
                          Slate rock? *(Aloud)*.
    Serv.   Yes!—
       Had your Lordship seen it, you must have
          remember'd
       The flight of steps, his children had worn up it
       With often climbing.
    Ord.   Well! It may be so.
    Serv. Nay, now I think on't, at this time of the year
       'Tis hid by vines.
    Ord. (To himself). The cavern—aye that cavern—
       But—how describe the place?—So—even so—
       He cannot fail to find it. *(To Servant)*. Where art
          going?
       Thou must deliver to this Isidore
       A letter.—Wait till I have written it. *(Exit servant)*.
       Well this was fortunate. The meddling friar
       Hath done me special service—against his will.
       Whate'er this insolent mountebank hath plotted
       I have now his life in keeping—Isidore's wife—
       Yes, it was she that pass'd me in the dell—
       She had newly left this Wizard! Treason! Treason!
       The scent lies strong on the ground! My *grateful*
          Isidore!
       "The stranger that lives nigh still picking weeds"—
       And this was his friend, his brother—his *sworn*
          brother
       Oh! I am grown a very simple stripling
       The wise men of this world make sport of me.
       By Heaven 'twas well contrived! In shame and
          terror
       I was to offer up my own life first,
       The atonement to my own offended conscience!
       And this False wizard—ha!—he was to pass

*Ord. (Checking the feeling of surprize, and forcing his
    tones into an expression of playful courtesy)*.
    Teresa? or the Phantom of Teresa?
Ter. Alas! the Phantom only, if in truth
    The substance of her Being, her Life's life,
    Have ta'en its flight thro' Alvar's death-wound—
(A pause).
                              Where—
    (Even coward Murder grants the dead a grave)
    O tell me, Valdez!—answer me, Ordonio!   120
    Where lies the corse of my betrothed husband?
Ord. There, where Ordonio likewise would fain lie!
    In the sleep-compelling earth, in unpierc'd darkness!
    For while we LIVE—
    An inward day that never, never sets,
    Glares round the soul, and mocks the closing eyelids!

    Over his rocky grave the Fir-grove sighs
    A lulling ceaseless dirge! 'Tis well with HIM!
*(Strides off in agitation towards the altar, but returns
as Valdez is speaking)*.
*Ter. (Recoiling with the expression appropriate to the
    passion)*.
    The rock! the fir-grove!
    (To Valdez).   Did'st thou hear him say it?
    Hush! I will ask him!
Val.   Urge him not—not now!   130
    This we *beheld*. Nor *He* nor I know more,

—————

    For Alvar's friend! He hath a trick of his manner.
    He was to tune his voice to honey'd sadness
    With lamentable tales of *her* dear Alvar,
    And *his* dear Alvar. And she wou'd have lov'd him.
    He that can sigh out in a woman's ear
    Sad recollections of her perish'd lover,—
    Can sob and smile with veering sympathy
    And now and then, as if by accident,
    Whisper just close enough to touch her cheek
    With timid lips. *He* takes the lover's place,
    He takes his place for certain! Dusky traitor!
    Were it not sport to whimper with thy mistress,
    Then steal way and roll upon my grave
    Till thy sides shook with laughter? Blood! Blood!
       Blood!
    They thirst for thy *blood!* Thy *blood* Ordonio!
    (Exit).
    [lines 175–6 in print version]

Than what the magic imagery reveal'd.
The assassin, who prest foremost of the three——
Ord. A tender-hearted, scrupulous, *grateful* villain,
Whom I will strangle!
*Val. (Looking with anxious disquiet at his Son, yet
attempting to proceed with his description).*
                              While his two companions—
Ord. Dead! dead already! what care we for the dead?
Val. (To Teresa). Pity him! soothe him! disenchant
    his spirit!
These supernatural shews, this strange disclosure,
And this too fond affection, which still broods
O'er Alvar's Fate, and still burns to avenge it—   140
These, struggling with his hopeless love for you,
Distemper him, and give reality
To the creatures of his fancy.
Ord.   Is it so?
Yes! yes! even like a child, that too abruptly
Rous'd by a glare of light from deepest sleep
Starts up bewilder'd and talks idly.
(Then mysteriously).   Father!
What if the Moors that made my brother's grave,
Even now were digging ours? What if the bolt,
Though aim'd, I doubt not, at the son of Valdez,
Yet miss'd its true aim when it fell on Alvar?   150
Val. Alvar ne'er fought against the Moors,—say rather,
He was their advocate; but you had march'd
With fire and desolation through their villages.—
Yet he by chance was captur'd.
Ord.   Unknown, perhaps,
Captur'd, yet as the son of Valdez, murder'd.
Leave all to me. Nay, whither, gentle Lady?
Val. What seek you now?
Ter.   A better, surer light
To guide me——
Both.   Whither?
Ter.   To the only place
Where life yet dwells for me, and ease of heart.
These walls seem threat'ning to fall in upon me!   160
Detain me not! a dim power drives me hence,
And that will be my guide.
Val.   To find a lover!
Suits that a high-born maiden's modesty?
O folly and shame! Tempt not my rage, Teresa!
Ter. Hopeless, I fear no human being's rage.
And am I hastening to the arms——O Heaven!

I haste but to the grave of my belov'd!
(Exit, Valdez following after her).
Ord. This, then, is my reward! and must I love her?
Scorn'd! shudder'd at! yet love her still? yes! yes!
By the deep feelings of Revenge and Hate   170
I will still love her—woo her—*win* her too!
(A pause).
Isidore safe and silent, and the portrait
Found on the wizard—he, belike, self-poison'd
To escape the crueller flames——My soul shouts
    triumph!
The mine is undermin'd! Blood! Blood! Blood!
They thirst for thy blood! *thy* blood, Ordonio!
(A pause).
The hunt is up! and in the midnight wood
With lights to dazzle and with nets they seek
A timid prey: and lo! the tyger's eye
Glares in the red flame of his hunter's torch!   180

To Isidore I will dispatch a message,
And lure him to the cavern! aye, that cavern!
He cannot fail to find it. Thither I'll lure him,
Whence he shall never, never more return!
(Looks through the side window).
A rim of the sun lies yet upon the sea,
And now 'tis gone! All shall be done to night. *(Exit).*

Act IV

Scene I: *A cavern, dark, except where a gleam
of moonlight is seen on one side at the further end
of it; supposed to be cast on it, from a crevice in
a part of the cavern out of sight. Isidore alone,
an extinguished torch in his hand.*

Isi. Faith 'twas a moving letter—very moving!
"His life in danger, no place safe but this!
'Twas his turn now to talk of gratitude."
And yet—but no! there can't be such a villain.
It can not be!
              Thanks to that little crevice,
Which lets the moonlight in! I'll go and sit by it.
To peep at a tree, or see a he goat's beard,
Or hear a cow or two breathe loud in their sleep—108

---
108 *To peep … sleep*: The Larpent version cuts lines 7–8.

Any thing but this crash of water drops!
These dull abortive sounds, that fret the silence   10
With puny thwartings and mock opposition!
So beats the death-watch to a sick man's ear.
(He goes out of sight, opposite to the patch of moonlight,
returns after a minute's elapse, in an exstacy of fear).
A hellish *pit!* The very same I dreamt of!
I was just in—and those damn'd fingers of ice
Which clutch'd my hair up! Ha!—what's that—it
    mov'd.
(Isidore stands staring at another recess in the cavern.
In the mean time, Ordonio enters with a torch, and
halloos to Isidore).
Isi. I swear that I saw something moving there!
The moonshine came and went like a flash of
    lightning—
I swear, I saw it move.
Ord. (Goes into the recess, then returns, and with great
    scorn).
                    A jutting clay stone
Drops on the long lank weed, that grows beneath:
And the weed nods and drips.
Isi. (Forcing a laugh faintly). A jest to laugh at!   20
It was not that which scar'd me, good my lord.
Ord. What scar'd you, then?
Isi.   You see that little reft?[109]
But first permit me!
(Lights his torch at Ordonio's, and while lighting it).
                    A lighted torch in the hand,
Is no unpleasant object here—one's breath
Floats round the flame, and makes as many colors,
As the thin clouds that travel near the moon.
You see that crevice there?
My torch extinguished by these water drops,
And marking that the moonlight came from thence,
I stept in to it, meaning to sit there;   30
But scarcely had I measured twenty paces—
My body bending forward, yea o'erbalanced
Almost beyond recoil, on the dim brink
Of a huge chasm I stept. The shadowy moonshine
Filling the Void so counterfeited Substance,
That my foot hung aslant adown the edge.
Was it my own fear?
                    Fear too hath its instincts!

---

[109] *reft*: a rare form of "rift," analogous with "cleft."

(And yet such dens as these are wildly told of,
And there are Beings that live, yet not for the eye)
An arm of frost above and from behind me,   40
Pluck'd up and snatcht me backward. Merciful
    Heaven!
You smile! alas, even smiles look ghastly here!
My lord, I pray you, go yourself and view it.
Ord. It must have shot some pleasant feelings
    through you.
Isi. If every atom of a dead man's flesh
Should creep, each one with a particular life,
Yet all as cold as ever—'twas just so!
Or had it drizzled needle-points of frost
Upon a feverish head made suddenly bald—[110]
Ord. (Interrupting him).   Why Isidore,
I blush for thy cowardice. It might have startled,   50
I grant you, even a *brave* man for a moment—
But such a panic—
Isi.   When a boy, my Lord!
I could have sate whole hours beside that chasm,
Push'd in huge stones and heard them strike and
    rattle
Against its horrid sides: then hung my head
Low down, and listen'd till the heavy fragments
Sank with faint crash in that still groaning well,
Which never thirsty pilgrim blest, which never
A living thing came near—unless, perchance,
Some blind-worm battens[111] on the ropy[112] mould   60
Close at its edge.
Ord.   Art thou more coward now?
Isi. Call him, that fears his fellow-man, a coward!
I fear not man—but this inhuman cavern,
It were too bad a prison-house for goblins.
Beside, (you'll smile, my lord) but true it is,

---

[110] *My body … bald*: The Larpent version replaces lines
32–48 with:
    Isi. Merciful Heaven! Do go! See it yourself.
    Ord. It must have shot some pleasant feelings thru'
        you.
    Isi. Had I been turn'd to Ice, and yet had felt
        Each single atom of my body creep
        With particular life! 'Twas even so!
        Or had it drizzl'd needle points of frost
        Upon a feverish head.
[111] *battens*: gluts itself.
[112] *ropy*: forming slimy threads.

My last night's sleep was very sorely haunted,
By what had pass'd between us in the morning.[113]
I saw you in a thousand fearful shapes,
And I entreat your lordship to believe me,
In my last dream—
Ord.   Well?
Isi.   I was in the act   70
Of falling down that chasm, when Alhadra
Wak'd me: she heard my heart beat.
Ord.   Strange enough!
Had you been here before?
Isi.   Never, my lord!
But mine eyes do not see it now more clearly,
Than in my dream I saw—that very chasm.
Ord. (Stands lost in thought, then after a pause).
I know not why it should be! yet it *is*—
Isi. What is, my lord?
Ord.   Abhorrent from our nature,
To kill a man.—
Isi.   Except in self-defence.
Ord. Why that's my case; and yet the soul recoils
    from it—
'Tis so with me at least. But you, perhaps,   80
Have sterner feelings?
Isi.   Something troubles you.
How shall I serve you? By the life you gave me,
By all that makes that life of value to me,
My wife, my babes, my honor, I swear to you,
Name it, and I will toil to do the thing,
If it be innocent! But this, my lord!
Is not a place where you could perpetrate,
No, nor propose, a wicked thing. The darkness,
When ten strides off we know 'tis chearful
    moonlight,
Collects the guilt, and crowds it round the heart.   90
It must be innocent.

*(Ordonio darkly, and in the feeling of self justification,
tells what he conceives of his own character and actions,
speaking of himself in the third person).*[114]
Ord.   Thyself be judge.
One of our family knew this place well.
Isi. Who? when? my lord?
Ord.   What boots it, who or when?
Hang up thy torch—I'll tell his tale to thee.
(They hang up their torches on some ridge in the cavern).
He was a man different from other men,
And he despis'd them, yet rever'd himself.
Isi. (Aside). He? *He* despised? Thou'rt speaking of
    thyself!
I am on my guard however: no surprize.
(Then to Ordonio). What, he was mad?
Ord.   All men seem'd mad to him!
Nature had made him for some other planet,   100
And press'd his soul into a human shape
By accident or malice. In this world
He found no fit companion.
Isi. (Aside). Of himself he speaks.[115]
                              Alas! poor wretch!
Mad men are mostly proud.
Ord.   He walk'd alone,
And phantom thoughts unsought for troubled him.
Something within would still be shadowing out
All possibilities; and with these shadows
His mind held dalliance. Once, as so it happen'd,
A fancy cross'd him wilder than the rest: 110
To this in moody murmur and low voice
He yielded utterance, as some talk in sleep.
The man who heard him.—
                              Why did'st thou look round?
Isi. I have a prattler three years old, my lord!
In truth he is my darling. As I went
From forth my door, he made a moan in sleep—
But I am talking idly—pray proceed!
And what did this man?
Ord.   With this human hand
He gave a substance and reality
To that wild fancy of a possible thing.—   120

---

113 The second edition of *Remorse* adds the following pas-
    sage:
        O sleep of horrors! Now run down and star'd at
        By Forms so hideous that they mock remem-
            brance—
        Now seeing nothing and imagining nothing,
        But only being *afraid*—stifled with Fear!
        While every goodly or familiar form
        Had a strange power of breathing terror round me!

---

114 *Ordonio … person*: For this stage direction, the Larpent
    version substitutes "*looking round the cavern*."
115 *speaks*: The Larpent version adds, "tis his own char-
    acter."

Well it was done! *(Then very wildly).*
                Why babblest thou of guilt?
The deed was done, and it pass'd fairly off.
And he whose tale I tell thee—dost thou listen?
Isi. I would my lord you were by my fire-side,
   I'd listen to you with an eager eye,
   Tho' you began this cloudy tale at midnight.
   But I do listen—pray proceed my lord—
Ord. Where was I?
Isi.   He of whom you tell the tale—
Ord. Surveying all things with a quiet scorn,
   Tam'd himself down to living purposes,   130
   The occupations and the semblances
   Of ordinary men—and such he seem'd!
   But that same over ready agent—he—
Isi. Ah! what of *him*, my lord?
Ord.   He prov'd a traitor,
   Betray'd the mystery to a brother traitor,
   And they between them hatch'd a damned plot
   To hunt him down to infamy and death.
   What did the Valdez? I am proud of the name
   Since he dar'd do it.—
(Ordonio grasps his sword, and turns off from Isidore, then after a pause returns).
                Our links burn dimly.
Isi. A dark tale darkly finish'd! Nay, my lord!   140
   Tell what he did.
Ord.[116]   That which his wisdom prompted—
   He made the Traitor meet him in this cavern,
   And here he kill'd the Traitor.
Isi.   No! the fool!
   He had not wit enough to be a traitor.
   Poor thick-ey'd beetle![117] not to have foreseen
   That he who gull'd thee with a whimper'd lie
   To murder his own brother, would not scruple
   To murder *thee*, if e'er his guilt grew jealous,
   And he could steal upon thee in the dark!
Ord. Thou would'st not then have come, if—

---

116 *Ord.*: The Larpent version indicates that Ordonio speaks *"fiercely."*

117 *thick-ey'd beetle*: This could come from the phrase "blind as a beadle," which comes to mean a kind of intellectual blindness; or perhaps from the heavy-weighted instrument used for driving in wedges from which was derived a sense of "beetle" as dullness or stupidity.

Isi.   Oh yes, my lord! 150
   I would have met him arm'd, and scar'd the coward.
(Isidore throws off his robe; shews himself armed, and draws his sword).
Ord. Now this is excellent and warms the blood!
   My heart was drawing back, drawing me back
   With weak and womanish scruples. Now my Vengeance
   Beckons me onwards with a Warrior's mien,
   And claims that life my pity robb'd her of—
   Now will I kill thee, thankless slave, and count it
   Among my comfortable thoughts hereafter.
Isi. And all my little ones fatherless—
                     Die thou first.
(They fight, Ordonio disarms Isidore, and in disarming him throws his sword up that recess opposite to which they were standing).
Isi. (Springing wildly towards Ordonio).
   Still I can strangle thee!
Ord.   Nay fool, stand off!
   I'll kill thee, but not so! Go fetch thy sword.[118]   160
(Isidore hurries into the recess with his torch, Ordonio follows him; a loud cry of "Traitor! Monster!" is heard from the cavern, and in a moment Ordonio returns alone).
Ord. I have hurl'd him down the Chasm! Treason for Treason.
   He *dreamt* of it: henceforward let him sleep,
   A dreamless sleep, from which no wife can wake him.
   His *dream* too is made out—Now for his friend.
   (Exit Ordonio).

Scene II:[119] *The interior Court of a Gothic or Saracenic Castle, with the vaulted Iron Door or Gate of a Dungeon low down, on one side.*

---

118 The second edition of *Remorse* deletes lines 159–60, and rewrites the stage directions as follows:
   (They fight, Ordonio disarms Isidore, and in disarming him throws his sword up that recess opposite to which they were standing. Isidore hurries into the recess with his torch, Ordonio follows him; a loud cry of "Traitor! Monster!" is heard from the cavern, and in a moment Ordonio returns alone).

119 *Scene II*: The Larpent version places this scene *"On a seacoast."* In the second edition of *Remorse*, Coleridge included a note that refers the reader to an appendix, which we include here:

The following Scene, as unfit for the Stage, was taken from the Tragedy, in the year 1797, and published in the Lyrical Ballads. But this work having been long out of print, and it having been determined, that this with my other Poems in that collection (the NIGHTIN-GALE, LOVE, and the ANCIENT MARINER) should be omitted in any future edition, I have been advised to reprint it, as a Note to the second Scene of Act the Fourth, p. 55.

(Enter Teresa and Selma).

Ter. 'Tis said, he spake of you familiarly,
  As mine and Alvar's common foster-mother.
Sel. Now blessings on the man, whoe'er he be,
  That join'd your names with mine! O my sweet
    Lady,
  As often as I think of those dear times,
  When you two little ones would stand, at eve,
  On each side of my chair, and make me learn
  All you had learnt in the day; and how to talk
  In gentle phrase; then bid me sing to you——
  'Tis more like heav'n to come, than what *has*
    been!   10
Ter. But that entrance, Selma?
Sel. Can no one hear? It is a perilous tale!
Ter. No one.
Sel.   My husband's father told it me,
  Poor old Sesina—angels rest his soul!
  He was a woodman, and could fell and saw
  With lusty arm. You know that huge round beam
  Which props the hanging wall of the old Chapel?
  Beneath that tree, while yet it was a tree,
  He found a baby wrapt in mosses, lin'd
  With thistle-beards, and such small locks of wool   20
  As hang on brambles. Well, he brought him
    home
  And rear'd him at the then Lord Valdez' cost.
  And so the babe grew up a pretty boy,
  A pretty boy, but most unteachable—
  And never learnt a prayer, nor told a bead,
  But knew the names of birds, and mock'd their
    notes,
  And whistled, as he were a bird himself:
  And all the autumn 'twas his only play
  To gather seeds of wild flowers, and to plant them
  With earth and water on the stumps of trees.   30
  A Friar, who gather'd simples in the wood,
  A grey-haired man, he lov'd this little boy:
  The boy lov'd him: and, when the friar taught him,

He soon could write with the pen; and from
    that time
Liv'd chiefly at the Convent or the Castle.
So he became a rare and learned youth:
But O! poor wretch! he read, and read, and read,
'Till his brain turn'd; and ere his twentieth year
He had unlawful thoughts of many things:
And though he pray'd, he never lov'd to pray   40
With holy men, nor in a holy place.
But yet his speech, it was so soft and sweet,
The late Lord Valdez ne'er was wearied with him.
And once, as by the north side of the chapel
They stood together, chain'd in deep discourse,
The earth heav'd under them with such a groan,
That the wall totter'd, and had well nigh fall'n
Right on their heads. My Lord was sorely
    frighten'd;
A fever seiz'd him, and he made confession
Of all the heretical and lawless talk   50
Which brought this judgment: so the youth
    was seiz'd,
And cast into that den. My husband's father
Sobb'd like a child—it almost broke his heart:
And once as he was working near this dungeon,
He heard a voice distinctly; 'twas the youth's,
Who sung a doleful song about green fields,
How sweet it were on lake or wide savannah
To hunt for food, and be a naked man,
And wander up and down at liberty.
He always doted on the youth, and now   60
His love grew desperate; and defying death,
He made that cunning entrance I describ'd,
And the young man escap'd.
Ter.   'Tis a sweet tale:
Such as would lull a list'ning child to sleep,
His rosy face besoil'd with unwip'd tears.
And what became of him?
Sel.   He went on shipboard
With those bold voyagers who made discovery
Of golden lands. Sesina's younger brother
Went likewise, and when he return'd to Spain,
He told Sesina, that the poor mad youth,   70
Soon after they arrived in that new world,
In spite of his dissuasion, seiz'd a boat,
And all alone set sail by silent moonlight
Up a great river, great as any sea,
And ne'er was heard of more: but 'tis suppos'd,
He liv'd and died among the savage men.

Ter. Heart-chilling Superstition! thou canst glaze,[120]
 Ev'n Pity's eye with her own frozen tear.
 In vain I urge the tortures that await him;
 Even Selma, reverend guardian of my childhood,
 My second mother, shuts her heart against me!
 Well, I have won from her what most imports
 The present need, this secret of the dungeon
 Known only to herself.—A Moor! a Sorcerer!
 No, I have faith, that nature ne'er permitted
 Baseness to wear a form so noble. True, 10
 I doubt not, that Ordonio had suborn'd him
 To act some part in some unholy fraud;
 As little doubt, that for some unknown purpose
 He hath baffled his suborner,[121] terror-struck him,
 And that Ordonio meditates revenge!
 But my resolve is fixed! myself will rescue him,
 And learn if haply he knew aught of Alvar.

(Enter Valdez).

Val. Still sad?—and gazing at the massive door
 Of that fell dungeon which thou ne'er had'st sight
  of,
 Save what, perchance, thy infant fancy shap'd it 20
 When the Nurse hush'd thy cries with unmeant
  Threats.
 Now by my faith, Girl![122] This same Wizard
  haunts thee!
 A stately man, and eloquent and tender— *(With a*
  sneer).
 Who then need wonder if a lady sighs
 Even at the thought of what these stern
  Dominicans—

Ter. (With solemn indignation). The horror of their
  ghastly punishments
 Doth so o'ertop the height of all compassion,
 That I should feel too little for mine enemy,
 If it were possible I could feel more,
 Even tho' the dearest inmates of our household 30
 Were doom'd to suffer them. That such things
  are——

Val. Hush, thoughtless woman!

Ter.   Nay, it wakes within me
 More than a woman's spirit.

Val.   No more of this—
 What if Monviedro or his creatures hear us!
 I dare not listen to you.

Ter.   My honor'd lord,
 These were my Alvar's lessons, and whene'er
 I bend me o'er his portrait, I repeat them,
 As if to give a voice to the mute Image.

Val. ————We have mourn'd for Alvar.
 Of his sad fate there now remains no doubt. 40
 Have I no other son?

Ter.   Speak not of him!
 That low imposture! That mysterious picture!
 If this be madness, must I wed a madman?
 And if not madness, there is mystery,
 And guilt doth lurk behind it.

Val.   Is this well?

Ter. Yes, it is truth: saw you his countenance?
 How rage, remorse, and scorn, and stupid fear,
 Displac'd each other with swift interchanges?
 O that I had indeed the sorcerer's power——
 I would call up before thine eyes the image 50
 Of my betrothed Alvar, of thy first-born.
 His own fair countenance, his kingly forehead,
 His tender smiles, love's day-dawn on his lips!
 That spiritual and almost heavenly light
 In his commanding eye—his mien heroic,
 Virtue's own native heraldry! to man
 Genial, and pleasant to his guardian angel.
 Whene'er he gladden'd, how the gladness spread
 Wide round him! and when oft with swelling tears,
 Flash'd through by indignation, he bewail'd 60
 The wrongs of Belgium's martyr'd patriots,[123]
 Oh, what a grief was *there*—for Joy to envy,
 Or gaze upon enamour'd!

       O my father!
 Recall that morning when we knelt together,
 And thou did'st bless our loves! O even now,
 Even now, my sire! to thy mind's eye present him
 As at that moment he rose up before thee,
 Stately, with beaming look! Place, place beside him
 Ordonio's dark perturbed countenance!
 Then bid me (Oh thou could'st not) bid me turn 70
 From him, the joy, the triumph of our kind!
 To take in exchange that brooding man, who never

---

120 *glaze*: to cover, to gloss over.
121 *suborner*: one who bribes another to commit perjury.
122 *and gazing ... Girl*: The Larpent version cuts this passage.

123 *Belgium's martyr'd patriots*: See note 27.

Lifts up his eye from the earth, unless to scowl.[124]
Val. Ungrateful woman! I have tried to stifle
An old man's passion! was it not enough,
That thou hast made my son a restless man,
Banish'd his health, and half unhing'd his reason;
But that thou wilt insult him with suspicion?
And toil to blast his honor? I am old,
A comfortless old man![125]   80
(Enter a Peasant and presents a letter to Valdez).
Val. (Reading it).
     "He dares not venture hither!" Why, what can this
         mean?
     "Lest the Familiars of the Inquisition,
     That watch around my gates, should intercept him;
     But he conjures me, that without delay
     I hasten to him—for my own sake entreats me
     To guard from danger him I hold imprison'd—
     He will reveal a secret, the joy of which
     Will even outweigh the sorrow."—Why what can
         this be?
Perchance it is some Moorish stratagem,
To have in me a hostage for his safety.   90
Nay, that they dare not! Ho! collect my servants!
I will go thither—let them arm themselves. *(Exit
     Valdez).*
Ter. (Alone). The moon is high in heaven, and all is
     hush'd.
Yet, anxious listener! I have seem'd to hear
A low dead thunder mutter thro' the night,
As 'twere a giant angry in his sleep.
O Alvar! Alvar! that they could return
Those blessed days that imitated heaven,
When we two wont[126] to walk at eventide;
When we saw nought but beauty; when we heard   100
The voice of that Almighty One who lov'd us
In every gale that breath'd, and wave that murmur'd!
O we have listen'd, even till high-wrought pleasure
Hath half assum'd the countenance of grief,

And the deep sigh seem'd to heave up a weight
Of bliss, that press'd too heavy on the heart.[127]
(A pause).
And this majestic Moor, seems he not one
Who oft and long communing with my Alvar,
Hath drunk in kindred lustre from his presence,
And guides me to him with reflected light?   110
What if in yon dark dungeon coward treachery
Be groping for him with envenom'd poignard
Hence womanish fears, traitors to love and duty—
I'll free him. *(Exit Teresa).*

     Scene III:[128] *The mountains by moonlight.*
*Alhadra alone in a Moorish dress; her eye fixed
on the earth. Then drop in one after another, from
different parts of the stage, a considerable number
of Morescoes, all in Moorish garments. They form
a circle at a distance around Alhadra. A Moresco,
Naomi, advances from out the circle.*

Naomi. Woman! May Alla and the prophet bless thee!
     We have obey'd thy call. Where is our chief?

---

[124]   *scowl*: The Larpent version adds, "For what new merit?
     For this late base Stratagem?"
[125]   The second edition of *Remorse* inserts the following:
     Ter.   O grief! to hear
        Hateful entreaties from a voice we love!
[126]   *wont*: were accustomed.

[127]   *heart*: The Larpent version cuts the rest of this scene.
[128]   The second edition of *Remorse* opens this scene as fol-
     lows:
             Scene III: *The mountains by moonlight.*
              Alhadra alone in a Moorish dress.
     Alh. Yon hanging woods, that touch'd by autumn
         seem
       As they were blossoming hues of fire and gold;
       The flower-like woods, most lovely in decay,
       The many clouds, the sea, the rock, the sands,
       Lie in the silent moonshine; and the owl,
       (Strange! very strange!) the screech-owl only wakes,
       Sole voice, sole eye of all this world of beauty!
       Unless, perhaps, she sing her screeching song
       To a herd of wolves, that skulk athirst for blood.
       Why such a thing am I?—Where are these men?
       I need the sympathy of human faces,
       To beat away this deep contempt for all things,
       Which quenches my revenge.—Oh! would to Alla,
       The raven, or the sea-mew, were appointed
       To bring me food! or rather that my soul
       Could drink in life from the universal air!
       It were a lot divine in some small Skiff
       Along some Ocean's boundless solitude,
       To float for ever with a careless course,

And why did'st thou enjoin[129] these Moorish
  garments?
Alh. (Lifting up eyes and looking round on the circle).
  Warriors of Mahomet! faithful in the battle!
  My countrymen! Come ye prepared to work
  An honourable deed? And would ye work it
  In the slave's garb? Curse on those christian robes!
  They are spell-blasted: and whoever wears them,
  His arm shrinks wither'd, his heart melts away,
  And his bones soften.
Naomi.   Where is Isidore?   10
Alh. (In a deep low voice). This night I went from
  forth my house, and left
  His children all asleep: and he was living!
  And I return'd and found them still asleep,
  But he had perished—
All Morescoes.   Perished?
Alh.   He had perished!
  Sleep on, poor babes! not one of you doth know
  That he is fatherless—a desolate orphan!
  Why shou'd we wake them? Can an infant's arm
  Revenge his murder?
One Moresco to another. Did she say his murder?
Naomi. Murder? Not murdered?
Alh.   Murder'd by a christian!
(They all at once draw their sabres).
Alh. (To Naomi, who advances from the circle).
  Brother of Zagri! fling away thy sword: 20
  This is thy chieftain's! *(He steps forward to take it).*
          Dost thou dare receive it?
  For I have sworn by Alla and the Prophet,
  No tear shall dim these eyes, this woman's heart

  And think myself the only Being alive!
  My children!—Isidore's children!—Son of Valdez,
  This hath new strung mine arm. Thou coward
    Tyrant!
  To stupify a Woman's Heart with anguish,
  Till she forgot—even that she was a Mother!
  (She fixes her eye on the earth. Then drop in one after
  another, from different parts of the stage, a considerable
  number of Morescoes, all in Moorish garments and
  Moorish armour. They form a circle at a distance round
  Alhadra, and remain silent till Naomi enters, distin-
  guished by his dress and armour, and by the silent obei-
  sance paid to him on his entrance by the other Moors).

129 *enjoin:* forbid.

Shall heave no groan, till I have seen that sword
Wet with the life-blood of the son of Valdez!
(A pause).
  Ordonio was your chieftain's murderer!
Naomi. He dies, by Alla!
All (Kneeling).   By Alla![130]
Alh. This night your chieftain arm'd himself,
  And hurried from me. But I follow'd him
  At distance till I saw him enter—*there!*   30
Naomi.[131] The cavern?
Alh.   Yes, the mouth of yonder cavern
  After a while I saw the son of Valdez
  Rush by with flaring torch: he likewise enter'd.
  There was another and a longer pause;
  And once, methought I heard the clash of swords!
  And soon the son of Valdez re-appear'd:
  He flung his torch towards the moon, in sport,
  And seem'd as he were mirthful! I stood listening,
  Impatient for the footsteps of my husband!
Naomi. Thou called'st him?
Alh.   I crept into the cavern—   40
  'Twas dark and very silent. *(Then wildly).*
              What said'st thou?
  No! no! I did not dare call, Isidore,
  Lest I should hear no answer! A brief while,
  Belike, I lost all thought and memory
  Of that for which I came! After that pause,
  O Heaven! I heard a groan, and follow'd it;
  And yet another groan, which guided me
  Into a strange recess—and there was *light*,
  A hideous light! his torch lay on the ground;
  Its flame burnt dimly o'er a chasm's brink.   50
  I spake; and whilst I spake, a feeble groan
  Came from that chasm! it was his last! his death-
    groan!
Naomi. Comfort her, Alla!
All.   Haste, let us seek the murderer![132]
Alh. I stood in unimaginable trance
  And agony that cannot be remember'd,
  Listening with horrid hope to hear a groan!
  But I had heard his last: my husband's death-groan!

---

130 *By Alla:* The Larpent version adds, "He dies."
131 *Alh.* The Larpent text identifies the speakers of this and
    the subsequent speech correctly, unlike the print text,
    which reverses them.
132 The second edition of *Remorse* removes this line.

Naomi. Haste! let us onward.

Alh.   I look'd far down the pit—
  My sight was bounded by a jutting fragment:
  And it was stain'd with blood. Then first I shriek'd,   60
  My eye-balls burnt, my brain grew hot as fire!
  And all the hanging drops of the wet roof
  Turn'd into blood—I saw them turn to blood!
  And I was leaping wildly down the chasm,
  When on the farther brink I saw his sword,
  And it said, Vengeance!—Curses on my tongue!
  The moon hath mov'd in Heaven, and I am here,
  And he hath not had vengeance! Isidore!
  Spirit of Isidore! thy murderer lives!
  Away! away!

All.   Away! away!   70
(She rushes off, all following).

Act V

Scene I:[133] *A Dungeon.*
Alvar (alone) rises slowly from a bed of reeds.

Alv. And this place my forefathers made for Man!
  This is the process of our Love and Wisdom
  To each poor brother who offends against us—
  Most innocent, perhaps—and what if guilty?
  Is this the only cure? Merciful God!
  Each pore and natural outlet shrivell'd up
  By Ignorance and parching Poverty,
  His energies roll back upon his heart,
  And stagnate and corrupt, 'till chang'd to poison,
  They break out on him, like a loathsome plague-spot!   10
  Then we call in our pamper'd mountebanks;[134]
  And this is their best cure! uncomforted
  And friendless Solitude, Groaning and Tears,
  And savage faces, at the clanking hour,
  Seen through the steam and vapours of his dungeon
  By the lamp's dismal twilight! So he lies
  Circled with evil, 'till his very soul

Unmoulds its essence, hopelessly deformed
By sights of evermore deformity!

With other ministrations thou, O Nature!   20
Healest thy wandering and distemper'd child:
Thou pourest on him thy soft influences,
Thy sunny hues, fair forms, and breathing sweets;
Thy melodies of woods, and winds, and waters,
Till he relent, and can no more endure
To be a jarring and a dissonant thing
Amid this general dance and minstrelsy;[135]
But, bursting into tears, wins back his way,
His angry spirit heal'd and harmoniz'd
By the benignant touch of love and beauty.   30

I am chill and weary! Yon rude bench of stone,
In that dark angle, the sole resting-place!
But the self-approving mind is its own light,
And life's best warmth still radiates from the heart,
Where love sits brooding, and an honest purpose.
(Retires out of sight. Enter Teresa with a taper).
Ter. It has chill'd my very life-blood! my own voice
    scares me;
  Yet when I hear it not, I seem to lose
  The substance of my being—my strongest grasp
  Sends inwards but weak witness that I am.
  I seek to cheat the echo.—How the half sounds   40
  Blend with this strangled light! Is he not here?
    (Looking round).
  O for one human face here—but to see
  One human face here to sustain me.—Courage!
  It is but my own fear! The life within me,
  It sinks and wavers like this cone of flame,
  Beyond which I scarce dare look onward! *(Shudders).*
  If I faint? If this inhuman den should be
  At once my death-bed and my burial vault?
  Ho! *(With a faint scream as Alvar emerges from the
    recess and moves hastily toward her).*
Alv. (Rushes towards her, and catches her as she is falling).
  O gracious heaven! it is, it is Teresa!   50
  Shall I reveal myself? The sudden shock
  Of rapture will blow out this spark of life,
  And Joy compleat what Terror has begun.
  O ye impetuous beatings here, be still!

---

133 *Scene I*: The Larpent version has a fuller stage direc-
    tion: "*(A dungeon feebly lighted. Alvar disc*ᵈ *on the
    ground).*" It then cuts the opening speech through line
    35, resuming with "*(Enter Teresa [with a Taper in her
    hand] at back of dungeon).*"
134 *mountebanks*: quacks, charlatans.

135 *minstrelsy*: singing.

Teresa, best belov'd! pale, pale, and cold!
Her pulse doth flutter! Teresa! my Teresa!
Ter. (Recovering, looks round wildly).
  I heard a voice; but often in my dreams
  I hear that voice! and wake and try—and try—
  To hear it waking! but I never could—
  And 'tis so now—even so! Well! he is dead—   60
  Murder'd perhaps! and I am faint, and feel
  As if it were no painful thing to die!
Alv. (Eagerly). Believe it not, sweet maid! Believe it not,
  Beloved woman! 'Twas a low imposture,
  Fram'd by a guilty wretch.
Ter. (Retires from him, and feebly supports herself
    against a pillar of the dungeon).
                        Ha! Who art thou?
Alv. (Exceedingly affected). Suborned by his brother—
Ter.   Didst *thou* murder him?
  And dost thou now repent? Poor troubled man,
  I do forgive thee, and may Heaven forgive thee!
Alv. Ordonio—he—
Ter.   If thou didst murder him—
  His spirit ever at the throne of God   70
  Asks mercy for thee: prays for mercy for thee,
  With tears in Heaven!
Alv.   Alvar was not murder'd.
  Be calm! Be calm, sweet maid!
Ter. (Wildly). Nay, nay, but tell me!
  (A pause, then presses her forehead). O 'tis lost again!
  This dull confused pain—
(A pause, she gazes at Alvar).
                        Mysterious man!
  Methinks I can not fear thee: for thine eye
  Doth swim with love and pity—Well! Ordonio—
  Oh my foreboding heart! And *he* suborn'd thee,
  And thou did'st spare his life? Blessings shower on
      thee,
  As many as the drops twice counted o'er   80
  In the fond faithful heart of his Teresa!
Alv. I can endure no more. The Moorish sorcerer
  Exists but in the stain upon his face.
  That picture—
Ter. (Advances toward him). Ha! speak on!
Alv.   Beloved Teresa!
  It told but half the truth. O let this portrait
  Tell all—that Alvar lives—that he is here!
  Thy much deceived but ever faithful Alvar.

(Takes her portrait from his neck, and gives it her).[136]
Ter. (Receiving the portrait). The same—it is the
    same. Ah! Who art thou?
  Nay, I will call thee, Alvar. *(She falls on his neck).*
Alv.   O joy unutterable!
  But hark! a sound as of removing bars   90
  At the dungeon's outer door. A brief, brief while
  Conceal thyself, my love! It is Ordonio.
  For the honour of our race, for our dear father;
  O for himself too (he is still my brother)
  Let me recall him to his nobler nature,
  That he may wake as from a dream of murder!
  O let me reconcile him to himself,
  Open the sacred source of penitent tears,
  And be once more his own beloved Alvar.
Ter. O my all-virtuous Love! I fear to leave thee   100
  With that obdurate man.
Alv.   Thou dost not leave me!
  But a brief while retire into the darkness:
  O that my joy could spread its sunshine round thee!
Ter. The sound of thy voice shall be my music!
(Retiring, she returns hastily and embracing Alvar).
  Alvar! my Alvar! am I sure I hold thee?
  Is it no dream? thee in my arms, my Alvar! *(Exit).*[137]
(A noise at the Dungeon door. It opens, and Ordonio
enters, with a goblet in his hand).
Ord. Hail, potent wizard! in my gayer mood
  I pour'd forth a libation to old Pluto,[138]
  And as I brimm'd the bowl, I thought on thee.
  Thou hast conspired against my life and honor,   110
  Hast trick'd me foully; yet I hate thee not.
  Why should I hate thee? this same world of ours,
  'Tis but a pool amid a storm of rain,
  And we the air-bladders[139] that course up and down,
  And joust and tilt in merry tournament;
  And when one bubble runs foul of another,
(Waving his hand to Alvar).
  The weaker needs must break.

---

136 *gives it her*: The Larpent version adds "*with great fond-*
    ness."
137 *Alvar ... arms, my Alvar*: The Larpent version cuts lines
    105–6.
138 *Pluto*: the Roman name for Hades, god of the under-
    world.
139 *air-bladders*: sacs filled with air in a plant or animal
    that help it float.

Alv.   I see thy heart!
There is a frightful glitter in thine eye,
Which doth betray thee. Inly-tortur'd man,
This is the wildness of a drunken anguish,   120
Which fain[140] would scoff away the pang of guilt,
And quell each human feeling.
Ord.   Feeling! feeling!
The death of a man—the breaking of a bubble—
'Tis true I cannot sob for such misfortunes;
But faintness, cold, and hunger—curses on me
If willingly I e'er inflicted them!
Come, take the beverage; this chill place demands it.
(Ordonio proffers[141] the goblet).
Alv. Yon insect on the wall,
Which moves this way and that, its hundred limbs,
Were it a toy of mere mechanic craft,   130
It were an infinitely curious thing!
But it has life, Ordonio! life, enjoyment!
And by the power of its miraculous will
Wields all the complex movements of its frame
Unerringly to pleasurable Ends!
Saw I that insect on this goblet's brim
I would remove it with an anxious pity!
Ord. What meanest thou?
Alv.   There's poison in the wine.
Ord. Thou hast guess'd right; there's poison in the wine.
There's poison in't—which of us two shall drink it?   140
For one of us must die!
Alv.   Whom dost thou think me?
Ord. The accomplice and sworn friend of Isidore.
Alv. I know him not.
And yet methinks, I have heard the name but lately.
Means he the husband of the Moorish woman?[142]
Isidore? Isidore?
Ord. Good! good! that Lie! by heaven it has restor'd me.
Now I am thy master!—Villain! thou shalt drink it,
Or die a bitterer death.
Alv.   What strange solution
Hast thou found out to satisfy thy fears,   150
And drug them to unnatural sleep?
(Alvar takes the goblet, and throws it to the ground).
                              My master!

Ord. Thou mountebank!
Alv.   Mountebank and villain!
What then art thou? For shame, put up thy sword!
What boots a weapon in a wither'd arm?
I fix mine eye upon thee, and thou tremblest!
I speak, and fear and wonder crush thy rage,
And turn it to a motionless distraction!
Thou blind self-worshipper! thy pride, thy cunning,
Thy faith in universal villainy,
Thy shallow sophisms, thy pretended scorn   160
For all thy human brethren—out upon them!
What have they done for thee? have they given
     thee peace?
Cur'd thee of starting in thy sleep? or made
The darkness pleasant when thou wak'st at
     midnight?
Art happy when alone? Can'st walk by thyself
With even step and quiet cheerfulness?
Yet, yet thou may'st be saved——
Ord. (Vacantly repeating the words). Sav'd? sav'd?
Alv.   One pang!
Could I call up one pang of true Remorse!
Ord. He told me of the babes that prattled to him,
His fatherless little ones! Remorse! Remorse!   170
Where got'st thou that fool's word? Curse on
     Remorse!
Can it give up the dead, or recompact[143]
A mangled body? mangled—dash'd to atoms!
Not all the blessings of an host of angels
Can blow away a desolate widow's curse!
And though thou spill thy heart's blood for
     atonement,
It will not weigh against an orphan's tear.
Alv. But Alvar—— *(Almost overcome by his feelings).*
Ord.   Ha! it choaks thee in the throat,
Even thee; and yet I pray thee speak it out—
Still Alvar!—Alvar!—howl it in mine ear!   180
Heap it like coals of fire upon my heart,
And shoot it hissing through my brain!
Alv.   Alas!
That day when thou didst leap from off the rock
Into the waves, and grasp'd thy sinking brother,
And bore him to the strand;[144] then, son of Valdez,
How sweet and musical the name of Alvar!

---

140 *fain*: willing, or even glad.
141 *proffers*: offers.
142 *And yet … woman*: The Larpent version cuts lines
     144–5.

---

143 *recompact*: join together again.
144 *strand*: shore.

Then, then, Ordonio, he was dear to thee,
And thou wert dear to him: heaven only knows
How very dear thou wert! Why did'st thou hate him?
O heaven! how he would fall upon thy neck,   190
And weep forgiveness!
Ord.   Spirit of the dead!
Methinks I know thee! ha! my brain turns wild
At its own dreams!—off—off—fantastic shadow!
Alv. (Seizing his hand). I fain would tell thee what I
    am; but dare not!
Ord. Cheat! villain! traitor! whatsoe'er thou be—
I fear thee, man!
Ter. (Rushing out and falling on Alvar's neck).
    Ordonio! 'tis thy brother!
*(Ordonio with frantic wildness runs upon Alvar with
his sword. Teresa flings herself on Ordonio and arrests
his arm).*
                    Stop, madman, stop!
Alv. Does then this thin disguise impenetrably
Hide Alvar from thee? Toil and painful wounds,
And long imprisonment in unwholesome dungeons,   200
Have marr'd perhaps all trait and lineament,[145]
Of what I was! But chiefly, chiefly, brother,
My anguish for thy guilt!
                    Ordonio—Brother!
Nay, nay, thou shalt embrace me.
*Ord. (Drawing back, and gazing at Alvar with a
    countenance of at once awe and terror).*
                                   Touch me not!
Touch not pollution, Alvar! I will die.
*(He attempts to fall on his sword, Alvar and Teresa
prevent him).*
Alv. We will find means to save your honor, live!
Oh live, Ordonio, for our Father's sake!
Spare his grey hairs!
Ter.   Oh, you may yet be happy.
Ord. O horror! not a thousand years in heaven
Could recompose this miserable heart,   210
Or make it capable of one brief joy!
Live! Live! Why yes! 'Twere well to live with you:
For is it fit a villain should be proud?
My Brother! I will kneel to you, my Brother!
    (Kneeling).
Forgive me, Alvar!——*Curse* me with forgiveness!

Alv. Call back thy soul, Ordonio, and look round thee!
Now is the time for greatness! Think that heaven—
Ter. O mark his eye! he hears not what you say.[146]
Ord. (Pointing at vacancy). Yes, mark his eye! there's
    fascination in it!
Thou said'st thou didst not know him—That is he!   220
He comes upon me!
Alv.   Heal, O heal him, heaven!
Ord. Nearer and nearer! and I can not stir!
Will no one hear these stifled groans, and wake me?
He would have died to save me, and I killed him—
A husband and a father!—
Ter.   Some secret poison
Drinks up his spirits!
Ord. (Fiercely recollecting himself). Let the Eternal
    Justice
Prepare my punishment in the obscure world—
I will not bear to live—to live—O agony!
And be myself alone my own sore torment!
*(The doors of the dungeon are broken open, and in
rush Alhadra, and the band of Morescoes).*
Alh. Seize first that man!   230
(Alvar presses onward to defend Ordonio).
Ord. Off, ruffians! I have flung away my sword.
Woman, my life is thine! to thee I give it!
Off! he that touches me with his hand of flesh,
I'll rend his limbs asunder! I have strength
With this bare arm to scatter you like ashes.
Alh. My husband—
Ord.   Yes, I murder'd him most foully.
Alv and Ter. O horrible![147]
Alh.   Why did'st thou leave his children?
Demon, thou should'st have sent thy dogs of hell
To lap their blood. Then, then I might have hardened
My soul in misery, and have had comfort.   240
I would have stood far off; quiet tho' dark,
And bade the race of men raise up a mourning
For the deep horror of a desolation,
Too great to be one soul's particular lot!
Brother of Zagri! let me lean upon thee.[148]

---

145 *lineament*: a portion of the body, particularly the face
    viewed in outline.

146 *he … say*: The Larpent version substitutes "there is fas-
    cination in it."

147 *O horrible!*: This half line is added from the second
    edition to complete the line.

148 *Brother … thee*: The Larpent version indicates this line
    is spoken "*to Naomi*."

(Struggling to suppress her feelings).
 The time is not yet come for woman's anguish,
 I have not seen his blood—Within an hour
 Those little ones will crowd around and ask me,
 Where is our father? I shall curse thee then!
 Wert thou in heaven, my curse would pluck thee   250
  thence!
Ter. He doth repent! See, see, I kneel to thee!
 O let him live! That aged man, his father!
Alh. (Sternly). Why had he such a son?
*(Shouts from the distance of RESCUE! RESCUE!
ALVAR! ALVAR! and the voice of Valdez heard)*.
Alh. Rescue?—and Isidore's Spirit unrevenged?
 The deed be mine! *(Suddenly stabs Ordonio)*.
      Now take *my* Life!
Ord. (Falling).   Atonement!
Alv. (While with Teresa supporting Ordonio). Arm of
  avenging Heaven!
 Thou hast snatch'd from me my most cherish'd
  hope—
 But go! my word was pledged to thee.
Ord.   Away!
 Brave not my Father's rage! I thank thee! Thou——
(The Moors hurry off Alhadra).[149]
 She hath aveng'd the blood of Isidore!   260
 I stood in silence like a slave before her
 That I might taste the wormwood[150] and the gall,
 And satiate this self-accusing heart
 With bitterer agonies than death can give.
 Forgive me, Alvar!—
    Oh!—could'st thou forget me! *(Dies)*.[151]
*(The stage fills with armed peasants, and servants,
Zulimez and Valdez at their head. Valdez rushes into
Alvar's arms)*.[152]

---

[149] *(The Moors hurry off Alhadra)*: The second edition of
Remorse does not include this stage direction, and in-
stead inserts: "*(Then turning his eyes languidly to
Alvar)*."

[150] *wormwood*: a plant proverbial for its bitter taste.

[151] *Dies*: The Larpent version handles the death of
Ordonio, lines 151–65, differently:
Ter. See! See! He doth repent! I kneel to thee!
 Be Merciful!
Alh.   Thou art young & innocent—
 'Twere merciful to kill thee! Yet I will not.
 And for thy sake none of this house shall die,
 Save only he.

Alv. Turn not thy face that way, my father! hide,
 Oh hide it from his eye! Oh let thy joy
 Flow in unmingled stream through thy first blessing.

Ter. O spare his life! They must not murder him!
Alh. To let him live—
  Were that a deep revenge!
All the band. No mercy! no mercy!
*(Naomi suddenly advances & stabs Ordonio. Alvar rushes
forward & catches him in his arms)*.
Ord.   'Tis well!
 Thou has aveng'd the Blood of Isidore!
 I stood in silence like a Slave before thee
 That I might taste the wormwood & the gall,
 And satiate this self accusing spirit
 With Bitterer agonies than death can give.
 For me Alvar! Oh cou'd'st thou forget me! *(Dies)*.
Shouts without. "Alvar! Alvar!"
(Enter a Moresco).
Mor. We are surprised. Away! Away! this instant
 The country is in Arms! Lord Valdez heads them
 And still cries out, "My son! My Alvar lives!"
 Haste to the Shore! they come the opposite road—
 Your wives & children are already safe—
 The boat is on the Shore! the vessel awaits.
Alh. Thou then art Alvar?—to my aid & safety
 Thy word stands pledged.
Alv. Arm of avenging heaven!
 I had two cherish'd hopes—the one remains
 The other thou has snatch'd from me—but my word
 Is pledg'd to thee—nor shall it be retracted.
*(The Moors surround Alhadra & hurry her off. Enter
arm'd Peasants with Valdez & Zulimez. Valdez rushes
into Alvar's arms)*.

[152] *(The stage … arms)*: The second edition of *Remorse* does
not include this stage direction, and instead inserts:
(Alvar and Teresa bend over the body of Ordonio).
Alh. (To the Moors). I thank thee, Heaven! thou hast
  ordained it wisely,
 That still extremes bring their own cure. That point
 In misery, which makes the oppressed Man
 Regardless of his own life, makes him too
 Lord of the Oppressor's—Knew I an hundred men
 Despairing, but not palsied by despair,
 This arm should shake the Kingdoms of the World,
 The deep foundations of iniquity
 Should sink away, earth groaning from beneath
  them;
 The strong-holds of the cruel men should fall,

(Both kneel to Valdez).

Val. My Son! My Alvar! bless, Oh bless him, heaven!

Ter. Me too, my Father?

Val.   Bless, Oh bless my children!   270

(Both rise).

Alv. Delights so full, if unalloy'd with grief,
    Were ominous. In these strange dread events,
    Just Heaven instructs us with an awful voice,
    That Conscience rules us e'en against our choice.
    Our inward Monitress to guide or warn,
    If listened to; but if repelled with scorn,
    At length as dire REMORSE, she reappears,
    Works in our guilty hopes, and selfish fears!
    Still bids, Remember! and still cries, Too late!
    And while she scares us, goads us to our fate.   280

EPILOGUE[153]

Oh! the procrastinating idle rogue,
The Poet has just sent his Epilogue;
Ay, 'tis just like him!—and the hand!
(Poring over the manuscript).   The stick!
I could as soon decipher Arabic!
But, hark! my wizard's own poetic elf
Bids me take courage, and make one myself!
An heiress, and with sighing swains in plenty
From blooming nineteen to full-blown five-and-
    twenty,
Life beating high, and youth upon the wing,   10
"A six years' absence was a heavy thing!"
Heavy!—nay, let's describe things as they are,
With sense and nature 'twas at open war—
Mere affectation to be singular.
Yet ere you overflow in condemnation,

Their Temples and their mountainous Towers
    should fall;
Till desolation seem'd a beautiful thing,
And all that were and had the Spirit of Life,
Sang a new song to her who had gone forth,
Conquering and still to conquer!
*(Alhadra hurries off with the Moors; the stage fills with
armed Peasants, and servants, Zulimez and Valdez at
their head. Valdez rushes into Alvar's arms).*

[153] Coleridge's epilogue, while being mentioned in contemporary reviews of the play, did not appear in the
first or second editions.

Think first of poor Teresa's education;
'Mid mountains wild, near billow-beaten rocks,
Where sea-gales play'd with her dishevel'd locks,
Bred in the spot where first to light she sprung,
With no Academies for ladies young—   20
Academies—(sweet phrase!) that well may claim
From Plato's sacred grove th' appropriate name![154]
No morning visits, no sweet waltzing dances—
And then for reading—what but huge romances,[155]
With as stiff morals, leaving earth behind 'em,
As the brass-clasp'd, brass-corner'd boards[156] that
    bind 'em.
Knights, chaste as brave, who strange adventures
    seek,
And faithful loves of ladies, fair as meek;
Or saintly hermits' wonder-raising acts,
Instead of—novels founded upon facts!   30
Which, decently immoral, have the art
To spare the blush, and undersap the heart!
Oh, think of these, and hundreds worse than these,
Dire disimproving disadvantages,
And grounds for pity, not for blame, you'll see,
E'en in Teresa's six years' constancy.

(Looking at the manuscript).

But stop! what's this?—Our Poet bids me say,
That he has woo'd your feelings in this Play
By no too real woes, that make you groan,
Recalling kindred griefs, perhaps your own,   40
Yet with no image compensate the mind,
Nor leave one joy for memory behind.
He'd wish no loud laugh, from the sly, shrewd sneer,
To unsettle from your eyes the quiet tear
That Pity had brought, and Wisdom would leave
    there.
Now calm he waits your judgment! (win or miss),
By no loud plaudits saved, damn'd by no factious
    hiss.

---

[154] *Academies … name*: The word "academy" comes from
the fact that Plato founded a school in a park on the
outskirts of Athens named for the hero Academus.

[155] *huge romances*: Coleridge's antipathy for long romance
novels, particularly of the Gothic variety such as those
written by Ann Radcliffe and Matthew Lewis, is well
known.

[156] *boards*: book covers.

Sketch of the New Melo-Dramatick Comick Pantomime called Harlequin and Humpo; or, Columbine by Candlelight!

Thomas John Dibdin

Thomas John Dibdin (1771–1841) was born out of wedlock to two important London theatrical figures, the elder Charles Dibdin and Harriet Pitt; his godfathers were David Garrick and the actor Francis Aickin. The Dibdin/Pitt family was, then, a powerful if illegitimate—in all senses of the word—force within the theater. His younger (also illegitimate) brother was the playwright Charles Isaac Mungo Dibdin, named for Isaac Bickerstaffe and his popular slave character Mungo from *The Padlock* (Drury Lane, 1768).

Thomas John Dibdin was introduced to the stage early on, when he was selected in 1775 to play Cupid to Mrs. Siddons' Venus for a Shakespeare Jubilee at Drury Lane. After some training with the choir at St. Paul's and with a classics tutor in Durham, he was apprenticed to Sir William Rawlings, Sheriff of London, but rebelled against his master's sense that the theater was no place for an apprentice. Under the alias of "Merchant," he joined the Dover circuit where he acted, painted scenery, and began to compose plays and songs. He moved on to the better paying Kent circuit, where he met his future wife, Ann Hilliar, and then to Liverpool and Manchester. By 1792, he claimed he could "sing 'Poor Jack,' paint scenes, play the fiddle, write a farce, get up a pantomime, attempt Sir Francis, Gripe, Apollo in 'Midas,' Mungo in the 'Padlock,' Darby in the 'Poor Soldier,' Captain Valentine in the 'Farmer,' and Polonius in 'Hamlet'; not to mention all dialects, as the Irishman in 'Rosina,' or any thing else, with French and German characters" (*Reminiscences of Thomas Dibdin*, 2 vols. [1827; rpt. New York: AMS Press, 1970] 1:162–3).

Dibdin met Ann Hilliar again in 1793 and married her, the two moving in 1794 to London, where he performed at Sadler's Wells, which also produced his first London play, *The Rival Loyalties; or, Shelah's Choice*. Patching up his differences with his former master Rawlings, he dropped his alias and began acting and writing under the name of Dibdin, penning sixteen productions for Sadler's Wells between 1794 and 1796 along with plays at various other minor theaters. Over the course of his career, he wrote more than 250 dramatic pieces, many prologues and epilogues, and more than 2,000 songs. His plays range from perhaps the most famous of pantomimes, *Harlequin and Mother Goose; or, The Golden Egg* (Covent Garden, 1806), to melodramas such as *Valentine and Orson* (Covent Garden, 1802), to adaptations of Joanna Baillie (*Constantine and Valeria; or, The Last of the Caesars* [Royal Circus, 1817]) and Coleridge (*Zopolya; or, The War Wolf* [Royal Circus, 1818]). He wrote a number of prose works—including *A Metrical History of England* (2 vols., 1813), his *Reminiscences* (1827), and *Bunyan's Pilgrim's Progress Metrically Condensed* (1834)—not to mention running the periodical *Tom Dibdin's Penny Trumpet*, and editing *The London Theatre, A Collection of the Most Celebrated Dramatic Pieces* (26 vols., 1815–18).

Dibdin's career as an actor and manager was equally rich and varied. He worked for the most part for Covent Garden from 1798 until 1807, acting in Richmond with his wife during the summers. In 1811–12, he managed the Surrey Theatre for Elliston and then became the prompter and writer of pantomimes for the new Drury Lane. In 1815, he became manager of Drury Lane and in 1816 of the Surrey as well. Elliston then fired him from Drury Lane, saying he could not manage two theaters at once, even though Dibdin had the support of members of the managing committee, including Byron who contributed a goodly sum to his closing benefit as well as "two hundred beautiful drawings of Turkish costume" (*Reminiscences*, 2:58). Although he had made large sums writing plays and was paid a seasonal salary of 520 pounds for his work at Drury Lane, he lost money on the Surrey and he was forced to close the theater in 1822. A brief period of managing and writing for the Haymarket brought his career to a close. He died on 16 September 1841 and was buried near his wife and his friend, the great pantomime clown Grimaldi.

Harlequin and Humpo; or, Columbine by Candlelight! opened at Drury Lane on 26 December 1812. It had a spectacular run of forty-eight nights, in spite of initial bad reviews (see the Appendix, pp. 383–85) and what appears to be the initial opposition of a rather well-organized community of "humpy men from the neighbourhood of the Temple" (*Reminiscences*, 2:7; Appendix), who feared the pantomime would be derogatory to dwarves. Most often paired with *Remorse* after Coleridge's play opened on 23 January 1813, *Harlequin and Humpo* can be seen as treating a number of the same subjects in spite of its radically different generic identity as Christmas pantomime. Through Owletta, the Fairy of the Night, Dibdin explores the same Gothic motifs drawn on by Coleridge as well as delighting in making metadramatic jokes about *Remorse*'s (and Drury Lane's) use of special lighting effects. Barred from seeing the sun until her eighteenth birthday, the Princess is trapped within a palace lit by an army of "Lanthorn Bearers, Candelabra men, and Extinguishers," just as Drury's audience found itself within the enclosed space of a theater lit by hundreds of candles whose sputtering and dripping wax forced theater personnel to be constantly at work snuffing and trimming. Just as Coleridge's character of Ordonio offers a critique of Napoleon as little usurper and would-be great man, so also does Dibdin's Humpo, king of the Dwarves, who stands in diminutive opposition to the quintessentially English Sir (and later, presumably, King) Arthur. Dibdin's pantomime, then, provides a telling example of the close ties between "literary" drama and theatrical spectacle, as well as demonstrating the self-conscious awareness with which technical innovations, popular styles such as the Gothic, and current political events could all be taken up in a single play.

Arriving at a copytext for Dibdin's pantomime has proven more difficult than with the other plays. The printed text, *Sketch of the New Melo-Dramatick Comick Pantomime, Called Harlequin and Humpo; or, Columbine by Candlelight!* (London: Lowndes & Hobbes, 1812), is, as it name suggests, merely an outline, providing fairly full descriptions of the action that frames the play but merely listing the scenes of the harlequinade proper. Our own text, therefore, draws most heavily upon the Larpent manuscript (Huntington Library LA 1750), which offers a particularly rich description for a pantomime. We have supplemented this with material from the printed text where it adds to our sense of what the performance would have offered. In addition, we have attempted to transcribe the (sometimes undecipherable) musical cues scrawled in the Larpent copy, since they provide a sense of how music functioned in the pantomime.

PRINCIPAL OPERATICK CHARACTERS:

Pomposso, (King of Phantasino)	Mr. Cooke
Punfunnidos (fool to the court)	Mr. Finn
Humpino (Prince of the Dwarfs, afterwards Lover)	Mr. Barnes
Humpo (King of the Dwarfs, afterwards Pantaloon)	Mr. West
Dumpo (Ambassador of the Dwarfs, afterwards Clown)	Mr. Kirby
Sir Arthur (a gallant Knight, afterwards Harlequin)	Mr. Hartland
Hugo (a Squire)	Mr. West
Princess of Phantasino	Miss Bew
Squinterina (her duenna)	Mr. Chatterley
Aquila (Spirit of Day)	Miss Poole
Owletta (Genius of Night)	Miss Horribow

PRINCIPAL PANTOMIME CHARACTERS:

Harlequin	Mr. Hartland
Monster of the Woods, Leaden Harlequin and Dancing Bear	Mr. Pack
Columbine	Miss Vallancy
Cupids	Misses J. Simpson, J. Scott, Pincott, Manning, Brown, Wright
Captain of the Candelabra Corps	Mr. West
Hornado (leader of the Lanthorn Bearers)	Mr. Aberdien
Putouto (Exempt of the Extinguishers)	Mr. Blower
Lanthorn Bearers, Candelabra Men, and Extinguishers	Messrs. Wilson, Douglas, Appleby, Cox, Staples, Perkins, Ellis, Newman, Billet, Seymour, Shade, Bynam, Pembery, Barnard, Parish, Reece, Booker, Robinson, &c. &c.

PRINCIPAL CHARACTERS IN THE BALLET

	Misses C. Bristow, Hohannot, Ruggles
Dancing Taper Bearers	Messrs. Mathews, Hope, Cost, Appleby, Brown, Vials, &c.
Dwarfs	Masters Tokely, Tuck, Connor, Hawker, Brown, Winstanley, Chittle, Buxton, Phillips, Cooke, Austin, Hammond, Baker, Tulip, I. Brown, Smythies, Lofthouse, Ryder, Dermot, Davis, Croker, Cross, Singleton, Shae Robinson, Stokes, T. Stokes, B. Cooke, Seymour, &c
	Misses Caffin, Carr, M. Carr, L. Carr, Curtis, Tokely, Bird, Carter, Bynam, Smith, Billet, Speke, F. Bynam, Appleby, Church, I. Simpson, I. Scott, Prescott, Manning, Brown, Wright, &c.
Giants	Monsieur Belletaille and Signor Montalto
Fiends	Mr. Austin, Mr. Jamieson
Applewoman	Mr. Hope
Coachmakers	Mr. Seymour, Mr. Williams
Plumbers	Mr. Stedman, Mr Willow
Landlord	Mr. Chapple
Genii of Light	Messrs. Danby, Caulfield, Whilmshurst, Ebbertson, Wallack, Cook, Jones, Dibble, Clarke, Oddwell, Mean, Wilson, Bennet, Dixon, &c.
	Mesdms. Chatterley, Minton, I. Boyce, Jones, Caulfield, S. Dennet, Scott, Corrie, Cook, E. Cooke, Horribow, &c.

The Ballet composed by Mr. Robert

The Comick Dances by Mr. Hartland

The Scenery designed by Mr. Greenwood, and executed by him, Messers. Gente, H. Smith, Latilla, &c &c and assistants.

The Machinery and Decorations by Messrs. Morris, Underwood, Drory, &c.

The Mechanical Changes by Messrs. Morris and Kirby

The Dresses by Mr. Banks, Miss Rein, Miss Robinson, and Assistants.

Scene I: *Exterior of a Palace of Black Marble enriched with Gold Entablatures[1] and Massy Architecture. No Windows visible. A Portal with steps descending into the Palace. Centinels[2] on Duty. Drums— Trumpets—Cannons and Loud Huzzas. Enter Punfunnidos & Mob.*

Mob. Hear him! hear him! hear him! Silence! Silence!

Punfunnidos. Friends & Countrymen of the Island of Phantasino—ye whose admiration of silence is proclaim'd with so much noise! Permit me most respectfully to ask what the devil's the matter with you?

Mob. We would fain know—

Pun. And so would I fain know where's the respect to my dignity—am not I Punfunnidos, Purveyor of Quips and Cranks[3] to Pomposso, King of Phantasino, Jester in Ordinary to the Solemn Council, relator of Stories extraordinary to the Maids of Honour, & universally allow'd to be the greatest fool at Court? Ha!! 10

2d. Mob. True, Sir—but one fool makes many & the entry of a Grand Ambassador at our Court has led us to inquire the cause.

Pun. I will unlock my knowledge box. Attend.—I needn't tell ye our King has a daughter, the fair Columbine, about whom Aquila and Owletta, two 20

fairies as opposite as Light and Darkness, quarrelled at her birth.

1st Mob. No, Sir, you needn't tell us that.

Pun. Nor do you want to hear how the black fairy decreed that should the Princess see daylight before completing the age of Eighteen, 'twou'd cost her life.

3d Mob. We know.

Pun. I know you do—nay more, you all can tell she will compleat her 18th year to-morrow & that from her Birth she has lived shut up within this dark Palace without more knowledge of the Sun than has a cucumber, attended by a Legion of Lanthorn[4] bearers, whole corps of Candle Snuffers, and such extraordinary stores of artificial Light as have melted all the wax in the country, rais'd the Price of Mutton,[5] and robb'd even Salads of their Oil. 30

1st Mob. Knowing all this—

Pun. Why do ye ask a fool to tell ye more—go— go—have ye not learn'd that it is necessary to keep even great folks in the dark—and do ye, Scum of the earth, expect Illumination—if ye do—home to your houses & from your windows view where Dumpo, Ambassador from Humpo, King of the Dwarfs, brings the Prince Humpino, his great Master's Son, to carry hence our Princess as his Bride—Hark! *(Martial Music).* Vanish!— *(Exit).* 40

(The Mob range on each side for Chorus. A March [Calculated for very short steps] introduces a Royal Banner of Humpo. Procession of Dwarfs [Children] Two & Two in superb habits, bearing little trophies.
Officer
Ambassador's Banner
Band of Jews' Harps or other Minikin[6] Musick
Officers bearing decorated Ensigns and the Ambassador's Credentials
The Ambassador
Ladies

---

[1] *Entablatures*: the architectural unit that sits above the columns, including the architrave, the frieze, and the cornice.

[2] *Centinels*: sentinels; guards.

[3] *Quips and Cranks*: after Milton, "L'Allegro," line 25; jokes and fanciful turns of speech.

---

[4] *Lanthorn*: lantern.

[5] *Price of Mutton*: Mutton is the meat taken from sheep; since it is rather fatty, mutton fat was used to make candles, the price of which is being raised by the demand made by the Princess's castle.

[6] *Minikin*: a small or insignificant thing; a diminutive person.

Officers
The Prince's Banner
A Car, with the Prince Humpino
Escorted by Two Giants
Officers).

Music: No. 1. March & Short Chorus during the
Procession.

He comes,
Beat Drums,
Sound Trump,
Gong Thump,   50
    Music play!

At yon Gate
On thy State,
Little great
Man we wait
    March away!

Valour's Pride!
Quickly ride
To thy Bride;
Time and Tide   60
    Never stay.

N.B.: as the Procession enters the Portal of the Sable
Palace, the Mob go off on separate sides.

Scene II: *Interior of the Marble Palace*
most brilliantly illuminated and adorned
with Pictures &c in Transparency.[7]

Music: No. 2. Andante. The Princess and her Ladies
discovered at various works—Musick—Cards and
amusements. Several Guards attending with large gold
Snuffers on their Shoulders—Flambeaux[8] *(not lit) for*
walking canes—Extinguishers for Caps—Flat
candlesticks as breakfast plates, or slung behind them,
and tinder boxes at their Cross belts—they snuff all the
Candles in three motions, to beat of drum.

---

7 *Transparency*: The theater made use of pictures on
   transparent materials through which a light was shone
   from behind.
8 *Flambeaux*: torches made of several thick wicks, dipped
   in wax and twisted together.

Music: No. 3. Dance in 3 movements from Calypso. A
group of elegantly dress'd dancers with little wax Tapers
come forward. The men first with their tapers lighted;
the women come forward, coquet[9] *with the men, a*
little, during the Dance—light their Tapers by those of
the Men—then each with a beautiful extinguisher puts
out her partner's light.—The men return the
compliment—they pretend to feel for each other in the
dark—miss each other and are in despair.—When a
troupe of little Cupids enter with Silver tinder boxes
and strike each a light—to Musick. Each Cupid then
draws a long match from his Quiver—lights it, relumes
the Tapers of the lovers, who dance off very much
delighted. The Princess rises in agitation and comes
forward—

Princess. Time, snuff the *wick* of my probation short
    Or else the *Oil* of Expectation wasted
    Will feed the lamp of look'd for day no more
    And hope *extinguished* by prolong'd delay
    Will turn existence *down* & put it out.
Duenna. Lustre of Ladies, Chandelier of Charms,
    Why dimly in the socket burn thy *Spirits*
    When they shou'd *blaze*? The Prince Humpino
        comes
    Fine as a Firescreen, and his mighty Heart
    Will at thy burning Beauties melt like wax.   10
Prin. His influence upon this Heart, compared
    With that of one I may not name, is scarce
    A Rushlight[10] to a Flambeaux! Leave me, Dame.
(Duenna retires up).
    Alas! I ne'er have seen Don Phoebus's[11] light
    The Glorious Sun, or Dian[12] snuff the moon
    Nor have the twinkling Stars, like little Sparks

---

9 *coquet*: flirt.
10 *Rushlight*: a rush-candle, a candle of feeble power made
    by dipping a rush in tallow or grease.
11 *Don Phoebus*: Phoebus Apollo is the Greek god of the
    sun, poetry, and healing. Here he is given the Spanish
    title that is used to precede one's Christian name—
    often, as here, used in literature in a humorous man-
    ner.
12 *Dian*: Diana, Greek goddess of the moon, chastity, and
    the hunt, and sister to Apollo.

Shot from a Catherine Wheel,[13] amaz'd my view,
Yet two such orbs as dear Sir Arthur's eyes
No Orrery[14] however well illumed
Has yet, in my opinion, ere produced.   20

Music: No. 4. Burlesque Air: Princess.
My feelings as firm were as wax in a frost,
    Till love took his bow by the handle;
Then soon I perceived how my pride was all lost,
    For he came like a thief in the candle.[15]

No taper exposed between two draughts of air,
    Such consumption of stamina suffers,
As I shall do, blown by the blast of despair,
    'Till fate cuts me off with her snuffers.[16]

Come lanthorn clad coldness and shield me once
        more,
    From love, of all ills the most grand ill;   30
Whose dart to the heart, is as perfect a bore,
    As to housewives, a thief in the Candle.

*Music: No. 5. Musick of Terror and Agitation. Enter
Sir Arthur with a Rose.*

*Music: No. 6. Just Like Love. Agitato. He throws
himself at the feet of the Princess and hides his face in
her robe.*

Prin. Why this despair, Sir Arthur, well I know
    The son of Humpo comes—yet sooner than with
        him

The day I'll share, I'll here remain with thee—
And love by lamplight—Lamplight did I say?
I would not fear e'en in the dark to stay.
(Trumpets).

*Music: No. 7. Short. Hurry. Enter the King, scarcely
leaving Sir Arthur time to hide behind some part of the
Building.*

Pomposso. Lo, Daughter! At the threshold of thy
        Palace
The Prince, thy Spouse that is to be, has learn'd
You dare prefer a simple Chamberlain,[17]   40
Yes, that Sir *Arthur* whom I twice have banished,
To him who offers Kingdoms with his hand.
Now mark in fear—if I Sir Arthur catch
He dies—for thee, as 'tis our custom here
That Princes shou'd not see their wives till after
The Knot is tied, prepare to be enclosed
In a State Palanquin[18] and with the Prince
Return.
Prin. Dread Sir, 'twere fatal; for my Eighteenth year
Is not as you supposed complete,[19] until   50
Another day has passed, should I go hence
And see the day ere yet the time's expired.
Pomp. 'Tis mere evasion—I've most deeply sworn
And you must hence—yet to prevent the worst
I'll have a carriage so contriv'd, no one
Shall open to a blush of day—two Suns
Revolving on thy Journey will secure
Thy safety, when arriv'd. Guards keep her safe
Till her departure—No words—Hence! Away!

---

13   *Catherine Wheel*: a kind of firework that burns while
     rotating; ultimately from a wheel with spikes project-
     ing from it, named in reference to the martyrdom of
     St. Catherine.
14   *Orrery*: a mechanical device that, through the use of a
     clockwork, represents the movement of the planets
     around the sun.
15   *a thief in the candle*: a proverbial expression, used by
     Dekker and Fletcher, for example, referring to a piece
     of the burning candlewick that, falling onto the
     grease, causes it to melt.
16   *snuffers*: a device for snuffing out candles; here it re-
     places the shears with which the Fates cut the thread
     of one's life or fate.

17   *Chamberlain*: a chamber attendant of a lord or king.
18   *Palanquin*: a covered conveyance for one person, con-
     sisting of a large box carried on two horizontal poles
     by four or six bearers, used in the Indian subcontinent
     and other Eastern countries.
19   *my Eighteenth year / Is not as you supposed complete*: The
     printed text, in indicating the confusion over whether
     the Princess is in or has passed her eighteenth year,
     notes that "the king, (perhaps on the Principle which
     so divided our opinions with respect to the termina-
     tion of the last Century) refuses to listen."

Music: No. 8. Affecting. The Princess kneels—The King won't listen—She is guarded off.

Music: No. 9. Presto forte. The King gives great charge & a Key to the Duenna—who is left alone.

Duen. Lo, the Princess *must* go—the Prince must not   60
see her till they be married—and when they *are*
she will be quite miserable; more fool she by my
modesty! I wish *I* had been born a Princess—I wish
I cou'd get a Prince for my husband. I shouldn't
be very particular about the means—Ah! There
was no Fairy, kind or unkind, to preside at my
nativity.

Music: No. 10. & Thunder. A Panel opens, and by means of a Parallel[20] cover'd with Clouds, Owletta is lower'd into the apartment and stands at the Duenna's side before she is aware. Music continuous.

Owletta. Yes, *I* presided and attend thy wishes.
Duen. (Screams). Who are you? Where did you come
from? and what do you want?   70
Owl. I am the great Owletta, a powerful fairy. I came
from a manufactory of mischief & want to help
all who are mischievously inclined—It was I who
pronounced a malediction on the Princess and
caused her confinement here—they have, as she
rightly inform'd her father, miscounted the
reckoning of her age—therefore do you
accompany her in the cover'd carriage they are now
preparing, and only contrive on the road to let its
daylight on her—She will then be transform'd to   80
an Owl, a shape I sometimes take myself; and you
will be carried forward as the Prince's Bride.

---

20 *A Panel opens, and by means of a Parallel*: The theater
of the period was known for its spectacular effects.
Here, a panel in a flat opens to reveal Owletta on a
parallel, i.e., a platform or pedestal to which other
smaller platforms could be attached. Owletta presumably occupied the central pedestal, surrounded by
clouds on the other pedestals that would open up to
reveal her. Her pedestal would sink under her weight
as a windlass operator pulled ropes attached to each
of the pedestals.

Duen. (Trembling). May I believe?
Owl. Dare not to doubt—Young Arthur dared to &
rejected my offer'd hand, & thus thro' thee I mean
to be revenged—Hence & prepare thee—fear not
my assistance. *(Sinks).*
Duen. No great revenge neither to give him a wife
like me,[21] methinks—wou'd she have had thee
marry an Owl.   90
(A who-o-o of an Owl is heard).
Mercy on us! She'll be at my elbow again if I don't
take care. *(Exit Duenna).*

Music: No. 11. Staccato. Enter Sir Arthur cautiously exploring his way out of the Palace. The stage is growing dark.

Sir Arthur. No outlet! no escape! Shou'd I be taken,
not only will the reputation of the Princess suffer,
but the Exempt[22] of the Extinguishers, the
Colonel of the Candelabra Corps, or a Lieutenant
of the Lanthorns will conduct me to my fate—Oh
Love! Love! When the cotton of our hearts is dipt
in thy—but hark!—they come!—is there no
guardian Fairy to protect me—it is quite dark   100
too—quite—quite—Ha!

Music: No. 12. Allegro Brilliante. The stage from having been made as dark as possible, is enlighten'd by a most brilliant cloud containing a Sun—in front of which stands the Fairy Aquila, who descends in a Parallel from the Panel opposite that which produced the other Fairy. She is most beautifully attired in Silver Armour—her Shield a Sun—an Eagle on her Helmet—in her hand a Bow—she approaches the astonish'd Knight and speaks. The orchestra (which had accompanied her descent with beautifully soft yet cheerful musick) ceases.

Aquila. Thou hast not wish'd in vain my gallant
Knight. Behold the guardian fairy of the Princess

---

21 *a wife like me*: A cancelled line in the Larpent version
of Owletta's preceding speech indicates that Prince
Humpino has rejected Owletta's hand, thus indicating why she would be seeking revenge on him as well.

22 *Exempt*: a lower officer in the cavalry.

whose bitter foe, the fiend Owletta, now contrives some hellish plot against her happiness—its nature I am not yet permitted to discover but this I know—the Sorceress delights to wear an Owl's form even as do I at times assume the Eagle's—disguis'd as the bird of night, She at this moment hovers round us—take this unerring bow, & aim [110] these shafts at ev'ry owl thou seest—should'st thou be fortunate and kill thy foe—the Princess will be thine. Hasten youth! No thanks—thou shalt pass hence invisible—thy Life were else in danger from the angry King.

Music: No. 13. Air: Aquila.[23]
Go gentle Knight
  Be fortunate, be free,
And 'midst each soft delight,
  Which love prepares for thee,
While hence I wing my airy flight, [120]
  Farewell! remember me.

(Lively Musick. Allegretto. Sir Arthur pays pantomime acknowledgements on one side as the Fairy ascends on the other. The Palace at the same time changes to):

Scene III: *A romantick Pass, near a ruin'd Tower.*

Music: No. 14. Distant March, then nearer, then characteristic pizzicato musick. Owletta enters in the foreground as if on the look out. Observes some figures on the distant Plain, and hides in a hollow tree. The March is resumed, and the Dwarf Procession, with the addition of the Princess's Guards, cross the stage preceding a handsome cover'd carriage on a Sledge, something in the form of a State Gondola or Barge. As it passes the Centre Owletta is seen to wave her wand.

Duen. (Is heard thro' a Gauze). Do have one peep, Madam; your Birthday is really past; you are mistaken in your reckoning and may see the Sun in safety.
Prin. If I were sure of that—

Duen. Sure! You may be sure! And if not, what worse can happen than to be forced to marry an ugly dwarf—there—I'll open the carriage.

Music: No. 15. Hurried but Piano. The Duenna opens a Slider[24] *in the roof of the Carriage.—Owletta waves her crutch. A Scream is heard from the carriage, from which a large Owl flies and perches on the ruin'd Tower. The Duenna puts her head out, laughs, kisses her hand to the Fairy, and the carriage moves off follow'd by the Guards.*

Owl. There Princess, stay till thy gay Knight has
    power to relieve thee.—
Nor ever hope to be Sir Arthur's wife [10]
Till he who loves thee best attempt thy life.

Music: No. 16. Air: Owletta.[25]
Revenge! I thank thee for thine aid,
  Rash Youth! to shun a Fairy's charms,
And thou, too, all-presumptuous Maid,
Soon shall thy fancied beauties fade,
  Nor live to bless the Traitor's arms. *(Exit).*

(A Staccato movement accompanied at the end of ev'ry three or four bars by notes resembling the mournful plaint of an owl, introduces Sir Arthur follow'd by a Squire, who carries a large Bag.)
Art. (Looking about). Is the Bag full, Hugo?
Squire. There's scarcely room for another, & if your worship goes on this way—the Race of Owls will be exterminated—bless me! There's a beauty! *(Sees* [20] *the Owl on the Tower).* Don't shoot her, Sir—She's too pretty to be killed.
Sir Arthur. (Looking). That is so very extraordinary a Bird that I feel a presentiment it must be the

---

24 *Slider*: a sliding door.

25 *Air: Owletta*: This song is not found in the Larpent version. However, there is a handwritten note in the British Museum's copy of the printed play: "'Revenge I Thank Thee' Sung by Miss Horribow in the same No. 16 N.S." No. 16 is the musical number indicated at this point in the Larpent version, so perhaps the song was added after the copy of the play was sent to Larpent for licensing.

---

23 *Air: Aquila*: This song is not found in the Larpent version.

fairy—for the Love of the Princess she comes down to a certainty—Fairies resume their natural forms when they die, so, Harkye,[26] Hugo! When I shoot, watch that Bird, & if she changes to a woman, chop her head off.

Music: No. 17 is No. 15 repeated. Sir Arthur lets fly an arrow. The Bird tumbles behind a Buttress of the Tower. A Scream is heard. Sir Arthur & Hugo run to the spot. The Princess is seen bleeding and supporting herself against the Tower. Hugo, who had been watching her with his Sword drawn, drops it, and says:

Hugo. Dear Master, I couldn't harm her for the Universe.

Art. Her! Who! O power of Love what has this hand 30 committed!

Music: No. 18. Agitato. Sir Arthur runs distracted to the Princess, who faints in his arms. Aquila suddenly appears.—Hugo runs away. The Fairy speaks:

Aqu. Courage! The wound is slight & was necessary to her disenchantment—since her life has been sought by him who loves her—behold my power can heal it. *(Touches the Princess with her wand— she recovers).* So, be united, Children, but as a Star of Night still frowns upon ye—till better times I give ye this disguise.

40

Music: No. 19. Short Presto. Changes them to Harlequin & Columbine and draws a wooden sword out of Sir Arthur's quiver which she gives him.

Aqu. This will protect you in my absence & when it changes to a bow & shaft, shoot at the first living object you behold, let it be whom it may, so shall your foes and mine be surely punished, your father reconciled, & all be happy.

Music: No. 20. The Lovers gratefully take leave of their Patroness, while she is singing the succeeding:

---

26 *Harkye:* "hark ye," or "listen you."

Air: Aquila.
    Trip, lightly trip,
    Of mirth unhurtful sip,
And guardian Genii[27] hov'ring round
    Shall still supply
    Their aid, while I,   50
Your friend, unchanging, will be found.

    Chorus of Spirits (behind—above—below—&c).
    Trip, lightly trip, &c.

(Harlequin & Columbine trip off on one side. Aquila goes off on the other.)

    Scene IV: *Grand Pavilion of the Dwarf King.*

Music: No. 21. Pomposo. The King, Prince, Ambassador, &c, &c, meet the cover'd carriage. The Duenna is led out veiled and dressed as the Princess. The Priest joins their hands. The Lady's veil being raised, all appear astonished. The Prince refuses to have her.

Music: No. 22. Presto. She bullies some, cuffs others, and kicks up a dust in the Palace—in the midst of the hubbub, the carriage changes to a car drawn by Owls—from which Owletta addresses the astonish'd court.

Owl. Peace fools, nor quarrel more among yourselves.
    But haste—o'ertake a pair of tripping elves
    Who have outwitted you & you and me.
    Take to deceive them, these *new forms* away.
    Your zeal in this our common cause display   5
    While thus I change the Scene to where you'll see
    The Game. Quick, put it up without delay.

Music: No. 23. Motto Staccato. Owletta waves her crutch and the King, Prince and Ambassador are transform'd to Pantaloon, Lover & Clown—and the Pavilion changes to:

---

27 *Genii:* plural of genius, where genius refers to the classical pagan belief of a spirit attending each individual or inhabiting a particular place; guardian spirits or spirits of the place.

V

Scene V:[28] *A Bower*

Scene VI: *A Coachmaker's Shop in London.*

Music: No. 24. Antic Danza. Several Carriages in various stages of building painted on the Scene. One completely finish'd, wheel'd on—and the body of another brought on and laid on the stage.

Music: No. 25. Pantaloon, Lover & Clown come on. Harlequin & Columbine dance on, trip round, and are pointed out to the Pantaloon, Lover & Clown, who commence a pursuit thro' the body of the Coach, which is repeated twice or thrice—till the Clown, fastening the farther door of the carriage, Harlequin and Columbine are stopp'd on that side & as they get in on the side of the audience, the Pursuers lock that door also and intimate that they have them secure. Harlequin waves his Sword out at the front windows and the Carriage moves away, leaving another where it stood—but this is not observ'd by Clown &c.

Music: No. 26. Hurry. The Clown in trying to stop the moving carriage, is carried round by the wheel. Pantaloon & Lover follow him off. When the stage is clear, Harlequin and Columbine come out of the carriage that was left behind and laugh at their opponents. They then go into the Coachmaker's Shop.

Music: No. 27. Rotatory tune. Clown returns, and as if still impelled by the Rotary motion of the wheel turns (a la Catherine Wheel) all round the Stage. Pantaloon & Lover follow, and have no small trouble to stop him. They then look about & are surprised at seeing a facsimile of the coach they had followed off still remaining on the stage.

Music: No. 28. Presto. They open the coach to look for Harlequin and Columbine, instead of which three figures like themselves come out of the coach and, after some confusion about which is which and some comic mimicry of each other, the false characters' drapes fly off & they change to blue devils or spitting Griffins[29] who chase them round the Stage till they take shelter in the coach body.—

Music: No. 29. Harlequin & Columbine reenter from the Coach maker's Shop. Harlequin waves his Sword. The windows of the coach body close, and the whole of it changes to a Balloon in which the Clown, Pantaloon and Lover are carried up & off. N.B.: To prevent its being really loaded, if the Coach body is over a Trap, the characters in it can descend below the stage unobserved by the audience before the Balloon rises. Harlequin & Columbine remain dancing on the stage till the Balloon is out of sight and then trip off together.

Scene VII: *A Romantick Forest Scene with two picturesque old trees.*

Music: No. 30. Allegro. Harlequin & Columbine enter. Are fatigued and each lean against a Tree.—Clown passes on, sees them and runs back to call his master. Harlequin perceives him, hides Columbine and takes shelter himself in the hollow of the tree opposite.

Music: No. 31. Lively. Pursuers enter, look about for the Lovers, beat Clown for false intelligence—when Harlequin is seen peeping thro' a hole in the upper part

---

28 *Scene V: A Bower.* This scene is not in the Larpent version, and the printed version merely lists the scenes in the harlequinade proper. However, *The Times*'s review speaks of a scene in which a boy contortionist "dressed in some savage character" is the central performer. *The European Magazine* identifies this boy as Mr. Pack, who plays the Monster of the Forest, the Leaden Harlequin (Scene XII), and the Dancing Bear (Scene XIV). Presumably the "savage character" is the Monster of the Forest; while it is possible that the Monster could appear in Scene VII (the "Romantick Forest" scene), this scene seems complete as described. It therefore appears that the boy's performance occurred in this undescribed scene as a set-piece incorporated into the pantomime at the last moment. See Appendix pages 384–85.

29 *to blue devils or spitting Griffins:* Blue was a favorite color for ghostly and demonic apparitions on stage. A griffin is a mythological creature normally depicted with the head and wings of an eagle and the body of a lion.

of the tree he had hid in. Clown points him out & runs into the hollow of the tree, and by the time he has climb'd up on the inside Harlequin appears in the tree next to Pursuers. Clown says, "I'm mistaken in the tree," comes down and gets into the other, when Harlequin appears in the first tree again—and nods to Clown as he appears in the upper part of the second— Clown makes signals to Pantaloon and Lover to guard the bottom of the Tree where Harlequin is, who, finding himself beset, climbs over the branches till out of sight.—Clown gets out of his tree & follows him— whilst he is partially hid by the branches.

Music: No. 32. Hushaby baby and Hurry. A great Crash is heard—and a Hallo! A branch breaks and a figure of the Clown falls out of the tree behind a part of the foliage &c——

Music: No. 33. Andante leg brokio. From whence the real Clown is brought piteously roaring and with all his bones broken.

Music: No. 34. Allegro. While Pantaloon and Lover are bringing him forward, Harlequin makes a forespring or Summerset[30] from the tree, fetches Columbine from her concealment and they run off unobserved— Pantaloon & Lover carry off the wounded Clown.

Scene VIII: *A Street.[31] On one side a Dutch Clockmaker's, on the Other, a Pastry Cook's.*

Music: No. 35. Allegro. Harlequin and Columbine enter, trip round, survey the Scene, and Harlequin buys Pastry for Columbine. They also notice some curious figures among the Dutch clock work.—Clown is heard to roar out. Harlequin & Columbine take shelter in the Clockmaker's Shop.

Music: No. 36. Andante comico. Clown enters, led on by Pantaloon & Lover and takes care to let the audience see that he is not really hurt. Sees the Pastry

cook's & begs for a little Wey[32]—which is given him— He then seems in great agony and begs for a Jelly—then a Tart, a Tongue, a Polony, a Plumbcake[33] &c &c— all of which he eats making but a mouthful of each. N.B.—They may be made on the Principle of blown up bladders & shrunk up to nothing on being emptied of their air. He however continues very bad and Pastry Cook runs for a Doctor.

Music: No. 37. Lively. In the meantime they are leading Clown in the Clock shop when Harlequin, from a window above, waves his sword, and all the figures on the Clocks become animated. The cuckoos sing—a cock crows—a Butcher, in knocking down an Ox, hits the Clown's head, as he is peeping close at it, with his pole ax. A Centinel walking before a Town fires his piece at Pantaloon, and a Gardener watering flowers plays a plentiful stream in the Lover's face. They cuff each other by mistake for these misfortunes—each supposing them to be inflicted by his neighbour—at length they see Harlequin laughing at the window— run into the shop leaving the Clown behind—who as soon as they are gone recovers the use of his legs and arms, steals a clock, and limps into the house with it.

Scene IX: *Inside of the Dutch Clockmaker's.*

Music: No. 38. Clock Tune. In the centre, a large Dutch Clock with workable Dutch Dolls on the top of it. Harlequin & Columbine enter—they hear the pursuers on the stairs.—Harlequin strikes the Clock—

---

30 *Summerset*: "somerset," somersault.

31 *A Street*: According to *The Times*'s review, this street is "in Cheapside," and there is an "antique fountain"; see Appendix page 384.

32 *Wey*: either "wey," a small measure, so that Clown is given a small amount, or "whey," the watery part of milk after the curds have been separated out.

33 *Jelly ... Tart ... Tongue ... Polony ... Plumbcake*: Clown's gluttony was a regular feature of the harlequinade. Here he eats a jellied sweet of some kind, like a jelly doughnut, a tart of baked pastry enclosing different ingredients, particularly fruit or cheese, a piece of animal tongue, a polony sausage made of partly cooked pork, and a plum-cake made of raisins, currants, and other preserved fruits. As the note in the text suggests, the trick of his eating so much is done by having the foodstuffs made of blown up "bladders" or balloons which can be immediately deflated as he "eats" them.

the figures on it turn into the Scene—the Clock opens—Harlequin & Columbine go into it—and appear immediately in Miniature (by two children) at the top, instead of the two figures. Clown comes on— looks about—sees no one—admires the Clockwork— produces the Clock he has stolen—sits down with it and introduces various tricks.[34] When Clown has play'd sufficient tricks with his Clock—he hears his master coming—and lies down as if very bad from his fall.—Pantaloon and Lover enter with a Pill box and 6 Phials.—The first containing a large bolus,[35] label'd "To be taken immediately." The Phials label'd—"To be taken every hour." The Clown objects to taking any of them—but his master and the Lover insist.—They first give him the Bolus, which is gilt—he pretends to take it, but sticks it on one of the clocks like a gilt-ornament. They then look what's o'clock—give him (much against his will) a draught.

Music: No. 39 Clown taking Physic. He has scarcely taken it, when Harlequin on the clock moves it an hour forward—Pantaloon sees the time and insists on Clown taking another, which is repeated as quickly and as often as the Physic will operate successfully on the audience. At last the Clown swells prodigiously and is laid on the back of two chairs, where he introduces a number of Pantomime tricks.[36]

Music: No. 40. Allegro. Presto comico. Harlequin & Columbine are intercepted trying to make their escape. Harlequin jumps thro' the clock. Clown in following him is hang'd to the Pendulum—and while the Lover and Pantaloon are fascinated[37] and forced to take the place of the two figures—Harlequin and Columbine run away at the bottom and the Scene closes.

Scene X: *Outside of a Country Public House. The Sign of the Bell. On one side, an Orchard wall with apples hanging over.*

Music: No. 41. Hornpipe[38] for Columbine. Harlequin & Columbine enter in quest of Refreshment.— Harlequin calls Landlord and orders wine;— Columbine also longs for some apples—and at her request Harlequin holds up his sword and apples fly from the tree on to the point of it. They have a half comic Pas deux[39] with the wine and apples—offering them alternately to each other—drinking to each other &c—but are interrupted by Clown—who is beaten off.

Music: No. 42. Bustle. Harlequin (to baulk the expected Pursuit) strikes the Wall—a flap from which turns over, and produces a collection of Ballads. Columbine turns round on a Centre into the wall[40]— a Basket chair comes round in her place and a profile table[41] with roasted apples.—Harlequin takes a dress from the Basket Chair and, assuming the appearance of an old applewoman, sits down, puts on a large pair of spectacles, & begins to knit.

Music: No. 43. Very Visual. Pizzicato.[42] Pursuers enter. They look in vain for Harlequin & Columbine—Pantaloon & Lover go into the Public House—Clown bargains for roasted apples—Steals some—burns his fingers—steals a Ballad and then the old woman's Spectacles to read it by. N.B. Here a Comic Song might be naturally enough introduced.

Music: No. 44. Pear Song. Clown gets beaten by the pretended Old Woman for his Roguery—and while

---

34 *various tricks*: The Larpent manuscript left space here for the tricks to be filled in, but they were never included. The best description of harlequinade tricks is found in David Mayer's *Harlequin in his Element*.

35 *Bolus*: a solid medicine to be swallowed, larger than a pill.

36 *Pantomime tricks*: Again, the Larpent copy left room to add descriptions of the tricks.

37 *fascinated*: hypnotized by the swinging Pendulum of the clock.

38 *Hornpipe*: a dance, identified with sailors, of a lively and vigorous manner, usually performed by one person.

39 *Pas deux*: "pas de deux," meaning a dance duet.

40 *turns round on a Centre into the wall*: In other words, the wall pivots to hide Columbine behind it, revealing the basket chair in her place.

41 *profile table*: A profile table is a flat piece of stage furniture cut out in outline.

42 *Pizzicato*: said of a note or passage played on a stringed instrument in which the strings are plucked with the finger instead of using the bow.

boxing with her, discovers the Harlequin dress under her disguise—calls out for assistance—Harlequin waves his sword, the bell on the public house sign begins making a devil of a noise, and while the Pantaloon, Lover, Clown & Landlord are staring at it—Harlequin waves in a real old applewoman who sits down in the Chair & Harlequin getting Columbine out from the wall, they run off. The enchanted bell ceases—Clown now tells his master that the applewoman is Harlequin—they all attack her—she calls out, "What strike a woman!" and pelts them with hot apples. Landlord and men from public house take her part. Lover and Pantaloon get well thrash'd, or perhaps pump'd at the Horse trough.—Clown slips out of the fray—eats all the apples and pockets all the Ballads—till at length he is kick'd off by his master and the Lover—for having given them false intelligence.

Scene XI: *View of a Sea-Port town, on one side the crane of a Store house.*[43]

Music: No. 45. Harlequin & Columbine enter—trip round & view the Scene—Sailors enter, are welcomed on shore by Harlequin & Columbine, and their girls propose a dance and perform a Hornpipe. Towards the end of it Clown comes on & is pointed out to the Sailors by Harlequin & beat off. Harlequin & Columbine dress as Sailor & Girl—the dance is resumed & they perform a double Hornpipe.

(Pursuers come on—a general rumpus ensues. Columbine is taken off by Pantaloon—Harlequin jumps over their heads—gets off—is pursued—brought back and cram'd into a sack and hung up in sight of the audience.)

Music: No. 46. Clown and Lover get great sticks to beat Harlequin (in the Bag) to atoms. At the first blow it is evident the sack is empty and Harlequin appears in the Warehouse over the Crane, waving his Sword. They are astonish'd—take down the Sack—turn it inside out—nothing appears there. Pantaloon re-enters

with Columbine. Lover tells him what has happened—and Clown is accused of having deceiv'd them with respect to Harlequin.—By way of punishment they propose putting him in the sack, and beating him. He resists & runs off, is brought back, put in the sack and hung up.

Music: No. 47. When they are going to beat him, Harlequin appears, waves his sword. The sack, from being evidently bulky, appears empty—and Clown suddenly pops on grinning at his masters' disappointment. They turn the sack inside out as before—nothing is there. They turn, see Clown laughing at them, run after him. Columbine, in the confusion, gives them the slip.—Runs to Harlequin, who keeps Pursuers at bay & escapes with Columbine. Pantaloon & Lover, still engaged with Clown, pop the sack over his head & beat him towards the Wing—just at the entrance the sack flies up and discovers a devil who hunts them off.

Scene XII: *Outside of a Plumber's Shop.*[44] *Various leaden figures (particularly a Harlequin and a Columbine) are standing in the window, also a swan and a sportsman with a gun—a black with a sundial &c &c.*

Music: No. 48. Contra danza. Harlequin & Columbine, hotly pursued, take refuge in the Plumber's shop. Pursuers pass across without seeing them. Harlequin & Columbine are going off when they observe their enemies returning. Harlequin strikes the leaden figures, which sink[45] *and Harlequin & Columbine assume their places.—Plumber comes on and directs his men to take down the figures of Harlequin & Columbine to be pack'd up. The Men lift the board down on which they stand, and they keep their attitudes as stiffly as possible while moving.—*

Music: No. 49. Brisk. Pursuers return—are going to seize Columbine. Plumbers interfere and intimate that the figures are new painted and will be spoil'd if touch'd. Harlequin with his sword tickles Plumber's

---

[43] *View … house*: The Larpent version indicates that this piece of scenery was placed in the front grooves, the tracks for scenery closest to the audience.

[44] *Plumber's Shop*: the shop of an artisan who works in lead, zinc, and tin.

[45] *sink*: via the trap doors on the stage.

ear, who thinking it done by the Clown bids him be quiet. A scuffle ensues, during which Harlequin hits several smart slaps, till Clown observes him, brings all the party forward & tells what he has seen. They get a net and sticks to catch them and beat Harlequin, who, while they are in consultation, trips off with Columbine, and, waving his sword as he goes, two figures rise instead of him and Columbine. Pursuers knock them down and they break. Plumbers insist on satisfaction. Harlequin peeps on & waves his sword— the swan plays water among them—the sportsman fires—the black and other leaden figures of Mercury, Fame[46] &c become animated and conclude the Scene with a comic dance.

Scene XIII: *A scene full of shops with practicable[47] signs projecting from the flats and wings. Viz. 1st an Optician's, the sign a large pair of spectacles 2nd a Gunsmith's, the sign a long gun 3rd a Cookshop, the sign a plumb pudding 4th a Hatter's, the sign an immense cock'd hat 5th a Shoemaker's,[48] the sign a large boot 6th Wine Vaults,[49] the sign a but[50] & bunch of grapes*

Music: No. 50. Morning in London Markets. Enter Harlequin & Columbine. They see Pursuers coming, who enter, and a pursuit takes place through all the different shops, till, while Pantaloon and Lover are looking for the fugitives, the Clown steals a telescope from the opticians, and, as the moon is just rising, peeps at it.

Music: No. 51. Tune Tyburn Tree. A gallows appears in the moon, which disappears when Clown ceases to look thro' the glass.

Music: No. 52. Horns of Bone. Lover enters, looks through, sees "Matrimony" and a pair of Horns[51] over it.

Music: No. 53. Round about the Maypole. Pantaloon enters, looks, and sees a miniature Harlequin & Columbine.

Music: No. 54. Clown gets in front of the telescope, the figures disappear and one like the Clown takes their place.

Music: No. 55. Presto. Harlequin from a window waves his sword. The telescope changes to a gun, goes off, shoots the Clown, who shams dead, & Pantaloon, with Lover, goes for assistance. They bring a Doctor. Clown peeps up, points to the cook shop as affording better medicine & kicks the doctor off.

Music: No. 56. Presto. Pantaloon & Lover see Harlequin & Columbine skipping off and go in pursuit of them. Clown eats a few dumplins[52] from Cook shop and steals a few more which he, on being watch'd, rams for concealment into the gun. Cook & Constable enter and are going to shoot him with the stolen dumplins. Gunsmith comes out, claims the gun and Clown pays the Cook for his pudding.[53] Harlequin enters, pursued, & leaps through one Eye of the Spectacles at the Opticians. Clown in following leaps through the other and their faces appear (painted) thro' each eye of the Barnacles,[54] which fall down like a yoke upon Pantaloon's neck, which stands in place of a nose to them. Harlequin brings Columbine out from the optician's &, to divert the Clown's attention (who follows him), he waves his sword. All the Signs descend. Pantaloon & Lover follow Harlequin & Columbine.

Music: No. 57. Brisk. The Clown remains with the signs, puts the Barrel for a Body, on the boot, the

---

46 *Mercury, Fame*: This suggests that there are various figures representing classical gods, including Fama and Mercury, the messenger god and protector of thieves.

47 *practicable*: said of stage props capable of actual use in the play, as distinct from things that are merely simulated.

48 *Shoemaker's*: The printed text identifies the shop as a bootmaker's.

49 *Wine Vaults*: The printed version identifies the shop as a spirit vendor's.

50 *but*: "butt," a cask for wine or ale.

---

51 *pair of Horns*: the sign of being a cuckold.

52 *dumplins*: dumplings.

53 *pudding*: here, a synonym for dumpling.

54 *Barnacles*: spectacles; from the meaning of barnacle as an instrument of torture, probably by way of the idea that ill-fitting glasses tortured the nose.

Plumb pudding on the Barrel for a head in which he sticks the Grapes for a nose. Puts the large Spectacles on them & the Cock'd Hat over all, sticks the long Gun on its Shoulder, and while he is admiring the figure he has form'd,[55] *it hops off after him, and turns round the long gun in all directions, overturns Pantaloon & Lover who are reentering, while Harlequin and Columbine return tripping over their prostrate opponents, and as they go off the scene closes.*

Scene XIV: *A Village.*[56]

Music: No. 58. Bear Tune Dronoso. Raree Shew[57] *man enters, follow'd by a Possee of Villagers & Children. They peep in while he sings them a comic chaunt of something temporary & whimsical, which they are supposed to see represented. He is accompanied by a Hurdygurdy*[58] *Woman who joins in the burthen of his ditty with her voice & instrument.*[59]

Music: No. 59. Trip Trip. Harlequin & Columbine enter, see pursuers at hand & change clothes with the Shew Man & Hurdygurdy woman who are paid by Harlequin for the loan of their shew box. Clown brings on his master and the Lover. They enquire of the pretended Shewman for Harlequin & Columbine.— Pantaloon & Lover are shewn off by their misdirection of Harlequin. Clown stays—asks to see the shew & dancers.

Music: No. 60. A comic Pas Trois[60] *with Harlequin & Columbine to the Hurdygurdy of the latter. Towards*

the end of the dance, Clown whips up the Shew Box and is going off with it, when Harlequin strikes it and it encloses Clown like a Box.

Music: No. 61. Comic. Shewman & woman return. Harlequin bids them take their Shew & Hurdygurdy again & Clown is carried off in the Box on one side roaring to the Hurdygurdy, which also accompanies the dance of Harlequin & Columbine who go laughing off on the other. Pursuers return—meet Clown with the Shew box hanging about him & fighting with the Shewman, who bangs him with his staff while the woman smashes her Hurdy Gurdy on his head & leaves it about his neck like a Collar.

Music: No. 62. Thunderato. Owletta enters. The Mob &c fly at sight of her. She beckons Pantaloon, Lover, and Clown to follow her in silence and all go off.

Scene XV: *Owletta's Den or the Cave of Night.*

Music: No. 63. No. 16 again. Harlequin & Columbine enter, are met and opposed by Owletta, Pantaloon, Lover, and Clown. Columbine is forcibly taken from Harlequin, who is left alone in the Caverns. Owls hoot & Spectres pass along in the Recesses of the Den. Harlequin throws himself on the ground, rises, recollects his sword, waves it, strikes the ground & rocks without effect, throws it from him angrily—it changes to a Bow and Arrow.

Music: No. 64. No. 15 again with 3 choruses. He recollects the Fairy's behest, runs and seizes the bow, looks about for an object, beholds Columbine entering an opening in the Rock, is going to her, hesitates, draws the Bow, pauses.—The words "Be Bold" appear in transparent letters in the Rock.[61] *He shoots—the figure falls. A Horrid yell—chains—gong—Thunder &c accompanying.*

Music: No. 65. Crash. The Dress of Columbine flies away and the hideous Owletta is seen sinking in the

---

55 *the figure he has form'd*: One of the famous tricks Clown performed was creating a creature out of various odds and ends.

56 *Scene XIV: A Village*: The Larpent version indicates that this set is placed in the front grooves.

57 *Raree Shew*: a travelling show, usually one that can be contained in a box; a peep show.

58 *Hurdygurdy*: an instrument in which strings make sounds as a wheel is rotated; a barrel-organ.

59 *Bear … instrument*: The review in *The Times* indicates that the man enters with a bear and the woman with a monkey, and the animals engage in a *pas de deux*. See Appendix page 384.

60 *Pas Trois*: "pas de trois," a dance trio.

61 *letters in the Rock*: These letters were likely written in phosphorous. The printed version indicates that these words are also spoken by an offstage voice.

arms of Fiends and into a chasm of Flames &c. The Rocks fall to pieces. Aquila is seen amid the Ruins with the real Columbine and the whole cave changes to:

Scene XVI: *Aquila's Palace; or, The Temple of Day.*[62]

Music: No. 66. Grand March. Where Aquila leads the Princess to the arms of her Lover. Beautiful Genii, the Hours, Loves, and Graces appear, accompanied by all possible Brilliancy, & celebrate the union of the Pantomime Pair with a:

Music: No. 67. Grand Dance and Finale. Chorus.
Sorrow away,
Night yield to Day,
    Joy to the Pair.

Quip, crank and smile.
Grief shall beguile,
    And banish dull care.

Chace sorrow away
And turn night to day.

                    FINIS.

---

62 *Temple of Day*: The printed version identifies this as the "Region of Light."

The Cenci: A Tragedy in Five Acts

Percy B. Shelley

Like Inchbald and Byron, Percy Bysshe Shelley (1792-1822) lived much of his adult life as an object of public speculation. The only son of Sussex aristocrats Timothy and Elizabeth Shelley, he stood to inherit his father's seat in Parliament and his grandfather's estate and baronetcy. Shelley thus was sent in 1804 to school at Eton, where he gained a reputation for eccentricity—he was often taunted by his schoolmates as "mad Shelley" and as "Shelley the atheist"—but also developed an early interest in writing and publishing. His father encouraged what he called his son's "printing freaks," and by the time he entered University College, Oxford in 1810, Shelley was already co-author (with his sister Elizabeth) of the anonymous *Original Poetry; by Victor and Cazire* (1810) and of the Gothic novel *Zastrozzi* (1810), written in imitation of Matthew Lewis and Charlotte Dacre. He continued to write and publish while at Oxford. *St. Irvyne; or, The Rosicrucian* (1811) shows him at first indulging, and then abandoning, Gothic fiction as a form, while the title of his joint production with college friend Thomas Jefferson Hogg, *Posthumous Fragments of Margaret Nicholson; Being poems found amongst the papers of that noted female who attempted the life of the King in 1786* (1810), nicely captures his fondness for literary pranks and political satire. However, Shelley's next production with Hogg in this vein, an anonymous pamphlet entitled *The Necessity of Atheism* (1811), had unforeseen and permanent repercussions. After being questioned by college authorities, both students were immediately expelled, and Shelley's refusal to repudiate the pamphlet resulted in a permanent break with his family.

Shelley's expulsion inaugurated a series of events over the next years that would make him notorious in his lifetime and an almost legendary figure among radicals after his tragic death by drowning in 1822.

In 1811 he eloped with the sixteen-year-old Harriet Westbrook, and over the next three years campaigned for radical causes in Ireland and Wales, published *Queen Mab* (1813), a poetical manifesto with philosophical notes, cultivated the friendships of London radicals Leigh Hunt and William Godwin, became estranged from Harriet, and eloped to the Continent with Godwin's daughter Mary in July of 1814. Accompanied by Mary's sister Jane "Claire" Claremont, Shelley and Mary returned after a few weeks and subsequently settled in London, where Shelley's improving financial health allowed them to cultivate their intellectual interests. The respite, however, was temporary. In the spring of 1816 Claire pursued and became the mistress of Lord Byron; and when Byron went into self-exile, she persuaded Shelley and Mary to travel to Lake Geneva, where the three met Byron and spent the summer with him. The summer ended the liaison, but in the next months Shelley and Mary were forced to cope with a series of family crises. The suicide of Mary's half-sister, Fanny Imlay, was quickly followed by that of Harriet Shelley, whose death in turn produced a legal battle that eventually resulted in Shelley's losing the custody of his and Harriet's two children, Ianthe and Charles, in 1818. In addition, Claire's affair had resulted in the birth of a daughter, Allegra. With Shelley serving as mediator between Claire and Byron, the family traveled to Italy, and after protracted negotiations Allegra was placed in a convent. The next years in Italy produced Shelley's most famous works, including *The Mask of Anarchy* (composed 1819, published 1832), *Prometheus Unbound* (1820), *Adonais* (1821), and *Julian and Maddalo*, published posthumously in 1824.

The Cenci (1819) was Shelley's only work to go through two authorized editions in his lifetime. Explicitly written for stage performance, it shows Shelley exploiting the vogue for the Gothic and for tragedy inaugurated by Samuel Coleridge's *Remorse* (Drury Lane, 1813) and established by Charles Robert Maturin's *Bertram* (Drury Lane, 1816). As with Shelley's long poem *Laon and Cythna* (published in 1817 as *The Revolt of Islam*), *The Cenci*'s focus on incest and patriarchal tyranny made it unpopular with reviewers; its subject matter also likely prevented London theater managers from considering it seriously. The play also, however, invokes many of the same themes as the "Lyrical Drama" Shelley produced contemporaneously with it, *Prometheus Unbound*. Like Prometheus, Beatrice is confronted with the problem of how to resist a potentially degrading tyranny without degrading herself. Unlike Prometheus, Beatrice must make her choices not in the visionary world of allegory but in what Shelley's Preface calls "sad reality." The play's considerable power—enough to have inspired George Bernard Shaw to overcome Victorian sexual taboos by staging it in 1883—stems from the ambiguity with which it handles Beatrice's situation. While Shelley's Preface rejects violence as a credible solution to social oppression, the play itself—particularly when we attend to the corruption of the papal government and Count Cenci's hints about venereal disease—gives Beatrice little choice.

The copytext for the play is *The Cenci; A Tragedy, in Five Acts* (London: C. & J. Ollier, 1819), as corrected from the errata leaf in the hand of Mary Shelley (Bodleian Library MS.don.d.130).

DEDICATION. To Leigh Hunt, Esq.[1]
My Dear Friend,

I inscribe with your name, from a distant country, and after an absence whose months have seemed years, this the latest of my literary efforts.

Those writings which I have hitherto published, have been little else than visions which impersonate my own apprehensions of the beautiful and the just.[2] I can also perceive in them the literary defects incidental to youth and impatience; they are dreams of what ought to be, or may be. The drama which I now present to you is a sad reality. I lay aside the presumptuous attitude of an instructor, and am content to paint, with such colours as my own heart furnishes, that which has been. 10

Had I known a person more highly endowed than yourself with all that it becomes a man to possess, I had solicited for this work the ornament of his name. One more gentle, honourable, innocent and brave; one of more exalted toleration for all who do and think evil, and yet himself more free from evil; one who knows better how to receive, and how to 20 confer a benefit though he must ever confer far more than he can receive; one of simpler, and, in the high-

---

[1] *Leigh Hunt, Esq.*: James Henry Leigh Hunt (1784–1859), English journalist, poet, and critic, who with his brother John launched the radical weekly newspaper *The Examiner*, which advocated abolition of the slave-trade, Catholic emancipation, and legal and parliamentary reform. Hunt continued to edit the paper even after being imprisoned in 1813 for attacks on the Prince Regent, and was celebrated as a champion of liberty. After his release in 1815, he published *The Story of Rimini* (1816), a retelling of the account of Paulo and Francesca in Canto II of Dante's *Inferno*. Hunt befriended John Keats and Shelley in 1816, and thereafter became a vocal supporter of the poetry of both writers: in many ways, he was Shelley's closest friend. His collaboration with Shelley and Lord Byron on the periodical *The Liberal* was broken up by Shelley's death in 1822 and subsequent quarrels with Byron. His best known critical essays appeared in *The Indicator* (1819–21) and *The Companion* (1828).

[2] *Those writings ... beautiful and the just*: Shelley most likely alludes here to his three long poems, *Queen Mab* (1813), *Alastor* (1816), and *Laon and Cythna* (1817).

est sense of the word, of purer life and manners I never knew: and I had already been fortunate in friendships when your name was added to the list.

In that patient and irreconcileable enmity with domestic and political tyranny and imposture which the tenor of your life has illustrated, and which, had I health and talents should illustrate mine, let us, comforting each other in our task, live and die.

And happiness attend you!

    Your affectionate friend,

      Percy B. Shelley.

Rome, May 29. 1819.

PREFACE.

A Manuscript was communicated to me during my travels in Italy which was copied from the archives of the Cenci Palace at Rome, and contains a detailed account of the horrors which ended in the extinction of one of the noblest and richest families of that city during the Pontificate of Clement VIII,[3] in the year, 1599. The story is, that an old man having spent his life in debauchery and wickedness, conceived at length an implacable hatred towards his children; which shewed itself towards one daughter under the form of an incestuous passion, aggravated by every circumstance of cruelty and violence. This daughter, after long and vain attempts to escape from what she considered a potential contamination both of body and mind, at length plotted with her mother-in-law[4] and brother to murder their common tyrant. The young maiden who was urged to this tremendous deed by an impulse which overpowered its horror, was evidently a most gentle and amiable being, a creature formed to adorn and be admired, and thus violently thwarted from her nature by the necessity of circumstance and opinion. The deed was quickly discovered

and in spite of the most earnest prayers made to the Pope by the highest persons in Rome the criminals were put to death. The old man had during his life repeatedly bought his pardon from the Pope for capital crimes of the most enormous and unspeakable kind, at the price of a hundred thousand crowns; the death therefore of his victims can scarcely be accounted for by the love of justice.[5] The Papal Government formerly took the most extraordinary precautions against the publicity of facts which offer so tragical a demonstration of its own wickedness and weakness; so that the communication of the M. S. had become, until very lately, a matter of some difficulty. Such a story, if told so as to present to the reader all the feelings of those who once acted it, their hopes and fears, their confidences and misgivings, their various interests, passions and opinions acting upon and with each other, yet all conspiring to one tremendous end, would be as a light to make apparent some of the most dark and secret caverns of the human heart.

On my arrival at Rome I found that the story of the Cenci was a subject not to be mentioned in Italian society without awakening a deep and breathless interest; and that the feelings of the company never failed to incline to a romantic pity for the wrongs, and a passionate exculpation of the horrible deed to which they urged her, who has been mingled two centuries with the common dust. All ranks of people knew the outlines of this history, and participated in the overwhelming interest which it seems to have the magic of exciting in the human heart. I had a copy of Guido's picture of Beatrice[6] which is preserved in the Colonna Palace, and my servant instantly recognized it as the portrait of *La Cenci*.

---

3 *Clement VIII*: Ippolito Aldobrandini (1536–1605), Pope from 1592 to 1605 and strong proponent of Counter-Reformative efforts.

4 *mother-in-law*: Well into the nineteenth century this word also could mean "stepmother."

5 Shelley's note: "The Pope, among other motives for severity, probably felt that whoever killed the Count Cenci deprived his treasury of a certain and copious source of revenue."

6 *Guido's picture of Beatrice*: the painting thought then to be of Beatrice Cenci painted by Guido Reni (1575–1642), now hanging in the Galleria Nazionale in Rome.

This national and universal interest which the story produces and has produced for two centuries and among all ranks of people in a great City, where the imagination is kept for ever active and awake, first suggested to me the conception of its fitness for a dramatic purpose. In fact it is a tragedy which has already received from its capacity of awakening and sustaining the sympathy of men, approbation and success. Nothing remained as I imagined, but to clothe it to the apprehensions of my countrymen in such language and action as would bring it home to their hearts. The deepest and the sublimest tragic compositions, King Lear and the two plays in which the tale of Oedipus is told, were stories which already existed in tradition, as matters of popular belief and interest, before Shakespeare and Sophocles[7] made them familiar to the sympathy of all succeeding generations of mankind.

This story of the Cenci is indeed eminently fearful and monstrous: any thing like a dry exhibition of it on the stage would be insupportable. The person who would treat such a subject must increase the ideal, and diminish the actual horror of the events, so that the pleasure which arises from the poetry which exists in these tempestuous sufferings and crimes may mitigate the pain of the contemplation of the moral deformity from which they spring.[8]

There must also be nothing attempted to make the exhibition subservient to what is vulgarly termed a moral purpose. The highest moral purpose aimed at in the highest species of the drama, is the teaching the human heart, through its sympathies and antipathies, the knowledge of itself;[9] in proportion to the possession of which knowledge, every human being is wise, just, sincere, tolerant and kind. If dogmas can do more, it is well: but a drama is no fit place for the enforcement of them. Undoubtedly, no person can be truly dishonoured by the act of another; and the fit return to make to the most enormous injuries is kindness and forbearance, and a resolution to convert the injurer from his dark passions by peace and love. Revenge, retaliation, atonement, are pernicious mistakes. If Beatrice had thought in this manner she would have been wiser and better; but she would never have been a tragic character: the few whom such an exhibition would have interested, could never have been sufficiently interested for a dramatic purpose, from the want of finding sympathy in their interest among the mass who surround them. It is in the restless and anatomizing casuistry[10] with which men seek the justification of Beatrice, yet feel that she has done what needs justification; it is in the superstitious horror with which they contemplate alike her wrongs and their revenge; that the dramatic character of what she did and suffered, consists.

I have endeavoured as nearly as possible to represent the characters as they probably were, and have sought to avoid the error of making them actuated

---

7 *Sophocles*: Sophocles (ca. 496–406 BC), Greek tragedian and author of 123 dramas, the best known of which is *Œdipus the King*. Only seven of his plays survive in their entirety. His formal artistry and attention to issues of character have made him the most critically acclaimed of the classical Greek dramatists.

8 *The person … from which they spring*: Shelley here appropriates a number of ideas current in eighteenth- and early nineteenth-century dramatic criticism about the pleasures and function of horror and tragedy. In particular, see Edmund Burke, "Of the Effects of Tragedy," in *A Philosophical Enquiry into the Origin of Our Ideas of the Sublime and Beautiful* (London: R. and J. Dodsley, 1757), part 1, section XV; David Hume, "Of Tragedy," in *Essays Moral, Political, and Literary*, ed. Thomas Hill Green and Thomas Hodge Grose, 2 vols.

(London, 1882), 1:258-65; Joanna Baillie, "Introductory Discourse" (Appendix, page 358); and *Eclectic Review* 10 (July-August 1813), 21–32.

9 *The highest moral purpose … the knowledge of the self*: See Joanna Baillie, "Introductory Discourse," on page 368 of the Appendix, which makes a similar case for the drama's ability to achieve a moral function by teaching through example.

10 *casuistry*: the science, art, or reasoning of the casuist, i.e., that person who studies and resolves cases of conscience or doubtful questions regarding duty and conduct.

by my own conceptions of right and wrong, false or true thus under a thin veil converting names and actions of the sixteenth century into cold impersonations of my own mind. They are represented as Catholics, and as Catholics deeply tinged with religion. To a Protestant apprehension there will appear something unnatural in the earnest and perpetual sentiment of the relations between God and man which pervade the tragedy of the Cenci. It will especially be startled at the combination of an undoubting persuasion of the truth of the popular religion with a cool and determined perseverance in enormous guilt. But religion in Italy is not, as in Protestant countries, a cloak to be worn on particular days; or a passport which those who do not wish to be railed at carry with them to exhibit; or a gloomy passion for penetrating the impenetrable mysteries of our being, which terrifies its possessor at the darkness of the abyss to the brink of which it has conducted him. Religion coexists, as it were, in the mind of an Italian Catholic with a faith in that of which all men have the most certain knowledge. It is interwoven with the whole fabric of life. It is adoration, faith, submission, penitence, blind admiration; not a rule for moral conduct. It has no necessary connexion with any one virtue. The most atrocious villain may be rigidly devout, and without any shock to established faith, confess himself to be so. Religion pervades intensely the whole frame of society, and is according to the temper of the mind which it inhabits, a passion, a persuasion, an excuse, a refuge; never a check. Cenci himself built a chapel in the court of his Palace, and dedicated it to St. Thomas the Apostle,[11] and established masses for the peace of his soul. Thus in the first scene of the fourth act Lucretia's design in exposing herself to the consequences of an expostulation with Cenci after having

administered the opiate, was to induce him by a feigned tale to confess himself before death; this being esteemed by Catholics as essential to salvation; and she only relinquishes her purpose when she perceives that her perseverance would expose Beatrice to new outrages.

I have avoided with great care in writing this play the introduction of what is commonly called mere poetry, and I imagine there will scarcely be found a detached simile or a single isolated description, unless Beatrice's description of the chasm appointed for her father's murder should be judged to be of that nature.[12]

In a dramatic composition the imagery and the passion should interpenetrate one another, the former being reserved simply for the full developement and illustration of the latter. Imagination is as the immortal God which should assume flesh for the redemption of mortal passion. It is thus that the most remote and the most familiar imagery may alike be fit for dramatic purposes which employed in the illustration of strong feeling, which raises what is low, and levels to the apprehension that which is lofty, casting over all the shadow of its own greatness. In other respects I have written more carelessly; that is, without an over-fastidious and learned choice of words. In this respect I entirely agree with those modern critics who assert that in order to move men to true sympathy we must use the familiar language of men.[13] And that our great ancestors the antient English poets are the writers, a study of

---

11 *St. Thomas the Apostle*: Saint Thomas (*d.* AD 53), one of the Twelve Apostles whose character is outlined in the Gospel according to John, particularly John 11:5–16. He is best known for the incredulity with which he received reports from his fellow apostles that Christ had risen, depicted in John 20:19–29.

12 Shelley's note: "An idea in this speech was suggested by a most sublime passage in 'El Purgatorio de San Patrieto' of Calderon: the only plagiarism which I have intentionally committed in the whole piece."

13 *those modern critics … familiar language of men*: See Joanna Baillie, "Introductory Discourse," in the Appendix to this volume, page 362. In addition, see William Wordsworth, Preface to *Lyrical Ballads* (1800), in *The Prose Works of William Wordsworth*, ed. W. J. B. Owen and Jane Worthington Smyser, 3 vols. (Oxford University Press, 1974), 1:123; and W. J. B. Owen, *Wordsworth as Critic* (London: Oxford University Press, 1969), 60–70.

whom might incite us to do that for our own age which they have done for theirs. But it must be the real language of men in general and not that of any particular class to whose society the writer happens to belong. So much for what I have attempted; I need not be assured that success is a very different matter; particularly for one whose attention has but newly been awakened to the study of dramatic literature.

I endeavoured whilst at Rome to observe such monuments of this story as might be accessible to a stranger. The portrait of Beatrice at the Colonna Palace is most admirable as a work of art: it was taken by Guido during her confinement in prison. But it is most interesting as a just representation of one of the loveliest specimens of the workmanship of Nature. There is a fixed and pale composure upon the features: she seems sad and stricken down in spirit, yet the despair thus expressed is lightened by the patience of gentleness. Her head is bound with folds of white drapery from which the yellow strings of her golden hair escape, and fall about her neck. The moulding of her face is exquisitely delicate; the eye brows are distinct and arched: the lips have that permanent meaning of imagination and sensibility which suffering has not repressed and which it seems as if death scarcely could extinguish. Her forehead is large and clear; her eyes which we are told were remarkable for their vivacity, are swollen with weeping and lustreless, but beautifully tender and serene. In the whole mien[14] there is a simplicity and dignity which united with her exquisite loveliness and deep sorrow are inexpressibly pathetic. Beatrice Cenci appears to have been one of those rare persons in whom energy and gentleness dwell together without destroying one another: her nature was simple and profound. The crimes and miseries in which she was an actor and a sufferer are as the mask and the mantle in which circumstances clothed her for her impersonation on the scene of the world.

The Cenci Palace is of great extent; and though in part modernized, there yet remains a vast and gloomy pile of feudal architecture in the same state as during the dreadful scenes which are the subject of this tragedy. The Palace is situated in an obscure corner of Rome, near the quarter of the Jews, and from the upper windows you see the immense ruins of Mount Palatine half hidden under their profuse overgrowth of trees. There is a court in one part of the palace (perhaps that in which Cenci built the Chapel to St. Thomas), supported by granite columns and adorned with antique friezes of fine workmanship and built up, according to the antient Italian fashion, with balcony over balcony of open work.[15] One of the gates of the palace formed of immense stones and leading through a passage, dark and lofty and opening into gloomy subterranean chambers, struck me particularly.

Of the Castle of Petrella, I could obtain no further information than that which is to be found in the manuscript.

DRAMATIS PERSONAE

Count Francesco Cenci
Giacomo, his Son
Bernardo, his Son
Cardinal Camillo
Orsino, a Prelate
Savella, the Pope's Legate
Olimpio, an Assassin
Marzio, an Assassin
Andrea, servant to Cenci
Nobles, Judges, Guards, Servants
Lucretia, Wife of Cenci, and step-mother of his
    children
Beatrice, his Daughter

---

14 *mien*: the air, bearing, or manner of a person, as expressive of character or mood.

15 *open work*: any architectural work, especially ornamental, characterized by perforations.

Scene: *Lies principally in Rome,*
but changes during the Fourth Act to Petrella,
a castle among the Apulian Apennines.

Time: *During the Pontificate of Clement VIII.*

Act I.

Scene I: *An apartment in the Cenci Palace.*
Enter Count Cenci, and Cardinal Camillo.

Camillo. That matter of the murder is hushed up
  If you consent to yield his Holiness
  Your fief that lies beyond the Pincian gate.—
  It needed all my interest in the conclave[16]
  To bend him to this point: he said that you
  Bought perilous impunity with your gold;
  That crimes like yours if once or twice
    compounded[17]
  Enriched the Church, and respited from hell
  An erring soul which might repent and live:—
  But that the glory and the interest   10
  Of the high throne he fills, little consist
  With making it a daily mart of guilt
  As manifold and hideous as the deeds
  Which you scarce hide from men's revolted eyes.
Cenci. The third of my possessions—let it go!
  Aye, I once heard the nephew of the Pope
  Had sent his architect to view the ground,
  Meaning to build a villa on my vines
  The next time I compounded with his uncle:
  I little thought he should outwit me so!   20
  Henceforth no witness—not the lamp—shall see
  That which the vassal threatened to divulge
  Whose throat is choked with dust for his reward.
  The deed he saw could not have rated higher
  Than his most worthless life:—it angers me!
  Respited me from Hell!—So may the Devil

Respite their souls from Heaven. No doubt Pope
    Clement,
  And his most charitable nephews, pray
  That the apostle Peter and the saints
  Will grant for their sake that I long enjoy   30
  Strength, wealth, and pride, and lust, and length
    of days
  Wherein to act the deeds which are the stewards
  Of their revenue.—But much yet remains
  To which they shew no title.
Cam.   Oh, Count Cenci!
  So much that thou migh'st honourably live
  And reconcile thyself with thine own heart
  And with thy God, and with the offended world.
  How hideously look deeds of lust and blood
  Through those snow white and venerable hairs!—
  Your children should be sitting round you now,   40
  But that you fear to read upon their looks
  The shame and misery you have written there.
  Where is your wife? Where is your gentle daughter?
  Methinks her sweet looks, which make all things else
  Beauteous and glad, might kill the fiend within you.
  Why is she barred from all society
  But her own strange and uncomplaining wrongs?
  Talk with me, Count,—you know I mean you well.
  I stood beside your dark and fiery youth
  Watching its bold and bad career, as men   50
  Watch meteors, but it vanished not—I marked
  Your desperate and remorseless manhood; now
  Do I behold you in dishonoured age
  Charged with a thousand unrepented crimes.
  Yet I have ever hoped you would amend,
  And in that hope have saved your life three times.
Cenci. For which Aldobrandino[18] owes you now
  My fief beyond the Pincian.—Cardinal,
  One thing, I pray you, recollect henceforth,
  And so we shall converse with less restraint.   60
  A man you knew spoke of my wife and daughter—
  He was accustomed to frequent my house;
  So the next day *his* wife and daughter came
  And asked if I had seen him; and I smiled:
  I think they never saw him any more.
Cam. Thou execrable man, beware!—
Cenci.   Of thee?

---

[16] *conclave*: the place in which the Cardinals meet in private for the election of a Pope; more generally, any private or closed assembly of an ecclesiastical character.

[17] *compounded*: having settled a debt by agreement of partial payment or compromise; having substituted money in lieu of another form of payment.

---

[18] *Aldobrandino*: the family name of Pope Clement VIII.

Nay this is idle:—We should know each other.
As to my character for what men call crime
Seeing I please my senses as I list,[19]
And vindicate that right with force or guile,   70
It is a public matter, and I care not
If I discuss it with you. I may speak
Alike to you and my own conscious heart—
For you give out that you have half reformed me,
Therefore strong vanity will keep you silent
If fear should not; both will, I do not doubt.
All men delight in sensual luxury,
All men enjoy revenge; and most exult
Over the tortures they can never feel—
Flattering their secret peace with others' pain.   80
But I delight in nothing else. I love
The sight of agony, and the sense of joy,
When this shall be another's, and that mine.
And I have no remorse and little fear,
Which are, I think, the checks of other men.
This mood has grown upon me, until now
Any design my captious[20] fancy makes
The picture of its wish, and it forms none
But such as men like you would start to know,
Is as my natural food and rest debarred   90
Until it be accomplished.
Cam.   Art thou not
Most miserable?
Cenci.   Why, miserable?—
No.—I am what your theologians call
Hardened;—which they must be in impudence,
So to revile a man's peculiar taste.
True, I was happier than I am, while yet
Manhood remained to act the thing I thought;
While lust was sweeter than revenge; and now
Invention palls:—Aye, we must all grow old—
And but that there remains a deed to act   100
Whose horror might make sharp an appetite
Duller than mine—I'd do,—I know not what.
When I was young I thought of nothing else
But pleasure; and I fed on honey sweets:
Men, by St. Thomas! cannot live like bees,
And I grew tired:—yet, till I killed a foe,
And heard his groans, and heard his children's groans,

Knew I not what delight was else on earth,
Which now delights me little. I the rather
Look on such pangs as terror ill conceals,   110
The dry fixed eye ball; the pale quivering lip,
Which tell me that the spirit weeps within
Tears bitterer than the bloody sweat of Christ.
I rarely kill the body which preserves,
Like a strong prison, the soul within my power,
Wherein I feed it with the breath of fear
For hourly pain.
Cam.   Hell's most abandoned fiend
Did never, in the drunkenness of guilt,
Speak to his heart as now you speak to me;
I thank my God that I believe you not.   120
(Enter Andrea).
Andrea. My Lord, a gentleman from Salamanca
Would speak with you.
Cenci.   Bid him attend me in
The grand saloon.[21] *(Exit Andrea).*
Cam.   Farewell; and I will pray
Almighty God that thy false, impious words
Tempt not his spirit to abandon thee. *(Exit Camillo).*
Cenci. The third of my possessions! I must use
Close husbandry, or gold, the old man's sword,
Falls from my withered hand. But yesterday
There came an order from the Pope to make
Fourfold provision for my cursed sons;   130
Whom I had sent from Rome to Salamanca,
Hoping some accident might cut them off;
And meaning if I could to starve them there.
I pray thee, God, send some quick death upon them!
Bernardo and my wife could not be worse
If dead and damned:—then, as to Beatrice—
(Looking around him suspiciously).
I think they cannot hear me at that door;
What if they should? And yet I need not speak
Though the heart triumphs with itself in words.
O, thou most silent air, that shalt not hear   140
What now I think! Thou, pavement, which I tread
Towards her chamber,—let your echoes talk
Of my imperious step scorning surprise,
But not of my intent!—Andrea!
(Enter Andrea).

---

[19] *list*: please, desire, or like.
[20] *captious*: designed to entrap or entangle by subtlety.

[21] *saloon*: also "salon," a large and lofty room for the reception of guests.

And. My lord?
Cenci. Bid Beatrice attend me in her chamber
    This evening:—no, at midnight and alone. *(Exeunt).*

          Scene II: *A Garden of the Cenci Palace.*
       Enter Beatrice and Orsino, as in conversation.

Beatrice. Pervert not truth,
    Orsino. You remember where we held
    That conversation;—nay, we see the spot
    Even from this cypress;—two long years are past
    Since, on an April midnight, underneath
    The moon-light ruins of mount Palatine,
    I did confess to you my secret mind.
Orsino. You said you loved me then.
Bea.   You are a Priest,
    Speak to me not of love.
Ors.   I may obtain
    The dispensation[22] of the Pope to marry.   10
    Because I am a Priest do you believe
    Your image, as the hunter some struck deer,
    Follows me not whether I wake or sleep?
Bea. As I have said, speak to me not of love;
    Had you a dispensation I have not;
    Nor will I leave this home of misery
    Whilst my poor Bernard, and that gentle lady
    To whom I owe life, and these virtuous thoughts,
    Must suffer what I still have strength to share.
    Alas, Orsino! All the love that once   20
    I felt for you, is turned to bitter pain.
    Ours was a youthful contract, which you first
    Broke, by assuming vows no Pope will loose.
    And thus I love you still, but holily,
    Even as a sister or a spirit might;
    And so I swear a cold fidelity.
    And it is well perhaps we shall not marry.
    You have a sly, equivocating vein
    That suits me not.—Ah, wretched that I am!
    Where shall I turn? Even now you look on me   30

As you were not my friend, and as if you
Discovered that I thought so, with false smiles
Making my true suspicion seem your wrong.
Ah! No, forgive me; sorrow makes me seem
Sterner than else my nature might have been;
I have a weight of melancholy thoughts,
And they forbode,—but what can they forbode
Worse than I now endure?
Ors.   All will be well.
    Is the petition yet prepared? You know
    My zeal for all you wish, sweet Beatrice;   40
    Doubt not but I will use my utmost skill
    So that the Pope attend to your complaint.
Bea. Your zeal for all I wish;—Ah me, you are cold!
    Your utmost skill...speak but one word...*(Aside).* Alas!
    Weak and deserted creature that I am,
    Here I stand bickering with my only friend!
    (To Orsino). This night my father gives a
        sumptuous feast,
    Orsino; he has heard some happy news
    From Salamanca, from my brothers there,
    And with this outward show of love he mocks   50
    His inward hate. 'Tis bold hypocrisy,
    For he would gladlier celebrate their deaths,
    Which I have heard him pray for on his knees:
    Great God! that such a father should be mine!
    But there is mighty preparation made,
    And all our kin, the Cenci, will be there,
    And all the chief nobility of Rome.
    And he has bidden me and my pale Mother
    Attire ourselves in festival array.
    Poor lady! She expects some happy change   60
    In his dark spirit from this act; I none.
    At supper I will give you the petition:
    Till when—farewell.
Ors.   Farewell. *(Exit Beatrice).*
                 I know the Pope
    Will ne'er absolve me from my priestly vow
    But by absolving me from the revenue
    Of many a wealthy see;[23] and, Beatrice,
    I think to win thee at an easier rate.

---

22 *dispensation*: the action of dispensing with a require-
    ment; an arrangement made by the administrator of
    the laws or canons of the church, granting, in special
    circumstances or in a particular case, an exemption
    from, or relaxation of, the penalty incurred by a breach
    of the law.

23 *see*: a seat or place of sitting; the office or position in-
    dicated by sitting in a particular chair; the territory
    under jurisdiction of a particular seat of government;
    a diocese.

Nor shall he read her eloquent petition:
He might bestow her on some poor relation
Of his sixth cousin, as he did her sister,   70
And I should be debarred from all access.
Then as to what she suffers from her father,
In all this there is much exaggeration:—
Old men are testy and will have their way;
A man may stab his enemy, or his vassal,
And live a free life as to wine or women,
And with a peevish temper may return
To a dull home, and rate[24] his wife and children;
Daughters and wives call this foul tyranny.
I shall be well content if on my conscience   80
There rest no heavier sin than what they suffer
From the devices of my love—A net
From which she shall escape not. Yet I fear
Her subtle mind, her awe-inspiring gaze,
Whose beams anatomize[25] me nerve by nerve
And lay me bare, and make me blush to see
My hidden thoughts.—Ah, no! A friendless girl
Who clings to me, as to her only hope:—
I were a fool, not less than if a panther
Were panic-stricken by the antelope's eye,   90
If she escape me. *(Exit)*.

Scene III: *A Magnificent Hall in the Cenci Palace.*
A Banquet. Enter Cenci, Lucretia, Beatrice,
Orsino, Camillo, Nobles.

Cenci. Welcome, my friends and Kinsmen; welcome ye,
Princes and Cardinals, pillars of the church,
Whose presence honours our festivity.
I have too long lived like an Anchorite,[26]
And in my absence from your merry meetings
An evil word is gone abroad of me;
But I do hope that you, my noble friends,
When you have shared the entertainment here,
And heard the pious cause for which 'tis given,
And we have pledged a health or two together,   10

---

24 *rate*: to chide, scold, or reprove angrily.

25 *anatomize*: to dissect or cut up; to lay open minutely;
   to analyze.

26 *Anchorite*: a person choosing to live withdrawn or se-
   cluded from the world, usually for religious purposes;
   a hermit.

Will think me flesh and blood as well as you;
Sinful indeed, for Adam made all so,
But tender-hearted, meek and pitiful.
1st Guest. In truth, my Lord, you seem too light of
   heart,
Too sprightly and companionable a man,
To act the deeds that rumour pins on you.
(To his Companion). I never saw such blithe and
   open cheer
In any eye!
2nd Guest.   Some most desired event,
In which we all demand a common joy,   20
Has brought us hither; let us hear it, Count.
Cenci. It is indeed a most desired event.
If, when a parent from a parent's heart
Lifts from this earth to the great Father of all
A prayer, both when he lays him down to sleep,
And when he rises up from dreaming it;
One supplication, one desire, one hope,
That he would grant a wish for his two sons
Even all that he demands in their regard—
And suddenly beyond his dearest hope,   30
It is accomplished, he should then rejoice,
And call his friends and kinsmen to a feast,
And task their love to grace his merriment,
Then honour me thus far—for I am he.
Bea. (To Lucretia). Great God! How horrible! Some
   dreadful ill
Must have befallen my brothers.
Lucretia.   Fear not, Child,
He speaks too frankly.
Bea.   Ah! My blood runs cold.
I fear that wicked laughter round his eye
Which wrinkles up the skin even to the hair.
Cenci. Here are the letters brought from Salamanca;   40
Beatrice, read them to your mother. God!
I thank thee! In one night didst thou perform,
By ways inscrutable, the thing I sought.
My disobedient and rebellious sons
Are dead!—Why, dead!—What means this
   change of cheer?
You hear me not, I tell you they are dead;
And they will need no food or raiment more:
The tapers that did light them the dark way
Are their last cost. The Pope, I think, will not
Expect I should maintain them in their coffins.   50

Rejoice with me—my heart is wondrous glad.
(Lucretia sinks, half fainting; Beatrice supports her).
Bea. It is not true!—Dear lady, pray look up.
  Had it been true, there is[27] a God in Heaven,
  He would not live to boast of such a boon.
  Unnatural man, thou knowest that it is false.
Cenci. Aye, as the word of God; whom here I call
  To witness that I speak the sober truth;—
  And whose most favouring Providence was shewn
  Even in the manner of their deaths. For Rocco
  Was kneeling at the mass, with sixteen others,   60
  When the church fell and crushed him to a
      mummy,[28]
  The rest escaped unhurt. Cristofano
  Was stabbed in error by a jealous man,
  Whilst she he loved was sleeping with his rival;
  All in the self-same hour of the same night;
  Which shows that Heaven has special care of me.
  I beg those friends who love me, that they mark
  The day a feast upon their calendars.
  It was the twenty-seventh of December:[29]
  Aye, read the letters if you doubt my oath.   70
(The Assembly appears confused; several of the guests rise).
1st Guest. Oh, horrible! I will depart—
2nd Guest.   And I.—
3rd Guest.   No, stay!
  I do believe it is some jest; though faith!
  'Tis mocking us somewhat too solemnly.
  I think his son has married the Infanta,[30]
  Or found a mine of gold in El Dorado;[31]
  'Tis but to season some such news; stay, stay!
  I see 'tis only raillery by his smile.
Cenci. (Filling a bowl of wine, and lifting it up).
  Oh, thou bright wine whose purple splendour leaps
  And bubbles gaily in this golden bowl

---

27 *there is*: as there is.
28 *mummy*: a pulpy substance or mass.
29 *twenty-seventh of December*: traditionally the feast day
    of John the Evangelist.
30 *Infanta*: a daughter of the king and queen of Spain or
    Portugal, especially the eldest daughter who is not heir
    to the throne.
31 *El Dorado*: the name of a fictitious country or city
    abounding in gold, believed by the Spaniards and by
    Sir Walter Raleigh to exist upon the Amazon River
    within the jurisdiction of the governor of Guiana.

Under the lamp light, as my spirits do,   80
To hear the death of my accursed sons!
Could I believe thou wert their mingled blood,
Then would I taste thee like a sacrament,
And pledge with thee the mighty Devil in Hell,
Who, if a father's curses, as men say,
Climb with swift wings after their children's souls,
And drag them from the very throne of Heaven,
Now triumphs in my triumph!—But thou art
Superfluous; I have drunken deep of joy
And I will taste no other wine to-night.   90
Here, Andrea! Bear the bowl around.
A Guest (Rising).   Thou wretch!
  Will none among this noble company
  Check the abandoned villain?
Cam.   For God's sake
  Let me dismiss the guests! You are insane,
  Some ill will come of this.
2nd Guest.   Seize, silence him!
1st Guest. I will!
3rd Guest.   And I!
Cenci. (Addressing those who rise with a threatening
    gesture).   Who moves? Who speaks?
  (Turning to the Company).   'tis nothing
  Enjoy yourselves.—Beware! For my revenge
  Is as the sealed commission of a king
  That kills, and none dare name the murderer.
(The Banquet is broken up; several of the Guests are
departing).
Bea. I do entreat you, go not, noble guests;   100
  What, although tyranny and impious hate
  Stand sheltered by a father's hoary hair?
  What, if 'tis he who clothed us in these limbs
  Who tortures them, and triumphs? What, if we,
  The desolate and the dead, were his own flesh,
  His children and his wife, whom he is bound
  To love and shelter? Shall we therefore find
  No refuge in this merciless wide world?
  O think what deep wrongs must have blotted out
  First love, then reverence in a child's prone mind   110
  Till it thus vanquish shame and fear! O, think!
  I have borne much, and kissed the sacred hand
  Which crushed us to the earth, and thought its stroke
  Was perhaps some paternal chastisement!
  Have excused much, doubted; and when no doubt
  Remained, have sought by patience, love, and tears

To soften him, and when this could not be
I have knelt down through the long sleepless nights
And lifted up to God, the Father of all,
Passionate prayers: and when these were not heard   120
I have still borne,—until I meet you here,
Princes and kinsmen, at this hideous feast
Given at my brothers' deaths. Two yet remain,
His wife remains and I, whom if ye save not,
Ye may soon share such merriment again
As fathers make over their children's graves.
Oh! Prince Colonna, thou art our near kinsman,
Cardinal, thou art the Pope's chamberlain,[32]
Camillo, thou art chief justiciary,[33]
Take us away!

*Cenci. (He has been conversing with Camillo during
    the first part of Beatrice's speech; he hears the
    conclusion, and now advances).*
                    I hope my good friends here   130
Will think of their own daughters—or perhaps
Of their own throats—before they lend an ear
To this wild girl.

Bea. (Not noticing the words of Cenci).
                    Dare no one look on me?
None answer? Can one tyrant overbear
The sense of many best and wisest men?
Or is it that I sue not in some form
Of scrupulous law, that ye deny my suit?
O God! That I were buried with my brothers!
And that the flowers of this departed spring
Were fading on my grave! And that my father   140
Were celebrating now one feast for all!

Cam. A bitter wish for one so young and gentle;
Can we do nothing?

Colonna.   Nothing that I see.
Count Cenci were a dangerous enemy:
Yet I would second any one.

A Cardinal.   And I.

Cenci. Retire to your chamber, insolent girl!

Bea. Retire thou, impious man! Aye, hide thyself
Where never eye can look upon thee more!
Wouldst thou have honour and obedience

---

32 *chamberlain*: a steward; the officer charged with the
    management of the private chambers of a sovereign.
33 *justiciary*: one who maintains or executes justice; an
    administrator of justice.

Who art a torturer? Father, never dream   150
Though thou mayst overbear this company,
But ill must come of ill.—Frown not on me!
Haste, hide thyself, lest with avenging looks
My brothers' ghosts should hunt thee from thy seat!
Cover thy face from every living eye,
And start if thou but hear a human step:
Seek out some dark and silent corner, there,
Bow thy white head before offended God,
And we will kneel around, and fervently
Pray that he pity both ourselves and thee.   160

Cenci. My friends, I do lament this insane girl
Has spoilt the mirth of our festivity.
Good night, farewell; I will not make you longer
Spectators of our dull domestic quarrels.
Another time.— *(Exeunt all but Cenci and Beatrice).*
                    My brain is swimming round;
Give me a bowl of wine!
(To Beatrice).   Thou painted viper!
Beast that thou art! Fair and yet terrible!
I know a charm shall make thee meek and tame,
Now get thee from my sight! *(Exit Beatrice).*
                            Here, Andrea,
Fill up this goblet with Greek wine. I said   170
I would not drink this evening; but I must;
For, strange to say, I feel my spirits fail
With thinking what I have decreed to do.—
(Drinking the wine). Be thou the resolution of
    quick youth
Within my veins, and manhood's purpose stern,
And age's firm, cold, subtle villainy;
As if thou wert indeed my children's blood
Which I did thirst to drink! The charm works well;
It must be done; it shall be done, I swear! *(Exit).*

ACT II.

Scene I: *An apartment in the Cenci Palace.*
    Enter Lucretia and Bernardo.

Luc. Weep not, my gentle boy; he struck but me
Who have borne deeper wrongs. In truth, if he
Had killed me, he had done a kinder deed.
O God, Almighty, do thou look upon us,
We have no other friend but only thee!
Yet weep not; though I love you as my own

I am not your true mother.
Bernardo.   O more, more,
  Than ever mother was to any child,
  That have you been to me! Had he not been
  My father, do you think that I should weep!   10
Luc. Alas! Poor boy, what else could'st thou have done?
(Enter Beatrice).
Bea. (In a hurried voice). Did he pass this way? Have
    you seen him, brother?
  Ah! No, that is his step upon the stairs;
  'Tis nearer now; his hand is on the door;
  Mother, if I to thee have ever been
  A duteous child, now save me! Thou, great God,
  Whose image upon earth a father is,
  Dost Thou indeed abandon me! He comes;
  The door is opening now; I see his face;
  He frowns on others, but he smiles on me,   20
  Even as he did after the feast last night.
(Enter a Servant).
  Almighty God, how merciful thou art!
  'Tis but Orsino's servant.—Well, what news?
Servant. My master bids me say, the Holy Father
  Has sent back your petition thus unopened.
        (Giving a paper).
  And he demands at what hour 'twere secure
  To visit you again?
Luc.   At the Ave Mary.[34] *(Exit Servant).*
  So, daughter, our last hope has failed; Ah me!
  How pale you look; you tremble, and you stand
  Wrapped in some fixed and fearful meditation,   30
  As if one thought were over strong for you:
  Your eyes have a chill glare; O, dearest child!
  Are you gone mad? If not, pray speak to me.
Bea. You see I am not mad: I speak to you.
Luc. You talked of something that your father did
  After that dreadful feast? Could it be worse
  Than when he smiled, and cried, "My sons are dead!"
  And every one looked in his neighbour's face
  To see if others were as white as he?
  At the first word he spoke I felt the blood   40
  Rush to my heart, and fell into a trance;
  And when it passed I sat all weak and wild;

---

[34] *At the Ave Mary*: at the time when bells are rung for
   the saying of the Ave Mary, i.e., the salutation to the
   Virgin Mary.

Whilst you alone stood up, and with strong words
  Checked his unnatural pride; and I could see
  The devil was rebuked that lives in him.
  Until this hour thus have you ever stood
  Between us and your father's moody wrath
  Like a protecting presence: your firm mind
  Has been our only refuge and defence:
  What can have thus subdued it? What can now   50
  Have given you that cold melancholy look,
  Succeeding to your unaccustomed fear?
Bea. What is it that you say? I was just thinking
  'Twere better not to struggle any more.
  Men, like my father, have been dark and bloody,
  Yet never—O! Before worse comes of it
  'Twere wise to die: it ends in that at last.
Luc. Oh, talk not so, dear child! Tell me at once
  What did your father do or say to you?
  He stayed not after that accursed feast   60
  One moment in your chamber.—Speak to me.
Ber. Oh, sister, sister, prithee, speak to us!
Bea. (Speaking very slowly with a forced calmness).
  It was one word, Mother, one little word;
  One look, one smile. *(Wildly)* Oh! He has
    trampled me
  Under his feet, and made the blood stream down
  My pallid cheeks. And he has given us all
  Ditch water, and the fever-stricken flesh
  Of buffaloes, and bade us eat or starve,
  And we have eaten.—He has made me look
  On my beloved Bernardo, when the rust   70
  Of heavy chains has gangrened his sweet limbs,
  And I have never yet despaired—but now!
  What could I say? *(Recovering herself)* Ah! No, 'tis
    nothing new.
  The sufferings we all share have made me wild:
  He only struck and cursed me as he passed;
  He said, he looked, he did;—nothing at all
  Beyond his wont, yet it disordered me.
  Alas! I am forgetful of my duty,
  I should preserve my senses for your sake.
Luc. Nay, Beatrice; have courage, my sweet girl,   80
  If any one despairs it should be I
  Who loved him once, and now must live with him
  Till God in pity call for him or me.
  For you may, like your sister, find some husband,
  And smile, years hence, with children round your
    knees;

Whilst I, then dead, and all this hideous coil[35]
  Shall be remembered only as a dream.
Bea. Talk not to me, dear lady, of a husband.
  Did you not nurse me when my mother died?
  Did you not shield me and that dearest boy?   90
  And had we any other friend but you
  In infancy, with gentle words and looks,
  To win our father not to murder us?
  And shall I now desert you? May the ghost
  Of my dead Mother plead against my soul
  If I abandon her who filled the place
  She left, with more, even, than a mother's love!
Ber. And I am of my sister's mind. Indeed
  I would not leave you in this wretchedness,
  Even though the Pope should make me free to live   100
  In some blithe place, like others of my age,
  With sports, and delicate food, and the fresh air.
  Oh, never think that I will leave you, Mother!
Luc. My dear, dear children!
(Enter Cenci, suddenly).
Cenci.   What, Beatrice here!
  Come hither!
(She shrinks back, and covers her face).
          Nay, hide not your face, 'tis fair;
  Look up! Why, yesternight you dared to look
  With disobedient insolence upon me,
  Bending a stern and an inquiring brow
  On what I meant; whilst I then sought to hide
  That which I came to tell you—but in vain.   110
Bea. (Wildly, staggering towards the door).
  O that the earth would gape! Hide me, O God!
Cenci. Then it was I whose inarticulate words
  Fell from my lips, and who with tottering steps
  Fled from your presence, as you now from mine.
  Stay, I command you—from this day and hour
  Never again, I think, with fearless eye,
  And brow superior, and unaltered cheek,
  And that lip made for tenderness or scorn,
  Shalt thou strike dumb the meanest of mankind;
  Me least of all. Now get thee to thy chamber!   120
  Thou too, loathed image of thy cursed mother,
  (To Bernardo). Thy milky, meek face makes me
    sick with hate!
(Exeunt Beatrice and Bernardo).

---

35 *coil*: fuss, bustle, or turmoil.

(Aside). So much has passed between us as must make
  Me bold, her fearful.—'Tis an awful thing
  To touch such mischief as I now conceive:
  So men sit shivering on the dewy bank,
  And try the chill stream with their feet; once in...
  How the delighted spirit pants for joy!
Luc. (Advancing timidly towards him).
  O husband! Pray forgive poor Beatrice.
  She meant not any ill.
Cenci.   Nor you perhaps?   130
  Nor that young imp, whom you have taught by rote
  Parricide[36] with his alphabet? Nor Giacomo?
  Nor those two most unnatural sons, who stirred
  Enmity up against me with the Pope?
  Whom in one night merciful God cut off:
  Innocent lambs! They thought not any ill.
  You were not here conspiring? You said nothing
  Of how I might be dungeoned as a madman;
  Or be condemned to death for some offence,
  And you would be the witnesses?—This failing,   140
  How just it were to hire assassins, or
  Put sudden poison in my evening drink?
  Or smother me when overcome by wine?
  Seeing we had no other judge but God,
  And he had sentenced me, and there were none
  But you to be the executioners
  Of his decree enregistered in heaven?
  Oh, no! You said not this?
Luc.   So help me God,
  I never thought the things you charge me with!
Cenci. If you dare speak that wicked lie again   150
  I'll kill you. What! It was not by your counsel
  That Beatrice disturbed the feast last night?
  You did not hope to stir some enemies
  Against me, and escape, and laugh to scorn
  What every nerve of you now trembles at?
  You judged that men were bolder than they are;
  Few dare to stand between their grave and me.
Luc. Look not so dreadfully! By my salvation
  I knew not aught that Beatrice designed;
  Nor do I think she designed any thing   160
  Until she heard you talk of her dead brothers.

---

36 *Parricide*: the crime of murdering one's father or either
    parent; more generally, the crime of murdering one's
    ruler or committing treason against one's country.

Cenci. Blaspheming liar! You are damned for this!
But I will take you where you may persuade
The stones you tread on to deliver you:
For men shall there be none but those who dare
All things—not question that which I command.
On Wednesday next I shall set out: you know
That savage rock, the Castle of Petrella:
'Tis safely walled, and moated round about:
Its dungeons underground, and its thick towers   170
Never told tales; though they have heard and seen
What might make dumb things speak.—Why do
    you linger?
Make speediest preparation for the journey! *(Exit
    Lucretia)*.
The all-beholding sun yet shines; I hear
A busy stir of men about the streets;
I see the bright sky through the window panes:
It is a garish, broad, and peering day;
Loud, light, suspicious, full of eyes and ears,
And every little corner, nook, and hole
Is penetrated with the insolent light.   180
Come darkness! Yet, what is the day to me?
And wherefore should I wish for night, who do
A deed which shall confound both night and day?
'Tis she shall grope through a bewildering mist
Of horror: if there be a sun in heaven
She shall not dare to look upon its beams;
Nor feel its warmth. Let her then wish for night;
The act I think shall soon extinguish all
For me: I bear a darker deadlier gloom
Than the earth's shade,[37] or interlunar air,[38]   190
Or constellations quenched in murkiest cloud,
In which I walk secure and unbeheld
Towards my purpose.—Would that it were done!
    (Exit).

Scene II: *A Chamber in the Vatican.*
Enter Camillo and Giacomo, in conversation.

Cam. There is an obsolete and doubtful law
By which you might obtain a bare provision
Of food and clothing—

Giacomo.   Nothing more? Alas!
Bare must be the provision which strict law
Awards, and aged, sullen avarice pays.
Why did my father not apprentice me
To some mechanic trade? I should have then
Been trained in no highborn necessities
Which I could meet not by my daily toil.
The eldest son of a rich nobleman   10
Is heir to all his incapacities;
He has wide wants, and narrow powers. If you,
Cardinal Camillo, were reduced at once
From thrice-driven[39] beds of down, and delicate
    food,
An hundred servants, and six palaces,
To that which nature doth indeed require?—
Cam. Nay, there is reason in your plea; 'twere hard.
Gia. 'Tis hard for a firm man to bear: but I
Have a dear wife, a lady of high birth,
Whose dowry in ill hour I lent my father   20
Without a bond or witness to the deed:
And children, who inherit her fine senses,
The fairest creatures in this breathing world;
And she and they reproach me not. Cardinal,
Do you not think the Pope would interpose
And stretch authority beyond the law?
Cam. Though your peculiar case is hard, I know
The Pope will not divert the course of law.
After that impious feast the other night
I spoke with him, and urged him then to check   30
Your father's cruel hand; he frowned and said,
"Children are disobedient, and they sting
Their fathers' hearts to madness and despair
Requiting years of care with contumely.
I pity the Count Cenci from my heart;
His outraged love perhaps awakened hate,
And thus he is exasperated to ill.
In the great war between the old and young
I, who have white hairs and a tottering body,
Will keep at least blameless neutrality."   40
(Enter Orsino).
You, my good Lord Orsino, heard those words.

---

37 *the earth's shade*: the shadow cast by the earth onto the
      moon during a lunar eclipse.
38 *interlunar air*: the dark period between an old and new
      moon.

39 *thrice-driven beds of down*: beds composed of only the
      lightest, softest, and finest down feathers. The term
      "driven" denotes the process by which lighter feathers
      are separated from the heavier ones by a current of air.

Ors. What words?

Gia.   Alas, repeat them not again!
   There then is no redress for me, at least
   None but that which I may atchieve myself,
   Since I am driven to the brink.—But, say,
   My innocent sister and my only brother
   Are dying underneath my father's eye.
   The memorable torturers of this land,
   Galeaz Visconti, Borgia, Ezzelin,[40]
   Never inflicted on the meanest slave   50
   What these endure; shall they have no protection?

Cam. Why, if they would petition to the Pope
   I see not how he could refuse it—yet
   He holds it of most dangerous example
   In aught to weaken the paternal power,
   Being, as 'twere, the shadow of his own.
   I pray you now excuse me. I have business
   That will not bear delay. *(Exit Camillo).*

Gia.   But you, Orsino,
   Have the petition: wherefore not present it?

Ors. I have presented it, and backed it with   60
   My earnest prayers, and urgent interest;
   It was returned unanswered. I doubt not
   But that the strange and execrable deeds
   Alledged in it—in truth they might well baffle
   Any belief—have turned the Pope's displeasure

Upon the accusers from the criminal:
   So I should guess from what Camillo said.

Gia. My friend, that palace-walking devil Gold
   Has whispered silence to his Holiness:
   And we are left, as scorpions ringed with fire.   70
   What should we do but strike ourselves to death?[41]
   For he who is our murderous persecutor
   Is shielded by a father's holy name,
   Or I would— *(Stops abruptly).*

Ors.   What? Fear not to speak your thought.
   Words are but holy as the deeds they cover:
   A priest who has forsworn the God he serves;
   A judge who makes truth weep at his decree;
   A friend who should weave counsel, as I now,
   But as the mantle of some selfish guile;
   A father who is all a tyrant seems,   80
   Were the profaner for his sacred name.

Gia. Ask me not what I think; the unwilling brain
   Feigns often what it would not; and we trust
   Imagination with such phantasies
   As the tongue dares not fashion into words,
   Which have no words, their horror makes them dim
   To the mind's eye.—My heart denies itself
   To think what you demand.

Ors.   But a friend's bosom
   Is as the inmost cave of our own mind
   Where we sit shut from the wide gaze of day,   90
   And from the all-communicating air.
   You look what I suspected—

---

[40] *Galeaz Visconti, Borgia, Ezzelin*: Gian Galeazzo Visconti (1351–1402), Milanese leader who brought the Visconti dynasty to the height of its power and almost succeeded in becoming the ruler of all northern Italy. His reign was marked by ruthless tactics, including the ambush and capture of his brother Bernabò, whom he may have subsequently poisoned. Cesare Borgia (ca. 1475–1507), Duke of Valentinois, natural son of Pope Alexander VI, who enhanced his father's papacy and tried to establish his own principality in central Italy. A number of political assassinations have been attributed to him, and his policies led Machiavelli to cite him as an example of the new "Prince." Ezzelino III da Romano (1194–1259), a soldier who became feudal mayor of Verona, Vicenza, and Padua, gained power over almost all of northeast Italy by aligning himself with the Holy Roman Emperor Frederick II and with the pro-imperial Ghibellines against the papist Guelfs. His cruelty earned him a place in Dante's *Inferno*.

[41] *as scorpions … ourselves to death?*: See Shelley, *Queen Mab; A Philosophical Poem: With Notes* (London: Privately printed by the author, 1813), page 74, part VI, lines 36–8; and Lord Byron, *The Giaour*, 1st ed. (London: John Murray, 1813), pages 8–9, lines 120–36; or 7th ed. (London: John Murray, 1813), page 21, lines 422–38. Byron's note to this passage reads as follows: "Alluding to the dubious suicide of the scorpion, so placed for experiment by gentle philosophers. Some maintain that the position of the sting, when turned towards the head, is merely a convulsive movement; but others have actually brought in the verdict 'Felo de se' [suicide]. The scorpions are surely interested in a speedy decision of the question, as, if once fairly established as insect Catos, they will probably be allowed to live as long as they think proper, without being martyred for the sake of an hypothesis."

Gia.   Spare me now!
   I am as one lost in a midnight wood,
   Who dares not ask some harmless passenger
   The path across the wilderness, lest he,
   As my thoughts are, should be—a murderer.
   I know you are my friend, and all I dare
   Speak to my soul that will I trust with thee.
   But now my heart is heavy and would take
   Lone counsel from a night of sleepless care.   100
   Pardon me, that I say farewell—farewell!
   I would that to my own suspected self
   I could address a word so full of peace.
Ors. Farewell!—Be your thoughts better or more bold.
(Exit Giacomo).

   I had disposed the Cardinal Camillo
   To feed his hope with cold encouragement:
   It fortunately serves my close designs
   That 'tis a trick of this same family
   To analyse their own and other minds.
   Such self-anatomy[42] shall teach the will   110
   Dangerous secrets: for it tempts our powers,
   Knowing what must be thought, and may be done,
   Into the depth of darkest purposes:
   So Cenci fell into the pit; even I,
   Since Beatrice unveiled me to myself,
   And made me shrink from what I cannot shun,
   Shew a poor figure to my own esteem,
   To which I grow half reconciled. I'll do
   As little mischief as I can; that thought
   Shall fee[43] the accuser conscience.
   (After a pause).   Now what harm   120
   If Cenci should be murdered?—Yet, if murdered,
   Wherefore by me? And what if I could take
   The profit, yet omit the sin and peril
   In such an action? Of all earthly things
   I fear a man whose blows outspeed his words;
   And such is Cenci: and while Cenci lives
   His daughter's dowry were a secret grave
   If a priest wins her.—Oh, fair Beatrice!
   Would that I loved thee not, or loving thee
   Could but despise danger and gold and all   130
   That frowns between my wish and its effect,
   Or smiles beyond it! There is no escape...

---

[42] *self-anatomy*: self-analysis.
[43] *fee*: to bribe.

Her bright form kneels beside me at the altar,
And follows me to the resort of men,
And fills my slumber with tumultuous dreams,
So when I wake my blood seems liquid fire;
And if I strike my damp and dizzy head
My hot palm scorches it: her very name,
But spoken by a stranger, makes my heart
Sicken and pant; and thus unprofitably   140
I clasp the phantom of unfelt delights
Till weak imagination half possesses
The self-created shadow. Yet much longer
Will I not nurse this life of feverous hours:
From the unravelled hopes of Giacomo
I must work out my own dear purposes.
I see, as from a tower, the end of all:
Her father dead; her brother bound to me
By a dark secret, surer than the grave;
Her mother scared and unexpostulating   150
From the dread manner of her wish atchieved:
And she!—Once more take courage, my faint heart;
What dares a friendless maiden matched with thee?
I have such foresight as assures success:
Some unbeheld divinity doth ever,
When dread events are near, stir up men's minds
To black suggestions; and he prospers best,
Not who becomes the instrument of ill,
But who can flatter the dark spirit, that makes
Its empire and its prey of other hearts   160
Till it become his slave...as I will do. *(Exit).*

ACT III.

Scene I: *An apartment in the Cenci Palace.*
Lucretia, to her enter Beatrice.

Bea. (She enters staggering, and speaks wildly).
   Reach me that handkerchief!—My brain is hurt;
   My eyes are full of blood; just wipe them for me...
   I see but indistinctly...
Luc.   My sweet child,
   You have no wound; 'tis only a cold dew
   That starts from your dear brow...Alas! Alas!
   What has befallen?
Bea.   How comes this hair undone?
   Its wandering strings must be what blind me so,
   And yet I tied it fast.—O, horrible!

The pavement sinks under my feet! The walls
Spin round! I see a woman weeping there,   10
And standing calm and motionless, whilst I
Slide giddily as the world reels.... My God!
The beautiful blue heaven is flecked with blood!
The sunshine on the floor is black! The air
Is changed to vapours such as the dead breathe
In charnel[44] pits! Pah! I am choked! There creeps
A clinging, black, contaminating mist
About me...'tis substantial, heavy, thick,
I cannot pluck it from me, for it glues
My fingers and my limbs to one another,   20
And eats into my sinews, and dissolves
My flesh to a pollution, poisoning
The subtle, pure, and inmost spirit of life!
My God! I never knew what the mad felt
Before; for I am mad beyond all doubt!
(More wildly). No, I am dead! These putrefying limbs
Shut round and sepulchre[45] the panting soul
Which would burst forth into the wandering air!
(A pause).
What hideous thought was that I had even now?
'Tis gone; and yet its burthen remains here   30
O'er these dull eyes...upon this weary heart!
O, world! O, life! O, day! O, misery!
Luc. What ails thee, my poor child? She answers not:
Her spirit apprehends the sense of pain,
But not its cause; suffering has dried away
The source from which it sprung...
Bea. (Franticly).   Like Parricide...
Misery has killed its father: yet its father
Never like mine...O, God! What thing am I?
Luc. My dearest child, what has your father done?
Bea. (Doubtfully). Who art thou, questioner? I have   40
    no father.
(Aside). She is the madhouse nurse who tends on me,
It is a piteous office.
(To Lucretia, in a slow, subdued voice).
                    Do you know
I thought I was that wretched Beatrice
Men speak of, whom her father sometimes hales[46]

---

44 *charnel*: pertaining to or characteristic of burial places;
   sepulchral, deathlike, or ghastly.
45 *sepulchre*: to entomb, bury, or serve as a burial-place for.
46 *hale*: to draw or pull.

From hall to hall by the entangled hair;
At others, pens up naked in damp cells
Where scaly reptiles crawl, and starves her there,
Till she will eat strange flesh. This woful story
So did I overact in my sick dreams,
That I imagined...no, it cannot be!   50
Horrible things have been in this wide world,
Prodigious mixtures, and confusions strange
Of good and ill; and worse have been conceived
Than ever there was found a heart to do.
But never fancy imaged such a deed
As... *(Pauses, suddenly recollecting herself).*
        Who art thou? Swear to me, ere I die
With fearful expectation, that indeed
Thou art not what thou seemest...Mother!
Luc.   Oh!
My sweet child, know you...
Bea.   Yet speak it not:
For then if this be truth, that other too   60
Must be a truth, a firm enduring truth,
Linked with each lasting circumstance of life,
Never to change, never to pass away.
Why so it is. This is the Cenci palace;
Thou art Lucretia; I am Beatrice.
I have talked some wild words, but will no more.
Mother, come near me: from this point of time,
I am... *(Her voice dies away faintly).*
Luc.   Alas! What has befallen thee, child?
What has thy father done?
Bea.   What have I done?
Am I not innocent? Is it my crime   70
That one with white hair, and imperious brow,
Who tortured me from my forgotten years,
As parents only dare, should call himself
My father, yet should be!—Oh, what am I?
What name, what place, what memory shall be
    mine?
What retrospects, outliving even despair?
Luc. He is a violent tyrant, surely, child:
We know that death alone can make us free;
His death or ours. But what can he have done
Of deadlier outrage or worse injury?   80
Thou art unlike thyself; thine eyes shoot forth
A wandering and strange spirit. Speak to me,
Unlock those pallid hands whose fingers twine
With one another.

Bea.   'Tis the restless life
Tortured within them. If I try to speak
I shall go mad. Aye, something must be done;
What, yet I know not...something which shall make
The thing that I have suffered but a shadow
In the dread lightning which avenges it;
Brief, rapid, irreversible, destroying   90
The consequence of what it cannot cure.
Some such thing is to be endured or done:
When I know what, I shall be still and calm,
And never anything will move me more.
But now!—O blood, which art my father's blood,
Circling thro' these contaminated veins,
If thou, poured forth on the polluted earth,
Could wash away the crime, and punishment
By which I suffer...no, that cannot be!
Many might doubt there were a God above   100
Who sees and permits evil, and so die:
That faith no agony shall obscure in me.

Luc. It must indeed have been some bitter wrong;
Yet what, I dare not guess. Oh, my lost child,
Hide not in proud impenetrable grief
Thy sufferings from my fear.

Bea.   I hide them not.
What are the words which you would have me
    speak?
I, who can feign no image in my mind
Of that which has transformed me. I, whose thought
Is like a ghost shrouded and folded up   110
In its own formless horror: of all words,
That minister to mortal intercourse,[47]
Which wouldst thou hear? For there is none to tell
My misery: if another ever knew
Aught like to it, she died as I will die,
And left it, as I must, without a name.
Death! Death! Our law and our religion call thee
A punishment and a reward...Oh, which
Have I deserved?

Luc.   The peace of innocence;
Till in your season you be called to heaven.   120
Whate'er you may have suffered, you have done
No evil. Death must be the punishment
Of crime, or the reward of trampling down

The thorns which God has strewed upon the path
Which leads to immortality.

Bea.   Aye; death...
The punishment of crime. I pray thee, God,
Let me not be bewildered while I judge.
If I must live day after day, and keep
These limbs, the unworthy temple of thy spirit,
As a foul den from which what thou abhorrest   130
May mock thee, unavenged...it shall not be!
Self-murder...no, that might be no escape,
For thy decree[48] yawns like a Hell between
Our will and it:—O! In this mortal world
There is no vindication and no law
Which can adjudge and execute the doom
Of that through which I suffer.

(Enter Orsino. She approaches him solemnly).
                          Welcome, Friend!
I have to tell you that, since last we met,
I have endured a wrong so great and strange,
That neither life or death can give me rest.   140
Ask me not what it is, for there are deeds
Which have no form, sufferings which have no
    tongue.

Ors. And what is he who has thus injured you?

Bea. The man they call my father: a dread name.

Ors. It cannot be...

Bea.   What it can be, or not,
Forbear to think. It is, and it has been;
Advise me how it shall not be again.
I thought to die; but a religious awe
Restrains me, and the dread lest death itself
Might be no refuge from the consciousness   150
Of what is yet unexpiated.[49] Oh, speak!

Ors. Accuse him of the deed, and let the law
Avenge thee.

Bea.   Oh, ice-hearted counsellor!
If I could find a word that might make known
The crime of my destroyer; and that done
My tongue should like a knife tear out the secret
Which cankers[50] my heart's core; ay, lay all bare
So that my unpolluted fame should be

---

47 *intercourse*: social communication between individuals.

48 *thy decree*: the decree that those committing suicide faced certain damnation.

49 *unexpiated*: unatoned for.

50 *canker*: to fester, corrode, rust, or tarnish.

With vilest gossips a stale mouthed story;
A mock, a bye-word, an astonishment:—   160
If this were done, which never shall be done,
Think of the offender's gold, his dreaded hate,
And the strange horror of the accuser's tale,
Baffling belief, and overpowering speech;
Scarce whispered, unimaginable, wrapt
In hideous hints...Oh, most assured redress!

Ors. You will endure it then?

Bea.   Endure?—Orsino,
It seems your counsel is small profit.
(Turns from him, and speaks half to herself).
                                Aye,
All must be suddenly resolved and done.
What is this undistinguishable mist   170
Of thoughts, which rise, like shadow after shadow,
Darkening each other?

Ors.   Should the offender live?
Triumph in his misdeed? and make, by use,
His crime, whate'er it is, dreadful no doubt,
Thine element; until thou mayst become
Utterly lost; subdued even to the hue
Of that which thou permittest?

Bea. (To herself).   Mighty death!
Thou double visaged shadow![51] Only judge!
Rightfullest arbiter! *(She retires absorbed in thought).*

Luc.   If the lightning
Of God has e'er descended to avenge...   180

Ors. Blaspheme not! His high Providence commits
Its glory on this earth, and their own wrongs
Into the hands of men; if they neglect
To punish crime...

Luc.   But if one, like this wretch,
Should mock, with gold, opinion, law, and
    power?
If there be no appeal to that which makes
The guiltiest tremble? If because our wrongs,

---

51   *Mighty death! / Thou double visaged shadow!*: Donald
Reiman and Neil Fraistat gloss these lines in their edition of *Shelley's Poetry and Prose* (2nd ed., New York
and London: W. W. Norton, 2002), page 168, note
3: "Shelley here associates the image of death with the
myth of Janus, the Roman god of beginnings and end-
ings, who is usually depicted with two faces, one to
the view the past and one the future."

For that they are, unnatural, strange, and monstrous,
Exceed all measure of belief? O God!
If, for the very reasons which should make   190
Redress most swift and sure, our injurer triumphs?
And we the victims, bear worse punishment
Than that appointed for their torturer?

Ors.   Think not
But that there is redress where there is wrong,
So we be bold enough to seize it.

Luc.   How?
If there were any way to make all sure,
I know not...but I think it might be good
To...

Ors.   Why, his late outrage to Beatrice;
For it is such, as I but faintly guess,
As makes remorse dishonour, and leaves her   200
Only one duty, how she may avenge:
You, but one refuge from ills ill endured;
Me, but one counsel...

Luc.   For we cannot hope
That aid, or retribution, or resource
Will arise thence, where every other one
Might find them with less need.

(Beatrice advances).

Ors.   Then...

Bea.   Peace, Orsino!
And, honoured Lady, while I speak, I pray,
That you put off, as garments overworn,
Forbearance and respect, remorse and fear,
And all the fit restraints of daily life,   210
Which have been borne from childhood, but
    which now
Would be a mockery to my holier plea.
As I have said, I have endured a wrong,
Which, though it be expressionless, is such
As asks atonement; both for what is past,
And lest I be reserved, day after day,
To load with crimes an overburthened soul,
And be...what ye can dream not. I have prayed
To God, and I have talked with my own heart,
And have unravelled my entangled will,   220
And have at length determined what is right.
Art thou my friend, Orsino? False or true?
Pledge thy salvation ere I speak.

Ors.   I swear
To dedicate my cunning, and my strength,

My silence, and whatever else is mine,
To thy commands.

Luc.   You think we should devise
His death?

Bea.   And execute what is devised,
And suddenly. We must be brief and bold.

Ors. And yet most cautious.

Luc.   For the jealous laws
Would punish us with death and infamy   230
For that which it became themselves to do.

Bea. Be cautious as ye may, but prompt. Orsino,
What are the means?

Ors.   I know two dull, fierce outlaws,
Who think man's spirit as a worm's, and they
Would trample out, for any slight caprice,
The meanest or the noblest life. This mood
Is marketable here in Rome. They sell
What we now want.

Luc.   To-morrow before dawn,
Cenci will take us to that lonely rock,
Petrella, in the Apulian Apennines.   240
If he arrive there...

Bea.   He must not arrive.

Ors. Will it be dark before you reach the tower?

Luc. The sun will scarce be set.

Bea.   But I remember
Two miles on this side of the fort, the road
Crosses a deep ravine; 'tis rough and narrow,
And winds with short turns down the precipice;
And in its depth there is a mighty rock,
Which has, from unimaginable years,
Sustained itself with terror and with toil
Over a gulph, and with the agony   250
With which it clings seems slowly coming down;
Even as a wretched soul hour after hour,
Clings to the mass of life; yet clinging, leans;
And leaning, makes more dark the dread abyss
In which it fears to fall: beneath this crag
Huge as despair, as if in weariness,
The melancholy mountain yawns...below,
You hear but see not an impetuous torrent
Raging among the caverns, and a bridge
Crosses the chasm; and high above there grow,   260
With intersecting trunks, from crag to crag,
Cedars, and yews, and pines; whose tangled hair
Is matted in one solid roof of shade

By the dark ivy's twine. At noon day here
'Tis twilight, and at sunset blackest night.[52]

Ors. Before you reach that bridge make some excuse
For spurring on your mules, or loitering
Until...

Bea.   What sound is that?

Luc. Hark! No, it cannot be a servant's step
It must be Cenci, unexpectedly   270
Returned...Make some excuse for being here.

Bea. (To Orsino, as she goes out).
That step we hear approach must never pass
The bridge of which we spoke. *(Exeunt Lucretia
and Beatrice).*

Ors.   What shall I do?
Cenci must find me here, and I must bear
The imperious inquisition of his looks
As to what brought me hither: let me mask
Mine own in some inane and vacant smile.

(Enter Giacomo, in a hurried manner).
How! Have you ventured hither? Know you then
That Cenci is from home?

Gia.   I sought him here;
And now must wait till he returns.

Ors.   Great God!   280
Weigh you the danger of this rashness?

Gia.   Aye!
Does my destroyer know his danger? We
Are now no more, as once, parent and child,
But man to man; the oppressor to the oppressed;
The slanderer to the slandered; foe to foe:
He has cast Nature off, which was his shield,
And Nature casts him off, who is her shame;
And I spurn both. Is it a father's throat
Which I will shake, and say, I ask not gold;
I ask not happy years; nor memories   290
Of tranquil childhood; nor home-sheltered love;
Though all these hast thou torn from me, and more;
But only my fair fame; only one hoard

---

52   *And winds ... blackest night* Reiman and Fraistat gloss
lines 243–265 as "contain[ing] the description which,
Shelley says in his Preface, he modeled on a passage near
the end of the second act of *El Purgatorio de San Patricio*
by the Spanish dramatist Pedro Calderón de la Barca
(1600–1681); in Calderón's play the description is that
of the entrance to Hell" (page 170, note 5).

Of peace, which I thought hidden from thy hate,
Under the penury heaped on me by thee,
Or I will...God can understand and pardon,
Why should I speak with man?

Ors.   Be calm, dear friend.

Gia. Well, I will calmly tell you what he did.
This old Francesco Cenci, as you know,
Borrowed the dowry of my wife from me,   300
And then denied the loan; and left me so
In poverty, the which I sought to mend
By holding a poor office in the state.
It had been promised to me, and already
I bought new clothing for my ragged babes,
And my wife smiled; and my heart knew repose.
When Cenci's intercession, as I found,
Conferred this office on a wretch, whom thus
He paid for vilest service. I returned
With this ill news, and we sate sad together   310
Solacing our despondency with tears
Of such affection and unbroken faith
As temper life's worst bitterness; when he,
As he is wont, came to upbraid and curse,
Mocking our poverty, and telling us
Such was God's scourge for disobedient sons.
And then, that I might strike him dumb with shame,
I spoke of my wife's dowry; but he coined
A brief yet specious tale, how I had wasted
The sum in secret riot; and he saw   320
My wife was touched, and he went smiling forth.
And when I knew the impression he had made,
And felt my wife insult with silent scorn
My ardent truth, and look averse and cold,
I went forth too: but soon returned again;
Yet not so soon but that my wife had taught
My children her harsh thoughts, and they all cried,
"Give us clothes, father! Give us better food!
What you in one night squander were enough
For months!" I looked, and saw that home was hell.   330
And to that hell will I return no more
Until mine enemy has rendered up
Atonement, or, as he gave life to me
I will, reversing Nature's law...

Ors.   Trust me,
The compensation which thou seekest here
Will be denied.

Gia.   Then...Are you not my friend?

Did you not hint at the alternative,
Upon the brink of which you see I stand,
The other day when we conversed together?
My wrongs were then less. That word parricide,   340
Although I am resolved, haunts me like fear.

Ors. It must be fear itself, for the bare word
Is hollow mockery. Mark, how wisest God
Draws to one point the threads of a just doom,
So sanctifying it: what you devise
Is, as it were, accomplished.

Gia.   Is he dead?

Ors. His grave is ready. Know that since we met
Cenci has done an outrage to his daughter.

Gia. What outrage?

Ors.   That she speaks not, but you may
Conceive such half conjectures as I do,   350
From her fixed paleness, and the lofty grief
Of her stern brow bent on the idle air,
And her severe unmodulated voice,
Drowning both tenderness and dread; and last
From this; that whilst her step-mother and I,
Bewildered in our horror, talked together
With obscure hints; both self-misunderstood
And darkly guessing, stumbling, in our talk,
Over the truth, and yet to its revenge,
She interrupted us, and with a look   360
Which told before she spoke it, he must die...

Gia. It is enough. My doubts are well appeased;
There is a higher reason for the act
Than mine; there is a holier judge than me,
A more unblamed avenger. Beatrice,
Who in the gentleness of thy sweet youth
Hast never trodden on a worm, or bruised
A living flower, but thou hast pitied it
With needless tears! Fair sister, thou in whom
Men wondered how such loveliness and wisdom   370
Did not destroy each other! Is there made
Ravage of thee? O, heart, I ask no more
Justification! Shall I wait, Orsino,
Till he return, and stab him at the door?

Ors. Not so; some accident might interpose
To rescue him from what is now most sure;
And you are unprovided where to fly,
How to excuse or to conceal. Nay, listen:
All is contrived; success is so assured
That...

(Enter Beatrice).

Bea.   'Tis my brother's voice! You know me not?   380

Gia. My sister, my lost sister!

Bea.   Lost indeed!

I see Orsino has talked with you, and
That you conjecture things too horrible
To speak, yet far less than the truth. Now, stay not,
He might return: yet kiss me; I shall know
That then thou hast consented to his death.
Farewell, farewell! Let piety to God,
Brotherly love, justice and clemency,
And all things that make tender hardest hearts
Make thine hard, brother. Answer not...farewell.   390

(Exeunt severally).

Scene II: *A mean Apartment in Giacomo's House.*
Giacomo alone.

Gia. 'Tis midnight, and Orsino comes not yet.

(Thunder, and the sound of a storm).

What! can the everlasting elements
Feel with a worm like man? If so the shaft
Of mercy-winged lightning would not fall
On stones and trees. My wife and children sleep:
They are now living in unmeaning dreams:
But I must wake, still doubting if that deed
Be just which is most necessary. O,
Thou unreplenished lamp! whose narrow fire
Is shaken by the wind, and on whose edge   10
Devouring darkness hovers! Thou small flame,
Which, as a dying pulse rises and falls,
Still flickerest up and down, how very soon,
Did I not feed thee, wouldst thou fail and be
As thou hadst never been! So wastes and sinks
Even now, perhaps, the life that kindled mine:
But that no power can fill with vital oil
That broken lamp of flesh. Ha! 'tis the blood
Which fed these veins that ebbs till all is cold:
It is the form that moulded mine that sinks   20
Into the white and yellow spasms of death:
It is the soul by which mine was arrayed
In God's immortal likeness which now stands
Naked before Heaven's judgement seat!

(A bell strikes).

                                    One! Two!

The hours crawl on; and when my hairs are white,

My son will then perhaps be waiting thus,
Tortured between just hate and vain remorse;
Chiding the tardy messenger of news
Like those which I expect. I almost wish
He be not dead, although my wrongs are great;   30
Yet...'tis Orsino's step...

(Enter Orsino).

                                    Speak!

Ors.   I am come
To say he has escaped.

Gia.   Escaped!

Ors.   And safe
Within Petrella. He passed by the spot
Appointed for the deed an hour too soon.

Gia. Are we the fools of such contingencies?
And do we waste in blind misgivings thus
The hours when we should act? Then wind and
    thunder,
Which seemed to howl his knell, is the loud laughter
With which Heaven mocks our weakness! I
    henceforth
Will ne'er repent of aught designed or done   40
But my repentance.

Ors.   See, the lamp is out.

Gia. If no remorse is ours when the dim air
Has drank this innocent flame, why should we quail
When Cenci's life, that light by which ill spirits
See the worst deeds they prompt, shall sink for ever?
No, I am hardened.

Ors.   Why, what need of this?
Who feared the pale intrusion of remorse
In a just deed? Although our first plan failed,
Doubt not but he will soon be laid to rest.
But light the lamp; let us not talk i' the dark.   50

Gia. (Lighting the lamp). And yet once quenched I
    cannot thus relume[53]
My father's life: do you not think his ghost
Might plead that argument with God?

Ors.   Once gone
You cannot now recall your sister's peace;
Your own extinguished years of youth and hope;
Nor your wife's bitter words; nor all the taunts
Which, from the prosperous, weak misfortune takes;
Nor your dead mother; nor...

---

53 *relume*: relight or rekindle.

Gia.   O, speak no more!
　　I am resolved, although this very hand
　　Must quench the life that animated it.   60
Ors. There is no need of that. Listen: you know
　　Olimpio, the castellan[54] of Petrella
　　In old Colonna's[55] time; him whom your father
　　Degraded from his post? And Marzio,
　　That desperate wretch, whom he deprived last year
　　Of a reward of blood, well earned and due?
Gia. I knew Olimpio; and they say he hated
　　Old Cenci so, that in his silent rage
　　His lips grew white only to see him pass.
　　Of Marzio I know nothing.
Ors.   Marzio's hate   70
　　Matches Olimpio's. I have sent these men,
　　But in your name, and as at your request,
　　To talk with Beatrice and Lucretia.
Gia. Only to talk?
Ors.   The moments which even now
　　Pass onward to-morrow's midnight hour
　　May memorize[56] their flight with death: ere then
　　They must have talked, and may perhaps have done,
　　And made an end...
Gia.   Listen! What sound is that?
Ors. The house-dog moans, and the beams crack:
　　　nought else.
Gia. It is my wife complaining in her sleep: 80
　　I doubt not she is saying bitter things
　　Of me; and all my children round her dreaming
　　That I deny them sustenance.
Ors.   Whilst he
　　Who truly took it from them, and who fills
　　Their hungry rest with bitterness, now sleeps
　　Lapped in bad pleasures, and triumphantly
　　Mocks thee in visions of successful hate
　　Too like the truth of day.
Gia.   If e'er he wakes
　　Again, I will not trust to hireling hands...

---

54 *castellan*: the governor or constable of a castle.
55 *old Colonna*: likely referring to Marcantonio Colonna
　　(1535–84), duke of Paliano, who commanded the pa-
　　pal forces in the battle of Lepanto (1571) against the
　　Turks.
56 *memorize*: to keep alive the memory of; memorialize.

Ors. Why, that were well. I must be gone; good-night!   90
　　When next we meet may all be done—
Gia.   And all
　　Forgotten—Oh, that I had never been! *(Exeunt).*

ACT IV.

Scene I: *An apartment in the Castle of Petrella.*
Enter Cenci.

Cenci. She comes not; yet I left her even now
　　Vanquished and faint. She knows the penalty
　　Of her delay: yet what if threats are vain?
　　Am I not now within Petrella's moat?
　　Or fear I still the eyes and ears of Rome?
　　Might I not drag her by the golden hair?
　　Stamp on her? Keep her sleepless till her brain
　　Be overworn? Tame her with chains and famine?
　　Less would suffice. Yet so to leave undone
　　What I most seek! No, 'tis her stubborn will   10
　　Which by its own consent shall stoop as low
　　As that which drags it down.
(Enter Lucretia).
　　　　　　　　　　　　Thou loathed wretch!
　　Hide thee from my abhorrence, Fly, begone!
　　Yet stay! Bid Beatrice come hither.
Luc.   Oh,
　　Husband! I pray for thine own wretched sake
　　Heed what thou dost. A man who walks like thee
　　Through crimes, and through the danger of his
　　　crimes,
　　Each hour may stumble o'er a sudden grave.
　　And thou art old; thy hairs are hoary gray;
　　As thou wouldst save thyself from death and hell,   20
　　Pity thy daughter; give her to some friend
　　In marriage: so that she may tempt thee not
　　To hatred, or worse thoughts, if worse there be.
Cenci. What! like her sister who has found a home
　　To mock my hate from with prosperity?
　　Strange ruin shall destroy both her and thee
　　And all that yet remain. My death may be
　　Rapid, her destiny outspeeds it. Go,
　　Bid her come hither, and before my mood
　　Be changed, lest I should drag her by the hair.   30
Luc. She sent me to thee, husband. At thy presence

She fell, as thou dost know, into a trance;
And in that trance she heard a voice which said,
"Cenci must die! Let him confess himself!
Even now the accusing Angel waits to hear
If God, to punish his enormous crimes,
Harden his dying heart!"

Cenci.   Why—such things are...
No doubt divine revealings may be made.
'Tis plain I have been favoured from above,
For when I cursed my sons they died.—Aye...so...   40
As to the right or wrong, that's talk...repentance...
Repentance is an easy moment's work
And more depends on God than me. Well...well...
I must give up the greater point, which was
To poison and corrupt her soul.

(A pause; Lucretia approaches anxiously, and then
shrinks back as he speaks).

                                        One, two;
Aye...Rocco and Cristofano my curse
Strangled: and Giacomo, I think, will find
Life a worse Hell than that beyond the grave:
Beatrice shall, if there be skill in hate
Die in despair, blaspheming: to Bernardo,   50
He is so innocent, I will bequeath
The memory of these deeds, and make his youth
The sepulchre of hope, where evil thoughts
Shall grow like weeds on a neglected tomb.
When all is done, out in the wide Campagna,[57]
I will pile up my silver and my gold;
My costly robes, paintings and tapestries;
My parchments and all records of my wealth,
And make a bonfire in my joy, and leave
Of my possessions nothing but my name;   60
Which shall be an inheritance to strip
Its wearer bare as infamy. That done,
My soul, which is a scourge,[58] will I resign

Into the hands of him who wielded it;
Be it for its own punishment or theirs,
He will not ask it of me till the lash
Be broken in its last and deepest wound;
Until its hate be all inflicted. Yet,
Lest death outspeed my purpose, let me make
Short work and sure... *(Going).*

Luc. (Stops him).   Oh, stay! It was a feint: 70
She had no vision, and she heard no voice.
I said it but to awe thee.

Cenci.   That is well.
Vile palterer[59] with the sacred truth of God,
Be thy soul choked with that blaspheming lie!
For Beatrice worse terrors are in store
To bend her to my will.

Luc.   Oh! to what will?
What cruel sufferings more than she has known
Canst thou inflict?

Cenci.   Andrea! Go call my daughter,
And if she comes not tell her that I come.
What sufferings? I will drag her, step by step,   80
Through infamies unheard of among men:
She shall stand shelterless in the broad noon
Of public scorn, for acts blazoned[60] abroad,
One among which shall be...What? Canst thou
     guess?
She shall become (for what she most abhors
Shall have a fascination to entrap
Her loathing will), to her own conscious self
All she appears to others; and when dead,
As she shall die unshrived[61] and unforgiven,
A rebel to her father and her God,   90
Her corpse shall be abandoned to the hounds;[62]
Her name shall be the terror of the earth;
Her spirit shall approach the throne of God
Plague-spotted with my curses. I will make
Body and soul a monstrous lump of ruin.

---

57 *Compagna*: Reiman and Fraistat provide the following
     gloss: "The Roman Compagna is the level valley of the
     Tiber River surrounding Rome; in Count Cenci's (and
     in Shelley's) day it was almost deserted because of its
     unhealthy climate—malaria was rife there—and be-
     cause Italian warlords, like the Orsini and Colonna
     families, had ravaged it" (page 176, note 9).

58 *scourge*: a whip or lash; a thing that is the object of
     divine chastisement.

59 *palterer*: an equivocator or haggler; one who plays fast
     and loose with serious matters.

60 *blazoned*: to paint in bright colors; to proclaim or make
     public in an unnecessarily loud or inappropriate man-
     ner.

61 *unshrived*: unconfessed.

62 *Her corpse shall be abandoned to the hounds*: See Jer-
     emiah 7:33 and 16:4.

(Enter Andrea).

And. The Lady Beatrice...

Cenci.   Speak, pale slave! What
    Said she?

And.   My Lord, 'twas what she looked; she said:
    "Go tell my father that I see the gulph
    Of Hell between us two, which he may pass,
    I will not." *(Exit Andrea).*

Cenci.   Go thou quick, Lucretia,   100
    Tell her to come; yet let her understand
    Her coming is consent: and say, moreover,
    That if she come not I will curse her. *(Exit Lucretia).*
                         Ha!
    With what but with a father's curse doth God
    Panic-strike armed victory, and make pale
    Cities in their prosperity? The world's Father
    Must grant a parent's prayer against his child,
    Be he who asks even what men call me.
    Will not the deaths of her rebellious brothers
    Awe her before I speak? For I on them   110
    Did imprecate[63] quick ruin, and it came.

(Enter Lucretia).

    Well; what? Speak, wretch!

Luc.   She said, "I cannot come;
    Go tell my father that I see a torrent
    Of his own blood raging between us."

Cenci. (Kneeling).   God!
    Hear me! If this most specious mass of flesh,
    Which thou hast made my daughter; this my blood,
    This particle of my divided being;
    Or rather, this my bane and my disease,
    Whose sight infects and poisons me; this devil
    Which sprung from me as from a hell, was meant   120
    To aught good use; if her bright loveliness
    Was kindled to illumine this dark world;
    If nursed by thy selectest dew of love
    Such virtues blossom in her as should make
    The peace of life, I pray thee for my sake,
    As thou the common God and Father art
    Of her, and me, and all; reverse that doom!
    Earth, in the name of God, let her food be
    Poison, until she be encrusted round
    With leprous stains! Heaven, rain upon her head   130

---

63   *imprecate*: pray for; invoke or call down evil or calam-
    ity upon a person.

The blistering drops of the Maremma's dew,[64]
    Till she be speckled like a toad; parch up
    Those love-enkindled lips, warp those fine limbs
    To loathed lameness! All-beholding sun,
    Strike in thine envy those life darting-eyes
    With thine own blinding beams!

Luc.   Peace! Peace!
    For thine own sake unsay those dreadful words.
    When high God grants He punishes such prayers.

Cenci. (Leaping up, and throwing his right hand
     towards Heaven).
    He does His will, I mine! This in addition,
    That if she have a child...

Luc.   Horrible thought!   140

Cenci. That if she ever have a child; and thou,
    Quick Nature! I adjure thee by thy God,
    That thou be fruitful in her, and encrease
    And multiply, fulfilling his command,
    And my deep imprecation! May it be
    A hideous likeness of herself, that as
    From a distorting mirror, she may see
    Her image mixed with what she most abhors,
    Smiling upon her from her nursing breast.
    And that the child may from its infancy   150
    Grow, day by day, more wicked and deformed,
    Turning her mother's love to misery:
    And that both she and it may live until
    It shall repay her care and pain with hate,
    Or what may else be more unnatural.
    So he may hunt her through the clamorous scoffs
    Of the loud world to a dishonoured grave.
    Shall I revoke this curse? Go, bid her come,
    Before my words are chronicled in Heaven. *(Exit*
     Lucretia).
    I do not feel as if I were a man,   160
    But like a fiend appointed to chastise
    The offences of some unremembered world.
    My blood is running up and down my veins;
    A fearful pleasure makes it prick and tingle:
    I feel a giddy sickness of strange awe;

---

64   *Maremma*: geographic region in central Italy rife with
    malaria. Drained by the Romans for agricultural pur-
    poses, it became a swampy marshland beginning in the
    sixth century.

My heart is beating with an expectation
Of horrid joy.
(Enter Lucretia).
               What? Speak!
Luc.   She bids thee curse;
And if thy curses, as they cannot do,
Could kill her soul...
Cenci.   She would not come. 'Tis well,
I can do both: first take what I demand,   170
And then extort concession. To thy chamber!
Fly ere I spurn thee: and beware this night
That thou cross not my footsteps. It were safer
To come between the tiger and his prey. *(Exit*
    Lucretia).
It must be late; mine eyes grow weary dim
With unaccustomed heaviness of sleep.
Conscience! Oh, thou most insolent of lies!
They say that sleep, that healing dew of heaven,
Steeps not in balm the foldings of the brain
Which thinks thee an impostor. I will go   180
First to belie thee with an hour of rest,
Which will be deep and calm, I feel: and then...
O, multitudinous Hell, the fiends will shake
Thine arches with the laughter of their joy!
There shall be lamentation heard in Heaven
As o'er an angel fallen; and upon Earth
All good shall droop and sicken, and ill things
Shall with a spirit of unnatural life
Stir and be quickened[65]...even as I am now. *(Exit).*

    Scene II: *Before the Castle of Petrella. Enter Beatrice*
        and Lucretia above on the ramparts.

Bea. They come not yet.
Luc.   'Tis scarce midnight.
Bea.   How slow
Behind the course of thought, even sick with speed,
Lags leaden-footed time!
Luc.   The minutes pass...
If he should wake before the deed is done?
Bea. O, mother! He must never wake again.
What thou hast said persuades me that our act
Will but dislodge a spirit of deep hell
Out of a human form.

---

[65] *quickened*: animated or stimulated.

Luc.   'Tis true he spoke
Of death and judgement with strange confidence
For one so wicked; as a man believing   10
In God, yet recking[66] not of good or ill.
And yet to die without confession!...
Bea.   Oh!
Believe that heaven is merciful and just,
And will not add our dread necessity
To the amount of his offences.
(Enter Olimpio and Marzio, below).
Luc.   See,
They come.
Bea.   All mortal things must hasten thus
To their dark end. Let us go down.
(Exeunt Lucretia and Beatrice from above).
Olimpio. How feel you to this work?
Marzio.   As one who thinks
A thousand crowns excellent market price
For an old murderer's life. Your cheeks are pale.   20
Oli. It is the white reflection of your own,
Which you call pale.
Mar.   Is that their natural hue?
Oli. Or 'tis my hate and the deferred desire
To wreak[67] it, which extinguishes their blood.
Mar. You are inclined then to this business?
Oli.   Aye.
If one should bribe me with a thousand crowns
To kill a serpent which had stung my child,
I could not be more willing.
(Enter Beatrice and Lucretia, below).
              Noble ladies!
Bea. Are ye resolved?
Oli.   Is he asleep?
Mar.   Is all
Quiet?
Luc.   I mixed an opiate with his drink: 30
He sleeps so soundly...
Bea.   That his death will be
But as a change of sin-chastising dreams,
A dark continuance of the Hell within him,
Which God extinguish! But ye are resolved?
Ye know it is a high and holy deed?

---

[66] *recking*: taking heed, care, or thought of something.
[67] *wreak*: to avenge or inflict retributive punishment on;
   also, to give vent or expression to.

Oli. We are resolved.

Mar. As to the how this act
Be warranted, it rests with you.

Bea. Well, follow!

Oli. Hush! Hark! What noise is that?

Mar. Ha! some one comes!

Bea. Ye conscience-stricken cravens,[68] rock to rest
Your baby hearts. It is the iron gate,   40
Which ye left open, swinging to the wind,
That enters whistling as in scorn. Come, follow!
And be your steps like mine, light, quick and
bold. *(Exeunt).*

Scene III: *An apartment in the Castle.*
Enter Beatrice and Lucretia.

Luc. They are about it now.

Bea. Nay, it is done.

Luc. I have not heard him groan.

Bea. He will not groan.

Luc. What sound is that?

Bea. List! 'tis the tread of feet
About his bed.

Luc. My God!
If he be now a cold stiff corpse...

Bea. O, fear not
What may be done, but what is left undone:
The act seals all.

(Enter Olimpio and Marzio).

Is it accomplished?

Mar. What?

Oli. Did you not call?

Bea. When?

Oli. Now.

Bea. I ask if all is over?

Oli. We dare not kill an old and sleeping man;
His thin gray hair, his stern and reverend brow,   10
His veined hands crossed on his heaving breast,
And the calm innocent sleep in which he lay,
Quelled me. Indeed, indeed, I cannot do it.

Mar. But I was bolder; for I chid Olimpio,
And bade him bear his wrongs to his own grave
And leave me the reward. And now my knife

---

68 *craven*: coward; one who is afraid of an opponent.

Touched the loose wrinkled throat, when the old
man
Stirred in his sleep, and said, "God! hear, O, hear,
A father's curse! What, art Thou not our Father?"
And then he laughed. I knew it was the ghost   20
Of my dead father speaking through his lips,
And could not kill him.

Bea. Miserable slaves!
Where, if ye dare not kill a sleeping man,
Found ye the boldness to return to me
With such a deed undone? Base palterers!
Cowards and traitors! Why, the very conscience
Which ye would sell for gold and for revenge
Is an equivocation: it sleeps over
A thousand daily acts disgracing men;
And when a deed where mercy insults heaven...   30
Why do I talk?

(Snatching a dagger from one of them and raising it).
Hadst thou a tongue to say,
"She murdered her own father," I must do it!
But never dream ye shall outlive him long!

Oli. Stop, for God's sake!

Mar. I will go back and kill him.

Oli. Give me the weapon. we must do thy will.

Bea. Take it! Depart! Return! *(Exeunt Olimpio and
Marzio).*
How pale thou art!
We do but that which 'twere a deadly crime
To leave undone.

Luc. Would it were done!

Bea. Even whilst
That doubt is passing through your mind, the world
Is conscious of a change. Darkness and Hell   40
Have swallowed up the vapour they sent forth
To blacken the sweet light of life. My breath
Comes, methinks, lighter, and the jellied blood
Runs freely through my veins. Hark!

(Enter Olimpio and Marzio).
He is...

Oli. Dead!

Mar. We strangled him that there might be no blood;
And then we threw his heavy corpse i' the garden
Under the balcony; 'twill seem it fell.

Bea. (Giving them a bag of coin). Here, take this
gold, and hasten to your homes.
And, Marzio, because thou wast only awed

By that which made me tremble, wear thou this!   50
(Clothes him in a rich mantle).
   It was the mantle which my grandfather
Wore in his high prosperity, and men
Envied his state: so may they envy thine.
Thou wert a weapon in the hand of God
To a just use. Live long and thrive! And, mark,
If thou hast crimes, repent: this deed is none.
(A horn is sounded).
Luc. Hark, 'tis the castle horn; my God! it sounds
   Like the last trump.[69]
Bea.   Some tedious guest is coming.
Luc. The drawbridge is let down; there is a tramp
   Of horses in the court; fly, hide yourselves!   60
(Exeunt Olimpio and Marzio).
Bea. Let us retire to counterfeit deep rest;
   I scarcely need to counterfeit it now:
   The spirit which doth reign within these limbs
   Seems strangely undisturbed. I could even sleep
   Fearless and calm: all ill is surely past. *(Exeunt).*

Scene IV: *Another apartment in the Castle. Enter on*
one side the Legate Savella, introduced by a servant,
and on the other Lucretia and Bernardo.

Savella. Lady, my duty to his Holiness
   Be my excuse that thus unseasonably
   I break upon your rest. I must speak with
   Count Cenci; doth he sleep?
Luc. (In a hurried and confused manner).
                  I think he sleeps;
Yet wake him not, I pray, spare me awhile,
He is a wicked and a wrathful man;
Should he be roused out of his sleep to-night,
Which is, I know, a hell of angry dreams,
It were not well; indeed it were not well.
Wait till day break... *(Aside).* O, I am deadly sick!   10
Sav. I grieve thus to distress you, but the Count
   Must answer charges of the gravest import,
   And suddenly; such my commission is.
Luc. (With increased agitation). I dare not rouse him:
   I know none who dare...

---

[69] *Like the last trump*: like the last trumpet, referring to
   the time when the archangel Gabriel's trumpet will
   announce the Last Judgment.

'Twere perilous;...you might as safely waken
A serpent; or a corpse in which some fiend
Were laid to sleep.
Sav.   Lady, my moments here
Are counted. I must rouse him from his sleep,
Since none else dare.
Luc. (Aside).   O, terror! O, despair!
   (To Bernardo). Bernardo, conduct you the Lord   20
      Legate[70] to
   Your father's chamber. *(Exeunt Savella and Bernardo).*
(Enter Beatrice).
Bea.   'Tis a messenger
   Come to arrest the culprit who now stands
   Before the throne of unappealable God.
   Both Earth and Heaven, consenting arbiters,
   Acquit our deed.
Luc.   Oh, agony of fear!
   Would that he yet might live! Even now I heard
   The Legate's followers whisper as they passed
   They had a warrant for his instant death.
   All was prepared by unforbidden means
   Which we must pay so dearly, having done.   30
   Even now they search the tower, and find the body;
   Now they suspect the truth; now they consult
   Before they come to tax us with the fact;
   O, horrible, 'tis all discovered!
Bea.   Mother,
   What is done wisely, is done well. Be bold
   As thou art just. 'Tis like a truant child
   To fear that others know what thou hast done,
   Even from thine own strong consciousness, and thus
   Write on unsteady eyes and altered cheeks
   All thou wouldst hide. Be faithful to thyself,   40
   And fear no other witness but thy fear.
   For if, as cannot be, some circumstance
   Should rise in accusation, we can blind
   Suspicion with such cheap astonishment,
   Or overbear it with such guiltless pride,
   As murderers cannot feign. The deed is done,
   And what may follow now regards not me.
   I am as universal as the light;
   Free as the earth-surrounding air; as firm
   As the world's centre. Consequence, to me,   50

---

[70] *Legate*: an ecclesiastic deputed to represent the Pope
   and armed with his authority.

Is as the wind which strikes the solid rock
But shakes it not.
(A cry within and tumult).
Voices.   Murder! Murder! Murder!
(Enter Bernardo and Savella).
Sav. *(To his followers).* Go search the castle round;
    sound the alarm;
    Look to the gates that none escape!
Bea.   What now?
Ber. I know not what to say...my father's dead.
Bea. How; dead! he only sleeps; you mistake,
    brother.
    His sleep is very calm, very like death;
    'Tis wonderful how well a tyrant sleeps.
    He is not dead?
Ber.   Dead; murdered.
Luc. *(With extreme agitation).*   Oh no, no
    He is not murdered though he may be dead;   60
    I have alone the keys of those apartments.
Sav. Ha! Is it so?
Bea.   My Lord, I pray excuse us;
    We will retire; my mother is not well:
    She seems quite overcome with this strange
      horror. *(Exeunt Lucretia and Beatrice).*
Sav. Can you suspect who may have murdered him?
Ber. I know not what to think.
Sav.   Can you name any
    Who had an interest in his death?
Ber.   Alas!
    I can name none who had not, and those most
    Who most lament that such a deed is done;
    My mother, and my sister, and myself.   70
Sav. 'Tis strange! There were clear marks of violence.
    I found the old man's body in the moonlight
    Hanging beneath the window of his chamber
    Among the branches of a pine: he could not
    Have fallen there, for all his limbs lay heaped
    And effortless; 'tis true there was no blood...
    Favour me, Sir; it much imports your house
    That all should be made clear; to tell the ladies
    That I request their presence. *(Exit Bernardo).*
(Enter Guards bringing in Marzio).
Guard.   We have one.
Officer. My Lord, we found this ruffian and another   80
    Lurking among the rocks; there is no doubt
    But that they are the murderers of Count Cenci:

Each had a bag of coin; this fellow wore
A gold-inwoven robe, which shining bright
Under the dark rocks to the glimmering moon
Betrayed them to our notice: the other fell
Desperately fighting.
Sav.   What does he confess?
Off. He keeps firm silence; but these lines found on him
    May speak.
Sav.   Their language is at least sincere.
    (Reads). "To the Lady Beatrice.   90
    That the atonement of what my nature
    Sickens to conjecture may soon arrive,
    I send thee, at thy brother's desire, those
    Who will speak and do more than I dare
    Write...Thy devoted servant,
                              Orsino."
(Enter Lucretia, Beatrice, and Bernardo).
    Knowest thou this writing, Lady?
Bea.   No.
Sav.   Nor thou?
Luc. *(Her conduct throughout the scene is marked by
    extreme agitation).*
    Where was it found? What is it? It should be
    Orsino's hand! It speaks of that strange horror
    Which never yet found utterance, but which made
    Between that hapless child and her dead father   100
    A gulph of obscure hatred.
Sav.   Is it so?
    Is it true, Lady, that thy father did
    Such outrages as to awaken in thee
    Unfilial hate?
Bea.   Not hate, 'twas more than hate:
    This is most true, yet wherefore question me?
Sav. There is a deed demanding question done;
    Thou hast a secret which will answer not.
Bea. What sayest? My Lord, your words are bold
    and rash.
Sav. I do arrest all present in the name
    Of the Pope's Holiness. You must to Rome.   110
Luc. O, not to Rome! Indeed we are not guilty.
Bea. Guilty! Who dares talk of guilt? My Lord,
    I am more innocent of parricide
    Than is a child born fatherless...Dear mother,
    Your gentleness and patience are no shield
    For this keen judging world, this two-edged lie,
    Which seems, but is not. What! will human laws,

Rather will ye who are their ministers,
Bar all access to retribution first,
And then, when Heaven doth interpose to do   120
What ye neglect, arming familiar things
To the redress of an unwonted[71] crime,
Make ye the victims who demanded it
Culprits? 'Tis ye are culprits! That poor wretch
Who stands so pale, and trembling, and amazed,
If it be true he murdered Cenci, was
A sword in the right hand of justest God,
Wherefore should I have wielded it? Unless
The crimes which mortal tongue dare never name
God therefore scruples to avenge.

Sav.   You own   130
That you desired his death?

Bea.   It would have been
A crime no less than his, if for one moment
That fierce desire had faded in my heart.
'Tis true I did believe, and hope, and pray,
Aye, I even knew...for God is wise and just,
That some strange sudden death hung over him.
'Tis true that this did happen, and most true
There was no other rest for me on earth,
No other hope in Heaven...now what of this?

Sav. Strange thoughts beget strange deeds; and here   140
    are both:
I judge thee not.

Bea.   And yet, if you arrest me,
You are the judge and executioner
Of that which is the life of life: the breath
Of accusation kills an innocent name,
And leaves for lame acquittal the poor life
Which is a mask without it. 'Tis most false
That I am guilty of foul parricide;
Although I must rejoice, for justest cause,
That other hands have sent my father's soul
To ask the mercy he denied to me.   150
Now leave us free; stain not a noble house
With vague surmises of rejected[72] crime;
Add to our sufferings and your own neglect
No heavier sum: let them have been enough:
Leave us the wreck we have.

---

71 *unwonted*: not usual or habitual; not commonly heard,
    seen, or practiced.
72 *rejected*: refused or repudiated.

Sav.   I dare not, Lady.
I pray that you prepare yourselves for Rome:
There the Pope's further pleasure will be known.

Luc. O, not to Rome! O, take us not to Rome!

Bea. Why not to Rome, dear mother? There as here
Our innocence is as an armed heel   160
To trample accusation. God is there
As here, and with his shadow ever clothes
The innocent, the injured and the weak;
And such are we. Cheer up, dear Lady, lean
On me; collect your wandering thoughts. My Lord,
As soon as you have taken some refreshment,
And had all such examinations made
Upon the spot, as may be necessary
To the full understanding of this matter,
We shall be ready. Mother; will you come?   170

Luc. Ha! they will bind us to the rack, and wrest
Self-accusation from our agony!
Will Giacomo be there? Orsino? Marzio?
All present; all confronted; all demanding
Each from the other's countenance the thing
Which is in every heart! O, misery!

(She faints, and is borne out).

Sav. She faints: an ill appearance this.

Bea.   My Lord,
She knows not yet the uses of the world.
She fears that power is as a beast which grasps
And loosens not: a snake whose look transmutes   180
All things to guilt which is its nutriment.
She cannot know how well the supine slaves
Of blind authority read the truth of things
When written on a brow of guilelessness:
She sees not yet triumphant Innocence
Stand at the judgement-seat of mortal man,
A judge and an accuser of the wrong
Which drags it there. Prepare yourself, my Lord;
Our suite will join yours in the court below. *(Exeunt).*

ACT V.

Scene I: *An Apartment in Orsino's Palace.*
Enter Orsino and Giacomo.

Gia. Do evil deeds thus quickly come to end?
O, that the vain remorse which must chastise
Crimes done, had but as loud a voice to warn

As its keen sting is mortal to avenge!
O, that the hour when present had cast off
The mantle of its mystery, and shewn
The ghastly form with which it now returns
When its scared game is roused, cheering the hounds
Of conscience to their prey! Alas! Alas!
It was a wicked thought, a piteous deed,   10
To kill an old and hoary-headed father.
Ors. It has turned out unluckily, in truth.
Gia. To violate the sacred doors of sleep;
To cheat kind nature of the placid death
Which she prepares for overwearied age;
To drag from Heaven an unrepentant soul
Which might have quenched in reconciling prayers
A life of burning crimes...
Ors.   You cannot say
I urged you to the deed.
Gia.   O, had I never
Found in thy smooth and ready countenance   20
The mirror of my darkest thoughts; hadst thou
Never with hints and questions made me look
Upon the monster of my thought, until
It grew familiar to desire...
Ors.   'Tis thus
Men cast the blame of their unprosperous acts
Upon the abettors of their own resolve;
Or anything but their weak, guilty selves.
And yet, confess the truth, it is the peril
In which you stand that gives you this pale sickness
Of penitence; Confess 'tis fear disguised   30
From its own shame that takes the mantle now
Of thin remorse. What if we yet were safe?
Gia. How can that be? Already Beatrice,
Lucretia and the murderer are in prison.
I doubt not officers are, whilst we speak,
Sent to arrest us.
Ors.   I have all prepared
For instant flight. We can escape even now,
So we take fleet occasion by the hair.
Gia. Rather expire in tortures, as I may.
What! will you cast by self-accusing flight   40
Assured conviction upon Beatrice?
She, who alone in this unnatural work,
Stands like God's angel ministered upon
By fiends; avenging such a nameless wrong
As turns black parricide to piety;
Whilst we for basest ends...I fear, Orsino,

While I consider all your words and looks,
Comparing them with your proposal now,
That you must be a villain. For what end
Could you engage in such a perilous crime,   50
Training me on with hints, and signs, and smiles,
Even to this gulf? Thou art no liar? No,
Thou art a lie! Traitor and murderer!
Coward and slave! But, no, defend thyself;
     (Drawing).
Let the sword speak what the indignant tongue
Disdains to brand thee with.
Ors.   Put up your weapon.
Is it the desperation of your fear
Makes you thus rash and sudden with a friend,
Now ruined for your sake? If honest anger
Have moved you, know, that what I just proposed   60
Was but to try you. As for me, I think,
Thankless affection led me to this point,
From which, if my firm temper could repent,
I cannot now recede. Even whilst we speak
The ministers of justice wait below:
They grant me these brief moments. Now if you
Have any word of melancholy comfort
To speak to your pale wife, 'twere best to pass
Out at the postern,[73] and avoid them so.
Gia. O, generous friend! How canst thou pardon me?   70
Would that my life could purchase thine!
Ors.   That wish
Now comes a day too late. Haste; fare thee well!
Hear'st thou not steps along the corridor? *(Exit
     Giacomo).*
I'm sorry for it; but the guards are waiting
At his own gate, and such was my contrivance
That I might rid me both of him and them.
I thought to act a solemn comedy
Upon the painted scene of this new world,
And to attain my own peculiar ends
By some such plot of mingled good and ill   80
As others weave; but there arose a Power
Which graspt and snapped the threads of my device
And turned it to a net of ruin...Ha!
(A shout is heard).
Is that my name I hear proclaimed abroad?
But I will pass, wrapt in a vile disguise;
Rags on my back, and a false innocence

---

73 *postern*: a side or back door or gate.

Upon my face, through the misdeeming crowd
Which judges by what seems. 'Tis easy then
For a new name and for a country new,
And a new life, fashioned on old desires,   90
To change the honours of abandoned Rome.
And these must be the masks of that within,
Which must remain unaltered...Oh, I fear
That what is past will never let me rest!
Why, when none else is conscious, but myself,
Of my misdeeds, should my own heart's contempt
Trouble me? Have I not the power to fly
My own reproaches? Shall I be the slave
Of...what? A word? which those of this false world
Employ against each other, not themselves;   100
As men wear daggers not for self-offence.
But if I am mistaken, where shall I
Find the disguise to hide me from myself,
As now I skulk from every other eye? *(Exit)*.

Scene II: *A Hall of Justice. Camillo, Judges etc.*
are discovered seated; Marzio is led in.

1st Judge. Accused, do you persist in your denial?
  I ask you, are you innocent, or guilty?
  I demand who were the participators
  In your offence? Speak truth and the whole truth.
Mar. My God! I did not kill him; I know nothing;
  Olimpio sold the robe to me from which
  You would infer my guilt.
2nd Judge.   Away with him!
1st Judge. Dare you, with lips yet white from the
    rack's kiss
  Speak false? Is it so soft a questioner,
  That you would bandy[74] lover's talk with it   10
  Till it wind out your life and soul? Away!
Mar. Spare me! O, spare! I will confess.
1st Judge.   Then speak.
Mar. I strangled him in his sleep.
1st Judge.   Who urged you to it?
Mar. His own son Giacomo, and the young prelate
  Orsino sent me to Petrella; there
  The ladies Beatrice and Lucretia
  Tempted me with a thousand crowns, and I

And my companion forthwith murdered him.
  Now let me die.
1st Judge.   This sounds as bad as truth.
  Guards, there,
  Lead forth the prisoner!
(Enter Lucretia, Beatrice, and Giacomo, guarded).
               Look upon this man;   20
  When did you see him last?
Bea.   We never saw him.
Mar. You know me too well, Lady Beatrice.
Bea. I know thee! How? where? when?
Mar.   You know 'twas I
  Whom you did urge with menaces and bribes
  To kill your father. When the thing was done
  You clothed me in a robe of woven gold
  And bade me thrive: how I have thriven, you see.
  You, my Lord Giacomo, Lady Lucretia,
  You know that what I speak is true.
(Beatrice advances towards him; he covers his face, and
shrinks back).
               Oh, dart
  The terrible resentment of those eyes   30
  On the dead earth! Turn them away from me!
  They wound: 'twas torture forced the truth. My
    Lords,
  Having said this let me be led to death.
Bea. Poor wretch, I pity thee: yet stay awhile.
Cam. Guards, lead him not away.
Bea.   Cardinal Camillo,
  You have a good repute for gentleness
  And wisdom: can it be that you sit here
  To countenance a wicked farce like this?
  When some obscure and trembling slave is dragged
  From sufferings which might shake the sternest heart   40
  And bade to answer, not as he believes,
  But as those may suspect or do desire
  Whose questions thence suggest their own reply:
  And that in peril of such hideous torments
  As merciful God spares even the damned. Speak now
  The thing you surely know, which is that you,
  If your fine frame were stretched upon that wheel,
  And you were told: "Confess that you did poison
  Your little nephew; that fair blue-eyed child
  Who was the lodestar[75] of your life":—and though   50

---

74 *bandy*: applying either to a ball or to words, to pass
  from one to another in a circle or group; to toss about.

75 *lodestar*: the polar or "guiding star"; figuratively, that
  on which one's attention or hopes are fixed.

All see, since his most swift and piteous death,
That day and night, and heaven and earth, and time,
And all the things hoped for or done therein
Are changed to you, through your exceeding grief,
Yet you would say, "I confess anything":
And beg from your tormentors, like that slave,
The refuge of dishonourable death.
I pray thee, Cardinal, that thou assert
My innocence.
Cam. (Much moved). What shall we think, my Lords?   60
    Shame on these tears! I thought the heart was frozen
    Which is their fountain. I would pledge my soul
    That she is guiltless.
Jud.   Yet she must be tortured.
Cam. I would as soon have tortured mine own nephew
    (If he now lived he would be just her age;
    His hair, too, was her colour, and his eyes
    Like hers in shape, but blue and not so deep)
    As that most perfect image of God's love
    That ever came sorrowing upon the earth.
    She is as pure as speechless infancy!   70
Jud. Well, be her purity on your head, my Lord,
    If you forbid the rack. His Holiness
    Enjoined us to pursue this monstrous crime
    By the severest forms of law; nay even
    To stretch a point against the criminals.
    The prisoners stand accused of parricide
    Upon such evidence as justifies
    Torture.
Bea.   What evidence? This man's?
Jud.   Even so.
Bea. (To Marzio). Come near. And who art thou
    thus chosen forth
    Out of the multitude of living men   80
    To kill the innocent?
Mar.   I am Marzio,
    Thy father's vassal.
Bea.   Fix thine eyes on mine;
    Answer to what I ask.
(Turning to the Judges).   I prithee mark
    His countenance: unlike bold calumny[76]

---

[76] *calumny*: false and malicious representation of the
    words or actions of others intended to injure their
    reputation; slanderous report; false witness.

Which sometimes dares not speak the thing it looks,
He dares not look the thing he speaks, but bends
His gaze on the blind earth.
(To Marzio).   What! wilt thou say
That I did murder my own father?
Mar.   Oh!
Spare me! My brain swims round...I cannot speak...
It was that horrid torture forced the truth.   90
Take me away! Let her not look on me!
I am a guilty miserable wretch;
I have said all I know; now, let me die!
Bea. My Lords, if by my nature I had been
    So stern, as to have planned the crime alleged,
    Which your suspicions dictate to this slave,
    And the rack makes him utter, do you think
    I should have left this two-edged instrument
    Of my misdeed; this man, this bloody knife
    With my own name engraven on the heft,   100
    Lying unsheathed amid a world of foes,
    For my own death? That with such horrible need
    For deepest silence, I should have neglected
    So trivial a precaution, as the making
    His tomb the keeper of a secret written
    On a thief's memory? What is his poor life?
    What are a thousand lives? A parricide
    Had trampled them like dust; and, see, he lives!
(Turning to Marzio).
    And thou...
Mar.   Oh, spare me! Speak to me no more!
    That stern yet piteous look, those solemn tones,   110
    Wound worse than torture.
(To the Judges).   I have told it all;
    For pity's sake lead me away to death.
Cam. Guards, lead him nearer the Lady Beatrice,
    He shrinks from her regard like autumn's leaf
    From the keen breath of the serenest north.
Bea. O thou who tremblest on the giddy verge
    Of life and death, pause ere thou answerest me;
    So mayst thou answer God with less dismay:
    What evil have we done thee? I, alas!
    Have lived but on this earth a few sad years,   120
    And so my lot was ordered, that a father
    First turned the moments of awakening life
    To drops, each poisoning youth's sweet hope; and
    then
    Stabbed with one blow my everlasting soul;

And my untainted fame; and even that peace
Which sleeps within the core of the heart's heart;
But the wound was not mortal; so my hate
Became the only worship I could lift
To our great father, who in pity and love,
Armed thee, as thou dost say, to cut him off;   130
And thus his wrong becomes my accusation;
And art thou the accuser? If thou hopest
Mercy in heaven, show justice upon earth:
Worse than a bloody hand is a hard heart.
If thou hast done murders, made thy life's path
Over the trampled laws of God and man,
Rush not before thy Judge, and say: "My maker,
I have done this and more; for there was one
Who was most pure and innocent on earth;
And because she endured what never any   140
Guilty or innocent endured before:
Because her wrongs could not be told, not thought;
Because thy hand at length did rescue her;
I with my words killed her and all her kin."
Think, I adjure you, what it is to slay
The reverence living in the minds of men
Towards our ancient house, and stainless fame!
Think what it is to strangle infant pity,
Cradled in the belief of guileless looks,
Till it become a crime to suffer. Think   150
What 'tis to blot with infamy and blood
All that which shews like innocence, and is,
Hear me, great God! I swear, most innocent,
So that the world lose all discrimination
Between the sly, fierce, wild regard of guilt,
And that which now compels thee to reply
To what I ask: Am I, or am I not
A parricide?
Mar.   Thou art not!
Jud.   What is this?
Mar. I here declare those whom I did accuse
Are innocent. 'Tis I alone am guilty.   160
Jud. Drag him away to torments; let them be
Subtle and long drawn out, to tear the folds
Of the heart's inmost cell. Unbind him not
Till he confess.
Mar.   Torture me as ye will:
A keener pang has wrung a higher truth
From my last breath. She is most innocent!
Bloodhounds, not men, glut yourselves well with me;

I will not give you that fine piece of nature
To rend and ruin. *(Exit Marzio, guarded).*
Cam.   What say ye now, my Lords?
Jud. Let tortures strain the truth till it be white   170
As snow thrice sifted by the frozen wind.
Cam. Yet stained with blood.
Jud. (To Beatrice).   Know you this paper, Lady?
Bea. Entrap me not with questions. Who stands here
As my accuser? Ha! wilt thou be he,
Who art my judge? Accuser, witness, judge,
What, all in one? Here is Orsino's name;
Where is Orsino? Let his eye meet mine.
What means this scrawl? Alas! ye know not what,
And therefore on the chance that it may be
Some evil, will ye kill us?
(Enter an Officer).
Off.   Marzio's dead.   180
Jud. What did he say?
Off.   Nothing. As soon as we
Had bound him on the wheel, he smiled on us,
As one who baffles a deep[77] adversary;
And holding his breath, died.
Jud.   There remains nothing
But to apply the question to those prisoners,
Who yet remain stubborn.
Cam.   I overrule
Further proceedings, and in the behalf
Of these most innocent and noble persons
Will use my interest with the Holy Father.
Jud. Let the Pope's pleasure then be done. Meanwhile   190
Conduct these culprits each to separate cells;
And be the engines[78] ready: for this night
If the Pope's resolution be as grave,
Pious, and just as once, I'll wring the truth
Out of those nerves and sinews, groan by groan.
    (Exeunt).

Scene III: *The cell of a prison. Beatrice is discovered
        asleep on a couch. Enter Bernardo.*

Ber. How gently slumber rests upon her face,
Like the last thoughts of some day sweetly spent
Closing in night and dreams, and so prolonged.

---

[77] *deep*: profound, penetrating, or difficult to overcome.
[78] *engine*: machine of torture.

After such torments as she bore last night,
How light and soft her breathing comes. Ay, me!
Methinks that I shall never sleep again.
But I must shake the heavenly dew of rest
From this sweet folded flower, thus...wake! awake!
What, sister, canst thou sleep?

Bea. (Awaking).   I was just dreaming
That we were all in Paradise. Thou knowest   10
This cell seems like a kind of Paradise
After our father's presence.

Ber.   Dear, dear sister,
Would that thy dream were not a dream! O God!
How shall I tell?

Bea.   What wouldst thou tell, sweet brother?

Ber. Look not so calm and happy, or even whilst
I stand considering what I have to say
My heart will break.

Bea.   See now, thou mak'st me weep:
How very friendless thou would'st be, dear child,
If I were dead. Say what thou hast to say.

Ber. They have confessed; they could endure no more   20
The tortures...

Bea.   Ha! What was there to confess?
They must have told some weak and wicked lie
To flatter their tormentors. Have they said
That they were guilty? O white innocence,
That thou shouldst wear the mask of guilt to hide
Thine awful and serenest countenance
From those who know thee not!

(Enter Judge with Lucretia and Giacomo, guarded).
                    Ignoble hearts!
For some brief spasms of pain, which are at least
As mortal as the limbs through which they pass,
Are centuries of high splendour laid in dust?   30
And that eternal honour which should live
Sunlike, above the reek of mortal fame,
Changed to a mockery and a bye-word?[79] What!
Will you give up these bodies to be dragged
At horses' heels, so that our hair should sweep
The footsteps of the vain and senseless crowd,
Who, that they may make our calamity
Their worship and their spectacle, will leave

The churches and the theatres as void
As their own hearts? Shall the light multitude   40
Fling, at their choice, curses or faded pity,
Sad funeral flowers to deck a living corpse,
Upon us as we pass to pass away,
And leave...what memory of our having been?
Infamy, blood, terror, despair? O thou,
Who wert a mother to the parentless,
Kill not thy child! Let not her wrongs kill thee!
Brother, lie down with me upon the rack,
And let us each be silent as a corpse;
It soon will be as soft as any grave.   50
'Tis but the falsehood it can wring from fear
Makes the rack cruel.

Gia.   They will tear the truth
Even from thee at last, those cruel pains:
For pity's sake say thou art guilty now.

Luc. O, speak the truth! Let us all quickly die;
And after death, God is our judge, not they;
He will have mercy on us.

Ber.   If indeed
It can be true, say so, dear sister mine;
And then the Pope will surely pardon you,
And all be well.

Jud.   Confess, or I will warp   60
Your limbs with such keen tortures...

Bea.   Tortures! Turn
The rack henceforth into a spinning-wheel!
Torture your dog, that he may tell when last
He lapped the blood his master shed...not me!
My pangs are of the mind, and of the heart,
And of the soul; aye, of the inmost soul,
Which weeps within tears as of burning gall
To see, in this ill world where none are true,
My kindred false to their deserted selves.
And with considering all the wretched life   70
Which I have lived, and its now wretched end,
And the small justice shewn by Heaven and Earth
To me or mine; and what a tyrant thou art,
And what slaves these; and what a world we make,
The oppressor and the oppressed...such pangs
    compel
My answer. What is it thou wouldst with me?

Jud. Art thou not guilty of thy father's death?

Bea. Or wilt thou rather tax high judging God
That He permitted such an act as that

---

79 *bye-word*: also byword, i.e., a person or thing who be-
    comes proverbial, as a type of specified characteristics;
    an object of scorn or contempt.

Which I have suffered, and which he beheld; 80
Made it unutterable, and took from it
All refuge, all revenge, all consequence,
But that which thou hast called my father's death?
Which is or is not what men call a crime,
Which either I have done, or have not done;
Say what ye will. I shall deny no more.
If ye desire it thus, thus let it be,
And so an end of all. Now do your will;
No other pains shall force another word.

Jud. She is convicted, but has not confessed. 90
Be it enough. Until their final sentence
Let none have converse with them. You, young Lord,
Linger not here!

Bea.　　　　　Oh, tear him not away!

Jud. Guards, do your duty.

Ber. (Embracing Beatrice). Oh! would ye divide
Body from soul?

Off.　　　　　That is the headsman's business.

(Exeunt all but Lucretia, Beatrice, and Giacomo).

Gia. Have I confessed? Is it all over now?
No hope! No refuge! O weak, wicked tongue
Which hast destroyed me, would that thou hadst
　　been
Cut out and thrown to dogs first! To have killed
My father first, and then betrayed my sister; 100
Aye, thee! the one thing innocent and pure
In this black guilty world, to that which I
So well deserve! My wife! my little ones!
Destitute, helpless, and I...Father! God!
Canst Thou forgive even the unforgiving,
When their full hearts break thus, thus!...

(Covers his face and weeps).

Luc.　　　　　　　　　O my child!
To what a dreadful end are we all come!
Why did I yield? Why did I not sustain
Those torments? Oh, that I were all dissolved
Into these fast and unavailing tears, 110
Which flow and feel not!

Bea.　　　　　　　What 'twas weak to do,
'Tis weaker to lament, once being done;
Take cheer! The God who knew my wrong, and
　　made
Our speedy act the angel of his wrath,
Seems, and but seems to have abandoned us.
Let us not think that we shall die for this.

Brother, sit near me; give me your firm hand,
You had a manly heart. Bear up! Bear up!
O, dearest Lady, put your gentle head
Upon my lap, and try to sleep awhile: 120
Your eyes look pale, hollow and overworn,
With heaviness of watching and slow grief.
Come, I will sing you some low, sleepy tune,
Not cheerful, nor yet sad; some dull old thing,
Some outworn and unused monotony,
Such as our country gossips sing and spin,
Till they almost forget they live: lie down!
So, that will do. Have I forgot the words?
Faith! They are sadder than I thought they were.

　　　　　　SONG.

False friend, wilt thou smile or weep 130
When my life is laid asleep?
Little cares for a smile or a tear,
The clay-cold corpse upon the bier!
　　Farewell! Heigho!
　　What is this whispers low?
There is a snake in thy smile, my dear;
And bitter poison within thy tear.

Sweet sleep, were death like to thee,
Or if thou couldst mortal be,
I would close these eyes of pain; 140
When to wake? Never again.
　　O World! Farewell!
　　Listen to the passing bell!
It says, thou and I must part,
With a light and a heavy heart.

(The scene closes).

Scene IV: *A Hall of the Prison.*
Enter Camillo and Bernardo.

Cam. The Pope is stern; not to be moved or bent.
He looked as calm and keen as is the engine
Which tortures and which kills, exempt itself
From aught[80] that it inflicts; a marble form,
A rite, a law, a custom: not a man.
He frowned, as if to frown had been the trick
Of his machinery, on the advocates

80　*aught*: anything whatsoever.

Presenting the defences, which he tore
And threw behind, muttering with hoarse, harsh
  voice:
"Which among ye defended their old father   10
Killed in his sleep?" Then to another: "Thou
Dost this in virtue of thy place; 'tis well."
He turned to me then, looking deprecation,
And said these three words, coldly: "They must die."

Ber. And yet you left him not?

Cam.   I urged him still;
Pleading, as I could guess, the devilish wrong
Which prompted your unnatural parent's death.
And he replied: "Paolo Santa Croce
Murdered his mother yester evening,
And he is fled. Parricide grows so rife   20
That soon, for some just cause no doubt, the young
Will strangle us all, dozing in our chairs.
Authority, and power, and hoary hair
Are grown crimes capital. You are my nephew,
You come to ask their pardon; stay a moment;
Here is their sentence; never see me more
Till, to the letter, it be all fulfilled."

Ber. O God, not so! I did believe indeed
That all you said was but sad preparation
For happy news. O, there are words and looks
To bend the sternest purpose! Once I knew them, 30
Now I forget them at my dearest need.
What think you if I seek him out, and bathe
His feet and robe with hot and bitter tears?
Importune him with prayers, vexing his brain
With my perpetual cries, until in rage
He strike me with his pastoral cross, and trample
Upon my prostrate head, so that my blood
May stain the senseless dust on which he treads,
And remorse waken mercy? I will do it!
O, wait till I return! *(Rushes out).*   40

Cam.   Alas! poor boy!
A wreck-devoted seaman thus might pray
To the deaf sea.

(Enter Lucretia, Beatrice, and Giacomo, guarded).

Bea.   I hardly dare to fear
That thou bring'st other news than a just pardon.

Cam. May God in heaven be less inexorable
To the Pope's prayers, than he has been to mine.
Here is the sentence and the warrant.

Bea. (Wildly).   Oh,
My God! Can it be possible I have

To die so suddenly? So young to go
Under the obscure, cold, rotting, wormy ground! 50
To be nailed down into a narrow place;
To see no more sweet sunshine; hear no more
Blithe voice of living thing; muse not again
Upon familiar thoughts, sad, yet thus lost —
How fearful! to be nothing! Or to be...
What? O, where am I? Let me not go mad!
Sweet Heaven, forgive weak thoughts! If there
  should be
No God, no Heaven, no Earth in the void world;
The wide, grey, lampless, deep, unpeopled world!
If all things then should be...my father's spirit, 60
His eye, his voice, his touch surrounding me;
The atmosphere and breath of my dead life!
If sometimes, as a shape more like himself,
Even the form which tortured me on earth,
Masked in gray hairs and wrinkles, he should come
And wind me in his hellish arms, and fix
His eyes on mine, and drag me down, down, down!
For was he not alone omnipotent
On Earth, and ever present? Even though dead,
Does not his spirit live in all that breathe,
And work for me and mine still the same ruin, 70
Scorn, pain, despair? Who ever yet returned
To teach the laws of death's untrodden realm?
Unjust perhaps as those which drive us now,
Oh, whither, whither?

Luc.   Trust in God's sweet love,
The tender promises of Christ: ere night,
Think we shall be in Paradise.

Bea.   'Tis past!
Whatever comes my heart shall sink no more.
And yet, I know not why, your words strike chill:
How tedious, false and cold seem all things. I
Have met with much injustice in this world; 80
No difference has been made by God or man,
Or any power moulding my wretched lot,
'Twixt good or evil, as regarded me.
I am cut off from the only world I know,
From light, and life, and love, in youth's sweet prime.
You do well telling me to trust in God,
I hope I do trust in Him. In whom else
Can any trust? And yet my heart is cold.

*(During the latter speeches Giacomo has retired
conversing with Camillo, who now goes out; Giacomo
advances).*

Gia. Know you not, Mother...Sister, know you not? 90
    Bernardo even now is gone to implore
    The Pope to grant our pardon.
Luc.   Child, perhaps
    It will be granted. We may all then live
    To make these woes a tale for distant years:
    Oh, what a thought! It gushes to my heart
    Like the warm blood.
Bea.   Yet both will soon be cold.
    O, trample out that thought! Worse than despair,
    Worse than the bitterness of death, is hope:
    It is the only ill which can find place
    Upon the giddy, sharp and narrow hour 100
    Tottering beneath us. Plead with the swift frost
    That it should spare the eldest flower of spring:
    Plead with awakening Earthquake, o'er whose couch
    Even now a city stands, strong, fair, and free;
    Now stench and blackness yawn, like death. Oh,
      plead
    With famine, or wind-walking Pestilence,
    Blind lightning, or the deaf sea, not with man!
    Cruel, cold, formal man; righteous in words,
    In deeds a Cain.[81] No, Mother, we must die:
    Since such is the reward of innocent lives; 110
    Such the alleviation of worst wrongs.
    And whilst our murderers live, and hard, cold men,
    Smiling and slow, walk through a world of tears
    To death as to life's sleep; 'twere just the grave
    Were some strange joy for us. Come, obscure Death,
    And wind me in thine all-embracing arms!
    Like a fond mother hide me in thy bosom,
    And rock me to the sleep from which none wake.
    Live ye, who live, subject to one another
    As we were once, who now...
(Bernardo rushes in).
Ber.   Oh, horrible! 120
    That tears, that looks, that hope poured forth in
      prayer,
    Even till the heart is vacant and despairs,
    Should all be vain! The ministers of death
    Are waiting round the doors. I thought I saw
    Blood on the face of one...what if 'twere fancy?

---

81 *Cain*: in Genesis, the name of the first murderer and
     fratricide; more generally, a fratricide; a murderer of
     one's siblings or countrymen.

Soon the heart's blood of all I love on earth
Will sprinkle him, and he will wipe it off
As if 'twere only rain. O, life! O, world!
Cover me! let me be no more! To see
That perfect mirror of pure innocence 130
Wherein I gazed, and grew happy and good,
Shivered[82] to dust! To see thee, Beatrice,
Who made all lovely thou didst look upon...
Thee, light of life...dead, dark! while I say, sister,
To hear I have no sister; and thou, Mother,
Whose love was as a bond to all our loves...
Dead! The sweet bond broken!
(Enter Camillo and Guards).
                 They come! Let me
Kiss those warm lips before their crimson leaves
Are blighted...white...cold. Say farewell, before
Death chokes that gentle voice! Oh, let me hear 140
You speak!
Bea.   Farewell, my tender brother. Think
    Of our sad fate with gentleness, as now:
    And let mild, pitying thoughts lighten for thee
    Thy sorrow's load. Err not in harsh despair,
    But tears and patience. One thing more, my child,
    For thine own sake be constant to the love
    Thou bearest us; and to the faith that I,
    Though wrapped in a strange cloud of crime and
      shame,
    Lived ever holy and unstained. And though
    Ill tongues shall wound me, and our common name 150
    Be as a mark stamped on thine innocent brow
    For men to point at as they pass, do thou
    Forbear, and never think a thought unkind
    Of those, who perhaps love thee in their graves.
    So mayest thou die as I do; fear and pain
    Being subdued. Farewell! Farewell! Farewell!
Ber. I cannot say, farewell!
Cam.   Oh, Lady Beatrice!
Bea. Give yourself no unnecessary pain,
    My dear Lord Cardinal. Here, Mother, tie
    My girdle for me, and bind up this hair 160
    In any simple knot; aye, that does well.
    And yours I see is coming down. How often
    Have we done this for one another; now
    We shall not do it any more. My Lord,
    We are quite ready. Well, 'tis very well.

---

82 *Shivered*: broken or shattered.

Sardanapalus; A Tragedy

Lord Byron

It has become a cliché that the life of Byron (1788–1824) is as well known as his poetry, but we are perhaps less familiar with how the drama and theater fit into both. Byron's love of the drama began early, during his school days at Harrow, where he had used Speech Days to showcase his prowess at dramatic declamation. He was an early frequenter of the London theaters and, during his years of fame, joined the committee that oversaw Drury Lane, where he urged Coleridge to submit a worthy successor to *Remorse*, lobbied for new productions of Baillie, and helped to get Maturin's *Bertram* staged. Between 1816 and his death in 1824 Byron wrote more dramas than any other of the canonical poets of the day, penning three history plays (*Marino Faliero, Doge of Venice*; *The Two Foscari*; and *Sardanapalus* [included here]) and four "mystery" plays (*Manfred, Cain, Heaven and Earth*, and *The Deformed Transformed*). While only *Marino Faliero* would be performed during his lifetime, his plays were a major force on the London stage throughout the nineteenth century.

George Gordon Byron was born in London to Captain John "Mad Jack" Byron and his second wife, Catherine Gordon. When Captain Byron, having run through their money, abandoned her in 1789, Byron's mother returned to her native Scotland. In 1798 when his great-uncle Baron Byron, the "wicked lord," died without issue, Byron suddenly inherited the title of the 6th Lord Byron. Mother and son moved to the ancestral home of Newstead Abbey. Derided for a clubfoot that had marked him since birth, Byron hated his school years at Harrow, but in the end managed to display his prowess on the cricket field and to lead a student revolt against a new headmaster. From Harrow he went to Cambridge, where he published his first book of poetry (*Hours of Idleness* [1807]) and went through various romantic infatua-

tions—not only for a series of cousins (Mary Duff, Margaret Parker, and Mary Chaworth) but also for a Cambridge choirboy (John Edleston).

Taking his MA from Cambridge in 1808, Byron first settled in London, publishing the satire *English Bards and Scotch Reviewers* (1809) before departing with his Cambridge friend John Cam Hobhouse in July on an eccentric Grand Tour, shaped by the Napoleonic wars, that led them to Portugal, Spain, Gibraltar, Malta, Albania, Greece, and Constantinople. Upon his return, he published the first two cantos of *Childe Harold's Pilgrimage* and took his seat in the House of Lords, where his first speech was in opposition to a bill calling for the death penalty for frame-smashers, the so-called "Luddites" who had engaged in industrial sabotage to protest the technological undermining of their livelihoods. Embraced by the Whigs in Parliament, Byron might have become an important political figure, had the literary fame of *Childe* not sent him on another course. Awakening one morning, in his own words, "to find himself famous," the young handsome Lord became the talk of the town. Audiences identified him with the charismatic yet cynical Harold as well as with the heroes of his subsequent "Oriental" tales, including *The Corsair* (1814), which sold ten thousand copies in a day. Sexual scandal followed literary celebrity, Byron involving himself in various high-profile affairs, most famously with Lady Caroline Lamb who found him "Mad—bad—and dangerous to know." However, it was his relationship with his half-sister Augusta Leigh, with whom he appears to have had a child in 1814, that shocked even the free-living aristocracy of the Regency. To repair his reputation and his debts, Byron in January 1815 married Annabella Milbanke, a marriage that produced a child but ended a year later amidst rumors of incest and charges of insanity.

In April 1816, Byron left England forever, traveling across Europe in a carriage modeled upon Napoleon's and visiting the battlefield of Waterloo, before settling for the summer in Geneva, where he resumed an affair with Jane "Claire" Clairmont and met her stepsister, Mary Godwin, and her lover, Percy Bysshe Shelley. The two poets would become important friends and allies, inspiring each other's verse; the summer meeting would result not only in Mary Shelley's *Frankenstein* and some of Percy Shelley's key lyrics, but also Byron's *Childe Harold III*, *Manfred*, and *The Prisoner of Chillon*, all published in 1816. Byron would move on to Italy, first to Venice and then to Ravenna, settling for a while as the recognized lover of Teresa Gamba Guiccioli, a woman nineteen years old yet married to a man three times her age. Byron continued to write in a range of forms and moods, but he also discovered Italian *otava rima*, suited to a satiric and comic vision that would blossom in *Beppo* (1818) and his masterpiece, *Don Juan* (1819–24). Involved through Teresa Guiccioli's family with efforts to throw off Austrian control within Italy, Byron followed the family into exile from Ravenna, settling in Pisa near the Shelleys. With Leigh Hunt, an old friend of both Byron and Shelley and a leader of London's left intelligentsia, the poets formed what their detractors called the "Pisan triumvirate" to produce the *Liberal*, but Shelley's sudden death and difficulties between Byron and Hunt led the journal to collapse after four issues. In July 1823, true to his love of the East and his dedication to revolutionary causes, Byron left for Greece to join the struggle against Turkey. On 19 April 1824, Byron died at the age of thirty-six, to be immediately hailed as a Greek national hero and to be confirmed in his status as the embodiment of the poetic and political moment that would come to be called romanticism.

Sardanapalus was written between January and May of 1821. *Marino Faliero* was at this time being acted in London, a performance to which Byron objected but about which he may have harbored hopes of success. While reports were inaccurate and mixed, Byron seems to have decided to devote considerable energy to the drama. *Sardanapalus* reflects his desire to create a "regular" English drama, but the play also contains extravagant gestures such as the final funeral pyre and has at its heart the eccentric character of Sardanapalus, the "Man-Queen," the pacifist leader of a warlike nation. The play evidences a wide range of influences, including Seneca's plays, Dryden's *All for Love*, and behind it Shakespeare (most obviously his *Antony and Cleopatra*), Alfieri (perhaps particularly his *Mirra*), and Grillparzer (perhaps particularly his *Sappho*). The play engages a wealth of key themes including orientalism and gender relations, and in the figure of Sardanapalus appears to offer a kind of counter-cultural riposte to the rulers of the day. *Sardanapalus* apparently had its first performance in Brussels in January 1834. It opened in London in a production by Macready at Drury Lane on 10 April 1834. With fine sets and great scenic effects, the play was a success, running for twenty-three nights. Drawing upon recent excavations in Nineveh and Babylon for his settings, Charles Kean revived the play in 1853 in a production that achieved ninety-three performances in two seasons; another production in 1875 was performed more than two thousand times across England within two years.

The copytext is Lord Byron, *Sardanapalus, a Tragedy; The Two Foscari, a Tragedy; Cain, a Mystery* (London: John Murray, 1821). We also have consulted the 1834 performance MS for *Sardanapalus*, located in the British Library; see *Plays from the Lord Chamberlain's Office*, Vol. X, Part II (1825), BL Add. MS. 42874(7) ff. 350–476.

DEDICATION.[1]

To the illustrious Goethe a Stranger presumes to offer the homage of a literary vassal to his liege-Lord—the first of existing masters;—who has created the literature of his own country—and illustrated that of Europe. The unworthy production which the author ventures to inscribe to him—is entitled "Sardanapalus."—

PREFACE.

In publishing the following Tragedies I have only to repeat that they were not composed with the most remote view to the stage.

On the attempt made by the Managers in a former instance, the public opinion has been already expressed.[2]

With regard to my own private feelings, as it seems that they are to stand for nothing, I shall say nothing.

For the historical foundation of the following compositions, the reader is referred to the Notes. 10

The Author has in one instance attempted to preserve, and in the other to approach the "unities";[3]

conceiving that with any very distant departure from them, there may be poetry, but can be no drama. He is aware of the unpopularity of this notion in present English literature;[4] but it is not a system of his own, being merely an opinion, which, not very long ago, was the law of literature throughout the world, and is still so in the more civilized parts of it. But "Nous 20 avons changé tout cela,"[5] and are reaping the advantages of the change. The writer is far from conceiving that any thing he can adduce by personal precept or example can at all approach his regular, or even irregular predecessors: he is merely giving a reason why he preferred the more regular formation of a structure, however feeble, to an entire abandonment of all rules whatsoever. Where he has failed, the failure is in the architect,—and not in the art.

PREFATORY NOTE TO *SARDANAPALUS*.

In this tragedy it has been my intention to follow the account of Diodorus Siculus,[6] reducing it, however, to such dramatic regularity as I best could, and trying to approach the unities. I therefore suppose the rebellion to explode and succeed in one day by a sudden conspiracy, instead of the long war of the history.

---

[1] *Dedication*: Byron's dedication to Goethe was first printed in 1823 in a second edition of *Sardanapalus* (this time without *The Two Foscari* and *Cain*) because Byron's publisher, John Murray, neglected to include it in the first edition. Byron was understandably annoyed and asked for a copy to be forwarded to Goethe. See *Byron's Letters and Journals*, 9:91 and 10:64.

[1] *On the attempt made ... expressed*: a reference to the production of Byron's *Marino Faliero* that opened at Drury Lane on 25 April 1821, against Byron's wishes. While Byron at first thought it had been hissed, it in fact had a fairly typical short run for a new tragedy.

[2] *"unities"*: referring to the doctrine that drama should be governed by "unities" of action, time, and place—i.e., that a drama should comprise a coherent series of events, that it should occur within a finite period (at most 24 hours), and that it take place in a single setting. The doctrine of the unities is usually ascribed to Aristotle (384–322 BCE), and is the product of the energetic reading and interpretation of the *Poetics* that occurred in Europe after 1500. See especially section eight of the *Poetics*: "the plot, as the imitation of an action, should imitate a single unified action—and ... the structure of the various sections of the events must

be such that the transposition or removal of any one section dislocates and changes the whole." Since 1500 the doctrine of the unities has been embraced by a number of British literary critics, including Sir Philip Sidney and Matthew Arnold. In seventeenth- and eighteenth-century France it enjoyed a special vogue, and influenced a number of playwrights Byron admired, including Dryden, Alfieri, and Grillparzer.

[4] *unpopularity of this notion in present English literature*: Byron presumably refers to the popularity of Shakespeare himself, who did not observe the unities, and to contemporary plays based on Elizabethan and Jacobean models such as Maturin's *Bertram* and Shelley's *The Cenci*.

[5] *Nous avons changé tout cela*: "We have changed all that"; Moliere, *Le Médicin malgré lui (The Doctor in Spite of Himself)*, II, iv.

[6] *Diodorus Siculus*: Born in Sicily, Diodorus was a Greek historian in the 1st century BCE. Byron consulted the second book of his *Bibliothecae Historicae* either in Greek or in *The Historical Library of Diodorus the Sicilian*, translated by G. Booth in 1700, which was in Byron's library.

DRAMATIS PERSONAE

Men:

Sardanapalus, King of Nineveh[7]
and Assyria,[8] &c.   Mr. Macready
Arbaces, the Mede[9] who
aspired to the Throne   Mr. Brindall
Beleses, a Chaldean[10] and
Soothsayer.   Mr. G. Bennett
Salemenes, the King's
Brother-in-law   Mr. Cooper

Altada, an Assyrian Officer
of the Palace
Pania   Mr. King
Zames
Sfero
Balea
Women:
Zarina, the Queen   Miss Phillips
Myrrha, an Ionian[11] female
Slave, and the Favourite
of Sardanapalus   Miss E. Tree
Women composing the Harem
of Sardanapalus, Guards,
Attendants, Chaldean
Priests, Medes, &c., &c.

Scene: *A Hall in the Royal Palace of Nineveh.*

Act I.

Scene I: *A Hall in the Palace.*

Salemenes (Solus). He hath wrong'd his queen, but
still he is her lord;
He hath wrong'd my sister, still he is my brother;
He hath wronged his people, still he is their
sovereign,
And I must be his friend as well as subject:
He must not perish thus. I will not see
The blood of Nimrod and Semiramis[12]
Sink in the earth, and thirteen hundred years
Of Empire ending like a shepherd's tale;

---

7 *Nineveh*: Lying opposite of modern Mosul, Nineveh
was one of the primary cities of Assyria, founded according to the Bible by Nimrod and in Greek sources
by Ninus (based on Tukulti-Ninurta, c. 1233-1197
BCE).

8 *Assyria*: a kingdom of northern Mesopotamia that became the center of one of the great empires of the ancient Middle East. It was located in what is now
northern Iraq and southeastern Turkey. Having been
a dependency of Babylonia and then the Mitanni kingdom, Assyria rose as an independent state in the 14th
century BCE. It had several periods of major power:
in the 13th century until the death of Tukulti-Ninurta
I (c. 1208 BCE), Assyria ruled in Mesopotamia, Armenia, and sometimes in northern Syria; in the 11th
century BCE Tiglath-pileser I briefly restored it to
prominence; in the 9th century BCE, and from the
mid-8th to the late 7th century BCE, a series of strong
Assyrian kings such as Tiglath-pileser III, Sargon II,
Sennacherib, and Esarhaddon brought most of the
Middle East, from Egypt to the Persian Gulf, under
their control. The last great Assyrian ruler was
Ashurbanipal (668–627 BCE), one of the prototypes
for the semi-mythical Sardanapalus.

9 *Mede*: The Medes were an Indo-European people akin
to the Persians who occupied a mountainous country
southwest of the Caspian Sea. Under Cyaxares (625–
585 BCE) and in alliance with Babylon, they defeated
the Assyrians, with Nineveh falling in 612 BCE.

10 *Chaldean*: Chaldea is a land in southern Babylonia, in
what is now southern Iraq. Chaldea was sometimes
under Assyrian control, though at other times Chaldea
ruled Babylonia. "Chaldean" also was used by several
ancient authors to denote the priests and other persons educated in the classical Babylonian literature,
especially in traditions of astronomy and astrology.

11 *Ionian*: Ionia was an ancient region comprising the
central sector of the western coast of Anatolia (now
in Turkey). It was the site of important Greek colonies. "Ionian" was sometimes used to refer to Greeks
in general.

12 *Nimrod and Semiramis*: Semiramis (perhaps the historical Sammu-ramat, reigned 811-807 BCE) was a
mythical Assyrian queen famed as a conqueror and
builder of cities. She was, according to Diodorus, married to Ninus, sometimes identified as the founder of
Nineveh. Since the Bible names Nimrod, "a mighty
hunter," as the founder of Nineveh (Genesis 10:9–11),
Byron identifies Nimrod with Ninus.

He must be roused. In his effeminate heart
There is a careless courage which corruption   10
Has not all quench'd, and latent energies,
Repress'd by circumstance, but not destroy'd—
Steep'd, but not drown'd, in deep voluptuousness.
If born a peasant, he had been a man
To have reach'd an empire;[13] to an empire born,
He will bequeath none; nothing but a name,
Which his sons will not prize in heritage:—
Yet, not all lost, even yet he may redeem
His sloth and shame, by only being that
Which he should be, as easily as the thing   20
He should not be and is. Were it less toil
To sway his nations than consume his life?
To head an army than to rule a harem?
He sweats in palling pleasures, dulls his soul,
And saps his goodly strength, in toils which yield
     not
Health like the chase, nor glory like the war—
He must be roused. Alas! there is no sound
(Sound of soft music heard from within).
     To rouse him short of thunder.
                      Hark! the lute,
The lyre, the timbrel; the lascivious tinklings
Of lulling instruments, the softening voices   30
Of women, and of beings less than women,
Must chime in to the echo of his revel,
While the great king of all we know of earth
Lolls crown'd with roses, and his diadem
Lies negligently by to be caught up
By the first manly hand which dares to snatch it.
Lo, where they come! already I perceive
The reeking odours of the perfumed trains,
And see the bright gems of the glittering girls,
At once his chorus and his council, flash   40
Along the gallery, and amidst the damsels,
As femininely garbed, and scarce less female,

The grandson of Semiramis, the man-queen.—[14]
He comes! Shall I await him? yes, and front him,
And tell him what all good men tell each other,
Speaking of him and his. They come, the slaves,
Led by the monarch subject to his slaves.

Scene II: *Enter Sardanapalus effeminately dressed,*
     his Head crown'd with Flowers, and his Robe
     negligently flowing, attended by a Train of
     Women and young Slaves.

Sardanapalus (Speaking to some of his attendants).
     Let the pavilion[15] over the Euphrates[16]
Be garlanded, and lit, and furnish'd forth
For an especial banquet; at the hour
Of midnight we will sup there: see nought wanting,

---

13   *If born … an empire*: Jerome J. McGann and Barry
     Weller suggest that there may be an allusion to
     Marlowe's Tamburlaine here, as an antitype of
     Sardanapalus. See *Byron: The Complete Poetical Works*
     (Clarendon Press, 1997), 6:612.

14   *man-queen*: The relevant source here is Diodorus
     Siculus (II. xxiii. 1-2): "For not to mention the fact
     that he was not seen by any man residing outside the
     palace, he lived the life of a woman, and spending his
     days in the company of his concubines and spinning
     purple garments and working the softest of wool, he
     had assumed the feminine garb and so covered his face
     and indeed his entire body with whitening cosmetics
     and the other unguents used by courtesans, that he
     rendered it more delicate than that of any luxury-lov-
     ing woman. He also took care to make even his voice
     to be like a woman's, and at his carousals not only to
     indulge regularly in those drinks and viands which
     could offer the greatest pleasure, but also to pursue the
     delights of love with men as well as with women; for
     he practiced sexual indulgence of both kinds without
     restraint, showing not the least concern for the disgrace
     attending such conduct" (quoted from McGann and
     Weller, 612).

15   *pavilion*: While Byron claimed in a letter to his pub-
     lisher (25 May 1821; *BLJ* VIII: 126–7) that his play
     made no allusions to contemporary events, as McGann
     and Weller point out, he draws attention to the word
     "pavilion," which might remind readers of the
     Brighton Pavilion the Regent had built for himself, and
     the word "queen," with Sardanapalus' strained relations
     with his queen perhaps echoing those between George
     IV and Queen Caroline.

16   *Euphrates*: Byron follows Diodorus in locating Nineveh
     on the Euphrates river, when it in fact was on the
     Tigris.

And bid the galley be prepared. There is
A cooling breeze which crisps the broad clear river:
We will embark anon. Fair nymphs, who deign
To share the soft hours of Sardanapalus,
We'll meet again in that the sweetest hour,
When we shall gather like the stars above us,   10
And you will form a heaven as bright as theirs;
Till then, let each be mistress of her time,
And thou, my own Ionian Myrrha,[17] choose,
Wilt thou along with them or me?
Myrrha.   My lord——
Sar. My lord, my life! why answerest thou so coldly?
  It is the curse of kings to be so answer'd.
  Rule thy own hours, thou rulest mine—say,
      wouldst thou
  Accompany our guests, or charm away
  The moments from me?
Myr.   The king's choice is mine.
Sar. I pray thee say not so: my chiefest joy   20
  Is to contribute to thine every wish.
  I do not dare to breathe my own desire,
  Lest it should clash with thine; for thou art still
  Too prompt to sacrifice thy thoughts for others.
Myr. I would remain: I have no happiness
  Save in beholding thine; yet——
Sar.   Yet! what YET?
  Thy own sweet will shall be the only barrier
  Which ever rises betwixt thee and me.
Myr. I think the present is the wonted[18] hour
  Of council; it were better I retire.   30
Sal. (Comes forward and says).
  The Ionian slave says well, let her retire.
Sar. Who answers? How now, brother?
Sal.   The *queen*'s brother,
  And your most faithful vassal, royal lord.
Sar. (Addressing his train). As I have said, let all
  dispose their hours

Till midnight, when again we pray your presence.
  (The court retiring).
(To Myrrha, who is going).
  Myrrha! I thought *thou* wouldst remain.
Myr.   Great King,
  Thou didst not say so.
Sar.   But *thou* lookedst it;
  I know each glance of those Ionic eyes,
  Which said thou wouldst not leave me.
Myr.   Sire! your brother——
Sal. His *consort*'s[19] brother, minion of Ionia!   40
  How darest *thou* name *me* and not blush?
Sar.   Not blush!
  Thou hast no more eyes than heart to make her
      crimson
  Like to the dying day on Caucasus,[20]
  Where sunset tints the snow with rosy shadows,
  And then reproach her with thine own cold
      blindness,
  Which will not see it. What, in tears, my Myrrha?
Sal. Let them flow on; she weeps for more than one,
  And is herself the cause of bitterer tears.
Sar. Cursed be he who caused those tears to flow!
Sal. Curse not thyself—millions do that already.   50
Sar. Thou dost forget thee: make me not remember
  I am a monarch.
Sal.   Would thou couldst!
Myr.   My sovereign,
  I pray, and thou too, prince, permit my absence.
Sar. Since it must be so, and this churl has check'd
  Thy gentle spirit, go; but recollect
  That we must forthwith meet: I had rather lose
  An empire than thy presence. *(Exit Myrrha).*[21]
Sal.   It may be,
  Thou wilt lose both, and both for ever!

---

17 Byron's note: "The Ionian name had been still more
  comprehensive, having included the Achaians and the
  Boeotians, who, together with those to whom it was
  afterwards confined, would make nearly the whole of
  the Greek nation, and among the orientals it was always the general name for the Greeks.—*Mitford's
  Greece*, vol. i p. 199."
18 *wonted*: customary.

19 *consort's*: A consort is a spouse.
20 *Caucasus*: a region and a mountain system lying between the Black and Azov seas on the west and the
  Caspian Sea on the east and occupied by Russia, Georgia, Azerbaijan, and Armenia. The Caucasus is part of
  the traditional dividing line between Europe and Asia.
21 *Exit Myrrha*: As McGann and Weller note, the scene
  between Sardanapalus and Salemenes that follows re-
  calls that between Antony and Ventidius in Dryden's
  All for Love, I: 375–80.

Sar.   Brother,
I can at least command myself, who listen
To language such as this; yet urge me not   60
Beyond my easy nature.
Sal.   'Tis beyond
That easy, far too easy, idle nature,
Which I would urge thee. Oh that I could rouse thee!
Though 'twere against myself.
Sar.   By the god Baal![22]
The man would make me tyrant.
Sal.   So thou art.
Think'st thou there is no tyranny but that
Of blood and chains? The despotism of vice—
The weakness and the wickedness of luxury—
The negligence—the apathy—the evils
Of sensual sloth—produce ten thousand tyrants,   70
Whose delegated cruelty surpasses
The worst acts of one energetic master,
However harsh and hard in his own bearing.
The false and fond examples of thy lusts
Corrupt no less than they oppress, and sap
In the same moment all thy pageant power
And those who should sustain it; so that whether
A foreign foe invade, or civil broil
Distract within, both will alike prove fatal:
The first thy subjects have no heart to conquer;   80
The last they rather would assist than vanquish.
Sar. Why, what makes thee the mouth-piece of the
          people?
Sal. Forgiveness of the queen, my sister's wrongs;
A natural love unto my infant nephews;
Faith to the king, a faith he may need shortly,
In more than words; respect for Nimrod's line;
Also, another thing thou knowest not.
Sar. What's that?
Sal.   To thee an unknown word.
Sar.   Yet speak it;
I love to learn.
Sal.   Virtue.
Sar.   Not know the word!
Never was word yet rung so in my ears—   90

Worse than the rabble's shout, or splitting trumpet;
I've heard thy sister talk of nothing else.
Sal. To change the irksome theme, then, hear of vice.
Sar. From whom?
Sal.   Even from the winds, if thou couldst listen
Unto the echoes of the nation's voice.
Sar. Come, I'm indulgent, as thou knowest, patient
As thou hast often proved—speak out, what
          moves thee?
Sal. Thy peril.
Sar.   Say on.
Sal.   Thus, then: all the nations,
For they are many, whom thy father left
In heritage, are loud in wrath against thee.   100
Sar. 'Gainst *me!* What would the slaves?
Sal.   A king.
Sar.   And what
Am I then?
Sal.   In their eyes a nothing; but
In mine a man who might be something still.
Sar. The railing drunkards! why, what would they have?
Have they not peace and plenty?
Sal.   Of the first
More than is glorious; of the last, far less
Than the king recks[23] of.
Sar.   Whose then is the crime,
But the false satraps,[24] who provide no better?
Sal. And somewhat in the monarch who ne'er looks
Beyond his palace walls, or if he stirs   110
Beyond them, 'tis but to some mountain palace,
Till summer heats wear down. O glorious Baal!
Who built up this vast empire, and wert made
A god, or at the least shinest like a God
Through the long centuries of thy renown,
This, thy presumed descendant, ne'er beheld
As king the kingdoms thou didst leave as hero,
Won with thy blood, and toil, and time, and peril!
For what? to furnish imposts[25] for a revel,
Or multiplied extortions for a minion.   120

---

22 *Baal*: a god worshiped in many ancient Middle East-
    ern communities, especially among the Canaanites; he
    was a fertility god, but also king of the gods.

23 *recks*: is aware.
24 *satraps*: A satrap was a provincial governor in the Per-
    sian empire, but it is used by extension to refer to sub-
    ordinate rulers, often suggesting that this rule is
    marked by tyranny or excess.
25 *imposts*: taxes or tributes.

Sar. I understand thee—thou wouldst have me go
    Forth as a conqueror. By all the stars
    Which the Chaldeans read! the restless slaves
    Deserve that I should curse them with their wishes,
    And lead them forth to glory.
Sal.   Wherefore not?
    Semiramis—a woman only—led
    These our Assyrians to the solar shores
    Of Ganges.[26]
Sar   'Tis most true. And *how* return'd?
Sal. Why, like a *man*—a hero; baffled, but
    Not vanquish'd. With but twenty guards, she made   130
    Good her retreat to Bactria.[27]
Sar.   And how many
    Left she behind in India to the vultures?
Sal. Our annals say not.
Sar.   Then I will say for them—
    That she had better woven within her palace
    Some twenty garments, than with twenty guards
    Have fled to Bactria, leaving to the ravens,
    And wolves, and men—the fiercer of the three,
    Her myriads of fond subjects. Is *this* glory?
    Then let me live in ignominy ever.
Sal. All warlike spirits have not the same fate.   140
    Semiramis, the glorious parent of
    A hundred kings, although she fail'd in India,
    Brought Persia, Media, Bactria, to the realm
    Which she once sway'd—and thou *might'st* sway.
Sar.   I *sway* them—
    She but subdued them.
Sal.   It may be ere long
    That they will need her sword more than your
        sceptre.
Sar. There was a certain Bacchus,[28] was there not?
    I've heard my Greek girls speak of such—they say

---

26 *Ganges*: the great river of the plains of northern In-
    dia, held sacred by people of the Hindu faith.
27 *Bactria*: an ancient country lying between the moun-
    tains of the Hindu Kush and the Amu Darya (ancient
    Oxus River) in what is now part of Afghanistan,
    Uzbekistan, and Tajikistan.
28 *Bacchus*: a name for Dionysus, god of wine and the
    center of an ecstatic religious cult. Among the many
    stories told of him are those about his campaigns to
    the East, with his victories in India perhaps modeled
    on those of Alexander the Great.

He was a god, that is, a Grecian god,
    An idol foreign to Assyria's worship,   150
    Who conquer'd this same golden realm of Ind[29]
    Thou prat'st of, where Semiramis was vanquish'd.
Sal. I have heard of such a man; and thou perceiv'st
    That he is deem'd a god for what he did.
Sar. And in his godship I will honour him—
    Not much as man. What, ho! my cup-bearer!
Sal. What means the king?
Sar.   To worship your new god
    And ancient conqueror. Some wine, I say.
(Enter Cupbearer).
Sar. (Addressing the Cupbearer).
    Bring me the golden goblet thick with gems,
    Which bears the name of Nimrod's chalice. Hence,   160
    Fill full, and bear it quickly. *(Exit Cupbearer).*
Sal.   Is this moment
    A fitting one for the resumption of
    Thy yet unslept-off revels?
(Re-enter Cupbearer, with wine).
Sar. (Taking the cup from him).   Noble kinsman,
    If these barbarian Greeks of the far shores
    And skirts of these our realms lie not, this Bacchus
    Conquer'd the whole of India, did he not?
Sal. He did, and thence was deem'd a deity.
Sar. Not so:—of all his conquests a few columns,
    Which may be his, and might be mine, if I
    Thought them worth purchase and conveyance, are   170
    The landmarks of the seas of gore he shed,
    The realms he wasted, and the hearts he broke.
    But here, here in this goblet is his title
    To immortality—the immortal grape
    From which he first express'd the soul, and gave
    To gladden that of man, as some atonement
    For the victorious mischiefs he had done.
    Had it not been for this, he would have been
    A mortal still in name as in his grave;
    And, like my ancestor Semiramis,   180
    A sort of semi-glorious human monster.
    Here's that which deified him—let it now
    Humanise thee; my surly, chiding brother,
    Pledge me to the Greek god!
Sal.   For all thy realms
    I would not so blaspheme our country's creed.

---

29 *Ind*: for India.

Sar. That is to say, thou thinkest him a hero,
That he shed blood by oceans; and no god,
Because he turn'd a fruit to an enchantment,
Which cheers the sad, revives the old, inspires
The young, makes Weariness forget his toil,   190
And Fear her danger; opens a new world
When this, the present, palls. Well, then *I* pledge thee
And *him* as a true man, who did his utmost
In good or evil to surprise mankind. *(Drinks).*
Sal. Wilt thou resume a revel at this hour?
Sar. And if I did, 'twere better than a trophy,
Being bought without a tear. But that is not
My present purpose: since thou wilt not pledge me,
Continue what thou pleasest.
    (To the Cupbearer).   Boy, retire.
    (Exit Cupbearer).
Sal. I would but have recall'd thee from thy dream: 200
Better by me awaken'd than rebellion.
Sar. Who should rebel? or why? what cause? pretext?
I am the lawful king, descend'd from
A race of kings who knew no predecessors.
What have I done to thee, or to the people,
That thou shouldst rail, or they rise up against me?
Sal. Of what thou hast done to me, I speak not.
Sar.   But
Thou think'st that I have wrong'd the queen: is't
    not so?
Sal. Think! Thou hast wrong'd her!
Sar.   Patience, Prince, and hear me.
She has all power and splendour of her station,   210
Respect, the tutelage of Assyria's heirs,
The homage and the appanage[30] of sovereignty.
I married her as monarchs wed—for state,
And loved her as most husbands love their wives.
If she or thou supposedst I could link me
Like a Chaldean peasant to his mate,
Ye knew nor me, nor monarchs, nor mankind.
Sal. I pray thee, change the theme; my blood disdains
Complaint, and Salemenes' sister seeks not
Reluctant love even from Assyria's lord!   220
Nor would she deign to accept divided passion
With foreign strumpets and Ionian slaves.
The queen is silent.

---

30 *appanage*: for apaganage, the provision made for the maintenance of the younger children of a king.

Sar.   And why not her brother?
Sal. I only echo thee the voice of empires,
Which he who long neglects not long will govern.
Sar. The ungrateful and ungracious slaves! they
    murmur
Because I have not shed their blood, nor led them
To dry into the desert's dust by myriads,
Or whiten with their bones the banks of Ganges;
Nor decimated them with savage laws,   230
Nor sweated them to build up pyramids,
Or Babylonian walls.[31]
Sal.   Yet these are trophies
More worthy of a people and their prince
Than songs, and lutes, and feasts, and concubines
And lavish'd treasures, and contemned[32] virtues.
Sar. Or for my trophies I have founded cities:
There's Tarsus and Anchialus,[33] both built
In one day—what could that blood-loving
    beldame,[34]
My martial grandam, chaste Semiramis,
Do more, except destroy them?

---

31 *pyramids … walls*: a reference to the famous pyramids of Egypt and walls of Babylon (with their Hanging Gardens), both among the Seven Wonders of the ancient world and both built with slave labor. The Hanging Gardens were usually thought to be built by King Nebuchadnezzar II, but they were sometimes seen as the work of Queen Sammu-ramat, here Semiramis.

32 *contemned*: despised.

33 *Tarsus and Anchialus*: Tarsus is an ancient city in south-central Turkey on the Tarsus River, about 12 miles from the Mediterranean coast. The birthplace of St. Paul and the site of the first meeting between Antony and Cleopatra, Tarsus first enters the historical record when it was rebuilt by the Assyrian king Sennacherib. Anchialus is a city on the Thracian coast, supposedly founded by Sardanapalus. In one of Byron's sources, *Mitford's Greece*, IX:311–13, we are told that the town contained a monument to Sardanapalus with the inscription, "Sardanapalus, son of Anacyndaraxes, in one day founded Anchialus and Tarsus. Eat, drink, play: all other human joys are not worth a fillip." See I, ii, 249–52.

34 *beldame*: a grandmother or more remote female ancestor.

Sal.   'Tis most true;   240
  I own thy merit in those founded cities,
  Built for a whim, recorded with a verse
  Which shames both them and thee to coming ages.
Sar. Shame me! By Baal, the cities, though well built,
  Are not more goodly than the verse! Say what
  Thou wilt 'gainst me, my mode of life or rule,
  But nothing 'gainst the truth of that brief record.
  Why, those few lines contain the history
  Of all things human: hear—"Sardanapalus,
  The king, and son of Anacyndaraxes,[35]   250
  In one day built Anchialus and Tarsus.
  Eat, drink, and love; the rest's not worth a fillip."[36]

---

[35] *Anacyndaraxes*: Anacyndaraxes is usually recorded as
    the father of Sardanapalus, though sometimes
    Anabaraxares is given as his father.

[36] Byron's note: "For this expedition he took only a small
    chosen body of the phalanx, but all his light troops. In
    the first day's march he reached Anchialus, a town said
    to have been founded by the king of Assyria,
    Sardanapalus. The fortifications, in their magnitude and
    extent, still, in Arrian's time, bore the character of great-
    ness, which the Assyrians appear singularly to have af-
    fected in works of the kind. A monument representing
    Sardanapalus was found there, warranted by an inscrip-
    tion in Assyrian characters, of course in the old Assyrian
    language, which the Greeks, whether well or ill, inter-
    preted thus: 'Sardanapalus, son of Anacyndaraxes, in
    one day founded Anchialus and Tarsus. Eat, drink, play:
    all other human joys are not worth a fillip.' Supposing
    this version nearly exact, (for Arrian says it was not quite
    so), whether the purpose has been to invite to civil or-
    der a people disposed to turbulence, rather than to rec-
    ommend immoderate luxury, may perhaps reasonably
    be questioned. What, indeed, could be the object of a
    king of Assyria in founding such towns in a country so
    distant from his capital, and so divided from it by an
    immense extent of sandy deserts and lofty mountains,
    and, still more, how the inhabitants could be at once in
    circumstances to abandon themselves to the intemper-
    ate joys, which their prince has been supposed to have
    recommended, is not obvious; but it may deserve obser-
    vation that, in that line of coast, the southern of Lesser
    Asia, ruins of cities, evidently of an age after Alexander,
    yet barely named in history, at this day astonish the ad-
    venturous traveller by their magnificence and elegance.
    Amid the desolation which, under a singularly barbar-

Sal. A worthy moral, and a wise inscription,
  For a king to put up before his subjects!
Sar. Oh, thou wouldst have me doubtless set up
    edicts—
  "Obey the king—contribute to his treasure—
  "Recruit his phalanx[37]—spill your blood at
    bidding—
  "Fall down and worship, or get up and toil."
  Or thus—"Sardanapalus on this spot
  "Slew fifty thousand of his enemies.   260
  "These are their sepulchres, and this his trophy."
  I leave such things to conquerors; enough
  For me, if I can make my subjects feel
  The weight of human misery less, and glide
  Ungroaning to the tomb; I take no license
  Which I deny to them. We all are men.
Sal. Thy sires have been revered as gods——
Sar.   In dust
  And death, where they are neither gods nor men.
  Talk not of such to me! the worms are gods;
  At least they banqueted upon your gods,[38]   270
  And died for lack of farther nutriment.
  Those gods were merely men;[39] look to their issue—

---

    ian government, has for so many centuries been daily
    spreading in the finest countries of the globe, whether
    more from soil and climate, or from opportunities for
    commerce, extraordinary means must have been found
    for communities to flourish there, whence it may seem
    that the measures of Sardanapalus were directed by
    juster views than have been commonly ascribed to
    him; but that monarch having been the last of a dy-
    nasty, ended by a revolution, obloquy on his memory
    would follow of course from the policy of his succes-
    sors and their partisans.

       The inconsistency of traditions concerning
    Sardanapalus is striking in Diodorus's account of him.—
    Mitford's Greece, vol. ix. pp. 311, 312, and 313."

[37] *phalanx*: a body of heavily armed infantry drawn up
    in close order, with their shields joined and long spears
    overlapping.

[38] *the worms … your gods*: McGann and Weller note that
    this echoes *Hamlet*, I.iii.21–25.

[39] *Those gods were merely men*: an allusion to the
    euhemerist interpretation of myth, in which the gods
    are seen as portraits of great men and myths are found
    to reflect human actions.

I feel a thousand mortal things about me,
But nothing godlike, unless it may be
The thing which you condemn, a disposition
To love and to be merciful, to pardon
The follies of my species, and (that's human)
To be indulgent to my own.

Sal.   Alas!
The doom of Nineveh is sealed.—Woe—woe
To the unrivall'd city!

Sar.   What dost dread?   280

Sal. Thou art guarded by thy foes: in a few hours
The tempest may break out which overwhelms thee,
And thine and mine; and in another day
What *is* shall be the past of Belus'[40] race.

Sar. What must we dread?

Sal.   Ambitious treachery,
Which has environ'd thee with snares; but yet
There is resource: empower me with thy signet
To quell the machinations, and I lay
The heads of thy chief foes before thy feet.

Sar. The heads—how many?

Sal.   Must I stay to number   290
When even thine own's in peril? Let me go;
Give me thy signet—trust me with the rest.

Sar. I will trust no man with unlimited lives.
When we take those from others, we nor know
What we have taken, nor the thing we give.

Sal. Wouldst thou not take their lives who seek for
    thine?

Sar. That's a hard question.—But, I answer Yes.
Cannot the thing be done without? Who are they
Whom thou suspectest?—Let them be arrested.

Sal. I would thou wouldst not ask me; the next moment   300
Will send my answer through thy babbling troop
Of paramours, and thence fly o'er the palace,
Even to the city, and so baffle all.—
Trust me.

Sar.   Thou knowest I have done so ever;
Take thou the signet. *(Gives the signet)*.

Sal.   I have one more request.—

Sar. Name it.

Sal.   That thou this night forbear the banquet
In the pavilion over the Euphrates.

Sar. Forbear the banquet! Not for all the plotters
That ever shook a kingdom! Let them come,
And do their worst: I shall not blench[41] for them;   310
Nor rise the sooner; nor forbear the goblet;
Nor crown me with a single rose the less;
Nor lose one joyous hour.—I fear them not.

Sal. But thou wouldst arm thee, wouldst thou not,
    if needful?

Sar. Perhaps. I have the goodliest armour, and
A sword of such a temper; and a bow
And javelin, which might furnish Nimrod forth:
A little heavy, but yet not unwieldy.
And now I think on't, 'tis long since I've used them,
Even in the chase. Hast ever seen them, brother?   320

Sal. Is this a time for such fantastic trifling?—
If need be, wilt thou wear them?

Sar.   Will I not?
Oh! if it must be so, and these rash slaves
Will not be ruled with less, I'll use the sword
Till they shall wish it turn'd into a distaff.[42]

Sal. They say thy Sceptre's turn'd to that already.

Sar. That's false! but let them say so: the old Greeks,
Of whom our captives often sing, related
The same of their chief hero, Hercules,
Because he loved a Lydian queen:[43] thou seest   330
The populace of all the nations seize
Each calumny they can to sink their sovereigns.

Sal. They did not speak thus of thy fathers.

Sar.   No;
They dared not. They were kept to toil and combat,
And never changed their chains but for their armour:
Now they have peace and pastime, and the license

---

[40] *Belus*: In Diodorus (I.xxviii:1), Belus is the son of
Poseidon and Libya who led the Egyptians to the
banks of the Euphrates and established the Chaldeans
as a priestly caste.

[41] *blench*: variant of blanch; turn pale (here, with fear).

[42] *distaff*: a cleft staff about three feet long used in ancient times for winding wool or flax for spinning; sym-
bolically, it comes to mean the female sex or female
authority.

[43] *Hercules … Lydian queen*: As punishment for killing
the sons of the king of Pylus, Hercules was commanded by the Delphic oracle to serve Omphale,
queen of Lydia, who, in some legends, dressed him in
women's clothes and had him work with her maids
spinning wool. He later was her lover.

To revel and to rail; it irks me not.
I would not give the smile of one fair girl
For all the popular breath that e'er divided
A name from nothing. What are the rank tongues   340
Of this vile herd, grown insolent with feeding,
That I should prize their noisy praise, or dread
Their noisome clamour?
Sal.   You have said they are men;
As such their hearts are something.
Sar.   So my dogs' are;
And better, as more faithful: but, proceed;
Thou hast my signet:[44]—since they are tumultuous,
Let them be temper'd, yet not roughly, till
Necessity enforce it. I hate all pain,
Given or received; we have enough within us,
The meanest vassal as the loftiest monarch,   350
Not to add to each other's natural burthen
Of mortal misery, but rather lessen,
By mild reciprocal alleviation,
The fatal penalties imposed on life;
But this they know not, or they will not know.
I have, by Baal! done all I could to soothe them:
I made no wars, I added no new imposts,
I interfered not with their civic lives,
I let them pass their days as best might suit them,
Passing my own as suited me.
Sal.   Thou stopp'st   360
Short of the duties of a king; and therefore
They say thou art unfit to be a monarch.
Sar. They lie.—Unhappily, I am unfit
To be aught save a monarch; else for me
The meanest Mede might be the king instead.
Sal. There is one Mede, at least, who seeks to be so.
Sar. What mean'st thou?—'tis thy secret; thou desirest
Few questions, and I'm not of curious nature.
Take the fit steps; and, since necessity
Requires, I sanction and support thee. Ne'er   370
Was man who more desired to rule in peace
The peaceful only; if they rouse me, better
They had conjured up stern Nimrod from his ashes,
"The Mighty Hunter." I will turn these realms
To one wide desert chase of brutes, who *were*,

But *would* no more, by their own choice, be human.
What they have found me, they belie; that *which*
They yet may find me—shall defy their wish
To speak it worse; and let them thank themselves.
Sal. Then thou at last canst feel?
Sar.   Feel! who feels not   380
Ingratitude?
Sal.   I will not pause to answer
With words, but deeds. Keep thou awake that energy
Which sleeps at times, but is not dead within thee,
And thou may'st yet be glorious in thy reign,
As powerful in thy realm. Farewell! *(Exit
    Salemenes).*
Sar. (Solus).   Farewell!
He's gone; and on his finger bears my signet,
Which is to him a sceptre. He is stern
As I am heedless; and the slaves deserve
To feel a master. What may be the danger,
I know not: he hath found it, let him quell it.   390
Must I consume my life—this little life—
In guarding against all may make it less?
It is not worth so much! It were to die
Before my hour, to live in dread of death,
Tracing revolt: suspecting all about me,
Because they are near; and all who are remote,
Because they are far. But if it should be so—
If they should sweep me off from Earth and Empire,
Why, what is Earth or Empire of the Earth?
I have loved, and lived, and multiplied my image;   400
To die is no less natural than those
Acts of this clay! 'Tis true I have not shed
Blood as I might have done, in oceans, till
My name became the synonyme of Death—
A terror and a trophy. But for this
I feel no penitence; my life is love:
If I must shed blood, it shall be by force.
Till now, no drop from an Assyrian vein
Hath flow'd for me, nor hath the smallest coin
Of Nineveh's vast treasures e'er been lavish'd   410
On objects which could cost her sons a tear:
If then they hate me, 'tis because I hate not;
If they rebel, 'tis because I oppress not.
Oh, men! ye must be ruled with scythes, not
    sceptres,
And mow'd down like the grass, else all we reap
Is rank abundance, and a rotten harvest

---

[44] *signet*: a small seal, usually on a finger-ring, used to give authorization to a document or to the official who carries it.

Of discontents infecting the fair soil,
Making a desert of fertility.—
I'll think no more.——Within there, ho!
(Enter an Attendant).
Sar.   Slave, tell
The Ionian Myrrha we would crave her presence.   420
Attendant. King, she is here.
(Myrrha enters).
Sar. (Apart to Attendant).   Away!
    (Addressing Myrrha)   Beautiful being!
Thou dost almost anticipate my heart;
It throbb'd for thee, and here thou comest: let me
Deem that some unknown influence, some sweet
    oracle,
Communicates between us, though unseen,
In absence, and attracts us to each other.
Myr. There doth.
Sar.   I know there doth, but not its name;
What is it?
Myr.   In my native land a God,
And in my heart a feeling like a God's,
Exalted; yet I own 'tis only mortal;   430
For what I feel is humble, and yet happy—
That is, it would be happy; but——*(Myrrha pauses).*
Sar.   There comes
For ever something between us and what
We deem our happiness: let me remove
The barrier which that hesitating accent
Proclaims to thine, and mine is seal'd.
Myr.   My lord!—
Sar. My lord—my king—sire—sovereign! thus it is—
For ever thus, address'd with awe. I ne'er
Can see a smile, unless in some broad banquet's
Intoxicating glare, when the buffoons   440
Have gorged themselves up to equality,
Or I have quaff'd me down to their abasement.
Myrrha, I can hear all these things, these names,
Lord—king—sire—monarch—nay, time was I
    prized them,
That is, I suffer'd them—from slaves and nobles;
But when they falter from the lips I love,
The lips which have been press'd to mine, a chill
Comes o'er my heart, a cold sense of the falsehood
Of this my station, which represses feeling
In those for whom I have felt most, and makes me   450
Wish that I could lay down the dull tiara,

And share a cottage on the Caucasus
With thee, and wear no crowns but those of flowers.
Myr. Would that we could!
Sar.   And dost *thou* feel this?—Why?
Myr. Then thou wouldst know what thou canst
    never know.
Sar. And that is——
Myr.   The true value of a heart;
    At least, a woman's.
Sar.   I have proved a thousand—
    A thousand, and a thousand.
Myr.   Hearts?
Sar.   I think so.
Myr. Not one! the time may come thou may'st.
Sar.   It will.
    Hear, Myrrha; Salemenes has declared—   460
    Or why or how he hath divined it, Belus,
    Who founded our great realm, knows more than I—
    But Salemenes hath declared my throne
    In peril.
Myr.   He did well.
Sar.   And say'st *thou* so?
    Thou whom he spurn'd so harshly, and now dared
    Drive from our presence with his savage jeers,
    And made thee weep and blush?
Myr.   I should do both
    More frequently, and he did well to call me
    Back to my duty. But thou spakest of peril—
    Peril to thee——
Sar.   Ay, from dark plots and snares   470
    From Medes—and discontented troops and nations.
    I know not what—a labyrinth of things—
    A maze of mutter'd threats and mysteries:
    Thou know'st the man—it is his usual custom.
    But he is honest. Come, we'll think no more on't—
    But of the midnight festival.
Myr.   'Tis time
    To think of aught save festivals. Thou hast not
    Spurn'd his sage cautions?
Sar.   What?—and dost thou fear?
Myr. Fear!—I'm a Greek, and how should I fear death?
    A slave, and wherefore should I dread my freedom? 480
Sar. Then wherefore dost thou turn so pale?
Myr.   I love.
Sar. And do not I? I love thee far—far more
    Than either the brief life or the wide realm,
    Which, it may be, are menaced;—yet I blench not.

Myr. That means thou lovest nor thyself nor me;
  For he who loves another loves himself,
  Even for that other's sake. This is too rash:
  Kingdoms and lives are not to be so lost.
Sar. Lost!—why, who is the aspiring chief who dared
  Assume to win them?
Myr.   Who is he should dread   490
  To try so much? When he who is their ruler
  Forgets himself, will they remember him?
Sar. Myrrha!
Myr.   Frown not upon me: you have smiled
  Too often on me not to make those frowns
  Bitterer to bear than any punishment
  Which they may augur.[45]—King, I am your subject!
  Master, I am your slave! Man, I have loved you!—
  Loved you, I know not by what fatal weakness,
  Although a Greek, and born a foe to monarchs—
  A slave, and hating fetters—an Ionian,   500
  And, therefore, when I love a stranger, more
  Degraded by that passion than by chains![46]
  Still I have loved you. If that love were strong
  Enough to overcome all former nature,
  Shall it not claim the privilege to save you?
Sar. Save me, my beauty! Thou art very fair,
  And what I seek of thee is love—not safety.
Myr. And without love where dwells security?
Sar. I speak of woman's love.
Myr.   The very first
  Of human life must spring from woman's breast,   510
  Your first small words are taught you from her lips,
  Your first tears quench'd by her, and your last sighs
  Too often breathed out in a woman's hearing,
  When men have shrunk from the ignoble care
  Of watching the last hour of him who led them.
Sar. My eloquent Ionian! thou speak'st music,
  The very chorus of the tragic song[47]
  I have heard thee talk of as the favourite pastime
  Of thy far father-land. Nay, weep not—calm thee.
Myr. I weep not.—But I pray thee, do not speak   520
  About my fathers or their land.

---

45 *augur*: to read auguries, to tell the future.
46 *King … chains*: McGann and Weller suggest lines 496–
   502 echo John Dryden's *All for Love*, II:7–15.
47 *tragic song*: a reference to the chorus in Greek tragedy.

Sar.   Yet oft
  Thou speakest of them.
Myr.   True—true: constant thought
  Will overflow in words unconsciously;
  But when another speaks of Greece, it wounds me.
Sar. Well, then, how wouldst thou *save* me, as thou
  saidst?
Myr. By teaching thee to save thyself, and not
  Thyself alone, but these vast realms, from all
  The rage of the worst war—the war of brethren.
Sar. Why, child, I loathe all war, and warriors;
  I live in peace and pleasure: what can man   530
  Do more?
Myr.   Alas! my lord, with common men
  There needs too oft the show of war to keep
  The substance of sweet peace; and for a king,
  'Tis sometimes better to be fear'd than loved.
Sar. And I have never sought but for the last.
Myr. And now art neither.
Sar.   Dost *thou* say so, Myrrha?
Myr. I speak of civic popular love, *self* love,
  Which means that men are kept in awe and law,
  Yet not oppress'd—at least they must not think so;
  Or if they think so, deem it necessary,   540
  To ward off worse oppression, their own passions.
  A king of feasts, and flowers, and wine, and revel,
  And love, and mirth, was never king of glory.
Sar. Glory! what's that?
Myr.   Ask of the gods thy fathers.
Sar. They cannot answer; when the priests speak for
  them,
  'Tis for some small addition to the temple.
Myr. Look to the annals of thine Empire's founders.
Sar. They are so blotted o'er with blood, I cannot.
  But what wouldst have? the Empire *has been*
  founded.
  I cannot go on multiplying empires.   550
Myr. Preserve thine own.
Sar.   At least I will enjoy it.
  Come, Myrrha, let us go on to the Euphrates;
  The hour invites, the galley is prepared,
  And the pavilion, deck'd for our return,
  In fit adornment for the evening banquet,
  Shall blaze with beauty and with light, until
  It seems unto the stars which are above us
  Itself an opposite star; and we will sit

Crown'd with fresh flowers like——

Myr.   Victims.

Sar.   No, like sovereigns,

The shepherd kings of patriarchal times,[48]   560

Who knew no brighter gems than summer wreaths,

And none but tearless triumphs. Let us on.

(Enter Pania).

Pania. May the king live for ever!

Sar.   Not an hour

Longer than he can love. How my soul hates

This language, which makes life itself a lie,

Flattering dust with eternity. Well, Pania!

Be brief.

Pan.   I am charged by Salemenes to

Reiterate his prayer unto the king,

That for this day, at least, he will not quit

The palace: when the general returns,   570

He will adduce such reasons as will warrant

His daring, and perhaps obtain the pardon

Of his presumption.

Sar.   What! am I then coop'd?

Already captive? can I not even breathe

The breath of heaven? Tell prince Salemenes,

Were all Assyria raging round the walls

In mutinous myriads, I would still go forth.

Pan. I must obey, and yet—

Myr.   Oh, Monarch, listen.—

How many a day and moon thou hast reclined

Within these palace walls in silken dalliance,   580

And never shown thee to thy people's longing;

Leaving thy subjects' eyes ungratified,

The satraps uncontroll'd, the gods unworshipp'd,

And all things in the anarchy of sloth,

Till all, save evil, slumber'd through the realm!

And wilt thou not now tarry for a day,

A day which may redeem thee? Wilt thou not

Yield to the few still faithful a few hours,

For them, for thee, for thy past fathers' race,

And for thy sons' inheritance?

Pan.   'Tis true!   590

From the deep urgency with which the Prince

Despatch'd me to your sacred presence, I

Must dare to add my feeble voice to that

Which now has spoken.

Sar.   No, it must not be.

Myr. For the sake of thy realm!

Sar.   Away!

Pan.   For that

Of all thy faithful subjects, who will rally

Round thee and thine.

Sar.   These are mere phantasies;

There is no peril: 'tis a sullen scheme

Of Salemenes, to approve his zeal,

And show himself more necessary to us.   600

Myr. By all that's good and glorious take this

    counsel.

Sar. Business to-morrow.

Myr.   Ay, or death to-night.

Sar. Why let it come then unexpectedly,

'Midst joy and gentleness, and mirth and love;

So let me fall like the pluck'd rose!—far better

Thus than be wither'd.

Myr.   Then thou wilt not yield,

Even for the sake of all that ever stirr'd

A monarch into action, to forego

A trifling revel.

Sar.   No.

Myr.   Then yield for *mine*;

For my sake!

Sar.   Thine, my Myrrha?

Myr.   'Tis the first   610

Boon which I e'er ask'd Assyria's king.

Sar. That's true, and wer't my kingdom must be

    granted.

Well, for thy sake, I yield me. Pania, hence!

Thou hear'st me.

Pan.   And obey. *(Exit Pania).*

Sar.   I marvel at thee.

What is thy motive, Myrrha, thus to urge me?

Myr. Thy safety; and the certainty that nought

Could urge the Prince thy kinsman to require

Thus much from thee, but some impending danger.

Sar. And if I do not dread it, why shouldst thou?

Myr. Because *thou* dost not fear, I fear for *thee*.   620

Sar. To-morrow thou wilt smile at these vain fancies.

Myr. If the worst come, I shall be where none weep,

And that is better than the power to smile.

And thou?

---

48   *shepherd kings of patriarchal times*: a reference to myths
of a golden age, a pastoral paradise, where man lived
in harmony with nature and even kings lived simply.

Sar.   I shall be king, as heretofore.

Myr. Where?

Sar.   With Baal, Nimrod, and Semiramis,
  Sole in Assyria, or with them elsewhere.
  Fate made me what I am—may make me nothing—
  But either that or nothing must I be;
  I will not live degraded.

Myr.   Hadst thou felt
  Thus always, none would ever dare degrade thee.   630

Sar. And who will do so now?

Myr.   Dost thou suspect none?

Sar. Suspect!—that's a spy's office. Oh! we lose
  Ten thousand precious moments in vain words,
  And vainer fears. Within there!—Ye slaves, deck
  The Hall of Nimrod for the evening revel;
  If I must make a prison of our palace,
  At least we'll wear our fetters jocundly;
  If the Euphrates be forbid us, and
  The summer dwelling on its beauteous border,
  Here we are still unmenaced. Ho! within there!   640
    (Exit Sardanapalus).

Myr. (Solus). Why do I love this man? My country's
    daughters
  Love none but heroes. But I have no country!
  The slave hath lost all save her bonds. I love him;
  And that's the heaviest link of the long chain—
  To love whom we esteem not. Be it so:
  The hour is coming when he'll need all love,
  And find none. To fall from him now were baser
  Than to have stabb'd him on his throne when highest
  Would have been noble in my country's creed;
  I was not made for either. Could I save him,   650
  I should not love *him* better, but myself;
  And I have need of the last, for I have fallen
  In my own thoughts, by loving this soft stranger:
  And yet methinks I love him more, perceiving
  That he is hated of his own barbarians,
  The natural foes of all the blood of Greece.
  Could I but wake a single thought like those
  Which even the Phrygians[49] felt when battling long

---

49 *Phrygians*: The Phrygians were a people occupying land
    to the east of Troy; they were known to the Assyrians.
    They are listed in the *Iliad* as part of the Trojan forces,
    and Byron seems to use the term as synonymous with
    Trojans.

'Twixt Ilion[50] and the sea, within his heart,
He would tread down the barbarous crowds, and   660
  triumph.
He loves me, and I love him; the slave loves
Her master, and would free him from his vices.
If not, I have a means of freedom still,
And if I cannot teach him how to reign,
May show him how alone a king can leave
His throne. I must not lose him from my sight.
    (Exit).

Act II

Scene I: *The Portal of the same Hall of the Palace.*

Beleses (Solus). The sun goes down: methinks he sets
  more slowly,
  Taking his last look of Assyria's empire.
  How red he glares amongst those deepening clouds,
  Like the blood he predicts. If not in vain,
  Thou sun that sinkest, and ye stars which rise,
  I have outwatch'd ye, reading ray by ray
  The edicts of your orbs, which make Time tremble
  For what he brings the nations, 'tis the furthest
  Hour of Assyria's years. And yet how calm!
  An earthquake should announce so great a fall—   10
  A summer's sun discloses it. Yon disk,
  To the star-read Chaldean, bears upon
  Its everlasting page the end of what
  Seem'd everlasting; but oh! thou true sun!
  The burning oracle of all that live,
  As fountain of all life, and symbol of
  Him who bestows it, wherefore dost thou limit
  Thy lore unto calamity? Why not
  Unfold the rise of days more worthy thine
  All-glorious burst from ocean? why not dart   20
  A beam of hope athwart the future years,
  As of wrath to its days? Hear me! oh! hear me!
  I am thy worshipper, thy priest, thy servant—
  I have gazed on thee at thy rise and fall,
  And bow'd my head beneath thy mid-day beams,
  When my eye dared not meet thee. I have watch'd
  For thee, and after thee, and pray'd to thee,

---

50 *Ilion*: another name for Troy; named for its founder
    Ilos.

And sacrificed to thee, and read, and fear'd thee,
And ask'd of thee, and thou hast answer'd—but
Only to thus much: while I speak, he sinks— 30
Is gone—and leaves his beauty, not his knowledge,
To the delighted west, which revels in
Its hues of dying glory. Yet what is
Death, so it be but glorious? 'Tis a sunset;
And mortals may be happy to resemble
The gods but in decay.

(Enter Arbaces by an inner door).

Arbaces.   Beleses, why
So wrapt in thy devotions? Dost thou stand
Gazing to trace thy disappearing god
Into some realm of undiscover'd day?
Our business is with night—'tis come.

Bel.   But not 40
Gone.

Arb.   Let it roll on—we are ready.

Bel.   Yes.
Would it were over!

Arb.   Does the Prophet doubt,
To whom the very stars shine victory?

Bel. I do not doubt of victory—but the victor.

Arb. Well, let thy science settle that. Meantime
I have prepared as many glittering spears
As will out-sparkle our allies—your planets.
There is no more to thwart us. The she-king,
That less than woman, is even now upon
The waters with his female mates. The order 50
Is issued for the feast in the pavilion.
The first cup which he drains will be the last
Quaff'd by the line of Nimrod.

Bel.   'Twas a brave one.

Arb. And is a weak one—'tis worn out—we'll mend it.

Bel. Art sure of that?

Arb.   Its founder was a hunter—
I am a soldier—what is there to fear?

Bel. The soldier.

Arb.   And the priest, it may be; but
If you thought thus, or think, why not retain
Your king of concubines? why stir me up?
Why spur me to this enterprise? your own 60
No less than mine?

Bel.   Look to the sky!

Arb.   I look.

Bel. What seest thou?

Arb.   A fair summer's twilight, and
The gathering of the stars.

Bel.   And midst them, mark
Yon earliest, and the brightest, which so quivers,
As it would quit its place in the blue ether.

Arb. Well?

Bel.   'Tis thy natal ruler—thy birth planet.[51]

Arb. (Touching his scabbard). My star is in this
scabbard: when it shines,
It shall out-dazzle comets. Let us think
Of what is to be done to justify
Thy planets and their portents. When we conquer, 70
They shall have temples—Ay, and priests—and thou
Shalt be the pontiff of—what gods thou wilt;
For I observe that they are ever just,
And own the bravest for the most devout.

Bel. Ay, and the most devout for brave—thou hast not
Seen me turn back from battle.

Arb.   No; I own thee
As firm in fight as Babylonia's captain,
As skilful in Chaldea's worship; now,
Will it but please thee to forget the priest,
And be the warrior?

Bel.   Why not both?

Arb.   The better; 80
And yet it almost shames me, we shall have
So little to effect. This woman's warfare
Degrades the very conqueror. To have pluck'd
A bold and bloody despot from his throne,
And grappled with him, clashing steel with steel,
That were heroic or to win or fall;
But to upraise my sword against this silkworm,
And hear him whine, it may be——

Bel.   Do not deem it:
He has that in him which may make you strife yet;
And were he all you think, his guards are hardy, 90
And headed by the cool, stern Salemenes.

Arb. They'll not resist.

Bel.   Why not? they are soldiers.

Arb.   True,
And therefore need a soldier to command them.

Bel. That Salemenes is.

---

51 *birth planet*: a reference to the astrological notion that
one's life is in some way determined by the influence
of the planet in the ascendant at one's birth.

Arb.   But not their king.
  Besides, he hates the effeminate thing that governs,
  For the queen's sake, his sister. Mark you not
  He keeps aloof from all the revels?
Bel.   But
  Not from the council—there he is ever constant.
Arb. And ever thwarted; what would you have more
  To make a rebel out of? A fool reigning,   100
  His blood dishonour'd, and himself disdain'd;
  Why, it is *his* revenge we work for.
Bel.   Could
  He but be brought to think so: this, I doubt of.
Arb. What, if we sound him?
Bel.   Yes—if the time served.
(Enter Balea).
Balea. Satraps! The king commands your presence at
  The feast to-night.
Bel.   To hear is to obey.
  In the pavilion?
Bal.   No; here in the palace.
Arb. How! in the palace? it was not thus order'd.
Bal. It is so order'd now.
Arb.   And why?
Bal.   I know not.
  May I retire?
Arb.   Stay.   110
Bel. (To Arbaces aside). Hush! let him go his way.
  (Alternately to Balea) Yes, Balea, thank the
    Monarch, kiss the hem
  Of his imperial robe, and say, his slaves
  Will take the crumbs he deigns to scatter from
  His royal table at the hour—was't midnight?
Bal. It was; the place, the Hall of Nimrod. Lords,
  I humble me before you, and depart. *(Exit Balea).*
Arb. I like not this same sudden change of place,
  There is some mystery; wherefore should he
    change it?
Bel. Doth he not change a thousand times a day?   120
  Sloth is of all things the most fanciful—
  And moves more parasangs[52] in its intents
  Than generals in their marches, when they seek
  To leave their foe at fault.—Why dost thou muse?

----

52 *parasang*: a Persian unit of measure equal to between
     3 and 3.5 miles.

Arb. He loved that gay pavilion,—it was ever
  His summer dotage.
Bel.   And he loved his queen—
  And thrice a thousand harlotry besides—
  And he has loved all things by turns, except
  Wisdom and Glory.
Arb.   Still—I like it not.
  If he has changed—why so must we: the attack   130
  Were easy in the isolated bower,
  Beset with drowsy guards and drunken courtiers;
  But in the hall of Nimrod——
Bel.   Is it so?
  Methought the haughty soldier fear'd to mount
  A throne too easily—does it disappoint thee
  To find there is a slipperier step or two
  Than what was counted on?
Arb.   When the hour comes,
  Thou shalt perceive how far I fear or no.
  Thou hast seen my life at stake—and gaily play'd
    for—
  But here is more upon the die—a kingdom.   140
Bel. I have foretold already—thou wilt win it:
  Then on, and prosper.
Arb.   Now were I a soothsayer,
  I would have boded so much to myself.
  But be the stars obey'd—I cannot quarrel
  With them, nor their interpreter. Who's here?
(Enter Salemenes).
Sal. Satraps!
Bel.   My prince!
Sal.   Well met—I sought ye both,
  But elsewhere than the palace.
Arb.   Wherefore so?
Sal. 'Tis not the hour.
Arb.   The hour—what hour?
Sal.   Of midnight.
Bel. Midnight, my lord!
Sal.   What, are you not invited?
Bel. Oh! yes—we had forgotten.
Sal.   Is it usual   150
  Thus to forget a sovereign's invitation?
Arb. Why—we but now received it.
Sal.   Then why here?
Arb. On duty.
Sal.   On what duty?
Bel.   On the state's.

We have the privilege to approach the presence;
But found the Monarch absent.

Sal. And I too
Am upon duty.

Arb. May we crave its purport?

Sal. To arrest two traitors. Guards! Within there!

(Enter Guards).

Sal. (Continuing) . Satraps,
Your swords.

Bel. (Delivering his). My lord, behold my scimitar.

Arb. (Drawing his sword). Take mine.

Sal. (Advancing). I will.

Arb. But in your
heart the blade—
The hilt quits not this hand.

Sal. (Drawing). How! dost thou brave me? 160
Tis well—this saves a trial, and false mercy.
Soldiers, hew down the rebel!

Arb. Soldiers! Ay—
Alone you dare not.

Sal. Alone! foolish slave—
What is there in thee that a prince should shrink
from
Of open force? We dread thy treason, not
Thy strength: thy tooth is nought without its
venom—
The serpent's, not the lion's. Cut him down.

Bel. (Interposing). Arbaces! Are you mad? Have I not
render'd
My sword? Then trust like me our sovereign's justice.

Arb. No—I will sooner trust the stars thou prat'st of 170
And this slight arm, and die a king at least
Of my own breath and body—so far that
None else shall chain them.

Sal. (To the Guards). You hear *him* and *me.*
Take him not,—kill.

*(The Guards attack Arbaces, who defends himself
valiantly and dexterously till they waver).*

Sal. Is it even so; and must
I do the hangman's office? Recreants![53] see
How you should fell a traitor. *(Salemenes attacks
Arbaces).*

(Enter Sardanapalus and Train).

---

[53] *Recreants*: cowards, even deserters.

Sar. Hold your hands—
Upon your lives, I say. What, deaf or drunken?
My sword! Oh fool, I wear no sword: here, fellow,
(To a Guard) Give me thy weapon.

*(Sardanapalus snatches a sword from one of the
soldiers, and rushes between the combatants—they
separate).*

Sar. In my very palace!
What hinders me from cleaving you in twain, 180
Audacious brawlers?

Bel. Sire, your justice.

Sal. Or—
Your weakness.

Sar. (Raising the sword). How?

Sal. Strike! so the blow's repeated
Upon yon traitor—whom you spare a moment,
I trust, for torture—I'm content.

Sar. What—him!
Who dares assail Arbaces?

Sal. I!

Sar. Indeed!
Prince, you forget yourself. Upon what warrant?

Sal. (Showing the signet). Thine.

Arb. (Confused). The king's!

Sal. Yes! and
let the king confirm it.

Sar. I parted not from this for such a purpose.

Sal. You parted with it for your safety—I
Employ'd it for the best. Pronounce in person. 190
Here I am but your slave—a moment past
I was your representative.

Sar. Then sheathe
Your swords.

*(Arbaces and Salemenes return their swords to the
scabbards).*

Sal. Mine's sheath'd: I pray you sheathe *not* yours:
'Tis the sole sceptre left you now with safety.

Sar. A heavy one; the hilt, too, hurts my hand. *(To a
Guard).*
Here, fellow, take thy weapon back. Well, sirs,
What doth this mean?

Bel. The Prince must answer that.

Sal. Truth upon my part, treason upon theirs.

Sar. Treason—Arbaces! treachery and Beleses!
That were an union I will not believe. 200

Bel. Where is the proof?

Sal.   I'll answer that, if once
  The king demands your fellow-traitor's sword.
Arb. (To Salemenes). A sword which hath been
    drawn as oft as thine
  Against his foes.
Sal.   And now against his brother,
  And in an hour or so against himself.
Sar. That is not possible: he dared not; no—
  No—I'll not hear of such things. These vain
    bickerings
  Are spawn'd in courts by base intrigues, and baser
  Hirelings, who live by lies on good men's lives.
  You must have been deceived, my brother.
Sal.   First   210
  Let him deliver up his weapon, and
  Proclaim himself your subject by that duty,
  And I will answer all.
Sar.   Why, if I thought so—
  But no, it cannot be; the Mede Arbaces—
  The trusty, rough, true soldier—the best captain
  Of all who discipline our nations—No,
  I'll not insult him thus, to bid him render
  The scimitar to me he never yielded
  Unto our enemies. Chief, keep your weapon.
Sal. (Delivering back the signet).
  Monarch, take back your signet.
Sar.   No, retain it;   220
  But use it with more moderation.
Sal.   Sire,
  I used it for your honour, and restore it
  Because I cannot keep it with my own.
  Bestow it on Arbaces.
Sar.   So I should:
  He never ask'd it.
Sal.   Doubt not, he will have it,
  Without that hollow semblance of respect.
Bel. I know not what hath prejudiced the prince
  So strongly 'gainst two subjects, than whom none
  Have been more zealous for Assyria's weal.
Sal. Peace, factious priest, and faithless soldier! thou   230
  Unit'st in thy own person the worst vices
  Of the most dangerous orders of mankind.
  Keep thy smooth words and juggling homilies
  For those who know thee not. Thy fellow's sin
  Is, at the least, a bold one, and not temper'd
  By the tricks taught thee in Chaldea.

Bel.   Hear him,
  My liege—the son of Belus! he blasphemes
  The worship of the land, which bows the knee
  Before your fathers.
Sar.   Oh! for that I pray you
  Let him have absolution. I dispense with   240
  The worship of dead men; feeling that I
  Am mortal, and believing that the race
  From whence I sprung are—what I see them—ashes.
Bel. King! Do not deem so: they are with the stars,
  And—
Sar.   You shall join them ere they will rise,
  If you preach farther—Why, *this* is rank treason.
Sal. My lord!
Sar.   To school me in the worship of
  Assyria's idols! Let him be released—
  Give him his sword.
Sal.   My lord, and king, and brother,
  I pray ye pause.
Sar.   Yes, and be sermonised,   250
  And dinn'd, and deafen'd with dead men and Baal,
  And all Chaldea's starry mysteries.
Bel. Monarch! respect them.
Sar.   Oh! for that—I love them;
  I love to watch them in the deep blue vault,
  And to compare them with my Myrrha's eyes;
  I love to see their rays redoubled in
  The tremulous silver of Euphrates' wave,
  As the light breeze of midnight crisps the broad
  And rolling water, sighing through the sedges
  Which fringe his banks: but whether they may be   260
  Gods, as some say, or the abodes of gods,
  As others hold, or simply lamps of night,
  Worlds, or the lights of worlds, I know nor care not.
  There's something sweet in my uncertainty
  I would not change for your Chaldean lore;
  Besides, I know of these all clay can know
  Of aught above it, or below it—nothing.
  I see their brilliancy and feel their beauty—
  When they shine on my grave I shall know neither.
Bel. For *neither*, Sire, say *better*.
Sar.   I will wait,   270
  If it so please you, pontiff, for that knowledge.
  In the mean time receive your sword, and know
  That I prefer your service militant
  Unto your ministry—not loving either.

Sal. (Aside). His lusts have made him mad. Then
    must I save him,
  Spite of himself.
Sar.   Please you to hear me, Satraps!
  And chiefly thou, my priest, because I doubt thee
  More than the soldier; and would doubt thee all
  Wert thou not half a warrior: let us part
  In peace—I'll not say pardon—which must be   280
  Earn'd by the guilty; this I'll not pronounce ye,
  Although upon this breath of mine depends
  Your own; and, deadlier for ye, on my fears.
  But fear not—for that I am soft, not fearful—
  And so live on. Were I the thing some think me,
  Your heads would now be dripping the last drops
  Of their attainted gore from the high gates
  Of this our palace into the dry dust,
  Their only portion of the coveted kingdom
  They would be crown'd to reign o'er—let that pass. 290
  As I have said, I will not *deem* ye guilty,
  Nor *doom* ye guiltless. Albeit better men
  Than ye or I stand ready to arraign you;
  And should I leave your fate to sterner judges,
  And proofs of all kinds, I might sacrifice
  Two men, who, whatsoe'er they now are, were
  Once honest. Ye are free, sirs.
Arb.   Sire, this clemency——
Bel. (Interrupting him). Is worthy of yourself; and,
    although innocent,
  We thank——
Sar.   Priest! keep your thanksgivings for Belus;
  His offspring needs none.
Bel.   But being innocent—— 300
Sar. Be silent.—Guilt is loud. If ye are loyal,
  Ye are injured men, and should be sad, not
    grateful.
Bel. So we should be, were justice always done
  By earthly power omnipotent; but innocence
  Must oft receive her right as a mere favour.
Sar. That's a good sentence for a homily,
  Though not for this occasion. Prithee keep it
  To plead thy Sovereign's cause before his people.
Bel. I trust there is no cause.
Sar.   No *cause*, perhaps;
  But many causers:—if ye meet with such   310
  In the exercise of your inquisitive function
  On earth, or should you read of it in heaven
In some mysterious twinkle of the stars,
Which are your chronicles, I pray you note,
That there are worse things betwixt earth and
    heaven[54]
Than him who ruleth many and slays none;
And, hating not himself, yet loves his fellows
Enough to spare even those who would not spare
    him
Were they once masters—but that's doubtful.
    Satraps!
Your swords and persons are at liberty   320
To use them as ye will—but from this hour
I have no call for either. Salemenes!
Follow me.
*(Exeunt Sardanapalus, Salemenes, and the Train, &c.,
leaving Arbaces and Beleses).*
Arb.   Beleses!
Bel.   Now, what think you?
Arb. That we are lost.
Bel.   That we have won the kingdom.
Arb. What? thus suspected—with the sword slung
    o'er us
But by a single hair,[55] and that still wavering
To be blown down by his imperious breath,
Which spared us—why, I know not.
Bel.   Seek not why;
  But let us profit by the interval.
  The hour is still our own—our power the same— 330
  The night the same we destined. He hath changed
  Nothing except our ignorance of all
  Suspicion into such a certainty
  As must make madness of delay.
Arb.   And yet——
Bel. What, doubting still?
Arb.   He spared our lives, nay, more,
  Saved them from Salemenes.
Bel.   And how long
  Will he so spare? till the first drunken minute.

---

54 *there ... heaven*: McGann and Weller suggest an echo
    of *Hamlet* I.v.167–8.
55 *sword ... single hair*: a reference to the Sword of
    Damocles. Damocles was a courtier of Dionysius I
    who excessively praised his master's happiness;
    Dionysius in return feasted him while a sword hung
    over his head held by a single hair to show him the
    actual nature of a tyrant's rule.

Arb. Or sober, rather. Yet he did it nobly;
  Gave royally what we had forfeited
  Basely——

Bel.   Say bravely.

Arb.   Somewhat of both, perhaps.   340
  But it has touch'd me, and, whate'er betide,
  I will no further on.

Bel.   And lose the world!

Arb. Lose any thing except my own esteem.

Bel. I blush that we should owe our lives to such
  A king of distaffs!

Arb.   But no less we owe them;
  And I should blush far more to take the grantor's!

Bel. Thou may'st endure whate'er thou wilt, the stars
  Have written otherwise.

Arb.   Though they came down,
  And marshall'd me the way in all their brightness,
  I would not follow.

Bel.   This is weakness—worse   350
  Than a scared beldam's dreaming of the dead,
  And waking in the dark.—Go to—go to.

Arb. Methought he look'd like Nimrod as he spoke,
  Even as the proud imperial statue stands
  Looking the monarch of the kings around it,
  And sways, while they but ornament, the temple.

Bel. I told you that you had too much despised him,
  And that there was some royalty within him—
  What then? he is the nobler foe.

Arb.   But we
  The meaner.—Would he had not spared us!

Bel.   So—   360
  Wouldst thou be sacrificed thus readily?

Arb. No—but it had been better to have died
  Than live ungrateful.

Bel.   Oh, the souls of some men!
  Thou wouldst digest what some call treason, and
  Fools treachery—and, behold, upon the sudden,
  Because for something or for nothing, this
  Rash reveller steps, ostentatiously,
  'Twixt thee and Salemenes, thou art turn'd
  Into—what shall I say?—Sardanapalus!
  I know no name more ignominious.

Arb.   But   370
  An hour ago, who dared to term me such
  Had held his life but lightly—as it is,

I must forgive you, even as he forgave us—[56]
  Semiramis herself would not have done it.

Bel. No—the queen liked no sharers of the kingdom,
  Not even a husband.

Arb.   I must serve him truly——

Bel. And humbly?

Arb.   No, sir, proudly—being honest.
  I shall be nearer thrones than you to heaven;
  And if not quite so haughty, yet more lofty.
  You may do your own deeming—you have codes,   380
  And mysteries, and corollaries of
  Right and wrong, which I lack for my direction,
  And must pursue but what a plain heart teaches.
  And now you know me.

Bel.   Have you finish'd?

Arb.   Yes—
  With you.

Bel.   And would, perhaps, betray as well
  As quit me?

Arb.   That's a sacerdotal[57] thought,
  And not a soldier's.

Bel.   Be it what you will—
  Truce with these wranglings, and but hear me.

Arb.   No—
  There is more peril in your subtle spirit
  Than in a phalanx.

Bel.   If it must be so—   390
  I'll on alone.

Arb.   Alone!

Bel.   Thrones hold but one.

Arb. But this is fill'd.

Bel.   With worse than vacancy—
  A despised monarch. Look to it, Arbaces:
  I have still aided, cherish'd, loved, and urged you;
  Was willing even to serve you, in the hope
  To serve and save Assyria. Heaven itself
  Seem'd to consent, and all events were friendly,
  Even to the last, till that your spirit shrunk
  Into a shallow softness; but now, rather
  Than see my country languish, I will be   400

---

56 *I must … us*: McGann and Weller suggest an echo of
  Colossians 3:13 and suggest this is the first of a series
  of links between Sardanapalus and Jesus as the "Prince
  of Peace."

57 *sacerdotal*: priestly.

Her saviour or the victim of her tyrant,
Or one or both, for sometimes both are one;
And, if I win, Arbaces is my servant.
Arb. Your servant!
Bel.   Why not? better than be slave,
The *pardon'd* slave of *she* Sardanapalus!
(Enter Pania).
Pan. My lords, I bear an order from the king.
Arb. It is obey'd ere spoken.
Bel.   Notwithstanding,
Let's hear it.
Pan.   Forthwith, on this very night,
Repair to your respective satrapies
Of Babylon and Media.
Bel.   With our troops?   410
Pan. My order is unto the satraps and
Their household train.
Arb.   But——
Bel.   It must be obey'd;
Say, we depart.
Pan.   My order is to see you
Depart, and not to bear your answer.
Bel. (Aside).   Ay!
Well, sir, we will accompany you hence.
Pan. I will retire to marshal forth the guard
Of honour which befits your rank, and wait
Your leisure, so that it the hour exceeds not. *(Exit
    Pania).*
Bel. Now then obey!
Arb.   Doubtless.
Bel.   Yes, to the gates
That grate the palace, which is now our prison,   420
No further.
Arb.   Thou hast harp'd the truth indeed!
The realm itself, in all its wide extension,
Yawns dungeons at each step for thee and me.
Bel. Graves!
Arb.   If I thought so, this good sword should dig
One more than mine.
Bel.   It shall have work enough:
Let me hope better than thou augurest;
At present, let us hence as best we may.
Thou dost agree with me in understanding
This order as a sentence?
Arb.   Why, what other
Interpretation should it bear? it is   430

The very policy of orient monarchs—
Pardon and poison—favours and a sword—
A distant voyage, and an eternal sleep.
How many satraps in his father's time—
For he I own is, or at least *was*, bloodless—
Bel. But *will* not, *can* not be so now.
Arb.   I doubt it.
How many satraps have I seen set out
In his sire's day for mighty vice-royalties,
Whose tombs are on their path! I know not how,
But they all sicken'd by the way, it was   440
So long and heavy.
Bel.   Let us but regain
The free air of the city, and we'll shorten
The journey.
Arb.   'Twill be shorten'd at the gates,
It may be.
Bel.   No; they hardly will risk that.
They mean us to die privately, but not
Within the palace or the city walls,
Where we are known and may have partisans:
If they had meant to slay us here, we were
No longer with the living. Let us hence.
Arb. If I but thought he did not mean my life—— 450
Bel. Fool! hence—what else should despotism alarm'd
Mean? Let us but rejoin our troops, and march.
Arb. Towards our provinces?
Bel.   No; towards your kingdom.
There's time, there's heart, and hope, and power,
    and means,
Which their half measures leave us in full scope.—
Away!
Arb.   And I even yet repenting must
Relapse to guilt!
Bel.   Self-defence is a virtue,
Sole bulwark of all right. Away, I say!
Let's leave this place, the air grows thick and choking,
And the walls have a scent of night-shade[58]—hence! 460
Let us not leave them time for further council.
Our quick departure proves our civic zeal;
Our quick departure hinders our good escort,
The worthy Pania, from anticipating

---

58 *night-shade*: belladonna or deadly nightshade, a plant
    with poisonous berries.

The orders of some parasangs from hence:
   Nay, there's no other choice, but——hence, I say.
(Exit with Arbaces, who follows reluctantly).
(Enter Sardanapalus and Salemenes).
Sar. Well, all is remedied, and without bloodshed,
   That worst of mockeries of a remedy;
   We are now secure by these men's exile.
Sal.   Yes,
   As he who treads on flowers is from the adder   470
   Twined round their roots.
Sar.   Why, what wouldst have me do?
Sal. Undo what you have done.
Sar.   Revoke my pardon?
Sal. Replace the crown now tottering on your temples.
Sar. That were tyrannical.
Sal.   But sure.
Sar.   We are so.
   What danger can they work upon the frontier?
Sal. They are not there yet—never should they be so,
   Were I well listen'd to.
Sar.   Nay, I *have* listen'd
   Impartially to thee—why not to them?
Sal. You may know that hereafter; as it is,
   I take my leave, to order forth the guard.   480
Sar. And you will join us at the banquet?
Sal.   Sire,
   Dispense with me—I am no wassailer:[59]
   Command me in all service save the Bacchant's.[60]
Sar. Nay, but 'tis fit to revel now and then.
Sal. And fit that some should watch for those who revel
   Too oft. Am I permitted to depart?
Sar. Yes——Stay a moment, my good Salemenes,
   My brother, my best subject, better prince
   Than I am king. You should have been the monarch,
   And I—I know not what, and care not; but   490
   Think not I am insensible to all
   Thine honest wisdom, and thy rough yet kind,
   Though oft-reproving sufferance of my follies.
   If I have spared these men against thy counsel,
   That is, their lives—it is not that I doubt
   The advice was sound; but, let them live: we will not

Cavil[61] about their lives—so let them mend them.
   Their banishment will leave me still sound sleep,
   Which their death had not left me.
Sal.   Thus you run
   The risk to sleep for ever, to save traitors—   500
   A moment's pang now changed for years of crime.
   Still let them be made quiet.
Sar.   Tempt me not:
   My word is past.
Sal.   But it may be recall'd.
Sar. 'Tis royal.
Sal.   And should therefore be decisive.
   This half-indulgence of an exile serves
   But to provoke—a pardon should be full,
   Or it is none.
Sar.   And who persuaded me
   After I had repeal'd them, or at least
   Only dismiss'd them from our presence, who
   Urged me to send them to their satrapies?   510
Sal. True; that I had forgotten; that is, sire,
   If they e'er reach their satrapies—why, then,
   Reprove me more for my advice.
Sar.   And if
   They do not reach them—look to it!—in safety,
   In safety, mark me—and security—
   Look to thine own.
Sal.   Permit me to depart;
   Their *safety* shall be cared for.
Sar.   Get thee hence, then;
   And, prithee, think more gently of thy brother.
Sal. Sire, I shall ever duly serve my sovereign. *(Exit*
   Salemenes).
Sar. *(Solus).* That man is of a temper too severe: 520
   Hard but as lofty as the rock, and free
   From all the taints of common earth—while I
   Am softer clay, impregnated with flowers.
   But as our mould is, must the produce be.
   If I have err'd this time, 'tis on the side
   Where error sits most lightly on that sense,
   I know not what to call it; but it reckons
   With me ofttimes for pain, and sometimes pleasure;
   A spirit which seems placed about my heart
   To count its throbs, not quicken them, and ask   530
   Questions which mortal never dared to ask me,

---

59 *wassailer*: reveller, from wassail, a spiced ale drunk at
    Christmas-time.
60 *Bacchant*: a participant in the orgiastic worship of
    Bacchus.

61 *Cavil*: raise frivolous objections.

Nor Baal, though an oracular deity—
Albeit his marble face majestical
Frowns as the shadows of the evening dim
His brows to changed expression, till at times
I think the statue looks in act to speak.
Away with these vain thoughts, I will be joyous—
And here comes Joy's true herald.
(Enter Myrrha).
Myr.   King! the sky
Is overcast, and musters muttering thunder,
In clouds that seem approaching fast, and show   540
In forked flashes a commanding tempest.
Will you then quit the palace?
Sar.   Tempest, sayst thou?
Myr. Ay, my good lord.
Sar.   For my own part, I should be
Not ill content to vary the smooth scene,
And watch the warring elements; but this
Would little suit the silken garments and
Smooth faces of our festive friends. Say, Myrrha,
Art thou of those who dread the roar of clouds?
Myr. In my own country we respect their voices
As auguries of Jove.[62]
Sar.   Jove!—ay, your Baal—   550
Ours also has a property in thunder,
And ever and anon some falling bolt
Proves his divinity, and yet sometimes
Strikes his own altars.
Myr.   That were a dread omen.
Sar. Yes—for the priests. Well, we will not go forth
Beyond the palace walls to-night, but make
Our feast within.
Myr.   Now, Jove be praised! that he
Hath heard the prayer thou wouldst not hear.
    The gods
Are kinder to thee than thou to thyself,
And flash this storm between thee and thy foes,   560
To shield thee from them.
Sar.   Child, if there be peril,
Methinks it is the same within these walls
As on the river's brink.
Myr.   Not so; these walls
Are high and strong, and guarded. Treason has

To penetrate through many a winding way,
And massy portal; but in the pavilion
There is no bulwark.
Sar.   No, nor in the palace,
Nor in the fortress, nor upon the top
Of cloud-fenced Caucasus, where the eagle sits
Nested in pathless clefts, if treachery be: 570
Even as the arrow finds the airy king,
The steel will reach the earthly. But be calm:
The men, or innocent or guilty, are
Banish'd, and far upon their way.
Myr.   They live, then?
Sar. So sanguinary?[63] *Thou!*
Myr.   I would not shrink
From just infliction of due punishment
On those who seek your life: wer't otherwise,
I should not merit mine. Besides, you heard
The princely Salemenes.
Sar.   This is strange;
The gentle and the austere are both against me,   580
And urge me to revenge.
Myr.   'Tis a Greek virtue.
Sar. But not a kingly one—I'll none on't; or
If ever I indulge in't, it shall be
With kings—my equals.
Myr.   These men sought to be so.
Sar. Myrrha, this is too feminine, and springs
From fear——
Myr.   For you.
Sar.   No matter—still 'tis fear.
I have observed your sex, once roused to wrath,
Are timidly vindictive to a pitch
Of perseverance, which I would not copy.
I thought you were exempt from this, as from   590
The childish helplessness of Asian women.
Myr. My lord, I am no boaster of my love,
Nor of my attributes; I have shared your splendour,
And will partake your fortunes. You may live
To find one slave more true than subject myriads:
But this the gods avert! I am content
To be beloved on trust for what I feel,
Rather than prove it to you in your griefs,
Which might not yield to any cares of mine.

62 *Jove*: Jupiter or Zeus, the king of the Greco-Roman
   Olympian gods.

63 *sanguinary*: bloodthirsty.

Sar. Grief cannot come where perfect love exists,   600
   Except to heighten it, and vanish from
   That which it could not scare away. Let's in—
   The hour approaches, and we must prepare
   To meet the invited guests who grace our feast.
        (Exeunt).

Act III.

Scene I: *The Hall of the Palace illuminated—
Sardanapalus and his Guests at Table—A Storm
without, and Thunder occasionally heard
during the Banquet.*

Sar. Fill full! Why this is as it should be: here
   Is my true realm, amidst bright eyes and faces
   Happy as fair! Here sorrow cannot reach.
Zames. Nor elsewhere—where the king is, pleasure
   sparkles.
Sar. Is not this better now than Nimrod's huntings,
   Or my wild grandam's chase in search of kingdoms
   She could not keep when conquer'd?
Altada.   Mighty though
   They were, as all thy royal line have been,
   Yet none of those who went before have reach'd
   The acmé[64] of Sardanapalus, who   10
   Has placed his joy in peace—the sole true glory.
Sar. And pleasure, good Altada, to which glory
   Is but the path. What is it that we seek?
   Enjoyment! We have cut the way short to it,
   And not gone tracking it through human ashes,
   Making a grave with every footstep.
Zam.   No;
   All hearts are happy, and all voices bless
   The king of peace, who holds a world in jubilee.
Sar. Art sure of that? I have heard otherwise;
   Some say that there be traitors.
Zam.   Traitors they   20
   Who dare to say so!—'Tis impossible.
   What cause?
Sar.   What cause? true,—fill the goblet up;
   We will not think of them: there are none such,
   Or if there be, they are gone.

---

64 *acmé*: the highest point, the culminating point of perfection.

Alt.   Guests, to my pledge!
   Down on your knees, and drink a measure to
   The safety of the king—the monarch, say I?
   The god Sardanapalus!
(Zames and the Guests kneel, and exclaim—)
               Mightier than
   His father Baal, the god Sardanapalus!
(It thunders as they kneel; some start up in confusion).
Zam. Why do you rise, my friends? In that strong peal
   His father gods consented.
Myr.   Menaced, rather.   30
   King, wilt thou bear this mad impiety?
Sar. Impiety!—nay, if the sires who reign'd
   Before me can be gods, I'll not disgrace
   Their lineage. But arise, my pious friends,
   Hoard your devotion for the thunderer there:
   I seek but to be loved, not worshipp'd.
Alt.   Both—
   Both you must ever be by all true subjects.
Sar. Methinks the thunders still increase: it is
   An awful night.
Myr.   Oh yes, for those who have
   No palace to protect their worshippers.   40
Sar. That's true, my Myrrha; and could I convert
   My realm to one wide shelter for the wretched,
   I'd do it.
Myr.   Thou'rt no god, then, not to be
   Able to work a will so good and general,
   As thy wish would imply.
Sar.   And your gods, then,
   Who can, and do not?
Myr.   Do not speak of that,
   Lest we provoke them.
Sar.   True, they love not censure
   Better than mortals. Friends, a thought has struck
   me:
   Were there no temples, would there, think ye, be
   Air worshippers—that is, when it is angry,   50
   And pelting as even now?
Myr.   The Persian prays
   Upon his mountain.[65]
Sar.   Yes, when the Sun shines.

---

65 *The Persian ... mountain*: an echo of Wordsworth's
Excursion IV:171–80. See also Byron's *Childe Harold's
Pilgrimage*, III, xci.

Myr. And I would ask if this your palace were
    Unroof'd and desolate, how many flatterers
    Would lick the dust in which the king lay low?
Alt. The fair Ionian is too sarcastic
    Upon a nation whom she knows not well;
    The Assyrians know no pleasure but their king's,
    And homage is their pride.
Sar.   Nay, pardon, guests,
    The fair Greek's readiness of speech.
Alt.   *Pardon!* sire: 60
    We honour her of all things next to thee.
    Hark! what was that?
Zam.   That! nothing but the jar
    Of distant portals shaken by the wind.
Alt. It sounded like the clash of—hark again!
Zam. The big rain pattering on the roof.
Sar.   No more.
    Myrrha, my love, hast thou thy shell[66] in order?
    Sing me a song of Sappho,[67] her, thou know'st,
    Who in thy country threw——
(Enter Pania, with his Sword and Garments bloody,
and disordered. The Guests rise in confusion).
Pan. (To the Guards)   Look to the portals;
    And with your best speed to the walls without.
    Your arms! To arms! The king's in danger. Monarch!   70
    Excuse this haste,—'tis faith.
Sar.   Speak on.
Pan.   It is
    As Salemenes fear'd; the faithless Satraps——
Sar. You are wounded—give some wine. Take
    breath, good Pania.
Pan. 'Tis nothing—a mere flesh wound. I am worn
    More with my speed to warn my sovereign,
    Than hurt in his defence.
Myr.   Well, Sir, the rebels.
Pan. Soon as Arbaces and Beleses reach'd
    Their stations in the city, they refused

To march; and on my attempt to use the power
    Which I was delegated with, they call'd   80
    Upon their troops, who rose in fierce defiance.
Myr. All?
Pan.   Too many.
Sar.   Spare not of thy free speech
    To spare mine ears the truth.
Pan.   My own slight guard
    Were faithful—and what's left of it is still so.
Myr. And are these all the force still faithful?
Pan.   No—
    The Bactrians, now led on by Salemenes,
    Who even then was on his way, still urged
    By strong suspicion of the Median chiefs,
    Are numerous, and make strong head against
    The rebels, fighting inch by inch, and forming   90
    An orb[68] around the palace, where they mean
    To centre all their force, and save the king.
    (He hesitates). I am charged to——
Myr.   'Tis no time for hesitation.
Pan. Prince Salemenes doth implore the king
    To arm himself, although but for a moment,
    And show himself unto the soldiers: his
    Sole presence in this instant might do more
    Than hosts can do in his behalf.
Sar.   What, ho!
    My armour there.
Myr.   And wilt thou?
Sar.   Will I not?
    Ho, there!—But seek not for the buckler;[69] 'tis   100
    Too heavy:—a light cuirass[70] and my sword.
    Where are the rebels?
Pan.   Scarce a furlong's length
    From the outward wall the fiercest conflict rages.
Sar. Then I may charge on horseback. Sfero, ho!
    Order my horse out.—There is space enough
    Even in our courts, and by the outer gate,
    To marshal half the horsemen of Arabia. *(Exit*
    Sfero for the armour).

---

66 *shell*: a lyre, from the legend that the first lyre was made
    from a tortoise shell.
67 *Sappho*: Sappho (ca. 612–580 BCE), Greek poet. As
    her date of birth coincides with the fall of Nineveh,
    Byron here engages in anachronism. McGann and
    Weller suggest an echo of Grillparzer's *Sappho*, which
    retells the legend that Sappho hurled herself into the
    sea after being rejected by Phaon.

68 *orb*: a sphere.
69 *buckler*: usually a small round shield, but here appar-
    ently a larger shield fastened by straps to the arms.
70 *cuirass*: a piece of armor, extending to the waist, con-
    sisting of a breastplate and a backplate that fasten to-
    gether.

Myr. How I do love thee!
Sar.   I ne'er doubted it.
Myr. But now I know thee.
Sar. (To his Attendant).   Bring down my spear too.—
    Where's Salemenes?
Pan.   Where a soldier should be,   110
    In the thick of the fight.
Sar.   Then hasten to him———Is
    The path still open, and communication
    Left 'twixt the palace and the phalanx?
Pan.   'Twas
    When I late left him, and I have no fear:
    Our troops were steady, and the phalanx form'd.
Sar. Tell him to spare his person for the present,
    And that I will not spare my own—and say,
    I come.
Pan.   There's victory in the very word. *(Exit*
        Pania).
Sar. Altada—Zames—forth, and arm ye! There
    Is all in readiness in the armoury.   120
    See that the women are bestow'd in safety
    In the remote apartments: let a guard
    Be set before them, with strict charge to quit
    The post but with their lives—command it, Zames.
    Altada, arm yourself, and return here;
    Your post is near our person.
(Exeunt Zames, Altada, and all save Myrrha. Enter
Sfero and others with the King's Arms, &c.).
Sfero.   King! your armour.
Sar. (Arming himself). Give me the cuirass—so: my
        baldric;[71] now
    My sword: I had forgot the helm, where is it?
    That's well—no, 'tis too heavy: you mistake, too—
    It was not this I meant, but that which bears   130
    A diadem around it.
Sfe.   Sire, I deem'd
    That too conspicuous from the precious stones
    To risk your sacred brow beneath—and, trust me,
    This is of better metal though less rich.
Sar. You deem'd! Are you too turn'd a rebel? Fellow!
    Your part is to obey: return, and—no—
    It is too late—I will go forth without it.

Sfe. At least, wear this.
Sar.   Wear Caucasus! why, 'tis
    A mountain on my temples.
Sfe.   Sire, the meanest
    Soldier goes not forth thus exposed to battle.   140
    All men will recognise you—for the storm
    Has ceased, and the moon breaks forth in her
        brightness.
Sar. I go forth to be recognised, and thus
    Shall be so sooner. Now—my spear! I'm arm'd.
(In going stops short, and turns to Sfero).
    Sfero—I had forgotten—bring the mirror.[72]
Sfe. The mirror, sire?
Sar.   Yes, sir, of polish'd brass,
    Brought from the spoils of India—but be speedy.
        (Exit Sfero).
Sar. Myrrha, retire unto a place of safety.
    Why went you not forth with the other damsels?
Myr. Because my place is here.
Sar.   And when I am gone——   150
Myr. I follow.
Sar.   *You!* to battle?
Myr.   If it were so,
    'Twere not the first Greek girl had trod the path.
    I will await here your *return.*
Sar.   The place
    Is spacious, and the first to be sought out,
    If they prevail; and, if it be so,
    And I return not——
Myr.   Still we meet again.
Sar. How?
Myr.   In the spot where all must meet at last—
    In Hades! if there be, as I believe,
    A shore beyond the Styx;[73] and if there be not,
    In ashes.
Sar.   Dar'st thou so much?
Myr.   I dare all things   160
    Except survive what I have loved, to be
    A rebel's booty: forth, and do your bravest.
(Re-enter Sfero with the mirror).

---

71 *baldric*: a belt, usually of leather and ornamented, worn
    over one shoulder, across the breast and under the op-
    posite arm, used to support a sword.

72 Byron's note: "Such the *mirror* Otho held / In the
    Illyrian field.—See *Juvenal*."
73 *Hades … Styx*: Hades is the classical underworld,
    reached by crossing the river Styx.

Sar. (Looking at himself).
This cuirass fits me well, the baldric better,
And the helm not at all. Methinks, I seem
(Flings away the helmet after trying it again).
Passing well in these toys; and now to prove them.
Altada! Where's Altada?
Sfe.   Waiting, Sire,
Without: he has your shield in readiness.
Sar. True; I forgot he is my shield-bearer
By right of blood, derived from age to age.
Myrrha, embrace me; yet once more—once more—   170
Love me, whate'er betide. My chiefest glory
Shall be to make me worthier of your love.
Myr. Go forth, and conquer!
(Exeunt Sardanapalus and Sfero).
                              Now, I am alone.
All are gone forth, and of that all how few
Perhaps return. Let him but vanquish, and
Me perish! If he vanquish not, I perish;
For I will not outlive him. He has wound
About my heart, I know not how nor why.
Not for that he is king; for now his kingdom
Rocks underneath his throne, and the earth yawns   180
To yield him no more of it than a grave;
And yet I love him more. Oh, mighty Jove!
Forgive this monstrous love for a barbarian,
Who knows not of Olympus:[74] yes, I love him
Now, now, far more than——Hark—to the war
  shout!
Methinks it nears me. If it should be so,
(She draws forth a small vial).
This cunning Colchian poison,[75] which my father
Learn'd to compound on Euxine[76] shores, and
  taught me
How to preserve, shall free me! It had freed me
Long ere this hour, but that I loved, until   190
I half forgot I was a slave:—where all

---

[74] *Olympus*: a mountain in Greece and home of the Greco-Roman gods.

[75] *Colchian poison*: Colchis, at the east end of the Black Sea south of the Caucasus mountains, was the legendary home of Medea, known for her command of witchcraft, including poisons.

[76] *Euxine*: The Euxine Sea is an ancient name for the Black Sea.

Are slaves save one, and proud of servitude,
So they are served in turn by something lower
In the degree of bondage, we forget
That shackles worn like ornaments no less
Are chains. Again that shout! and now the clash
Of arms—and now—and now—
(Enter Altada).
Alt.   Ho, Sfero, ho!
Myr. He is not here; what wouldst thou with him? How
  Goes on the conflict?
Alt.   Dubiously and fiercely.
Myr. And the king?
Alt.   Like a king. I must find Sfero,   200
And bring him a new spear with his own helmet.
He fights till now bare-headed, and by far
Too much exposed. The soldiers knew his face,
And the foe too; and in the moon's broad light,
His silk tiara and his flowing hair
Make him a mark too royal. Every arrow
Is pointed at the fair hair and fair features,
And the broad fillet[77] which crowns both.
Myr.   Ye gods,
Who fulmine[78] o'er my fathers' land, protect him!
Were you sent by the king?
Alt.   By Salemenes,   210
Who sent me privily upon this charge,
Without the knowledge of the careless sovereign.
The king! the king fights as he revels! ho!
What, Sfero! I will seek the armoury,
He must be there. *(Exit Altada).*
Myr.   'Tis no dishonour—no—
'Tis no dishonour to have loved this man.
I almost wish now, what I never wish'd
Before, that he were Grecian. If Alcides
Were shamed in wearing Lydian Omphale's
She-garb,[79] and wielding her vile distaff; surely   220
He, who springs up a Hercules at once,
Nurs'd in effeminate arts from youth to manhood,
And rushes from the banquet to the battle,

---

[77] *fillet*: headband.

[78] *fulmine*: literally, to thunder (to fulminate), but by extension to speak out loudly and fiercely. See Milton, *Paradise Regained*, IV:270.

[79] *Alcides … She-garb*: Alcides is another name for Hercules. See note 44.

As though it were a bed of love, deserves
That a Greek girl should be his paramour,
And a Greek bard his minstrel, a Greek tomb
His monument. How goes the strife, sir?
(Enter an Officer).

Officer.   Lost,
Lost almost past recovery. Zames! Where
Is Zames?

Myr.   Posted with the guard appointed
To watch before the apartment of the women.   230
        (Exit Officer).

Myr. (solus). He's gone; and told no more than that
        all's lost!
What need have I to know more? In those words,
Those little words, a kingdom and a king,
A line of thirteen ages, and the lives
Of thousands, and the fortune of all left
With life, are merged; and I, too, with the great,
Like a small bubble breaking with the wave
Which bore it, shall be nothing. At the least
My fate is in my keeping: no proud victor
Shall count me with his spoils.
(Enter Pania).

Pan.   Away with me,   240
Myrrha, without delay; we must not lose
A moment—all that's left us now.

Myr.   The king?

Pan. Sent me here to conduct you hence, beyond
The river, by a secret passage.

Myr.   Then
He lives——

Pan.   And charged me to secure your life,
And beg you to live on for his sake, till
He can rejoin you.

Myr.   Will he then give way?

Pan. Not till the last. Still, still he does whate'er
Despair can do; and step by step disputes
The very palace.

Myr.   They are here, then:—ay,   250
Their shouts come ringing through the ancient halls,
Never profaned by rebel echoes till
This fatal night. Farewell, Assyria's line!
Farewell to all of Nimrod! Even the name
Is now no more.

Pan.   Away with me—away!

Myr. No; I'll die here!—Away, and tell your king
I loved him to the last.

(Enter Sardanapalus and Salemenes with Soldiers.
Pania quits Myrrha, and ranges himself with them).

Sar.   Since it is thus,
We'll die where we were born—in our own halls.
Serry[80] your ranks—stand firm. I have despatch'd
A trusty satrap for the guard of Zames,   260
All fresh and faithful; they'll be here anon.
All is not over.—Pania, look to Myrrha.
(Pania returns towards Myrrha).

Sal. We have breathing time: yet once more charge,
        my friends—
One for Assyria!

Sar.   Rather say for Bactria!
My faithful Bactrians, I will henceforth be
King of your nation, and we'll hold together
This realm as province.

Sal.   Hark! they come—they come.
(Enter Beleses and Arbaces with the Rebels).

Arb. Set on, we have them in the toil. Charge! Charge!

Bel. On! on!—Heaven fights for us and with us.—On!
(They charge the King and Salemenes with their
Troops, who defend themselves till the Arrival of Zames
with the Guard before mentioned. The Rebels are then
driven off, and pursued by Salemenes, &c. As the King
is going to join the pursuit, Beleses crosses him).

Bel. Ho! tyrant—I will end this war.

Sar.   Even so,   270
My warlike priest, and precious prophet, and
Grateful and trusty subject: yield, I pray thee.
I would reserve thee for a fitter doom,
Rather than dip my hands in holy blood.

Bel. Thine hour is come.

Sar.   No, thine.—I've lately read,
Though but a young astrologer, the stars;
And ranging round the zodiac, found thy fate
In the sign of the Scorpion, which proclaims
That thou wilt now be crush'd.

Bel.   But not by thee.
(They fight; Beleses is wounded and disarmed).

Sar. (Raising his sword to despatch him, exclaims—)
Now call upon thy planets, will they shoot   280
From the sky to preserve their seer and credit?
(A party of Rebels enter and rescue Beleses. They assail
the King, who, in turn, is rescued by a Party of his
Soldiers, who drive the Rebels off).

---

80 *Serry:* close up, press close together.

The villain was a prophet after all.
Upon them—ho! there—victory is ours. *(Exit in
        pursuit).*
Myr. (To Pania). Pursue! Why stand'st thou here,
        and leavest the ranks
Of fellow-soldiers conquering without thee?
Pan. The king's command was not to quit thee.
Myr.   Me!
Think not of me—a single soldier's arm
Must not be wanting now. I ask no guard,
I need no guard: what, with a world at stake,
Keep watch upon a woman? Hence, I say,   290
Or thou art shamed! Nay, then, *I* will go forth,
A feeble female, 'midst their desperate strife,
And bid thee guard me *there*—where thou
        shouldst shield
Thy sovereign. *(Exit Myrrha).*
Pan.   Yet stay, damsel! She is gone.
If aught of ill betide her, better I
Had lost my life. Sardanapalus holds her
Far dearer than his kingdom, yet he fights
For that too; and can I do less than he,
Who never flash'd a scimitar till now?
Myrrha, return, and I obey you, though   300
In disobedience to the monarch. *(Exit Pania).*
(Enter Altada and Sfero by an opposite door).
Alt.   Myrrha!
What, gone? yet she was here when the fight raged,
And Pania also. Can aught have befallen them?
Sfe. I saw both safe, when late the rebels fled:
They probably are but retired to make
Their way back to the harem.
Alt.   If the king
Prove victor, as it seems even now he must,
And miss his own Ionian, we are doom'd
To worse than captive rebels.
Sfe.   Let us trace them;
She cannot be fled far; and, found, she makes   310
A richer prize to our soft sovereign
Than his recover'd kingdom.
Alt.   Baal himself
Ne'er fought more fiercely to win empire, than
His silken son to save it: he defies
All augury of foes or friends; and like
The close and sultry summer's day, which bodes
A twilight tempest, bursts forth in such thunder
As sweeps the air and deluges the earth.
The man's inscrutable.
Sfe.   Not more than others.
All are the sons of circumstance; away—   320
Let's seek the slave out, or prepare to be
Tortured for his infatuation, and
Condemn'd without a crime. *(Exeunt).*
(Enter Salemenes and Soldiers, &c.).
Sal.   The triumph is
Flattering: they are beaten backward from the palace,
And we have open'd regular access
To the troops station'd on the other side
Euphrates, who may still be true; nay, must be,
When they hear of our victory. But where
Is the chief victor? where's the king?
(Enter Sardanapalus, cum suis,[81] *&c., and Myrrha).*
Sar.   Here, brother.
Sal. Unhurt, I hope.
Sar.   Not quite; but let it pass.   330
We've clear'd the palace——
Sal.   And I trust the city.
Our numbers gather; and I've order'd onward
A cloud of Parthians,[82] hitherto reserved,
All fresh and fiery, to be pour'd upon them
In their retreat, which soon will be a flight.
Sar. It is already, or at least they march'd
Faster than I could follow with my Bactrians,
Who spared no speed. I am spent; give me a seat.
Sal. There stands the throne, Sire.
Sar.   'Tis no place to rest on,
For mind nor body; let me have a couch,   340
(They place a seat).
A peasant's stool, I care not what: so—now
I breathe more freely.
Sal.   This great hour has proved
The brightest and most glorious of your life.
Sar. And the most tiresome. Where's my cup-bearer?
Bring me some water.
Sal. (Smiling).   'Tis the first time he
Ever had such an order: even I,
Your most austere of counsellors, would now

---

81 *cum suis*: with his suite.
82 *Parthians*: Parthia was an ancient land corresponding
    roughly to the modern region of Khorasan in Iran. The
    Parthian empire stood from 247 BCE–224 CE.

Suggest a purpler beverage.

Sar.   Blood—doubtless.
But there's enough of that shed; as for wine,
I have learn'd to-night the price of the pure element: 350
Thrice have I drank of it, and thrice renew'd,
With greater strength than the grape ever gave me,
My charge upon the rebels. Where's the soldier
Who gave me water in his helmet?

One of the Guards.   Slain, Sire!
An arrow pierced his brain, while, scattering
The last drops from his helm, he stood in act
To place it on his brows.

Sar.   Slain! unrewarded!
And slain to serve my thirst: that's hard, poor slave!
Had he but lived, I would have gorged him with
Gold: all the gold of earth could ne'er repay   360
The pleasure of that draught; for I was parch'd
As I am now.

(They bring water—he drinks).

                    I live again—from henceforth
The goblet I reserve for hours of love,
But war on water.

Sal.   And that bandage, sire,
Which girds your arm?

Sar.   A scratch from brave Beleses.

Myr. Oh! he is wounded!

Sar.   Not too much of that;
And yet it feels a little stiff and painful,
Now I am cooler.

Myr.   You have bound it with——

Sar. The fillet of my diadem: the first time
That ornament was ever aught to me,   370
Save an incumbrance.

Myr. (To the Attendants). Summon speedily
A leech[83] of the most skilful: pray, retire;
I will unbind your wound and tend it.

Sar.   Do so,
For now it throbs sufficiently: but what
Know'st thou of wounds? yet wherefore do I ask.
Know'st thou, my brother, where I lighted on
This minion?[84]

Sal.   Herding with the other females,
Like frighten'd antelopes.

Sar.   No: like the dam
Of the young lion, femininely raging,
(And femininely meaneth furiously,   380
Because all passions in excess are female),[85]
Against the hunter flying with her cub,
She urged on with her voice and gesture, and
Her floating hair and flashing eyes,[86] the soldiers,
In the pursuit.

Sal.   Indeed!

Sar.   You see, this night
Made warriors of more than me. I paused
To look upon her, and her kindled cheek;
Her large black eyes, that flash'd through her long
    hair
As it stream'd o'er her; her blue veins that rose
Along her most transparent brow; her nostril   390
Dilated from its symmetry; her lips
Apart; her voice that clove through all the din,
As a lute's pierceth through the cymbal's clash,
Jarr'd but not drown'd by the loud brattling; her
Waved arms, more dazzling with their own born
    whiteness
Than the steel her hand held, which she caught up
From a dead soldier's grasp; all these things made
Her seem unto the troops a prophetess
Of victory, or Victory herself,
Come down to hail us hers.

Sal. (Aside).   This is too much.   400
Again the love-fit's on him, and all's lost,
Unless we turn his thoughts. *(Aloud).* But pray
    thee, Sire,
Think of your wound—you said even now 'twas
    painful.

Sar. That's true, too; but I must not think of it.

Sal. I have look'd to all things needful, and will now
Receive reports of progress made in such
Orders as I had given, and then return
To hear your further pleasure.

Sar.   Be it so.

---

83 *leech*: a physician.

84 *minion*: both a favorite in the sense of one who owes
    everything to a sovereign, and one specially beloved
    or favored, a lover.

85 *femininely ... female*: McGann and Weller suggest an
    echo of *Hamlet*, III.ii.165–6.

86 *floating hair and flashing eyes*: an echo of Coleridge's
    "Kubla Khan," line 50.

Sal. (In retiring). Myrrha!

Myr.   Prince.

Sal.   You have shown a
    soul to-night,

    Which, were he not my sister's lord——But now   410
    I have no time: thou lov'st the king?

Myr.   I love
    Sardanapalus.

Sal.   But wouldst have him king still?

Myr. I would not have him less than what he should be.

Sal. Well, then, to have him king, and yours, and all
    He should, or should not be; to have him *live*,
    Let him not sink back into luxury.
    You have more power upon his spirit than
    Wisdom within these walls, or fierce rebellion
    Raging without: look well that he relapse not.

Myr. There needed not the voice of Salemenes   420
    To urge me on to this: I will not fail.
    All that a woman's weakness can—

Sal.   Is power
    Omnipotent o'er such a heart as his;
    Exert it wisely. *(Exit Salemenes).*

Sar.   Myrrha! what, at whispers
    With my stern brother? I shall soon be jealous.

Myr. (Smiling). You have cause, sire; for on the earth
    there breathes not
    A man more worthy of a woman's love—
    A soldier's trust—a subject's reverence—
    A king's esteem—the whole world's admiration!

Sar. Praise him, but not so warmly. I must not   430
    Hear those sweet lips grow eloquent in aught
    That throws me into shade; yet you speak truth.

Myr. And now retire, to have your wound look'd to,
    Pray, lean on me.

Sar.   Yes, love! but not from pain.
    (Exeunt omnes).

Act IV.

Scene I: *Sardanapalus discovered sleeping
upon a Couch, and occasionally disturbed
in his Slumbers, with Myrrha watching.*

Myr. (sola,[87] *gazing).* I have stolen upon his rest, if
    rest it be,

---

87 *sola*: alone.

Which thus convulses slumber: shall I wake him?
No, he seems calmer. Oh, thou God of Quiet![88]
Whose reign is o'er seal'd eyelids and soft dreams,
Or deep, deep sleep, so as to be unfathom'd,
Look like thy brother, Death—so still—so stirless—
For then we are happiest, as it may be, we
Are happiest of all within the realm
Of thy stern, silent, and unwakening twin.
Again he moves—again the play of pain   10
Shoots o'er his features, as the sudden gust
Crisps the reluctant lake that lay so calm
Beneath the mountain shadow; or the blast
Ruffles the autumn leaves, that drooping cling
Faintly and motionless to their loved boughs.
I must awake him—yet not yet: who knows
From what I rouse him? It seems pain; but if
I quicken him to heavier pain? The fever
Of this tumultuous night, the grief too of
His wound, though slight, may cause all this, and   20
    shake
Me more to see than him to suffer. No:
Let Nature use her own maternal means,—
And I await to second, not disturb her.

Sar. (Awakening). Not so—although ye multiplied
    the stars,
And gave them to me as a realm to share
From you and with you! I would not so purchase
The empire of eternity. Hence—hence—
Old hunter of the earliest brutes! and ye,
Who hunted fellow-creatures as if brutes;
Once bloody mortals—and now bloodier idols,   30
If your priests lie not! And thou, ghastly beldame!
Dripping with dusky gore, and trampling on
The carcasses of Inde—away! away!
Where am I? Where the spectres? Where——
    No—that
Is no false phantom: I should know it 'midst
All that the dead dare gloomily raise up
From their black gulf to daunt the living. Myrrha!

Myr. Alas! thou art pale, and on thy brow the drops
    Gather like night dew. My beloved, hush—

---

88 *God of Quiet*: The Greco-Roman god of sleep was
   Hypnos in Greek, Somnus in Latin. He was the son
   of Nyx (Night) and the brother of Thanatos (Death),
   as indicated in line 6.

Calm thee. Thy speech seems of another world,   40
And thou art lord of this. Be of good cheer;
All will go well.
Sar.   Thy *hand*—so—'tis thy hand;
'Tis flesh; grasp—clasp—yet closer, till I feel
Myself that which I was.
Myr.   At least know me
For what I am, and ever must be—thine.
Sar. I know it now. I know this life again.
Ah, Myrrha! I have been where we shall be.
Myr. My lord!
Sar.   I've been i' the grave—where worms
    are lords,
And kings are——But I did not deem it so;
I thought 'twas nothing.
Myr.   So it is; except   50
Unto the timid, who anticipate
That which may never be.
Sar.   Oh, Myrrha! if
Sleep shows such things, what may not death
    disclose?
Myr. I know no evil death can show, which life
Has not already shown to those who live
Embodied longest. If there be indeed
A shore, where mind survives, 'twill be as mind,
All unincorporate: or if there flits
A shadow of this cumbrous clog of clay,
Which stalks, methinks, between our souls and   60
    heaven,
And fetters us to earth—at least the phantom,
Whate'er it have to fear, will not fear death.
Sar. I fear it not; but I have felt—have seen—
A legion of the dead.
Myr.   And so have I.
The dust we tread upon was once alive,
And wretched. But proceed: what hast thou seen?
Speak it, 'twill lighten thy dimm'd mind.
Sar.   Methought——
Myr. Yet pause, thou art tired—in pain—exhausted; all
Which can impair both strength and spirit: seek
Rather to sleep again.
Sar.   Not now—I would not   70
Dream; though I know it now to be a dream
What I have dreamt:—and canst thou bear to
    hear it?
Myr. I can bear all things, dreams of life or death,

Which I participate with you, in semblance
Or full reality.
Sar.   And this look'd real,
I tell you: after that these eyes were open,
I saw them in their flight—for then they fled.
Myr. Say on.
Sar.   I saw, that is, I dream'd myself
Here—here—even where we are, guests as we were,
Myself a host that deem'd himself but guest,   80
Willing to equal all in social freedom;
But, on my right hand and my left, instead
Of thee and Zames, and our custom'd meeting,
Was ranged on my left hand a haughty, dark,
And deadly face—I could not recognise it,
Yet I had seen it, though I knew not where;
The features were a giant's, and the eye
Was still, yet lighted; his long locks curl'd down
On his vast bust, whence a huge quiver rose
With shaft-heads feather'd from the eagle's wing,   90
That peep'd up bristling through his serpent hair.
I invited him to fill the cup which stood
Between us, but he answer'd not—I fill'd it—
He took it not, but stared upon me, till
I trembled at the fix'd glare of his eye:
I frown'd upon him as a king should frown—
He frown'd not in his turn, but look'd upon me
With the same aspect, which appall'd me more,
Because it changed not; and I turn'd for refuge
To milder guests, and sought them on the right,   100
Where thou wert wont to be. But—— *(He pauses).*
Myr.   What instead?
Sar. In thy own chair—thy own place in the banquet—
I sought thy sweet face in the circle—but
Instead—a grey-hair'd, wither'd, bloody-eyed,
And bloody-handed, ghastly, ghostly thing,
Female in garb, and crown'd upon the brow,
Furrow'd with years, yet sneering with the passion
Of vengeance, leering too with that of lust,
Sate:—my veins curdled.
Myr.   Is this all?
Sar.   Upon
Her right hand—her lank, bird-like right hand—   110
    stood
A goblet, bubbling o'er with blood; and on
Her left, another, fill'd with—what I saw not,
But turn'd from it and her. But all along

The table sate a range of crowned wretches,
Of various aspects, but of one expression.
Myr. And felt you not this a mere vision?
Sar.   No:
It was so palpable, I could have touch'd them.
I turn'd from one face to another, in
The hope to find at last one which I knew
Ere I saw theirs: but no—all turn'd upon me,   120
And stared, but neither ate nor drank, but stared,
Till I grew stone, as they seem'd half to be,
Yet breathing stone, for I felt life in them,
And life in me: there was a horrid kind
Of sympathy between us, as if they
Had lost a part of death to come to me,
And I the half of life to sit by them.
We were in an existence all apart
From heaven or earth——And rather let me see
Death all than such a being!
Myr.   And the end?   130
Sar. At last I sate marble as they, when rose
The hunter, and the crew; and smiling on me—
Yes, the enlarged but noble aspect of
The hunter smiled upon me—I should say,
His lips, for his eyes moved not—and the woman's
Thin lips relax'd to something like a smile.
Both rose, and the crown'd figures on each hand
Rose also, as if aping their chief shades—
Mere mimics even in death—but I sate still:
A desperate courage crept through every limb,   140
And at the last I fear'd them not, but laugh'd
Full in their phantom faces. But then—then
The hunter laid his hand on mine: I took it,
And grasp'd it—but it melted from my own,
While he too vanish'd, and left nothing but
The memory of a hero, for he look'd so.
Myr. And was: the ancestor of heroes, too,
And thine no less.
Sar.   Ay, Myrrha, but the woman,
The female who remain'd, she flew upon me,
And burnt my lips up with her noisome[89] kisses;   150
And, flinging down the goblets on each hand,
Methought their poisons flow'd around us, till
Each form'd a hideous river. Still she clung;
The other phantoms, like a row of statues,

Stood dull as in our temples, but she still
Embraced me, while I shrunk from her, as if,
In lieu of her remote descendant, I
Had been the son who slew her for her incest.[90]
Then—then—a chaos of all loathsome things
Throng'd thick and shapeless: I was dead, yet   160
    feeling—
Buried, and raised again—consumed by worms,
Purged by the flames, and wither'd in the air!
I can fix nothing further of my thoughts,
Save that I long'd for thee, and sought for thee,
In all these agonies, and woke and found thee.
Myr. So shalt thou find me ever at thy side,
Here and hereafter, if the last may be.
But think not of these things—the mere creations
Of late events acting upon a frame
Unused to toil, yet over-wrought by toil   170
Such as might try the sternest.
Sar.   I am better.
Now that I see *thee once* more, *what was seen*
Seems nothing.
(Enter Salemenes).
Sal.   Is the king so soon awake?
Sar. Yes, brother, and I would I had not slept;
For all the predecessors of our line
Rose up, methought, to drag me down to them.
My father was amongst them, too; but he,
I know not why, kept from me, leaving me
Between the hunter-founder of our race,
And her, the homicide and husband-killer,   180
Whom you call glorious.
Sal.   So I term you also,
Now you have shown a spirit like to hers.
By day-break I propose that we set forth,
And charge once more the rebel crew, who still
Keep gathering head, repulsed, but not quite quell'd.
Sar. How wears the night?
Sal.   There yet remain some hours
Of darkness: use them for your further rest.
Sar. No, not to-night, if 'tis not gone: methought
I pass'd hours in that vision.

---

89 *noisome*: harmful, noxious.

90 *son … incest*: For this aspect of Semiramis' story, E. H.
Coleridge cites Book I, chapter ii of the works of the
Roman historian Justinus; McGann and Weller suggest
Byron may have known Voltaire's *Semiramis* (1748).

Myr.   Scarcely one;
  I watch'd by you: it was a heavy hour,   190
  But an hour only.
Sar.   Let us then hold council;
  To-morrow we set forth.
Sal.   But ere that time,
  I had a grace to seek.
Sar.   'Tis granted.
Sal.   Hear it
  Ere you reply too readily; and 'tis
  For *your* ear only.
Myr.   Prince, I take my leave.
    (Exit Myrrha).
Sal. That slave deserves her freedom.
Sar.   Freedom only!
  That slave deserves to share a throne.
Sal.   Your patience—
  'Tis not yet vacant, and 'tis of its partner
  I come to speak with you.
Sar.   How! of the queen?
Sal. Even so. I judged it fitting for their safety,   200
  That, ere the dawn, she sets forth with her children
  For Paphlagonia,[91] where our kinsman Cotta[92]
  Governs; and there at all events secure
  My nephews and your sons their lives, and with them
  Their just pretensions to the crown in case——
Sar. I perish—as is probable: well thought—
  Let them set forth with a sure escort.
Sal.   That
  Is all provided, and the galley ready
  To drop down the Euphrates; but ere they
  Depart, will you not see——
Sar.   My sons? It may   210
  Unman my heart, and the poor boys will weep;
  And what can I reply to comfort them,
  Save with some hollow hopes, and ill-worn smiles?
  You know I cannot feign.
Sal.   But you can feel;
  At least, I trust so: in a word, the queen

Requests to see you ere you part—for ever.
Sar. Unto what end? what purpose? I will grant
  Aught—all that she can ask—but such a meeting.
Sal. You know, or ought to know, enough of women,
  Since you have studied them so steadily,   220
  That what they ask in aught that touches on
  The heart, is dearer to their feelings or
  Their fancy, than the whole external world.
  I think as you do of my sister's wish;
  But 'twas her wish—she is my sister—you
  Her husband—will you grant it?
Sar.   'Twill be useless:
  But let her come.
Sal.   I go. *(Exit Salemenes).*
Sar.   We have lived asunder
  Too long to meet again—and *now* to meet!
  Have I not cares enow,[93] and pangs enow,
  To bear alone, that we must mingle sorrows,   230
  Who have ceased to mingle love?
(Re-enter Salemenes and Zarina).
Sal.   My sister! Courage:
  Shame not our blood with trembling, but remember
  From whence we sprung. The queen is present, sire.
Zar. I pray thee, brother, leave me.
Sal.   Since you ask it.
    (Exit Salemenes).
Zarina. Alone with him! How many a year has passed,
  Though we are still so young, since we have met,
  Which I have worn in widowhood of heart.
  He loved me not: yet he seems little changed—
  Changed to me only—would the change were
    mutual!
  He speaks not—scarce regards me—not a word—   240
  Nor look—yet he *was* soft of voice and aspect,
  Indifferent, not austere. My lord!
Sar.   Zarina!
Zar. No, *not* Zarina—do not say Zarina.
  That tone—that word—annihilate long years,
  And things which make them longer.
Sar.   'Tis too late

---

91 *Paphlagonia*: an ancient district of Anatolia adjoining
    the Black Sea, bounded by Bithynia in the west,
    Pontus in the east, and Galatia in the south.
92 *Cotta*: Diodorus (II.xxvi:8) indicates he is the gover-
    nor of Paphlagonia and "the most loyal" of
    Sardanapalus' subjects.

93 *enow*: for enough. McGann and Weller suggest that
    the meeting between Sardanapalus and his wife both
    echoes the meeting of Antony and Octavia in Act III
    of Dryden's *All for Love* and presents an imaginary re-
    union between Byron and Lady Byron.

To think of these past dreams. Let's not reproach—
That is, reproach me not—for the *last* time——
Zar. And *first.* I ne'er reproach'd you.
Sar.   'Tis most true;
And that reproof comes heavier on my heart
Than——But our hearts are not in our own power.   250
Zar. Nor hands; but I gave both.
Sar.   Your brother said,
It was your will to see me, ere you went
From Nineveh with—— *(He hesitates).*
Zar.   Our children: it is true.
I wish'd to thank you that you have not divided
My heart from all that's left it now to love—
Those who are yours and mine, who look like you,
And look upon me as you look'd upon me
Once——but they have not changed.
Sar.   Nor ever will.
I fain would have them dutiful.
Zar.   I cherish
Those infants, not alone from the blind love   260
Of a fond mother, but as a fond woman.
They are now the only tie between us.
Sar.   Deem not
I have not done you justice: rather make them
Resemble your own line, than their own sire.
I trust them with you—to you: fit them for
A throne, or, if that be denied——You have heard
Of this night's tumults?
Zar.   I had half forgotten,
And could have welcomed any grief, save yours,
Which gave me to behold your face again.
Sar. The throne—I say it not in fear—but 'tis   270
In peril: they perhaps may never mount it:
But let them not for this lose sight of it.
I will dare all things to bequeath it them;
But if I fail, then they must win it back
Bravely—and, won, wear it wisely, not as I
Have wasted down my royalty.
Zar.   They ne'er
Shall know from me of aught but what may honour
Their father's memory.
Sar.   Rather let them hear
The truth from you than from a trampling world.
If they be in adversity, they'll learn   280
Too soon the scorn of crowds for crownless princes,
And find that all their father's sins are theirs.
My boys!—I could have borne it were I childless.

Zar. Oh! do not say so—do not poison all
My peace left, by unwishing that thou wert
A father. If thou conquerest, they shall reign,
And honour him who saved the realm for them,
So little cared for as his own; and if——
Sar. 'Tis lost, all earth will cry out thank your father!
And they will swell the echo with a curse.   290
Zar. That they shall never do; but rather honour
The name of him, who, dying like a king,
In his last hours did more for his own memory
Than many monarchs in a length of days,
Which date the flight of time, but make no annals.
Sar. Our annals draw perchance unto their close;
But at the least, whate'er the past, their end
Shall be like their beginning—memorable.
Zar. Yet, be not rash—be careful of your life,
Live but for those who love.
Sar.   And who are they?   300
A slave, who loves from passion—I'll not say
Ambition—she has seen thrones shake, and loves;
A few friends, who have revell'd till we are
As one, for they are nothing if I fall;
A brother I have injured—children whom
I have neglected, and a spouse——
Zar.   Who loves.
Sar. And pardons?
Zar.   I have never thought of this,
And cannot pardon till I have condemn'd.
Sar. My wife!
Zar.   Now blessings on thee for that word!
I never thought to hear it more—from thee.   310
Sar. Oh! thou wilt hear it from my subjects. Yes—
These slaves, whom I have nurtured, pamper'd, fed,
And swoln with peace, and gorged with plenty, till
They reign themselves—all monarchs in their
    mansions—
Now swarm forth in rebellion, and demand
His death, who made their lives a jubilee;
While the few upon whom I have no claim
Are faithful! This is true, yet monstrous.
Zar.   'Tis
Perhaps too natural; for benefits
Turn poison in bad minds.
Sar.   And good ones make   320
Good out of evil. Happier than the bee,
Which hives not but from wholesome flowers.

Zar.   Then reap
  The honey, nor inquire whence 'tis derived.
  Be satisfied—you are not all abandon'd.
Sar. My life insures me that. How long, bethink you,
  Were not I yet a king, should I be mortal;
  That is, where mortals *are*, not where they must be?
Zar. I know not. But yet live for my—that is,
  Your children's sake!
Sar.   My gentle, wrong'd Zarina!
  I am the very slave of circumstance   330
  And impulse—borne away with every breath!
  Misplaced upon the throne—misplaced in life.
  I know not what I could have been, but feel
  I am not what I should be—let it end.
  But take this with thee: if I was not form'd
  To prize a love like thine, a mind like thine,
  Nor dote even on thy beauty—as I've doted
  On lesser charms, for no cause save that such
  Devotion was a duty, and I hated
  All that look'd like a chain for me or others,   340
  (This even rebellion must avouch); yet hear
  These words, perhaps among my last—that none
  E'er valued more thy virtues, though he knew not
  To profit by them—as the miner lights
  Upon a vein of virgin ore, discovering
  That which avails him nothing: he hath found it,
  But 'tis not his—but some superior's, who
  Placed him to dig, but not divide the wealth
  Which sparkles at his feet; nor dare he lift
  Nor poise it, but must grovel on upturning   350
  The sullen earth.
Zar.   Oh! if thou hast at length
  Discover'd that my love is worth esteem,
  I ask no more—but let us hence together,
  And *I*—let me say *we*—shall yet be happy.
  Assyria is not all the earth—we'll find
  A world out of our own—and be more blest
  Than I have ever been, or thou, with all
  An empire to indulge thee.
(Enter Salemenes).
Sal.   I must part ye—
  The moments, which must not be lost, are passing.
Zar. Inhuman brother! wilt thou thus weigh out   360
  Instants so high and blest?
Sal.   Blest!
Zar.   He hath been

So gentle with me, that I cannot think
  Of quitting.
Sal.   So—this feminine farewell
  Ends as such partings end, in *no* departure.
  I thought as much, and yielded against all
  My better bodings. But it must not be.
Zar. Not be?
Sal.   Remain, and perish——
Zar.   With my husband——
Sal. And children.
Zar.   Alas!
Sal.   Hear me, sister, like
  My sister:—all's prepared to make your safety
  Certain, and of the boys too, our last hopes.   370
  'Tis not a single question of mere feeling,
  Though that were much—but 'tis a point of state:
  The rebels would do more to seize upon
  The offspring of their sovereign, and so crush——
Zar. Ah! do not name it.
Sal.   Well, then, mark me: when
  They are safe beyond the Median's grasp, the rebels
  Have miss'd their chief aim—the extinction of
  The line of Nimrod. Though the present king
  Fall, his sons live for victory and vengeance.
Zar. But could not I remain, alone?
Sal.   What! leave   380
  Your children, with two parents and yet orphans—
  In a strange land—so young, so distant?
Zar.   No—
  My heart will break.
Sal.   Now you know all—decide.
Sar. Zarina, he hath spoken well, and we
  Must yield awhile to this necessity.
  Remaining here, you may lose all; departing,
  You save the better part of what is left,
  To both of us, and to such loyal hearts
  As yet beat in these kingdoms.
Sal.   The time presses.
Sar. Go, then. If e'er we meet again, perhaps   390
  I may be worthier of you—and, if not,
  Remember that my faults, though not atoned for,
  Are *ended.* Yet, I dread thy nature will
  Grieve more above the blighted name and ashes
  Which once were mightiest in Assyria—than——
  But I grow womanish again, and must not;
  I must learn sternness now. My sins have all

Been of the softer order——*hide* thy tears—
I do not bid thee *not* to shed them—'twere
Easier to stop Euphrates at its source   400
Than one tear of a true and tender heart—
But let me not behold them; they unman me
Here when I had remann'd myself. My brother,
Lead her away.

Zar.   Oh, god! I never shall
Behold him more!

Sal. (Striving to conduct her). Nay, sister, I *must* be
obeyed.

Zar. I must remain—away! you shall not hold me.
What, shall he die alone?—*I* live alone?

Sal. He shall *not die alone*; but lonely you
Have lived for years.

Zar.   That's false! I knew *he* lived,
And lived upon his image—let me go!   410

Sal. (Conducting her off the stage).
Nay, then, then, I must use some fraternal force,
Which you will pardon.

Zar.   Never. Help me! Oh!
Sardanapalus, wilt thou thus behold me
Torn from thee?

Sal.   Nay—then all is lost again,
If that this moment is not gain'd.

Zar.   My brain turns—
My eyes fail—where is he? *(She faints)*.

Sar. (Advancing).   No—set her down—
She's dead—and you have slain her.

Sal.   'Tis the mere
Faintness of o'er-wrought passion: in the air
She will recover. Pray, keep back.—*(Aside)* I must
Avail myself of this sole moment to   420
Bear her to where her children are embark'd,
I' the royal galley on the river. *(Salemenes bears her off)*.

Sar. (Solus).   This, too—
And this too must I suffer—I, who never
Inflicted purposely on human hearts
A voluntary pang! But that is false—
She loved me, and I loved her. Fatal passion!
Why dost thou not expire *at once* in hearts
Which thou hast lighted up at once? Zarina!
I must pay dearly for the desolation
Now brought upon thee. Had I never loved   430
But thee, I should have been an unopposed

Monarch of honouring nations. To what gulfs
A single deviation from the track
Of human duties leads even those who claim
The homage of mankind as their born due,
And find it, till they forfeit it themselves!

(Enter Myrrha).

Sar. You here! Who call'd you?

Myr.   No one—but I heard
Far off a voice of wail and lamentation,
And thought——

Sar.   It forms no portion of your duties
To enter here till sought for.

Myr.   Though I might,   440
Perhaps, recal some softer words of yours
(Although they *too were chiding*), which reproved me,
Because I ever dreaded to intrude;
Resisting my own wish and your injunction
To heed no time nor presence, but approach you
Uncall'd for: I retire.

Sar.   Yet, stay—being here.
I pray you pardon me: events have sour'd me
Till I wax peevish—heed it not: I shall
Soon be myself again.

Myr.   I wait with patience,
What I shall see with pleasure.

Sar.   Scarce a moment   450
Before your entrance in this hall, Zarina,
Queen of Assyria, departed hence.

Myr. Ah!

Sar.   Wherefore do you start?

Myr.   Did I do so?

Sar. 'Twas well you enter'd by another portal,
Else you had met. That pang at least is spared her!

Myr. I know to feel for her.

Sar.   That is too much,
And beyond nature—'tis nor mutual
Nor possible. You cannot pity her,
Nor she aught but——

Myr.   Despise the favourite slave?
Not more than I have ever scorn'd myself.   460

Sar. Scorn'd! what, to be the envy of your sex,
And lord it o'er the heart of the world's lord?

Myr. Were you the lord of twice ten thousand worlds—
As you are like to lose the one you sway'd—
I did abase myself as much in being
Your paramour, as though you were a peasant—

Nay, more, if that the peasant were a Greek.
Sar. You talk it well——
Myr.   And truly.
Sar.   In the hour
  Of man's adversity all things grow daring
  Against the falling; but as I am not   470
  Quite fall'n, nor now disposed to bear reproaches,
  Perhaps because I merit them too often,
  Let us then part while peace is still between us.
Myr. Part!
Sar.   Have not all past human beings parted,
  And must not all the present one day part?
Myr. Why?
Sar.   For your safety, which I will have look'd to,
  With a strong escort to your native land;
  And such gifts, as, if you had not been all
  A queen, shall make your dowry worth a kingdom.
Myr. I pray you talk not thus.
Sar.   The queen is gone: 480
  You need not shame to follow. I would fall
  Alone—I seek no partners but in pleasure.
Myr. And I no pleasure but in parting not.
  You shall not force me from you.
Sar.   Think well of it—
  It soon may be too late.
Myr.   So let it be;
  For then you cannot separate me from you.
Sar. And will not; but I thought you wish'd it.
Myr.   I!
Sar. You spoke of your abasement.
Myr.   And I feel it
  Deeply—more deeply than all things but love.
Sar. Then fly from it.
Myr.   'Twill not recal the past—   490
  'Twill not restore my honour, nor my heart.
  No—here I stand or fall. If that you conquer,
  I live to joy in your great triumph; should
  Your lot be different, I'll not weep, but share it.
  You did not doubt me a few hours ago.
Sar. Your courage never—nor your love till now;
  And none could make me doubt it save yourself.
  Those words——
Myr.   Were words. I pray you, let the proofs
  Be in the past acts you were pleased to praise
  This very night, and in my further bearing,   500
  Beside, wherever you are borne by fate.

Sar. I am content; and, trusting in my cause,
  Think we may yet be victors and return
  To peace—the only victory I covet.
  To me war is no glory—conquest no
  Renown. To be forced thus to uphold my right
  Sits heavier on my heart than all the wrongs
  These men would bow me down with. Never, never
  Can I forget this night, even should I live
  To add it to the memory of others.   510
  I thought to have made mine inoffensive rule
  An era of sweet peace 'midst bloody annals,
  A green spot amidst desert centuries,
  On which the future would turn back and smile,
  And cultivate, or sigh when it could not
  Recal Sardanapalus' golden reign.
  I thought to have made my realm a paradise,
  And every moon an epoch of new pleasures.
  I took the rabble's shouts for love—the breath
  Of friends for truth—the lips of woman for   520
  My only guerdon[94]—so they are, my Myrrha:
  (He kisses her). Kiss me. Now let them take my
    realm and life!
  They shall have both, but never thee!
Myr.   No, never!
  Man may despoil his brother man of all
  That's great or glittering—kingdoms fall—hosts
    yield—
  Friends fail—slaves fly—and all betray—and, more
  Than all, the most indebted—but a heart
  That loves without self-love! 'Tis here—now
    prove it.
(Enter Salemenes).
Sal. I sought you.—How! *she* here again?
Sar.   Return not
  Now to reproof: methinks your aspect speaks   530
  Of higher matter than a woman's presence.
Sal. The only woman whom it much imports me
  At such a moment now is safe in absence—
  The queen's embark'd.
Sar.   And well? say that much.
Sal.   Yes.
  Her transient weakness has past o'er; at least,
  It settled into tearless silence: her
  Pale face and glittering eye, after a glance

_____

94 *guerdon*: reward.

Upon her sleeping children, were still fix'd
Upon the palace towers as the swift galley
Stole down the hurrying stream beneath the star-   540
   light;
But she said nothing.

Sar.   Would I felt no more
Than she has said.

Sal.   'Tis now too late to feel!
Your feelings cannot cancel a sole pang;
To change them, my advices bring sure tidings
That the rebellious Medes and Chaldees, marshall'd
By their two leaders, are already up
In arms again; and, serrying their ranks,
Prepare to attack: they have apparently
Been join'd by other satraps.

Sar.   What! more rebels?
Let us be first, then.

Sal.   That were hardly prudent   550
Now, though it was our first intention. If
By noon to-morrow we are join'd by those
I've sent for by sure messengers, we shall be
In strength enough to venture an attack,
Ay, and pursuit too; but till then, my voice
Is to await the onset.

Sar.   I detest
That waiting; though it seems so safe to fight
Behind high walls, and hurl down foes into
Deep fosses,[95] or behold them sprawl on spikes
Strew'd to receive them, still I like it not—   560
My soul seems lukewarm; but when I set on them,
Though they were piled on mountains, I would have
A pluck at them, or perish in hot blood!—
Let me then charge!

Sal.   You talk like a young soldier.

Sar. I am no soldier, but a man: speak not
Of soldiership, I loathe the word, and those
Who pride themselves upon it; but direct me
Where I may pour upon them.

Sal.   You must spare
To expose your life too hastily; 'tis not
Like mine or any other subject's breath: 570
The whole war turns upon it—with it; this
Alone creates it, kindles, and may quench it—
Prolong it—end it.

---

[95] *fosses*: trenches or pits.

Sar.   Then let us end both!
'Twere better thus, perhaps, than prolong either;
I'm sick of one, perchance of both.

(A trumpet sounds without).

Sal.   Hark!

Sar.   Let us
Reply, not listen.

Sal.   And your wound?

Sar.   'Tis bound—
'Tis heal'd—I had forgotten it. Away!
A leech's lancet would have scratch'd me deeper;
The slave that gave it might be well ashamed
To have struck so weakly.

Sal.   Now, may none this hour   580
Strike with a better aim!

Sar.   Ay, if we conquer;
But if not, they will only leave to me
A task they might have spared their king. Upon
   them!

(Trumpet sounds again).

Sal. I am with you.

Sar.   Ho, my arms! again, my arms!

   (Exeunt).

Act V.

Scene I: *The same Hall of the Palace.*
Myrrha and Balea.

Myr. (At a window). The day at last has broken.
   What a night
Hath usher'd it! How beautiful in heaven!
Though varied with a transitory storm,
More beautiful in that variety!
How hideous upon earth! where peace and hope,
And love and revel, in an hour were trampled
By human passions to a human chaos,
Not yet resolved to separate elements.—
'Tis warring still! And can the sun so rise,
So bright, so rolling back the clouds into   10
Vapours more lovely than the unclouded sky,
With golden pinnacles, and snowy mountains,
And billows purpler than the ocean's, making
In heaven a glorious mockery of the earth,
So like we almost deem it permanent;
So fleeting, we can scarcely call it aught

Beyond a vision, 'tis so transiently
Scatter'd along the eternal vault: and yet
It dwells upon the soul, and soothes the soul,
And blends itself into the soul, until   20
Sunrise and sunset form the haunted epoch
Of sorrow and of love; which they who mark not,
Know not the realms where those twin genii
(Who chasten and who purify our hearts,
So that we would not change their sweet rebukes
For all the boisterous joys that ever shook
The air with clamour), build the palaces
Where their fond votaries repose and breathe
Briefly;—but in that brief cool calm inhale
Enough of heaven to enable them to bear   30
The rest of common, heavy, human hours,
And dream them through in placid sufferance;
Though seemingly employ'd like all the rest
Of toiling breathers in allotted tasks
Of pain or pleasure, *two* names for *one* feeling,
Which our internal, restless agony
Would vary in the sound, although the sense
Escapes our highest efforts to be happy.
Bal. You muse right calmly: and can you so watch
The sunrise which may be our last?
Myr.   It is   40
Therefore that I so watch it, and reproach
Those eyes, which never may behold it more,
For having look'd upon it oft, too oft,
Without the reverence and the rapture due
To that which keeps all earth from being as fragile
As I am in this form. Come, look upon it,
The Chaldee's god,96 which, when I gaze upon,
I grow almost a convert to your Baal.
Bal. As now he reigns in heaven, so once on earth
He sway'd.
Myr.   He sways it now far more, then; never   50
Had earthly monarch half the peace and glory
Which centres in a single ray of his.
Bal. Surely he is a god!
Myr.   So we Greeks deem too;

---

96 *The Chaldee's god*: The peoples of Mesopotamia did not
    have a sun-centered pantheon, and Baal (in the next
    line) is a god of fertility and the earth, not the sun.
    The "Chaldees," as a semi-historical group, however,
    were supposedly adept at studying the heavens.

And yet I sometimes think that gorgeous orb
Must rather be the abode of gods than one
Of the immortal sovereigns. Now he breaks
Through all the clouds, and fills my eyes with light
That shuts the world out. I can look no more.
Bal. Hark! heard you not a sound?
Myr.   No, 'twas mere fancy;
They battle it beyond the wall, and not   60
As in late midnight conflict in the very
Chambers: the palace has become a fortress
Since that insidious hour; and here within
The very centre, girded by vast courts
And regal halls of pyramid proportions,
Which must be carried one by one before
They penetrate to where they then arrived,
We are as much shut in even from the sound
Of peril as from glory.
Bal.   But they reach'd
Thus far before.
Myr.   Yes, by surprise, and were   70
Beat back by valour; now at once we have
Courage and vigilance to guard us.
Bal.   May they
Prosper!
Myr.   That is the prayer of many, and
The dread of more: it is an anxious hour;
I strive to keep it from my thoughts. Alas!
How vainly!
Bal.   It is said the king's demeanour
In the late action scarcely more appall'd
The rebels than astonish'd his true subjects.
Myr. 'Tis easy to astonish or appal
The vulgar mass which moulds a horde of slaves;   80
But he did bravely.
Bal.   Slew he not Beleses?
I heard the soldiers say he struck him down.
Myr. The wretch was overthrown, but rescued to
Triumph, perhaps, o'er one who vanquish'd him
In fight, as he had spared him in his peril;
And by that heedless pity risk'd a crown.
Bal. Hark!
Myr.   You are right; some steps approach, but
slowly.
*(Enter Soldiers, bearing in Salemenes wounded, with a
broken Javelin in his Side; they seat him upon one of
the Couches which furnish the Apartment).*

Myr. Oh, Jove!

Bal.   Then all is over.

Sal.   That is false.
 Hew down the slave who says so, if a soldier.

Myr. Spare him—he's none: a mere court butterfly,   90
 That flutter in the pageant of a monarch.

Sal. Let him live on, then.

Myr.   So wilt thou, I trust.

Sal. I fain would live this hour out, and the event,
 But doubt it. Wherefore did ye bear me here?

Soldier. By the king's order. When the javelin struck
     you,
 You fell and fainted; 'twas his strict command
 To bear you to this hall.

Sal.   'Twas not ill done:
 For seeming slain in that cold dizzy trance,
 The sight might shake our soldiers—but—'tis vain,
 I feel it ebbing!

Myr.   Let me see the wound;   100
 I am not quite skilless: in my native land
 'Tis part of our instruction. War being constant,
 We are nerved to look on such things.

Sol.   Best extract
 The javelin.

Myr.   Hold! no, no, it cannot be.

Sal. I am sped, then!

Myr.   With the blood that fast must follow
 The extracted weapon, I do fear thy life.

Sal. And I *not* death. Where was the king when you
 Convey'd me from the spot where I was stricken?

Sol. Upon the same ground, and encouraging
 With voice and gesture the dispirited troops   110
 Who had seen you fall, and falter'd back.

Sal.   Whom heard ye
 Named next to the command?

Sol.   I did not hear.

Sal. Fly, then, and tell him, 'twas my last request
 That Zames take my post until the junction,
 So hoped for, yet delay'd, of Ofratanes,
 Satrap of Susa.[97] Leave me here: our troops
 Are not so numerous as to spare your absence.

Sol. But, prince——

---

[97] *Susa*: modern Shush, Susa was the capital of Elam and
    administrative capital of the Achaemenian king Darius
    I and his successors from 522 BCE.

Sal.   Hence, I say! Here's a courtier and
 A woman, the best chamber company.
 As you would not permit me to expire   120
 Upon the field, I'll have no idle soldiers
 About my sick couch. Hence! and do my bidding!
     (*Exeunt the Soldiers*).

Myr. Gallant and glorious spirit! must the earth
 So soon resign thee?

Sal.   Gentle Myrrha, 'tis
 The end I would have chosen, had I saved
 The monarch or the monarchy by this;
 As 'tis, I have not outlived them.

Myr.   You wax paler.

Sal. Your hand; this broken weapon but prolongs
 My pangs, without sustaining life enough
 To make me useful: I would draw it forth   130
 And my life with it, could I but hear how
 The fight goes.

(*Enter Sardanapalus and Soldiers*).

Sar.   My best brother!

Sal.   And the battle
 Is lost?

Sar. (*Despondingly*). You see *me* here.

Sal.   I'd rather see you *thus*!

(*He draws out the weapon from the wound, and dies*).

Sar. And *thus* I will be seen; unless the succour,
 The last frail reed of our beleagur'd hopes,
 Arrive with Ofratanes.

Myr.   Did you not
 Receive a token from your dying brother,
 Appointing Zames chief?

Sar.   I did.

Myr.   Where's Zames?

Sar. Dead.

Myr.   And Altada?

Sar.   Dying.

Myr.   Pania? Sfero?

Sar. Pania yet lives; but Sfero's fled or captive.   140
 I am alone.

Myr.   And is all lost?

Sar.   Our walls,
 Though thinly manned, may still hold out against
 Their present force, or aught save treachery:
 But i' the field——

Myr.   I thought 'twas the intent
 Of Salemenes not to risk a sally
 Till ye were strengthen'd by the expected succours.

Sar. I overruled him.

Myr.   Well, the fault's a brave one.

Sar. But fatal. Oh, my brother! I would give
 These realms, of which thou wert the ornament,
 The sword and shield, the sole-redeeming honour,   150
 To call back——But I will not weep for thee;
 Thou shalt be mourn'd for as thou wouldst be
   mourn'd.
 It grieves me most that thou couldst quit this life
 Believing that I could survive what thou
 Hast died for—our long royalty of race.
 If I redeem it, I will give thee blood
 Of thousands, tears of millions, for atonement,
 (The tears of all the good are thine already).
 If not, we meet again soon, if the spirit
 Within us lives beyond:—thou readest mine,   160
 And dost me justice now. Let me once clasp
 That yet warm hand, and fold that throbless heart
(Embraces the body)
 To this which beats so bitterly. Now, bear
 The body hence.

Sol.   Where?

Sar.   To my proper chamber.
 Place it beneath my canopy, as though
 The king lay there: when this is done, we will
 Speak further of the rites due to such ashes.

*(Exeunt Soldiers with the body of Salemenes. Enter
Pania).*

Sar. Well, Pania! have you placed the guards, and
   issued
 The orders fix'd on?

Pan.   Sire, I have obey'd.

Sar. And do the soldiers keep their hearts up?

Pan.   Sire?   170

Sar. I'm answer'd! When a king asks twice, and has
 A question as an answer to *his* question,
 It is a portent. What! they are dishearten'd?

Pan. The death of Salemenes, and the shouts
 Of the exulting rebels on his fall,
 Have made them——

Sar.   Rage—not droop—it should
   have been.
 We'll find the means to rouse them.

Pan.   Such a loss
 Might sadden even a victory.

Sar.   Alas!
 Who can so feel it as I feel? but yet,

Though coop'd within these walls, they are strong,   180
   and we
 Have those without will break their way through
   hosts,
 To make their sovereign's dwelling what it was—
 A palace; not a prison, nor a fortress.

(Enter an Officer, hastily).

Sar. Thy face seems ominous. Speak!

Officer.   I dare not.

Sar.   Dare not?
 While millions dare revolt with sword in hand!
 That's strange. I pray thee break that loyal silence
 Which loathes to shock its sovereign; we can hear
 Worse than thou hast to tell.

Pan.   Proceed, thou hearest.

Off. The wall which skirted near the river's brink
 Is thrown down by the sudden inundation[98]   190
 Of the Euphrates, which now rolling, swoln
 From the enormous mountains where it rises,
 By the late rains of that tempestuous region,
 O'erfloods its banks, and hath destroy'd the bulwark.

Pan. That's a black augury! it has been said
 For ages, "That the city ne'er should yield
 "To man, until the river grew its foe."[99]

Sar. I can forgive the omen, not the ravage.
 How much is swept down of the wall?

Off.   About
 Some twenty stadii.[100]

Sar.   And all this is left   200
 Pervious to the assailants?

Off.   For the present
 The river's fury must impede the assault;
 But when he shrinks into his wonted channel,
 And may be cross'd by the accustom'd barks,
 The palace is their own.

Sar.   That shall be never.
 Though men, and gods, and elements, and omens,

---

98   *inundation*: flooding.

99   *That the city ... foe*: Diodurus (II.xxvi:9) tells of the
      fulfillment of the prophecy, though it occurred only
      in the third year of the siege of Nineveh (II.xxvii:1).

100 *stadii*: plural of "stadium," an ancient Greek and Roman
      measure of varying length, most commonly equal to 600
      Greek or Roman feet, or 1/8 of a Roman mile. In the
      King James Bible, "stadium" is translated as "furlong."

Have risen up 'gainst one who ne'er provoked them,
My fathers' house shall never be a cave
For wolves to horde and howl in.
Pan.   With your sanction
I will proceed to the spot, and take such measures   210
For the assurance of the vacant space
As time and means permit.
Sar.   About it straight,
And bring me back as speedily as full
And fair investigation may permit
Report of the true state of this irruption
Of waters. *(Exeunt Pania and the Officer).*
Myr.   Thus the very waves rise up
Against you.
Sar.   They are not my subjects, girl,
And may be pardon'd, since they can't be punish'd.
Myr. I joy to see this portent shakes you not.
Sar. I am past the fear of portents: they can tell me   220
Nothing I have not told myself since midnight:
Despair anticipates such things.
Myr.   Despair!
Sar. No; not despair precisely. When we know
All that can come, and how to meet it, our
Resolves, if firm, may merit a more noble
Word than this is to give it utterance.
But what are words to us? we have well nigh done
With them and all things.
Myr.   Save *one deed*—the last
And greatest to all mortals; crowning act
Of all that was—or is—or is to be—   230
The only thing common to all mankind,
So different in their births, tongues, sexes, natures,
Hues, features, climes, times, feelings, intellects,
Without one point of union save in this,
To which we tend, for which we're born, and thread
The labyrinth of mystery, call'd life.
Sar. Our clew[101] being well nigh wound out, let's be
cheerful.
They who have nothing more to fear may well
Indulge a smile at that which once appall'd;
As children at discover'd bugbears.
(Re-enter Pania).
Pan.   'Tis   240
As was reported: I have order'd there

A double guard, withdrawing from the wall
Where it was strongest the required addition
To watch the breach occasion'd by the waters.
Sar. You have done your duty faithfully, and as
My worthy Pania! further ties between us
Draw near a close. I pray you take this key: *(Gives
a key)*
It opens to a secret chamber, placed
Behind the couch in my own chamber. (Now
Press'd by a nobler weight than e'er it bore—   250
Though a long line of sovereigns have lain down
Along its golden frame—as bearing for
A time what late was Salemenes). Search
The secret covert[102] to which this will lead you;
'Tis full of treasure; take it for yourself
And your companions: there's enough to load ye,
Though ye be many. Let the slaves be freed, too;
And all the inmates of the palace, of
Whatever sex, now quit it in an hour.
Thence launch the regal barks, once form'd for   260
pleasure,
And now to serve for safety, and embark.
The river's broad and swoln, and uncommanded
(More potent than a king) by these besiegers.
Fly! and be happy!
Pan.   Under your protection!
So you accompany your faithful guard.
Sar. No, Pania! that must not be; get thee hence,
And leave me to my fate.
Pan.   'Tis the first time
I ever disobey'd: but now——
Sar.   So all men
Dare beard me now, and Insolence within
Apes Treason from without. Question no further;   270
'Tis my command, my last command. Wilt *thou*
Oppose it? *thou!*
Pan.   But yet—not yet.
Sar.   Well, then,
Swear that you will obey when I shall give
The signal.
Pan.   With a heavy but true heart,
I promise.
Sar.   'Tis enough. Now order here
Faggots, pine-nuts, and wither'd leaves, and such

---

101 *clew:* a ball of thread, particularly that used to guide
one through a labyrinth (see V.i.236).

102 *covert:* hiding place.

Things as catch fire and blaze with one sole spark;
Bring cedar, too, and precious drugs, and spices,
And mighty planks, to nourish a tall pile;
Bring frankincense and myrrh,[103] too, for it is   280
For a great sacrifice I build the pyre;
And heap them round yon throne.

Pan.   My lord!

Sar.   I have said it,
  And *you* have *sworn*.

Pan.   And could keep my faith
  Without a vow. *(Exit Pania)*.

Myr.   What mean you?

Sar.   You shall know
  Anon—what the whole earth shall ne'er forget.

(Enter Pania, returning with a Herald).

Pan. My king, in going forth upon my duty,
  This herald has been brought before me, craving
  An audience.

Sar.   Let him speak.

Herald.   The *King* Arbaces——

Sar. What, crown'd already?—But, proceed.

Her.   Beleses,
  The anointed high-priest——

Sar.   Of what god, or demon?   290
  With new kings rise new altars. But, proceed;
  You are sent to prate your master's will, and not
  Reply to mine.

Her.   And Satrap Ofratanes——

Sar. Why, *he* is ours.

Her. (Showing a ring). Be sure that he is now
  In the camp of the conquerors; behold
  His signet ring.

Sar.   'Tis his. A worthy triad!
  Poor Salemenes! thou hast died in time
  To see one treachery the less: this man
  Was thy true friend and my most trusted subject.
  Proceed.

Her.   They offer thee thy life, and freedom   300
  Of choice to single out a residence
  In any of the further provinces,
  Guarded and watch'd, but not confined in person,
  Where thou shalt pass thy days in peace; but on

Condition that the three young princes are
  Given up as hostages.

Sar. (Ironically).   The generous victors!

Her. I wait the answer.

Sar.   Answer, slave! How long
  Have slaves decided on the doom of kings?

Her. Since they were free.

Sar.   Mouthpiece of mutiny!
  Thou at the least shalt learn the penalty   310
  Of treason, though its proxy only. Pania!
  Let his head be thrown from our walls within
  The rebels' lines, his carcass down the river.
  Away with him!

(Pania and the Guards seizing him).

Pan.   I never yet obey'd
  Your orders with more pleasure than the present.
  Hence with him, soldiers! do not soil this hall
  Of royalty with treasonable gore;
  Put him to rest without.

Her.   A single word:
  My office, king, is sacred.

Sar.   And what's *mine*?
  That thou shouldst come and dare to ask of me   320
  To lay it down?

Her.   I but obey'd my orders,
  At the same peril if refused, as now
  Incurr'd by my obedience.

Sar.   So there are
  New monarchs of an hour's growth as despotic
  As sovereigns swathed in purple, and enthroned
  From birth to manhood!

Her.   My life waits your breath.
  Yours (I speak humbly)—but it may be—yours
  May also be in danger scarce less imminent:
  Would it then suit the last hours of a line
  Such as is that of Nimrod, to destroy   330
  A peaceful herald, unarm'd, in his office;
  And violate not only all that man
  Holds sacred between man and man—but that
  More holy tie which links us with the gods?

Sar. He's right.—Let him go free.—My life's last act
  Shall not be one of wrath. Here, fellow, take

(Gives him a golden cup from a table near)

  This golden goblet, let it hold your wine,
  And think of *me*; or melt it into ingots,
  And think of nothing but their weight and value.

---

103 *frankincense and myrrh*: Both are aromatic gum resins
     used as incense; both are brought by the Wise Men as
     gifts to the infant Jesus.

Her. I thank you doubly for my life, and this   340
    Most gorgeous gift, which renders it more precious.
    But must I bear no answer?
Sar.   Yes,—I ask
    An hour's truce to consider.
Her.   But an hour's?
Sar. An hour's: if at the expiration of
    That time your masters hear no further from me,
    They are to deem that I reject their terms,
    And act befittingly.
Her.   I shall not fail
    To be a faithful legate[104] of your pleasure.
Sar. And, hark! a word more.
Her.   I shall not forget it,
    Whate'er it be.
Sar.   Commend me to Beleses;   350
    And tell him, ere a year expire, I summon
    Him hence to meet me.
Her.   Where?
Sar.   At Babylon.[105]
    At least from thence he will depart to meet me.
Her. I shall obey you to the letter. *(Exit Herald).*
Sar.   Pania!—
    Now, my good Pania—quick—with what I order'd.
Pan. My lord,—the soldiers are already charged.
    And see! they enter.
(Soldiers enter, and form a Pile about the Throne, &c.).
Sar.   Higher, my good soldiers,
    And thicker yet; and see that the foundation
    Be such as will not speedily exhaust
    Its own too subtle flame; nor yet be quench'd   360
    With aught officious aid would bring to quell it.
    Let the throne form the *core* of it; I would not
    Leave that, save fraught with fire unquenchable,
    To the new comers. Frame the whole as if
    'Twere to enkindle the strong tower of our
    Inveterate enemies. Now it bears an aspect!
    How say you, Pania, will this pile suffice
    For a king's obsequies?[106]

---

104 *legate*: an ambassador or messenger.
105 *Beleses … Babylon*: Diodorus (II.xxviii:2) records that
    Beleses asked for the governorship of Babylon.
    McGann and Weller suggest an echo of Shakespeare's
    Julius Caesar's promise to see Brutus at Philippi
    (IV.iii.281–6).
106 *obsequies*: funeral rites.

Pan.   Ay, for a kingdom's.
    I understand you, now.
Sar.   And blame me?
Pan.   No—
    Let me but fire the pile, and share it with you.   370
Myr. That duty's mine.
Pan.   A woman's!
Myr.   'Tis the soldier's
    Part to die *for* his sovereign, and why not
    The woman's with her lover?
Pan.   'Tis most strange!
Myr. But not so rare, my Pania, as thou think'st it.
    In the mean time, live thou.—Farewell! the pile
    Is ready.
Pan.   I should shame to leave my sovereign
    With but a single female to partake
    His death.
Sar.   Too many far have heralded
    Me to the dust already. Get thee hence;
    Enrich thee.
Pan.   And live wretched!
Sar.   Think upon   380
    Thy vow;—'tis sacred and irrevocable.
Pan. Since it is so, farewell.
Sar.   Search well my chamber,
    Feel no remorse at bearing off the gold;
    Remember, what you leave you leave the slaves
    Who slew me: and when you have borne away
    All safe off to your boats, blow one long blast
    Upon the trumpet as you quit the palace.
    The river's brink is too remote, its stream
    Too loud at present to permit the echo
    To reach distinctly from its banks. Then fly,—   390
    And as you sail, turn back; but still keep on
    Your way along the Euphrates: if you reach
    The land of Paphlagonia, where the queen
    Is safe with my three sons in Cotta's court,
    Say what you *saw* at parting, and request
    That she remember what I *said* at one
    Parting more mournful still.
Pan.   That royal hand!
    Let me then once more press it to my lips;
    And these poor soldiers who throng round you, and
    Would fain die with you!
*(The Soldiers and Pania throng round him, kissing his
hand and the hem of his robe).*

Sar.   My best! my last friends!   400
    Let's not unman each other—part at once:
    All farewells should be sudden, when for ever,
    Else they make an eternity of moments,
    And clog the last sad sands of life with tears.
    Hence, and be happy: trust me, I am not
    Now to be pitied; or far more for what
    Is past than present;—for the future, 'tis
    In the hands of the deities, if such
    There be: I shall know soon. Farewell—farewell.
(Exeunt Pania and Soldiers).
Myr. These men were honest: it is comfort still   410
    That our last looks should be on loving faces.
Sar. And *lovely* ones, my beautiful!—but hear me!
    If at this moment, for we now are on
    The brink, thou feel'st an inward shrinking from
    This leap through flame into the future, say it:
    I shall not love thee less; nay, perhaps more,
    For yielding to thy nature: and there's time
    Yet for thee to escape hence.
Myr.   Shall I light
    One of the torches which lie heap'd beneath
    The ever-burning lamp that burns without,   420
    Before Baal's shrine, in the adjoining hall?
Sar. Do so. Is that thy answer?
Myr.   Thou shalt see. *(Exit
    Myrrha).*
Sar. *(Solus).* She's firm. My fathers! whom I will rejoin,
    It may be, purified by death from some
    Of the gross stains of too material being,
    I would not leave your ancient first abode
    To the defilement of usurping bondmen;
    If I have not kept your inheritance
    As ye bequeath'd it, this bright part of it,
    Your treasure, your abode, your sacred relics   430
    Of arms, and records, monuments, and spoils,
    In which *they* would have revell'd, I bear with me
    To you in that absorbing element,
    Which most personifies the soul as leaving
    The least of matter unconsumed before
    Its fiery workings:—and the light of this
    Most royal of funereal pyres shall be
    Not a mere pillar form'd of cloud and flame,
    A beacon in the horizon for a day,
    And then a mount of ashes, but a light   440
    To lesson ages, rebel nations, and

    Voluptuous princes. Time shall quench full many
    A people's records, and a hero's acts;
    Sweep empire after empire, like this first
    Of empires, into nothing; but even then
    Shall spare this deed of mine, and hold it up
    A problem few dare imitate, and none
    Despise—but, it may be, avoid the life
    Which led to such a consummation.
*(Myrrha returns with a lighted Torch in one Hand,
and a Cup in the other.)*
Myr.   Lo!
    I've lit the lamp which lights us to the stars.   450
Sar. And the cup?
Myr.   'Tis my country's custom to
    Make a libation to the gods.
Sar.   And mine
    To make libations amongst men. I've not
    Forgot the custom; and although alone,
    Will drain one draught in memory of many
    A joyous banquet past.
    *(Sardanapalus takes the cup, and after drinking and
        tinkling the reversed cup, as a drop falls,
        exclaims—)*   And this libation
    Is for the excellent Beleses.
Myr.   Why
    Dwells thy mind rather upon that man's name
    Than on his mate's in villany?
Sar.   The other
    Is a mere soldier, a mere tool, a kind   460
    Of human sword in a friend's hand; the other
    Is master-mover of his warlike puppet:
    But I dismiss them from my mind.—Yet pause,
    My Myrrha! dost thou truly follow me,
    Freely and fearlessly?
Myr.   And dost thou think
    A Greek girl dare not do for love, that which
    An Indian widow braves for custom?[107]
Sar.   Then
    We but await the signal.
Myr.   It is long
    In sounding.
Sar.   Now, farewell; one last embrace.

---

107 *Indian widow braves for custom*: a reference to the
    Hindu practice of suttee, in which a widow immolates
    herself on the funeral pyre of her husband.

Myr. Embrace, but *not* the last; there is one more.   470
Sar. True, the commingling fire will mix our ashes.
Myr. And pure as is my love to thee, shall they,
    Purged from the dross of earth, and earthly passion,
    Mix pale with thine. A single thought yet irks me.
Sar. Say it.
Myr.   It is that no kind hand will gather
    The dust of both into one urn.
Sar.   The better:
    Rather let them be borne abroad upon
    The winds of heaven, and scatter'd into air,
    Than be polluted more by human hands
    Of slaves and traitors; in this blazing palace,   480
    And its enormous walls of reeking ruin,
    We leave a nobler monument than Egypt
    Hath piled in her brick mountains, o'er dead kings,
    Or *kine*,[108] for none know whether those proud piles
    Be for their monarch, or their ox-god Apis:[109]
    So much for monuments that have forgotten
    Their very record!
Myr.   Then farewell, thou earth!

And loveliest spot of earth! farewell Ionia!
    Be thou still free and beautiful, and far
    Aloof from desolation! My last prayer   490
    Was for thee, my last thoughts, save *one*, were of thee!
Sar. And that?
Myr.   Is yours.
(The trumpet of Pania sounds without).
Sar.   Hark!
Myr.   *Now!*
Sar.   Adieu, Assyria!
    I loved thee well, my own, my fathers' land,
    And better as my country than my kingdom.
    I satiated thee with peace and joys; and this
    Is my reward! and now I owe thee nothing,
    Not even a grave. *(He mounts the pile).*
             Now, Myrrha!
Myr.   Art thou ready?
Sar. As the torch in thy grasp. *(Myrrha fires the pile).*
Myr.   'Tis fired! I come.
(As Myrrha springs forward to throw herself into the flames, the Curtain falls).

---

108 *kine*: cows.
109 *Apis*: in ancient Egyptian religion, a sacred bull deity
    worshiped at Memphis.

Appendix: Contemporary Reviews and Commentary

1. Review of Hannah Cowley, *A Bold Stroke for a Husband*. *The Morning Chronicle and Weekly Advertiser* No. 4298 (26 February 1783), page 3. Extract. A slightly altered version of this review also appeared in *The General Evening Post* No. 7648 (25–27 February 1783), page 3; *The Whitehall Evening-Post* No. 5556 (25–27 February 1783), page 3; and *The London Chronicle* No 4095 (25–27 February 1783), page 199.

This comedy is the production of Mrs. Cowley, whose prolific Muse has given birth to a larger number of dramatic offspring within the same length of time, than any dramatic author of the present century, Mr. Foote only excepted. The comedies of *Which is the Man? The Belle's Stratagem, The Runaway*, and the farce of *Who's the Dupe?* from the time of their first representation have continued to be popular pieces, and we are happy to be able to say, that *A Bold Stroke for a Husband* promises to be as much a favourite of the town as any one of the beforementioned productions.

The scene of this Comedy lies in Spain. The incidents and business of it arise from a double plot, or rather from two fables ingeniously interwoven: in one of them a strong moral interest is held out; in the other, though less seriously important, the mind is not less attached from vivacity of character, humour of situation, and power of comic effect. [The Reviewer provides a plot synopsis].

This Comedy is light, interesting, and entertaining. Without pretensions to a place in the first rank of dramatic productions, it does honour to the second. The fable is ingeniously contrived, its conduct managed with adroitness, and its denouement naturally unfolded. The characters are in general well discriminated, and though not original, have in their situation and disposition a sufficient shape of merit to excuse and hold attention. The dialogue is neat, full of shrewd observation and well-applied pleasantry; in some places witty, and in others elevated and poetic. The situations are frequently comic, and easily and accountably produced. The play is rather too long, and the character of Victoria, which, in a moral point of view, must be deemed the heroine, is not rendered sufficiently important. Olivia is brought more forward on the canvas, and consequently the risible faculties of the audience are oftener interested than their sensibility and their regard for virtue in distress; a matter that operates as a recommendation within the theatre, though it demands a notice from the critic. Upon the whole, however, the play is such as does honour to its author, and will, we doubt not, prove essentially serviceable to the theatre.

The characters of Olivia and Victoria were, we understand, originally cast to Mrs. Abington[1] and Miss Younge.[2] Ill health, and the dread of not being able to go through the run, Mrs. Cowley's comedies generally obtain, obliged the former most admirable actress to decline her character. Miss Younge is now an invalid, and possibly the same cause induced her to give up Victoria. Be that matter as it may, Mrs. Mattocks gave ample proof of her abilities in Olivia, which she played well in general, and in some of the scenes excellently. Mrs. Robinson, for a young actress, bustled tolerable well through Victoria. In the pathetic parts she spoke with an obvious impression of feeling, in the lighter situations of her character

---

1 *Mrs. Abington*: Mrs. James Abington, Frances, née Barton (1737–1815), actress and mainstay of the Dublin (1759–65), Drury Lane (1765–82) and Covent Garden (1782–90) stages. Famous for her elegance and whimsicality, she was best known as the original Lady Teazle in Sheridan's *The School for Scandal*. She retired suddenly in February 1790; just as suddenly she came out of retirement in 1797 after the death of Mrs. Pope (Elizabeth Younge) to act until 1799.

2 *Miss Younge*: Mrs. Alexander Pope the first, Elizabeth, née Younge (1740?–97). See the Glossary of Actors and Actresses for more information.

with an easy gayety; a little more force would, however, do service in bringing forward both the lights and shades of her character. Mrs. Wilson played the latter part of Minette incomparably. She deserves great praise for throwing a novelty of manner into those of her scenes, in which the Maid appears the Mistress. The situation is by no means a new one to the stage; to colour it therefore so as to give it the appearance of originality is a real merit. Mr. Quick, in the early part of the play, seemed frozen; his words came out coldly, as drops of melting ice. Towards the middle of it, he had obtained possession of himself, and played, as he always does, when he is not embarrassed, with great comic effect. Mr. Wroughton was interesting throughout the character of Carlos, and Mr. Lewis extremely pleasant in Julio. Edwin, if more articulate and intelligible, would play Vincentio inexceptionably. Mr. Whitfield made the most of Garcia, and Mrs. Whitfield shewed by her performance of Laura, that she is equal to a better cast of characters than she at present possesses. Wilson had no great scope for the exercise of his talents in Gasper.

The two new street scenes were produced in the course of the representation that had a good effect. The dresses of Mr. Wroughton, Mr. Lewis, Mr. Edwin, Mr. Whitfield, and Mrs. Mattocks, were new, and extremely elegant. Mrs. Mattocks, however, should put on a better hoop. Though an elegant-made woman, yet being short, her figure, when full dressed, requires some of that nicety of attention to ornament, which she has as good a taste in displaying, as any actress on the stage.

The Prologue had some good turns in it upon the different species of *bold strokes*, than could be adduced, as instances of modern manners. It was well delivered by Mr. Whitfield.

The epilogue spoke of the plenty of husbands the peace would afford the ladies, and contained, some popular allusions to personal bravery of those who fought to obtain it. It ended in a long descriptive of the life of a lady, in the different stages of her progress, from her girlish days to those of her becoming a married woman; the song went to a very pretty tune. The epilogue was adroitly spoken, and agreeably sung, by Mrs. Mattocks.

The *Bold Stroke for a Husband* was received by a numerous audience with loud and universal applause, and as we have before said, promises to become a popular play.

---

2. **Review of Hannah Cowley, *A Bold Stroke for a Husband*. *Monthly Review* 70 (February 1784), pages 136-9. Extract.**

This comedy, as the Author herself observes at the conclusion, exhibits "TWO *bold strokes*—one to *reclaim* a husband, the other to *get* one." The several adventurers in these *bold strokes* are consequently females.

The principal heroine, whose aim is to *get* a husband, in order to enforce her bold stroke, has recourse to a *Belle's Strategem* (like other belles' strategems, not very *new*), assuming the character of a termagant, in order to baffle the matches proposed by her father, and to disgust the suitors whom she dislikes.

The secondary heroine, who wishes to *reclaim* a husband, effects her purpose by two *bold* strokes indeed;— by disguising herself as a man, she engages the affections of the mistress to the husband who has deserted her; and, by disguising a servant as his kinsman, she recovers an estate settled by her husband on that mistress. Neither of these *bold strokes* are, we think, conducted with address, or founded in probability.

The *Characters* of this play have no greater excellence than the *Fable*. None of them are marked with those discriminating touches, that distinguish the drawings of able dramatists. *Vincentio* is a miserable sketch of a *Conoscente*. Don *Caesar* is not without pleasantry. He possesses, indeed, almost all the humour of the piece. The Dialogue is pert and flippant, and (like the incidents) calculated for the meridian of the shelves of a circulating Library: the whole Drama, indeed, is in the style of a common Modern Novel.

In order to counteract, as much as possible the seeming severity in the preceding strictures, we give, as a specimen of the comedy, one of the scenes which, we apprehend, the fair Authoress ranks among the very best: [The Reviewer quotes III.iii].

Prefixed to the comedy is "A Prologue, written by Two gentlemen": a prologue which affords no proof that TWO *heads are better than* ONE. The Epilogue is meant to be poetical and musical, and may be sung or said with equal advantage.

---

3. Review of Hannah Cowley, *A Bold Stroke for a Husband*. *Critical Review* 57 (March 1784), pages 201-5. Extract.

Mrs. Cowley's Comedies are generally rather interesting and agreeable, than regular and original. The attention is engaged by a lively dialogue, and peculiar situations: without an appeal to the reason. We seldom meet with a new character, and the old ones are scarcely distinguished by a discriminating feature: the usual passions are excited by the usual causes; and, if the author has surveyed human nature out of her common walks, she has dropped the pencil either from timidity or despair. If we were to pursue this severity, we might observe, that Mrs. Cowley is a plagiarist, both from others, and even from herself; or, that the narrow circle within which she confines her prospects, renders her necessarily uniform in her conduct, and tinctures her incidents with little variety. But we are not yet so deaf to the general applause; age has not yet steeled our hearts with such a listless apathy, as to induce us to refuse a leaf or laurel to the wreath which common consent has crowned her. We can readily allow merit, though it has not plumed itself with the ornaments of Terence[3] or Moliere; and we can approve of a play, though the rules of Aristotle or Horace[4] may be neglected. The present comedy is indeed highly interesting:—the attention, even in the closet, seldom fails; in the theatre it is "tremblingly alive." This magic is worth a host of criticisms, and arises from an acute perception of those feelings whose influence we can never escape, and of that kind of expectation which must be gratified. When all the events, thus artfully connected, are related in language easy and elegant, lively and familiar, we are not surprised that our minds are hurried on at the will of the author; that we forget every "wise saw" of criticism, every "modern instance," and join in the usual acclamations.

As we have thus given a general opinion of Mrs. Cowley's merit, we should descend to a particular examination of the conduct of the piece, if it were not that a skeleton would, as usual, give an unfavourable and unjust idea of the spirit which animated the individual. If we were to be allowed a criticism on any part of her Dialogue, we might suggest that she has been rather unfavourable to her own sex. If she has described our

> 'Fancies as more giddy and infirm,
> More longing, wavering, sooner lost and worn
> Than women's are:'

Or, if she described the ladies as gay and fickle, 'lightly wooed or won,' she might have pleaded precedent and custom, for trite sentiments, and common-place raillery. But we think the following passage has a worse tendency, since it inculcates, and from a woman's pen, that levity and neglect are as powerful advocates as flattery. [The Reviewer quotes Victoria's speech in which she describes how she wooed Laura in Act II, Scene ii].

Another error is giving English manners to the inhabitants of Spain. The peculiarities of that nation are very little attended to; and the costume, on the whole, very carelessly preserved: but this will not diminish the pleasure of the spectator, though the reader perceives it with regret.

---

3 *Terence*: Publius Terentius Afer (195–159 BCE), after Plautus considered the greatest Roman comic dramatist, and the author of six verse comedies that have long been regarded as the basis of the modern comedy of manners.

4 *Molière ... Aristotle or Horace*: Molière (full name Jean-Baptiste Poquelin 1622–73), French actor and playwright, often considered the most important writer of French comedy; Aristoteles (384–322 BCE), ancient Greek philosopher and author of the *Poetics*; Quintus Horatius Flaccus (65–8 BCE), Latin poet and satirist, author of *The Art of Poetry*.

We shall insert a lively scene, as a specimen of our author's talents. The *Bold Stroke* is rather a *Belle's Strategem*: to gain the lover she likes, Olivia assumes those dispositions which she thinks least agreeable to her other admirers. [The Reviewer provides an extract from I.ii, and ends without summary comments.]

———

4. Inchbald, Elizabeth, "Remarks on *A Bold Stroke for a Husband*." *The British Theatre*. Ed. Elizabeth Inchbald. 25 vols. London: Longman, Hurst, Rees, and Orme, 1808. Volume 19. Pages 3-5.[5]

Although "The Bold Stroke for a Husband," by Mrs. Cowley, does not equal "The Bold Stroke for a Wife," by Mrs. Centlivre,[6] either in originality of design, wit, or humour, it has other advantages more honourable to her sex, and more conducive to the reputation of the stage.

Here is contained no oblique insinuation, detrimental to the cause of morality—but entertainment and instruction unite, to make a pleasant exhibition at a theatre, or give an hour's amusement in the closet.

Plays, where the scene is placed in a foreign country, particularly when that country is Spain, have a license to present certain improbabilities to the audience, without incurring the danger of having them called such; and the authoress, by the skill with which she has used this dramatic permittance, in making the wife of Don Carlos pass for a man, has formed a most interesting plot, and embellished it with lively, humourous, and affecting incident.

Still there is another plot, of which Olivia is the heroine, as Victoria is of the foregoing; and this more comic fable, in which the former is chiefly concerned, seems to have been the favourite story of the authoress, as from this she has taken her title.

But if Olivia makes a bold stroke to obtain a husband, surely Victoria makes a still bolder stroke to preserve one; and there is something less honourable in the enterprises of a young maiden, in order to renounce her state, than in those of a married woman to avert the dangers that are impending over hers.

Whichever of those females becomes the most admired subject with the reader, he will not be insensible to the trials of the other, or to the various interests of the whole dramatis personae, to whom the writer has artfully given a kind of united influence; and upon a happy combination it is, that, sometimes, the success of a drama more depends, than upon the most powerful support of any particularly prominent, yet insulated, character.

The part of Don Vincentio was certainly meant as a moral satire upon the extravagant love, or the foolish affectation, of pretending to love, to extravagance—music. This satire was aimed at so many, that the shaft struck none. The charm of music still prevails in England, and the folly of affected admirers.

Vincentio talks music, and Don Julio speaks poetry. Such, at least, is his fond description of his mistress Olivia, in that excellent scene in the third act, where she first takes off her veil, and fascinates him at once by the force of her beauty.

In the delineation of this lady, it is implied that she is no termagant, although she so frequently counterfeits the character. This insinuation the reader, if he pleases, may trust—but the man who would venture to marry a good impostor of this kind, could not excite much pity, if his helpmate was often induced to act the part which she had heretofore, with so much spirit, assumed.

The impropriety of making fraud and imposition necessary evils, to counteract tyranny and injustice, is the fault of all Spanish dramas—and perhaps the only one which attaches to the present comedy.

---

5 *Pages 3–5*: Each play within *The British Theatre* carries its own pagination. Within Volume 19, *A Bold Stroke for a Husband* is the fifth play.

6 *Mrs. Centlivre*: Susannah Centlivre (1669?–1723), English dramatist and arguably the most successful female playwright of the eighteenth century. Besides *A Bold Stroke for a Wife* (Lincoln's Inn Fields, 1718), her plays *The Gamester* (Lincoln's Inn Fields, 1705), *The Busie Body* (Drury Lane, 1709), and *The Wonder* (Drury Lane, 1714) were mainstays of London repertory theater throughout the eighteenth century.

5. Baker, David Erkine; Reed, Isaac; Jones, Stephen. "Cowley, Mrs. Hannah." *Biographia Dramatica; or, A Companion to the Playhouse.* 3 vols. London: Longman, Hurst, Rees, Orme, and Brown, 1812. Volume 1, Part 1, pages 152-4. Extract.

Her genius may seem to have been hereditary; her grandmother by the father's side having been first cousin to the celebrated poet Gray; by whom she was held in such high estimation, that he passed a considerable portion of his time at her house in Barnstaple... In the different characters of daughter, wife, and mother, Mrs. Cowley's conduct was most exemplary. Her manners were lively and unassuming, and her countenance was peculiarly animated and expressive. Though public as a genius, yet private as a woman, she wore her laurels gracefully veiled: at the theatres, except to oblige others by accompanying them, she was never seen; frequently, for years together, she was not there at all. Her dramatic pieces were brought out under the superintendence of her husband; except, we believe, the last two; he having then joined his regiment in India. In her writings, nothing was laboured; all was spontaneous effusion: she had nothing of the drudge of literature; and fame was not half so much her object as the pleasure of composition. When her fancy had prompted her to the amusement of dramatic writing, so little sanguine was she in her expectation that her comedy would be accepted by Mr. Garrick, to whom it was sent, that it was not until about twelve months afterwards, that he was informed who had sent it to him, or was asked what his opinion was. The comedy alluded to was *The Runaway*; it was written in a fortnight, and its remarkable success many will recollect...However anxious Mrs. Cowley might be at the moment of writing, her work was no sooner out, than she became regardless of it. It was to domestic life, as we have before observed, that her mind was given; fame appeared to be not at all essential to her happiness. *The Siege of Acre*[7] would never have appeared,

had it not been heard of, asked for, and made a present of to a respectable bookseller, who was a stranger to her. In the course of the last ten years of her life she wrote a few slight poems, in friendship with the families of Lady Carew,[8] Lady Duntze,[9] Mrs. Wood,[10] and other ladies in her neighbourhood, which probably are yet extant. In her latter years, on account of her dislike of cards, and the dress and trouble of evening amusements, she declined all invitations; but received very large parties at her own house. She established a singular custom, of throwing open her house, one morning in a week, for ladies only, and was on those occasions attended by a crowd...

Besides the poems of *The Maid of Arragon*,[11] and *The Siege of Acre*, which we have incidentally mentioned, this lady produced a third, excellent in its kind, called *The Scottish Village*.[12]

The last time her pen was thus employed, was on a slight poem, given to a poor sexton of the parish, who was distressed by the loss of his property, in the then late floods, and which was restored to him by the douceurs of those to whom he showed the poem for perusal.

To the above we should add, that Mrs. Cowley was the "Anna Matilda," who so long maintained a celebrated poetical newspaper correspondence with "Della Crusca" (the late Mr. Merry);[13] though the parties were, personally, total strangers to each other.

---

7   *The Siege of Acre*: referring to Hannah Cowley, *The Siege*

of Acre: A Poem, in Four Books (London: G. Wilkie and J. Robinson, 1810).

8   *Lady Carew*: member of a prominent family in South Wales and Devon from the 14th century.

9   *Lady Duntze*: probably the wife of Sir John Duntze, M.P. and merchant from Devon.

10   *Mrs. Wood*: unidentified member of a Devon family.

11   *Maid of Arragon*: referring to Hannah Cowley, *The Maid of Arragon: A Tale* (London: L. Davis and 12 others, 1780).

12   *The Scottish Village*: referring to Hannah Cowley, *The Scottish Village: Or, Pitcairn Green: A Poem* (London: G. G. J. and J. Robinson, 1786).

13   *"Anna Matilda" ... "Della Crusca" (the late Mr. Merry)*: poetic pseudonym used by Hannah Cowley for the poems she published in *The World* newspaper from 1787 to 1789, most famous for her poetic correspondence with "Della Crusca," the pen name of Robert Merry (1755–98).

6. *The Works of Mrs. Cowley.* 3 vols. London: Wilkie and Robinson, 1813. Volume 1, pages 392-3. Extract.

The Author had hitherto confined herself within the range of English manners; but now, for Variety, she takes her flight to other realms, and customs differing from our own.

This play came out in the year 1783. Its schemes are so numerous, that almost every Character forms a plot. It has certainly considerable whim and fancy, to give an air of Probability to which, distance of Time or distance of Place was requisite; the Author has chosen the latter, and the Scene is laid in Spain, where to the romantic the mind readily gives credit.

It was intended that VICTORIA, amiably employed in reclaiming her Husband, and CARLOS should be the Leading Characters in this Drama, the vivacious adventures of JULIO and OLIVIA enlivening the serious business in which the Moral of the Play is enforced. This is clear from the Prologue, and from the Play itself. On the Stage the Author's intention ought to be fulfilled; but, from the way in which the Comedy is sometimes cast, that intention is controuled, the piece is thrown into a class of comedies merely lively, and deprived of half its Strength.

This arises from the frequent custom, whilst the most brilliant talents of the theatre are called forth in JULIO, OLIVIA, and MINETTE, of allotting CARLOS, VICTORIA, and LAURA to inferior performers. Yet there are situations enough of great Interest, throughout the adventures of CARLOS and VICTORIA, to bear out any talents that may be exerted in them. And no inferior performer can do Justice to the strongly drawn character of the degraded LAURA; particularly in the first scene of the Fifth Act, at the moment when she is deluded to destroy the Deed, and thereby to preserve VICTORIA and her Children from destruction.

At the Theatre generally the Third Scene of the Third Act, to the end of the act, is omitted from brevity, and DON CAESAR, in the Second Scene of the Fourth Act, comes in without MARCELLA, and commences with the fifth speech. MARCELLA, who is only introduced by the author in these two scenes, in the latter of which she speaks but once, and VASQUEZ her Father who is only introduced in the first of them, form thus no part of the *Dramatis Personae* on the Stage. But this causes no Confusion; for the LETTER in the second Scene of the Fourth Act explains to the audience every thing contained in the closet, at the Theatre their absence is advantageous; because, on account of the slight importance of the characters, none but very inferior performers can be expected in them, by whom the current of the action is checked.

In their absence the adventures of OLIVIA and her Lovers proceed, as they should to give them their full effect, in one unbroken current of Vivacity.

7. Boaden, James. *Memoirs of Mrs. Siddons. Interspersed with Anecdotes of Authors and Actors.* 2 vols. London: Henry Colburn, 1827. Volume 2, pages 9-11. Extract.

It is very natural for a lady addicted to dramatic composition, to look to the authors of her own sex with partiality. It is thus we see the Bold Stroke for a *Wife*, of Mrs. Centlivre, suggesting to Mrs. Cowley a Bold Stroke for a *Husband*—a comedy which she brought out at Covent Garden Theatre on the 25th of February, 1783. This play labours with two distinct interests, which a very little attention might have woven into each other. One of them is the common girlish expedient of *disgusting* a variety of known suitors in favour of one unknown. The pleasantest point here, was the father locking the daughter up, and upon his leaving the room, her lover starting suddenly from his concealment...The other is a trite experiment (I mean on the stage, for in real life, nothing perhaps of the sort has ever occurred), of a neglected wife going *en cavalier* to her husband's mistress, to learn *how to captivate.* The mistress naturally falling in love with this wife, who can play to the life any part but her own, in her fondness, possesses her of all the *conveyances* which her husband had made to the prejudice of his family.

It is a common observation that the writings of the ladies do not shun the broadest latitude taken by the other sex; and so indifferent, for the most part, do they seem to their peculiar interests, that they luxuriate in the description of a gay agreeable profligate. They would inspire constancy, but they paint the rover: in their most perfect characters the heart always pants for pleasure. But this I learn is the *creed*, as well as practice, among the dramatists of the fair sex. The female friend who sketches the character of Mrs. Behn,[14] speaks out upon the subject. "She was a woman of SENSE, and *consequently* a lover of pleasure." We have had four ladies eminent among our comic writers—Behn, Centlivre, Cowley, and Inchbald; and a not very rigid moralist would strike out much from the writings of each of them.

———————

8. Daniels, George. *"A Bold Stroke for a Husband." Cumberland's British Theatre.* 48 vols. London: John Cumberland, 1829-75. Volume 36, pages 3-7. Extract.

COSTUME.

DON JULIO.—White satin Spanish doublet, trimmed with silver and slashed with blue satin—white scarf—full slashed trunks—white silk tights—white shoes, with blue rosettes—lace collar—ornaments round the neck—sword and belt—white hat, and ostrich feathers.

DON CARLOS.—White kerseymere[15] doublet, cloak, and trunks—white hose—russet boots—black Spanish hat, with white ostrich feathers and diamond loop—sword, ruff, &c. The dress slashed with pink, and trimmed with silver lace and buttons.

DON CAESAR.—Black velvet and gold doublet, trunks, and cloak—red hose—russet shoes—hat and ostrich feathers—sword and ruff.

DON VINCENTIO.—White kerseymere doublet, cloak, and pantaloons, slashed with white satin, and trimmed with silver lace—russet boots—hat to match—ruff, chain, and sword.

DON GARCIA.—Scarlet and silver doublet, cloak, and pantaloons—ruff—black hat and feathers—sword—russet boots.

DON VASQUEZ.—Plum-coloured doublet, trunks, cloak, and hat, slashed with purple satin—collar—red hose—russet shoes.

GASPER.—*First dress*: Black and orange doublet, trunks, and cloak—collar—red hose—russet shoes—gray hairs. *Second dress*: Purple satin and silver doublet, trunks, and cloak—several orders round the neck—red ribbon, and eye-glass—cane, collar, &c.

PEDRO.—Brown and scarlet doublet, trunks, and cloak—blue hose—russet shoes—collar.

DONNA OLIVIA.—White satin and silver Spanish dress—white satin shoes—several ornaments, feathers, &c.

DONNA VICTORIA.—*First dress*: White satin Spanish dress, veil, &c. *Second dress, as a Cavalier*: Canary Spanish tunic—collar—black hat and ostrich feathers—white silk stockings—white lace-up boots—sword, &c.

DONNA LAURA.—Blue satin and silver Spanish dress.

DONNA MARCELLA.—Pink satin and lace dress—white veil.

MINETTE.—Claret-coloured petticoat—black velvet body—blue Spanish apron—white slip—black satin shoes—the dress trimmed with small bell-buttons and pink and blue ribbon.

INIS.—Orange-coloured petticoat, ditto.

SANCHA.—Blue silk petticoat, ditto.

———————

14 *Mrs. Behn*: Aphra Behn (1640?–89), English dramatist, translator, poet, and novelist. Author of several plays, including *The Rover* (Duke's Theatre, 1677) and *The Lucky Chance* (Drury Lane, 1686), she is considered to be the first professional woman writer.

15 *kerseymere*: a twilled fine woolen cloth of a peculiar texture, one-third of the warp being always above and two-thirds below each shoot of the weft.

9. Review of Elizabeth Inchbald, *Every One Has His Fault. The Morning Herald* No. 4,329 (30 January 1793), page 3. Extract.

Covent Garden. A new Comedy, called "EVERY ONE HAS HIS FAULT"; was presented at this Theatre, last night. [The Reviewer lists the characters and actors and summarizes the plot].

It will appear from this recapitulation, that some parts of the story, are rendered interesting, by the shew of probable misery; and some are ludicrous, more than was intended, by the course of events, perhaps, too far incongruous and improbable.—But, though the scenes are not all naturally produced, there are few, which do not compensate for a faulty introduction, by a dialogue abounding with interesting sentiment, or lively repartee. Some of the scenes between Captain *Irwin*, and his family or friends, are very tenderly wrought; and those, in which Sir *Robert Ramble* appears, have a sort of gaiety, which, if it does not reach the purity of wit, is never debased by buffoonery.

The characters, except that of *Placid*, which is from FOOTE,[16] have, at least, as much novelty, as can be expected at the present day; and that of *Harmony* is, perhaps, entirely new. In the general conduct of the Play there is this distinguishing merit, that the incidents are not produced, or heightened by any mechanic contrivances or efforts of *manual wit*, without which so few comedies have of late been ventured upon the stage. Upon the whole, this is a piece, with some scenes of forceful interest, some of elegant manners, and some of well-tempered ridicule;—a polite Comedy, after the mode, which was called French, while any thing like literature, or manners remained in France.

The House was filled with a very fashionable audience, who received it with unanimous and frequent applause; so that it promises to be the favourite Comedy of the season. The author, we understand, is Mrs. INCHBALD, who gave it a Prologue and Epilogue, which were very well spoken by FARREN and Mrs. MATTOCKS.

---

10. Review of Elizabeth Inchbald, *Every One Has His Fault. The Star* No. 1,476 (30 January 1793), page 2. Extract.

Covent-Garden. A new Comedy, called *Every One has his Fault*, was presented at this Theatre last night. [The Reviewer lists the characters and actors].

This piece may more properly be called a dramatized Novel than a Comedy. It has much distress, much fine sentiment, and some interest, but little nature and less humour.

There is little originality of character in the Comedy, if we except the part given to MUNDEN, which is that of a whimsical Philanthropist, the sole business of whose life it is to reconcile his jarring friends one towards another, by the means of little insinuations behind the other's back.—Though this sort of character may not be found very frequently in nature,—it may furnish out a good moral hint to such as are of a quite contrary disposition—

"More studious to divide than to unite."[17]
And we give the author credit for the sketch, though made from fancy than reality. MUNDEN played it, as he does every thing, admirably. The part given to QUICK he made the most of, but he could not make much. The rest of the good acting was with Mr. and Mrs. POPE, LEWIS,

---

16 *FOOTE*: Samuel Foote (1720–77), English actor and prolific dramatist, best known for his farces, which satirized public figures and events through topical allusions and mimicry. Elizabeth Inchbald included his *The Author* (Drury Lane, 1757), *The Minor* (Haymarket, 1760), *The Mayor of Garratt* (Drury Lane, 1764), and *The Lyar* (Haymarket, 1764) in her seven-volume *Collection of Farces and Other Afterpieces* (1815).

17 *"More studious to divide than to unite"*: quoted from Alexander Pope, *An Essay on Man*, Epistle 2, line 72.

Mrs. MATTOCKS, FARREN, and Mrs. ESTEN.—
FAWCETT, though a good player, was not well suited
with a character.

The play was received with applause by a very full
house. The company in the boxes and pit was almost entirely in mourning.[18]

The Prologue and Epilogue were delivered by Mr.
FARREN and Mrs. MATTOCKS.

----

11. Review of Elizabeth Inchbald, *Every One Has His Fault The True Briton* No. 26 (30 January 1793), page 2. Extract.

[The Reviewer introduces the piece, lists the characters
and actors, and summarizes the plot].

The piece, well as it went off, is very exceptionable.
Can it be conceived that a Military Officer, whose detestation of Cowardice, under his supposed insanity, made
him shudder at the commission of Suicide, would become
a foot-pad,[19] with the instrument of self-destruction in
his hand, and commit a robbery in the public street?

It has another tendency, and that highly objectionable. Allusions are made to the dearness of provisions in
the Metropolis; and in several sentences the *Democrat* displays a cloven foot.

The Audience are kept alive throughout the whole
of the performance, alternately moved either by the pathetic or the ludicrous, which were most unaccountably
blended. The emotion excited by a tender scene had not
time to subside, when the Spectator was half convulsed
with laughter by a new effort of the comic Muse.

We are at a loss what to term this new species of composition; 'tis neither Comedy, nor Tragi-Comedy, but
something anomalous in which the two are jumbled together.

----

18   *almost entirely in mourning*: Louis XVI was executed on 21
    January 1793. The news reached England a few days later.
19   *foot-pad*: a highwayman who robs on foot.

The Performers were very successful, and more perfect
than could have been expected at a first representation.

The MARGRAVE and MARGRAVINE of
ANSPACH,[20] made a part of a very crowded and respectable Audience.

----

12. Review of Elizabeth Inchbald, *Every One Has His Fault. The World* No. 1900 (30 January 1793), page 3. Extract.

We have been so long been accustomed to behold our
Theatres disgraced by performances under the false title
of comedy, that we sit down with the greater pleasure to
recommend the production of last night, which, if its success be equivalent with its merit, must be beneficial, in a
very extraordinary degree, to the interest of the Manager.

Mrs. INCHBALD has amused, and what redounds
more to her honour, instructed the town in more instances
than one. To her pen are we indebted for the present
Comedy, which she has introduced to the public under
the title of *Every one has his fault*.

[The Reviewer provides the names of the characters
and actors, and summarizes the plot].

This is the groundwork of the plot; though there are
various other characters which, if not absolutely connected

----

20   *MARGRAVE and MARGRAVINE of ANSPACH*: Elizabeth
    Berkeley Craven (1750–1828) and her second husband,
    Christian Fredric, the Margrave of Anspach and nephew
    of Frederic the Great. She originally married Lord Craven
    in 1767, and as Lady Craven moved in social and literary
    circles that included Johnson, Reynolds and Walpole.
    Sheridan brought forth her play *The Miniature* at Drury
    Lane in 1780. She separated from her husband in 1783
    and met the Margrave while traveling in Europe. They
    married after the death of her husband in 1791, moved to
    England, and purchased Brandenburgh House, which fea-
    tured a private theater where she produced her plays for
    more than a decade. In addition to her plays, she wrote
    an account of her journeys, a novel, and her memoirs.

with the story, are not so far removed to authorise any reason of complaint.

Mr. Harmony is a character as singular as it is benevolent. Totally regardless of his own advantages or felicities, he seeks only to comfort the dejected, reconcile those at variance, and make every body happy he has any concern with: his mode of burying animosity, by expressing to the opposite parties the respect which they secretly entertain for each other, is whimsical enough; but from so frequent a repetition it becomes stale and insipid.

Solus and *Placid* are well opposed—the one made to *enter*, the other eager to *retire* from the marriage state; the eccentricities of the former contrive to keep the audience in an uninterrupted roar of laughter the whole time he is on stage.

Lord *Norland*, stern, haughty, and inflexible, comes directly from *Dorriforth*, in the "*Simple Story*";[21]—and indeed the circumstance of his taking under his particular protection the son of Lady *Elinor*, cannot be disputed to derive its source from the same Novel. Plagiarism is always a fault—but perhaps not quite so enormous when the Author robs only from herself.

Character, Mrs. INCHBALD has evidently taken great pains to delineate—and it must be confessed she has not missed her aim. Mrs. *Placid* is the only one we cannot acknowledge to take its exact origin from nature—it certainly is rather overdrawn.

The distresses of *Irving*, are such as *told*, if we may use the expression, to the feelings of every one present, not absolutely dead to pity and humanity—the absurd and dangerous tendency of overstrained etiquette and ceremony, are very well, and very properly exposed. Many an honest man has sunk beneath its rigour—and when the punctilios of form are suffered to crush the indigent and worthy—who is there that will not unite to remedy their increase?

The language is what might be expected from so elegant an Author—but if it were deprived of a few expressions which *may* be converted into a *double entendre*, we should like it the better. We say *may*, because there are a set of beings, who, to the disgrace of British gallantry, grasp at any thing; which by the horrible additions of their conceit, may be rendered a matter of imputation on the decency of the female Author. These literary *Monsters*, for nothing else can they be called, seem to glory in attempting the disrepute of the fair part of our countrymen; but to their confusion be it spoken, the talents of a BARBAULD,[22] a COWLEY, a MORE,[23] and an INCHBALD, will be the ornament and boast of Great Britain; notwithstanding the mean and unjust attacks of ignorance and envy.

The performers we have not time to mention. The Prologue and Epilogue were well delivered by FARREN, and Mrs. MATTOCKS.

POLLIO.

---

13. Review of Elizabeth Inchbald, *Every One Has His Fault. Critical Review*, **new series 7 (Feb. 1793), pages 223-4.**

A minute account of this comedy would lead to a disquisition of too much length for the limits of our Review; and, perhaps, a general criticism will be much more satisfactory. We might select some of the striking scenes, in order to exhibit the dramatic art with which they are constructed,

---

21 *Dorriforth, in the "Simple Story"*: referring to the primary male character in Elizabeth Inchbald's novel *A Simple Story* (1791).

22 *BARBAULD*: Anna Laetitia Barbauld (1743–1825), English essayist, poet, literary critic, and children's author. The title of her 50-volume series, *The British Novel* (1810), is obviously indebted to Inchbald's 25-volume *The British Theatre* (1808), and constitutes a similarly impressive achievement.

23 *MORE*: Hannah More (1745–1833), English essayist, dramatist, poet, and religious and educational writer, author of *The Search after Happiness* (1773), *The Inflexible Captive* (Drury Lane, 1774), *Percy* (Drury Lane, 1777), *The Fatal Falsehood* (1779), and *Sacred Dramas for Young Persons* (1782).

and the elegant, yet natural, turn of the dialogue. That method, however, seems to us too much hackneyed; and besides, all specific beauties, either of plot or composition, are relative, depending entirely upon their place, their connection, their relation to what preceded; and the consequences, which follow like effects from their causes. For this reason it is that detached scenes seldom make the impression for the sake of which they are selected. We shall, therefore, content ourselves with stating, upon the whole, what sort of a play Mrs. Inchbald has presented to the public.

The very title develops her subject, and indicates a dramatic genius. Comedy, it must be observed, has been distinguished into different classes, arising from the practice of modern poets. The critics have enumerated the several species, such as, comedy of intrigue, comedy of character, the pathetic comedy (*comedie larmoyante*), genteel comedy, and the lower comedy (*comedie bourgeose*). The comedy of intrigue, depending upon surprize, and a rapid succession of incidents, has often succeeded on the stage. Of late years it seems to have been chiefly cultivated by our present race of authors. It is unnecessary to mention the pieces that have given *a cheap* delight in the representation, but have left in the mind of the loudest applauders not one trace of sentiment or observation on the manners. Of such performances we may say, with Horace, that they are addressed to the eye, not to the ear.—Mrs. Inchbald, undismayed by the reigning taste, has had the courage to aim at useful mirth and moral instruction. She has produced a variety of characters, well marked, and well contrasted, all tending to explain and prove the maxim which forms the title of her play. She has cultivated the noblest province of the drama, which consists in true delineation of character. She has not selected her dramatis personae from books written for circulating libraries. She has looked at life, and, to use Dryden's expression, her play is the theft of a comic writer's from mankind.[24]

---

[24] *Dryden's expression, her play is the theft of a comic writer's from mankind*: From John Dryden, Preface to *An Evening's Love* (King's Theatre, 1671): "For to write humour in Comedy (which is the theft of Poets from mankind) little of fancy is requir'd; the Poet observes only what is ridiculous, and pleasant folly, and by judging exactly what is so, he pleases in the representation of it."

The piece before us is a comedy of character, with an intermixture of that, which has been called pathetic comedy. Irwin has his fault, but a fault that springs from delicate sensibility and a generous disposition. It must be acknowledged that his producing a pistol, as the instrument which is to relieve him from misery, is a circumstance that shocks even in the reading; but he atones for it when he says, "And yet I want the courage to be a villain." Mrs. Irwin is a beautiful specimen of true affection and conjugal fidelity. Comic humour and the pathetic are happily blended in this play, and are so managed as to succeed each other with the most pleasing vicissitude. The man who, after his career of folly, has seen the merit of a valuable woman, from whom he had been divorced, has occurred in the course of human transactions. Mr. Solus, who is tired of solitude, and wishes to enter into the married state, but is deterred by the imperious spirit of Mrs. Placid, is an agreeable compound of sense and folly, or, properly speaking, of the ridiculous absurd.— The play, upon the whole, is a picture of life; the fable is well conducted, and the plot is artfully brought to a conclusion. It must, therefore, be said of Mrs. Inchbald, that the praise of aiming at the true ends of comedy must be fairly allowed to her. Her success in so arduous an undertaking needs not to be mentioned; the public suffrage is loud in her favour at every repetition of her play.

---

14. Review of *Every Man Has His Fault*. *The Thespian Magazine* 1 (March 1793), pages 220-1. Extract.

This comedy is avowedly the production of Mrs. Inchbald, and indeed one may easily perceive, as Foigard says, that "she has robb'd herself"; for most of the characters may be traced in her Next Door Neighbours, I'll tell you what, Appearance is against them, &c. However it is on the whole a very entertaining play, and we doubt not will have a long and successful run—to the performers she is considerably indebted, particularly to Mr. Lewis, who by his excellent acting makes an indifferent character stand very forward on the canvas—Mr. and

Mrs. Pope and Mrs. Grist played home to the feelings; we never witnessed an audience so visibly affected by the "art and cunning of the scene," as at the exquisite pathetic performance of the latter-mentioned lady in the last act.—Had not it been for the whimsical appearance of Quick, we should have thought ourselves at a tragedy (not a *modern* one); but the instant this little disciple of Momus made his entree in his bridegroom dress, all sorrow vanished, and some minutes elapsed before the peals of laughter, he occasioned, would permit the play to proceed—his acting was of the best sort. Munden, Mrs. Mattocks, and Mrs. Esten received many flattering marks of approbation.

---

15. "Dramatic Criticisms. Every One Has His Fault. Mrs. Inchbald." *The Thespian Magazine* 1 (March 1793), pages 234-5.

In the decline of dramatic genius, the world is indebted to Mrs. Inchbald for contributing her share of support; and it is a powerful argument in favour of female capability, that at present, the soft sex are the chief support: it is the argument of experience. The present piece is not a strict comedy. It has a double—we had almost said a triple plot; at least there are three separate interests...The characters are well-conceived and such as nature may own. The peer and the philanthropist form a fine contrast, and the more so as it does not appear a studied one: they are placed in such different situations that it is not till towards the close that we are permitted to view them in conjunction; then indeed we are surprised. The man of fashion we pronounce to be the best and nearest to real life, that has been drawn for some time; we may recognise the original every day. The philanthropist presents an amiable moral; had his mode of reconciliation been better correspondent with veracity, it might have been more so. These, with the batchelor, are the characters the author may claim. We give her great credit for her representation of Irvin after he has committed the robbery; it

is the scene of nature and of feeling, and shows a wonderful knowledge of the human heart. The language is perspicuous and just; wit has no share in the piece. There is an error which the general of our plays abound with, and which has not entirely escaped: it is conceived that comedy should represent eccentricities, which is encroaching upon farce: this we think is done in the answer of Placid to Mrs. Placid; he had said that he had lost his appetite; she insists he shall be hungry, and he answers: "O yes, I have an excellent appetite, I shall eat prodigiously."—It is not consistent with the character of the peer that he should be so easily softened by the flattery which the philanthropist offers him: we may almost say of him that "his is too proud to be vain." Some of the others are easier wrought upon than we conceive to be natural. We do not approve of making the names of the persons expressive of their characters; it anticipates novelty. Upon the whole this piece has so much to praise and so little to censure that we think it a considerable acquisition to the fame of the fair author, and the drama of her country.

CENSOR DRAMATICUS.

---

16. Inchbald, Elizabeth. "Remarks on *Every One Has His Fault*." *The British Theatre*. Ed. Elizabeth Inchbald. 25 vols. London: Longman, Hurst, Rees, and Orme, 1808. Volume 23. Pages 3-4.

There is at present an opinion prevailing, in regard to dramatic works, which, if just, is wholly contradictory to every proof of *cause* and *effect*, which has been applied to the rise and fall of other arts and sciences.

It is said, that modern dramas are the worst that ever appeared on the English stage,—yet it is well known, that the English theatres never flourished as they do at present.

When it is enquired, why painting, poetry, and sculpture, decline in England? "Want of encouragement" is the sure reply—but this reply cannot be given to the question, "Why dramatic literature fails?" for never was there such high remuneration conferred upon every person, and every work, belonging to the drama.

A new play, which, from a reputed wit of former times, would not, with success, bring him a hundred pounds, a manager will now produce, from a reputed blockhead, at the price of near a thousand; and sustain all risk whether it be condemned or not.

Great must be the attraction of modern plays to repay such speculation.

It follows, then, if the stage be really sunk so low as it is said to be, that patronage and reward have ruined, instead of having advanced, genius. Or, it is not more likely, that public favour has incited the envious to rail; or, at best, raised up minute enquirers into the excellences of that amusement, which charms a whole nation; and criticism sees faults, as fear sees ghosts—whenever they are looked for.

It is a consolation to the dramatist of the present age, that, while his plays are more attractive than ever those of former writers were, those authors had their contemporary critics as well as he, though less acute and less severe, indeed, than the present race. As a testimony—they often had not satire sharp enough to avert that bitterest punishment to an ambitious author—neglect.

Of this play, "Every One has his Fault," nothing, in modesty, can be said, beyond mere matter of fact. It has been productive both to the manager and the writer, having, on its first appearance, run, in the theatrical term, near thirty nights; during which, some of the audience were heard to laugh, and some were seen to weep—it may likewise with truth be added, that, whatever critics may please to say against the production, they cannot think more humbly of its worth, than

THE AUTHOR.

17. **Baker, David Erkine; Reed, Isaac; Jones, Stephen.** *"Every One Has His Fault." Biographia Dramatica; or, A Companion to the Playhouse.* **London: Longman, Hurst, Rees, Orme, and Brown, 1812. Part 2, pages 205-6. Extract.**

An attack upon this piece[25] produced the following letter to the printer of *The Diary* (Mr. William Woodfall):[26] "Sir, after the most laborious efforts to produce a dramatic work deserving the approbation of the town; after experiencing the most painful anxiety till that approbation was secured; a malicious falsehood, aimed to destroy every advantage arising from my industry, has been circulated in a print called *The True Briton*; in which I am accused of conveying seditious sentiments to the public. This charge I considered of little importance, while an impartial audience were, every evening, to judge of its truth;— but my accuser having, in this day's paper, taken a different mode of persecution, saying I have expunged those sentences which were of dangerous tendency, the play can, now, no longer be its own evidence. I am therefore compelled to declare, in contradiction to this assertion, that not one line, or one *word*, has been altered or omitted since the first night of representation. As a further proof of the injustice with which I have been treated, had I been so unfortunate in my principles, or blind to

---

25 *An attack upon this piece*: In his *Censorship of English Drama 1737–1824* (San Marino, CA: Huntington Library, 1975), 84, L. W. Conolly states, "Government newspapers (especially the *True Briton*) took great exception to some parts of the play, particularly to references to the high cost and scarcity of provisions in London, and Mrs. Inchbald felt obliged publicly to defend herself against the charge that the play contained 'dangerous or seditious expressions.'"

26 *The Diary (Mr. William Woodfall)*: referring to *The Diary; or, Woodfall's Register*, which ran 1452 issues from Monday, 30 March 1789 to Saturday, 31 August 1793. William Woodfall (1746–1803), London printer best known in the 1790s and 1800s for printing "impartial reports" of debates for Parliament and for the East India Company.

my own interest, as to have written any thing of the nature of which I am accused, I most certainly should not have presented it for reception to the manager of Covent Garden theatre.   E. INCHBALD.

Leicester Square,

Feb. 1, 1793."

———

18. Boaden, James. *Memoirs of the Life of John Philip Kemble, Esq. Including a History of the Stage, from the Time of Garrick to the Present Period.* **2 vols. London: Longman, Hurst, Rees, Orme, Brown, and Green, 1825. Volume 2, pages 78-80. Extract.**

We were making hasty strides to realise the new species of comedy. On the 29th of this month [January], the tragi-comedy of *Every One Has His Fault*, by Mrs. Inchbald, was acted with great applause at Covent Garden. The interest here is in a Captain Irvin, who, having married the daughter of Lord Norland, betakes himself to America to repair his circumstances, and comes back desperate at his ill success. His mind settles upon suicide, and he goes to a coffee-house to commit the act; but his better genius holds his hand, and in his way back to his lodging, he merely robs his father-in-law of his pocket-book, and a large quantity of stage bank-notes which it contains. But he is irresolute as to property he had been with regard to life, and returns the stolen goods by a servant...The peer is relentless, and resolves to prosecute...After many vain attempts to reconcile this unhappy family, Mr. Harmony succeeds by a pretended letter from the daughter, announcing her husband's death. The old blockhead repents of his cruelty, and poetical justice is achieved by a *compromise of the felony.* Whether the search after great strength of interest, such as the above, has had a tendency to refine or debase the national taste, is a question which I have no right to determine. Pure comedy cannot be written on easier terms, than much observation of character and manners, and an elegant and pointed dialogue, if the portion of wit should fall below the abundance of Congreve[27] and Sheridan.[28] The German drama, however, was happily at hand to solve this and all other doubts as to dramatic composition, and settle us in a region of monstrous incidents and false morals, from which our escape is little to be expected. Satisfied with our new masters, we have learned to invent in their taste, and indeed our original productions might be almost taken for translations. The melo-drama, pure from the German, or the germanised French stages, is the principal ornament of our splendid national theatres.

———

19. Daniels, George. *"Every One Has His Fault." Cumberland's British Theatre...Printed from the Acting Copies, as Performed at the Theatres Royal, London.* **48 vols. London: John Cumberland, 1829-75. Volume 7, pages 5-8. Extract.**

COSTUME.

LORD NORLAND.—Full dress suit.

SIR ROBERT RAMBLE.—Blue coat, white waistcoat, buff pantaloons, silk stockings, and shoes.

SOLUS.—First dress—Brown suit. Second dress—White cloth suit, trimmed with silver, wedding favours, &c.

HARMONY.—Plain brown suit.

PLACID.—Brown coat, white waistcoat, and white breeches.

———

27   *Congreve*: William Congreve (1670–1729), English dramatist noted for his brilliant comic dialogue and his satirical portrayal of fashionable society, author of *The Old Batchelour* (Drury Lane, 1693), *The Mourning Bride* (Lincoln's Inn Fields, 1693), *The Double-Dealer* (Drury Lane, 1693), *Love for Love* (Lincoln's Inn Fields, 1695), and *The Way of the World* (Lincoln's Inn Fields, 1700).

28   *Sheridan*: Richard Brinsley Sheridan (1751–1816), Whig politician and statesman, playwright, and proprietor of Drury Lane Theatre, best known for his plays *The Rivals* (Covent Garden, 1775), *The School for Scandal* (Drury Lane, 1777), *The Critic* (Drury Lane, 1779), and *Pizarro* (Drury Lane, 1798).

EDWARD.—Drab-coloured jacket, white waistcoat, and white trowsers.

HAMMOND.—Suit of black.

LADY ELEANOR IRWIN.—Dark sarsnet[29] dress, trimmed with white.

MRS. PLACID.—Pink gauze dress, trimmed with white lace.

MISS WOOBURN.—White muslin dress, trimmed with white satin riband.

MISS SPINSTER.—First dress—Grey silk gown. Second dress—White silk gown and petticoat, trimmed with white satin.

————————

20. Letter to the Lord Chamberlain.[30] *The Monthly Mirror* 1 (December 1795), pages 40-2.

MY LORD,

A Writer less presumptuous than myself would, perhaps, lose much time in search of a proper selection of ceremonious *terms* and *phrases*, before he ventured to address an OFFICER OF STATE, so elevated as your Lordship; but as I am not about to write a dedication of panegyric on your Lordship's talents, nor to supplicate a situation in your Lordship's gift, I may as well forego all unnecessary compliment, and enter upon my subject boldly and *at once*.

MY LORD, it is to *one* particular duty of your high office only I mean to confine myself; and that is, to your *control over the* STAGE. The subject is indeed a comprehensive, and, as far as it relates to the general *manners* and *improvement* of a NATION, assuredly a most serious and *important* one. The authority with which your Lordship is vested is so unlimited, that unless great care be taken, the STAGE will soon groan under as desperate a tyranny as in some countries of which we have heard *religious opinion* does at this moment. When *Sir* ROBERT WALPOLE, in alarm about a poor stupid performance which exhibited a minister in a darker garb than he wished to be seen in, shackled the STAGE with the political *fetter* which has since galled it so unmercifully, he never once thought of the abuses to which absolute power is liable even in hands the most impartial. Surely if he had, he would not have neglected to clog the LICENSER[31] with a few wholesome restrictions; so that in the remedy of particular evils, he might not affect the general good; that in rescinding the EXUBERANCES, he might not injure the *step*.

MY LORD, it seems to me that it never entered into the conception of the ministry, that it was necessary for a LICENSER to be a *man of talent*. I don't presume to know what talent may be requisite to make an *officer of state*, but the *drama*, MY LORD, it should be recollected, is a species of literature, one of the most useful and valuable, perhaps, we possess. I would not be thought wantonly to stigmatize the taste or discriminating powers of any person: but, MY LORD, prejudice may carry a man a great way; and when his vision is clouded by the mists of policy, he may imagine that to be a *libel on government*, which is in reality nothing more than a *moral sentiment*.

The stage, MY LORD, is at this moment in such a deplorable condition, that every attempt to trace the different causes of its degeneracy is to be considered in the most flattering light. I shall commence in the following month *a series of letters to the* LICENSER, in conformity to the promise made in our preface, wherein I mean to explain the use, necessity, and duties of such a character: his influence on dramatic writing in general: and the

—————

29 *sarsnet*: i.e., "sarsenet" or "sarcenet," a very fine and soft silk material made both plain and twilled, in various colors, used chiefly for linings and dresses.

30 *Lord Chamberlain*: a chief officer who shares, with the Lord Steward, the Master of the House, and the Mistress of the Robes, the oversight of all officers of the Royal Household. He appoints the royal professional men and tradesmen, has control of the actors at the royal theaters, and is the licenser of plays.

31 *LICENSER*: i.e., the Licenser of Plays, an office created in 1737 through the Licensing Act, which decreed that all new plays must be inspected and approved by the Lord Chamberlain's Office.

qualifications requisite to the due discharge of his office. The utility of this research is unquestionable. If the *waters*, MY LORD, are unwholesome, we look to the *fountain*. The *tree* does not wither till its *root* is dessicated. The LICENSER has in charge the *morals* as well as the *politics* of the Stage. Nothing comes before the public without his sanction and authority: of course he is accountable in part for all the trash, vulgarity, and impiety, which, under a thousand shapes, are soliciting the public *imitation*.

If, in the prosecution of this subject, I should speak with some boldness, your Lordship will take into consideration that my views are directed immediately to the *public good*; that I am not attacking a *private*, but a *legislative* character;[32] and therefore, should my zeal chance to carry me to any *extreme*, I shall be acquitted of any intentional irreverence to your Lordship's person.

> I have the honour to be,
>> My Lord,
>>> Your Lordship's
>>>> Most obedient
>>>>> Humble Servant,
>>>>>> HONESTIUS.

---

21. "The Coalition of Managers!!" *The Monthly Mirror* 1 (January 1796), pages 181-4. Extract.

When a country feels itself too weak to oppose the menaced vengeance of a formidable enemy, it is a trick of policy to call in the aid of neighbouring powers, that they may be able to effect, by a junction of interests, what separately they could never hope to achieve. Managers of theatres, as well as of nations, are properly objects of suspicion and distrust. What then are the public to imagine when they find parties, professedly and necessarily inimical to each other uniting themselves on a sudden in one band of apparent amity and good will, conferring reciprocal favours; and, unexpectedly, exercising the duties of social and moral virtue? What, but that despairing of completing a system of arbitrary control over the stage and all its co-relative and consequent operations, while on influence is perpetually thwarting another; they have at length resolved to enter into a regular compact, and by *one concentric effort*, establish a DRAMATIC DESPOTISM. If the people so far forget their duty to suffer this abominable league, the consequences may be dreadful. The stage, instead of a public benefit, will become a source of mere private emolument; all the spirited exertions resulting from fair and honourable competition, will instantly be lost; the improvements which we owe to emulative, industry, and ingenuity will be interrupted; there will be a total stagnation of liberality and enterprise; and the caprices and absurdities of managers will make their undisputed way through the channel of public amusement.

It is to the paucity of theatres, and consequently the confined advantages of competition, that half the evils of which we daily complain are attributable; but if this triple alliance, with which we are managed, should take place, and continue, how would these evils be increased! The public would no longer command, but obey; they must then intreat as a favour, what now they may demand as a right. Interference will be as impertinent as unavailable.—Let the managers once agree to support each other's machinations, and the noble independence of British audiences is at an end. If now we have reason to be dissatisfied with the company or entertainments of one theatre, we can go to another for superior amusement. If the manager of Covent-Garden, by a sordid parsimony, neglects to provide handsomely for the public, they can withdraw their countenance from that theatre, and give it to Drury-Lane, where the expenditure may be more liberal. In short, while the interests of the proprietors are divided, the people have the redress of their grievances in their own hands; but if a junto[33] should be established, the people have NO will—NO prerogative—NO patron-

---

32 *private, but a legislative character.* The author makes this distinction because of his anxiety over libel laws.

33 *junto*: a body of men joined for a common purpose, especially of a political character.

age. The company of comedians may still be *called* the servants of the public, but how empty and ridiculous will appear this nominal compliment, when the public are become the servants of managers. It is scarcely possible to enumerate all the mischiefs which would spring from a coalition of this nature. There would not only be a relaxation of effort in managers, but authors and actors would become still more than they are the slaves of their will. For instance, should Mr. Colman refuse his sanction to any production, however brilliant or excellent, the author would present it to Mr. Sheridan and Mr. Harris[34] in vain. The will of one manager would be the will of all. The young and enterprising actor, with no other recommendation than his own merit, would stand little chance of an engagement during the existence of such a compact; for who does not see, at once, the system that will be pursued? The companies of each theatre will be formed from *reciprocal presentations*. In the winter season Mr. Colman shall supply his friends Harris and Sheridan, and those gentlemen shall requite the obligation in the summer. Again, if Mr. Harris will give an engagement to Miss L————, he shall participate in the Haymarket stock of amusement. If Mr. Sheridan will engage Mrs. G————, he shall also come in for *his share*. The emulation of some actors will be destroyed, and the ambition of others subdued; for instance, is it to be supposed that a proprietor will be at the expense of fifteen or sixteen pounds per week for a performer, in a certain cast, when he can have the occasional assistance of an established favourite for nothing?

[The author thinks through a number of scenarios with different actors].

The stage, alas! is declining, too rapidly to need any disposition on the part of managers to precipitate its ruin. Our degeneracy, indeed, is said to be general; and some go so far as to affirm, that we are of necessity and un-

avoidably approximating to a state of comparative fatuity; that as, in all matters of taste, there is a progressive improvement; a consummation or *ne plus ultra*,[35] and a decline; so, from a candid review of literature it is pretty evident the *acmé* has long since been gained, and every succeeding generation will be more and more inert and stupid. If this be the case, the managers have some plea to offer in excuse for the miserable trash they are perpetually foisting on the public; but alas! if they are unable to stem the torrent of nonsense which is pouring down so rapidly from every quarter; they surely need not lend a helping hand to expedite its progress;—if they cannot communicate genius to their authors, nor judgment to their players, they can at least keep the channels of theatrical information, clear and unobstructed. To check the ardour of enterprise is to shut the door against probable improvement. Where there is no encouragement, there can be no effort. In short, LET THE MANAGERS COALESCE, AND ALL THE PURPOSES OF THE DRAMA ARE COMPLETELY ANNIHILATED.

———

22. "To the Licenser." *The Monthly Mirror* 1 (January 1796), pages 184-5.

It is to the *use*, *necessity*, and *duties* of your situation, that I mean to direct my attention. You may probably feel its *importance* too well to be reminded of it; but, in investigating the state of the BRITISH STAGE, it is impossible to overlook a character placed by the hand of power at its head, to direct and regulate its conduct.

It is in many countries, not less liberal or enlightened than our own, a matter of complete astonishment, that the guidance of our drama should be intrusted to ONE MAN: the absurdity, indeed, is so glaring, that, were we not convinced that such was actually the case, we should be inclined to treat it as the chimera of a dis-

---

34 *Mr. Harris*: Thomas Harris (*d.* 1820), proprietor and manager of Covent Garden Theatre, first in partnership with George Colman and then alone, from 1767 until his death in 1820. In his own time he was often accused of privileging spectacle over the best interests of the drama.

35 *ne plus ultra*: the utmost limit to which one can go or has gone; the acme or final culmination.

turbed imagination: for what *individual* was ever known to possess such a combination of talents and virtues which one cannot but connect in idea, with a character that requires the exercise of both in more perfection than human nature, in its most exalted state, is adequate to?

But if foreigners are astonished that a superintendent, like this, should *exist*, how much more will they be surprised when they are told, that Englishmen, more jealous of their rights than any other people in the universe, sit tamely under the exercise of his authority, and so far from regretting their subjection, never think proper even to inquire into the nature of the office. It may be urged that this indolent insensibility arises from their not feeling any ill effects from a LICENSER's jurisdiction: but the fact is, they are not acquainted with the extent of his power, and I question whether *one twentieth* part of the British nation have any idea what a LICENSER is. I hope, however, in the course of these letters, to prove, that not only the DRAMA, but *men* and *manners* in general, are very materially affected and injured by his authority, notwithstanding it is by some supposed to be merely *nominal*, and by others more *beneficial* than otherwise to the interests of the stage.

It is not to be imagined that any arguments which an obscure individual may advance, however sound or rational, can tend to the *abolition* of an office which has been established by parliamentary edict, and to which *fees and perquisites are attached*. But we all know that it is not essential to a party's being placed in a situation under government, that he should be apprized of its *duties*, and YOU, Sir, very probably may have omitted to make a proper estimate of such as belong to *your own*; since it rarely happens that a man, eager after the *profits*, stops short to think of the *qualifications* of his office. In my opinion, however, *one* should be proportionate to the *other*, and though I cannot pretend to ascertain what the former *may be*,[36] I shall attempt accurately to distinguish

what the latter *ought to be*. Perhaps, Sir, like some men who, though too idle to go in quest of provision, are very willing to eat when it is *set before them*, you may have no objection *to be taught* what you would not take the trouble *to learn*. Be that as it may, the writer will think *his* trouble amply requited, should any effort of his be the means of enforcing the DUE DISCHARGE OF YOUR DUTY: it matters not who *plants the tree*, so that THE PUBLIC enjoy the *fruits*. The waters of the *Nile* were not less fertilizing, because its sources were *unknown*.

I am, Sir, &c.

HONESTIUS.

––––––––––

23. "To the Licenser: Letter II." *Monthly Mirror* 2 (September 1796), pages 302-3.

Sir,

I look upon a LICENSER to be neither more nor less than a dramatic *inquisitor*; and I do not regret his arbitrary exercise of power, merely as tending to destroy the *freedom* of the BRITISH STAGE, but as *encroaching* on a privilege still dearer and more important to Englishmen, THE LIBERTY OF THE PRESS. In a subsequent letter I shall attempt to point out the manner in which that liberty is affected. I mean at present to inquire into the *utility of your office*, and to see whether the end of its original establishment has been answered.

The government of all nations is entitled to respect; and it is essentially necessary that the legislative authority should be secure from the wanton attacks of faction and disloyalty. To prevent, therefore, the propagation of seditious sentiments, through the medium of a public stage, the appointment of a situation like yours, I grant,

––––––––––

36 *what the former may be*: See *List of Plays Licensed by John Larpent*, 2 vols. (1801–1815; 1816–1824), Huntington Library Manuscript 19926. The memorandum book does not have figures for 1795, the year the author writes. Between 1801 and 1810, however, Larpent charged a standard fee of two guineas (£2, 2*s*) per play, and charged one guinea (£1, 1*s*) for occasional addresses to be spoken at the theater. In these same years, his average income from these fees was £74, 14*s*, 2*d* per year.

was expedient; but to make *one man* the SOLE ARBITER of dramatic proceedings, must strike every considerate person as an act of egregious folly: and Sir Robert Walpole, instead of meriting the thanks and gratitude of his countrymen, which he would have been justly entitled to, had his plan been properly digested, is remembered only, on this subject, to be despised for his negligence. If that minster's judgment had been *oracular*, indeed, and he could have prognosticated the *infallibility* of every man who should be appointed to the office of LICENSER, his establishment would be less objectionable; but we know very well that a Lord Chamberlain may exercise his peculiar functions as a statesman, without inquiring at all into the nature of the *drama*, and that he appoints under him a LICENSER, or an *examiner of all plays*, as that annually-enlarging volume, the *red book*,[37] styles it, not because he may be better acquainted with the subject than himself, but, because the *salary* and *fees* annexed to the *place*, are worthy the acceptance of a man he may wish to oblige.

The effusions of dramatic genius are, therefore, exposed to every kind of perversion; the blundering supervisor may stumble on a spirited passage, and imagine it to be politically libellous, because he can comprehend neither its beauty nor its tendency. With this impression, he has nothing to do but to strike it out with his pen. *Morality* immediately becomes *defamation*, and *metaphor* involves (for ought he knows) all sorts of *treason* and *illegality*. Ignorance may start objections to one passage, and caprice to another, till the piece be thought unfit for representation, or permitted to be acted only in such a state as that inevitable condemnation must ensue.

I do not charge *you*, Sir, with having so misconceived, and so mangled the productions which come before you in your official capacity; it is a sufficient argument for my purpose, that to such misconceptions, and such wanton expunctions, a dramatic author is subject. You may probably know your duty, and know also how to discharge it

---

37 *red book*: the Red Book of the Exchequer, a miscellaneous volume, containing copies of charters, statutes, surveys, etc.

(though a few circumstances which have lately come within my knowledge have left a few doubts on my mind) but you cannot answer for the talents of your *successor*— no more than your predecessor could answer for *you*. The qualifications of a LICENSER are not defined like those of a physician, a lawyer, or any other professional character; he goes through no examination before his formal instalment into office: he has no claims to make but those of his patron; interest, not merit, is his initiation and his warranty.

Thus then, I conceive, the *utility* of the office is at an end, since its ostensible holder is not *necessarily* a man of competent ability to execute it, he has *great power* and is liable to *abuse* it, he has UNLIMITED POWER, and may therefore be a *dangerous character*.

I am, &c.

HONESTIUS.

---

24. **Review of opening night performance of *Blue-Beard*. *The Morning Chronicle* No. 8,939 (17 January 1798), page 3.**

Drury-Lane. A new spectacle, under the title of *Blue Beard*, and founded on the old Christmas tale that has so long amused children, was brought out last night with much splendor of dress, decoration and machinery; but so imperfect, particularly in the latter part, that it was impossible to form a fair judgment of its merits.

The procession over the Mountains is exquisitely beautiful, and the delusion of the perspective is new to the Stage. But the scene of the most powerful interest is that where *Fatima* is relieved by the approach of the *Spahis*;—the Music of the Quartetto has a passion that is irresistible. To give effect to this Romance, and that the taste and expence so lavishly bestowed on the decoration may not be lost, a great part of the dialogue, which is unsufferably tedious, must be cut away. The whole part of Mr. SUETT, after his first scene, contributed nothing to the interest, but became tedious from its insipidity. In a Spectacle of Action like this, where every thing is addressed to the eye and the ear, and so little to the judgment or the heart, there is nothing so material to success as rapidity in the progress of the plot. The scene should never flag. The charming PARISOT made her appearance, and danced in her peculiar stile; but there was no spirit in the music adapted to her *entrée*, and the applause was therefore feeble. A sentence of SUETT—"Oh what a fine thing it is to be a great Minister whom no one dares to turn out,"[38] seized upon by the audience as a political allusion to the present day, and produced a mixed acclamation of applause and censure, as political allusions always do. Perhaps in the present instance it was not intended by the author.

---

25. Review of opening night performance of *Blue-Beard*. *The Morning Herald* No. 5,406 (17 January 1798), page 2.

Drury-Lane. A Dramatic Romance, called *Blue Beard*, translated from the French by Mr. COLMAN, was performed last night, for the first time. It is taken from the old story, and, as a dramatic production, possesses a sufficient share of interest to render it attractive; but its chief pretensions to public favour rest neither on the story, which is too romantic to be considered at all probable, nor upon the dialogue, which is weak and incoherent. Its merit consists in the beauty of the music, the splendor of the scenery, and the ingenuity of the machinery. These, indeed, form a powerful aid to the piece, and will not fail to bear it through in popular triumph.—The spectacle is of the most magnificent description. The procession of *Blue Beard* to the house of *Ibrahim*, to bring home his intended bride, *Fatima*, exceeds any thing of the kind we have for a long time witnessed; and the scenic decorations are beyond any thing the English stage has lately exhibited. Of the music too much cannot be said; it is at once grand, simple, and scientific,[39] and adds a fresh laurel to the musical fame of KELLY.—An elephant, two camels, and several horses, all artificial, are introduced in the pageantry, and produce the most pleasant effect. In the course of the representation, many blunders in working the scenery, which are unavoidable in the first representation of this nature, occurred, and the delays which took place were consequently very great. The gratification which the audience experienced from the exhibition, however, amply compensated for the inconvenience attendant upon those protractions, and the whole went off with great *eclat*. It was 12 o'clock before the curtain dropped, owing to the frequent interruptions caused by the magnitude of the scenery, and the difficulty of erecting some parts of it; but these obstacles will of course be obviated by repetition, and we have no doubt but that *Blue Beard* will long continue to attract crowded Houses. The expence of getting it up is said to be not less than two thousand pounds. Most of the songs were deservedly *encored*, and some of the sentiments highly applauded: the serious part of the dialogue is by far the best: the wit is, for the most part, very *mediocre*. A political allusion, "that it was a fine thing to be a great man in office, when no one could turn him out," was well received, although a long contention, in which the ayes had decidedly the advantage, arose in consequence of it.—PALMER, KELLY, Mrs. CROUCH, and Miss DE CAMP, exerted their abilities throughout with the happiest effect. Mrs. CROUCH looked divinely, and her dress, which was becoming and decent, formed a striking contrast to the indelicacy to which Miss De Camp had recourse, to display the symmetry of her person.

---

38 *"Oh … out"*: Apparently the audience considered this line a reference to Prime Minister William Pitt; their ambivalent response gives some sense of Pitt's level of popularity in 1798.

---

39 *scientific*: theoretically artful or methodical in a pleasing way; technically learned, skillful, elegant.

26. Review of opening night performance of *Blue-Beard*. *The Oracle and Public Advertiser* No. 19,833 (17 January 1798), page 3. Extract.

BLUE BEARD, was represented for the first time. The dialogue, such as it is, comes from the pen of COLMAN; the music from KELLY; and the machinery from JOHNSTONE.

[The Reviewer lists the characters and actors].

The scene of the Drama is laid in *Asiatic Turkey*, and BLUE BEARD, a character whose history must be well known to our Readers, is a Bashaw of Three Tails. Except in this circumstance, and the transposition of the scene, very little alteration is made in the main incidents of the original fable. But the story of *Blue Beard* is calculated chiefly to excite commiseration and terror. In the present piece, all that can charm the scenic eye, and delight the musical ear, the beautiful and the terrific, are combined to render it a superb and an interesting spectacle.

[The Reviewer summarizes the plot]

The conclusion was ill managed and too abrupt. The stage was several times left totally unoccupied, and the conduct of the whole betrayed a want of practice in the business of the evening, which the necessary attentions of a repetition will remove. In the *Blue Room*, or Charnel House, where the ashes of *Blue Beard's* Wives are deposited, the whole contrivances were thrown into ridicule by the want of celerity in the intended transitions. KELLY attempted in vain to remove the Spectre of Death. In the height of his indignation he pummelled it several times, thinking to force it to abscond from the public eye. The Spectre remained, however, incorrigible; and shewed uncommon attention to the audience, by the most polite *bows* we ever witnessed from a *Spectre!* The spectators could not resist the temptation, and laughed very heartily at this *phenomenon*.

The performers acquitted themselves with as happy an effect as the part alloted to them would permit. PALMER, in *Blue Beard*, "fretted and strutted his hour on the stage,"[40] with much commendable anxiety for the success of the drama. KELLY, in *Selim*, evinced a bold and dignified manner when about to be crushed by the superior powers of *Blue Beard*. BANNISTER, jun. in *Shacabac*, was very pleasant. Mrs. CROUCH and Miss DECAMP were very successful; and the former demonstrated astonishing powers in the pathetic; the *Trio*, from the Castle, by these three was as happy a combination of distress and sound as to be found in few places.

The Dialogue was *la! la!*[41]

The Music, for which KELLY deserves the greatest encomiums, is very pleasing, though not all strictly original. Almost all the Airs were encored, and a *quartetto* in the first Act most deservedly so.

BANNISTER sung a pleasant song in the first Act, on the idea of men *guillotining* their *wives* to prevent strife, cutting off argument and head together, in a manner that was much applauded. There was also a very pleasant duet in the same act, between him and Mrs. BLAND.

BLUE BEARD was given for a second representation with the loudest plaudits.

---

27. Review of opening night performance of *Blue-Beard*. *The True Briton* No. 1,581 (17 January 1798), page 3. Also printed in *The Sun* No. 1659 (17 January 1798), page 2. Reprinted in slightly altered form in *The Whitehall Evening Post* No. 7985 (16-18 January 1798), page 2. Extract.

Drury-Lane. The long-expected Dramatic Romance of *Blue Beard*, or *Female Curiosity*, was represented at this Theatre last night, before as large an audience as the house would admit.

[The Reviewer provides the names of the characters and actors, and summarizes the plot].

---

40 *"fretted and strutted his hour on the stage"*: referring to William Shakespeare's *Macbeth* V.v.25.

41 *la! la!*: The reviewer here refers to fashionable slang of young women in the late eighteenth century. See, for example, Liska's statement in *Timour the Tartar* I.i: "La! Father, how can you snub one so!"

Such is the manner in which Mr. Colman has drama-
tised this well known Story. Some of the situations are
terrific, but it is, on the whole, much too long.

The Piece is diversified by character, and enlivened
with many humorous points in the dialogue. The Scenery is highly splendid. The opening Scene, of a fine land-
scape, and the rising of the Sun, is very beautiful. The
Anti-chamber, or Hall, in the castle, is superb.—The Sepulchre, with the skeleton, the birds of prey flitting over
the tomb, and the Shades of the departed wives, form an
awful spectacle. There is also a beautiful scene of an illuminated Garden with a Cascade. In this scene Parisot appeared, and displayed all her graces to delight Fatima.

Upon the whole, this Romance is very well calculated
for the season of the year, and affords an amusement that
is pleasing in itself, and interesting, as it recals to the mind
the story that delighted it in the days of childhood.

The Music is principally composed by Kelly, and it
is a strong proof of his taste, fancy, and science,[42] as a
Musician. Several of the Airs were *encored*; and a
Quartetto, by Kelly, Suett, Miss De Camp, and Mrs.
Crouch, received warm and repeated applause.

The acting was altogether very good: Palmer, Suett,
Young Bannister, and Kelly, all merit particular notice.
Miss De Camp played with her usual spirit, and Mrs.
Crouch shewed powers of acting that deserve the notice
of the Managers, distinct from her musical abilities.

There were one or two passages in the dialogue,
which however harmless in intention, admitted of a Political application, and should consequently be omitted,
as they excited applause on the one hand, and censure on
the other, which may hereafter lead to turbulence and
confusion.

The Procession of the Bashaw over the mountain,
with the camels and the elephant, ought not to pass without notice; it was natural and magnificent.

There were impediments in the management of the
scenery, which might be expected in so complicated a
work; but the whole should be shortened, and it will go
off very well. The awful impression of the interior of the

sepulchre, was mingled with ludicrous sensations, by the
staggering motion of the *Skeleton*, who seemed as if, to
guard against the *damps* of the place, he had taken *a drop
too much.*

**28. Review of *Blue-Beard*. *The Monthly Mirror* 5 (Jan-
uary 1798), 45.**

After the *Country Girl*,[43] the basis of Mrs. Jordan's[44] reputation as a comic actress, a *grand dramatic* Romance, under the above title, was brought forward in a style of
splendour and magnificence almost equal to *Lodoiska* or
Richard Coeur de Lion.[45] The story is known to every
child in the kingdom, from three years old to fourscore;
and, as nothing material is added to, or taken from it, it
will be unnecessary to relate the incidents. The dialogue
is beneath contempt; and this will be easily credited when
we assure the reader that it is in the very worst style of
Colman's very worst productions. A quibble—a pun—a
simile—a metaphor—a conceit—and there is the *dialogue*.
It is, from beginning to end, a patchwork of buffoonery
and bombast, put together, as it should seem, for the express purpose of retarding the action, and harrassing the
mind of every unfortunate spectator, whom chance or
curiosity might bring into the theatre. There is no shut-
ting one's ears to all this insipidity; for we can come at
no sight of the *show* without being dinned with the jar-

---

42 *science*: knowledge acquired by learning, study, and mastery.

43 *Country Girl*: David Garrick's *Country Girl* premiered at
Drury Lane in 1766; Dorothea Jordan had her first London performance in the role on 18 October 1785.
44 *Mrs. Jordan's*: referring to Dorothea Jordan (1761–1816),
English actress, especially famed for her high-spirited comedy and for cross-dressing and tomboy roles.
45 *Lodoiska or Richard Coeur de Lion*: John Philip Kemble's
and Stephen Storace's "escape" opera *Lodoiska* had its premier at Drury Lane in 1794; Lieutenant-General John
Burgoyne's *Richard Coeur de Lion* had its premiere at Drury
Lane in 1786. Both were popular afterpieces that required
extravagant sets.

gon of the *showman*. The *spectacle* is, of itself, grand in the extreme. The *procession* of *Blue-beard* to the house of his father-in-law is one of the finest and best regulated objects the stage has produced. The *music*, too, proves Kelly (what his former efforts, except the two pieces in the Castle Spectre, have, in our opinion, *not* done) a musician of great taste and fancy. The quartettos in both acts are finished compositions, and the *quick movement* which De Camp commences on the battlement is equal to anything we ever heard.

These are the chief excellences of Bluebeard. The scenery is not uniformly well painted; the castle, in particular, is offensive to the eye of taste. The fable is conducted without art or ingenuity, and all the interest of the fiction is entirely smothered and subdued by the imbecility of the author.

Mrs. Crouch—Kelly—De Camp—the *arms* and *legs* of Parisot—the *head* of the skeleton—and the *wings* of the hobgoblins—not forgetting the *horses* and the *elephants*, performed their parts to admiration.

<hr>

29. Review of *Blue-Beard*. *Monthly Review*, 2nd series 26 (May 1798), 95.

The author of this piece professes that, a pantomime not being forthcoming at Drury Lane for the Christmas holidays, he was induced, expressly for that season, to supply the place of Harlequinade. We shall not enter into a regular examination of either the fable or the incidents; for, in fact, we know no rules by which our criticism should be directed. We have heard, and believe, that Mr. Colman has executed his design with considerable ability; but we are sorry that such abilities should be employed in the service of the Smithfield Muses.[46] We wish to see that

gentleman renounce entirely the province of the marvellous incredible legends, and the whole monstrous offspring of extravagant fancy, in which truth and nature are never observed. From some specimens of his genius, we think that we have a right to expect better things from his pen, whenever he shall choose to return to the verge of human life.

Respicere exemplar vitae morumque jubebo
Doctum imitatorem, et veras hinc ducere voces.[47]

<hr>

30. Review of the 1811 revival of *Blue-Beard*. *The Morning Post* No. 12,497 (19 February 1811), page 3. Extract.

Covent Garden. This Theatre boasted an overflow last night at a very early hour. Before the rising of the curtain, every box was full, and the pit and galleries were crowded with as much as they could have been, had a second Young Roscius[48] been announced in the bills of the day.

The cause of this eager anxiety was the revival of the dramatic Romance of *Blue Beard*, which has long been in preparation, and which has at length been produced in a style of splendour, of which it is impossible to form an adequate idea without paying a visit to the Theatre.

It has been understood for some time past, that it was the intention of the Managers to introduce real horses in the revival of this piece. Many sneers have been thrown out on the subject, and many more may be expected to follow the performance of last night. We are no advocates for such innovations on the stage or in politics as to go to explode what has hitherto been regarded as good, and

<hr>

46 *Smithfield Muses*: referring to the poorer areas of London around Smithfield Market; thus, "Smithfield Muses" refers to those muses who inspire the lowest popular entertainments (as opposed to legitimate comedy and tragedy).

47 *Respicere … voces* Horace, *Ars Poetica* 317: "I should direct the learned imitator to have a regard to nature and manners, and draw his expressions from life."

48 *Young Roscius*: referring to William Henry West Betty (1791–1874), known as "Master Betty" or "the Young Roscius," an English actor who won instant success as a child prodigy in 1804 and performed until 1808, when he entered Christ's College, Cambridge.

which experience has proved beneficial to the community at large. We can never approve of any system that may go to exclude SHAKESPEARE, to make way for pantomimes in five acts, or which may give to unmeaning noise and gaudy *spectacle*, that time which might afford as rational pleasure and dignified amusement in the works of our best dramatists. In favour of so vicious a system we can never lift our voice; yet still we do not see any reason for that alarm which some of our contemporaries profess to feel on the present occasion. We do not see that SHAKESPEARE is likely to be trampled under foot by the horses introduced in an after-piece at Covent-garden Theatre, and without meaning any thing disrespectful to the present company of performers, we do not see that one in any way disgraced by such auxiliaries. If pantomimes are at all to be tolerated at the National Theatres, we can see no reason why the managers should be forbidden to get them up in as splendid a manner as they are got up elsewhere, and though much may be said of the tendency of such spectacles to vitiate public taste; we are of opinion that very little injury need be dreaded from them, at a time when that is most prized which is most ridiculous, and when *Hamlet Travestied* is more eagerly followed that *Hamlet* itself.

Of the intrinsic merits of the piece last night revived, it is unnecessary for us now to speak. The object of attraction was less the merits of the romance itself than the embellishments of which rumour had spoken. Of these, though much had been said, there certainly is no reason to complain of exaggeration.—The scenery throughout is most superb, and if all the parts are not to be praised as appropriate, those who most disapprove of the spectacle, so finished, must of necessity confess it magnificent. The march over the mountains is well managed. A miniature procession, as formerly at Drury-lane Theatre, is seen at a distance. The music is heard as being also a great way off. The procession gradually approaches, and the music is heard more distinctly, till at length the cavalcade[49] reaches the stage. The display of the wealth of

---

49   *cavalcade*: a procession on horseback, especially on a festive or solemn occasion.

Abomelique is very grand, and the whole was so well arranged that no disorder appeared throughout the scene. The illuminated garden was excessively brilliant. The devices there exhibited reflect great honour on the taste and ingenuity of those by whom they were contrived; and these, with the admirable dancing of Mrs. PARKER, closed the first act with great *eclat*.

In the early part of the second act, the horses made their first appearance, and were greeted with universal applause: the beauty of the animals filled every one with admiration, and when they were seen ascending the heights with the greatest velocity imaginable, the audience were perfectly in raptures.

The scene of the Blue Chamber was most deservedly admired: its singular beauty was sufficient to justify the curiosity of *Fatima*. The paintings which adorn it have a most beautiful effect, and the dreadful change which takes place on the fatal key being applied to the door, is similar to that contrived at Drury-lane, but more striking and impressive.

We should despair of being able to do justice to the last scene in description, if our time and our limits would admit of the attempt. After a general battle in front of the stage, which is in some parts managed very well, though the whole is a good deal confused, the contending parties appear on the draw-bridge of the castle. The bridge breaks down. The cavalry opposed to the tyrant are below, and are here seen to charge up the broken bridge, which is in a direction almost perpendicular. *Abomelique* is conquered. The castle is fired, men and horses are seen dying on the stage, and a variety of interesting objects presenting themselves to the eye, form a *coup d'œil*, which we again declare ourselves unable to describe.

[The reviewer comments in passing on individual performances].

The Piece was announced for repetition with thunders of applause. Louder acclamations we never heard. In its progress it was twice greeted with three regular cheers. Upon the whole, from the warm gratification expressed by the audience—from the beauty of the music which is composed and selected by Mr. KELLY—from the excessive splendour with which it has been brought forward, and from the interest excited by the story notwithstanding its extravagance, we think it likely to become *the rage* a second time, and we should not be greatly surprised if it were to have even a greater run than it had when it first came out.

———————

31. Review of the 1811 revival of *Blue-Beard*. *The Times* No. 8224 (19 February 1811), page 3. Extract.

Covent-Garden Theatre. Last night, after "Every Man in his Humour,"[50] *Blue Beard* was exhibited. This beautiful afterpiece was a distinguished favorite in its earlier day, and will be so again, if decoration and magnificence can make any thing a favourite.

It has often surprised us, that with the single source of Eastern Tales open to Managers, they should ever have turned away from the rich, the fantastic, and the varied, to such unmeaning pieces of dulness as *Mother Goose* and *Asmodeus*.[51] *Blue Beard* is not the only story among the treasures of Arabian and Persian romance which might form an interesting drama. There is scarcely one among the multitude of those which we have admired in our childhood for their wild and strange beauty, and valued in our more mature age as memorials of national manners, that might not be capable of dramatic form, and dramatic delight.

The scenery and dresses of the present performance are extremely shewy. In the procession scene, the passage of the troops, and whole proud attendance of an eastern Satrap in its march through the hills, was singularly picturesque. The banquet scene in the garden, the blue chamber, and the Bashaw's castle, were admirable efforts of the artist: but the storming of the palace was a collection of every thing that could be gathered into one scene to make it striking. As the Spahis rushed forward to attack the gate, the drawbridge was let down, and a detachment of horses were seen fording the moat. They successively sprung upon the stage, and the whole depth of the scene was filled with combatants, foot and horse. The passing of the cavalry under the arches of the rampart, and their charge up the drawbridge, might be almost taken for the subject of a painting. Some of the horses were wounded, and they fell on the stage, fainting gradually under their wounds. One horse who had thrown off his rider, and was dying, on hearing the report of a pistol, sprung up to "join the battle hour once more," and, after a single effort, fell as if totally exhausted. The sagacity and spirit of those fine animals were carried to a height which we could scarcely have conceived.

The whole performance was received with shouts of applause.

[The reviewer selects some performances for applause and censure before finishing the review by noting some "slight inaccuracies" in the costumes.]

———————

32. [Hunt, James Henry Leigh]. "Application to Parliament for a Third Theatre." *The Examiner* No. 168 (17 March 1811). Pages 161-2.

The reader will be startled perhaps at seeing this subject under the head of politics; but matters of taste and literature are more connected with the political character of the times than most people imagine or than the Pittites[52] and their friends can allow; and the stage, in particular, is of importance to it, and felt to be so. It is for this reason that the Chamberlain of the Household,[53] though an officer of very

———————

50 *"Every Man in his Humour"*: referring to Ben Jonson, *Every Man in His Humour* (first acted by the Lord Chamberlain's Men, 1598).

51 *Mother Goose and Asmodeus*: referring to *Harlequin and Mother Goose* (Covent Garden, 1806), by Thomas John Dibdin, and *Harlequin and Asmodeus; or, Cupid on Crutches* (Covent Garden, 1810).

52 *Pittites*: Hunt appears to be punning here as a way of further connecting politics and theater. "Pittite" can signify either an adherent of the policies of English statesman William Pitt (1759–1806), or one who occupies a seat in the pit of a theater.

53 *Chamberlain of the Household*: See note 30.

doubtful authority in this respect, has always taken care to keep his eyes upon the drama, ever since chance threw it in their way. CHARLES the 1st, who was fond of letters, used to correct plays for performance with his own hand: his successors, agreeably to the STUART policy, which was at once cunning and short-sighted, paid as great, though not a similar, attention to the stage: and the French Emperor,[54] smitten with a regard for its interests equal to that which he entertains for the Press, has taken the Parisian theatres under his peculiar care; so peculiar indeed in every item attending their conduct, that to his other titles, he might fairly add that of Manager-General of the French stage. In his dominions, this is natural enough, and consistent with the stage of things; but in England, it is not easy to see why the stage should not be put upon a footing with the press, and rendered responsible to the laws only, instead of being at the nod of one of his Majesty's servants,—a situation which tends to make both actors and authors servile, or at best, submissive. I do not say, that this power is exercised at present to any very obnoxious degree, for certainly it is not; but the chance of such an abuse is wrong in a free country. At any rate, as courtiers are apt to think every thing better for their master's interests than freedom of speech, they naturally incline to the encouragement of shew and spectacle in preference to the higher drama; and thus far the controul has an undoubted tendency to injure the public taste.—But I am wandering from the main subject.

The Public are aware, that a Petition from a number of gentlemen—chiefly merchants in the city, I believe—requesting permission to erect a third theatre in the metropolis, is to be considered for the second time tomorrow in the House of Commons; and that a petition for a charter for this purpose was refused by his MAJESTY[55] some little time back. The petitioners make their request upon

the *sole* ground of the *increase* of London and Westminster, the population of which, it is stated, has nearly doubled during the course of his Majesty's reign: and certainly, if this is really the sole ground upon which the petitioners could apply, and if his MAJESTY had no better argument for them presented to his mind, the refusal, which he was advised to give, was not very wonderful. But if such a ground, in itself, was no conclusive reason for granting what they asked, the counter-petitions presented from the other Theatres,—from the Managers of Covent-Garden, from Mr. SHERIDAN and his theatrical connexions, from Messrs. GREVILLE and ARNOLD, from Mr. TAYLOR of the *Opera*, and lastly, from Mr. ELLISTON of the *Circus*, were altogether absurd in the reasons they advanced against it. The Covent-Garden Managers, whether from a consciousness of their Mother Geese and their Blue Beards, I know not, took it for granted that a new theatre, professing to respect the legitimate drama, would be their ruin; and pathetically reminded his MAJESTY of the countenance he had so often shewn them by his Royal presence. Mr. SHERIDAN also, though he, of all men, ought to know what enriches and ruins a theatre, affects the same conviction; appeals to the humanity of the KING and his Council; says that the patent granted to his predecessors by Charles 2d, gives him the right of monopoly on the occasion; and supposing, for the sake of argument, that a third theatre might be necessary, talks of another patent, which he has in his possession ready for the purpose, and which he calls a reserved patent, that is to say, in plain terms, a dormant and departed one.—The petition of Messrs. GREVILLE and ARNOLD are founded principally upon what is represented as a prior claim, which is in fact nothing more than a licence from the Chamberlain; and both these gentlemen run into the common mistake that an additional theatre must of necessity injure the rest, because it *is* additional. This reasoning is carried to its height of absurdity by Messrs. TAYLOR and ELLISTON, the former of whom, in contemplating the success of another English theatre, fears for the attractions of his Italian one; while the latter is equally alarmed lest a little more of the legitimate drama should entice away the class of people who

---

54 *French Emperor*: Napoleon Bonaparte (1769–1821), French general, First Consul (1799–1804), and Emperor of France (1804–1814, 1815).

55 *his MAJESTY*: George III (1738–1820), King of Great Britain from 1760 to 1820. From 5 February 1811 until his death, George III's son (later George IV) ruled as regent for his father, who had become insane.

visit him;—as if those who can sit out Italian operas, will have much inclination for good English plays; or those who delight in the vulgar medley of Mr. ELLISTON's Circus, will be led way to see pieces of a higher order and actors of a less paltry ambition. The person, who is to be heard on this occasion with most respect, is Mrs. RICHARDSON, the widow of one of the Drury-lane proprietors, who finds herself with four daughters in a state of great distress in consequence of the late destruction of that theatre. But when this lady and her friends treat the application of the Petitioners as an inhumanity towards those who suffered by that event, they forget that the application looks to a public effect, and should therefore be judged on public grounds; and in short, it is not to be concealed that the distress of the renters of Drury-lane theatre originates in the bad habits of Mr. SHERIDAN himself, and that it is as ridiculous as it is pitiable to hear him making so much noise about a concern, which he has already ruined and never can restore. Ask his own renters and performers; and hear what they say on this subject, with bitterness of regret.

It is useless however to enter into this part of the subject, and into disputes about patents and prerogatives, which have already been discussed before the Privy Council. These are matters that do not affect the main point of the *expediency* of erecting a new theatre; and if the reader has any curiosity to see them, he will find them at large in an account of the proceedings published last year. Will it be believed that in this account,—in this pamphlet detailing the arguments and petitions for and against, and published by the petitioners themselves with an evident feeling of conscious right,—will it be believed, that, in such a publication, the only argument, which is of real importance to the question of expediency, should be *omitted*? And yet, so it is; and with an apparent studiousness, that is unaccountable. This argument, which appears conclusive to every body whose opinion I have heard on the subject, is the necessity of exciting a greater spirit of *emulation* among theatrical managers.—The fact of an increase in population is well enough; but if the counter-petitioners can shew that the theatres still remain unfilled in spite of this increase, they do away the argument as far as any arithmetical con-

sequence is to be deduced. This however does not affect the necessity of a new stimulus to *emulation*; for it is very easy to prove, that even if the population of London and Westminster were only half as much as it is now said to be, a third theatre would be necessary on the same ground. The counter-petitioners very justly state that it is not of want of room the public complain: no, indeed; they complain that there is too much room in *one spot*; they complain, that *instead of one or two great theatres, in which sense and sound are lost, there are not four or five small ones, in which every body could see and hear;—in which the actor could convey his painting, and the dramatist his poetry, to the remotest corner of the house*:—in a word, they complain that a theatrical monopoly, in the hands of one or two parties, enables any persons, into whose hands it may fall, to care for nothing but their own selfish views of profit; to defy the taste of the few; corrupt the taste, perhaps the morals, of the many; and thus degrade the spirit and reputation of their countrymen.

See how completely this is borne out by facts. The Messrs. HARRIS of Covent-Garden, and the Messrs SHERIDAN of Drury-lane, have respectively been bad managers,—the former from want of taste, and the latter from want of economy. Both of them, fancying themselves secure in their monopoly, or to use their own cant, supposing that nobody else could be so inhuman upon their industry and expenses as to question it, did as they pleased with the town. They *left us no choice* between staying away from the theatre, and going to one where we might see and hear nothing: They left us, generally speaking, no choice between staying away, and witnessing a succession of foolish "novelties," melodramas, and over-grown farces, which have since rendered our dramatic character a bye word in Europe; and lastly, they left us no choice between keeping our wives and daughters from the rational entertainment that occasionally presented itself, and suffering them to run the gauntlet through a multitude of wretched beings,[56] who make the theatre a place of open resort. Nay, the bagnios[57] and theatres arise equally renovated, in every respect, from

---

56 *wretched beings*: Hunt here likely refers to prostitutes, as his subsequent reference to "bagnios" makes clear.
57 *bagnios*: houses of prostitution.

their respective conflagrations; and while the former rear their unblushing fronts in the same spot in which they fell, the latter re-appear with additional conveniences, and a new luxuriance of invitation, for the confluence of evening debauchery. It may be safely said, that a more *evident* desire to attract was shewn, in the construction of the new theatre at Covent-Garden, towards those who do *not* come to see the play, than to those who do. In Paris, where nothing ought to exist that could put an Englishman to the blush for his country, the drama is confessedly superior at present to ours; and setting aside the national slavishness, the conduct of the theatres doubly comfortable and respectable. To what are these advantages owing? Simply, to the number of the theatres, which produces emulation; and to the removal, out of sight of all that can offend the modesty, or raise the apprehensions, of decent families. Upon this latter point, which though it is certainly capable of exaggeration, is of real and considerable importance, Mr. SHERIDAN affects to doubt the intentions of the Petitioners, and at best to consider them as puritanic. For my own part, if any attention is due on this subject to an humble individual who has been no inattentive observer of the drama for some years past, I can safely say, that nothing but my duty as a journalist could induce me to visit the theatres, in their present condition, unless attracted by some excellent revival or sterling novelty; and even then I should be obliged to take much preparatory trouble in order to get a seat in which I could see and hear, and in which the females, who might happen to be with me, should not be shocked and terrified.—I sincerely regret that other subjects, pressing upon my attention, have prevented me from attending just now to the present one, till it was too late for me to do it the least justice;—but every gentleman in the House of Commons, who is prepared to regard it in its just importance to the taste and morals of the community, will, it is hoped, declare his sentiments tomorrow night; and at any rate, do his utmost to prevent the question from dropping into one of those indifferent matters of accommodation, in which the corrupt of all sides are happy to *oblige* any celebrated partizan who happens to have an interest in its defeat.

33. [Hunt, James Henry Leigh], Review of the 1811 revival of *Blue-Beard*. *The Examiner* No. 169 (24 March 1811). Reprinted in *Leigh Hunt's Dramatic Criticism 1808-1831*. Ed. Lawrence Huston Houtchens and Carolyn Washburn Houtchens. New York: Columbia University Press, 1949. Pages 45-9.

Mr. Colman's melodrama of *Blue Beard*, one of those wretched compounds of pun and parade, which serve to amuse the great babies of this town and to frighten the less, still forms the nightly boast of this "classical" theatre. With the jokes about troopers *trooping* off, and persons unable to keep a secret because their teeth *chatter*, the reader is no doubt well acquainted, and quite willing, I trust, to have no further acquaintance; and it is needless to point out the gross want of costume [*sic*] which the author has manifested from beginning to end, not only in the incidents, but in the language and the habits of thinking. In one of the songs a Turkish girl is made to talk of her lover's "ringlets," which said lover, agreeably to truth, is represented on the stage with a turban and no hair at all. But the stage is not so judiciously inconsistent in other parts of the story; and it has been well remarked in the *Times* that the introduction and paintings in a room is contrary to the religion as well as customs of the Mahometans. It may be observed, in fine, that the story has not even the usual moral of childish tales: there is, it is true, the "punishment of curiosity," and the curiosity may be a wrong one; but the excitation of it is at the same time wanton, the discovery it makes hurtful to the infant spectator, and the punishment itself unjust. The production indeed is unworthy of criticism, and would not have been noticed in this paper but for a singular novelty that has lately been added to the representation. That actors should make beasts of themselves is no new thing; but the *gravis Esopus*[58] of our Stage, Mr. Kemble, must turn beasts into actors; and accordingly, after having had dog actors at Drury-Lane, and jack-ass

---

[58] *gravis Esopus*: i.e., "solemn Aesop."

actors (emblematic wags!) at Sadler's Wells, we are now presented with horse actors at "classical" Covent-Garden. These prepossessing palfreys appear to be about twenty in number, and come prancing on the Stage into rank and file with as much orderliness as their brethren at the Horse Guards, facing directly to the spectators, and treating them with a few preparatory curvettings,[59] indicative of ardour, so that when the riders draw their swords, the appearance is not a little formidable, and seems to threaten a charge into the pit. After this, and a few picturesque gallopings over a bridge, they do not appear till the last scene, when all their powers are put forth, and *Blue Beard* and his myrmidons[60] utterly eclipsed. Firstly, the aforesaid gallopings are repeated over mound and bridge, till every steed has reappeared often enough to represent ten or a dozen others; then one or two of them get interestingly entangled in a crowd; then a drawbridge, breaking down, is scaled by three or four at full gallop, which calls down the thunder of the galleries; then a duel ensues between a couple of the horsemen, of whose desperate blows the reader may have a lively idea if he has ever seen the impassioned images that tap the hour on Saint Dustan's.[61] The excessive politeness, indeed, manifested by these duellists, and the delicate attention they pay to each other's convenience, reminds one of the celebrated battle of Fontenoy,[62] where the officers of the French and English guards, coming together, pulled off their hats to each other and mutually insisted upon giving up the honour of the first fire. The only difference is that the consistency of the thing, the qualis ab incepto,[63] was not so well

kept up in the latter instance. Lastly, comes the grand display, the dying scene; and here it is difficult to say which is more worthy of admiration, the sensibility or science of these accomplished quadrupeds. When I saw them, there seemed to be but three who performed this part of the ceremony, and it may safely be asserted, that never did horses die with so much resignation. If I knew their names (let us suppose they are *Twitcher*, *Twirler*, and *Whitenose*), I should say that *Twitcher* and *Twirler*, who were parties in the duel, had most emulation, and *Whitenose* most coolness. The two former seemed to be aware that they were in battle; the latter manifested an indifference to his situation, almost amounting to disdain. *Twitcher* and his antagonist were, if I may so speak, about the pitch of Brunton[64] and Claremont,[65] easy but majestic, and amiably severe; but the presence of mind displayed by *Whitenose* was equal, at least, to that of Liston.[66] Lord Grizzle[67] himself, in his dying moments, could not surpass his philosophic preparation and finished demise. While the other two were occupied with their own rencontre,[68] he entered the stage with as much indiffer-

---

59 *curvettings*: leapings by a horse with the forelegs raised and together, and with the hind legs leaving the ground before the forelegs reach the ground again.

60 *myrmidons*: unscrupulously faithful servants or hirelings; hired ruffians.

61 *Saint Dustan's*: a London church located on the Strand, famous for its clock, whose figures stiffly and sedately hammer out the time each hour.

62 *battle of Fontenoy*: confrontation of 11 May 1745 that led to the French conquest of Flanders during the War of the Austrian Succession.

63 *qualis ab incepto*: the quality (of something) from the beginning.

---

64 *Brunton*: probably John Brunton (1775–1849), who made his debut in 1782 at the age of seven at Bristol and then acted at Norwich from 1795–1800. He debuted at Covent Garden on 22 September 1800 in *Lover's Vows*. In 1804, he became manager of the theater at Brighton and later managed theaters at Norwich, Birmingham, and Lynn; in 1823, he was manager of the West London Theatre.

65 *Claremont*: William Claremont (d. 1832), actor, born William Cleaver to a shop assistant and a delivery man, according to the *Authentic Memoirs of the Green Room*. Having been apprenticed to a linen draper, he decided to pursue a career on stage and thus changed his name. He joined the company at Margate in 1792 and Covent Garden in 1793–94, playing many small parts there through the 1804–5 season until he moved to Drury Lane, where he remained at least through the 1821–2 season.

66 *Liston*: John Liston (1776?–1846), who was one of the most popular (and the most highly paid) comic actors of his day and who appeared at Covent Garden, Drury Lane, and the Olympic but perhaps had his greatest successes at the Haymarket.

67 *Lord Grizzle*: a character from Henry Fielding's *Tom Thumb, a Tragedy* (Haymarket, 1730).

68 *rencontre*: encounter.

ence as if nothing had happened, though it was soon evident that he had received his mortal wound, for after a little meditation he began to die, bending his knees one after the other, like a camel stooping to be loaded, and then turning upon his side and becoming motionless, just as a human actor does upon his back. The other horses, by this time, are disposed also in their respective attitudes; the dismounted warriors are seen fighting across their bodies; drums, trumpets, smoke, and confusion complete the effect; and the close of the scene lets loose a thousand exclamations of praise of the new performers.

Joking apart, it is no doubt interesting to see of what so noble an animal as the horse is capable; and it is still more agreeable to be relieved from those miserable imitations of him, which come beating time on the Stage with human feet, and with their hind knees the wrong way. If it were possible to present the public with such exhibitions and at the same time cherish a proper taste for the Drama, they might even be hailed as a genuine improvement in representation; for if men, and not puppets, act men, there seems to be no dramatic reason why horses should not act horses. But there are always two very strong objections, staring this kind of novelty in the face—one respecting public taste, and the other the poor beasts themselves. The success of such exhibitions is not only allowed to be a mark of corrupted taste with regard to better things, but it materially helps to produce that corruption. They are too powerful a stimulus to the senses of the common order of spectators, and take away from their eyes and ears all relish for more delicate entertainment. The managers and the public thus corrupt each other; but it is the former who begin the infection by building these enormous theatres in which a great part of the spectators must have noise and shew before they can hear or see what is going forwards. In time these spectators learn to like nothing else; and then the managers must administer to their depraved appetite, or they cannot get rich. Are these the persons to cry out against the erection of a new and smaller theatre?

But the animals themselves are to be considered, with regard to *their* comfort. A sprightly horse has a profusion of graceful and active movements; and it is his nature per-haps to be fond of a certain kind of exertion. He delights, when in health and vigour, in scouring[69] the fields; and feels, we are told, an emulous ardour in the race; but then the fields and the raceground are proper places for him; the turf incites him to activity, and the open air breathes health and pleasure into his veins. On the other hand, it will take a great deal to persuade a rational spectator at the theatre that the closeness of a stage, the running round and round, the bending of knees, the driving up steep boards, and above all, the mimicry of absolute death, do not give the animal considerable pain, and have not cost a hundred times as much in the training. It is a common observation respecting these horses at Covent-Garden, that in galloping about the stage, they exhibit a manifest constraint and timidity; and when they pretend to come in at full speed, have a jumping and feeble motion resembling that of rabbits. We all know by what merciless practices bears and camels are taught to dance; and anybody who has been at a country fair and seen the wretched mode in which dogs and birds are worried through their feats will be slow to believe that the docility necessary for such purposes is obtained by good usage. The Arabs, it is true, and other nations, whose uncivilized state brings the animal and his master into familiarity from their birth, can teach their horses to perform a thousand surprising feats with no other means than habit and kind treatment; but this is a very different case; the sphere of action is different, and the animal is put upon no other action than it is natural and pleasant to him to perform. The Managers of Covent-Garden should know that what is said by many, and thought by most people, of the training of these horses, is not favourable to the humanity of their masters; and till there is some explicit statement on the subject it will be as difficult to think otherwise as it is impossible to applaud their introduction at all.

---

69 *scouring*: moving about hastily or energetically.

34. Daniels, George, *"Blue Beard." Cumberland's British Theatre...Printed from the Acting Copies, as Performed at the Theatres Royal, London.* 48 vols. London: John Cumberland, 1829-75. Volume 36. Pages 5-10. Extract.

COSTUME.

ABOMELIQUE.—Blue velvet robe, richly embroidered, trimmed with ermine, and lined with white satin—amber satin vest, richly embroidered—rich satin scarf, embroidered and trimmed with bullion—white satin trousers—yellow boots—rich turban—a blue beard.

IBRAHIM.—*First dress*: Brown Turkish suit. *Second dress*: A richly embroidered robe.

SELIM.—Blue striped jacket and trousers—crimson fly, trimmed with brown fur—turban—yellow boots.

SHACABAC.—Red striped jacket and trousers—brown fly—turban—red slippers.

HASSAN.—White jacket and trousers—red slippers—turban.

SPAHIS.—Striped trousers and jackets—scarlet flies—turbans.

BLUE BEARD'S SOLDIERS.—Crimson robes—white jackets and trousers—yellow boots—turbans.

FATIMA.—*First dress*: Blue Turkish robe—white muslin under dress and trousers—turban. *Second dress*: White satin, richly spangled with gold—superb turban.

IRENE.—*First dress*: Yellow Turkish robe—white muslin under dress and trousers—turban. *Second dress*: White satin, richly spangled with silver—splendid turban.

BEDA.—Buff robe, trimmed with blue—silver spangled under dress.

35. Adolphus, John. *Memoirs of John Bannister*, 2 vols. London: Richard Bentley, 1839. Volume 2, pages 11-16.

Not less [than Matthew Lewis's *The Castle Spectre*] was the success (and it is not necessary to put their merit into balance) of Colman's "Blue Beard," performed with all the operatic strength of the company, and with all the aids that scenery, decoration, and stage contrivance could bestow (16th January). Colman was particularly happy in adapting this cherished nursery fable to the stage: he had full license to throw loose the reins of his imagination; and so long as he kept the darlings of our infancy,—Blue Beard, his wife, and sister Ann, the mysterious chamber and the enchanted tell-tale key,—before us, he had unlimited discretion as to whatever else he might choose to introduce: he was welcome to have three-tailed bashaws and spahis, and as many pasteboard horses and elephants as the stage could hold.

Colman says, as an apology for having had recourse to this nursery story, that the children, both old and young, being accustomed to expect a pantomime at Christmas, and the house having provided no other, he had prepared this trifle to supply the place of a harlequinade. The apology is unworthy of him: the piece was not acted until nearly a month after Christmas, when the holidays were over, and the young misses and masters returned to their "*Fables choisies*" and their "*Excerpta.*"[70] A pantomime on the subject of Blue Beard had been unsuccessful some winters before; the French had made a dramatic essay on the story, under the name of "*Raoul Barbe Bleue,*" and this was in fact the basis of the piece. Kelly discloses the truth with such characteristic *naïvete*, that he shall tell it here in his own words. "After the success of 'The Castle Spectre,'" he says, "I determined to endeavour to get the French programme of 'Blue Beard,' which I had brought from Paris, dramatized. I accordingly called upon my valued friend, George

---

70 "*Fables choisies*" *and their* "*Excerpta*": i.e., "chosen fables" and "excerpts."

Colman, and told him that I had brought him the outline of a French romance, which I believed, if he would undertake to write it, would prove highly successful: I told him moreover that my object was to endeavour to establish my name as a composer by furnishing the music for it; that I was perfectly sure a week's work would accomplish the literary part of the two acts, for which I would give him a couple of hundred pounds. After having discussed the subject and two bottles of wine, the witty dramatist agreed to my terms, and I promised to accompany him to his country-house and remain with him for a week. I did so, and, before the week was ended, the piece was complete; and those who have seen it—and who has not?—will bear testimony to the admirable manner in which he executed his task."

If in the writing of "Blue Beard" there is not a sufficient portion of wit,—if the poetry of the songs is not of a quality to justify the high approbation of the town,—yet the beauty of the scenery, the aptness (after the first night) of the machinery, and, above all, the exquisite and well-employed talent of the performers, were calculated to win approbation from the indifferent, or even the churlish: not one part could have been better filled. Palmer condescended to perform the savage Bashaw; he gave to his love the proper haughtiness, and roared out his impatience to fill up the number of his murders with characteristic force. Dicky Suett, as Ibrahim, father-in-law of Blue Beard, punned, exulted, shivered, and ran away, with his usual drollery. Kelly put forth his best powers to give effect to his own music; and even the little part of a little negro, brought on merely to waste a few minutes, was made of value by Hollingsworth. Bannister, in Shacabac, the honest and reluctant confidant of a villainous master, highly increased his reputation. The workings of his mind when indignation at the past murders of his patron, and a desire to prevent that which was then in contemplation, were ill restrained by fear, and by a knowledge that Abomelique "wore a charmed life," gave scope to his fine display of blended tragic and comic power; while his gay, frolicksome, innocent love, won all hearts, and made many envy Beda.

Adverting to the ladies: it is not possible to praise too highly the exquisite feeling with which Mrs. Crouch played and sung the oppressed and unfortunate Fatima. Mrs. Bland, always happy as the sweetheart of Jack Bannister, embellished Beda with her sweetest notes. Her song, "His sparkling eyes were dark as jet," and the duet, "Tink-a-tink," which she performed with Bannister, were among her most popular exertions. But Miss de Camp (Mrs. Charles Kemble) excelled all her former excellences, and rose to the highest pitch of scenic charm in Irene. A firm and an immovable affection for her sister Fatima, impaired only by the urgency of female curiosity, which makes her unintentionally involve her beloved relative in so much peril; a pert self-confidence, shown somewhat saucily toward her father, were forcibly displayed: but the crown, the high achievement of the character, was her interesting grief at the menaced woeful catastrophe; and in the quartette, where, following the nursery fable, the author places her at the top of a tower, to "look out if she can see anybody coming," her advance from an infant hope to a full-grown assurance of aid, her progressive animation from the moment when she sees "a cloud of dust arise," to that when she sees "them galloping," her scream of joy, and the agitation of her whole frame when she "waves her handkerchief,"—all these constituted the high perfection of the dramatic art; and there was not in the house an eye nor a hand which did not give signs of sensibility, and pay a tribute of applause.

Kelly's pleasing and effective music, the delight of the audience, afforded some ground for invidious carping; but it could not be depreciated by the criticisms of the envious. Men who delight in trumpeting forth their sagacity, by disclosing what never was a mystery, told us that the celebrated "tink-a-tink" was a Russian melody; Kelly never concealed or denied it. They further alleged that the beautiful March in the first act was not his; but the assertion was not more illiberal than unfounded: he demonstrated the fact; and his assertion was corroborated by Mr. Eley, the master of the band of the Horse Guards, to whom these sagacious persons had attributed the composition...But such facts and such supposition gave rise to the charge that he was not the author of his own works; and formed a foundation of Sheridan's joke when Kelly commenced business as a wine-merchant: "Write over your door, 'Michael Kelly, composer of wine, and importer of music.'"

———

36. George Colman the Younger, "[On the Size of the Theatres]," quoted in Richard Brinsley Peake, *Memoirs of the Colman Family, including their Correspondence with the most Distinguished Personages of their Time*, 2 vols. London: Richard Bentley, 1841. Volume 2, pages 224-7.

It is curious to observe how, after a certain time, the moderns of Drury Lane and Covent Garden reverted all at once to this magnificence of the ancients of Greece and Rome; for immediately after my father's demise,[71] I opened the Haymarket Theatre in 1795, with an occasional piece,[72] which contains a ridicule, a good-natured one I hope, on the extended dimensions of the two principal London Play-houses, wherein I say, in a song alluding to them:

> When people appear
> Quite unable to hear,
> 'Tis undoubtedly needless to talk;

and that,

> 'Twere better they began
> On the new invented plan,
> And with Telegraphs transmitted us the plot:

The new Large Houses soon found the necessity of recurring to that "magnificence of spectacle"...they introduced White Oxen, Horses, Elephants, both sham and real; and the song above quoted ends with the following verse:

> But our House here's so small
> That we've no need to bawl,
> And the summer will rapidly pass,
> So we hope you'll think fit
> To hear the Actors a bit,
> Till the Elephants and Bulls come from grass:
> Then let Shakspeare and Jonson go hang, go hang!
> Let your Otways and Drydens go drown!
> Given them Elephants and White bulls enough,
> And they'll take in all the town,
> > Brave boys!

No doubt, the vastness of the two Theatres above mentioned must disappoint many who go thither for all that complete gratification arising from the intellectual repast which the whole round of our drama professes to give.

There are no certain rules of architecture for the conveyance of sound; but an actor, by pitching his voice according to its various powers of modulation, may do much to counteract the impediments in a building; the drawback, therefore, upon his inflections of tone appears to be a good deal less than the deductions from his countenance. To produce in very large theatres the desired and instantaneous effects of the voice, more is requisite, though much may be gained by practice than there ought to be; but to send post-haste intelligence in a smile, to forward dispatches by a glance, to print, as it were, a Gazette in the face, that it may reach eager politicians, so far distant from the spot whence information must be transmitted, is a much more arduous undertaking. Still, even this difficulty may, it is presumed, be in some measure surmounted; for, since the adoption of the present scale of the principal theatres, there have been and are performers, both tragic and comic, whose sudden turns of countenance have commanded general applause; but whether such effects may not often be produced by daubing, by exaggeration, and distortions of the visage, like scenes painted in distemper, is a question.

Garrick, always tremblingly alive to his great celebrity, and judicious in nursing his fame, would not probably have risked his powers in theatres of the present magnitude, particularly in the sublimer walk of tragedy.

---

71   *my father's demise*: George Colman the Elder, proprietor of the Haymarket Theatre, died in 1794.

72   Peake's Note: "'New Hay at the Old Market;' the first scene of which is still acted under the title of 'Sylvester Daggerwood.'"

His talents must have suffered a paralysis, a loss of half their vitality, when the rapid and astonishing transitions of his eye and his features could not instantly, by their close fidelity to nature, electrify all who witnessed them.

On the whole, if a sweeping decision can be formed from these loose remarks, it may be said, that the principal London theatres are too large for all the purposes they should accomplish; too large for the perfect convenience of vision, and for an easy modulation of speech; too large to

"Hold the mirror up to nature,"[73]

so as to give a full and just reflection of her delicate features and proportions; and theatrical proprietors seem to be of this opinion, by giving of late more into spectacle, melo-drama, and opera, which may be better seen and heard at a distance, than those representations which have been quaintly termed the Legitimate Drama. The proprietors may possibly plead, that there is a dearth of legitimate dramatists, and it may be so; it has been averred to by the case in all ages; but few regular shoemakers are inclined to take the trouble of making shoes, when they find so much encouragement given to them for cobbling. Between managers and the town, who leads or who drives is a problem of difficult solution; do they not by turns lead and drive each other?

---

37. Review of *Timour the Tartar*. *The Morning Chronicle* No. 13,096 (30 April 1811), page 2.

Covent-Garden Theatre.—The greatest actors who have of late obtained so much celebrity, made their appearance again last night at this Theatre, in a new piece manufactured expressly for them; and if horse-actors are to be the rage, why should not they, as well as biped performers, have characters made for them to show them off to the best advantage. This new species of bathos must, however, sometimes, involve the writers, or manufacturers, of

---

73 *"Hold the mirror up to nature"*: quoted from William Shakespeare, *Hamlet* III.ii.22.

dramatic compositions for horses, in a whimsical sort of embarrassment. One may conceive the number of parenthesis of direction he must introduce, as thus—"Here the horse runs at the adversary of his master, so as to give the appearance of saving his disarmed owner from death. In the mean time the latter regains his sword. The adversary in a rage stabs the horse, who dies with great dignity. The master of the horse avenges the death of the noble animal, by killing the man who slew him."

Of such a description was the Romantic Melo-Drame (as it is called in the bills) of last night, and which is entitled *Timour the Tartar*. Of course, none of those who went to see it expected any plot; there was, however, to do the thing justice, something like a plot, but the great object was the quadruped actors. Had the audience been polled upon the subject, we think we may venture to say that three-fourths of them came to see the horses—the horses—and nothing but the horses. Some few amongst the audience, perhaps jealous of the fame of these most wonderful animals, or perhaps solicitous for the restoration of what audiences now a-days seem to consider a *bore*, taste and refinement, ventured to hiss when these great four-legged characters made their appearance. But these hisses, which might have had the effect of woefully lengthening the face of a dramatic author (a character not much known now) whose piece was under the ordeal, merely gave rise to a number of deafening Bravoes! and Huzzas! and cries of "Turn them out!" which completely overwhelmed the hisses. The majority were determined that the horses should tread the stage in triumph, and the horses had the day.

Amidst the clattering of hoofs, the clangor of swords and spears, and the shouts of an enraptured audience, it is scarcely possible, or perhaps hardly worth while, for criticism to attempt to speak. If gaudy spectacle is to be the order of the night, and horses the masters of the ceremonies, it is beneath the dignity of criticism to scan the performance; and to grooms may be left the task of reciting the feats of the horses which they manage.

Some part of the piece may be considered as a satire upon a neighbouring Emperor. *Timour* is an usurper, and raises his needy relations to princely dignity. There are a few jokes in this part of it, but the greater part of them were made to depend upon the short stature of little Mrs. LISTON; and if that lady should unfortunately be taken ill, and rendered unable to perform, the jokes would be rather in a bad way. There was also a song or two, but, from the indifference with which they were heard, it seemed as if the greater part of the audience considered them as quite secondary to the grand equestrian performance that was to follow. The scenery is very beautiful, and, with one or two exceptions, was well managed. The horses certainly performed extraordinary feats; they scaled walls, leaped through breaches, plunged into the water, and galloped about as if they were quite at home in their parts. Mrs. H. JOHNSTON was the heroine of the piece, and her horse very politely knelt down for her to mount and alight. *Timour's* fortress was at last stormed; himself and his followers overpowered, and thus ended this romantic melo-drame. *Timour* was enacted with appropriate fierceness by FARLEY; Mrs. H. JOHNSTON played the heroine well, and made a bold leap into the water (at least such water as the Theatre affords) to escape from *Timour*. Her rescue by her little son, (Master CHAPMAN), who plunges after her on horseback, excited a tumult of applause. FAWCETT, who played the Father of the Usurper, came forward, at the conclusion of the piece, to announce, we suppose, its repetition for this evening; but the huzzas were so loud that not a word he said could be heard; he made his bow and retired. Some hissing was then heard, but it was again overwhelmed by most determined and deafening shouts of applause.

38. Review of *Timour the Tartar*. *The Sun* No. 5,814 (30 April 1811), page 3. Extract.

Covent-Garden. After the representation *The Comedy of Errors*, which was very well supported in its characters, a new grand Melo-Drama was brought forward last night at this Theatre, under the title *Timour, the Tartar*.

[The Reviewer lists the characters and actors, and summarizes the plot].

This drama is perhaps, altogether, one of the most splendid that has ever been seen on the English Stage. The author has evidently intended to have some reference to the Usurper of France in the character and elevation of the Tartar Chief. Timour, like him, has forced himself, by artifice and villainy, into the seat of power, and like him exalts his beggarly connections to situations of Royalty. The fable is well calculated for a display of various and striking incidents and scenery. After the *Horses*, who are of course the chief Performers of the piece, FAWCETT, FARLEY, Mrs. H. JOHNSTON, and Master CHAPMAN, deserve particular commendation. They respectively exerted themselves with great effect. Mrs. H. JOHNSTON, indeed, appears to more advantage in this Equestrian exhibition than she does in general in the more regular drama.

As we have mentioned the chief incidents in the outline of the fable, it is not necessary that we should describe the detail, as our Readers may easily conceive that the most striking of those incidents form the subjects for representation on the Stage. We have only to add, that as far as it is possible in so complicated a drama, the piece was very accurately exhibited last night. In fact, the first public representation of pieces of this nature may be considered as the last rehearsal. The audience received the drama with great applause, and though some expressions of discontent were apparent, they were soon overpowered, and effectually silenced by the general tumult of applause, which sanctioned its repetition this evening, when announced by Mr. FAWCETT.

39. Review of *Timour the Tartar*. *The Dramatic Censor* (May, 1811), pages 241-5. Extract. A truncated version of this appeared in *The Times* No. 8,283 (30 April 1811), page 4. Extract.

May 1. Covent-Garden Theatre.—This evening was represented the Tragedy of *Douglas*, with the degrading romantic Melo-Drama, called

TIMOUR THE TARTAR.

[The Reviewer lists Dramatis Personae].

The ruinous success of *Blue Beard* hath encouraged the managers of this Theatre to make another Vandal[74] experiment on the public taste for scenery, horsemanship, and mummery. *Timour the Tartar*, which, to lose nothing by want of dignity in the title, is called a Grand Romantic Melo-drama, is one display of splendour and equitation from beginning to end. [The Reviewer proceeds to summarize the plot].

This is the worst attempt at that exploded thing called "plot," that we recollect to have seen in even an after-piece. The anxiety of a mother for her child may be introduced, with effect, into those more delicate efforts of the drama which allow time for thoughts and tears; but it is too fine for pantomime: it was the prominence which is necessary to give it effect, in that broad beam of glare and glitter, "neighing steeds and fighting men." The whole piece was sedulously contrived for shew, and nothing could be more beautiful than some of the scenery. The court of the castle, with the triumphal chariot, and its three spotted coursers, turned and winded as they were with a grace and dexterity that must throw the "*Primores*,"[75] of the Four-in-hand Club[76] into utter despair; the mother-of-pearl chamber; and the closing scene, a fine compound of cataract and castle, deserve all the praise that can be given to the scene-painter. This last scene, and its whole gorgeous exhibition, is worth being commemorated by itself: after the Georgians have threatened to storm the castle, and *Timour* has retorted by threatening to stab the Princess, she glides from his hand, and springs from a height, which really appeared too perilous to give pleasure to the spectators. She is seen struggling with the waves of the cataract, and her child plunges in on horseback to save her. After rising from wave to wave, the Princess and her son gain the land, and ascend the cascade on horseback. They are received at its summit with shouts of joy by the Georgians, and the castle is attacked. The walls are beaten down by a battering-ram, the cavalry rush through the breach at full gallop, and the curtain falls amid the clash of arms, the braying of trumpets, and the blaze of blue lights!

The piece is, on the whole, as shewy as it could be made by the most lavish profusion of theatrical pomp: but the horses are the principal performers.[77] Some displeasure appeared to have been predetermined on by the critics in the pit: but the *unaffected* zeal and *natural acting* of the horses gradually softened the asperity of their enemies; and the melo-drama concluded with a roar of approbation!

In regard to the general effect of this piece, we are bound in justice to allow, that it is the most superb spectacle we have ever seen. It is not only very far superior, in shew, to *Blue Beard*, but it is superior to *Tarare*, which is yet considered by the Parisians as the most splendid Drama that has been produced in Paris! The scenery was superb, and extremely well managed for a first representation.

On considering the merits of the performers, Mr.

---

74 *Vandal*: likely referring to the Vandals, a Germanic people who maintained a kingdom in North Africa from AD 429 to 534 and who sacked Rome in 455. Their name has remained a synonym for willful desecration or destruction.

75 "*Primores*": literally, "firsts," here meaning premier.

76 *Four-in-hand Club*: an association of wealthy young men dedicated to driving around town in expensive carriages rebuilt like stagecoaches while attired as very well-dressed coachmen. The fad was satirized by Percy Shelley in line 97 of *Peter Bell the Third* (referring to them as the "driving schism") and by Thomas Love Peacock through his character Sir Telegraph Paxarett in *Melincourt* (1818).

77 At this point in the review, *The Dramatic Censor* footnotes a long letter from "Oliver Old Times" complaining about his experience at the opening night of *Timour*, and comparing degraded British taste to that of the Romans in the final days of the empire. See Appendix, pp. 347–48.

FAWCETT ranks in the first order; but his zeal to do all that he can on every novel occasion, reflects credit on his disposition as well as his ability. Mrs. H. JOHNSTON acted with sensibility and spirit, and looked on horseback like another *Thalestris*.[78] Miss BOLTON was meek and charming; and little CHAPMAN was honored by a general sentiment of approbation. It is our opinion that this boy will ripen into excellence, if he is well tutored.

There is a tournament, in which two champions contend for the fair hand of *Selima*, which was ably sustained, in a spirit of chivalry, by Messieurs MAKEEN and CROSSMAN, in which the latter is victorious; but he is a lover of the true old breed, for his affection is wholly manifested by actions, as he doth not condescend to utter one word.

> How arts improve in this aspiring age!
> *Peers* mount the box! and *horses* mount the stage!
> While waltzing females, with unblushing face,
> Disdain to dance but in—a man's embrace!
> How arts improve, when modesty is dead,
> And sense and taste are, like our bullion, fled?

---

40. Letter to the Editor. *The Dramatic Censor* (May, 1811), page 244n.

To the Editor of the DRAMATIC CENSOR.

Sir,—After an absence of seven years, being obliged to come to town upon business, I went the other evening to Covent-Garden—the play was the *Knight of Snowdoun*,[79] which, to tell you the truth, about the third act, threw me

into a sound sleep, from which I was roused by the clattering of the hoofs of the Princess of Mingrelia's palfry—you may judge I was during the rest of the representation of Timour kept broad awake, by the bray of kettle drums, the galloping of horses, and the clangour of the trumpets—this greatly shocked and surprised me who remembered Garrick's time, when a fine Tragedy was succeeded by an entertaining Farce, and the audience dispersed not merely *amused*, but I verily believe *improved* by the night's entertainment;—but I will confess to you that still more than the mummery astonished me, was to witness *the shouting and delirious acclamation* that prevailed, and my hearing many grave men and women exclaim, *delightful! charming! wonderful!* and, in a word, curvet[80] round the whole circle of superlatives with as much alacrity as *Bluebeard*'s charger.— This, I own, puzzled me—I went home to my coffee-house, took a tumbler of brandy and water, and still could not solve this phenomenon of bad taste. After a night's rather disturbed rest, in the morning at breakfast a sort of solution of the difficulty occurred to me, which I beg permission to communicate to you—*We are becoming a warlike people*, Mr. Editor. We had wars in Queen Anne's time, but then we fought by *a sort of proxy*—at present the case is different, and the military spirit is diffused from the cot to the throne. Thanks to Bonaparte's threats of invasion, *every man* now is *a soldier*, and therefore naturally becomes enamoured of "the pomp, pride, and circumstances of glorious war,"[81] and amongst them "*the neighing steed*"[82] of course holds a conspicuous place in his affections—the field of battle is become "familiar to his thoughts," and what before he would have turned from in disgust, he now contemplates with pleasure. It was just so in Rome, it was not till after the time of Terence, who was the friend of Scipio[83] and

---

78 *Thalestris*: legendary queen of the Amazons and lover of Alexander the Great, dramatized in John Weston's (fl. 1667) *The Amazon Queen, or, the Amours of Thalestris to Alexander the Great: A Tragi-Comedy* (London: Hen. Herringman, 1667). Alexander Pope appropriated the name to represent Gertrude Morely in *The Rape of the Lock* (1714).

79 *Knight of Snowdoun*: Thomas Morton's *The Knight of Snowdoun: A Musical Drama, in Three Acts* premiered at Covent Garden on 5 February 1811.

80 *curvet*: See note 59.

81 "*the pomp, pride, and circumstances of glorious war*": misquoted from William Shakespeare, *Othello* III.iii.354: "Pride, pomp, and circumstance of glorious war!"

82 "*the neighing steed*": quoted from William Shakespeare, *Othello* III.iii.351

83 *Scipio*: Scipio Aemilianus, also called Scipio Africanus Minor (185/184–129 BCE), Roman general famed both for his exploits during the Third Punic War (149–146 BCE)

Laelius,[84] that the Romans took so violently to *gladiatorial exhibitions*; nor did they prefer them to his comedies till, like us, they were *at war with the whole world*. Caesar, in the true feeling of a *martial* critic, blames Terence for his want of *spirit*, and adds a wish, in which, I am sure, as applied to our modern dramatists, every playgoer of the present day heartily joins—

> *Lenibus* atque utinam scriptis,
> adjuncta foret *vis comica*.[85]

This spirit-stirring observation of Caesar's is I am certain the opinion of every *Militia and Volunteer Colonel* throughout the nation—no wonder then that a body of *such weight* should have an influence in turning the scale of national taste.

There is another, and a very strong concurring cause for this partiality towards equestrian performers—need I say that I allude to that respectable fraternity called the *Four-in-Hand Club*, who with a laudable veneration for antiquity, are trying, *as far as in them lies*, to revive the glories of the Olympic Games in the *exalted* characters of *mail coachmen*—excellent members, not merely of the *community*, but of *Parliament!* they are preparing themselves to superintend the great scheme of the *Post Office Conveyances* (invented by Mr. Palmer,[86] who, unfortu-

nately for himself, did not, like Lord Liverpool,[87] *make his bargain sure*), and to obtain a *personal* knowledge of all the *turnpike* and *bye-roads* in the kingdom.

> Go on brave youths, till in some future age
> *Whips* shall become the *Senatorial badge*,
> And England see her thronging Senators
> Meet all at Westminster in *boots* and *spurs*;
> Of *bets* and *taxes* learnedly debate,
> And guide, with *equal* reins, *a steed or state*.

Yes, Mr. Editor, it is to the prevalence of the *military spirit* and *the four-in-hand* that I ascribe this passion for *equestrian mummery*—and while I hail the *cause*, I cannot but say I am heartily grieved at the *effects*. But I have already trespassed too long on your time. I must now take my leave, and subscribe myself

> Your obedient Servant,
> OLIVER OLD TIMES.

————————

41. "Timour the Tartar." *Bell's Weekly Messenger* No. 787 (5 May 1811), page 137.

Bonaparte was certainly never in a more miserable condition than he is at present.—So true is the proverb that "All a man's misfortunes fall on him at once."—Lord Wellington has defeated him in Portugal; General Graham has routed him at Barrosa;[88] and Mr. Kemble, not to be behindhand with his illustrious countrymen, is making a

and for his subjugation of Spain (134–133 BCE). He received the name Africanus and a "triumph" in Rome after his destruction of Carthage (146 BCE).

84 *Laelius*: Gaius Laelius Sapiens the Younger (fl. 2nd century BCE), Roman soldier and politician, friend of Scipio Aemilianus, and one of the speakers in Cicero's *De Senectute* ("On Old Age"), *De Amicitia* ("On Friendship"; also called *Laelius*), and *De Republica* ("On the Republic").

85 *Lenibus atque utinam scriptis, adjuncta foret vis comica*: The quotation is from Suetonio, *De Poetis*, and is a line of poetry (doubtfully) attributed to Caesar, meaning "and I wish that there was some comic force added to your [Terence's] gentle verses."

86 *Post Office Conveyances (invented by Mr. Palmer)*: John Palmer (1742–1818), proprietor of the theaters in Bath and Bristol who in the 1780s began a reform of the postal service that greatly improved it by, among other things, replacing postboys on tired horses with stage coaches; he entered into a dispute with the government over remuneration for his services that was not settled until 1813.

87 *Lord Liverpool*: Robert Banks Jenkinson (1770–1828), British prime minister 1812–27, who, despite his long tenure of office, was overshadowed by the greater political imaginativeness of his colleagues, George Canning and Viscount Castlereagh, and by the military prowess of the Duke of Wellington.

88 *Lord Wellington ... Barrosa*: referring to the Peninsular War (1808–11), in which British forces successfully defended themselves against the French armies, the Duke of Wellington eventually winning control of Portugal and General Thomas Graham winning a key victory at Barrosa in Spain on 5 March 1811.

most spirited campaign against him at Covent-Garden; borrowing the cavalry of Astley,[89] and bringing to bear on him the whole park of artillery of the Playhouse, he has attacked him in his own palace, and battered his St. Cloud[90] over his ears. Mr. Kemble deserves as much praise for his poetry, as for his pageantry; for though some persons have expressed an ill-natured doubt whether Mr. Kemble be really in earnest, and whether, in the production of this Piece, he did not rather look to his own interest than the interest of the nation, we, for our own parts are perfectly persuaded, as well from the gravity of this Piece, as from its spirit of poetry and magnificence, that Mr. Kemble fully intended it as a national boon; and in his attack on Bonaparte, he is as much in earnest as General Graham himself. We have only to express our hopes, that this spirit of patriotism and ingenious allegorical representation will extend beyond the walls of Covent-Garden-house. The season of the country fairs is now coming round; we hope, therefore, *Punch*[91] will do his duty, and that Richardson[92] and Saunders[93] will rival Kemble and the Cortes[94] in holding up the great usurper, the Timour of Europe, to universal execration. There is one thing in Timour the Tartar, the ingenuity of which we particularly admire, and that is, the representation of the Empress of France in the person of Mrs. H. Johnston, as *Princess of Mongreilia*; if a man is to be soundly rated, there is both life and nature by putting it in the mouth of his wife—the Empress accordingly does not spare Bonaparte.

---

42. [Hunt, James Henry Leigh], Review of *Timour the Tartar. The Examiner* No. 176 (12 May 1811), pages 299-300.

Covent-Garden. It is a pity, considering their very equal merits, that Mr. Arnold's opera[95] and the new melodrama of *Timour the Tartar* cannot be seen together, sympathizing in each other's ill-success. But this perhaps would be too much.—Who the author of this plagiarism from Mr. ASTLEY may be, I have not heard; but whoever he is, he need not awaken the jealousy of that gentleman:—the pageantry is indeed gaudy, and the rabbit-palfreys[96] vivacious; but the spectators are not satisfied; and the town seems beginning to think that one stage is quite enough for the public torture of these poor animals. For the rest of it, the melodrama appears to be a most awful, but at the same time insidious attack on the reputation of BONAPARTE. *Timour*, better known among us by the appellation of *Tamerlane*, is here represented as a chief altogether and barbarous, with a vulgar father and sister about him, and treating for marriage with a foreign princess who insults and disdains him in the act of promising to be his wife. This is very like TIMOUR, to be sure, and still more like BONAPARTE, who is perfectly shocked, no doubt; to hear of these terrible proceedings against him in "the finest theatre in Europe!"

---

89 *Astley*: Philip Astley (1742–1814), English trick rider who opened Astley's Amphitheatre, the first modern circus.

90 *St. Cloud*: probably referring to the royal château and Parc de Saint-Cloud, located just west of Paris and famous for its artificial cascade. The château was destroyed in 1870 during the Franco-Prussian War.

91 *Punch*: a hooknosed, humpbacked character, the most popular of marionettes and glove puppets and the chief figure in the Punch-and-Judy puppet show.

92 *Richardson*: probably John Richardson (1766–1836), showman, who initially established himself as a publican in 1796 at the Harlequin across from Drury Lane. He produced plays at the Bartholomew and Greenwich Fairs.

93 *Saunders*: possibly Master Saunders (fl. 1800–1807), who performed on the tightrope at the Royal Circus and who was sometimes called "The Infant Equestrian Phenomenon." Among his specialties were leaping through two hoops at full speed on a horse and leaping over platforms and pyramids of light.

94 *Cortes*: the name of the legislative assemblies in Portugal and Spain; the reference is to the struggle against Napoleon in the Peninsular War, mentioned above.

95 *Mr. Arnold's opera*: *The Americans*, which *The Examiner* in the previous article had just condemned as "hopelessly and ludicrously bad."

96 *rabbit-palfreys*: i.e., "rabbit-horses"; here "rabbit" functions both as an expression of contempt (meaning a poor performer) and as an exact term, a "rabbit-horse" being a horse that runs "in and out," i.e., not in a straight line.

43. Review of *Timour the Tartar*. *European Magazine* 59 (May 1811), pages 377-8.[97] Extract.

May 1. A new Grand Romantic Melo-Drama, written by M. G. Lewis, Esq. was produced for the first time at Covent-Garden, under the title of "TIMOUR THE TARTAR."

Before the commencement of the piece, it was evident that there was a strong party against it. The opposition threw a great number of hand-bills from the upper boxes, containing (as we understood) some declamations against equestrian performances being introduced at the regular theatre. These, however, met with a very unfavourable reception; most of them were torn to pieces with indignation, and those who had dispersed them were loudly hissed. [The Reviewer then provides a summary of the plot].

Such is the outline of this piece, which surpasses in splendour any thing of the kind that we have seen on the stage. As a literary work it will not rank very high; but as a dramatic production, rich in contrivance and incident, and above all, interest, it is entitled to great praise. the situations are good; and the characters well supported. In every part there is something to strike and to please; and with all the grandeur it has none of the fatiguing dullness usually attendant on stage pageantry.

In the first act, a splendid combat scene exceeded all that we had previously witnessed. The opening of the second act charmed us with a scene representing a chamber in the castle of *Timour*.—Than this display of eastern grandeur nothing could be more superb. The last scene, in which the castle of *Timour*, and a beautiful water-fall, are the most conspicuous objects, would be injured in its effect by too minute a description. It is impossible to conceive any thing more striking; and the exertions of the horses have a wonderful effect. The white horse which carried the heroine (Mrs. H. Johnston) plays admirably.

He kneels, leaps, tumbles, dances, fights, dashes into water and up precipices, in a very superior style of acting, and completely astonished the audience. His fellow labourers in the scene also displayed much ability, and lived, died, climbed up walls perpendicularly, or scampered up longitudinally, with the greatest ingenuity. On the piece being announced for repetition, some hissing at the horses was heard; but was overwhelmed by most determined and deafening shouts of applause; and *Timour* has crowded the house ever since.

It has been asked, how the stage is degraded by the introduction of these noble and beautiful beasts? If pasteboard and wicker-work animals are allowed, against which we do not remember any declamation from the time of the *Tatler* to the present, can it be any degradation to follow the example of the ancients, and to introduce the living horse in all the evolutions of real action?

---

44. Daniels, George. "*Timour the Tartar*." *Cumberland's British Theatre...Printed from the Acting Copies, as Performed at the Theatres Royal, London*. 48 vols. London: John Cumberland, 1829-75. Volume 29, pages 5-9. Extract.

COSTUME.
    TIMOUR.—Crimson fly—puce tunic—yellow satin shirt—red trousers—green boots—turban—dagger: all richly ornamented—chains, and beads for the neck.
    AGIB.—Body—crimson fly—white trousers—turban—slippers: all richly ornamented.
    BERMEDDIN.—White trousers—white body—yellow tunic—sash—sword—cap.
    ABDALLAR.—Ibid.—Boots.
    OCTAR.—Purple fly—crimson shirt—white trousers—turban—boots—sword.
    KERIM.—White chain armour—skirt—red trousers—cap to match the armour—boots—sword—chain.
    SANBALLAT.—Green chain armour—puce fly—red striped trousers—turban—boots.

---

97 *Review ... 377–8*: This review is a longer and more substantial version of a review that appeared originally in *The Morning Post* No. 12,558 (30 April 1811), page 3.

ORASMIN.—Blue satin tunic—green velvet fly—white trousers—boots—turban.

OGLOU.—Puce fly—yellow tunic—white trousers—fleshings[98]—turban.

THE TROOP.—Ibid, of various colours.

ZORILDA.—*First dress*: Breast-plate and helmet—elegant white satin petticoat, richly ornamented—long crimson train—yellow boots. *Second dress*: Plain white muslin.

SELIMA.—Pink and white satin dress—white satin trousers and turban—red morocco boots—beads.

LISKA.—Crimson and white Turkish dress—turban—trousers—boots—beads, &c.

THE AMAZONS.—Breast-plates—helmets—blue satin petticoats—swords—fleshings—blue morocco boots.

———————

45. Review of *The Quadrupeds of Quedlinburgh*. *The Times* **No. 8357 (27 July 1811), page 3. Reprinted in** *The Evening Mail* **No. 3,751 (26-29 July 1811), page 3.**

A new Satire on Equestrian Theatricals, and a powerful rival to the "Quadrupeds," was produced last night. It is the German play of the *Anti-Jacobin*, with a prologue, an introductory scene between the manager and the author, and a concluding exhibition of battles, blue lights,[99] and cavalry. The cavalry were Centaurs of a new description, half man and half *basket*-work; and their appearance and spirit were admirable. They performed the usual stage manœuvres of cavalry—they plunged into rapid streams, ascended rushing cataracts, and scaled embattled towers: some died, and some fled; and the victors, the vanquished, and the slain performed their respective functions with a truth, a nature, and a vivacity, which did them all equal and infinite humour.

The performance had one fault—the most inauspicious fault of a new performance—it was intolerably long; and the hisses which were occasionally heard, proceeded, perhaps, as much from the weariness as from the discrimination of the critics. As a burlesque, the *Rovers of Weimar* is amusing; for it fastens on the tangible absurdities of the German drama, and fastens on them laughably; but the laugh is at a thing of other days: the German drama is past and gone,—it is beyond the reach of ridicule,—its absurdities cannot be revived,—and they cannot now furnish matter for even the slight ridicule of a passing burlesque. But excepting this erroneous choice of a material of laughter and of satire, the present burlesque has considerable merit. We think it not inferior to any piece of ridicule since the "Critic";[100] and we think, that with a few more songs, which might be ingenious parodies of popular poetry, and a few more points scattered through the dialogue, which ought to turn on absurdities of our own day, the "Rovers of Weimar" would have a full share of public approbation.

———————

46. Review of *The Quadrupeds of Quedlinburgh*. *The Morning Post* **No. 12,634 (27 July 1811), page 3.**

Haymarket.—Last night was produced at this Theatre, as a grand dressed rehearsal of Tragico, Comico-Anglo-Germanico-Hippo-Ono-Dramatico-Romance, a new piece in two acts, called *The Quadrupeds of Quedlinburgh*, or *the Rovers of Weimar*.

This entertainment is said to be furnished to the Theatre by Mr. COLMAN. For the truth of this we cannot pretend to vouch; but we must confess, that from the description given of the family of *Mr. Bathos* in the first scene, without any previous information on the subject, we should have thought it exceedingly probable that the

———

98 *fleshings*: flesh-colored tights.
99 *blue lights*: pyrotechnical compositions that burn with a blue flame, used also at sea as a night-signal.

100 *the "Critic"*: referring to Richard Brinsley Sheridan, *The Critic, or A Tragedy Rehearsed, a dramatic piece in three acts* (Drury Lane, 1779).

piece was from the pen of the author of "Sylvester Daggerwood."[101] The romance which is rehearsed is taken from the admired burlesque on the German School, which some ten or twelve years ago[102] appeared in *The Anti-Jacobin*, and which has been frequently attributed to Mr. CANNING.[103]—The first act went off exceedingly well. The meeting of *Matilda Pottingen* and *Cecilia Muckenfield*, called forth loud bursts of laughter from all parts of the Theatre, and the song of the captive *Rogero* about the happy days he passed at the

"U-

"Niversity of Gottingen,"

told with the happiest effect, and closed the scene with universal applause. The latter part of the romance was less successful. The force of the satire was not always felt, and in some instances where it was felt, its propriety was not acknowledged. The scene of *Pizzaro*,[104] in which Rolla

releases *Alonzo* from prison, is ridiculed in a manner too plain to be misunderstood: *Casimere* (Munden) releases *Rogero* (Liston), by getting into the prison in the disguise of an apothecary, and giving the sentinel (a Monk with a firelock[105]) two seven-shilling pieces. The idea was instantly taken, and the scene had a strong effect on the risible muscles of the audience. Laughter, however, is not always a symptom of good humour, and in the present instance, far from proving to be such, it was but the harbinger of loud disapprobation. The romance concludes with a grand battle, in which the last scene of *Timour: the Tartar* is closely imitated and burlesqued, in the first style of extravagance. Basket horses are seen on the ramparts of a castle, and prancing about in all directions. A battering ram is introduced as in *Timour*, and with similar effect. The last scene of *The Exile*[106] is then travestied, and the piece concludes in the *fashionable style*, so that

"The understanding traces it in vain,
Lost and bewilder'd in a fruitless search;
Nor sees with how much art the winding runs,
Nor where the regular confusion ends."[107]

The piece, although much applauded at its commencement, was strongly opposed in its progress towards its close. Like most of the new afterpieces, it is much too long, but its gravest fault is, it is produced at the wrong time. It is not every dramatic piece that will *keep* (behind the scenes) any length of time; and this is one which ought to have been performed as soon as it could have been snatched from the

---

101   *"Sylvester Daggerwood"*: pseudonym of George Colman the Younger for his *Memoirs of Sylvester Daggerwood, comedian &c. deceased; including many years of provincial vicissitudes, interspersed with genuine anecdotes of many eminent persons, and several deceased and living actors and managers*, 2 vols. (London: M. Allen, 1806). Also, the nineteenth-century title of Colman the Younger's *New Hay at the Old Market* (Haymarket, 1795).

102   *ten or twelve years ago*: The original installments of *The Rovers* appeared in *The Anti-Jacobin: or Weekly Examiner* 30-1 (4–11 June 1798), pages 235–9, 242–6.

103   *Mr. CANNING*: George Canning (1770–1827), British statesman who served as foreign secretary (1807–09, 1822–27) and as prime minister (1827). In 1797, he helped found *The Anti-Jacobin: or Weekly Examiner* (1797–98), a periodical dedicated to exposing and attacking revolutionary sentiment in Britain and abroad. It quickly became known for its raucous satires of "corrupt" literatures, attacking (most notoriously) Erasmus Darwin, Johann Wolfgang von Goethe, August von Kotzebue, Friedrich Schiller, and Robert Southey.

104   *Pizzaro*: Here the reviewer mistakenly attributes the scene to Richard Brinsley Sheridan's *Pizarro* (adapted from August von Kotzebue's *Die Spanier in Peru*), which debuted at Drury Lane on 24 May 1799 and was performed 67 times in its first 14 months. Given that the original publication dates of *The Rovers* in *The Anti-Jacobin* (4 June and 11 June 1798) precede Sheridan's play by nearly a year, the

scene cannot be ridiculing *Pizarro*. More likely, the scene is ridiculing Friedrich Schiller's *Die Raüber* and Matthew Lewis's *The Castle Spectre* (Drury Lane, 14 December 1797).

105   *firelock*: a flint-lock, i.e., a gun in which the gun-lock consists of a flint screwed to the cock, which is struck against the hammer and produces sparks, which ignite the priming in the flash-pan.

106   *The Exile*: referring to Frederick Reynolds, *The Exile, or the Deserts of Siberia: an operative play, in three acts* (King's Theatre, 1808).

107   *"The understanding … confusion ends"*: slightly misquoted from Joseph Addison, *Cato*, I.i.51–4.

pen of its author, or of its projector.[108] It is the same in principle as *The Rehearsal*[109] and *The Critic*, but it is, as a whole, much inferior to both. The *Mr. Bathos* in this does not deserve to rank with the *Bays* and *Puff* of *The Rehearsal* of the Duke of BUCKINGHAM, and "*The Critic*" of SHERIDAN. The distinguished merits of those pieces caused "*The Quadrupeds of Quedlinburgh*" to appear very poor to those conversant with theatrical affairs, and to others its point was lost; its satire not understood. ELLISTON was completely lost in the Poet. His presence during the rehearsal rather injured than heightened its effect; and if the piece is to be continued, we should think it would be better to set both him and Mr. EYRE at liberty after the opening scene, than to keep them in the way of the actors on the stage, where, though both are laughed at, neither can gain applause.

---

47. Review of *The Quadrupeds of Quedlinburgh*. *Bell's Weekly Messenger* No. 777 (24 February 1811), pages 61-2. Extract.

Hay-Market. The Quadrupeds of Quedlinburgh, or Rovers of Weimar, a satire upon the taste of the town for equestrian spectacle, was produced at this Theatre, and as the Piece was announced with more than ordinary tone, a more than ordinary expectation was excited by it.

The object of the Play was the ridicule of German language, plot, and sentiment—of those unnatural transitions of passion, and combinations of humour and character, which are no where found but on the German Stage. The general plot to it, we believe, is in a witty raillery of the style of Southey,[110] in the *Anti-Jacobin*. The

morals of the German Drama are as tedious and unnatural, as their plots and characters. They were very well characterised in the Prologue, as sentimental pickpockets, heroic highwaymen, and innocent adulteresses.

Such was the object of the Drama, and certainly the wishes of the audience went with its success. The question now is as to the execution.

There are chiefly two forms of comic ridicule—the one is the heightening of folly or absurdity, by increasing as it were its effect and dimensions, by putting it forth under circumstances calculated to exhibit its deviation from nature. This may be termed comic caricature. The following is an instance of it. The Germans are very extravagant in their feelings and sympathies and sentiments; it is a ridicule of this extravagance; two Ladies are introduced as passengers in the Brunswick waggon. They talk together about three minutes, and then perceiving their congenial natures propose an eternal friendship, and deluge each other's neck with tears. Now, there is no objection to this kind of caricature, as long as it has a show of ridicule—as long as it is a parody of a similar absurdity. By itself, however, and independent of any aim at ridicule, it is sheer nonsense. Lords *Puddingfield* and *Beefington* were in this latter predicament. They were absolute fools, and without any original in ridicule.

The second kind of ridicule is burlesque; which is of two kinds, the high burlesque, which parodies low images and affairs in a lofty style, and the low burlesque, which degrades what is serious and lofty, by low and buffoonish appendages. Both these kinds of humour were employed in this Piece, but occasionally without an attention to their nature. Buffoonery was introduced without an aim, and without any possible nature or probability; and the high burlesque was frequently mere grave stupidity and arrant nonsense.

Upon the whole, however, *The Rovers* had a great and uncommon merit, a portion of wit and meaning which would be sought in vain in most other modern plays.

[The reviewer prints the Prologue].

This Piece, produced at the Little Theatre, in the Hay-market, on Friday night, by the Author's previous avowal, is taken from an admirable SATIRE upon the rage

---

108 *projector*: one who puts forth a project; also, a schemer or speculator.

109 *The Rehearsal*: referring to George Villiers, Duke of Buckingham, *The Rehearsal, a Comedy* (Drury Lane, 1671).

110 *Southey*: Robert Southey (1774–1843), British poet and prose writer known in the 1790s for his radicalism, which he later recanted. He was Poet Laureate from 1813 to 1843.

for the German Drama, published in the ANTI-JACOBIN Paper about 12 years ago. It is a piece of most exquisite humour, and is attributed to Mr. Canning—It is well worthy of his powers, and, though a work of temporary ridicule, deserves to be preserved. We have therefore republished the first part in our Paper of this day, and shall give the remainder in our next.

Mr. Colman has changed the title of the Piece, which had the name of the ROVERS, or DOUBLE ARRANGEMENT.

[The reviewer prints the plot and first act of *The Rovers*].

---

48. [Hunt, James Henry Leigh]. Review of *The Quadrupeds of Quedlinburgh. The Examiner* 187 (28 July 1811), pages 485-6.

Haymarket. The new piece at this theatre, in contribution to the general ridicule against the KEMBLE horses,—was produced on Friday evening instead of Monday, in consequence of the old disputes between the Proprietors. It is called the *Quadrupeds of Quedlinburgh, or the Rovers of Weimar*; and that no explanations may be wanting to the learned, or mysterious attraction to the vulgar, is described as a Tragico-Comico-Anglo-Germanico-Hippo-*Ono*-Dramatico Romance. Like its rival at the Lyceum however it is an old acquaintance of the public, being little else, in fact as its name advertised, but Mr. CANNING's well-known mock drama on the German taste, brought forward for the first time, I believe, on the stage, and introduced by a scene in the old way between author and manager. A paragraph to this effect was added, I see, to the play bill of yesterday,[111] most probably in consequence of the disapprobation expressed by a considerable part of the audience on the first night of its representation. "The ground-work," says the advertisement, "and some scenes, with alterations, of this drama, are extracted from a celebrated and witty periodical publication commenced in London towards the close of the last century, and now discontinued. The piece has long been in preparation, and the public is respectfully informed that every effort has been strained to *surpass Nature!*" It may be asked why Mr. COLMAN himself, who has shewn himself well skilled in low humour, has not presented us with a satire of his own on this occasion? but the neglect is of a piece with his usual concern for the interests of his theatre; and perhaps we have no reason to regret the loss, considering how he has sunk of late into the common-place of our dramatic punsters.

The induction of the present piece is not calculated to recover his former reputation. It is a collection of puns about horses and legs, such as four legs, last legs, left legs, and right legs; and is polluted by that vile and unfeeling substitute for humour which raises a laugh at personal deformity, the supposed author, *Dr. Bathos*, lamenting the humps and rickets of his sickly children. The alterations of the piece itself, and the remarks which are made upon it by the author and manager (ELLISTON and EYRE) who overlook the performance as in the *Critic* and the *Rehearsal*, are in a better taste, and therefore more suitable to the work, but they are still unnecessary and unseasonable, and serve for little but to render it tedious. In fact, no good has been done to the work itself by introducing it on the stage under the present circumstances. Its burlesque, in the first place, demands a continual reference in the minds of the audience to the nonsense of the German dramas, which is no longer before the pub-

---

111 *the play bill of yesterday*: The insertion to which Hunt refers was actually not added for the play's second night, but in fact was present in playbills and advertisements beginning 20 July 1811. The playbill for 27 July, however, does add the following note placed at the end: "The Public is respectfully inform'd that the QUADRUPEDS OF QUEDLINBURGH, was perform'd Yesterday Evening, for the first time, to an overflowing Audience; was received with the loudest Applause, and roars of laughter;—and will be repeated every Night, till further notice." Later playbills repeat this note (with slight alterations, and noting "encreased roars of laughter").

lic, at least is no longer familiar to them; and in the second, it is really in too good a taste, generally speaking, to please a mixed audience; not that an audience now-a-days has not taste enough to be pleased with what is good, but because the popular mind is formed to judge of nature alone and of what is seen and felt in the world at large; and burlesque, of any delicacy, implies an acquaintance with artificial contrasts and combinations, which are quite out of the way of common apprehension. It is for this reason that the *Rehearsal* is no longer performable; and the *Critic* would probably be laid on the shelf with it, were it not for its excellent first act, which exhibits a general character that every body can understand,—an irritable author pretending to disregard criticism and courting a frankness that puts him to the rack. In proportion as the application becomes more general, and the burlesque more gross, the common perception enlightens towards it. Thus *Tom Thumb*,[112] with its alehouse sentiment, is the most popular piece of its kind; and even the *Tailors*, which is now performing at the Lyceum, is more favoured by the audience than the piece before us, to which it is infinitely inferior. It is not to be concealed however that the *Rovers* is far from being complete of its kind. It is objectionable for a common fault on these subjects,—a confusion of burlesque and mock-heroic, which are in reality very distinct things, the former being a degradation of what is great, the latter an elevation of what is little; and besides, the ground of its ridicule is not always well chosen. The sentimental ladies and wild youths are proper game; but the imprisonment of a man in chains for a series of years, however unwarrantably tragedized by the Germans, is, to say the least of it, no joke; caricaturing it is almost as violent an assault upon our feelings one way, as exaggerating its misery is in another.

The representation is far from good. Indeed, with the exception of Mr. MUNDEN, who is quite lost in the hero of the piece, the only good performer is Mr. Linton, who acts *Rogero*, and he does not seem at his ease on the occa-

sion. A song evidently perplexes him, especially if it taxes his voice to any height; and accordingly he makes poor work of the celebrated ditty about the *University of Gottingen*; but one or two of his ineffable ogles make up for every thing. The last scene, which in fact is the only one that has any thing to do with *quadrupeds*, presents us with the customary battle; and the steeds consist of cloaked wicker-work adapted before and behind to the bodies of the performers, by which means every man is enabled to be his own horse, and also to caper and twist about with a rapidity that would certainly be the death of an ordinary palfrey. The only living quadruped is a solitary jackass, bestridden by MUNDEN, so that the scene is in every respect inferior to that at the other little theatre; for the Haymarket burlesque makes a grand mistake in imitating the fine clothes and plumed helmets of the Covent-garden combatants, and in bringing *real* Knights and *real* Captains to the contest:—the object is not to copy in little, but to degrade in little, and this is properly done by the ragged warriors and the sticks and staves of the Lyceum.

It is to be hoped that the disputes at this Theatre, whether owing to the negligent habits of Mr. COLMAN or in the litigiousness of his partners, are no longer to annoy the public. One may certainly feel for the situation of the Lord Chancellor,[113] when he complains of being made the manager of operas and summer theatres. It is a pity however that his Lordship should think it becoming or facetious in him to repeat his summary criticisms on players in general, and to be continually telling us that

---

112 *Tom Thumb*: referring to [Henry Fielding], *Tom Thumb. A tragedy. As it is acted at the theatre in the Hay-Market. Written by Scriblerus Secundus* (London: J. Roberts, 1730).

---

113 *Lord Chancellor*: also called the Chancellor of England and Lord High Chancellor, considered the highest officer of the crown, and an important member of the cabinet. He is the highest judicial functionary in the kingdom, and ranks above all peers spiritual and temporal, except only princes of the blood and the archbishop of Canterbury; he is keeper of the Great Seal, is styled "Keeper of his Majesty's conscience," and is president and prolocutor of the House of Lords. He presides in what was the Court of Chancery; appoints all justices of peace; is the general guardian of infants, lunatics, and idiots; is visitor of hospitals and colleges of royal foundation; and is patron of all church livings under twenty marks in value.

he would not give five shillings to hear the finest singers in London. If he cannot, as he assures us, go with comfort into any place of public amusement in consequence of broaching these opinions, why does he recall them to mind? And above all, why does he go to places which he holds in contempt? The opinions, whatever he may think of them, are certainly not necessary to his reputation or seasonable to his judicial speeches. Nobody, I believe, accuses his Lordship of having a taste of any kind, much less for things that delighted such men as DRYDEN and MILTON,[114] and still less for wantonly spending his five shillings;—then why should he think it necessary to defend himself from the imputation? Besides, it is not fair on his part to take such advantage of the stage, whatever annoyance it may give him with its concerns. What would he say to a singer, who in consequence of being chagrined by his Lordship's strictures, should think proper to introduce a philippic upon him in a solo, or quote at him those memorable lines,—

> "The man that has not music in his soul
> "Nor is not mov'd with concord of sweet sounds,
> "Is fit for treasons," &c. &c.[115]

---

49. "Cursory Thoughts on the Decline of TRAGEDY." *The Thespian Magazine* 1 (February 1793), pages 197-8. Extract.

It is with regret I observe that the noblest of all theatrical exhibitions, that of Tragedy, is considerably on the decline; this I the more sincerely lament, as there is no part of the entertainments of the theatre so capable of softening the ferocity and improving the minds of the lower classes of people, than the frequent exhibition of Tragedies, in which the distress is carried to the highest extreme, and the moral is at once affecting and instructive. There are many thousands who cannot read for instruction; or if they could, they have neither time nor inclination to do, and there are many likewise who are too volatile to listen to the rigid lessons of a parental monitor; but in the exhibition of moral Tragedies they can listen to instruction under the mask of pleasure. Were the Theatre under certain regulations we might enter it with as much propriety as we do a church: what I mean by its being under certain regulations, is, that licentious Comedy and Pantomime buffoonery should be entirely banished from it, and nothing introduced but what has a real moral effect. By these means virtue and vice might be represented to the audience, as each receiving their due rewards; and benevolence, justice, heroism, and the propriety of moderating the passions, might be forcibly recommended to those uncultivated persons who have no inclination to listen to instruction, did it not present itself in the form of a pleasing amusement. There are certainly many Tragedies of more sublime and loftier language, but few better calculated to deter the lower order of people from entering into such scenes of villainy than the *Tragedy of George Barnwell*. Illiterate minds cannot comprehend the sublime beauties of blank verse; but the simple and unaffected language of Lillo,[116] is perfectly intelligible to the lowest intellects—I have not the least doubt but this play has saved many persons from an ignominious end, and as such, ought to be more frequently represented, however it may be despised by the fashionable world.

---

114 *DRYDEN and MILTON*: referring to John Dryden (1631–1700) and John Milton (1608–74), generally considered among the greatest seventeenth-century British poets.

115 "*The man ... &c. &c.*: quoted from William Shakespeare, *The Merchant of Venice*, V.i.83–5.

116 *Tragedy of George Barnwell ... Lillo*: referring to the didactic tragedy, *The London Merchant: or, the History of George Barnwell* (1731), by George Lillo (1693–1739), which depicts a young apprentice's descent into vice and ruin. In the late eighteenth and early nineteenth centuries, the play traditionally was performed with the Christmas pantomime on Boxing Day (26 December), when London's apprentices would be given a holiday from work.

50. Baillie, Joanna. "Introductory Discourse." *A Series of Plays: In Which It Is Attempted to Delineate the Stronger Passions of the Mind, Each Passion Being the Subject of a Tragedy and a Comedy.* **London: T. Cadell, Jun. and W. Davies, 1798. Pages 1-72. Extract.**

...Before I explain the plan of this work, I must make a demand upon the patience of my reader, whilst I endeavour to communicate to him those ideas regarding human nature, as they in some degree affect almost every species of moral writings, but particularly the Dramatic, that induced me to attempt it; and, as far as my judgment enabled me to apply them, has directed me in the execution of it.

From that strong sympathy which most creatures, but the human above all, feel for others of their kind, nothing has become so much an object of man's curiosity as man himself. We are all conscious of this within ourselves, and so constantly do we meet with it in others, that like every circumstance of continually repeated occurrence, it thereby escapes observation. Every person, who is not deficient in intellect, is more or less occupied in tracing, amongst the individuals he converses with, the varieties of understanding and temper which constitute the characters of men; and receives great pleasure from every stroke of nature that points out to him those varieties. This is, much more than we are aware of, the occupation of children, and of grown people also, whose penetration is but lightly esteemed; and that conversation which degenerates with them into trivial and mischievous tattling, takes its rise not unfrequently from the same source that supplies the rich vein of the satirist and the wit. That eagerness so universally shewn for the conversation of the latter, plainly enough indicates how many people have been occupied in the same way with themselves. Let any one, in a large company, do or say what is strongly expressive of his peculiar character, or of some passion or humour of the moment, and it will be detected by almost every person present. How often may we see a very stupid countenance animated with a smile, when the

learned and the wise have betrayed some native feature of their own minds! and how often will this be the case when they have supposed it to be concealed under a very sufficient disguise! From this constant employment of their minds, most people, I believe, without being conscious of it, have stored up in idea the greater part of those strongly marked varieties of human character, which may be said to divide it into classes; and in one of those classes they involuntarily place every new person they become acquainted with.

I will readily allow that the dress and the manners of men, rather than their characters and dispositions are the subjects of our common conversation, and seem chiefly to occupy the multitude. But let it be remembered that it is much easier to express our observations upon these. It is easier to communicate to another how a man wears his wig and cane, what kind of house he inhabits, and what kind of table he keeps, than from what slight traits in his words and actions we have been led to conceive certain impressions of his character: traits that will often escape the memory, when the opinions that were founded upon them remain. Besides, in communicating our ideas of the characters of others, we are often called upon to support them with more expence of reasoning than we can well afford, but our observations on the dress and appearance of men, seldom involve us in such difficulties. For these, and other reasons too tedious to mention, the generality of people appear to us more trifling than they are: and I may venture to say that, but for this sympathetick curiosity towards others of our kind, which is so strongly implanted within us, the attention we pay to the dress and manners of men would dwindle into an employment as insipid, as examining the varieties of plants and minerals, is to one who understands not natural history.

In our ordinary intercourse with society, this sympathetick propensity of our minds is exercised upon men, under the common occurrences of life, in which we have often observed them. Here vanity and weakness put themselves forward to view, more conspicuously than the virtues: here men encounter those smaller trials, from which they are not apt to come off victorious; and here, consequently, that which is marked with the whimsical and ludicrous will strike us most forcibly, and make the strongest impression on our memory. To this sympathetick propensity of our minds, so exercised, the genuine and pure comick of every composition, whether drama, fable, story, or satire is addressed.

If man is an object of so much attention to man, engaged in the ordinary occurrences of life, how much more does he excite his curiosity and interest when placed in extraordinary situations of difficulty and distress? It cannot be any pleasure we receive from the sufferings of a fellow-creature which attracts such multitudes of people to publick execution, though it is the horrour we conceive for such a spectacle that keeps so many more away. To see a human being bearing himself up under such circumstances, or struggling with the terrible apprehensions which such a situation impresses, must be the powerful incentive, which makes us press forward to behold what we shrink from, and wait with trembling expectation for what we dread.[117] For though few at such a spectacle can get near enough to distinguish the expression of face, or the minuter parts of a criminal's behaviour, yet from a considerable distance will they eagerly mark whether he steps firmly; whether the motions of his body denote agitation or calmness; and if the wind does but ruffle his garment, they will, even from that change upon the outline of his distant figure, read some expression connected with his dreadful situation. Though there is a greater proportion of people in whom this strong curiosity will be overcome by other dispositions and motives; though there are many more who will stay away from such a sight than will go to it; yet there are very few who will not be eager to converse with a person who has beheld it; and to learn, very minutely, every circumstance connected with it, except the very act itself of inflicting death. To lift up the roof of his dungeon, like the *Diable boiteux*,[118] and look upon a criminal the night before he suffers, in his still hours of privacy, when all that disguise, which respect for the opinion of others, the strong motive by which even the lowest and wickedest of men still continue to be moved, would present an object to the mind of every person, not withheld from it by great timidity of character, more powerfully attractive than almost any other.

Revenge, no doubt, first began amongst the savages of America that dreadful custom of sacrificing their prisoners of war. But the perpetration of such hideous cruelty could never have become a permanent national custom, but for this universal desire in the human mind to behold man in every situation, putting forth his strength against the current of adversity, scorning all bodily anguish, or struggling with those feelings of nature, which, like a beating stream, will oft'times burst through the artificial barriers of pride. Before they begin those terrible rites they treat their prisoners kindly; and it cannot be supposed that men, alternately enemies and friends to so many neighbouring tribes, in manners and appearance like themselves, should so strongly be actuated by a spirit of publick revenge. This custom, therefore, must be considered as a grand and terrible game, which every tribe plays against another; where they try not the strength of the arm, the swiftness of the feet, nor the acuteness of the eye, but the fortitude of the soul. Considered in this light, the excess of cruelty exercised upon their miserable victim, in which every hand is described as ready to inflict its portion of pain, and every head ingenious in the contrivance of it, is no longer to be wondered at. To put into his measure of misery one agony less, would be, in some degree, betraying the honour of their nation: would be doing a species of injustice to every hero of their own tribe who had already sustained it, and to those who might be called upon to do so; amongst whom each of

---

117 Baillie's note: "In confirmation of this opinion I may venture to say, that of the great numbers who go to see a publick execution, there are but very few who would not run away from, and avoid it, if they happened to meet with it unexpectedly. We find people stopping to look at a procession, or any other uncommon sight, they may have fallen with accidentally, but almost never an execution. No one goes there who has not made up his mind for the occasion; which would not be the case, if any natural love of cruelty were the cause of such assemblies."

118 *Diable boiteux*: referring to the *Diable Boiteux* (1707, *The Devil upon Two Sticks*) of Le Sage (1668–1747), where Asmodeus, the demon, places Don Cleofas on an elevated situation, and unroofs the houses for inspection.

these savage tormentors has his chance of being one, and has prepared himself for it from his childhood. Nay, it would be a species of injustice to the haughty victim himself, who would scorn to purchase his place amongst the heroes of his nation at an easier price than his undaunted predecessors.

Amongst the many trials to which the human mind is subjected, that of holding intercourse, real or imaginary, with the world of spirits: of finding itself alone with a being terrifick and awful, whose nature and power are unknown, has been justly considered as one of the most severe. The workings of nature in this situation, we all know, have ever been the object of our most eager enquiry. No man wishes to see the Ghost himself, which would certainly procure him the best information on the subject, but every man wishes to see one who believes that he sees it, in all the agitation and wildness of that species of terrour. To gratify this curiosity how many people have dressed up hideous apparitions to frighten the timid and superstitious! and have done it at the risk of destroying their happiness or understanding for ever. For the instances of intellect being destroyed by this kind of trial are more numerous, perhaps, in proportion to the few who have undergone it than by any other.

How sensible are we of this strong propensity within us, when we behold any person under the pressure of great and uncommon calamity! Delicacy and respect for the afflicted will, indeed, make us turn ourselves aside from observing him, and cast down our eyes in his presence; but the first glance we direct to him will involuntarily be one of the keenest observation, how hastily soever it may be checked; and often will a returning look of enquiry mix itself by stealth with our sympathy and reserve.

But it is not in situations of difficulty and distress alone, that man becomes the object of this sympathetick curiosity; he is no less so when the evil he contends with arises in his own breast, and no outward circumstance connected with him either awakens our attention or our pity. What human creature is there, who can behold a being like himself under the violent agitation of those passions which all have, in some degree, experienced, without feeling himself most powerfully excited by the

sight? I say, all have experienced; for the bravest man on earth knows what fear is as well as the coward; and will not refuse to be interested for one under the dominion of this passion, provided there be nothing in the circumstances attending it to create contempt. Anger is a passion that attracts less sympathy than any other, yet the unpleasing and distorted features of an angry man will be more eagerly gazed upon, by those who are no wise concerned with his fury or the objects of it, than the most amiable placid countenance in the world. Every eye is directed to him; every voice hushed to silence in his presence; even children will leave off their gambols as he passes, and gaze after him more eagerly than the gaudiest equipage. The wild tossings of despair; the gnashings of hatred and revenge; the yearnings of affection, and the softened mien of love; all that language of the agitated soul, which every age and nation understands, is never addressed to the dull nor inattentive.

It is not merely under the violent agitations of passion, that man so rouses and interests us; even the smallest indications of an unquiet mind, the restless eye, the muttering lip, the half-checked exclamation, and the hasty start, will set our attention as anxiously upon the watch, as the first distant flashes of a gathering storm. When some great explosion of passion bursts forth, and some consequent catastrophe happens, if we are at all acquainted with the unhappy perpetrator, how minutely will we endeavour to remember every circumstance of his past behaviour! and with what avidity will we seize upon every recollected word or gesture, that is in the smallest degree indicative of the supposed state of his mind, at the time when they took place. If we are not acquainted with him, how eagerly shall we listen to similar recollections from another! Let us understand, from observation or report, that any person harbours in his breast, concealed from the world's eye, some powerful rankling passion of what kind soever it may be, we shall observe every word, every motion, every look, even the distant gait of such a man, with a constancy and attention bestowed upon no other. Nay, should we meet him unexpectedly on our way, a feeling will pass across our minds as though we found ourselves in the neighborhood of some secret and fearful thing. If invisible, would we not follow him into his lonely haunts, into his closet, into the midnight silence of his chamber? There is, perhaps, no employment which the human mind will with so much avidity pursue, as the discovery of concealed passion, as the tracing the varieties and progress of a perturbed soul.

It is to this sympathetick curiosity of our nature, exercised upon mankind in great and trying occasions, and under the influence of the stronger passions, when the grand, the generous, the terrible attract our attention far more than the base and depraved, that the high and powerfully tragick, of every composition, is addressed.

This propensity is universal. Children begin to shew it very early; it enters into many of their amusements, and that part of them too, for which they shew the keenest relish. It tempts them many times, as well as the mature in years, to be guilty of tricks, vexations, and cruelty; yet God Almighty has implanted in us, as well as all our other propensities and passions, for wise and good purposes. It is our best and most powerful instructor. From it we are taught the proprieties and decencies of ordinary life, and are prepared for distressing and difficult situations. In examining others we know ourselves. With limbs untorn, with head unsmitten, with senses unimpaired by despair, we know what we ourselves might have been on the rack, on the scaffold, and in the most afflicting circumstances of distress. Unless when accompanied with passions of the dark and malevolent kind, we cannot well exercise this disposition without becoming more just, more merciful, more compassionate; and as the dark and malevolent passions are not the predominant inmates of the human breast, it hath produced more deeds—O many more! of kindness than of cruelty. It holds up for our example a standard of excellence, which, without its assistance, our inward consciousness of what is right and becoming might never have dictated. It teaches us, also, to respect ourselves, and our kind; for it is a poor mind, indeed, that from this employment of its faculties, learns not to dwell upon the noble view of human nature rather than the mean.

Universal, however, as this disposition undoubtedly is, with the generality of mankind it occupies itself in a passing and superficial way. Though a native trait of character or of passion is obvious to them as well as to the sage, yet to their minds it is but the visitor of a moment; they look upon it singly and unconnected: and though this disposition, even so exercised, brings instruction as well as amusement, it is chiefly by storing up in their minds those ideas to which the instructions of others refer, that it can be eminently useful. Those who reflect and reason upon what human nature holds out to their observation, are comparatively but few. No stroke of nature which engages their attention stands insulated and alone. Each presents itself to them with many varied connections; and they comprehend not merely the immediate feeling which gave rise to it, but the relation of that feeling to others which are concealed. We wonder at the changes and caprices of men; they see in them nothing but what is natural and accountable. We stare upon some dark catastrophe of passion, as the Indians did upon an eclipse of the moon; they, conceiving the track of ideas through which the impassioned mind has passed, regard it like the philosopher who foretold the phenomenon. Knowing what situation of life he is about to be thrown into, they perceive in the man, who, like Hazael, says, "is thy servant a dog that he should do this thing?"[119] the foul and ferocious murderer. A man of this contemplative character partakes, in some degree, of the entertainment of the Gods, who were supposed to look down upon this world and the inhabitants of it, as we do upon a theatrical exhibition; and if he is of a benevolent disposition, a good man struggling with, and triumphing over adversity, will be to him, also, the most delightful spectacle. But though this eagerness to observe their fellow-creatures in every situation, leads not the generality of mankind to reason and reflect; and those strokes of nature which they are so ready to remark, stand single and unconnected in their minds, yet they may be easily induced to do both: and there is no mode of instruction which they will so eagerly pursue, as that which lays open before them, in a more enlarged and connected view, than their individual

---

119 *"is thy servant a dog that he should do this thing?"*: quoted from II Kings 8.13.

observations are capable of supplying, the varieties of the human mind. Above all, to be well exercised in this study will fit a man more particularly for the most important situations of life. He will prove for it the better Judge, the better Magistrate, the better Advocate; and as a ruler or conductor of other men, under every occurring circumstance, he will find himself the better enabled to fulfil his duty, and accomplish his designs. He will perceive the natural effect of every order that he issues upon the minds of his soldiers, his subjects, or his followers; and he will deal to others judgment tempered with mercy; that is to say truly just; for justice appears to us severe only when it is imperfect.

In proportion as moral writers of every class have exercised within themselves this sympathetick propensity of our nature, and have attended to it in others, their works have been interesting and instructive. They have struck the imagination more forcibly, convinced the understanding more clearly, and more lastingly impressed the memory. If unseasoned with any reference to this, the fairy bowers of the poet, with all his gay images of delight, will be admired and forgotten; the important relations of the historian, and even the reasonings of the philosopher, will make a less permanent impression.

The historian points back to the men of other ages, and from the gradually clearing mist in which they are first discovered, like the mountains of a far distant land, the generations of the world are displayed to our mind's eye in grand and regular procession. But the transactions of men become interesting to us only as we are made acquainted with men themselves. Great and bloody battles are to us battles fought in the moon, if it is not impressed upon our minds, by some circumstances attending them, that men subject to like weaknesses and passions with ourselves, were the combatants.[120] The establishments of

policy make little impression upon us, if we are left ignorant of the beings whom they affected. Even a very masterly drawn character will but slightly imprint upon our memory the great man it belongs to, if, in the account we receive of his life, those lesser circumstances are entirely neglected, which do best of all point out to us the dispositions and tempers of men. Some slight circumstance characteristick of a particular turn of a man's mind, which at first sight seems but little connected with the great events of his life, will often explain some of those events more clearly to our understanding, than the minute details of ostensible policy. A judicious selection of those circumstances which characterise the spirit of an associated mob, paltry and ludicrous as some of them may appear, will oftentimes convey to our minds a clearer idea why certain laws and privileges were demanded and agreed to, than a methodical explanation of their causes. An historian who has examined human nature himself, and likewise attends to the pleasure which developing and tracing it, does ever convey to others, will employ our understanding as well as our memory with his pages; and if

---

General be less scientifick, and the soldiers less dauntless. Let them go into the field for a cause that is dear to them, and fight with the ardour which such motives inspire; till discouraged with the many deaths around them, and the renovated pressure of the foe, some unlooked-for circumstance, trifling in itself, strikes their imagination at once; they are visited with the terrors of nature; their national pride, the honour of soldiership, is forgotten; they fly like a fearful flock. Let some beloved chief then step forth, and call upon them by the love of their country, by the memory of their valiant fathers, by every thing that kindles in the bosom of man the high and generous passions: they stop; they gather round him; and, goaded by shame and indignation, returning again to the charge, with the fury of wild beasts rather than the courage of soldiers, bear down every thing before them. Which of these two battles will interest us the most? and which of them shall we remember the longest? The one will stand forth in the imagination of a reader like a rock of the desert, which points out to the far-removed traveller the country through which he has passed, when its lesser objects are obscured in the distance; whilst the other leaves no traces behind it, but in the minds of the scientifick in war."

---

120 Baillie's note: "Let two great battles be described to us with all the force and clearness of the most able pen. In the first let the most admirable exertions of military skill in the General, and the most unshaken courage in the soldiers, gain over an equal or superiour number of brave opponents a compleat and glorious victory. In the second let the

this is not done, he will impose upon the latter a very difficult task, in retaining what she is concerned with alone.

In argumentative and philosophical writings, the effect which the author's reasoning produces on our minds depends not entirely on the justness of it. The images and examples that he calls to his aid, to explain and illustrate his meaning, will very much affect the attention we are able to bestow upon it, and consequently the quickness with which we shall apprehend, and the force with which it will impress us. These are selected from animated and unanimated nature, from the habits, manners, and characters of men; and though that image or example, whatever it may be in itself, which brings out his meaning most clearly, ought to be preferred before every other, yet of two equal in this respect, that which is drawn from the most interesting source will please us the most of the time, and most lastingly take hold of our minds. An argument supported with vivid and interesting illustration, will long be remembered when many equally important and clear are forgotten; and a work where many such occur will be held in higher estimation by the generality of men, than one its superior, perhaps, in acuteness, perspicuity, and good sense.

Our desire to know what men are in the closet as well as in the field, by the blazing hearth, and at the social board, as well as in the council and the throne, is very imperfectly gratified by real history; romance writers, therefore, stepped boldly forth to supply the deficiency; and tale writers, and novel writers, of many descriptions, followed after. If they have not been very skilful in their delineations of nature; if they have represented men and women speaking and acting as men and women never did speak or act; if they have caricatured both our virtues and our vices; if they have given us such pure and unmixed, or such heterogeneous combinations of character as real life never presented, and yet have pleased and interested us, let it not be imputed to the dulness of man in discerning what is genuinely natural in himself. There are many inclinations belonging to us, besides this great master-propensity of which I am treating. Our love of the grand, the beautiful, the novel, and above all of the mar-

vellous, is very strong; and if we are richly fed with what we have a good relish for, we may be weaned to forget our native and favourite aliment. Yet we can never so far forget it, but that we will cling to, and acknowledge it again, whenever it is presented before us. In a work abounding with the marvellous and unnatural, if the author has any how stumbled upon an unsophisticated genuine stroke of nature, we will immediately perceive and be delighted with it, though we are foolish enough to admire at the same time, all the nonsense with which it is surrounded. After all the wonderful incidents, dark mysteries, and secrets revealed, which an eventful novel so liberally presents to us; after the beautiful fairy ground, and even the grand and sublime scenes of nature with which the descriptive novel so often enchants us; those works which most strongly characterize human nature in the middling and lower classes of society, where it is to be discovered by stronger and more unequivocal marks, will ever be the most popular. For though great pains have been taken in our higher sentimental novels to interest us in the delicacies, embarrassments, and artificial distresses of the more refined part of society, they have never been able to cope in the publick opinion with these. The one is a dressed and beautiful pleasure-ground, in which we are enchanted for a while, amongst the delicate and unknown plants of artful cultivation; the other is a rough forest of our native land; the oak, the elm, the hazel, and the bramble are there; and amidst the endless varieties of its paths we can wander for ever. Into whatever scenes the novelist may conduct us, what objects soever he may present to our view, still is our attention most sensibly awake to every touch faithful to nature; still are we upon the watch for every thing that speaks to us of ourselves.

The fair field of what is properly called poetry, is enriched with so many beauties, that in it we are often tempted to forget what we really are, and what kind of beings we belong to. Who in the enchanted regions of simile, metaphor, allegory and description, can remember the plain order of things in this every-day world? From heroes whose majestic forms rise like a lofty tower, whose eyes are lightning, whose arms are irresistible, whose course is like the storms of heaven, bold and exalted sentiments we will readily receive; and will not examine them very accurately by that rule of nature which our own breast prescribes to us. A shepherd whose sheep, with fleeces of purest snow, browze the flowery herbage of the most beautiful vallies; whose flute is ever melodious, and whose shepherdess is ever crowned with roses; whose every care is love, will not be called very strictly to account for the loftiness and refinement of his thoughts. The fair Nymph, who sighs out her sorrows to the conscious and compassionate wilds; whose eyes gleam like the bright drops of heaven; whose loose tresses stream to the breeze, may say what she pleases with impunity. I will venture, however, to say, that amidst all this decoration and ornament, all this loftiness and refinement, let one simple trait of the human heart, one expression of passion genuine and true to nature, be introduced, and it will stand forth alone in the boldness of reality, whilst the false and unnatural around it, fade away upon every side, like the rising exhalations of the morning. With admiration, and often with enthusiasm we proceed on our way through the grand and the beautiful images raised to our imagination by the lofty Epic muse; but what even here are those things that strike upon the heart; that we feel and remember? Neither the descriptions of war, the sound of the trumpet, the clanging of arms, the combat of heroes, nor the death of the mighty, will interest our minds like the fall of the feeble stranger, who simply expresses the anguish of his soul, at the thoughts of that far-distant home which he must never return to again, and closes his eyes amongst the ignoble and forgotten; like the timid stripling goaded by the shame of reproach, who urges his trembling steps to the fight, and falls like a tender flower before the first blast of winter. How often will some simple picture of this kind be all that remains upon our minds of the terrifick and magnificent battle, whose description we have read with admiration? How comes it that we relish so much the episodes of an heroick poem? It cannot merely be that we are pleased with a resting-place, where we enjoy the variety of contrast; for were the poem of the simple and familiar kind, and an episode after the heroick style introduced into it, ninety readers out of an hundred would pass over it altogether. Is it not that

we meet such a story, so situated, with a kind of sympathetick good will, as in passing through a country of castles and of palaces, we should pop unawares upon some humble cottage, resembling the dwellings of our own native land, and gaze upon it with affection? The highest pleasures we receive from poetry, as well as from the real objects which surround us in the world, are derived from the sympathetick interest we all take in beings like ourselves; and I will even venture to say, that were the grandest scenes which can enter into the imagination of man, presented to our view, and all reference to man completely shut out from our thoughts, the objects that composed it would convey to our minds little better than dry ideas of magnitude, colour, and form; and the remembrance of them would rest upon our minds like the measurement and distances of the planets.

If the study of human nature then, is so useful to the poet, the novelist, the historian, and the philosopher, of how much greater importance must it be to the dramatick writer? To them it is a powerful auxiliary, to him it is the centre and strength of the battle. If characteristick views of human nature enliven not their pages, there are many excellences with which they can, in some degree, make up for the deficiency, it is what we receive from them with pleasure rather than demand. But in his works no richness of invention, harmony of language, nor grandeur of sentiment will supply the place of faithfully delineated nature. The poet and the novelist may represent to you their great characters from the cradle to the tomb. They may represent them in any mood or temper, and under the influence of any passion which they see proper, without being obliged to put words into their mouths, those great betrayers of the feigned and adopted. They may relate every circumstance, however trifling and minute, that serves to develope their tempers and dispositions. They tell us what kind of people they intend their men and women to be, and as such we receive them. If they are to move us with any scene of distress, every circumstance regarding the parties concerned in it, how they looked, how they moved, how they sighed, how the tears gushed from their eyes, how the very light and shadow fell upon them, is carefully described, and the few things that are given to them to say along with all this assistance, must be very unnatural indeed if we refuse to sympathize with them. But the characters of the drama must speak directly for themselves. Under the influence of every passion, humour, and impression; in the artificial veilings of hypocrisy and ceremony, in the openness of freedom and confidence, and in the lonely hour of meditation they speak. He who made us hath placed within our breasts a judge that judges instantaneously of every thing they say. We expect to find them creatures like ourselves; and if they are untrue to nature, we feel that we are imposed upon; as though the poet had introduced to us for brethren, creatures of a different race, beings of another world.

As in other works deficiency in characteristick truth may be compensated by excellences of a different kind, in the drama characteristick truth will compensate every other defect. Nay, it will do what appears a contradiction; one strong genuine stroke of nature will cover a multitude of sins even against nature herself. When we meet in some scene of a good play a very fine stroke of this kind, we are apt to become so intoxicated with it, and so perfectly convinced of the author's great knowledge of the human heart, that we are unwilling to suppose the whole of it has not been suggested by the same penetrating spirit. Many well-meaning enthusiastic criticks have given themselves a great deal of trouble in this way; and have shut their eyes most ingeniously against the fair light of nature for the very love of it. They have converted, in their great zeal, sentiments palpably false, both in regard to the character and situation of the persons who utter them, sentiments which a child or a clown would detect, into the most skilful depictments of the heart. I can think of no stronger instance to shew how powerfully this love of nature dwells within us.[121]

Formed as we are with these sympathetick propensities in regard to our own species, it is not at all wonderful that theatrical exhibition has become the grand and favourite amusement of every nation into which it has been introduced. Savages will, in the wild contortions of the dance, shape out some rude story expressive of character or passion, and such a dance will give more delight to their companions than the most artful exertions of agility. Children in their gambols will make out a mimic representation of the manners, characters, and passions of grown men and women, and such a pastime will animate and delight them much more than a treat of the daintiest sweetmeats, or the handling of the gaudiest toys. Eagerly as it is enjoyed by the rude and the young, to the polished and the ripe in years it is still the most interesting amusement. Our taste for it is durable as it is universal. Independently of those circumstances which first introduced it, the world would not have long been without it. The progress of society would soon have brought it forth; and men in the whimsical decorations of fancy would have displayed the characters and actions of their heroes, the folly and absurdity of their fellow-citizens, had no Priest of Bacchus ever existed.[122]

---

121 Baillie's note: "It appears to me a very strong testimony of the excellence of our great national Dramatist, that so many people have been employed in finding out obscure and refined beauties, in what appear to ordinary observation his very defects. Men, it may be said, do so merely to shew their own superiour penetration and ingenuity. But grant-

ing this; what could make other men listen to them, and listen so greedily too, if it were not that they have received from the works of Shakspeare, pleasure far beyond what the most perfect poetical compositions of a different character can afford?"

122 Baillie's note: "Though the progress of society would have given us the Drama, independently of the particular cause of its first commencement, the peculiar circumstances connected with its origin, have had considerable influence upon its character and style, in the ages through which it has passed even to our days, and still will continue to affect it. Homer had long preceded the dramatick poets of Greece; poetry was in a high state of cultivation when they began to write; and their style, the construction of their pieces, and the characters of their heroes were different from what they would have been, had theatrical exhibitions been the invention of an earlier age and a ruder people. Their works were represented to an audience, already accustomed to hear long poems rehearsed at their publick games, and the feasts of their gods. A play, with the principal characters of which they were previously acquainted;

In whatever age or country the Drama might have taken its rise, tragedy would have been the first-born of its children. For every nation has its great men, and its great events upon record; and to represent their own forefathers struggling with those difficulties, and braving those dangers, of which they have heard with admiration, and the effects of which they still, perhaps, experience, would certainly have been the most animating subject for the poet, and the most interesting for his audience, even independently of the natural inclination we all so universally shew for scenes of horrour and distress, of passion and heroick exertion. Tragedy would have been the first child of the Drama, for the same reasons that have made

---

in which their great men and heroes, in the most beautiful language, complained of their rigorous fate, but piously submitted to the will of the Gods; in which sympathy was chiefly excited by tender and affecting sentiments; in which strong bursts of passion were few; and in which whole scenes frequently passed, without giving the actors any thing to do but to speak, was not too insipid for them. Had the Drama been the invention of a less cultivated nation, more of action and passion would have been introduced into it. It would have been more irregular, more imperfect, more varied, more interesting. From poor beginnings it would have advanced in a progressive state; and succeeding poets, not having those polished and admired originals to look back upon, would have presented their respective contemporaries with the produce of a free and unbridled imagination. A different class of poets would most likely have been called into existence. The latent powers of men are called forth by contemplating those works in which they find any thing congenial to their own peculiar talents; and if the field, wherein they could have worked, is already enriched with a produce unsuited to their cultivation, they think not of entering it at all. Men, therefore, whose natural turn of mind led them to labour, to reason, to refine, and exalt, have caught their animation from the beauties of the Grecian Drama, and they who, perhaps, ought only to have been our Criticks have become our poets. I mean not, however, in any degree to depreciate the works of the ancients; a great deal we have gained by those beautiful compositions; and what we have lost by them it is impossible to compute. Very strong genius will sometimes break through every disadvantage of circumstances: Shakspeare has arisen in this country, and we ought not to complain."

heroick ballad, with all its battles, murders, and disasters, the earliest poetical compositions of every country.

We behold heroes and great men at a distance, unmarked by those small but distinguishing features of the mind, which give a certain individuality to such an infinite variety of similar beings, in the near and familiar intercourse of life. They appear to us from this view like distant mountains, whose dark outlines we trace in the clear horizon, but the varieties of whose roughened sides, shaded with heath and brushwood, and seamed with many a cleft, we perceive not. When accidental anecdote reveals to us any weakness or peculiarity belonging to them, we start upon it like a discovery. They are made known to us in history only, by the great events they are connected with, and the part they have taken in extraordinary or important transactions. Even in poetry and romance, with the exception of some love story interwoven with the main events of their lives, they are seldom more intimately made known to us. To Tragedy it belongs to lead them forward to our nearer regard, in all the distinguishing varieties which nearer inspection discovers; with the passions, the humours, the weaknesses, the prejudices of men. It is for her to present to us the great and magnanimous hero, who appears to our distant view as a superior being, as a God, softened down with those smaller frailties and imperfections that enable us to glory in, and claim kindred to his virtues. It is for her to exhibit to us the daring and ambitious man, planning his dark designs, and executing his bloody purposes, mark'd with those appropriate characteristicks, which distinguish him as an individual of that class; and agitated with those varied passions, which disturb the mind of man when he is engaged in the commission of such deeds. It is for her to point out to us the brave and impetuous warrior struck with those visitations of nature, which, in certain situations, will unnerve the strongest arm, and make the boldest heart tremble. It is for her to shew the tender, gentle, and unassuming mind animated with that fire which, by the provocation of circumstances, will give to the kindest heart the ferocity and keenness of a tiger. It is for her to present to us the great and striking characters that are to be found amongst men, in a way which the poet, the novelist, and the historian can but imperfectly attempt. But above all, to her, and to her only it belongs to unveil to us the human mind under the dominion of those strong and fixed passions, which, seemingly unprovoked by outside circumstances, will from small beginnings brood within the breast, till all the better dispositions, all the fair gifts of nature are borne down before them. Those passions which conceal themselves from the observation of men; which cannot unbosom themselves even to the dearest friend; and can, often times, only give their fulness vent in the lonely desert, or in the darkness of midnight. For who hath followed the great man into his secret closet, or stood by the side of his nightly couch, and heard those exclamations of the soul which heaven alone may hear, that the historian should be able to inform us? and what form of story, what mode of rehearsed speech will communicate to us those feelings, whose irregular bursts, abrupt transitions, sudden pauses, and half-uttered suggestions, scorn all harmony of measured verse, all method and order of relation?

On the first part of this task her Bards have eagerly exerted their abilities: and some amongst them, taught by strong original genius to deal immediately with human nature and their own hearts, have laboured in it successfully. But in presenting to us those views of great characters, and of the human mind in difficult and trying situations which peculiarly belong to Tragedy, the far greater proportion, even of those who may be considered as respectable dramatick poets, have very much failed. From the beauty of those original dramas to which they have ever looked back with admiration, they have been tempted to prefer the embellishments of poetry to faithfully delineated nature. They have been more occupied in considering the works of the great Dramatists who have gone before them, and the effects produced by their writings, than the varieties of human character that first furnished materials for those works, or those principles in the mind of man by means of which such effects were produced. Neglecting the boundless variety of nature, certain strong outlines of character, certain bold features of passion, certain grand vicissitudes, and striking dramatick situations have been repeated from one gen-

eration to another; whilst a pompous and solemn gravity, which they have supposed to be necessary for the dignity of tragedy, has excluded almost entirely from their works those smaller touches of nature, which so well develope the mind; and by shewing men in their hours of state and exertion only, they have consequently shewn them imperfectly. Thus, great and magnanimous heroes, who bear with majestic equanimity every vicissitude of fortune; who in every temptation and trial stand forth in unshaken virtue, like a rock buffeted by the waves; who, encompast with the most terrible evils, in calm possession of their souls, reason upon the difficulties of their state; and, even upon the brink of destruction, pronounce long eulogiums[123] on virtue, in the most eloquent and beautiful language, have been held forth to our view as objects of imitation and interest; as though they had entirely forgotten that it is only for creatures like ourselves that we feel, and therefore, only from creatures like ourselves that we receive the instruction of example.[124] Thus, passionate and impetuous warriors, who are proud, irritable, and vindictive, but generous, daring, and disinterested; setting their lives at a pin's fee for the good of others, but incapable of curbing their own humour of a moment to gain the whole world for themselves; who

---

123 *eulogiums*: laudatory discourses; formal expressions of praise.

124 Baillie's note: "To a being perfectly free from all human infirmity our sympathy refuses to extend. Our Saviour himself, whose character is so beautiful, and so harmoniously consistent; in whom, with outward proofs of his mission less strong than those that are offered to us, I should still be compelled to believe, from being utterly unable to conceive how the idea of such a character could enter into the imagination of a man, never touches the heart more nearly than when he says, "Father, let this cup pass from me." Had he been represented to us in all the unshaken strength of these tragick heroes, his disciples would have made fewer converts, and his precepts would have been listened to coldly. Plays in which heroes of this kind are held forth, and whose aim is, indeed, honourable and praiseworthy, have been admired by the cultivated and refined, but the tears of the simple, the applauses of the young and untaught have been wanting."

will pluck the orbs of heaven from their places, and crush the whole universe in one grasp, are called forth to kindle in our souls the generous contempt of everything abject and base; but with an effect proportionably feeble, as the hero is made to exceed in courage and fire what the standard of humanity will agree to.[125] Thus, tender and pathetick lovers, full of the most gentle affections, the most amiable dispositions, and the most exquisite feelings; who present their defenceless bosoms to the storms of this rude world in all the graceful weakness of sensibility, are made to sigh out their sorrows in one unvaried strain of studied pathos, whilst this constant demand upon our feelings makes us absolutely incapable

of answering it.[126] Thus, also, tyrants are represented as monsters of cruelty, unmixed with any feelings of humanity; and villains as delighting in all manner of treachery and deceit, and acting upon many occasions for the very love of villainy itself; though the perfectly wicked are as ill fitted for the purposes of warning, as the perfectly virtuous are for those of example.[127] This spirit of imitation, and attention to effect, has likewise confined them very much in their choice of situations and events to bring their great characters into action: rebellions, conspiracies, contentions for empire, and rivalships in love have alone been thought worthy of trying these heroes; and palaces and dungeons the only places magnificent or solemn enough for them to appear in.

They have, indeed, from this regard to the works of preceding authors, and great attention to the beauties of composition, and to dignity of design, enriched their plays

---

125 Baillie's note: "In all the burlesque imitations of tragedy, those plays in which the hero is pre-eminent, are always exposed to bear the great brunt of the ridicule; which proves how popular they have been, and how many poets, and good ones too, have been employed upon them. That they have been so popular, however, is not owing to the intrinsick merit of the characters they represent, but their opposition to those mean and contemptible qualities belonging to human nature, of which we are most ashamed. Besides, there is something in the human mind, independently of its love of applause, which inclines to boast. This is ever the attendant of that elasticity of soul, which makes us bound up from the touch of oppression; and if there is nothing in the accompanying circumstances to create disgust, or suggest suspicions of their sincerity, (as in real life is commonly the case), we are very apt to be carried along with the boasting of others. Let us in good earnest believe that a man is capable of achieving all that human courage can achieve, and we will suffer him to talk of impossibilities. Amidst all their pomp of words, therefore, our admiration of such heroes is readily excited, (for the understanding is more easily deceived than the heart), but how stands our sympathy affected? As no caution nor foresight, on their own account, is ever suffered to occupy the thoughts of such bold disinterested beings, we are the more inclined to care for them, and to take an interest in their fortune through the course of the play: yet, as their souls are unappalled by any thing; as pain and death are not at all regarded by them; and as we have seen them very ready to plunge their own swords into their own bosoms, on no very weighty occasion, perhaps, their death distresses us but little, and they commonly fall unwept."

126 Baillie's note: "Were it not, that in tragedies where these heroes preside, the same soft tones of sorrow are so often repeated in our ears, till we are perfectly tired of it, they are more fitted to interest us than any other: both because in seeing them, we own the ties of kindred between ourselves and the frail mortals we lament; and sympathise with the weakness of mortality unmixed with any thing to degrade or disgust; and also, because the misfortunes, which form the story of the play, are frequently of the more familiar and domestic kind. A king driven from his throne, will not move our sympathy so strongly, as a private man torn from the bosom of his family."

127 Baillie's note: "I have said nothing here in regard to female character, though in many tragedies it is brought forward as the principal one of the piece, because what I have said of the above characters is likewise applicable to it. I believe there is no man that ever lived, who has behaved in a certain manner on a certain occasion, who has not had amongst women some corresponding spirit, who on the like occasion, and every way similarly circumstanced, would have behaved in the like manner. With some degree of softening and refinement, each class of tragick heroes I have mentioned has its corresponding one amongst the heroines. The tender and pathetick no doubt has the most numerous, but the great and magnanimous is not without it, and the passionate and impetuous boasts of one by no means inconsiderable in numbers, and drawn sometimes to the full as passionate and impetuous as itself."

with much striking, and sometimes sublime imagery, lofty thoughts, and virtuous sentiments; but in striving so eagerly to excell in those things that belong to tragedy in common with many other compositions, they have very much neglected those that are peculiarly her own. As far as they have been led aside from the first labours of a tragick poet by a desire to communicate more perfect moral instruction, their motive has been respectable, and they merit our esteem. But this praiseworthy end has been injured instead of promoted by their mode of pursuing it. Every species of moral writing has its own way of conveying instruction, which it can never, but with disadvantage, exchange for any other. The Drama improves us by the knowledge we acquire of our own minds, from the natural desire we have to look into the thoughts, and observe the behaviour of others. Tragedy brings to our view men placed in those elevated situations, exposed to those great trials, and engaged in those extraordinary transactions, in which few of us are called upon to act. As examples applicable to ourselves, therefore, they can but feebly affect us; it is only from the enlargement of our ideas in regard to human nature, from that admiration of virtue, and abhorrence of vice which they excite, that we can expect to be improved by them. But if they are not represented to us as real and natural characters, the lessons we are taught from their conduct and their sentiments will be no more to us than those which we receive from the pages of the poet or the moralist.

But the last part of the task which I have mentioned as peculiarly belonging to tragedy, unveiling the human mind under the dominion of those strong and fixed passions, which seemingly unprovoked by outward circumstances, will from small beginnings brood within the breast, till all the better dispositions, all the fair gifts of nature are borne down before them, her poets in general have entirely neglected, and even her first and greatest have but imperfectly attempted. They have made use of the passions to mark their several characters, and animate their scenes, rather than to open to our view the nature and portraitures of those great disturbers of the human breast, with whom we are all, more or less, called upon to contend. With their strong and obvious features, therefore, they have been presented to us, stripped almost entirely of those less obtrusive, but not less discriminating traits, which mark them in their actual operation. To trace them in their rise and progress in the heart, seems but rarely to have been the object of any dramatist. We commonly find the characters of tragedy affected by the passions in a transient, loose, unconnected manner; or if they are represented as under the permanent influence of the more powerful ones, they are generally introduced to our notice in the very height of their fury, when all that timidity, irresolution, distrust, and a thousand delicate traits, which make the infancy of every great passion more interesting, perhaps, than its full-blown strength, are fled. The impassioned character is generally brought into view under those irresistible attacks of their power, which it is impossible to repell; whilst those gradual steps that lead him into this state, in some of which a stand might have been made against the foe, are left entirely in the shade. These passions that may be suddenly excited, and are of short duration, as anger, fear, and oftentimes jealousy, may in this manner be fully represented; but those great masters of the soul, ambition, hatred, love, every passion that is permanent in its nature, and varied in progress, if represented to us but in one stage of its course, is represented imperfectly. It is a characteristick of the more powerful passions that they will increase and nourish themselves on very slender aliment;[128] it is from within that they are chiefly supplied with what they feed on; and it is in contending with opposite passions and affections of the mind that we best discover their strength, not with events. But in tragedy it is events more frequently than opposite affections which are opposed to them; and those often of such force and magnitude that the passions themselves are almost obscured by the splendour and importance of the transactions to which they are attached. Besides being thus confined and mutilated, the passions have been, in the greater part of our tragedies, deprived of the very power of making themselves known. Bold and figurative language belongs peculiarly to them. Poets, admiring those

---

128 *aliment*: that which nourishes or feeds; food.

bold expressions which a mind, labouring with ideas too strong to be conveyed in the ordinary forms of speech, wildly throws out, taking earth, sea, and sky, every thing great and terrible in nature to image forth the violence of its feelings, borrowed them gladly, to adorn the calm sentiments of their premeditated song. It has therefore been thought that the less animated parts of tragedy might be so embellished and enriched. In doing this, however, the passions have been robbed of their native prerogative; and in adorning with their strong figures and lofty expressions the calm speeches of the unruffled, it is found that, when they are called upon to raise their voice, the power of distinguishing themselves has been taken away. This is an injury by no means compensated, but very greatly aggravated by embellishing, in return, the speeches of passion with the ingenious conceits and complete similes of premeditated thought.[129] There are many other things regarding the manner in which dramatick poets have generally brought forward the passions in tragedy, to the great prejudice of that effect they are naturally fitted to produce upon the mind, which I forbear to mention, lest they should too much increase the length of this discourse; and leave an impression on the mind of my reader, that I write more in the spirit of criticism, than becomes one who is about to bring before the publick a work, with, doubtless, many faults and imperfections on its head.

From this general view, which I have endeavoured to communicate to my reader, of tragedy, and those principles in the human mind upon which the success of her efforts depends, I have been led to believe, that an attempt to write a series of tragedies, of simpler construction, less embellished with poetical decorations, less constrained by that lofty seriousness which has so generally been consid-

ered as necessary for the support of tragick dignity, and in which the chief object should be to delineate the progress of the higher passions in the human breast, each play exhibiting a particular passion, might not be unacceptable to the publick. And I have been the more readily induced to act upon this idea, because I am confident, that tragedy, written upon this plan, is fitted to produce stronger moral effect than upon any other. I have said that tragedy in representing to us great characters struggling with difficulties, and placed in situations of eminence and danger, in which few of us have any chance of being called upon to act, conveys its moral efficacy to our minds by the enlarged views which it gives to us of human nature, by the admiration of virtue, and execration of vice which it excites, and not by the examples it holds up for our immediate application. But in opening to us the heart of man under the influence of those passions to which all are liable, this is not the case. Those strong passions that, with small assistance from outward circumstances, work their way in the heart, till they become the tyrannical masters of it, carry on a similar operation in the breast of the Monarch, and the man of low degree. It exhibits to us the mind of man in that state when we are most curious to look into it, and is equally interesting to all. Discrimination of character is a turn of mind, tho' more common than we are aware of, which every body does not possess; but to the expressions of passion, particularly strong passion, the dullest mind is awake; and its true unsophisticated language the dullest understanding will not misinterpret. To hold up for our example those peculiarities in disposition, and modes of thinking which nature has fixed upon us, or which long and early habit has incorporated with our original selves, is almost desiring us to remove the everlasting mountains, to take away the native land-marks of the soul; but representing the passions brings before us the operation of a tempest that rages out its time and passes away. We cannot, it is true, amidst its wild uproar, listen to the voice of reason, and save ourselves from destruction; but we can foresee its coming, we can mark its rising signs, we can know the situations that will most expose us to its rage, and we can shelter our heads from the coming blast. To change a cer-

---

129 Baillie's note: "This, perhaps, more than any thing else has injured the higher scenes of tragedy. For having made such free use of bold hyperbolical language in the inferiour parts, the poet when he arrives at the highly-impassioned sinks into total inability: or if he will force himself to rise still higher on the wing, he flies beyond nature altogether, into the regions of bombast and nonsense."

tain disposition of mind which makes us view objects in a particular light, and thereby, oftentimes, unknown to ourselves, influences our conduct and manners, is almost impossible; but in checking and subduing those visitations of the soul, whose causes and effects we are aware of, every one may make considerable progress, if he proves not entirely successful. Above all, looking back to the first rise, and tracing the progress of passion, points out to us those stages in the approach of the enemy, when he might have been combated most successfully; and where the suffering him to pass may be considered as occasioning all the misery that ensues.

Comedy presents to us men as we find them in the ordinary intercourse of the world, with all the weaknesses, follies, caprice, prejudices, and absurdities which a near and familiar view of them discovers. It is her task to exhibit them engaged in the busy turmoil of ordinary life, harassing and perplexing themselves with the endless pursuits of avarice, vanity, and pleasure; and engaged with those smaller trials of mind, by which men are most apt to be overcome, and from which he, who could have supported with honour the attack of great occasions, will oftentimes come off the most shamefully foiled. It belongs to her to shew the varied fashions and manners of the world, as, from the spirit of vanity, caprice, and imitation, they go on in swift and endless succession; and those disagreeable or absurd peculiarities attached to particular classes and conditions in society. It is for her also to represent men under the influence of the stronger passions; and to trace the rise and progress of them in the heart, in such situations, and attended with such circumstances as take off their sublimity, and the interest we naturally take in a perturbed mind. It is hers to exhibit those terrible tyrants of the soul, whose ungovernable rage has struck us so often with dismay, like wild beasts tied to a post, who growl and paw before us, for our derision and sport. In pourtraying the characters of men she has this advantage over tragedy, that the smallest traits of nature, with the smallest circumstances which serve to bring them forth, may by her be displayed, however ludicrous and trivial in themselves, without any ceremony. And in developing the passions she enjoys a similar advantage; for

they often more strongly betray themselves when touched by those small and familiar occurrences which cannot, consistently with the effect it is intended to produce, be admitted into tragedy.

As tragedy has been very much cramped in her endeavours to exalt and improve the mind, by that spirit of imitation and confinement in her successive writers, which the beauty of her earliest poets first gave rise to, so comedy has been led aside from her best purposes by a different temptation. Those endless changes in fashions and in manners, which offer such obvious and ever-new subjects of ridicule; that infinite variety of tricks and manœuvres by which the ludicrous may be produced, and curiosity and laughter excited: the admiration we so generally bestow upon satirical remark, pointed repartee, and whimsical combinations of ideas, have too often led her to forget the warmer interest we feel, and the more profitable lessons we receive from genuine representations of nature. The most interesting and instructive class of comedy, therefore, the real characteristick, has been very much neglected, whilst satirical, witty, sentimental, and, above all, busy or circumstantial comedy have usurped the exertions of the far greater proportion of Dramatick Writers...

––––––––––

51. Baillie, Joanna. "To the Reader." *A Series of Plays.* 3 vols. London: Cadell and Davies, 1812. Volume 3, pages iii-xxxi. Extract.

After an interval of nine years, I offer to the Public a third volume of the "Series of Plays"; hoping that it will be received, as the preceding volumes have been, with some degree of favour and indulgence. This, I confess, is making very slow progress in my promised undertaking; and I could offer some reasonable excuse for an apparent relaxation of industry, were I not afraid it might seem to infer a greater degree of expectation or desire, on the part of my readers, to receive the remainder of the work, than I am at all entitled to suppose.

With the exception of a small piece, in two acts, at the end of the book, this volume is entirely occupied with different representations of one passion; and a passion, too, which has been supposed to be less adapted to dramatic purposes than any other—Fear. It has been thought that, in Tragedy at least, the principal character could not possibly be actuated by this passion, without becoming so far degraded as to be incapable of engaging the sympathy and interest of the spectator or reader. I am, however, inclined to think, that even Fear, as it is under certain circumstances and to a certain degree a universal passion (for our very admiration of Courage rests upon this idea), is capable of being made in the tragic drama, as it often is in real life, very interesting, and consequently not abject.

The first of these plays is a Tragedy of five acts, the principal character of which is a woman, under the dominion of Superstitious Fear; and that particular species of it, (the fear of ghosts, or the returning dead), which is so universal and inherent in our nature, that it can never be eradicated from the mind, let the progress of reason or philosophy be what it may. A brave and wise man of the 19th century, were he lodged for the night in a lone apartment where murder has been committed, would not so easily believe, as a brave and wise man of the 14th century, that the restless spirit from its grave might stalk round his bed and open his curtains in the stillness of midnight: but should circumstances arise to impress him with such a belief, he would feel the emotions of Fear as intensely, though firmly persuaded that such beings have no power to injure him. Nay, I am persuaded that, could we suppose any person with a mind so constituted as to hold intercourse with such beings entirely devoid of Fear, we should turn from him with repugnance as something unnatural—as an instance of mental monstrosity. If I am right then in believing this impression of the mind to be so universal, I shall not be afraid of having so far infringed on the dignity of my heroine, as to make her an improper object to excite dramatic interest. Those, I believe, who possess strong imagination, quick fancy, and keen feeling, are most easily affected by this species of Fear: I have, therefore, made Orra a lively, cheerful, buoyant character, when not immediately under its influence; and even extracting from her supersti-

tious propensity a kind of wild enjoyment, which tempts her to nourish and cultivate the enemy that destroys her. The catastrophe is such as Fear, I understand, does more commonly produce than any other passion. I have endeavoured to trace the inferior characters of the piece with some degree of variety, so as to stand relieved from the principal figure; but as I am not aware that any particular objection is likely to be made to any of them, they shall be left entirely to the mercy of my reader.

But if it has been at all necessary to offer any apology for exhibiting Fear as the actuating principle of the heroine of the first play, what must I say in defence of a much bolder step in the one that follows it? in which I have made Fear, and the fear of Death too, the actuating principle of a hero of Tragedy. I can only say, that I believed it might be done, without submitting him to any degradation that would affect the sympathy and interest I intended to excite. I must confess, however, that, being unwilling to appropriate this passion in a serious form to my own sex entirely, when the subjects of all the other passions, hitherto delineated in this series, are men, I have attempted what did indeed appear at first sight almost impracticable. This *esprit de corps* must also plead my excuse for loading the passion in question with an additional play. The fear of Death is here exhibited in a brave character, placed under such new and appalling circumstances as might, I supposed, overcome the most courageous; and as soon as he finds himself in a situation like those in which he has been accustomed to be bold, viz. with arms in his hand and an enemy to encounter, he is made immediately to resume all his wonted[130] spirit. Even after he believes himself to be safe, he returns again to attack, in behalf of his companion, who beseeches him to fly, and who is not exposed to any personal danger, a force so greatly superior to his own as to leave himself scarcely a chance for redemption.

That great active courage in opposing danger, and great repugnance from passive endurance and unknown change which are independent of our exertions, are per-

---

130 *wonted*: accustomed.

fectly consistent, is a point, I believe, very well ascertained. Soldiers, who have distinguished themselves honourably in the field, have died pusillanimously on the scaffold; while men brought up in peaceful habits, who, without some very strong excitement, would have marched with trepidation to battle, have died under the hands of the executioner with magnanimous composure. And, I believe, it has been found by experience, that women have always behaved with as much resolution and calmness in that tremendous situation as men; although I do not believe that women, in regard to uncertain danger, even making allowance for their inferior strength and unfavourable habits of life, are so brave as men. I have therefore supposed that, though active and passive courage are often united, they frequently exist separately, and independently of each other. Nor ought we to be greatly surprised at this when we consider, that a man, actively brave, when so circumstanced that no exertion of strength or boldness is of any avail, finds himself in a new situation, contrary to all former experience; and is therefore taken at greater disadvantage than men of a different character. He, who has less of that spirit which naturally opposes an enemy, and still hopes to overcome while the slightest probability remains of success, has often before, in imagination at least, been in a similar predicament, and is consequently better prepared for it. But it is not want of fortitude to bear bodily sufferings, or even deliberately inflicted death, under the circumstances commonly attending it, that the character of Osterloo exhibits. It is the horror he conceives on being suddenly awakened to the imagination of the awful retributions of another world, from having the firm belief of them forced at once upon his mind by extraordinary circumstances, which so miserably quells an otherwise undaunted spirit. I only contend for the consistency of brave men shrinking from passive sufferings and unknown change, to shew, that so far from transgressing, I have, in this character, kept much within the bounds which our experience of human nature would have allowed me. If I am tediously anxious to vindicate myself on this subject, let my reader consider, that I am urged to it from the experience I have had of the great reluctance with which people generally receive characters which are not drawn agreeably to the received rules of dramatic dignity, and common-place heroism.

It may be objected that the fear of Death is in him so closely connected with Superstitious Fear, that the picture traced in this play bears too near a resemblance to that which is shewn in the foregoing. But the fears of Orra have nothing to do with apprehension of personal danger, and spring solely from a natural horror of supernatural intercourse: while those of Osterloo arise, as I have already noticed, from a strong sense of guilt, suddenly roused within him by extraordinary circumstances; and the prospect of being plunged, almost immediately by death, into an unknown state of punishment and horror. Not knowing by what natural means his guilt could be brought to light, in a manner so extraordinary, a mind the least superstitious, in those days, perhaps I may even say in these, would have considered it to be supernatural; and the dreadful consequences, so immediately linked to it, are surely sufficiently strong to unhinge the firmest mind, having no time allowed to prepare itself for the tremendous change. If there is any person, who, under such circumstances, could have remained unappalled, he does not belong to that class of men, who, commanding the fleets and armies of their grateful and admiring country, dare every thing by flood and by field that is dangerous and terrific for her sake; but to one far different, whom hard drinking, opium, or impiety have sunk into a state of unmanly and brutish stupidity. It will probably be supposed that I have carried the consequences of his passion too far in the catastrophe to be considered as natural; but the only circumstance in the piece that is not entirely invention, is the catastrophe. The idea of it I received from a story told to me by my mother, many years ago, of a man condemned to the block, who died in the same manner; and since the play has been written, I have had the satisfaction of finding it confirmed by a circumstance very similar, related in Miss Plumtre's interesting account of the atrocities committed in Lions by the revolutionary tribunals...[131]

[Baillie then describes the other plays in the volume].

---

131 Baillie's note: "Plumptre's *Residence in France*, vol. i. p. 339."

Having said all that appears to me necessary in regard to the contents of the volume, I should now leave my reader to peruse it without further hindrance; but as this will probably be the last volume of Plays I shall ever publish, I must beg to detain him a few moments longer. For I am inclined to think, he may have some curiosity to know what is the extent of my plan in a task I have so far fulfilled; and I shall satisfy it most cheerfully. It is my intention, if I live long enough, to add to this work the passions of Remorse, Jealousy, and Revenge. Joy, Grief, and Anger, as I have already said, are generally of too transient a nature, and are too frequently the attendants of all our other passions to be made the subjects of an entire play. And though this objection cannot be urged in regard to Pride and Envy, two powerful passions which I have not yet named; Pride would make, I should think, a dull subject, unless it were merely taken as the ground-work of more turbulent passions; and Envy, being that state of mind, which, of all others, meets with least sympathy, could only be endured in Comedy or Farce, and would become altogether disgusting in Tragedy. I have besides, in some degree, introduced this latter passion into the work already, by making it a companion or rather a component part of Hatred. Of all our passions, Remorse and Jealousy appear to me to be the best fitted for representation. If this be the case, it is fortunate for me that I have reserved them for the end of my task; and that they have not been already published, read, and very naturally laid aside as unfit for the stage, because they have not been produced upon it.

My reader may likewise wish to know why, having so many years ago promised to go on publishing this work, I should now intend to leave it off, though I still mean to continue writing till it shall be compleated; and this supposed wish, I think myself bound to gratify.—The Series of Plays was originally published in the hope that some of the pieces it contains, although first given to the Public from the press, might in time make their way to the stage, and there be received and supported with some degree of public favour. But the present situation of dramatic affairs is greatly against every hope of this kind; and should they ever become more favourable, I have now good reason to believe, that the circumstance of these plays having been already published, would operate strongly against their being received upon the stage. I am therefore strongly of opinion that I ought to reserve the remainder of the work in manuscript, if I would not run the risk of entirely frustrating my original design. Did I believe that their having been already published would not afterwards obstruct their way to the stage, the untowardness of present circumstances should not prevent me from continuing to publish.

Having thus given an account of my views and intentions regarding this work, I hope that, should no more of it be published in my lifetime, it will not be supposed I have abandoned or become weary of my occupation, which is in truth as interesting and pleasing to me now as it was at the beginning.

But when I say, present circumstances are unfavourable for the reception of these Plays upon the stage, let it not be supposed that I mean to throw any reflection upon the prevailing taste for dramatic amusements. The Public have now to chuse between what we shall suppose are well-written and well-acted Plays, the words of which are not heard, or heard but imperfectly by two thirds of the audience, while the finer and more pleasing traits of the acting are by a still greater proportion lost altogether, and splendid pantomime, or pieces whose chief object is to produce striking scenic effect, which can be seen and comprehended by the whole. So situated, it would argue, methinks, a very pedantic love indeed, for what is called legitimate Drama, were we to prefer the former. A love for active, varied movement in the objects before us; for striking contrasts of light and shadow; for splendid decorations and magnificent scenery, is as inherent in us as the interest we take in the representation of the natural passions and characters of men: and the most cultivated minds may relish such exhibitions, if they do not, when both are fairly offered to their choice, prefer them. Did our ears and our eyes permit us to hear and see distinctly in a Theatre so large as to admit of chariots and horsemen, and all the "pomp and circumstance of war,"[132] I

---

132 *"pomp and circumstance of war"*: See note 81.

see no reason why we should reject them. They would give variety, and an appearance of truth to the scenes of heroic Tragedy, that would very much heighten its effect. We ought not, then, to find fault with the taste of the Public for preferring an inferior species of entertainment, good of its kind, to a superior one, faintly and imperfectly given.

It has been urged, as a proof of this supposed bad taste in the Public, by one[133] whose judgment on these subjects is and ought to be high authority, that a play,[134] possessing considerable merit, was produced some years ago on Drury-Lane stage, and notwithstanding the great support it received from excellent acting and magnificent decoration, entirely failed. It is very true that, in spite of all this, it failed, during the eight nights it continued to be acted, to produce houses sufficiently good to induce the Managers to revive it afterwards. But it ought to be acknowledged, that that piece had defects in it as an acting Play, which served to counterbalance those advantages; and likewise that, if any supposed merit in the writing ought to have redeemed those defects, in a theatre, so large and so ill calculated to convey sound as the one in which it was performed, it was impossible this could be felt or comprehended by even a third part of the audience.

The size of our theatres, then, is what I chiefly allude to, when I say, present circumstances are unfavourable for the production of these Plays. While they continue to be of this size, it is a vain thing to complain

either of want of taste in the Public, or want of inclination in Managers to bring forward new pieces of merit, taking it for granted that there are such to produce. Nothing can be truly relished by the most cultivated audience that is not distinctly heard and seen, and Managers must produce what will be relished. Shakespeare's Plays, and some of our other old Plays, indeed, attract full houses, though they are often repeated, because, being familiar to the audience, they can still understand and follow them pretty closely, though but imperfectly heard; and surely this is no bad sign of our public taste. And besides this advantage, when a piece is familiar to the audience, the expression of the actors' faces is much better understood, though seen imperfectly; for the stronger marked traits of feeling which even in a large theatre may reach the eyes of a great part of the audience, from the recollection of finer and more delicate indications, formerly seen so delightfully mingled with them in the same countenances during the same passages of the Play, will, by association, still convey them to the mind's eye, though it is the mind's eye only which they have reached.

And this thought leads me to another defect in large theatres, that ought to be considered.

Our great tragic actress, Mrs. Siddons, whose matchless powers of expression have so long been the pride of our stage, and the most admired actors of the present time, have been brought up in their youth in small theatres, where they were encouraged to enter thoroughly into the characters they represented; and to express in their faces that variety of fine fleeting emotion which nature, in moments of agitation, assumes, and the imitation of which we are taught by nature to delight in. But succeeding actors will only consider expression of countenance as addressed to an audience removed from them to a greater distance; and will only attempt such strong expression as can be perceived and have effect at a distance. It may easily be imagined what exaggerated expression will then get into use; and I should think, even this strong expression will not only be exaggerated but false. For, as we are enabled to assume the outward signs of passion, not by mimicking what we have beheld in others, but by internally assuming, in some degree, the passion itself; a

---

133 *one*: probably the reviewer in *The British Critic*, who in a May 1810 review of Baillie's *The Family Legend* declared "when there is an author living who is capable of giving to the public such scenes as are here printed, there should be no feeling or wish in the Managers of the London theatres, or their audiences to give her honourable employment. This but too fully explains the latent cause of our former complaints. The British Public is not at present worthy of good Dramas; fighting horses and dancing dogs fill up all their wishes for theatrical amusement; and scenes, of which our best poets would have been proud, would be recited before such hearers like tales told to a dead Ass" (XXXV:53).

134 *a play*: *De Monfort*, which opened at Drury Lane 29 March 1800.

mere outline of it cannot, I apprehend, be given as an outline of figure frequently is, where all that is delineated is true though the whole is not filled up. Nay, besides having it exaggerated and false, it will perpetually be thrust in where it ought not to be. For real occasions of strong expression not occurring often enough, and weaker being of no avail, to avoid an apparent barrenness of countenance, they will be tempted to introduce it where it is not wanted, and thereby destroy its effect where it is.—I say nothing of expression of voice, to which the above observations obviously apply. This will become equally, if not in a greater degree, false and exaggerated, in actors trained from their youth in a large theatre.

But the department of acting that will suffer most under these circumstances, is that which particularly regards the gradual unfolding of the passions, and has, perhaps, hitherto been less understood than any other part of the art—I mean Soliloquy. What actor in his senses will then think of giving to the solitary musing of a perturbed mind that muttered, imperfect articulation which grows by degrees into words; that heavy, suppressed voice as of one speaking through sleep; that rapid burst of sounds which often succeeds the slow languid tones of distress; those sudden, untuned exclamations which, as if frightened at their own discord, are struck again into silence as sudden and abrupt, with all the corresponding variety of countenance that belongs to it;—what actor, so situated, will attempt to exhibit all this? No; he will be satisfied, after taking a turn or two across the front of the stage, to place himself directly in the middle of it; and there, spreading out his hands as if he were addressing some person whom it behoved him to treat with great ceremony, to tell to himself, in an audible uniform voice, all the secret thoughts of his own heart. When he has done this, he will think, and he will think rightly, that he has done enough.

The only valuable part of acting that will then remain to us, will be expression of gesture, grace and dignity, supposing that these also shall not become affected by being too much attended to and studied.

It may be urged against such apprehensions that, though the theatres of the metropolis should be large, they will be supplied with actors, who have been trained to the stage in small country-theatres. An actor of ambition (and all actors of genius are such) will practise with little heart in the country what he knows will be of no use to him on a London stage; not to mention that the style of acting in London will naturally be the fashionable and prevailing style elsewhere. Acting will become a less respectable profession than it has continued to be from the days of Garrick; and the few actors, who add to the natural advantages requisite to it, the accomplishments of a scholar and a gentleman, will soon be wed away by the hand of time, leaving nothing of the same species behind them to spring from a neglected and sapless root.

All I have said on this subject, may still in a greater degree be applied to actresses; for the features and voice of a woman, being naturally more delicate than those of a man, she must suffer in proportion from the defects of a large theatre.

The great disadvantage of such over-sized buildings to natural and genuine acting, is, I believe, very obvious; but they have other defects which are not so readily noticed, because they, in some degree, run counter to the common opinion of their great superiority in every thing that regards general effect. The diminutive appearance of individual figures, and the straggling poverty of grouping, which unavoidably takes place when a very wide and lofty stage is not filled by a great number of people, is very injurious to general effect. This is particularly felt in Comedy, and all plays on domestic subjects; and in those scenes also of the grand drama, where two or three persons only are produced at a time. To give figures who move upon it proper effect, there must be depth as well as width of stage; and the one must bear some proportion to the other, if we would not make every closer or more confined scene appear like a section of a long passage, in which the actors move before us, apparently in one line, like the figures of a magic lanthorn.

It appears to me, that when a stage is of such a size that as many persons as generally come into action at one time in our grandest and best-peopled plays, can be produced on the front of it in groups, without crowding together more than they would naturally do any where else for the convenience of speaking to one another, all is gained in point of general effect that can well be gained. When modern gentlemen and ladies talk to one another in a spacious saloon, or when ancient warriors and dames conversed together in an old baronial hall, they do not, and did not stand further apart than when conversing in a room of common dimensions; neither ought they to do so on the stage. All width of stage beyond what is convenient for such natural grouping, is lost; and worse than lost, for it is injurious. It is continually presenting us with something similar to that which always offends us in a picture, where the canvas is too large for the subject; or in a face, where the features are too small for for the bald margin of cheeks and forehead that surrounds them.

Even in the scenes of professed shew and spectacle, where nothing else is considered, it appears to me that a very large stage is in some degree injurious to general effect. Even when a battle is represented in our theatres, the great width of the stage is a disadvantage; for as it never can nor ought to be represented but partially, and the part which is seen should be crowded and confused, opening a large front betrays your want of numbers; or should you be rich enough in this respect to fill it sufficiently, imposes upon you a difficulty seldom surmounted, viz. putting the whole mass sufficiently in action to sustain the deception.[135] When a moderate number of combatants, so as to make one connected groupe, are fighting on the front of a moderately wide stage, which they sufficiently occupy, it is an easy thing, through the confusion of their brandished weapons and waving banners, to give the appearance of a deep active battle beyond them, seen, as it were, through a narrow pass; and beholding all the tumult of battle in the small view opened before us, our imagination supplies what is hid. If we open a wider view, we give the imagination less to do and supply what it would have done less perfectly. In narrowing our battle, likewise, we could more easily throw smoke or an appearance of dust over the back ground, and procure for our fancy an unlimited space.

In processions, also, the most pleasing effect of our imaginations is, when the marshalled figures are seen in long perspective which requires only depth of stage; and the only advantage a wide stage has on such occasions is containing the assembled mass of figures, when the moving line stops and gathers itself together on the front. The rich confusion of such a crowd is indeed very brilliant and pleasing for a short time, but it is dearly purchased at the price of many sacrifices.

On those occasions too, when many people are assembled on the front of the stage to give splendour and importance to some particular scene, or to the conclusion of a piece, the general effect is often injured by great width of stage. For the crowd is supposed to be attracted to the spot by something which engages their attention; and, as they must not surround this object of attention, (which would be their natural arrangement), lest they should conceal it from the audience, they are obliged to spread themselves out in a long straight line on each side of it: now the shorter those lines or wings are, spreading out from the centre figures, the less do they offend against natural arrangement, and the less artificial and formal does the whole scene appear.

In short, I scarcely know of any advantage which a large stage possesses over one of a moderate size without great abatements, even in regard to general effect, unless it be when it is empty, and scenery alone engages our attention, or when figures appear at a distance on the back ground only. Something in confirmation of what I have

---

135 Baillie's note: "The objections above do not apply to scenes where sieges are represented; for then the more diminished the actors appear, the greater is the importance and magnitude given to the walls or castle which they attack, while the towers and buttresses, &c. sufficiently occupy the width and height of the stage, and conceal the want of numbers and general activity in the combatants. And the managers of our present large theatres have, in my opinion, shewn great judgement in introducing into their mixed pieces of late so many good scenes of this kind, that have, to my fancy at least, afforded a grand and animating shew. Nor do they fairly apply to those combats or battles into which horses are introduced; for a moderate number of those noble animals may be made to occupy and animate, in one connected groupe, the front of the widest stage that we are in danger of having, and to conceal the want of a numerous host and tumultuous battle behind them."

been saying, has, perhaps, been felt by most people on entering a grand cathedral, where, figures moving in the long aisles at a distance, add grandeur to the building by their diminished appearance; but in approaching near enough to become themselves distinct objects of attention, look stunted and mean, without serving to enlarge by comparison its general dimensions.

There is also, I apprehend, greater difficulty, in a very wide and lofty stage, to produce variety of light and shadow; and this often occasions the more solemn scenes of Tragedy to be represented in a full, staring, uniform light that ought to be dimly seen in twilight uncertainty; or to have the objects on them shewn by partial gleams only, while the deepened shade around gives a sombre indistinctness to the other parts of the stage, particularly favourable to solemn or terrific impressions. And it would be more difficult, I imagine, to throw down light upon the objects on such a stage, which I have never indeed seen attempted in any theatre, though it might surely be done in one of moderate dimensions with admirable effect. In short, a great variety of pleasing effects from light and shadow might be more easily produced on a smaller stage, that would give change and even interest to pieces otherwise monotonous and heavy; and would often be very useful in relieving the exhausted strength of the chief actors, while want of skill in the inferior could be craftily concealed.[136]

---

136 Baillie's note: "That strong light cast up from lamps on the front of the stage which has long been in use in all our theatres, is certainly very unfavourable to the appearance and expression of individual actors, and also to the general effect of their grouped figures. When a painter wishes to give intelligence and expression to a face, he does not make his lights hit upon the under part of his chin, the nostrils, and the under curve of the eyebrows, turning of course all the shadows upwards. He does the very reverse of all this; that the eye may look hollow and dark under the shade of its brow; that the shadow of the nose may shorten the upper lip, and give a greater character of sense to the mouth; and that any fulness of the under chin may be the better concealed. From this disposition of the light in our theatres, whenever an actor, whose features are not particularly sharp and pointed, comes near the front of the

On this part of the subject, however, I speak with great diffidence, not knowing to what perfection machinery for the management of light may be brought in a large

---

stage, and turns his face fully to the audience, every feature immediately becomes shortened and snub, and less capable of any expression, unless it be of the ludicrous kind. This at least will be the effect produced to those who are seated under or on the same level with the stage, making now a considerable proportion of an audience; while to those who sit above it, the lights and shadows, at variance with the natural bent of the features, will make the whole face appear confused, and (compared to what it would have been with light thrown upon it from another direction) unintelligible.——As to the general effect of grouped figures: close groupes or crowds, ranged on the front of the stage, when the light is thrown up upon them, have a harsh flaring appearance; for the foremost figures catch the light, and are too much distinguished from those behind, from whom it is intercepted. But when the light is thrown down upon the objects, this cannot be the case: for then it will glance along the heads of the whole crowd, even to the very bottom of the stage, presenting a varied harmonious mass of figures to the eye, deep, mellow and brilliant.

It may, perhaps, be objected to these last observations, that the most popular of our night-scenes in nature, and those which have been most frequently imitated by the painter, are groupes of figures with strong light thrown up upon them, such as gypsies or banditti round a fire, or villagers in a smith's forge, &c. But the striking and pleasing effect of such scenes is owing to the deep darkness which surrounds them; while the ascending smoke, tinged with flame-colour in the one case, and the rafters or higher parts of the wall catching a partial gleam in the other, connect the brilliant colouring of the figures with the deep darkness behind them, which would else appear hard and abrupt, and thus at the same time produce strong contrast with harmonious gradation. I need scarcely mention, for it is almost too obvious, that the effect of the light so thrown on the faces of those figures abundantly confirms my first observations, regarding the features and expression of individuals' faces. Yet I do not mean to say that light thrown up from the front of a stage, where light is also admitted from many other quarters, can have so strong an effect upon the countenances as in such situations.

Groupes of gypsies, &c. are commonly composed but of one circle of figures; for did they amount to any thing like a deepened groupe or crowd, the figures behind would

theatre. But at the same time, I am certain that, by a judicious use of light and scenery, an artificial magnitude may be given to a stage of a moderate size, that would, to the eye, as far as distance in perspective is concerned, have an effect almost equal to any thing that can be produced on a larger stage: for that apparent magnitude arising from succession of objects, depends upon the depth of the stage, much more than its width and loftiness, which are often detrimental to it; and a small or moderate sized theatre may have, without injury to proportion, a very deep stage.

It would be, I believe, impertinent to pursue this subject any farther: and I beg pardon for having obtruded it

---

be almost entirely lost. But those grand night-scenes containing many figures which we admire in nature or in painting,—processions by torch-light or in an illuminated street,—crowds gathered to behold a conflagration, &c. always have the light thrown down upon them.—It may be urged indeed that the greater part of our stage-scenes are meant to represent day and not night, so that the observations above are but partially applicable. It is very true that stage-scenes generally are supposed to be seen by day-light; but day-light comes from heaven, not from the earth; even within-doors our whitened ceilings are made to throw down reflected light upon us, while our pavements and carpets are of a darker colour.

In what way this great defect of all our theatres could be rectified, I am not at all competent to say. Yet, I should suppose, that by bringing forward the roof of the stage as far as its boards or floor, and placing a row of lamps with reflectors along the inside of the wooden front-piece, such a light as is wanted might be procured. The green curtain in this case behoved not to be let down, as it now is, from the front-piece, but some feet within it; and great care taken that nothing should be placed near the lamps capable of catching fire. If this were done, no boxes, I suppose, could be made upon the stage; but the removal of stage-boxes would in itself be a great advantage. The front-piece at the top; the boundary of the stage from the orchestra at the bottom; and the pilasters on each side, would then represent the frame of a great moving picture, entirely separated and distinct from the rest of the theatre: whereas, at present, an unnatural mixture of audience and actors, of house and stage takes place near the front of the stage, which destroys the general effect in a very great degree."

so far where it may not appear naturally to be called for. I plead in my excuse an almost irresistible desire to express my thoughts, in some degree, upon what has occupied them considerably; and a strong persuasion that I ought not, how unimportant soever they may be, entirely to conceal them.

I must now beg leave to return my thanks to the Public for that indulgent favour which for so many years has honoured and cheered my labour; and whether more or less liberally dealt to me, has at all times been sufficient to prevent me from laying down my pen in despair. Favour, which has gratified me the more sensibly, because I have shared it with contemporary writers of the highest poetic genius, whose claims to such distinction are so powerful.

---

52. Review of Joanna Baillie, *A Series of Plays* volumes 1-3 (1798-1812); *Miscellaneous Plays* (1804); and *The Family Legend* (1810). *Eclectic Review* 10 (July-August 1813), 21-32, 167-86. Extract.

Most of our readers know that, about fifteen years ago, Miss Baillie published the first volume of a series of Plays upon the Passions, in which it was intended to make each stronger passion the subject of both a tragedy and a comedy; and that she has been proceeding in her undertaking with two more volumes, suffering, however, the series to be interrupted, once by a volume of Miscellaneous Plays, and again by a single tragedy, called the Family Legend. It is our intention, in the present article, to speak of all her works together.

Before we enter upon the consideration of the plays themselves, however, we must detain our readers a little upon an old question, which Miss Baillie has brought forward anew in the preface to her first volume; viz. how it comes to pass that tragedy can be agreeable?

[The Reviewer quotes from Richard Hurd, David Hume, Edmund Burke, and Mark Akenside before closing the first half of the review by arguing that Baillie's sense of audience pleasure in tragedy depends upon voyeurism and sympathetic curiosity with those undergoing situations and torments that no one would want to go through themselves].

Miss Baillie is decidedly of the good old school of English drama: and, therefore, we must warn all the admirers of the monotonous declamation of French tragedy, all the lovers of Melpomene[137] in hoop-petticoats, and high-heeled shoes, to look elsewhere. They will find little to their taste here. The personages are not always ranting or whining, in the extasies of love, or the agonies of despair, or the madness of rage: they really do talk, (we do not blush for our fair author), like men and women of this world,—men and women who have some other bond of connection with the reader besides speaking the same language, and acknowledging the same rules of prosody.

[The reviewer then complains of the bareness of her plots, and provides examples of impractical stage directions].

Are these, we say, really meant as stage-directions? If so, Miss B. would surely require "a kingdom for a stage." But we are convinced, in truth, that the very attempt to represent such things would turn the tragedy into burlesque. The fact is, that Miss B. relies too much upon her marginal notices; her pages are sometimes a tissue of mingled narrative and dialogue. To say nothing of the awkwardness of this, its effect in drawing the mind from the work to the author is truly lamentable. After being thrown into a fine glow by an eloquent oration or a generous sentiment, we are all at once damped again by being advertised of the look and gesture with which it is to be accompanied. There appears to be a mysterious importance in some of her directions, as

> 'Enter Count Zaterloo, Rayner, Sebastian, and four others of the band, armed, and a few of them bearing in their hands dark lanthorns. *It is particularly requested* if this play should be ever

acted, that no light be permitted on the stage but that which proceeds from the lanterns only.'[138]

Miss Baillie's incidents are not only few but trivial. After all that may be said of the familiarlity to which tragedy may very properly descend, she is never to become childish, and lisp and totter. We, therefore, object to a catastrophe's being produced by a man's dressing himself up like a spectre-knight, and frightening a poor girl into madness. This is even beneath comedy, as, we think, Miss B. has sufficiently shewn in her "second marriage."[139] That a tragedy villain should be discovered by his underling in a fit of spite, for having been deceived by a bribe of false brilliants, is equally reprehensible. Neither have we any praise to bestow upon the catastrophe of Rayner, where the hero is saved from the axe, by a negro slave, whose good offices he had obtained by giving him his cloak on a cold night, and who, in return, saws the main prop of the scaffold across

> 'So that the headsman mounting first, the platform
> Fell with a crash—'

and Rayner is saved long enough to hear of a pardon.

We wish, therefore, that Miss Baillie would oftener take her subjects from history. She has succeeded sufficiently well in "Constantine Paleologus" to go forward vigorously in that path;—though even here the introduction of a mock conjurer and his insignia, puts one too much in mind of Cadwallader Crabtree,[140] and his cats.

One word more, and we have done with the fables of Miss B. We think that they are sometimes conducted too *historically*. She begins at the beginning and goes strait on. This may be in part owing to her plan of giving entire the rise and progress of a passion in a play; but, besides this, she

---

[137] *Melpomene*: in Greek religion, one of the nine Muses, patron of tragedy and lyre playing.

[138] *'Enter … lanterns only'*: The reviewer refers to Baillie's stage directions to *Rayner* II.i, published in *Miscellaneous Plays* (1804).

[139] *"second marriage"*: *The Second Marriage* was published in the second volume of Baillie's *A Series of Plays* (1802).

[140] *Cadwallader Crabtree*: referring to a character in Tobias Smollett's *The Adventures of Peregrine Pickle* (1751).

has no skill, (if we may borrow an expression from painting,) in *fore-shortening*, in so adjusting a few parts of the piece, that it may be lengthened in the reader's imagination,—that he may seem to see the whole from what she may find it expedient to lay before him.

We proceed to the characters. Here the author has great merit. It is peculiarly difficult to unfold tragic or heroic character. It is in general from very minute and even ludicrous circumstances, that the novelist and the comedian depict their personages; and in avoiding these, as beneath the dignity of his subject, the tragedian is too apt to exceed on the other side, and give his characters no discriminating strokes at all. Miss B. has managed this with great skill. Her characters are strongly marked, and yet highly poetical, frail and infirm, and yet very interesting. De Monfort, brave and generous and manly, struggling with an infernal passion, bearing up and making head against it, and at length finally borne down by it, and brought to the perpetration of a deed cowardly, ungenerous, and unmanly; Constantine, the soft, the domestic, the effeminate, rouzed to action, to deeps of war and terror, by the best passions of the soul, love and pity for his subjects, standing out bravely with his little band of followers in the midst of a ruined and desolate city, and yet sometimes almost sinking back into luxury and love;— Valeria, beautiful and tender, full of love and full of fears, yet, when collected in herself, dignified and majestic;— these are characters conceived in the true spirit of poetry, and touched and finished with the hand of a master.

[The Reviewer then praises her domestic scenes, her descriptions, her poetry, and her songs].

We cannot take our leave of Miss B. however, without expressing our regret, at the resolution she has taken of keeping whatever plays she may henceforward write, "intra penetralia vestae."[141] Whey should the public be deprived of so great, and (judging by the editions that her works have gone through,) so highly prized an entertainment, because forsooth, the *managers of playhouses* have

not thought fit to bring her tragedies forward on the stage? We have on so many former occasions entered our solemn protest against the *acted* drama, that to repeat it here seems needless. In criticising Miss Baillie's plays we have regarded them solely as dramatic *writings*. We have considered them as furnishing a high intellectual entertainment, totally unconnected with the grossness of the theatre, and its long inseparable train of evils. The fair author's partiality for *the boards* appears to us a weakness much to be regretted: for we are well convinced it has had, in many instances, an unhappy effect on her genius, in making her address the senses rather than the imagination, and in placing before her the mimic representations of things rather than the realities themselves.

———

53. "Remarks on the Plays on the Passions, by Joanna Baillie." *Edinburgh Magazine* (previously *The Scots Magazine*), new series, 2 (June 1818), 517-20. Extract.

These plays have now been before the public twenty years. The author has informed us, in an introductory discourse, in which she has given a luminous explication of the laws of the drama, that they were intended for the stage. As few of them, however, have been brought upon the stage at all, and these have not kept their play there long, it will be the object of this paper to examine wherein lies the fault,—whether with the public, or the directors of our theatrical entertainments, or in the dramas themselves. Joanna Baillie was one of the earliest of the luminaries who have adorned this age of poets; and, splendid as the march of some of them has been, she is not yet, perhaps, surpassed in many of the most unequivocal attributes of poetical excellence. We know not if there be a sex in soul, but in the perusal of these plays we remark much of the energy and sublimity that have been thought to belong to one sex, with the delicacy and purity peculiar to the other. The living poets have, with a few exceptions, written from the fancy rather than the imagination and the heart. They seem to have forgotten that "the proper study

141 *"intra penetralia vestae"*: literally, "within the interior of her hearth"; here meaning "within the private quarters of her house."

of mankind is man";[142] and have fetched their subjects from the land of fairies, or witches, or apparitions, or demons, rather than from the habitations of man, or, when they have deigned to introduce him into their pictures, it has been with a view of illustrating some factitious state of society, in which he had deviated as far from nature as possible. They are always in extremes. With them passion is the hurricane of the soul, or a sentimental babyism that is perpetually puling to the moonlight. Joanna Baillie has risen above all these faults, and does not owe one iota of her glory to sacrificing to a false taste, to which fashion has given currency; and her characters are always, in general, native, and do not seek to attract notice by the singularity of their costume,—by rusty helms, or antique armour, nor by eccentricity in their actions, nor by an overstrained strength of passion, or the whine of simplicity. She is above such affectations, and has risen into fame by the fidelity of her delineations of human character, and the manly energy of her poetry, relieved, as it is, by a sweetness and a tenderness truly feminine.

The Greek tragedians have reared a goodly structure from the simple elements of man, that will probably outlive, not only the beautiful marble which the genius of their sculptors has inspired with life and passion, but all the other glories of their country, Homer alone excepted. The Romans, whatever may be their claim to literary distinction, in other respects, have no tragedy; and the French, with all their boasting on the subject, have copied the Greek tragedy in all its faults, rather than its spirit; and to such a slavish length have they carried their imitation that there is little original in their tragic drama, but its insipidity, and its absolute destitution of poetry and nature. In passing, we can only bow in reverence before the throne of Shakespeare, and mark the glance of that eye that scans the universe of man, which he pictures on a canvas of celestial texture, and in the hues of Eden. Some of his contemporaries, and one or two of his successors, would have exalted any other nation to the pinnacle of dramatic glory, but in the splendour of his reputation, every other fame is obscured; and while his name is

pronounced as that of a tutelary deity, in the cottage, and in the palace, and in the dwellings of all the intermediate classes, we seldom think even of Otway, but when we go to the representation of Venice Preserved.[143] Joanna Baillie, though certainly far beneath Shakespeare, may bear no unfavourable comparison with any other dramatist of this country. The question again recurs, why are her plays not added to the stock of the English stage? This we are now to consider, and we shall do so as candidly and as dispassionately as we can. With all our deference to her name, and all our admiration for her genius, we cannot help thinking that the plan of devoting a play exclusively to one passion is unfortunate, as it not only narrows the limits of dramatic representation, but otherwise subjects her to great inconvenience. It is true, that, in some of our best tragedies, one passion is predominant, and its excess leads to the catastrophe, as the jealousy of Othello, and the ambition of Lady Macbeth; but no one, except our author, ever thought of giving, in the form of a drama, an anatomical analysis,—a philosophical dissection of a passion. Her highly poetical mind and fine conception of human character, and her glorious elevation of moral sentiment, would have risen above every difficulty but this. To make this plain by an example in Othello, though jealousy is the poisoned fountain from which all the calamities of the piece flow, we never think of it abstracted from the character of the Moor. It is the consummate art and villainy by which Iago kindles up his generous and unsuspecting mind the fires that are to consume him, and his giving to "trifles light as air" the hues of importance, and his well feigned friendship, while he is seeking his undoing;—it is the terrible workings, and the overwhelming eruptions of this volcanic passion, and the powerful sympathy we feel for the gentle and pure Desdemona, that form the charm of this great drama, and the passion is interesting only as it influences the fortunes of the prime actors. In Miss Baillie the characters and the incidents are merely a mirror in which to contemplate the passions, or rather a microscope, by means of which she seems to think that she has brought within the sphere of our vision things

142 *"the proper study of mankind is man"*: quoted from line 2 of Epistle II of Alexander Pope's *An Essay on Man* (1733).

143 *Otway … Venice Preserved*: referring to Thomas Otway's *Venice Preserved* (Duke's Theatre, 1677).

too minute for the naked intellectual eye. This is, we think, the radical defect of her plays, and casts an air of restraint and formality over the whole of her performances; yet there are in them many delightful redeeming qualities, and we shall have much more pleasure in dilating upon these than in the discovery of faults, where there is so much to admire.

As far as we remember, the best plays, ancient and modern, are founded either on historical facts, or on legends, which, in all probability, had their origin in real events, that had undergone considerable changes by the inaccuracy, or even the genius of the narrators. This is to follow the order of nature, and in this case the action is seldom confined to the developement of one passion. All the Greek, and the greater number of Shakespeare's tragedies, have been so constituted. Miss Baillie's plan was therefore a bold innovation on a long and universally established practice; but it is time to think of its execution. Independently of this fundamental mistake, we think she has sometimes erred in the delineation of her characters, and the developement of her fables...

[The Reviewer comments on *De Monfort* and *Basil*]

For these reasons, we cannot help lamenting that ever Miss Baillie thought of fettering herself by a false system, instead of looking into life, and drawing her subjection thence unshackled by prepossessions of any kind. There was in the idea a certain air of originality that was seductive to an ardent and ingenious mind, and she incautiously followed its splendour, not considering whither it would lead her. In her preface, she even boasts of it; and, as it is the only claim she makes on our approbation, we regret that we cannot grant it; yet, in these dramas, there is much left for us to admire.

In an age of great poets, she has acquired, by her dramatic writings, a distinguished station in the literature of her country, yet we are almost tempted to wish that she had written epic rather than dramatic poetry, for which her powers of description, and loftiness of her conceptions, have eminently qualified her. If a tragedy written for the stage is not received there with an enthusiasm of delight, or if the applause is bestowed on any thing foreign to the characters and their fortunes, the author may be said to have failed in his aim. Miss Baillie's ambition was the stage, this

she has herself told us, and, indeed, we believe it is the aim of every person who writes a drama, whatever name he choose to give it,—she has submitted to the judgment from which there is no appeal; every thing has been done for her that the talents of the most distinguished actors could achieve;—a Siddons and a Kemble have been enlisted in her cause;—she has been heard with favour and applause, and partiality has even turned aside the edge of criticism;—her plays have had their run, yet they have been quietly laid aside on the shelves of the prompter, and we now hear of them as a part of our acted drama, no more than if they had never enjoyed a stage existence. This is a death-blow to the hopes of the candidate for dramatic glory, and perhaps more mortifying than the tumultuous condemnation of a first night, where a few noisy and malicious people may prevail over the good sense of the more judicious part of the house. The fault in this case cannot be with the public, for they had read the Plays on the Passions with feelings of delight before any of them were acted, and went to the representation with partiality in their favour;—it can hardly be with the managers of our theatres, for it is likely that they will bring the plays most frequently forward that draw the fullest houses. There is then only one other alternative, and in it we fear that we shall find the cause. These dramas possess poetical merit of so extraordinary a kind, and in many instance dramatic merit too, that we cannot help regretting the cause deeply wherever it may lie.

No species of literature is so constantly under the eye of the public as the acted drama:—every London apprentice has Shakespeare by heart; nor is there any which is in so great danger of being forgotten as an unacted play. Ford[144] and Massinger[145] were till lately left to the obscurity of black letter, and the libraries of the curious. Yet if this admirable woman has failed in aught, she has failed where

---

144 *Ford*: John Ford (1586–1639?), English dramatist of revenge tragedies, including *The Lover's Melancholy* (published 1629), *The Broken Heart* (published 1633), *'Tis Pity She's a Whore* (published 1633), and *Perkin Warbeck* (published 1634).

145 *Massinger*: Philip Massinger (1583–1639/40), English dramatist noted for his satirical comedies, including *A New Way to Pay Old Debts* (1624) and *The City Madam* (1632).

few but Shakespeare have succeeded. If she has not always been faithful even to the delineation of her favourite passions, and has not always made men and women pass in review before us in the unquestionable attributes and the universal features of nature,—if there is often wanting a link in that mysterious chain, that leads men as by the irresistible impulse of fate to the perpetration of crimes; yet has she exhibited many fine conceptions of character, and many scenes truly dramatic,—of an elevating energy, or a melting tenderness. If she had never portrayed another character than Jane De Monfort,—and never written another scene than that betwixt her and De Monfort, after the perpetration of the murder of Rezenvelt, these alone would have raised her to a high rank among the dramatists of her country. She has here finely conceived and beautifully expressed the purity and the ardour of sisterly affection,—all those holy ties that link the heart of a sister to a brother, and which not even infamy can dissolve. In this character every lineament is so completely filled up,—all the most amiable feelings of our nature flow so spontaneously,—it exhibits such a lofty moral tone in union with such tenderness, and there is withal so little of effort in its production, that we are confident that it is not the offspring of the imagination, but the unstudied effusion of her own spirit. Who would not venerate such a character as Jane De Monfort, and if in this beautiful portrait Miss Baillie has unawares perhaps drawn herself, who would not erect a shrine alike to her virtues and her genius?

_____

54. Review of T. Dibdin, *Harlequin and Humpo; or, Columbine by Candlelight. The Times* No. 8795 (28 December 1812), page 3.

Drury-Lane Theatre. On Saturday a new Pantomime, entitled *Harlequin and Humpo*, was exhibited at this Theatre. *George Barnwell* took the lead, by right of custom; and after the lagging morality of this banker's clerk, and the coarse temptations of his mistress, a Pantomime may be a natural relief. It is perhaps upon some such strag-

gling analogy, that Theatres have ventured on the curious mixture of the *utile* and the *dulce*,[146] that is to be found in the fall of *George Barnwell*, and the triumphant tricks of *Harlequin*,—the hanging of the one, and the marriage of the other. However they may draw their conclusions upon a point of such difficulty, the Managers of Drury-Lane were certainly unfortunate in the medium by which they undertook to dry up the sorrows of the audience on Saturday. Whatever depression of spirit might have been produced by the sudden death of the city hero, was scarcely elevated by the threatening mortality of his successor; and unless hisses can be construed into a specific[147] for tears, the Pantomime did but little to restore the fallen gaiety of its Christmas audience. "*Harlequin and Humpo*" is professedly the work of Mr. T. DIBDIN; and from the quantity of character which its Author had at stake upon the stage, and from the due notice which it is to be presumed he might have had of the general approach of Christmas about the end of the year, we might have expected the full exertion of all his practised ability. Whether he was inclined to this vigorous display, or was content only to give a sketch of what was to be hereafter wondered at,—whether he "checked his thunders in mid-volley,"[148] or at once exploded his whole magazine,—must be explained upon higher authority than ours: but it is certain, that if his object were to amuse the audience, he amused them only by his failure. The Pantomime opens with an *exposé* of the plot by a *fool*,—a clumsy contrivance, but rendered perfectly necessary from the confusion of the Pantomime. The first display was the procession of the Ambassador of the Dwarfs, to ask in marriage, for the heir-apparent, a Princess who had never been permitted to see the day. This procession of little

_____

146 *utile and the dulce*: utility and sweetness, from Horace's *Ars Poetica*.

147 *specific*: a specific remedy.

148 "*checked his thunders in mid-volley*": perhaps quoted from Thomas Green Fessenden, *Terrible Tractoration!!: A poetical petition against tractorising trumpery, and the Perkinistic institution: in four cantos, most respectfully addressed to the Royal College of Physicians by Christopher Caustic* (London: T. Hurst and J. Ginger, 1803), III:272.

figures, with immense faces and turbands, weighed down with finery, was amusing enough. The interior of the palace, in which the absence of day-light was compensated by a profusion of tapers and torches, was extremely showy: the attendants, of course, partook of the character of the place; and all bore some implements which might be termed of "the first necessity" in an establishment, where to let in the sun, was to be death to their mistress. Troops of lantern bearers,—men capped with enormous extinguishers,—dancers with tapers—, were not unnatural attendants; and, so far, the Pantomime had its share of applause; but from this forth, all was dulness, awkwardness, and misfortune. The dwarfs wandered backwards and forwards in great innocence and perplexity. The enchantments of the Princess were libels upon magic; harlequin lost the power of his sword; and to all its slaps and circlings, the scenery remained inexorable. Chaos came again;—solid walls walked up and down the stage in the deepest distress,—whole houses went astray.—pistols and cannons missed fire with "malice prepense,"[149]—an antique fountain, spouting volumes of water, pushed its presence into a watchmaker's shop in Cheapside, and staid there with apparent satisfaction. A plumber's shop dancing away, was interrupted in the height of its gaiety by a roar from all parts of the theatre, and the whole leaden assemblage of birds and beasts carried off in the arms of the stage servants. *Harlequin* himself seemed to feel the influence of the roar, and calmly exchanged somersets and springs for the gentler amusement of climbing. The same spirit spread downwards, and even the brutes sympathised. After much persuasion, a thing intended for a Bear rolled forward, and, after a few gambols, commenced a *pas de deux* with the most deplorable of Monkies. However, the creature gradually rose beyond his species; and after a few curvets[150] on his hind legs, forgot that it was the lot of Bears to move on four. To reconcile the audience to this sudden elevation, it pulled off a piece of its cuticle, slipped the fur from one side of his face, and shewed, that if it

was not entirely a man, it was at least but moderately a bear. This was at length hissed off. The Monkey was left behind, unable to move, and was finally carried away by the stage servants, who were the great magicians of the night. The whole was disaster upon disaster,—the *Clown* was clownish beyond all the necessities of his profession,—*Harlequin's* customary capers were cut in heaviness of heart,—*Pantaloon* and his friends were kicked in the usual quantity, but even their sufferings and struggles did not tell. One performer alone deserved to be exempted from the general condemnation. This was a boy dressed in some savage character. His slight figure was fitted for activity; but his activity surpassed all that we have ever seen of human distortion. He gave an extraordinary idea of the powers that lie concealed in the human frame. Practice has brought this boy to such command of his limbs, that to walk on his hands, or his head, or his back, or his feet, seems almost equal to him. He ran rapidly round the stage on his hands and feet, with his belly upwards; he bounded from shoulder to shoulder; he sprung from lying flat upon the ground with a frightful suppleness of a serpent. The fabric and contignation[151] of our bodies is wonderful. We lose more than half their powers by the indolent and sluggish neglect of modern education. No other animal possesses so fine, so intimate, and so applicable a union of agility and strength. The spring and dart of a tiger could scarcely be more rapid than the plunges of this boy: but the pantomime could not live upon the efforts of a single exhibitor, and the audience had already expressed their dissatisfaction in terms not to be misunderstood. The hissing grew more relentless towards the close; and when the curtain fell, and an attempt was made to give out the pantomime again, the cries of "off, off," drowned the voice of the delegate upon this occasion.

Mr. DIBDIN had decorated this *chef-d'oeuvre*[152] with some songs, but he had resigned them into hands that did them no peculiar honour. A Miss HORRIBOW had the merit of delivering one in a stile which, we be-

---

149 *"malice prepense"*: considered and planned beforehand; premeditated, purposed; intentional, deliberate.

150 *curvets*: See note 59.

151 *contignation*: a term usually used in carpentry, meaning the condition or manner of being joined together.

152 *chef-d'oeuvre*: masterwork.

lieve, has been seldom heard within the walls of a theatre. This lady's speaking and singing tones seem in some want of cultivation. Nothing could be imagined more natively *Vandalic*.[153] Miss BEW also sung a meagre song, in a stile most righteously proportioned to its deservings. The music was said to be by Mr. KELLY: but even this favourite selector's skill in borrowing, was involved in the presiding spirit of the piece, and the music excited no attention.

---

55. Review of T. Dibdin, *Harlequin and Humpo; or, Columbine by Candlelight.* **Bell's Weekly Messenger No. 875, (3 January 1813), page 1.**

DRURY-LANE.—The Managers of this Theatre presented the public with the usual treat, in a New Pantomime, *Columbine by Candlelight.* The scenery is good, and the story tolerable; but there is a little too much trouble in making Harlequin and Columbine, and the latter is not worth the making. We are sorry to have to speak in this manner of any single performer, but it is injustice to ourselves, and to the public, to allow in silence of such Columbines. Why not one of the Giroux, or any one but this. For our own parts, we have so much pleasure in seeing a good Pantomime, that we feel unusually disappointed when we miss it by the fault of the actors. The owl, too, is very indifferently managed, and there is a deficiency of rural scenery, and too many chairs and tables, and shops. When will Mother Goose be equalled?—good scenery, good music, and natural humour. But, to say the truth, the Pantomime entertained us, and therefore, perhaps, we are bound to speak well of it.

56. Review of T. Dibdin, *Harlequin and Humpo; or, Columbine by Candlelight.* **European Magazine 63 (January 1813), page 45. Extract.**

DRURY-LANE, *Dec.* 26.—A new Pantomime, by Mr. T. Dibdin, was produced at this Theatre, entitled "HARLEQUIN AND HUMPO; or, *Columbine by Candlelight.*"

The fable informs us, that the Princess Columbine is confined by the malediction of a fairy, who subjects her to the danger of death should she behold day-light till she attains her eighteenth year. The piece opens with the *Court Fool*, who announces the arrival of an Ambassador from the *King of the Dwarfs*, to ask the hand of Columbine for the young Prince. The Princess is in love with Sir Arthur; and urges the danger of being removed to the Dwarfish Court, lest she should be exposed to see daylight. The Duenna conspires against the Princess who is entrusted to her care, and opens the place where she is enclosed, and the Princess is consequently transformed into an owl. Sir Arthur, who is under the influence of the good fairy, appears as Harlequin, and the Princess is restored to him as Columbine.

This piece was, on the whole, favourably received, though, in point of fun and humour, it falls short of many pantomimes which we have seen. The attraction of such entertainments depends upon their scenery, the pleasantry of their tricks, and the accompanying music. So far as scenery can recommend a Piece, that of the present harlequinade deserves much commendation; but the tricks are dull, and afford little that is new. The *Monster of the Woods* was the chief novelty. Pack represented the character, and was deservedly and loudly applauded.

[The rest of the review borrows from *The Times* review of the same play].

---

[153] *Vandalic*: barbarous, ignorantly destructive.

57. [Hunt, James Henry Leigh], "[On Pantomime],"
The Examiner Nos. 158 and 161 (5 January 1817 and
26 January 1817). Reprinted in *Leigh Hunt's Dramatic
Criticism 1808-1831*. Ed. Lawrence Huston Houtchens
and Carolyn Washburn Houtchens. New York: Columbia University Press, 1949. Pages 140-5.

We must indulge ourselves a little this season on the subject of Pantomimes—a species of drama, for which, at
whatever hazard of our critical reputation, we must acknowledge a great predilection. There is no such thing as
modern comedy, tragedy, nor even farce, since Mr.
Colman has left off writing it; but Pantomime flourishes
as much as ever, and makes all parties comfortable; it enchants the little holiday folks; it draws tenfold applauding thunder from the gods; it makes giggle all those who
can afford to be made giggle; and finally, it brings out
the real abilities of our dramatic writers, who would be
very pleasant fellows if they would not write comedy.

Yes, there is something *real* in Pantomime: there is
animal spirit in it. A comedy may be, and often is, a gross
piece of effort from beginning to end, both in dialogue
and performance, and so may a tragedy: in either case you
have no sensation, very often, but one of the most painful in the world, that of seeing a number of people pretending to be what they are not, the actors affecting an
interest, while they are deploring their bad parts, and the
author thinking himself wise, and shewing at every sentence that he is foolish. Nobody pleases, and nobody is
pleased. But in Pantomime, who so busy and full of glee
as the understrappers[154] and Banbury-cake men?[155]
What so clever, in their way as the heels of Harlequin and
the jaws of the Clown? And what so gay and eternal as

the music, which runs merrily through the whole piece,
like the pattern of a watered gown?

Let us recollect the delights of the three principal
personages—the *Clown*, *Harlequin*, and *Colombine*. The
others have their merits, particularly *Pantaloon*, who is a
prodigiously dull old gentleman, and does not spoil the
effect of his native stupidity with unskilful speaking. He
is so dull that we lose all uneasy sympathy with him as
an animal, and only retain sufficient to give zest to the
tripping up of his heels. *Pantaloon*, together with the other
characters, originates in Italian comedy, where he performs
his part of the old gentleman of the second class in ours.
The *Clown*, or as he used to be called, *Scaramouch*, is a
descendant of the famous Italian comedian
Scaramaccia,[156] who began a sort of dynasty of
humourous servants, and gave his name to them as Caesar did to the Roman Emperors. It was said of him that
he had a very talkative countenance; and certainly nothing of the eloquence has been lost in that of the present
potentate—Mr. Grimaldi,[157] who is assuredly

"No tenth transmitter of a foolish face."[158]

But more of these particulars by and by. The Clown is a
delightful fellow to tickle our self-love with. He is very
stupid, mischievous, gluttonous, and cowardly, none of
which, of course, any of us are, especially the first; and
as in these respects, we feel a lofty advantage over him,
so he occasionally aspires to our level by a sort of glimmering cunning and jocoseness, of which he thinks so
prodigiously himself as to give us a still more delightful

---

154 *understrappers*: subordinates or underlings.

155 *Banbury-cake men*: A Banbury tart or cake was often tri-
angular and filled with fruit, especially raisins; the suggestion would seem to be that pantomime makes full use of
the stage hands necessary for the special effects and bakers
who supply the sweets that Clown devours.

156 *Scaramouch ... Scaramaccia*: a stock character in Italian
farce, a boastful poltroon, who is constantly being cudgeled
by Harlequin.

157 *Mr. Grimaldi*: Joseph Grimaldi (1778–1837), the greatest
harlequinade clown, who revolutionized the role and,
through it, English pantomime. His greatest achievement
was in *Harlequin and Mother Goose; or, The Golden Egg*,
written by Thomas Dibdin as the Christmas pantomime
in 1806; running for 92 nights to packed houses, it was
the most famous Christmas entertainment of the nineteenth century. His memoirs were put into the third person and published by Dickens.

158 *"No tenth transmitter of a foolish face"*: from Richard Savage's "The Bastard's Lot," line 8.

notion of our superiority. When he shakes his shoulders therefore at the dullest trick in the world, we laugh with equal enjoyment; when he pilfers from the cake-man, and looks the most outrageous lies in the latter's face, we love the profligate wag who so unambitiously amuses us at another's expense; and when he trips up his poor old master, whose face comes on the ground like a block of wood, we shout with rapture to see the lesser stupid thus overturn the greater. Nor is all this to be quarrelled with. We have a right to enjoy a good notion of ourselves in a pleasant way, and as long as we are all merry together; and here we enjoy it with all the advantages of harmlessness. We imagine our superiority, and that is enough; and we can relieve ourselves at any time from the more tragic delights, by calling to mind that the trips up and thumps are not real. Nay, even if they were, we reflect that they would be but so many fugitive bodily pains, with which no human spirit is wounded. But our philosophy will be getting grave.

See then who comes here to give us a new kind of pleasure, in which animal spirits are everything! It is the party-coloured[159] descendant of the famous Arlequin,[160] another real comedian, who has bequeathed his name to a class of theatrical beings. *Harlequin*, in the Italian comedy, is generally a servant, messenger, or other person in low life, active, cunning, and impudent. In the English pantomime, as perfected by Rich[161] and others, he is always a lover who has eloped with his mistress, and this gives him a tastier and pleasanter air with us, while it not only leaves him all his alacrity, but gives him every possible reason for it. Activity indeed at least shares his passion with love. He is the perpetual motion personified. At his very first appearance, he seems ambitious to shew you all his powers, from head to feet. He wriggles about, he capers, he takes a circuit, he nods, he wags his wooden sword, as a dog does his tail, he draws and prophetically flourishes it, he gives a jump sideways with both his knees, like a toy; and lastly, to convince the uncharitable that those who have good heels have good heads also, he begins grinding about his pericranium[162] in that remarkable manner, gradually getting it into proper rotatory pursuasiveness, till the whole head is whirling like a ventilator. Who does not wish such a fellow success with his mistress, and see moreover that he must gain it?

And here whirls in the damsel herself, fit companion for that vivacious fugitive, and an epitome of all that is trim and chaceable. What an amiable airiness, slender without weakness, and plump without inactivity! "Sir," as Dr. Johnson[163] might have said, after having taken his bottle of wine at the Mitre, "these are such figures as we may imagine Pan or Phoebus to have hunted in the woods." *Colombine* in the Italian comedy is the mistress of *Harlequin*, as well as in our Pantomime, and performs the part of lady's-maids or the sprightly servants. Her name signifies the little dove; and such is she in her beauty, her ready flight, her elegance, and her amorousness. The Managers should always select as graceful a girl for this part as possible, who could indulge in all the feats of activity and dancing without trenching on the ladylike; for all the above qualities should lift her into that. We remember seeing the late Mrs. Heathcote a few years back in the character, when Miss Searle;[164] and then for

---

159 *party-coloured*: i.e., parti-colored, variegated; marked patches, squares, or spots of different colors.

160 *Arlequin*: presumably Francisque Moylin (fl. 1715–51), the actor-manager whose troupe arrived in London in 1718 and were engaged by manager John Rich to perform at Lincoln's Inn Fields Theatre. Moylin was received with such acclaim, particularly as Harlequin, that the engagement was extended through March 1719. He is additionally credited with being the first to bring Molière to London audiences.

161 *Rich*: John Rich (1682–1761), English theater manager and actor, the popularizer of English pantomime and founder of Covent Garden Theatre.

162 *grinding about his pericranium*: working the skull hard; in this case, Hunt refers both to the act of thinking hard and to the mimetic performance of thinking hard by moving the head around in circles faster and faster.

163 *Dr. Johnson*: Samuel Johnson (1709–84), English critic, biographer, essayist, poet, and lexicographer. The reviewer here likely refers to Johnson's prefatory essay to his edition of Shakespeare (1765).

164 *Mrs. Heathcote … Miss Searle*: Caroline Searle (b. 1799), later Mrs. Heathcote, actress and dancer.

the first time began to wonder what the world and its axis had been at, since its inhabitants had made a fable of the Golden Age, and turned from the best things and virtues in it to the pursuit of all sorts of imaginary possessions, which only serve to set them against each other.

The three general pleasures of a Pantomime are its bustle, its variety, and its sudden changes. We have already described the unceasing vivacity of the music. The stage is never empty or still; either Pantaloon is hobbling about, or somebody is falling flat, or somebody else is receiving an ingenious thump on the face, or the Clown is jolting himself with jaunty dislocations, or Colombine is skimming across like a frightened pigeon, or Harlequin is quivering hither and thither, or gliding out of a window, or slapping something into a metamorphosis.

But the Pantomime, at present, is also the best medium of dramatic satire. Our farces and comedies spoil the effect of their ridicule by the dull mistakes of the author; but the absence of dialogue in Pantomime saves him this contradiction, and leaves the spectators, according to their several powers, to imagine what supplement they please to the mute caricature before them. Thus the grotesque mimicry of Mr. Grimaldi has its proper force; and the bullies or coxcombs whom he occasionally imitates come in one respect still nearer to the truth than in the best dialogue, being in actual life very dull persons who have little or nothing to say. Harlequin's sword also, besides being a thing very pleasant in the imagination to handle, is excellent at satirical strokes. Lissom[165] as a cane, and furnishing all that little supply of conscious power which a nervous mind requires, and which is the secret of all button-pulling, switch-carrying, seal twirling, and glove twirling, it is not possible to witness its additional possession of a magic power without envy. We always think, when we see it, what precious thumps we should like to give some persons—that is to say, provided we could forget our own infirmities for the occasion. We would have a whole train of them go by at proper distances, like boys coming to be confirmed—the worldly, the hypocritical, the selfish, the self-sufficient, the gossip-

ing, the traitorous, the ungrateful, the vile-tempered, the ostentatious, the canting, the oppressing, the envious, the sulky, the money-scraping, the prodigiously sweet-voiced, the over-cold, the over-squeezing, the furious, the resenter of inconvenience who has inconvenienced, the cloaker of conscious ill by accusation, the insolent in return for sparing. What fine work for a winter's morning, with a good broad set of backs to operate upon! We would have looking-glasses put before the patients, in order that they might know themselves when transformed into their essential shapes; after which they might recover; and then the wisest, the least presuming, and most generous person among the spectators, such a one as was agreed by his most veracious companions to know himself best, and to be the most able to bear objection, should set a glass before ourselves, and give us a thump equally informing.

———————

58. Dibdin, Thomas John. *The Reminiscences of Thomas Dibdin.* 2 vols. London: Henry Colburn, 1837. Volume 2, pages 7-8.

The [New Drury Lane] theatre opened on the 10th of October, 1812, under happier auspices than the New Covent-Garden had done: Mr. Elliston recited Lord Byron's prize address on the occasion; and for several nights after, the audience were annoyed by unsuccessful candidates, who disputed the judgment of the Committee appointed to select the address from the immense number offered; and one gentleman, who came on the stage, and insisted on reciting his rejected offspring, was only restrained from doing so by being taken into custody. I produced a pantomime at Drury-Lane, which proved a very fortunate speculation, bearing the name of "Harlequin and Humpo, or Colombine by Candlelight." The night previous to its representation brought me an anonymous letter, stating that three hundred humpy men from the neighbourhood of the Temple had determined on opposing the piece. As there was no ridicule of deformed folks in the pantomime, I had no apprehensions of those whose

———————

165 *Lissom*: supple, limber, agile, and lithesome.

backs were so awfully *up*, and had the pleasure to see the curtain fall unaccompanied by a single token of disapprobation; and the pantomime was acted forty-eight nights, which is more than I can say of the farce I produced at Covent-Garden under the title of "Schniederkins," which was soon withdrawn.

---

59. Review of Samuel Coleridge, *Remorse. Morning Chronicle* No. 13,641 (24 January 1813), page 3. Extract.

[The Reviewer lists the actors and characters, and then summarizes the plot].

The story of this play, of which our readers will be able to form a tolerably correct idea from the foregoing outline, affords an admirable opportunity for the display of those powers of natural description and sentiment, which Mr. COLERIDGE is so well known to possess. The author's name stands high for the reputation of genius, and he has very successfully employed that genius in the production of a dramatic work, which is fraught with beauty and interest. In the progress of the fable, the wild and romantic scenery of Spain, the manners and superstitions of the age, are described with a grace of poetic fancy, which, while it brings the objects before us by a magic charm, forwards the development of the plot, and gives peculiar interest to the characters and the tragic muse. In the judicious appropriation, as well as in the richness and beauty of his decorations, we have no hesitation in saying that Mr. COLERIDGE has highly succeeded. His images are not less striking from their originality, and a peculiar felicity of expression, than from their intrinsic merit. Among many other passages we might notice the description of *Alvar*'s love for music when a child, the sorcerer's invocation, and the song in the third act; and the beautiful and impassioned apostrophe on life, near the conclusion of the play. The conduct of the story does not involve any violent transitions, or gross improbabilities. In executing this part of his task, the author discovers equal judgment and

skill. The interest is kept alive by a succession of situations and events, which call forth the finest sensibilities of the human breast, without shocking the imagination by an accumulation of hopeless and unmerited suffering. The artful management by which, in the distribution of poetical justice, the punishment of guilt is effected by the guilty, or devolves on a fierce and uncontroulable spirit of revenge, in the person of *Alhadra*, so as to leave no stain on the more perfect and interesting characters of the play, deserves the highest praise. In the conception and delineation of character, Mr. COLERIDGE has shewn a powerful imagination, as well as deep reflection on the general principles which regulate and modify our stronger passions. The characters of *Alhadra*, *Isidore*, and *Ordonio* are the most marked and prominent. The last of these appears the most studied, and most complex and refined, and is, we should suspect, the author's favourite. Besides the obvious features, and stronger working of the passions in this character, there are many traits of a more subtle nature which, we trust, will not escape the nice observation of an enlightened audience, though they may be regarded as too metaphysical for tragedy. The character of *Ordonio*, as Mr. COLERIDGE has described it, is that of a man of originally strong understanding, and morbid feelings; whose reason points out to him a high and severe standard of unattainable perfection, while his temperament urges him on to a violation of all the ordinary distinction of right and wrong; whose pride finds consolation for its vices in its contempt for the dull virtues, or perhaps hypocritical pretences of the generality of men: whose conscience seeks a balm for its wounds in theoretical speculations on human depravity, and whose moody and preposterous self love, by an habitual sophistry, exaggerates the slightest affront, or even a suspicion of possible injury, into solid reasons for the last acts of hatred and revenge. A lie is with him a sufficient provocation of a murder, and the destruction of his supposed enemy, from which he shrinks as an assassination, is instantly converted into an act of heroism by the attempt of his antagonist to defend himself. Thus he says to *Alvar*, whom he suspects of deceiving him—"I thank thee for that lie, it has restored me! Villain, now I am thy master, and thou shalt die." And again to *Isidore*, when he reluctantly draws his sword in the cavern scene,—"now this is excellent, and warms the blood. My heart was drawing back with weak and womanish scruples. Now my vengeance beckons me onward with a warrior's mien, and claims that life my pity robbed her of. Now I will kill thee, thankless slave, and count it among my comfortable thoughts hereafter."—There are many instances of the same kind, by which the Author has carried on what may be called the underplot of the character, and which shew the hand of a master. We have insisted the longer on this excellence, because of its rarity, for, except SHAKE-SPEARE, who is every where full of these double readings and running accompaniments to the ruling passion, there is scarcely any other dramatic writer who has so much as attempted to describe the involuntary, habitual reaction of the passions, and understanding on each other:—We say, the involuntary, or unconscious reaction which takes place, for as to the known, conscious opposition and struggle for master between reason and passion, duty and inclination, there is no want of rhetorical declamation, of profound calculations, and able casuistry on the subject in the generality of dramatic writers, ancient or modern, foreign or domestic.—The gradation of confidence in villainy, corresponding with the rank and power of the guilty, is very pointedly marked in the character of *Isidore*, the accomplice of *Ordonio*. There is a selfish, calculating cunning, a servile meanness, a cowardly superstitious hesitating scrupulousness in his conduct, corresponding with his subordination in crime, and which the stronger will and self-originating passions of his employer almost totally subdue in him. The two principal female characters, *Alhadra* and *Teresa*, have a very beautiful effect, as contrasted with each other. The dauntless activity, ever mindful of her wrongs, full of fears, and ready for revenge. Her natural temperament, the spirit of her religion, the persecution she has suffered, her husband's death, combine in working her up to a pitch of heroic energy and frenzied passion, which is finely relieved by the tender sensibility, the meek piety, and resigned fortitude of the orphan ward of the *Marquis Valdez*. The scene at the beginning of the first act, in which *Teresa* is introduced defending her *widowed* attachment to her first love, is full of a dignified sorrow, mingled with an artless simplicity of nature, which has been seldom equalled. In some parts of this character, however, there is something of a German cast,[166] of that sentimental whine and affectation of fine feeling, of which we have had a full quantity at second-hand, and in translations. There are also some occasional words and phrases, which are too often repeated, and which savour too much of a particular style, to be perfectly to our taste.... The language is in general rich, bold, elegant, natural,—and the verse unites to the studied harmony of metrical composition, a variety of cadence, an ease and flexibility, by which it can be adapted, without effort, to the characteristic expression and sudden transitions of impassioned declamation.

It has been observed, that dramatic writings may be divided into two classes, that SHAKESPEARE alone gives the substance of tragedy, and expresses the very soul of the passions, while all other writers convey only a general description or shadowy outline of them—that his is the real text of nature, and the rest but paraphrases and commentaries on it, rhetorical, poetical, and sentimental. If Mr. COLERIDGE has not been able to break the spell, and to penetrate the inmost circle of the heart, he has approached nearer than almost any other writer, and has produced a very beautiful representation of human nature, which will vie with the best and most popular of our sentimental dramas.

Too much praise cannot be bestowed on the exertions of the actors. Mr. ELLISTON's representation of *Don Alvar* preserved a tone of solemn and impressive dignity, suited to the elevation of the character. Mr. RAE, by the force of his action, and by the striking changes both of his voice and countenance, pourtrayed, with admirable effect, the conflict of passions in the bosom of *Ordonio*. The management of the scenery, decorations, &c. gave every possible assistance to the success of the play. The *coup-d'oeil*[167] of the invocation scene was one

---

166 *something of a German cast*: referring to the immense popularity of German drama, and especially the plays of Auguste von Kotzebue, which enjoyed a vogue on the London stage between 1797 and 1800.

167 *coup-d'oeil*: a view or scene as it strikes the eye at a glance.

of the most novel and picturesque we remember to have witnessed.—The play might, perhaps, be reduced to a more convenient length by omitting some of the scenes in the third act, after the entrance of the Inquisitors, which retard the progress of the story, without heightening the interest or developing the characters. The remonstrances between *Valdez* and *Teresa*, on the subject of her love, become tedious from repetition; and the contrast between the pictures of the brothers is too evidently copied from the well-known passage in SHAKESPEARE.[168] We are decidedly of opinion, that the entrance of the Moors, and their assassination of *Ordonio*, ought to precede the final reconciliation between him and his brother. "The quality of mercy" ought not to be "strained,"[169]— especially on the stage. The duty of forgiveness, however amiable in itself, is not a dramatic virtue; and a tragic writer ought rather to effect his purpose by appealing to the passions of his audience, than to their goodness. The play was received throughout with marks of the deepest attention, and reiterated bursts of applause, and announced for a second representation amidst the acclamation of the audience.

[The Reviewer ends by quoting a passage of the invocation from III.i].

―――――――

60. [Barnes, Thomas], Review of Samuel Coleridge, *Remorse. The Examiner* No. 266 (31 January 1813), **pages 73-4. Extract.**

Drury-Lane. Dunces have so long kept exclusive possession of the stage, and by a sort of intelligent consciousness rather inconsistent with their general want of apprehension, are so unanimous in their praise and support of each other, that we almost despaired to see a man

of genius step forward to dispute their (from its long existence) almost sacred title. It is one of the pains as well as pleasures of genius,—by which term we mean powerful intellect combined with strong feeling—to be tenderly delicate and exquisitely alive to ridicule and censure: though eagerly fond of praise, it shuns the bustle of public competition, and wishes rather to appeal to a few similarly-constructed minds. As that timidity is founded on pride, not on modesty, it is easily convertible into a less amiable feeling: though every sneer tortures the very heart's core, self-approbation presents a highly convincing firmness against every attack; and as the bashfulness of an awkward school-boy speedily degenerates into hard-faced impudence, so the shrinking man of genius, by a short process, becomes an insolent, overweening being, despising the opinions of all men out of his own partial circle, and looking upon all the rest of mankind as "mere dung o' the soil."[170] We have thrown out these preliminary remarks, to explain at once the general absence of men of genius from the stage, and the few exceptions. Mr. COLERIDGE, whose poetic talents are undisputed, though they are deformed by sentimentalities, and whines, and infant lispings, has, it appears, hardened by the public ordeal which he has for some years undergone, manfully disregarded the pelting scorn of many a critic, and ventures now to lay his claims before a mixed multitude. Instead of the heart-expressed approbation of refined and feeling taste, he courts the applause of unsmirched artificers, young unintellectual citizens, and of those negatives of feeling and of thought, who, by a term more opprobrious than any which satire ever invented, call themselves people of fashion. His appeal has been crowned, as the French say, with complete success, and we will now examine a little how far it deserved it.

[The Reviewer provides a summary of the plot].

Such is the story, which we dismiss with little care, as in most dramas, and especially in this, it is a thing of

―――――――

168 *the well-known passage in SHAKESPEARE*: See William Shakespeare, *Hamlet* I.ii.139–59.

169 *"quality of mercy" ought not to be "strained"*: See William Shakespeare, *The Merchant of Venice* IV.i.184.

170 *"mere dung o' the soil"*: apparently misquoted from Jeremiah 9:22: "Speak, Thus saith the Lord, Even the carcasses of men shall fall as dung upon the open field, and as the handful after the harvest man, and none shall gather them."

minor importance: a very poor story, well-conducted, may excite the highest interest, and here Mr. COLERIDGE has excelled. The fable is managed and developed with a rapidity which never languishes, an intelligibility which a child might follow, and a surprize which would keep awake the most careless attention. The skill indeed with which the situations are disposed, so as to create effect, would have done honour to a veteran dramatist; for this we suppose Mr. COLERIDGE is indebted to his acquaintance with the German drama, which, in the hands of SCHILLER[171] at least, redeems all its faults by its excellence, and among its other striking beauties, abounds in the picturesque. We never saw more interest excited in a theatre than was expressed at the sorcery-scene in the third act. The altar flaming in the distance, the solemn invocation, the pealing music of the mystic song, altogether produced a combination so awful, as nearly to overpower reality, and make one half believe the enchantment which delighted our senses.

The characters most laboured by the author are *Ordonio* and *Alhadra*. The first is a philosophic misanthrope, a *Hamlet* corrupted by bad passions—a man of distempered feelings and perverted intellect; who reasons not to subdue, but to excuse his bad appetites; who satisfies his conscience that assassination is a mere bagatelle;—nay, more, that it is praiseworthy, because man is an air-bladder, a bubble, and because the death of a man gives occasion for the birth of 10,000 worms, who of course having equal capacity for happiness, are equally happy with the displaced gentleman. This last reasoning might appear conclusive to a jury of worms, but we think no beings else, not even twelve metaphysicians, could be found who would acquit *Ordonio*. We do not object to it as immoral, but as silly, and not consistent with the powerful intellect ascribed to this bad man.—The character of *Alhadra* deserves unmixed praise: it is an impressive,

high-wrought picture of a strongly-feeling, noble-spirited woman, whom tenderness supplies with energy, and whose daring springs from the gentlest affections,—maternal and conjugal love.—Such a woman, if her lot had been happy, would have been an example of virtue: but misery converts her into a revengeful murderer. Both these characters are developed with a force of thinking, and a power of poetry, which have been long strangers to the stage, and the return of which we hail as the omen of better days. Indeed, in none of his works has Mr. C. exhibited so much of his sentimental and descriptive power, so little deformed with his peculiar affectations. His images have his usual truth and originality without their usual meanness: his tenderness is as exquisite as in his best pieces, and does not degenerate into his usual whining. There are many passages to which we could refer as instances of his poetical excellence: the invocation of *Alvar*, in the 3d act, is indeed a strain of a higher mood: so is *Alhadra*'s description of her feelings, when she rushed into the cavern where her husband was murdered, yet feared to speak lest no voice should answer. Nor were we less pleased with *Teresa*'s delineation of the two brothers, though it brought to our minds *Hamlet*'s contrasted pictures of his father and his uncle.

The piece does not owe much to its acting. Mrs. GLOVER, indeed, suprised us:—with a face comic in every feature, with a person which engaged no interest, with a voice whose every tone in unpleasing, she contrived to present to us one of the most impressive portraitures of strong passion that we ever recollect to have seen:—

"Before such merit all objections fly,
    PRITCHARD's genteel, and GARRICK's six
        feet high."[172]

Mr. RAE, in the last scene, shewed that his face was capable of expressing the most complex workings of the soul. Mr. ELLISTON was animated, and that is all. Of Miss SMITH, we would rather say nothing.

---

171 *SCHILLER*: Friedrich von Schiller (1759–1805), German dramatist, poet, and literary theorist, best remembered for such dramas as *Die Räuber* (1781; *The Robbers*), the *Wallenstein* trilogy (1800–01), *Maria Stuart* (1801), and *Wilhelm Tell* (1804).

172 *"Before … high"*: See Charles Churchill, *The Rosciad* (1761), lines 851–2.

61. Review of *The Cenci, a Tragedy in Five Acts. The Literary Gazette* No. 167 (1 April 1820), pages 209-10. Extract.

Of all the abominations which intellectual perversion, and poetical atheism, have produced in our times, this tragedy appears to us to be the most abominable. We have much doubted whether we ought to notice it; but, as watchmen place a light over the common sewer which has been opened in a way dangerous to passengers, so have we concluded it to be our duty to set up a beacon on this noisome and noxious publication. We have heard of Mr. Shelley's genius; and were it exercised upon any subject not utterly revolting to human nature, we might acknowledge it. But there are topics so disgusting...and this is one of them; there are themes so vile...as this is; there are descriptions so abhorrent to mankind...and this drama is full of them; there are crimes so beastly and demoniac...in which *The Cenci* riots and luxuriates, that no feelings can be excited by their obtrusion but those of detestation at the choice, and horror at the elaboration. We protest most solemnly, that when we reached the last page of the play, our minds were so impressed with its odious and infernal character, that we could not believe it to be written by a mortal being for the gratification of his fellow-creatures on this earth: it seemed to be the production of a fiend, and calculated for the entertainment of devils in hell.

That monsters of wickedness have been seen in the world, is too true; but not to speak of the diseased appetite which would delight to revel in their deeds, we will affirm that depravity so damnable as that of Count Cenci, in the minute portraiture of which Mr. S. takes so much pains, and guilt so atrocious as that which he paints in every one of his dramatic personages, never had either individual or aggregate existence. No; the whole design, and every part of it, is a libel upon humanity; the conception of a brain not only distempered, but familiar with infamous images, and accursed contemplations. What adds to the shocking effect is the perpetual use of the sa-

cred name of God, and incessant appeals to the Saviour of the universe. The foul mixture of religion and blasphemy, and the dreadful association of virtuous principles with incest, parricide, and every deadly sin, form a picture which, "To look upon we dare not."

Having said, and unwillingly said, this much on a composition which we cannot view without inexpressible dislike, it will not be expected from us to go into particulars farther than is merely sufficient to enforce our warning. If we quote a passage of poetic power, it must be to bring tenfold condemnation on the head of the author—for awful is the responsibility where the head condemns the heart, and the gift of talent is so great, as to remind us of Satanic knowledge and lusts, and of "archangel fallen."

[The review then quotes from the Preface, summarizes the plot, and quotes I.iii.1-273].

This single example, which is far from being the most obnoxious, unnatural, and infernal in the play, would full justify the reprobation we have pronounced. Mr. Shelley, nor no man, can pretend that any good effect can be produced by the delineation of such diabolism; the bare suggestions are a heinous offence; and whoever may be the author of such a piece, we will assert, that Belzebub alone is fit to be the prompter. The obscenity too becomes more refinedly vicious when Beatrice, whose "crimes and miseries," forsooth, "are as the mask and the mantle in which *circumstances clothed her* for her impersonation on the scenes of the of the world"[173] is brought prominently forward. But we cannot dwell on this. We pass to a quotation which will prove that Mr. Shelley is capable of powerful writing: the description of sylvan scenery would be grand, and Salvator-like,[174] were it not put into the mouth of a child pointing

---

173 Reviewer's Note: "Preface, xiii., and a sentence, which, if not nonsense, is a most pernicious sophistry. There is some foundation for the story, as the Cenci family were devoured by a terrible catastrophe; and a picture of the daughter by Guido, is still in the Colonna Palace."

174 *Salvator-like*: referring to the style of the paintings of Salvator Rosa (1615–73), Italian painter and etcher remembered for his wildly romantic and sublime landscapes, marine paintings, and battle pictures.

out a site for the murder of the author of her being, "unfit to live, but more unfit to die."

[The review quotes III.i.243-72].

It will readily be felt by our readers why we do not multiply our extracts. In truth there are very few passages which will bear transplanting to a page emulous of being read in decent and social life. The lamentable obliquity of the writer's mind pervades every sentiment, and "corruption mining all within,"[175] renders his florid tints and imitations of beauty only the more loathsome. Are loveliness and wisdom incompatible? Mr. Shelley makes one say of Beatrice, that

> Men wondered how such loveliness and wisdom
> Did not destroy each other!

Cenci's imprecation of his daughter, though an imitation of Lear, and one of a multitude of direct plagiarisms, is absolutely too shocking for perusal; and the dying infidelity of that paragon of parricides, is all we dare to venture to lay before the public.

[The review quotes V.iv.78-89].

We now most gladly take leave of this work; and sincerely hope, that should we continue our literary pursuits for fifty years, we shall never need again to look into one so stamped with pollution, impiousness, and infamy.

---

62. [Scott, John], Review of *The Cenci, a Tragedy in Five Acts. London Magazine* 1 (May 1820), pages 546-555. Extract.

[The review opens with several paragraphs arguing that to write on a perverse subject is an act of personal vanity].

These remarks are (not altogether) but principally, suggested, by the Preface, Poems, and Dedication, contained in the volume under our review:—yet it is no more than fair towards Mr. Shelley to state, that the *style* of his writings betrays but little affectation, and that their mat-

ter evinces much real power of intellect, great vivacity of fancy, and a quick, deep, serious feeling, responding readily, and harmoniously, to every call made on the sensibility by the imagery and incidents of this variegated world. So far Mr. Shelley has considerable advantages over some of those with whom he shares many grave faults. In the extraordinary work now under notice, he, in particular, preserves throughout a vigorous, clear, manly turn of expression, of which he makes excellent use to give force, and even sublimity, to the flashes of passion and of phrenzy,—and wildness and horror to the darkness of cruelty and guilt. His language, as he travels through the most exaggerated incidents, retains its correctness and simplicity;—and the most beautiful images, the most delicate and finished ornaments of sentiment and description, the most touching tenderness, graceful sorrow, and solemn appalling misery, constitute the very genius of poesy, present and powerful in these pages, but, strange and lamentable to say, closely connected with signs of a depraved, nay mawkish, or rather emasculated moral taste, craving after trash, filth, and poison, and sickening at wholesome nutriment. There can be but little doubt that *vanity* is at the bottom of this, and that weakness of *character* (which is a different thing from what is called weakness of *talent*) is also concerned. Mr. Shelley likes to carry about with him the consciousness of his own peculiarities; and a tinge of disease, probably existing in a certain part of his constitution, gives to these peculiarities a very offensive cast. This unlucky tendency of his, is at once his pride and his shame: he is tormented by more than suspicions that the general sentiment of society is against him—and, at the same time, he is induced by irritation to keep harping on sore subjects. Hence his stories, which he selects or contrives under a systematic predisposition as it were,—are usually marked by some anti-social, unnatural, and offensive feature:—whatever "is not to be named amongst men," Mr. Shelley seems to think has a peculiar claim to celebration in poetry;—and he turns from war, rapine, murder, seduction, and infidelity,—the vices and calamities of which our common nature and common experience permit the generality of persons to sympathise,—to cull some morbid or maniac sin of rare and

---

175 *"corruption mining all within"*: See William Shakespeare, *Hamlet* III.iv.148.

doubtful occurrence, and sometimes to found a *system* of practical purity and peace on violations which it is disgraceful even to contemplate.

His present work (*The Cenci*) we think a case in point. We shall furnish the reader with the story on which this Drama is founded, as it is given by Mr. Shelley in his preface:—

[The review quotes the preface, and then dismisses the history provided by Shelley as improbable and unnatural].

[H]is object, he says, is "*the teaching the human heart the knowledge of itself*, in proportion to the possession of which knowledge every human being is wise, sincere, *tolerant*, and kind." p. ix. He therefore considers that his work, *The Cenci*, is "subservient to a moral purpose." We think he is mistaken in every respect. His work does not teach the human heart, but insults it:—a father who invites guests to a splendid feast, and then informs them of the events they are called together to celebrate, in such lines as the following, has neither heart nor brains, neither human reason nor human affections, nor human passions of any kind;—nothing, in short of human about him but the external form, which, however, in such a state of demoniac frenzy, must flash the wild beast from its eyes rather than the man.

[The review quotes I.iii.77-89].

In this way, Mr. Shelley proposes to *teach* the human heart, and thus to effect "*the highest moral purpose!*" His precepts are conveyed in the cries of Bedlam; and the outrage of a wretched old maniac, long passed the years of appetite, perpetrated on the person of his miserable child, under motives that are inconsistent with reason, and circumstances impossible in fact, is presented to us as a mirror in which we may contemplate a portion, at least, of our common nature! How far this disposition to rake in the lazar-house[176] of humanity for examples of human life and action, is consistent with a spirit of *tolerance* for the real faults and infirmities of human nature, on which Mr. Shelley lays so much stress, we may discover in one of his own absurd allusions. The murder of the Count Cenci he

---

176 *lazar-house*: a house for lazars or diseased persons, especially lepers.

suggests, in the first quotation we have given from his preface, was punished by the Pope, *chiefly* because the numerous assassinations committed by this insane man were a copious source of the papal revenue, which his death dried-up for ever. The atrocity involved in this supposition, is, we hesitate not to say, extravagant and ridiculous. That a Pope of these times might be inclined to make money of a committed murder, is not only likely, but consistent with history: but at what epoch, under what possible combination of the circumstances of government and society, could it be a rational speculation in the breast of a ruler to preserve a particular nobleman with peculiar care, that his daily murders, committed in the face of the public, he himself, in the mean time, walking about a crowded city, might continue to be a source of personal profit to the sovereign! Nor would the paltriness of such a calculation, contrasted with its excessive guilt, permit it to be seriously made in any breast that can justly be adduced as an example of the heart of man. It would be intolerable to the consciousness of any one invested with the symbols of dignity and the means for absolute authority. It would be for such an one to commit murders himself, not to wait in sordid expectation of the bribery to follow their commission by others. It requires the "*enlarged liberality*" of Mr. Shelley and his friends, to fashion these chimeras of infamy, and then display them as specimens of Princes, Priests, and Ministers. The truth is, that we see few or no signs of their *toleration*, but in regard to cases of incest, adultery, idleness, and improvidence:—towards a class of abuses and enormities, falling too surely within the range of human nature and human history, but from which they are far removed by the circumstances of their conditions in life, and equally so, perhaps, by the qualities of their personal characters, they have neither tolerance nor common sense. Their sympathies then lead them to degrade and misrepresent humanity in two ways: by extenuating the commission of unnatural vices, and aggravating the guilt of natural ones:—and as it forms of their principal objects to dissipate all the "dogmas" of religion, it is further to be observed, that they thus leave the nature of man bare and defenceless, without refuge or subterfuge— let them call it which they please. They render miserable man accountable for all his acts; his soul is the single source of all that occurs to him; he is forbidden to derive hope either from his own weakness or the strength of a great disposing authority, presiding over the world, and guiding it on principles that have relation to the universe. This is a very different basis from that of the Ancient Drama:—in it, the blackness and the storms suspended over the head of man, and which often discharged destruction on his fairest possessions, *hung from Heaven*, and above them there was light, and peace, and intelligence.

The radical foulness of moral complexion, characterizing such compositions as this one now before us, we shall never let escape unnoticed or unexposed, when examples of it offer themselves. It is at once disgusting and dangerous; our duty, therefore, is here in unison with our tastes. In The Cenci, however, the fault in question is almost redeemed, so far as literary merit is concerned, by uncommon force of poetical sentiment, and very considerable purity of poetical style. There are gross exceptions to the latter quality, and we have quoted one; but the praise we have given will apply generally to the work. The story on which it is founded has already been explained. We shall proceed to give, by some extracts from the Drama itself, an idea of its execution.

[The review quotes I.i.34-56, 81-91; I.ii.47-63; I.iii.36-50, 90-8, 137-40, 160-78; II.i.1-128; III.i.1-32; IV.i.39-45; IV.iii.1-7; V.iv.141-65].

Here the Drama closes, but our excited imaginations follow the parties to the scaffold of death. This tragedy is the production of a man of great genius, and of a most unhappy moral constitution.

---

63. Review of *The Cenci, a Tragedy*. *New Monthly Magazine* 13 (May 1820), pages 550-3. Extract.

Whatever may be the variety of opinion respecting the poetical genius displayed in this work, there can be but one sentiment of wonder and disgust, in every honest heart, at the strange perversity of taste which selected its theme. It is the story of a wretch grown old in crime, whose passions are concentrated at last in quenchless hate towards his children, especially his innocent and lovely daughter, against whom he perpetrates the most fearful of outrages, which leads to his death by her contrivance, and her own execution for the almost blameless parricide. The narrative, we believe, is "extant in choice Italian," but this is no excuse for making its awful circumstances the groundwork of a tragedy. If such things have been, it is the part of a wise moralist decently to cover them. There is nothing in the circumstances of a tale being true which renders it fit for the general ear. The exposure of a crime too often pollutes the very soul which shudders at its recital, and destroys that unconsciousness of ill which most safely preserves its sanctities. There can be little doubt that the horrible details of murder, which are too minutely given in our public journals, lead men to dwell on horrors till they cease to petrify, and gradually prepare them for that which once they trembled to think on.

[The review continues to catalogue crimes better left unrepresented].

If the story of the drama before us is unfit to be told as mere matter of historic truth, still further is it from being suited to the uses of poetry. It is doubtless one of the finest properties of the imagination to soften away the asperities of sorrow, and to reconcile by its mediating power, the high faculties of man and the mournful vicissitudes and brief duration of his career in this world. But the distress which can thus be charmed away, or even rendered the source of pensive joy, must not be of a nature totally repulsive and loathsome. If the tender hues of the fancy cannot blend with those of the grief to which they are directed, instead of softening them by harmonious influence, they will only serve to set their blackness in a light still more clear and fearful. Mr. Shelley acknowledges that "any thing like a dry exhibition of his tale on the stage would be insupportable," and that "the person who would treat such a subject must increase the ideal, and diminish the actual horror of the events, so that the pleasure which arises from the poetry which exists in these stupendous sufferings and crimes, may mitigate the pain of the contemplation of the moral deformity from which they spring." But in the most prominent of these sufferings and crimes there is no poetry, nor can poetry do aught to lessen the weight of superfluous misery they cast on the soul. Beauties may be thrown around them; but as they cannot mingle with their essence they will but increase their horrors, as flowers fantastically braided round a corpse, instead of lending their bloom to the cheek, render its lividness more sickening. In justice to Mr. Shelley we must observe, that he has not been guilty of attempting to realize his own fancy. There is no attempt to lessen the horror of the crime, no endeavour to redeem its perpetrator by intellectual superiority, no thin veil thrown over the atrocities of his life. He stands, base as he is odious, and, as we have hinted already, is only thought of as a man, when he softens into a murderer.

We are far from denying that there is great power in many parts of this shocking tragedy. Its author has at least shown himself capable of leaving these cold abstractions which he has usually chosen to embody, and of endowing human characters with life, sympathy, and passion. With the exception of Cenci, who is half maniac and half fiend, his persons speak and act like creatures of flesh and blood, not like the problems of strange philosophy set in motion by galvanic art. The heroine Beatrice is, however, distinguished only from the multitude of her sex by her singular beauty and sufferings. In destroying her father she seems impelled by madness rather than will, and in her fate, excites pity more by her situation than her virtues. Instead of avowing the deed, and asserting its justice, as would be strictly natural for one who had committed such a crime from such a cause—she tries to avoid death by the meanest arts of falsehood, and encourages her accomplices to endure the extremities of torture rather than implicate her by confession. The banquet given by Cenci to all the cardinals and nobles of Rome, in order to give expression to his delight on the violent deaths of his sons, is a wanton piece of absurdity, which could have nothing but its improbability to recommend it for adoption. The earlier scenes of the play are tame— the middle ones petrifying—and the last scene of all, affecting and gentle. Some may object to the final speech of Beatrice, as she and her mother are going out to die, where she requests the companion of her fate to "tie her girdle for her, and bind up her hair in any simple knot," and refers to the many times they had done this for each other, which they should do no more, as too poor and trifling for the close of a tragedy. But the play, from the commencement of the third act, is one catastrophe, and the quiet pathos of the last lines is welcome as breaking the iron spell which so long has bound the currents of sympathy.

The diction of the whole piece is strictly dramatic— that is, it is nearly confined to the expression of present feeling, and scarcely ever overloaded with imagery which the passion does not naturally create. The following beautiful description of the chasm appointed by Beatrice for the murder of her father, is truly asserted by the author to be the only instance of isolated poetry in the drama:

[The review quotes III.i.242-64].

The speeches of Cenci are hardly of this world. His curses on his child—extending, as they do, the view of the reader beyond the subject into a frightful vista of polluting horrors—are terrific,[177] almost beyond example, but we dare not place them before the eyes of our readers. There is one touch, however, in them, singularly profound and sublime, to which we may refer. The wretch, debased as he is, asserts his indissoluble relation of father, as giving him a potency to execrate his child, which the universe must unite to support and heaven allow—leaning upon this one sacred right which cannot sink from under him, even while he curses! The bewildered ravings of Beatrice are awful,[178] but their subject will not allow of their quotation. We give the following soliloquy of Cenci's son, when he expects to hear news of his father's murder, because, though not the most striking, it is almost the only unexceptionable instance which we can give of Mr. Shelley's power to develop human passions.

[The review quotes III.ii.1-31].

We must make one more remark on this strange instance of perverted genius, and we shall then gladly fly from its remembrance for ever. It seems at first sight wonderful, that Mr. Shelley, of all men, should have perpe-

---

177 *terrific*: Here, the word means inspiring terror.
178 *awful*: Here, the word means inspiring awe.

trated this offence against taste and morals. He professes to look almost wholly on the brightest side of humanity—to "bid the lovely scenes of distance hail"—and live in fond and disinterested expectation of a "progeny of golden years" hereafter to bless the world. We sympathize with him in these anticipations, though we differ widely from him as to the means by which the gradual advancement of the species will be effected. But there is matter for anxious enquiry, when one, richly gifted, and often looking to the full triumph of happiness and virtue, chooses to drag into public gaze the most awful crimes, and luxuriates in the inmost and most pestilential caverns of the soul. To a mind, thus strangely inconsistent, something must be wanting. The lamentable solution is, that Mr. Shelley, with noble feelings, with far-reaching hopes, and with a high and emphatic imagination, has no power of religious truth fitly to balance and rightly to direct his energies. Hence a restless activity prompts him to the boldest and most fearful excursions—sometimes almost touching on the portals of heaven, and, at others, sinking a thousand fathoms deep in the cloudy chair of cold fantasy, into regions of chaos and eternal night. Thus will he continue to vibrate until he shall learn that there are sanctities in his nature as well as rights, and that these venerable relations which he despises, instead of contracting the soul, nurture its most extended charities, and cherish the purest aspirations for universal good. Then will he feel that his imaginations, beautiful as ever in shape, are not cold, but breathing with genial life, and that the most ravishing prospects of human improvement, can only be contemplated steadily from those immortal pillars which Heaven has provided for Faith to lean on.

64. [Lockhart, John Gibson], Review of *Sardanapalus, a Tragedy; The Two Foscari, a Tragedy; and Cain, a Mystery. Blackwood's Edinburgh Magazine* 11 (January 1822), pages 90-2. Extract.

Upon the whole, we imagine this will be reckoned rather a heavy volume; and certainly it could not sell the better for coming out on the same day with the Pirate.[179] Mr. Murray and Mr. Constable should understand each other a little better, and each would serve his own interest, by not being too anxious to interfere with the interest of his rival. It is bad policy to bring out the Edinburgh[180]— the dull, stupid, superannuated, *havering*[181] Edinburgh— and the Quarterly[182]—the cold, well-informed, heartless, witless, prosing, pedantic Quarterly—both in the same week. And although we should be very sorry to compare the first writers of their time with *such folks* as the "clever old body"[183] and the "sour little gentleman,"[184] we cannot help saying, that Lord Byron and the Author of Waverley[185] might quite as well choose different months for favouring the public with their visits—which are rather more pleasant, to be sure, but quite as regular and as expensive as if they were two tax gatherers.

It would be highly ridiculous to enter, at this time of day, into any thing like a formal review, *here*, of Lord Byron's new volume. We have not happened to meet with any two

---

179 *Pirate*: novel by Walter Scott, published by John Constable in 1821.
180 *Edinburgh*: the *Edinburgh Review*, published by Constable.
181 *havering*: talking garrulously and foolishly; talking nonsense.
182 *Quarterly*: the *Quarterly Review*, published by John Murray.
183 *"clever old body"*: Francis Jeffrey, editor of the *Edinburgh Review*.
184 *"sour little gentleman"*: William Gifford, editor of the *Quarterly Review*.
185 *Author of Waverley*: Walter Scott, who, beginning with his first novel *Waverley* in 1814, published his enormously popular fiction anonymously. The author of the novels quickly took on the appellation of "the author of *Waverley*."

individuals who expressed two different opinions about it and its contents. There is a great deal of power in Sardanapalus: (the Sardanapalus of David Lyndsay[186] is weighed in the balance, and found wanting, when compared with it) but as a play, it is an utter failure; and, in God's name, why call a thing a tragedy, unless it be meant to be a play? What would people say to a new song of Tom Moore's,[187] prefaced with an earnest injunction on many, woman, and child, never to think of singing it? A tragedy, *not meant to be acted*, seems to us to be just about as reasonable an affair as a song not meant to be sung. But even as *a poem*, Sardanapalus is *not* quite worthy of its author. Let any one just think, for a moment, of the magnificent story of Sardanapalus, and then imagine what a thing Lord Byron might have made of it, had he chosen the fiery narrative pace of Lara, or the Giaour[188]—instead of this lumbering, and lax, and highly *undramatic* blank-verse dialogue.

[The rest of the review addresses Byron's feud with the Poet Laureate, Robert Southey].

———

65. [Jeffrey, Francis], Review of *Sardanapalus, a Tragedy; The Two Foscari, a Tragedy; and Cain, a Mystery. Edinburgh Review* 36 (February 1822), pages 413-52. Extract.

It must be a more difficult thing to write a good play—or even a good dramatic poem—than we had imagined. Not that we should, *a priori*, have imagined it to be very easy; but it is impossible not to be struck with the fact, that, in comparatively rude times, when the resources of the art had been less carefully considered, and Poetry certainly had not collected all her materials, success seems to have been more frequently, and far more easily obtained. From the middle of Elizabeth's reign till the end of James's, the drama formed by far the most brilliant and beautiful part of our poetry,—and indeed of our literature in general. From that period to the Revolution, it lost a part of its splendour and originality; and still continued to occupy the most conspicuous and considerable place in our literary annals. For the last century; it has been quite otherwise—our poetry has ceased almost entirely to be dramatic; and, though men of great name and great talent have occasionally adventured into this once fertile field, they have reaped no laurels, and left no trophies behind them. The genius of Dryden[189] appears nowhere to so little advantage as in his tragedies; and the contrast is truly humiliating when, in a presumptuous attempt to heighten the colouring, or enrich the simplicity of Shakespeare, he bedaubs with obscenity, or deforms with rant, the genuine passion and profligacy of Antony and Cleopatra—or intrudes on the enchanted solitude of Prospero and his daughter, with the tones of worldly gallantry, or the caricatures of affected simplicity. Otway, with the sweet and mellow diction of the former age, had none of its force, variety, or invention. Its decaying fires burst forth in some strong and irregular flashes, in the disorderly scenes of Lee;[190] and sunk at last in the ashes and scarcely glowing embers of Rowe.[191]

Since his time—till very lately—the school of our ancient dramatists has been deserted: and we can scarcely say that any new one has been established. Instead of the irregular and comprehensive plot—the rich discursive dialogue—the ramblings of fancy—the magic creations

---

186   *Sardanapalus of David Lyndsay*: See David Lyndsay, *Dramas of the Ancient World* (Edinburgh: W. Blackwood, 1822).

187   *Tom Moore's*: Thomas Moore (1779–1852), Irish poet, satirist, composer, and musician, best known for his *Poems of the Late Thomas Little, Esq.* (1801), *Lalla Rookh* (1817), and *Irish Melodies* (1807–34).

188   *Lara, or the Giaour*: referring to two long poems published by Byron in 1814 and 1813, respectively.

189   *Dryden*: John Dryden (1631–1700), English poet, dramatist, and literary critic.

190   *Lee*: Nathaniel Lee (1649–92), English playwright, best known for his play *The Rival Queens* (King's Theatre, 1677).

191   *Rowe*: Nicholas Rowe (1674–1718), English dramatist, best known for his plays *Tamerlane* (1701), *The Fair Penitent* (1703), *The Tragedy of Jane Shore* (1714), and *The Tragedy of the Lady Jane Grey* (1715).

of poetry—the rapid succession of incidents and characters—the soft, flexible, and evervarying diction—and the flowing, continuous, and easy versification which characterized those masters of the golden time, meagre stories—few personages—characters decorous and consistent, but without nature or spirit—a guarded, timid, classical diction—ingenious and methodical disquisitions—turgid or sententious declamations—and a solemn and monotonous strain of versification. Nor can this be ascribed, even plausibly, to any decay of genius among us; for the most remarkable failures have fallen on the highest talents. We have already hinted at the miscarriages of Dryden. The exquisite taste and fine observation of Addison,[192] produced only the solemn mawkishness of Cato. The beautiful fancy and generous affections of Thomson,[193] were chilled and withered as soon as he touched the verge of the Drama, where his name is associated with a mass of verbose puerility, which it is difficult to conceive could ever have proceeded from the author of the Seasons and the Castle of Indolence. Even the mighty intellect, the eloquent morality, and lofty diction of Johnson, which gave too tragic and magnificent tone to his ordinary discourse, failed altogether to support him in his attempt to write actual tragedy; and Irene is not only unworthy of the imitator of Juvenal and the author of Rassalas and the Lives of the Poets, but is absolutely, and in itself, nothing better than a tissue of wearisome and unimpassioned declamations. We have named the most celebrated names in our literature, since the decline of the drama almost to our days; and if *they* have neither lent any new honours to the stage, nor borrowed any from it, it is needless to say, that those who adventured with weaker powers had no better fortune. The Mourning Bride of Congreve, the Revenge of Young, and the Douglas of Home[194] [we cannot add the Mysterious Mother of Walpole—even to please Lord Byron],[195] are almost the only tragedies of the last age that are familiar to the present; and they are evidently the works of a feebler and more effeminate generation—indicating, as much by their exaggerations as by their timidity, their own consciousness of inferiority to their great predecessors—whom they affected, however, not to imitate, but to supplant.

But the native taste of our people was not thus to be seduced and perverted; and when the wits of Queen Anne's time[196] had lost the authority of living authors, it asserted itself by a fond recurrence to its original standards, and a resolute neglect of the more regular and elaborate dramas by which they had been succeeded. Shakespeare, whom it had been the fashion to decry and even ridicule, as the poet of a rude and barbarous age,[197]

---

192 *Addison*: Joseph Addison (1672–1719), English essayist and dramatist, best known for *The Spectator*; his tragedy *Cato* (Drury Lane, 1713) was a resounding success.

193 *Thomson*: James Thomson (1700–48), Scottish poet and author of *The Seasons* (1726–30) and *The Castle of Indolence* (1748). In 1730 his tragedy *Sophonisba* was performed at Drury Lane.

194 *The Mourning Bride of Congreve, the Revenge of Young, and Douglas of Home*: referring to plays by William Congreve (Lincoln's Inn Fields, 1697), Edward Young (Drury Lane, 1721), and William Home (Covent Garden, 1757).

195 *we cannot add … Byron*: referring to Byron's defense of Horace Walpole in the preface to *Marino Faliero* (1821): "It is the fashion to underrate Horace Walpole, first, because he was a nobleman, and secondly, because he was a gentleman; but to say nothing of the composition of his incomparable letters, and of the *Castle of Otranto*, he is the 'Ultimus Romanorum' [the last of the Romans], the author of the *Mysterious Mother*, a tragedy of the highest order, and not a puling love-play. He is the father of the first romance, and of the last tragedy in our language, and surely worthy of a higher place than any living writer, be he who he may."

196 *Queen Anne's time*: Queen Anne ruled Great Britain from 1702 to 1714.

197 Jeffrey's Note: "It is not a little remarkable to find such a man as Goldsmith joining in this pitiful sneer. In his Vicar of Wakefield, he constantly represents his famous town ladies, Miss Carolina Amelia Wilhelmina Skeggs, and the other, as discoursing about 'high life, *Shakespeare*, and the musical glasses!'—And, in a more serious passage, he introduced a player as astonishing the Vicar, by informing him that 'Dryden and Rowe's manner were quite out of fashion—our taste has gone back a whole century; Fletcher, Ben Jonson, and, above all, the *plays of Shakespeare*, are the

was reinstated in his old supremacy: and when his legitimate progeny could no longer be found at home, his spurious issue were hailed with rapture from foreign countries, and invited and welcomed with the most eager enthusiasm on their arrival. The German imitations of Schiller and Kotzebue,[198] caricatured and distorted as they were by the aberrations of a vulgar and vitiated taste, had still so much of the raciness and vigour of the old English drama, from which they were avowedly derived, that they instantly became more popular in England than any thing that her own artists had recently produced; and served still more effectually to recall our affections to their native and legitimate rulers. Then followed republications of Massinger, and Beaumont and Fletcher,[199] and Ford, and their contemporaries—and a host of new tragedies, all written in avowed and elaborate imitation of ancient models. Miss Baillie, we rather think, had the merit of leading the way in this return to our old allegiance—and then came a volume of plays by Mr. Chenevix,[200] and a

succession of single plays, all of considerable merit, from Mr. Coleridge, Mr. Maturin, Mr. Wilson, Mr. Cornwall, and Mr. Milman.[201] The first and the last of these names are the most likely to be remembered; but none of them, we fear, will ever be ranked with the older worthies; nor is it conceivable that any age should ever class them together.

We do not mean, however, altogether to deny, that there may be some illusion, in our habitual feelings, as to the merits of the great originals—consecrated as they are, in our imaginations, by early admiration, and associated, as all their peculiarities, with the mere accidents and oddities of their diction now are, with the recollection of their intrinsic excellences. It is owing to this, we suppose, that we can scarcely venture to ask ourselves, what reception one of Shakespeare's irregular plays—the Tempest for example, or the Midsummer Night's Dream—would be likely to meet with, if it were *now* to appear for the first time, without name, notice, or preparation? Nor can we pursue the hazardous supposition through all the possibilities to which it invites us, without something like a sense of impiety and profanation. Yet, though some little superstition may mingle with our faith, we must still believe it to be the true one. Though time may have hallowed many things that were at first but common, and accidental associations imparted a charm to much that was in itself indifferent, we cannot but believe that there was an original sanctity which time only matured and extended—and an inherent charm from which the association derived all its power. And when we look candidly and calmly to the works of our early dramatists, it is impossible, we think, to dispute, that after criticism has done its worst on them—after all deductions for impossible plots and fantastical characters, unaccountable

only things that go down.' 'How!' says the Vicar, 'is it possible that the present age can be pleased with *that antiquated dialect*, that *obsolete humour*, and those *overcharged characters* which abound in the works you mention?' No writer of name, who was not aiming at paradox, would venture to say this now."

198 *Kotzebue*: Auguste Friedrich Ferdinand von Kotzebue (1761–1819), German dramatist, perhaps the most popular and influential playwright of the late-eighteenth and early-nineteenth centuries. Among his many plays to appear on the London stage after 1797, his *Spanier in Peru* was adapted by Sheridan as *Pizarro* (Drury Lane, 1798), while his *Das Kind der Liebe* was adapted by Inchbald as *Lovers' Vows* (Covent Garden, 1798).

199 *Beaumont and Fletcher*: Francis Beaumont (1585?–1616) and John Fletcher (1579–1625), playwriting duo who collaboratively produced *The Woman Hater* (1606); *Philaster* (1608–10); *The Coxcombe* (1608–10); *The Maide's Tragedy* (1608–11); *The Captaine* (1609–12); *A King and No King* (1611); *Cupid's Revenge* (1611); *The Scornful Ladie* (1613–17); *Love's Pilgrimage* (1616?); and *The Noble Gentleman* (1625?).

200 *Mr. Chenevix*: Richard Chenevix (1774–1830), *Two Plays* [*Mantuan Revels, a Comedy* and *Henry the Seventh, an Historical Tragedy*] (London: Joseph Johnson, 1812).

201 *Coleridge … Milman*: Samuel Coleridge, *Remorse, a Tragedy* (Drury Lane, 1813); Charles Maturin, *Bertram* (Drury Lane, 1816); Barry Cornwall, *Mirandola, a Tragedy* (London: J. Warren, 1821); Arthur Wilson, *The Inconstant Lady: A Play in Verse* (Oxford: Samuel Collingwood, 1814); and Henry Hart Milman, *Fazio, a Tragedy* (Covent Garden, 1818).

forms of speech, and occasional extravagance, indelicacy and horrors—there is a facility and richness about them, both of thought and of diction—a force of invention, and a depth of sagacity—an originality of conception, and a play of fancy—a nakedness and energy of passion, and, above all, a copiousness of imagery, and a sweetness and flexibility of verse, which is altogether unrivalled, in earlier or in later times;—and places them, in our estimation, in the very highest and foremost place among ancient or modern poets.

It is in these particulars that the inferiority of their recent imitators is most apparent—in the want of ease and variety—originality and grace. There is, in all their attempts, whatever may be their other merits or defects, an air of anxiety and labour—and indications, by far too visible, at once of timidity and ambition. This may arise, in part, from the fact of their being, too obviously and consciously, imitators. They do not aspire so much to rival the genius of their originals, as to copy their manner. They do not write as *they* themselves would have written in the present day, but as they imagine themselves would have written two hundred years ago. They emulate the quaint familiarities of that classical period—and wonder that they are not mistaken for new incarnations of its departed poets! One great cause why they are not, is, that they speak an unnatural dialect, and are constrained by a masquerade habit; in neither of which it is possible to display that freedom, and those delicate traits of character, which are the life of the drama, and were among the chief merits of those who once exalted it so highly. Another bad effect of imitation, and especially of the imitation of unequal and irregular models in a critical age, is, that nothing is thought fit to be copied but the exquisite and shining passages;—from which it results, in the *first* place, that all our rivalry is reserved for occasions in which its success is most hopeless; and, in the *second* place, that instances, even of occasional success, want their proper grace and effect, by being deprived of the relief, shading and preparation, which they would naturally have received in a less fastidious composition; and, instead of the warm and native and ever-varying graces of a spontaneous effusion, the work acquires the false and feeble brilliancy

of a prize essay in a foreign tongue—a collection of splendid patches of different texture and pattern.

[The review then attributes the current mediocrity in dramatic productions to want of courage and unreasonable dread of criticism].

Lord Byron, in some respects, may appear not to have been wanting in intrepidity. He has not certainly been very tractable in advice, nor very patient of blame. But this, in him, we fear, is not superiority to censure, but aversion to it; and, instead of proving that he is indifferent to detraction, shows only, that the dread and dislike of it operate with more than common force on his mind. A critic, whose object was to give pain, would desire no better proof of the efficacy of his inflictions, than the bitter scorn and fierce defiance with which they are encountered; and the more vehemently the noble author protests that he despises the reproaches that have been bestowed on him, the more certain it is that he suffers from their severity, and would be glad to escape if he cannot overbear them. But however this may be, we think it is certain that his late dramatic efforts have not been made carelessly, or without anxiety. To us, at least, they seem very elaborate and hard-wrought compositions; and this indeed we take to be their leading characteristic, and the key to most of their peculiarities.

Considered as Poems, we confess they appear to us to be rather heavy, verbose, and inelegant—deficient in the passion and energy which belongs to the other writings of the noble author—and still more in the richness of imagery, the originality of thought, and the sweetness of versification for which he used to be distinguished. They are for the most part solemn, prolix, and ostentatious—lengthened out by large preparations for catastrophes that never arrive, and tantalizing us with slight specimens and glimpses of a higher interest scattered thinly up and down many weary pages of pompous declamation. Along with the concentrated pathos and homestruck sentiments of his former poetry, the noble author seems also, we cannot imagine why, to have discarded the spirited and melodious versification in which they were embodied, and to have formed to himself a measure equally remote from the spring and vigour of his former compositions, and from the softness and inflexibility of the ancient masters of the drama. There are some sweet lines, and many of great weight and energy; but the general march of the verse is cumbrous and unmusical. His lines do not vibrate like polished lances, at once strong and light, in the hands of his persons, but are wielded like clumsy batons in a bloodless affray. Instead of the graceful familiarity and idiomatical melodies of Shakespeare, it is apt, too, to fall into clumsy prose, in its approaches to the easy and colloquial style; and, in the loftier passages, is occasionally deformed by low and common images that harmonize but ill with the general solemnity of the diction.

As Plays, we are afraid we must also say that the pieces before us are wanting in interest, character, and action:—at least we must say this of the two last of them—for *there is* interest in Sardanapalus—and beauties besides, that make us blind to its other defects. There is, however, throughout, a want of dramatic effect and variety; and we suspect there is something in the character and habit of Lord B.'s genius which will render this unattainable. He has too little sympathy with the ordinary feelings and frailties of humanity, to succeed well in their representation—"His soul is like a star, and dwells apart." It does not "hold the mirror up to nature," nor catch the hues of surrounding objects; but, like a kindled furnace, throws out its intense glare and gloomy grandeur on the narrow scene which it irradiates. He has given us, in his other works, some glorious pictures of nature—some magnificent reflections, and some inimitable delineations of character: But the same feelings prevail in them all; and his portraits in particular, though a little varied in the drapery and attitude, seem all copied from the same original. His Childe Harold, his Giaour, Conrad, Lara, Manfred, Cain, and Lucifer,—are all one individual. There is the same varnish of voluptuousness on the surface—the same canker of misanthropy at the core, of all he touches. He cannot draw the changes of many-coloured life, nor transport himself into the condition of the infinitely diversified characters by whom a stage should be peopled. The very intensity of his feelings—the loftiness of his views—the pride of his nature or his genius, without him from this

identification; so that in personating the heroes of the scene, he does little but repeat himself. It would be better for him, we think, if it were otherwise. We are sure it would be better for his readers. He would get more fame, and things of far more worth than fame, if he would condescend to a more extended and cordial sympathy with his fellow-creatures; and we should have more variety of fine poetry, and, at all events, better tragedies. We have no business to read him a homily on the sinfulness of pride and uncharity; but we have a right to say, that it argues a poorness of genius to keep always to the same topics and persons; and that the world will weary at last of the most energetic pictures of misanthropes and madmen—outlaws and their mistresses!

[The review then exhorts Byron to think of the example of Shakespeare].

But we must now look at the Tragedies; and on turning again to SARDANAPALUS, we are half inclined to repent of the severity of some of our preceding remarks, or to own at least that they are not strictly applicable to this performance. It is a work beyond all question of great beauty and power; and though the heroine has many traits in common with the Medoras and Gulnares of Lord Byron's undramatic poetry, the hero must be allowed to be a new character in his hands. He has, indeed, the scorn of war, and glory, and priestcraft, and regular mortality, which distinguishes the rest of his Lordship's favourites; but he has no misanthropy, and very little pride—and may be regarded, on the whole, as one of the most truly good-humoured, amiable and respectable voluptuaries to whom we have ever been presented. In this conception of his character, the author has very wisely followed nature and fancy rather than history. *His* Sardanapalus is not an effeminate, worn-out debauchee, with shattered nerves and exhausted senses, the slave of indolence and vicious habits; but a sanguine votary of pleasure, a princely epicure, indulging, revelling in boundless luxury while he can, but with a soul so inured to voluptuousness, so saturated with delights, that pain and danger, when they come uncalled for, give him neither concern nor dread; and he goes forth, from the banquet to the battle, as to a dance or measure, attired by the Graces, and with youth, joy, and love for his guides. He dallies with Bellona as her bridegroom—for his sport and pastime; and the spear or fan, the shield or shining mirror, become his hands equally well. He enjoys life, in short, and triumphs in death; and whether in prosperous or adverse circumstances, his soul smiles out superior to evil. The Epicurean philosophy of Sardanapalus gives him a fine opportunity, in his conferences with his stern and confidential adviser, Salemenes, to contrast his own imputed and fatal vices of ease and love of pleasure with the boasted virtues of his predecessors, War and Conquest; and we may as well begin with a short specimen of this characteristic discussion.

[The review quotes I.ii.208-78].

But the chief charm and vivifying angel of the piece is MYRRHA, the Greek slave of Sardanapalus—a beautiful, heroic, devoted, and ethereal being—in love with the generous and infatuated monarch—ashamed of loving a barbarian—and using all her influence over him to ennoble as well as to adorn his existence, and to arm him against the terrors of its close. Her voluptuousness is that of the heart—her heroism of the affections. If the part she takes in the dialogue be sometimes too subdued and submissive for the lofty daring of her character, it is still such as might become a Greek slave—a lovely Ionian girl, in whom the love of liberty and the scorn of death, was tempered by the consciousness of what she regarded as a degrading passion, and an inward sense of fitness and decorum with reference to her condition. The development of this character and its consequences, form so material a part of the play, that most of the citations with which we shall illustrate our abstract of it, will be found to bear upon it.

[The review then summarizes the plot, quoting I.ii.464-562, III.i.94-162, III.i.200-39, III.i.339-433, IV.i.102-58, IV.i.491-531, V.i.400-22, V.i.450-99, before treating *The Two Foscari*, *Cain*, and the immoral tendencies of Byron's poetry].

66. [Gifford, William], Review of *Marino Faliero, Doge of Venice, an Historical Tragedy* and *Sardanapalus, a Tragedy; The Two Foscari, a Tragedy; and Cain, a Mystery. Quarterly Review* 27 (July 1822), pages 476-524. Extract.

Several years have passed away since we undertook the review of any of Lord Byron's Poetry. Not that we have been inattentive observers of that genius whose fertility is, perhaps, not the least extraordinary of its characteristics, of whose earlier fruits we were among the first and warmest eulogists, and whose later productions—though hardly answering the expectation which he once excited—would have been, of themselves, sufficient to establish the renown of many scores of ordinary writers. Far less have we been able to witness, without deep regret and disappointment, the systematic and increasing prostitution of those splendid talents to the expression of feelings, and the promulgation of opinions, which, as Christians, as Englishmen, and even as men, we were constrained to regard with abhorrence. But it was from this very conflict of admiration and regret;—this recollection of former merits and sense of present degradation;—this reverence for talent and scorn of sophistry, that we remained silent. The little effect which our advice had, on former occasions, produced, still further tended to confirm us in our silence,—a silence of which the meaning could hardly, as we conceived, be misunderstood, and which we wished Lord Byron himself to regard as an appeal, of not the least impressive kind,—to his better sense and taste and feelings. We trusted that he would himself, ere long, discover that wickedness was not strength, nor impiety courage, nor licentiousness warmheartedness, nor an aversion to his own country philosophy; and that riper years, and a more familiar acquaintance with that affliction to which all are heirs, and those religious principles by which affliction is turned into a blessing, would render him not only almost but altogether such a poet as virgins might read, and Christians praise, and Englishmen take pride in.

[The review catalogues Byron's recent publications up to *Marino Faliero*].

In this hope we have not been disappointed. Whatever may be the other merits of his tragedies, on the score of morals they are unimpeachable. His females, universally, are painted in truer and worthier colors than we have been accustomed to witness from his pencil, and the qualities which he holds up, in his other characters, to admiration and to pity, are entirely unmingled with those darker and disgusting tints, from which even Childe Harold was not free, and which he appears to have thought necessary to excite any interest in such characters as Manfred, Lara, Alp, and the Giaour. Even the Mystery of Cain, wicked as it may be, is the work of a nobler and more daring wickedness than that which delights in insulting the miseries, and stimulating the evil passions, and casting a cold-blooded ridicule over all the lofty and generous feelings of our nature: and it is better that Lord Byron should be a manichee, or a deist,[202]—nay, we would almost say, if the thing were possible, it is better that he should be a moral and argumentative atheist, than the professed and systematic poet of seduction, adultery and incest; the contemner of patriotism, the insulter of piety, the raker into every sink of vice and wretchedness to disgust and degrade the hearts of his fellow-creatures.

[The review then treats *Cain* before taking up the question of Byron's support of the "Unities" of time, place, and action].

That Shakspeare and his continental rivals have written in very different styles, is a fact sufficiently evident. That different names should be given to these different styles is not only natural but convenient and desirable. That the high-sounding titles of "the drama," or "the regular drama," should be applied to the one, while the more homely but not less expressive designation of "play" is left for the other, is an arrangement which (if it affords any comfort to the admirers of the Parisian school) we, for our part, might cheerfully acquiesce in. But, if we are to be pelted with the epithets of "incorrect," "uncivilized," and we know not what, for saying that we prefer a *play* of Shakspeare's to a *drama* of Racine's[203] or Alfieri's;[204] if all merit or beauty is to be appreciated by a French critic in a Grecian mask, and if the noblest models of writing are to be abandoned and despised, because they do not tally with rules arbitrarily imposed, and customs which no more concern us than the droit d'aubaine;[205] when, lastly, these usurpations find an advocate in one who is himself among the most illustrious living ornaments of English poetry, it is time to make up our minds, either to defend the national laws, or to submit to the "Code of Napoleon";[206] and to examine whether there be really, in favour of this last, so much extrinsic authority or so much intrinsic excellence, as to call on us to adopt it, in place of that ancient licence of pleasing and being pleased in the manner most effectual and most natural, which the poets and audiences of England have, till now, considered as their birthright.

Nor is this all. We have, we confess it, an additional and private reason for our grudge against the regular school, inasmuch as we cannot but believe that an adherence to its forms in the works now before us, has robbed the world of no inconsiderable quantity of beautiful

---

202 *manichee, or a deist*: Strictly considered, a manichee is one adhering to a religious system widely accepted from the third to the fifth century, composed of Gnostic Christian, Mazdean, and pagan elements. The special feature of the system which the name chiefly suggests to modern readers is the dualistic theology, according to which Satan was represented as co-eternal with God. A deist is one who acknowledges the existence of a God upon the testimony of reason, but rejects revealed religion.

203 *Racine's*: Jean Racine (1633–99), French dramatist and historiographer renowned for his classical tragedies, notably *Andromaque* (1667), *Britannicus* (1669), *Bérénice* (1670), *Bajazet* (1672), and *Phèdre* (1677).

204 *Alfieri's*: Conte Vitorio Alfieri (1749–1803), Italian dramatist, best-known for his tragedies *Filippo*, *Antigone*, *Oreste*, *Mirra*, and *Saul*, his masterpiece.

205 *droit d'aubaine*: right of French kings whereby they claimed the property of every stranger who died in their country without being naturalized; it was abolished by the National Assembly in 1790, re-established by Napoleon, and finally annulled July 14, 1819.

206 *"Code of Napoleon"*: French civil code enacted in 1804 and still extant, with revisions; it has been the main influence in the nineteenth-century civil codes of most countries of continental Europe and Latin America.

poetry. We are not, indeed, from the present specimens, by any means justified in supposing that the genius of Lord Byron is eminently dramatic, or that, *even* if he had condescended to take Shakspeare as a model, his "irregularities" would have equalled the "woodnotes wild" of his predecessor. But, feeling this as we do,—and while we bear in mind his own modest and candid protest against imputing to any defect in the art what he would rather have us consider as a failure in the architect, we cannot but perceive that to run a race in chains (though those chains may be voluntary) is too much for the speed of Achilles himself; and that the beauties (for many and great beauties are, undoubtedly to be met within the works which we have undertaken to examine) are rather in spite than in consequence of the rules which their author has adopted.

[The review then argues that no English playwright except Addison adopted the Unities, that the drama of Spain is equally irregular, and that Britain has contributed more to art and learning in the last hundred years than any other country].

This is, however, by the way; and its connexion with the real merits of the case is, certainly, by no means vital. A doctrine may be sound though the majority of the world reject it; and the consent of the greatest and most overwhelming majority, though it may be a *presumption*, is still not a *proof* of its soundness. Let us examine, then, the principles on which Lord Byron's dramatic canons depend, and the arguments which are usually advanced to prove their necessity. In this task we are sensible that we can supply but little which Johnson has not already said far better,—but even Johnson himself will be found, in some few instances, to have made a larger admission to modern prejudice than either the reason of the case or the truth of literary history would warrant.

The first, if not the most important of the arguments in favor of the dramatic unities, is the alleged practice and authority of the ancients. The French drama assumes to itself, exclusively, the name of "regular" and "classical," and the critics and poets of other nations have been, for the most part, sufficiently courteous to admit the accuracy of this designation, and to take it for granted that plays

of which the scene is never changed; of which the action is grave and stately, without intermixture of comedy or lighter dialogue; and whose heroes and heroines decorously retire behind the curtain to die, are not only after the manner of Paris, but of Rome and Athens, and (at least in ancient times) of all "the more civilized parts of the world."[207]

Now, suppose it were admitted that this view of the subject was correct, it might still be asked on what grounds (if the practice and precedent of antiquity are to decide the question) the French copy of the ancient drama is so partial and imperfect? If they think it necessary to be classical, why are they not so altogether? Why has so important, so essential, so dignified and beautiful a feature of the ancient tragedy as the *chorus* been altogether discarded from their theatres? Why have singing and recitative given place to declamation? Or why are the vizard[208] and the cothurnus[209] abandoned in favour of rouge and kid slippers? If we are answered, (as we doubtless shall be), that these changes arise from the different habits of our audiences and the different construction of our theatres; that they are nearer approaches to nature, and get rid of unnecessary difficulties while they detract nothing from the power of pleasing; it is surely as reasonable to say that, on the same principles, we have innovated a little farther. We may surely plead that the unity of place and time, which was convenient and desirable on a stage open to the sky, and where changes of scene were, in a great measure, rendered impossible, is no longer necessary in playhouses of the modern form, and furnished with modern machinery. We may plead this same imitation of nature which discarded the chorus and the mask, has induced us to adopt a less sustained and a more varied tone of dialogue; and that we see not sufficient reason for denying to our poets and actors the opportunity

---

207 *"the more civilized parts of the world"*: misquoted from Byron's own preface to *Sardanapalus*.
208 *vizard*: a mask or visor.
209 *cothurnus*: a thick-soled boot reaching to the middle of the leg, worn by tragic actors in the ancient Athenian drama; a buskin.

of displaying the human character in the most moving and terrible of all situations, because Horace (of whom more anon) is alleged as disapproving the representation of all death on the theatre.

But the supporters of dramatic liberty need not stop here. Not only do the French critics fail in proving that the authority of the ancients can oblige us to imitate them—they are wrong in point of *fact*, inasmuch as there are few circumstances belonging to the ancient drama at the present day more generally recognized among scholars than that the Greeks did not adhere to, and apparently knew nothing of those canons to which so confident an appeal is made.

[The review then looks to the work of Aeschylus, and argues that neither Aristotle's *Poetics* nor Horace's *Art of Poetry* provide explicit defenses of the Unities. It then attributes the weaknesses of Corneille's dramas and Byron's *The Two Foscari* to their following the Unities].

But we had really supposed that the question of scenic illusion had long since been too generally and too correctly understood, to make it necessary, at this time of day, to renew its discussion. We hardly could have thought it needful to prove, that the spectator of a drama does not actually imagine himself an assistant in the Venetian senate, or a witness of the capture of Nineveh. For ourselves, we confess, we resort to the theatre to hear and see a story told in dialogue, and illustrated by dresses and scenery. We may be more *moved*, but we are not more *deceived* by what we witness there, than if we read the same poem in a book with prints; and the change of scene, or a supposed interval between the scenes, produces no other effect on our minds than the turning over of a new page, or the opening of a second volume. Nor can we conceive a greater instance of the efficacy of system to blind the most acute perception, than the fact that Lord Byron, in works avowedly and exclusively intended for the closet, has piqued himself on the observance of rules, which (be their advantage on the stage what it may) are evidently, off the stage, a matter of perfect indifference. The only object of adhering to the unities is to preserve the illusion of the scene. To the reader they are obviously useless.

[The review then treats *Marino Faliero*, arguing that Shakespeare would have improved the play by beginning its action much earlier].

In Sardanapalus he has been far more fortunate, inasmuch as his subject is one eminently adapted not only to tragedy in general, but to that peculiar kind of tragedy which Lord Byron is anxious to recommend. The history of the last of the Assyrian kings is at once sufficiently well-known to awaken that previous interest which belongs to illustrious names and early associations; and sufficiently remote and obscure to admit of any modification of incident or character which a poet may find convenient. All that we know of Nineveh and its sovereigns is majestic, indistinct, and mysterious. We read of an extensive and civilized monarchy erected in the ages immediately succeeding the deluge, and existing in full might and majesty while the shores of Greece and Italy were unoccupied, except by roving savages. We read of an empire whose influence extended from Samarcand to Troy, and from the mountains of Judah to those of Caucasus, subverted, after a continuance of thirteen hundred years, and a dynasty of thirty generations, in an almost incredibly short space of time, less by the revolt of two provinces than by the anger of Heaven and the predicted fury of natural and inanimate agents. And the influence which both the conquests and the misfortunes of Assyria appear to have exerted over the fates of the people for whom, of all others in ancient history, our strongest feelings are (from religious motives) interested, throws a sort of sacred pomp over the greatness and the crimes of the descendants of Nimrod, and a reverence which no other equally remote portion of profane history is likely to obtain with us. At the same time all which we know is so brief, so general, and so disjointed, that we have few of those preconceived notions of the persons and facts represented which in classical dramas, if servilely followed, destroy the interest, and if rashly departed from, offend the prejudices of the reader of the auditor. An outline is given of the most majestic kind; but it is an outline only, which the poet may fill up at pleasure; and in ascribing, as Lord Byron has done for the sake of his favourite unities, the destruction of the Assyrian empire to the treason of one night, instead of the war of several years, he has neither shocked our better knowledge, nor incurred any conspicuous improbability.

[The review then notes that tragedies where the chief cause of calamity is war or the wrath of the Gods are better suited to the constraint of Unity of Time than plays where tragic heroes cause their own downfalls].

Accordingly his Sardanapalus is pretty nearly such a person as the Sardanapalus of history may be supposed to have been, making due allowance for the calumnies to which an unfortunate prince is liable from his revolted subjects. Young, thoughtless, spoiled by flattery and unbounded self-indulgence, but with a temper naturally amiable, and abilities of a superior order, he affects to undervalue the sanguinary renown of his ancestors as an excuse for inattention to the most necessary duties of his rank; and flatters himself, while he is indulging his own sloth, that he is making his people happy. Yet, even in his fondness for pleasure, there lurks a love of contradiction. It is because he is schooled by Salamenes and his queen that he runs with more eagerness to dissipation: and he enjoys his follies the more from a sense of the witty and eloquent sophistry with which he is able to defend them. He feels that his character is under-rated; he suspects that he is himself the cause of this degradation; but he is elevated by the knowledge that he understands himself better than those around him. He has been so gorged with flattery that he rates it at its true value; yet his social hours are passed with flatterers, and he is not displeased with flattery the wildest and most impious, because he derives a satisfaction from knowing that he is not deceived by it.

The same peculiarity runs throughout his character. He forgives the disaffected satraps, though internally convinced of their guilt, with a frankness that would have been generosity, if it were not that he is too indolent to inquire, and too proud to condemn them on the mere authority of Salamenes. He professes to have slighted his queen for no other reason than because his love was there a duty; and even his passion for Myrrha is a feeling of superiority and possession, not of admiration and service. It is made up of kisses and compliments. He keeps her by him as a child does a plaything, and is interested and amused by her eloquence, her courage, and her powerful understanding, as with a plaything more singular and attractive than any he has enjoyed before. But he mocks her touching piety; he rallies her just apprehensions and manly counsels; he is less unwilling than he ought to be to admit her as a sharer in his funeral pile; he speaks of her as "a slave who loves from passion," and he, perhaps, speaks the truth when he says that he should love her more if she were something less heroic.

With all this, sufficient elevation of courage and sentiment is mingled here to prove the natural strength of his mind, and just sufficient warmth of feeling to evince his natural kindliness of disposition. Though he shrinks from the ordinary exertions of a sovereign, he feels a delightful stimulus in the novelty and dignity of danger. With Salamenes, with his soldiers, with the herald of the rebel host, his demeanour is magnanimous and kingly. Except in the too great eagerness which prompts his nocturnal sally, he discharges, with coolness and ability, the duties not only of a warrior but a general. He exults, when alone and expecting the fatal torch, in that ancestry which he had before affected to despise, but whose martial fame his own end is not to detract from—and in his interview with Zarina; in his expressions of tenderness by the dead body of his brother-in-law, and when receiving the last homage of his faithful guard, he betrays in a natural and touching manner the knowledge that his estimate of life and of mankind has been wrong, and abundantly redeems himself from that contempt to which an unqualified selfishness would have consigned him.

Yet, of the whole picture, selfishness is the prevailing feature—selfishness admirably drawn indeed; apologized for by every palliating circumstance of education and habit, and clothed in the brightest colours of which it is susceptible from youth, talents, and placability. But it is selfishness still, and we should have been tempted to quarrel with the art which made vice and frivolity thus amiable, if Lord Byron had not at the same time pointed out with much skill the bitterness and weariness of spirit which inevitably wait on such a character; and if he had not given a fine contrast to the picture in the accompanying portraits of Salamenes and of Myrrha.

Salamenes is the direct opposite to selfishness; and the character, though slightly sketched, displays little less ability than that which we have just been reviewing. He is a stern, loyal, plain-spoken soldier and subject; clear-sighted, just and honourable in his ultimate views, though not more punctilious about the means of obtaining them than might be expected from a respectable satrap of ancient Nineveh, or a respectable vizier[210] of the modern Turkish empire. To his king, in spite of personal neglect and family injuries, he is, throughout, pertinaciously attached and punctiliously faithful. To the king's rebels he is inclined to be severe, bloody, and even treacherous—an imperfection, however, in his character, to want which would, in his situation, be almost unnatural, and which is skilfully introduced as a contrast to the indolence of his master. Of the satrap, however, the faults as well as the virtues are alike the offspring of disinterested loyalty and patriotism. It is for his country and his king that he is patient of injury; for them that he is valiant; for them cruel. He has no ambition of personal power, no thirst for individual fame. In battle and in victory "Assyria!" is his only war-cry. When he sends off the queen and princes, he is less anxious for his nephews and sister than for the preservation of the line of Nimrod; and in his last moments it is the supposed flight of his sovereign which alone distresses and overcomes him.

Myrrha is a female Salamenes, in whom, with admirable skill, attachment to the individual Sardanapalus is substituted for the gallant soldier's loyalty to the descendant of kings; and whose energy of expostulation, no less than the natural high tone of her talents, her courage, and her Grecian pride, is softened into a subdued and winning tenderness by the constant and painful recollection of her abasement as a slave in the royal harem; and still more by the lowliness of perfect womanly love in the presence of and towards the object of her passion. No character can be drawn more natural than hers; few ever have been drawn more touching and amiable. Of course she is not, nor could be, a Jewish or a Christian heroine; but she is a model of Grecian piety and nobility of spirit, and she is one whom a purer faith would have raised to the level of a Rebecca or a Miriam.

With such leading personages as these, it may be well expected that Lord Byron has given a drama of no common force and beauty; and, in fact, though there are some obvious reasons which render it unfit for the English stage, we regard it as, on the whole, the most splendid specimen which our language affords of that species of tragedy which the author admires so greatly on the Parisian theatres. It has, indeed, more force, more vivacity, and more interest than is possessed in general by the continental drama; and while it is less stiff and rigid than Alfieri, it frequently reminds us of some of his noblest productions. There are some instances, indeed, in which, as we think, notwithstanding our late admission, his beloved unities have cramped his powers, and where he has lost something of effect by a needless departure from the historical outline of Diodorus. Even in respect of plot, however, Sardanapalus deserves considerable praise.

[The review then summarizes the plot, and moves on to *The Two Foscari* and *Cain*].

---

67. Review of *Sardanapalus*. *The Morning Chronicle* No. 20,164 (11 April 1834), page 2.

Drury-Lane Theatre. Sardanapalus, by Lord BYRON, was presented to an audience last night, under every possible advantage of acting, scenery, and costume. If, therefore, it turns out not a very successful experiment, the fault lies in the work, and not in the management—unless, indeed, it be an error to have attempted the performance of it at all. The author was aware that it could not become popular; he never contemplated the acting of it when he wrote it, and he composed it upon a plan, and with a severity of rule, that has never been adopted with success upon our stage. He vindicated this course in his preface; but

---

210   *vizier*: in the Turkish empire, Persia, or other Muslim country: a high state official or minister, frequently one invested with vice-regal authority; a governor or viceroy of a province; subsequently the chief minister of the sovereign.

the fact was, that Lord BYRON was not a poet of imagination in the highest and truest sense of the word; there is no instance of a bitter satirist being a poet of imagination. Independently of his first, the best portions of all his productions, and even of the Tragedy before us, are satirical. Hence his avowed dislike of SHAKESPEARE, and of the system (as far as system it can be called) he pursued in his plays, and hence the opposite course which Lord BYRON invariably recommended both by precept and example. It is impossible that the romantic drama should ever be superseded in this country. Our neighbours of Germany have borne willing testimony in its favour, and our neighbours of France are every day more and more evincing their disposition to shake off the fetters of the unities. Certainly the tragedy of *Sardanapalus* will gain no converts to the classic drama—at least when publicly represented—and though it may be read with great satisfaction as a poem, it wants incident and even interest as a play. In the original the scene lies only in a great chamber of the palace, but in the alteration it is once changed, and the three last acts are supposed to pass in the hall of Nimrod. Thus, some little violence has been done to the piece as it was written, and so far from meaning to complain of it, we should have thought the person who prepared *Sardanapalus* for the stage fully justified, had he taken such parts of Lord BYRON's tragedy as suited his purpose, and had endeavoured to lighten the weight of the scenes by a variation of the place of action. Lord BYRON has not scrupled to introduce into act 3, the absurdity of a battle in the very hall where *Sardanapalus*, in the opening of the next act, is discovered asleep, which surely is doing greater violence to probability than trusting to the imagination of the spectator, and changing the scene; this absurdity has been judiciously avoided by the adapter, only we would have recommended him to have gone in this respect considerably farther. For the same reason we do not object to the introduction of two chorusses in the first and third acts; they are decided improvements, are extremely appropriate to the situations, and add considerably to the life of the performance. In other respects, with certain omissions of speeches that do not advance the plot, however they may serve to illustrate character,

the tragedy was exhibited last night much as Lord BYRON wrote it. After all that has been done for it, it remains a heavy lingering performance, the action of which is single, and not of a kind to excite strongly the feelings of a popular assembly. The situation and overthrow of *Sardanapalus*, even with the aid of *Ionian Myrrha*, produce little sympathy, and the scene with his wife is a mere piece of gratuitous grief which in no way contributes to the general design.

It is very clear that Lord BYRON, in this Tragedy, as in nearly all his other works, has had an eye to himself—he has drawn *Sardanapalus* exactly what he would himself have been under similar circumstances, "effeminately vanquished," not effeminate, or, to use his own words, "soft, but not fearful." He was a being merely selfish—devoted to his own indulgence, luxurious by nature, and only roused to action by the compulsion of circumstances. There was a resemblance even in the situation of the two persons, for *Sardanapalus* had cast away his wife, and doated upon a slave, who in turn doated upon him, though we have no record to show that *Myrrha*, like the Guiccioli, made a boast of her lawless intimacy, and consented that it should be proclaimed to the world in notes to the life of her paramour, the materials for which were furnished in her own hand writing.

One great object with Lord BYRON in writing *Sardanapalus*, seems to have been to lash priest-craft in the person of *Beleses*, and many passages tending to this purpose might be collected in the course of the tragedy. As it was, perhaps, supposed that in these times such passages would be peculiarly welcome, and might be turned against the Established Church, most of them were omitted. Thus we found no trace of the exclamation of *Salamenes*, the brother of the hero, when addressing *Beleses*—

"Peace, factious priest and faithless soldier! thou
Unit'st in thine own person the worst vices
Of the most dangerous orders of mankind."

But the mode in which it would have been received was pretty obvious from the rounds of applause which followed the subsequent moderate imputation by *Sardanapalus*, addressed to the same personage:—

"—————————Please you to hear me, Satraps!
And chiefly thou, my priest, because I doubt thee
More than the soldier; and would doubt thee all,
Wert thou not half a warrior."

ELLEN TREE and MACREADY came on together,
in what the author designates as his second scene, but it
is, in fact, his first. Testimonies of esteem and admiration
were showered down upon both most profusely, but from
peculiar circumstances, we may say that they were especially meant for the lady, who has been placed in a situation of some difficulty and delicacy. First, the part of
Myrrha was put into the hands of Mrs. PHILLIPS; then
it was transferred to those of Miss E. TREE; and subsequently taken from Miss E. TREE, to be given to Mrs.
MARDYN, who was said to have studied under Lord
BYRON, and to have received the "delicate touches" of
the Noble Poet. Mrs. MARDYN, however, was suddenly
taken ill, and again ELLEN TREE was required to appear as *Myrrha*, and we may add, that she went through
the undertaking greatly to the satisfaction of the house.
We, perhaps, think that she might have done better had
she done worse; but she was apparently so afraid of over-
charging the part, that she kept down some points that
might have been rendered more prominent. What she said
and did would have been fully understood and appreciated in a smaller theatre, but in our large houses it is absolutely necessary to "overstep the modesty of nature,"[211]
or the performer fails to produce any effect. Hence the
rarity with which quiet points tell, and an audience is
never made to feel them but by an actor of consummate
skill and great experience. The truth of this observation
we are sure no one will pretend to deny. This was ELLEN
TREE's error—an error easily avoided, and an error for
which we admire her. She looked most interestingly, and
played most sweetly; but we think her figure would have
shown better without the light-blue drapery which concealed, in a great degree, the graceful flow of her person.
MACREADY's *Sardanapalus*, we do not scruple to say,
was a faultless performance; yet this is saying nothing: it

was not only faultless but admirable in every respect,
whether we take into view the conception of the poet, or
the efforts of the actor not only to embody the conception, but to carry it farther in perfect consistency with
original design. Many passages were finely delivered, but
none more finely than the reproof to *Arbaces* and *Beleses*
in Act II. The narrative of the dream in Act IV was powerful, but the subject is so disagreeable that the force of
the actor only increased its deformity. In noticing the alterations of the piece, we ought to have mentioned that
that part of the scene where *Sardanapalus* hastily arms,
and calls for a mirror to survey his beauty, was omitted,
and we think rightly. Lord BYRON, indeed, justified it
by a passage in *Juvenal* relating to *Otho*; but what might
be very natural in the Roman, might be very unnatural
in the Assyrian; and at such a moment, when the utmost
dispatch is necessary, nothing could be more preposterous than to introduce such an incident. Here, again, Lord
BYRON was thinking—not of what *Sardanapalus* would
have done—but of his own personal beauty, and what he
should have done. It was a piece with his anxiety about
his tooth-powder, and his vexation at the defect in his
foot, because it interfered with his self-love. COOPER
was an excellent *Salamenes*. It was just a part to which he
was equal; not requiring any polish of deportment, or
peculiar discrimination, the nature of the character being distinctly marked, and without variety. He died by
an arrow, and not by a javelin, as in the original, which
was a bad change; inasmuch as the drawing out of so small
an instrument, would not occasion a sudden, large effusion of blood, and instant death. The other actors—
KING, BRINDALL, and G. BENNETT—who had the
parts of *Pania, Arbaces, Beleses*, were sufficient; but
YARNOLD's flourishing mode of making his exit in one
of the scenes occasioned a general laugh.

The same effect was produced, we hardly know why,
when in the last scene a body of soldiers came on loaded
with wood, &c. for the pyre; perhaps because the masses
of real wood would have been heavier than any two could
have carried. The operation is preparatory to the catastrophe, which is very well managed. *Myrrha* lights the pile,
then joins *Sardanapalus*, who has mounted his burning

---

211 *"overstep the modesty of nature"*: quoted from William
Shakespeare, *Hamlet*, III.ii.19.

throne, and they are both soon involved in flames, and overwhelmed by the ruins of the falling palace. The walls give way, and open a view of Nineveh in one general blaze, and the whole city is red hot in the shortest possible time. The curtain descends, not the usual act-drop, but a view of Newstead Abbey,[212] obviously a hasty production, and not doing as much credit as usual to Stanfield's[213] pencil. Lord BYRON is represented sitting in a boat on the lake reading, some time after he had made away with his patrimony. Hence the scene was not very appropriate; and the recollection, that after so many ages the Abbey had passed into another family, could not be very grateful. ELLEN TREE and MACREADY were called for, and they duly made their obeisances hand-in-hand. COOPER announced the tragedy for repetition to-morrow, in the midst of loud applauses.

---

68. Review of *Sardanapalus*. *The Times* No. 15,449 (11 April 1834), page 2. Extract.

Drury Lane. Last night Lord Byron's beautifully written tragedy of *Sardanapalus* was performed on the boards of this theatre, and with a success which perfectly justifies the production, in spite of the noble author's repugnance, so frequently expressed, to having it acted. Acutely sensitive as the noble lord was, amidst all his affected misanthropy, to public opinion, it was natural for him to feel apprehensive that his reputation might be prejudiced by the performance of a play written solely for the closet, and which the preservation of the "unities" seemed to render unfit for representation before an English audi-

ence. It is undoubtedly true that this strict adherence to the ancient models, the maintenance of which has obliged the author to depart from the truth of history, and make a rebellion which occupied a considerable period of time explode and succeed in one day, does detract from the merit of the tragedy as an acting drama, and causes the latter scenes especially to flag; but the manner in which the performance of last night was received proves that there is sufficient dramatic interest in the plot, and in the characters of the piece, to render it successful. The tragedy, as performed last night, is, we understand, an adaptation of Mr. Macready. It is considerably curtailed, some scenes in the original being totally omitted. For instance, the battle which takes place in the palace in the 3d act, between the King's troops and the rebels, is left out; as is also the little incident of the mirror, brought at Sardanapalus's command, that he may admire himself when clothed in his armour. The chief character in the piece, that of Sardanapalus, was sustained by Mr. Macready with ability. It struck us, however, that he was not so successful in the representation of Sardanapalus, surrounded by his favourites, and revelling in the pleasures of his palace, as when, roused by rebellion, he assumes the man, and leads forth his adherents to battle and to victory. In this part of the performance he did not express all that lightness of heart, and buoyancy of spirits, which Sardanapalus is represented as possessing; but in the latter portion of the drama Mr. Macready was much more effective, and portrayed the bold, yet fickle, character of the monarch with perfect truth to nature. The description of the dream in the fourth act was admirably given by him, and called forth general marks of approbation from the audience. The character of Myrrha was excellently performed by Miss E. Tree. For some time past it had been announced that this part was to be filled by Mrs. Mardyn, for whom, as the play-bills said, it was intended by the noble author. However much we may lament the cause of this lady's absence, which we understand is severe indisposition, we must say that in our opinion the public have been gainers by it, as Miss Ellen Tree, who supplied her place, is an infinitely better actress than Mrs. Mardyn ever was, and

---

212 *Newstead Abbey*: Byron's hereditary seat, located in Nottinghamshire, sold by Byron in 1818.
213 *Stanfield's*: Clarkson Stanfield, R.A. (1793–1867), English artist who made a successful career as a scene-painter for Edinburgh and London theaters, and who was also considered one of England's finest marine painters. He is best known for his *Battle of Trafalgar* (1863).

in personal appearance much more fitted to represent the "Ionian Myrrha" than that lady can be now,—may we not add, ever could have been? Indeed, it would be difficult to select among living actresses one who could fill the character more efficiently in all respects than the lady by whom it was personated last night, though we must presume that she has had but a short time allowed for preparation. In the earlier scenes of the play, which, develop the gentle and affectionate character of Myrrha, Miss Tree most successfully embodied the poet's idea. In every action and expression of countenance her devoted love for Sardanapalus shone forth; bursting through the melancholy which seemed to hang over her, because she "loved whom she esteemed not." On her entrances Miss Tree was hailed most enthusiastically by the audience, and her reception at the close was as flattering as it was deserved. The insignificant part of Zarina was assigned to Miss Phillips, who did as much for it as we believe any actress could do. We regret that Miss Phillips had not a better opportunity afforded her of displaying her talents. Mr. Cooper took the part of Salamenes, and showed by his correct delivery, and not injudicious acting, that he had studied it carefully. At the fall of the curtain the applause was unequivocal in favour of the repetition of the piece, previous to which, however, we would recommend some alteration in a few of the subordinate arrangements. The exits and entrances of the inferior actors, and the grouping of the soldiery, were in some instances so awkwardly managed as to create laughter. The erection of the funeral pile on the stage has also a very ludicrous effect, and is prejudicial to the interest of the drama. Trifles like these have often assisted in the condemnation of really good productions, and they ought not, therefore, to be overlooked. There is some good scenery in the piece, among which is a very splendid representation of a banquet; and a new drop scene, representing a view of Newstead Abbey, has been painted for the occasion. The conflagration of the funeral pile, when once erected, was capitally managed. In accordance with the modern fashion, Mr. Macready, and Miss E. Tree were at the fall of the curtain called for, and on their appearance loudly cheered by the audience.

Glossary of Actors and Actresses

Bannister, Charles (1741–1804), 4th Spahi in *Blue-Beard*, was a popular actor whose accomplishments would be overshadowed by those of his son John. Initially turned down by Garrick, he began his career on the Norwich-Ipswich circuit and did a stint with Samuel Foote at the Haymarket; he finally joined the Drury Lane company in the 1767–68 season, performing at the Haymarket in the summers and sometimes defecting to Covent Garden. A popular actor during his prime, he was known for his voice and his skill at mimicry.

Bannister, John (1760–1836), Shacabac in *Blue-Beard*, the son of the comic actor Charles Bannister, entered the theater against his father's wishes, having his debut at Garrick's urging at his father's benefit at Drury Lane on 27 August 1778. He debuted in tragedy opposite Mary Robinson, playing Saphana to her Palmira in *Mahomet* on 11 November 1778. The father and son were popular at both Drury Lane and the Haymarket; John was also a popular actor in the provinces. Respected within the profession, he played some 425 characters.

Barnes, Mr., Humpino in *Harlequin and Humpo*, is perhaps **John Barnes (died 1841)**, who had his London debut at the Haymarket in 1811. He was in New York by 1816 and later managed the Richmond Hill Theatre there. His wife, Mary Greenhill, is known to have performed at Drury Lane in 1815.

Bew, Jemima Maria (fl. 1810–1814), the Princess of Fantasino in *Harlequin and Humpo*, was the daughter of the actor Charles Bew, or perhaps the daughter of John Henry Johnstone, another actor who may have been involved with her mother before she married Bew. Jemima Maria Bew acted in the Drury Lane company between 1810 and 1814. She married the actor Frederick Vining in 1814 and continued to act for a while under her married name.

Bland, Mrs. George, Maria Theresa Catherine, née Tersi (called Romani and Romanzini) (1770–1838), Beda in *Blue-Beard*, an actress and singer who began performing when she was four. By age eleven she was given a role at the King's Theatre on 5 June 1781; she debuted at Drury Lane the following season. While she trained at the Royal Circus, most of her career was spent at Drury Lane, often performing at the Haymarket in the summers. She was unhappily married to George Bland and conducted an open affair with the actor Thomas Caulfield. Known as a singer in the English ballad style, she could be quite impressive, as in her performance of the incantation scene in Coleridge's *Remorse*.

Chapman, Master, who played Agib in *Timour the Tartar*, cannot be positively identified. He may be **William Chapman (fl. 1770?–1820?)**, who was an actor, singer, and possible descendant of comedian Thomas Chapman, but we know little about him, and if he in fact began performing around 1770, it is unlikely he would be listed as "Master" Chapman at the time of the performance of *Timour*. There is a Chapman acting at the Haymarket in the early 1800s (who may be William), as well as one at Covent Garden. There was also a Chapman who tutored the actress Miss Chester. Master Chapman may have been an equestrian borrowed for the performance from a company such as Astley's.

Chatterley, Mr., Squinterina in *Harlequin and Humpo*, is perhaps **Robert E. Chatterley (fl. 1792–1818)**, a messenger and prompter at Drury Lane who also secured minor acting parts. His most frequent parts were waiters and bailiffs; there is at least one cross-dressed role in a listing of his habitual parts at Drury Lane. His wife is also carried on the Drury Lane accounts for 1795–96 and then again from 1807 through 1818–19. She played small parts such as maids. In *Harlequin and Humpo*, she seems to have played a Genii of Light. There is a slight chance that Squinterina was played by their son, the more famous William Simmonds Chatterley, though he appears to have been away from London at the time of the production.

Cooke, James (fl. 1791–1825), Pomposso in *Harlequin and Humpo*, was a singer and actor who played at Drury Lane from the 1790–91 season until at least 1816–17; he had his debut on 1 January 1791. He was known for his good bass voice.

Crossman, John (fl. 1787–1817), Kerim in *Timour the Tartar*, was an equestrian, one of the "two greatest Equestrian Performers of the time," according to Charles Dibdin. He began performing at Astley's Amphitheatre in 1787, moving to the competition at the Royal Circus in 1793. He was involved in a venture to bring circuses to venues throughout England and Ireland and was a partner in the rebuilt Astley's Amphitheatre beginning in 1804.

Crouch, Mrs. Rawlings Edward, Ann Maria, née Phillips (1763–1805), Fatima in *Blue-Beard*, an actress known for her beauty and her voice, joined the Drury Lane company in 1780, studying under the music master Thomas Linley and debuting on 11 November in Arne's opera *Artaxerxes*. She remained at Drury Lane throughout her career, performing at various venues in the summer. While officially married to a Navy lieutenant, Rawlings Edward Crouch, for seven years beginning in 1785, she was involved with the actor/singer Michael Kelly (Selim in *Blue-Beard*) from 1787. In addition to being a favorite singer on stage, she and Kelly were successful as vocal teachers.

Davenett, Mrs., née Harriett Pitt (1748?–1814), Sancha in *A Bold Stroke for a Husband*, was the daughter of the London and provincial comedic actress, Ann Pitt. Harriett Pitt began public performance as early as 25 August 1758 when she spoke an epilogue at Bristol's Jacob Wells Theatre. Accomplished as a dancer, she took various roles until 1762 when she became employed as a dancer at Covent Garden for the next five seasons, making her acting debut as Jacinta in *The Mistake* on 6 February 1766. While there remains no record of her appearing on the London stage for another 14 years, she did join Drury Lane in the 1778–79 season and remained until the end of the 1779–80 season. In 1780–81, Pitt transferred to Covent Garden and until 1793 was awarded minor roles in comedy, after which time she once again dropped from sight.

De Camp, Maria Theresa, later Mrs. Charles Kemble (1775–1838), Irene in *Blue-Beard*, was a popular actress, dancer, and singer, and also a playwright. Born in Vienna to a musical family (her father joined Covent Garden's oratorio band in 1777), she started performing as a dancer at the age of eight. She was with the Royal Circus until the Prince of Wales recommended her to Colman, who debuted her at the Haymarket on 14 June 1786. She debuted at Drury Lane on 24 October 1786 and continued to play there and at the Haymarket. She had her first major success as Macheath in the *Beggar's Opera* in 1792. Known for her voice, beauty, and charm, she was given key singing parts. She was attacked for the immodesty of her dress in *Blue-Beard*. In 1806, she finally married Charles Kemble after a long engagement and over the protests of the Kemble family; she did, however, move from Drury Lane to Covent Garden with the rest of the Kemble clan that year. Her play *Smiles and Tears; or, The Widow's Stratagem* opened at Covent Garden on 12 December 1815. She was the mother of Fanny Kemble.

De Camp, Vincent (1779–1830), Isidore in *Remorse*, was an actor and singer, and brother to Maria Theresa De Camp. He debuted in a juvenile part on 5 November 1792 with the Drury Lane company at King's Theatre but joined the troupe only in 1794; he was also a regular at the Haymarket. After 1814, he moved to various provincial theaters and then to North America. He may have died in Houston, Texas.

Dignum, Charles (1765?–1827), 1st Spahi in *Blue-Beard* (he would play Selim in a later production), was a singer, actor, and composer who had his debut at

Drury Lane in 1784 where he was a popular tenor for close to thirty years. He played many leading and secondary roles in operas and musical romances as well as filling a number of minor parts in Shakespeare's works. He was a favorite singer with audiences and also composed songs. Though sometimes criticized for his corpulent stature, he earned a significant amount of money as a lead singer in Drury Lane's March oratorios.

Edwin, John (1749–1790), Don Vincentio in *A Bold Stroke for a Husband*, began his acting career at the age of 15 at the Falcon, a club in Fetter Lane. Edwin soon became engaged at Manchester and later at Smock Alley, Dublin, in the fall of 1765 where he first appeared as Sir Philip Modelove in *A Bold Stroke for a Wife*. He joined the Bath company in 1768 and played there off and on until 1779. His first professional appearances in London were at the Haymarket in 1776. On 24 September 1779 at Covent Garden, where he became a chief attraction until his death in 1790, Edwin played Touchstone in *As You Like It*. He proved a talented comic actor who was a particular favorite with the audiences, known not only for his acting but also for his occasional songs "in character" and his *entr'acte* singing.

Elliston, Robert William (1774–1831), Bartholomew Bathos in *The Quadrupeds of Quedlinburgh* and Don Alvar in *Remorse*, was an actor, singer, manager, and playwright, and one of the key theatrical figures of the day. Trained for the clergy, he pursued a theatrical career instead, acting in the provinces, including Tate Wilkinson's York circuit. In 1796, he married, had his London debut at Haymarket on 25 June, and then acted at Covent Garden on 21 September. He was absent from London between 1797 and 1803; among other engagements at this time, he tried to open a theater in either Oxford or London. He was back at the Haymarket in 1803 and debuted at Drury Lane in 1804, where he remained through the 1808–9 season. In 1809, he purchased the Royal Circus, which he refitted and renamed the Surrey in 1810. He also purchased the Croyden and Manches-

ter theaters, as well as a book trade business; in 1812, he bought the Olympic Pavilion, and he also sought to buy Vauxhall Gardens and the Crow Street Theatre in Dublin. He rejoined Drury Lane from 1812 to 1815. In 1819, he realized one dream when he obtained the lesseeship of Drury Lane, but by 1826 he had lost £30,000 and had to return the theater to a committee of proprietors. Beyond his attempts at running a theater, Elliston was an important actor in comedies and melodramas; some felt he was a comic genius, with Leigh Hunt, for example, comparing him to Garrick. He also wrote a number of plays, including *The Venetian Outlaw* (1805).

Esten, Mrs. James, Harriet Pye, née Bennett, later Mrs. John Scott-Warring (1765?–1865), Miss Wooburn in *Every One Has His Fault*, was an actress, pianist, singer, and dancer. Harriett Pye Bennett was the daughter of Agnes Maria Bennett, an author of several popular novels. Harriet married James Esten, a lieutenant in the Royal Navy, in 1784. Issues with creditors sent him to France and then later to Santo Domingo. To support her children, Mrs. Esten turned to the stage. Her mother arranged for a meeting with Thomas Harris of Covent Garden who encouraged her to gain some experience in the provinces. She began her career at Bristol on 19 June 1786 as Alicia in *Jane Shore*. Mrs. Esten enjoyed success at Bath and Bristol. However, she did not get along with William Dimond, and thus she moved to Smock Alley, Dublin, in 1788–89. She was the first to play the *Forte-Piano* in the Edinburgh Theatre and throughout her career indulged her musical abilities whenever possible. Harris engaged Mrs. Esten at Covent Garden for the 1790–91 season, where she seems to have worked without a salary for the first year. While Harris at first did not engage her full-time, influential friends secured her a place by 1792; between her second and third season with Covent Garden she won a contract to manage the Edinburgh Theatre, a contract she later sold to Kemble. She ended her career very successfully at Edinburgh in 1802–03.

Eyre, Edmund John (1767–1816), the Manager in *The Quadrupeds of Quedlinburgh*, was an actor and playwright. He began as a solid actor in the provinces, which led him to the Drury Lane company from 1806 to 1811 before joining the theater in Edinburgh. His plays include *The Dreamer Awake* (Covent Garden, 1791), *The Maid of Normandy* (denied a license by Larpent but performed in Dublin and elsewhere), *The Vintagers* (Haymarket, 1809) and *High Life in the City* (Haymarket, 1811). He was one of the petitioners in 1810 seeking to open a new theater.

Farley, Charles (1771–1859), Timour in *Timour the Tartar*, began his career as a callboy at Covent Garden Theatre and went on to be an actor, singer, dancer, choreographer and playwright. He first acted at Covent Garden on 11 October 1784 at the age of 13. By 1800, he was an important figure in designing pantomimes (he even instructed Grimaldi) and ballets; the first original work wholly ascribed to him is *Raymond and Agnes; or, the Castle of Lindenbergh* (Covent Garden, 1797), an adaptation from Lewis's *The Monk*. He also acted in the summers at the Haymarket and was with Drury Lane from 1808 to 1814 and again during the 1821–22 season. Farley was primarily admired for his voice and his acting in melodramas; Timour was considered one of his best roles. He was also in charge of organizing the action for the play.

Farren, William (1754–1795), Lord Norland in *Every One Has His Fault*, was a journeyman actor. He was the son of a tallow chandler in Clerkenwell who spent much of his youth in London. There is some dispute about his initial apprenticeship(s), but after his father died he was apprenticed at the age of 18 to Richard Yates, an actor at Drury Lane. Initially, he worked with Yates in Birmingham and then made his debut at Drury Lane on 20 March 1775 as Jason in *Medea*. Farren continued at Drury Lane, playing primarily supporting roles, through 1783–84, but he desired bigger roles and more money. He broke with Drury Lane to join the company at Covent Garden where he had sometimes been called upon to act when some unforeseen circumstance left a part vacant. Farren remained at Covent Garden for a decade where he continued playing supporting roles and occasionally a major role until he died. Farren was not especially appreciated by the critics, who thought him dull.

Fawcett, John (1768–1837), Mr. Placid in *Every One Has His Fault* and Oglou in *Timour the Tartar*, was an actor, singer, playwright and stage manager. He was born into a theatrical family, but his parents sought to keep him from the stage; he ran away to join a Margate theatrical company under the name of Foote, then moved to Tunbridge Wells to act under his own name, where he came to the attention of the playwright Richard Cumberland who recommended him to Tate Wilkinson, manager of the important York circuit. Fawcett first tried to succeed as a tragedian, but his true talent lay in farce. In 1788, Fawcett married the actress Susan Moore; she died in 1797, and in 1806 Fawcett married the actress/singer Anne Gaudry. He joined the Covent Garden company for the 1791–92 season, where he rapidly became one of the most popular performers; he was also a mainstay of the summer season at the Haymarket. Fawcett weathered many storms at Covent Garden to become the treasurer and trustee of its retirement fund in 1808 and then stage manager from 1818 to 1828. He retired from the stage in 1830 to great applause. He was also a playwright, his most interesting piece being *Obi; or, Three Finger'd Jack* (Haymarket, 1800).

Fearon, James (1746–1789), Vasquez in *A Bold Stroke for a Husband*, lived an obscure life prior to his London debut in 1771, though he acted between 1768 and 1771 in Glasgow and in Edinburgh at the New Concert Hall and the Theatre Royal. He began his eighteen-year London career at the Haymarket Theatre on 17 May 1771, playing the part as Kitely in *Every Man in his Humour*, and remained with the theatre over the summer season. He then went on to play at the Crow Street Theatre, Dublin, at Cooper's Hall in King Street, and again at the Haymarket, playing a wide variety of roles, mostly in comedy and farce.

On 19 September 1774, Fearon played the Steward in *All's Well That Ends Well* in his first appearance at Covent Garden, where he would remain for 14 years.

Feron, Miss, Liska in *Timour the Tartar,* is perhaps **Elizabeth Feron (1793/95–1853)**, a singer and actress who was brought out at Vauxhall as a child. She performed in London, but by 1828 was playing at the Park Theatre, New York. She married the theatrical manager Joseph Glossop, moved to Italy, and then six years later returned to England as Madame Feron.

Field, Mr., Orasmin in *Timour the Tartar,* is perhaps **J. Field (fl. 1792?–1811?)**, a minor actor who may have performed in Dublin in 1792, at Chester in 1794, at the Haymarket in 1794, in Manchester in 1796, and at Plymouth in 1798. There was a J. Field at the Haymarket for the summers of 1803–5 who was also on the paylist at Covent Garden from 1803 to 1811.

Finn, Mr., the Waiter at Weimar in *The Quadrupeds of Quedlinburgh* and Punfunnidos in *Harlequin and Humpo,* is perhaps **Henry James William Finn (1787–1840)**, a comic actor, playwright, and son to George Finn, a retired officer of the British Navy; he was born in Nova Scotia and reared in New York. He perhaps attended Princeton but did not graduate. He studied law in New York and then visited England where he began to act; we know he worked at the Haymarket in small parts in 1811 and 1812. He appeared in Philadelphia in 1817 in his first known American performance. He debuted in New York in 1818. He returned to England in 1821, doing painting and provincial acting until he obtained a position at the Surrey Theatre. He returned to America and the Boston stage in 1822. He wrote several plays, including a successful melodrama, *Montgomery; or, The Falls of Montmorency* (1825). In 1825, he became a partner in Boston's Federal Street Theatre. He died when the steamboat *Lexington* burned in Long Island Sound.

Gibbs, Maria, née Logan, later the second Mrs. George Colman the Younger (b. 1770; fl. 1783–1844), Cecilia Muckinfield in *The Quadrupeds of Quedlinburgh,* appeared at the Haymarket as "A Very Young Lady" as early as 1783 and became part of the company at Palmer's ill-fated Royalty Theatre. In 1788, she was at Drury Lane with Palmer but then disappears for five years; she was perhaps blacklisted for her part in the attempt to create a rival to the patent theaters. With the Palmers restored to good graces after 1789, she returned to the Haymarket where she became a star, perhaps only second to Dorothy Jordan as a comedienne. In 1794, she returned to Drury Lane and then moved to Covent Garden; she would continue to alternate between the theaters throughout her career, with the summer Haymarket theater always providing her with her best venue. She may or may not have married someone named Gibbs; by 1795, she became Colman's lover and perhaps married him; they remained devoted throughout the rest of their lives.

Glover, Mrs. Samuel, Juliana, née Betteron (1779–1850), Matilda Pottingen in *The Quadrupeds of Quedlinburgh* and Alhadra in *Remorse,* was the daughter of an acting family who began performing early in life in Ireland and then on the York circuit. She had her London debut at Covent Garden on 12 October 1797 and was already felt to be a promising actress. Her abusive father is said to have sold her to Samuel Glover for £1000; in any event, she married him. In 1810, she moved to the Drury Lane company, where her performance as Alhadra—not a typical part for this comic actress—was widely praised. As she aged, her roles changed, but she could be seen performing a line of old women at the Covent Garden, Drury Lane, Haymarket, Lyceum, Strand, and Olympic theaters into the 1830s; she was, in fact, still on stage in the year of her death.

Grist, Harriet, later Mrs. Berry, then Mrs. Thomas Ludford Bellamy (c.1777–?), Edward in *Every One Has His Fault,* was the daughter of the actor Thomas Grist who worked in the provinces after leaving London in 1777. She began her career as a child actress. Her first known appearance was as Jenny Diver in *The Beggar's Opera* on 19 January 1792 at Edinburgh. She made her debut at Covent Garden on 11

October 1792 as Sophia in *The Road to Ruin*. She returned to Covent Garden for the 1793–94 season but disappears from the paylist in December to marry Mr. Berry. As Mrs. Berry, she performed at Richmond, Edinburgh, and Margate, finally making an appearance at the Haymarket in 1797. Afterwards she enjoyed some success in Ireland. In 1799, she married Thomas Ludford Bellamy, stage manager at the Crow Theatre and, later, proprietor of a theater in Manchester. After leaving Manchester, Mrs. Bellamy acted in Belfast where her husband was a proprietor of the Arthur Street Theatre. They both returned to London in 1807 where Mrs. Bellamy took an engagement at the Haymarket in 1808. Nothing is known of her after her husband's death, except that she claimed his estate.

Grove, Mr., Puddingfield in *The Quadrupeds of Quedlinburgh*, is perhaps the **Mr. Grove (fl. 1793–1803)** mentioned in Thomas Gilliland's *Dramatic Mirror* (1808).

Hartland, Mr., Harlequin in *Harlequin and Humpo*, is perhaps **Frank or Frederick Hartland (1783?–1852)**, who is listed in a single-word obituary as a pantomimist; there is a portrait of him in the Harvard Theatre Collection.

Hollingsworth, Thomas (1748–1814), Hassan in *Blue-Beard*, the son of Covent Garden house servants but raised by the actor Joseph Younger after his father's death in 1767, became an actor, singer, and dancer. While playing some parts as a youth, he is first mentioned in a performance at Covent Garden on 22 May 1773 as Daniel in *The Conscious Lovers*. From 1775 to 1787, he played at various provincial theaters, before joining Sheridan's Drury Lane. He left Drury Lane at the end of the 1803–4 season, playing at the Royal Circus, the Royalty, and the Surrey as well as in the provinces. A regular performer in pantomimes and in comic roles, he was never popular with the critics.

Jeffries, Mr., Octar in *Timour the Tartar*, is perhaps **Tom Jeffries (fl. 1787?–1822)**. There is a Mr. Jeffries who was a dancer at the Royal Circus as early as 1787, the "Young Jeffries" who came to be known as an equestrian, and the clown Jeffries who performed at Astley's in the early 1790s. There was a Jeffries on the Covent Garden paylist from 1804 until at least 1815; he was in the Drury Lane company at least from 1820 to 1822. Playbills for Astley's Amphitheatre and the Royal Circus emphasize their Mr. Jeffries' ability to perform fabulous equestrian feats, presumably put to good use in *Timour*.

Johnston, Mrs. Henry Erskine, the first, Nannette, née Parker (b. 1782), Zorilda in *Timour the Tartar*, was the daughter of a pantomime player and equestrian producer. She performed as Miss Parker at Sadler's Wells in 1793 and 1794 and at the Royal Circus in 1795. While at school in Edinburgh, where her father was proprietor of the Circus, she met and married (1796) the popular actor Henry Erskine Johnston. The couple went to Dublin in 1797; he joined the company at Covent Garden for the 1797–98 season. Mrs. Johnston played Ophelia to her husband's Hamlet at the Haymarket on 3 September 1798 and joined the Covent Garden company beginning with the 1798–99 season. She separated from her husband in 1811 to live with Henry Harris, the manager of Covent Garden; she retired from the stage when she and Harris broke in 1814. She was known as a stunningly beautiful woman, a pleasing singer, a talented comedienne, and a fine actress of tragedy. The role of Zorilda enabled her to draw upon the equestrian skills she had learned from her father.

Kelly, Michael (1762–1826), Selim in *Blue-Beard* as well as the composer of the music, was an important composer and musical director as well as an actor, singer, and manager. Born in Dublin where he had his first performances as a singer, he traveled to Italy and Vienna to study music, where he met Hayden, worked with Gluck, and befriended Mozart. He created the roles of Basilio and Don Curzio in Mozart's *Le nozze di Figaro*. He made his London debut at Drury Lane on 20 April 1787 in *A School for Fathers*. He lived with Mrs. Anna Maria Crouch from

1785 until her death in 1805. Kelly frequently wrote music for Drury Lane (including for Lewis' *Castle Spectre* and Baillie's *De Monfort*) and performed there and at the opera house, the King's Theatre. In the early 1790s, his radical tendencies and interest in French theater took him to Paris on several occasions. From 1794 on, he was the stage manager at the King's Theatre.

Kirby, Mr., Dumpo and then Clown in *Harlequin and Humpo*, is perhaps **James Kirby (d. 1826)**, who made his debut in London at the Royalty Theatre. He was known for playing the part of Clown in New York, where he debuted at the Broadway Circus. He drowned in Brooklyn in 1826.

King, Matthew Peter (1773–1823), the composer for *Timour the Tartar* and perhaps Abdalec, was a pianist and composer who wrote music for melodramas, farces, and comic operas at Covent Garden, Drury Lane, the Sans Souci, and the Lyceum. He played one of his own piano compositions at Covent Garden on 16 May 1793 after the mainpiece. There is some indication that he performed on stage when his music was being sung, so he may have had a part in *Timour*.

Lewis, William Thomas (c. 1746–1811), Don Julio in *A Bold Stroke for a Husband* and Sir Robert Ramble in *Everyone Has His Fault*, was born in Ormskirk, Lancashire. He made his first recorded stage appearance in 1751–52 as the page Robin in *The Merry Wives of Windsor*. He acted with the Smock Alley Theatre and the Crow Street Theatre in Dublin, before he was noticed by Richard Cumberland as Belcour in *The West Indian* at the Capel Street Theatre. While Cumberland recommended Lewis to Garrick, it was George Colman who hired him for Covent Garden, where he acted for 35 consecutive seasons, playing at least 194 parts and creating 85 original roles in diverse genres. Between 1782 and 1803, Lewis became the acting manager or deputy of Covent Garden and continued acting mostly in roles of mannered comedy and farce. After giving his farewell performance on 29 May 1809 as Roger in *The Ghost* and as the Copper Captain in *Rule a Wife*

and Have a Wife, Lewis affectionately told the audience that after 36 years on the London stage, he could not remember having "once fallen under your displeasure."

Liston, John (1776?–1846), Rogero in *The Quadrupeds of Quedlinburgh*, was a popular comic actor known particularly for playing old men and bumpkins. He had made a name for himself in the provinces, particularly on the York circuit, and was brought to London by Colman to play at the Haymarket in 1805 where he would act almost every summer until 1830; he joined Covent Garden in 1806, and he continued to play there until 1822 (when he moved to Drury Lane before joining Madame Vestris at the Olympic). Beloved by everyone from Hazlitt and Hunt to George IV, he created a number of memorable roles including "Paul Pry" and was the highest paid comedian of his day.

Liston, Mrs. John, née Tyer (d. 1854), Liska in *Timour the Tartar*, married the popular comic actor John Liston in 1807; they performed at Covent Garden until 1822, when she retired from the stage. She possessed a good ballad voice, according to Leigh Hunt.

Maddocks, Walter (d. 1823), 2nd slave in *Blue-Beard*, was an actor and singer who moved from Norwich to Liverpool, Manchester, and Birmingham before he came to Drury Lane in 1789. He played there for three decades as a tenor chorus singer and minor actor. His wife (d. 1834) played a female peasant in *Blue-Beard*; they had been together in Norwich, but she joined the company at Drury Lane in 1794.

Mallinson, Mr., Beefington in *The Quadrupeds of Quedlinburgh*, is perhaps **Joseph Mallinson (fl. 1811)**, who was an actor in London at the time of this performance.

Martin, Mr., Doctor Pottingen in *The Quadrupeds of Quedlinburgh*, is perhaps **Mr. Martin (fl. 1791–96)**, who was at the Haymarket at least in 1791 and 1796.

Mattocks, Mrs. George, Isabella, née Hallam (1746–1826), Olivia in *A Bold Stroke for a Husband* and Mrs. Placid in *Every One Has His Fault*, was descended from a long line of actors and actresses and born into a family closely connected with the Rich family of Covent Garden Theatre. While her debut occurred at Covent Garden on 2 October 1752, in the children's role as the Duke of York in *Richard III*, Isabella made her first "adult" appearance at Covent Garden when she was 15 as Juliet in *Romeo and Juliet*. Although she became renowned for her comic ability, she also played a number of tragic roles and was known as an excellent singer in oratorios, concerts, and comic operas. Although she was a favorite of the audiences, critical opinion of her talents frequently varied until late in her career when she won the admiration of such critics as Leigh Hunt and James Boaden.

Morris, Catherine, later Mrs. George Colman the first (fl. 1777–1784), Marcella in *A Bold Stroke for a Husband*, appeared first as a "Lilliputian" in Garrick's *Lilliput*. Although her acting career was short, it was active, performing over 60 parts in tragedy, comedy and comic opera at both the Haymarket and Covent Garden before 1784. She married the playwright and manager George Colman the Younger, from whom she later separated due to his affair with the actress Maria Gibbs. Nothing is known about her life prior to or following her acting career.

Munden, Joseph Shepherd (1758–1833), Mr. Harmony in *Every One Has His Fault* and Casimere in *The Quadrupeds of Quedlinburgh*, an actor, singer, and manager, was born in Brook's Market, Leather Lane, Holborn. Initially, he was apprenticed to an apothecary but eventually moved on to work for a lawyer. His first appearance on stage occurred in 1775 at either Rochdale or Liverpool. He stayed on at Liverpool, acting supernumerary roles and otherwise supporting himself as a scrivener. Munden's first appearance in London was at the Haymarket Theatre in 1779. After making a few appearances, he withdrew to the provinces where he developed a reputation as a player of comic pieces. At this time, he also obtained some shares in the Austin & Whitlock Company, but he seems to have tired of management and by 1790 was engaged at Covent Garden. Most of Munden's roles were those connected with comic pieces of the day. He received a good deal of notice, with Byron praising his role as Polonius in *Hamlet* and Lamb writing of his comic countenance and ludicrous gestures. A quarrel with the management at Covent Garden ended his career there. By 1813, he was engaged by Drury Lane where he spent the final years of his career. He ended his life as a poor, embittered recluse, having suffered financial losses in his investments.

Noble, Mr., the Duke of Saxe Weimar in *The Quadrupeds of Quedlinburgh*, is perhaps **William Noble (fl. 1799–1813)**, an actor attached to the Haymarket from 1804 until at least 1809 but probably until 1812 when he appears in Edinburgh. He had previously acted in the provinces and was part of a group James Wilson had gathered in 1799 to play in a company in Richmond.

Palmer, Jack (also known as "Plausible Jack") (1744–1798), Abomelique in *Blue-Beard*, was one of the period's most popular and versatile actors and singers. The son of Robert Palmer, a minor functionary at Drury Lane, he made his debut at the Haymarket on 28 April 1762 in *The Orators*, and then played briefly at Drury Lane and in the provinces before joining the company at Drury Lane in 1766–67. Taking over the parts of "Gentleman John" Palmer (no relation), he went on to command over 350 different roles. His offstage efforts were not as successful: his marriage was tumultuous and his attempt at forming a fourth major London theater, the Royalty, was blocked by the patent theaters and resulted in a debt from which Palmer never recovered. He died on stage (2 August 1798) from an attack of apoplexy during the fourth act of Kotzebue's *The Stranger*.

Platt, Miss or Mrs. S. J. (1743–1800), Inis in *A Bold Stroke for a Husband*, was the daughter of Bartholomew Platt, a singer, and a mother who was also a performer. At age five, Miss Platt spoke a prologue at Phillips's New Theatre on Bowling Green, Southwark. While she appeared once again in 1763, playing Corinna in *The Citizen* at the Haymarket

Theatre on 18, 22, and 29 July, she was afterwards absent for five more years until 1768 when she joined the Drury Lane company. Having borne a child out of wedlock, she took the name of Mrs. Platt. In addition to working with the Drury Lane Theatre, Miss Platt also acted at the Haymarket Theatre during her 37-year adult acting career. She acted in farce and Shakespearean comedy and was a very versatile actress, singing, playing in pantomime, and retaining younger roles until her death at age 57.

Poole, Miss, Aquila in *Harlequin and Humpo*, cannot be identified. One is tempted to identify her with **Maria Dickons, née Poole (1770–1833)**, who was known for her voice and thus could have played this role; she was also at Drury Lane around this time, but she was then performing under her married name (she had married in 1800). Maria Dickons debuted at Covent Garden in 1793 before moving to the provinces and then retiring upon her marriage. Her husband's financial difficulties, however, brought her back to Covent Garden in 1807 and then to Drury Lane in 1811. She left England for Paris with Mrs. Catalani in 1816, and then had some success in Italy, before returning to London in 1818. She retired from the stage in 1820.

Pope, Alexander (1762–1835), Mr. Irwin in *Every One Has His Fault* and Marquis Valdez in *Remorse*, actor and playwright, was trained as a portrait painter in Ireland where he also did some acting. He debuted at Covent Garden on 8 January 1785. He married the actress Elizabeth Younge in 1785. A key repertory actor, Pope was mostly at Covent Garden until being dismissed after the 1808–9 season. He joined Drury Lane in 1812 and stayed there through the 1826–27 season. Leigh Hunt found Pope to be an actor "without face, expression, or delivery," a judgment oftentimes echoed by other critics.

Pope, Mrs. Alexander the first, Elizabeth, née Younge (c. 1740–1797), Lady Eleanor Irwin in *Every One Has His Fault*, was one of the more powerful actresses of her day. Little is known of Mrs. Pope's youth. Purportedly, she came from a good family and was well educated. Her parents died early in her life. At some point she came into contact with Garrick, who needed a woman with enough talent to challenge Mrs. Barry. Mrs. Pope began her career at Drury Lane on 22 October 1768 as Imogen in *Cymbeline*. After the 1769–70 season, she failed to come to terms with Garrick and spent the following season at the Capel Street Theatre in Dublin where she enjoyed considerable success. In 1771 she returned to Drury Lane where she remained engaged for eight seasons and fully established herself as a leading actress in both comedy and tragedy. In 1779, again because of salary disputes, she moved on, this time to Covent Garden where she spent the remainder of her career. Mrs. Pope married Alexander Pope in 1785. She was the only woman to become an honorary member of the "School of Garrick" and died with an estate worth £7,000.

Powell, John (1755–1836), Monviedro in *Remorse*, got his start as an actor in the provinces, including Bath where he met and married his wife around 1775. He had his Drury Lane debut on 20 October 1798 and remained with the theater until 1828. He died in Canada in 1836.

Powell, Sparks (d. 1798), Hammond in *Every One Has His Fault*, was an actor, singer, and manager. Powell was reportedly the son of a cook of George III. As a young man he was at sea for several years and thereafter a traveler in Asia and the East Indies. In 1776 he joined Fox's company at Brighton; by 1782, Powell was engaged at Bath and continued there and at Bristol for six years, but was discharged from Bath for acting at Salisbury without permission. Powell appeared at Covent Garden on 26 April 1788 for a benefit and a year later was engaged by Harris to fill the roles of old men in comedies. He played some 47 parts during his first year at Covent Garden, a testament to the experience he must have had in the provinces. Powell remained at Covent Garden for another ten years. He was then hired by Cobb, the proprietor at Brighton, to manage that theater. The theater lost £200 that season and Powell returned to

Covent Garden. While playing a cottager at Covent Garden in 1798, Powell suddenly took ill and died the next day.

Quick, John (1748–1831), Don Caesar in *A Bold Stroke for a Husband* and Mr. Solus in *Every One Has His Fault*, began his acting career in the provinces in Kent and Surrey at the age of 12, and, as early as age 14, he appeared at Croydon as Altamount in *The Fair Penitent*. His London debut on 18 June 1766 as Folly in *The Minor* and Jasper in *Miss in Her Teens* led to his employment first at the Haymarket and later with Covent Garden. At Covent Garden, Quick acted in modest roles until 1773, when he played Tony Lumpkin in the premiere of *She Stoops to Conquer*, a performance that received much critical acclaim. While working at Covent Garden for 31 consecutive years, Quick, known best for his comedic ability, acted in more than 70 original roles, and eventually became one of the highest paid performers in the Covent Garden company.

Rae, Alexander (1782–1820), Ordonio in *Remorse*, was originally trained to join the East India Company. In 1806, he joined the theater at Bath, having been recommended by Richard Cumberland. His London premiere was at the Haymarket on 9 June 1806 as Octavian in *The Mountaineers*. He then joined the Liverpool company for four years. On 14 November 1812, he appeared at Drury Lane in his favorite part, Hamlet. After a stint as stage manager for Drury Lane, he left to manage the Royalty Theatre in 1820, but the attempt failed and he died later that year. Known for his good looks and elegance, he was sometimes criticized for his voice and lack of energy.

Robinson, Mrs. Thomas, Mary, née Darby (1758–1800), Victoria in *A Bold Stroke for a Husband*, was a famous actress, mistress, and one of the most important poets of the period. She was introduced at the age of 15 to David Garrick, then in his final season as an actor at the Drury Lane Theatre, who offered to train her and allow her to play Cordelia in his own *Lear*. Mary, however, given her family's ruinous financial situation, was forced to marry that year, and her husband proved to be a gambler and womanizer. In order to support herself and her daughter, she finally made her debut on 10 December 1776 when she, after extensive coaching by Garrick, played Juliet at the Drury Lane Theatre. She was an immediate hit. Her strong performance as Perdita in *Florizel and Perdita*, Garrick's adaptation of Shakespeare's *The Winter's Tale*, won her the nickname "Perdita" Robinson and the admiration of the Prince of Wales. She became his mistress in 1779, which opened her to attacks, particularly after he abandoned her the next year. She was saved from financial ruin by Charles James Fox, and became involved with Colonel Banastre Tarleton, a decorated and controversial officer during the American revolutionary war. The scandal and a six-month excursion to Paris ended her reign at Drury Lane; when she returned to the stage for the 1782–83 season it was at Covent Garden. Paralyzed from the waist down by a badly handled miscarriage in 1783, she left the stage (returning briefly in 1787 at Edinburgh) and concentrated on her writing, which included a poetical correspondence as "Laura" and "Laura Maria" with Robert Merry's "Della Crusca"; several collections of poetry, including *Poems* (1791), *Sappho and Phaon* (1796), and *Lyrical Tales* (1800); eight novels, including *Hubert De Sevrac* (1796), and a formidable body of non-fiction prose, including essays supporting the French Revolution, *Thoughts on the Condition of Women and on the Injustice of Mental Insubordination* (1799), and *Memoirs of the Late Mrs. Robinson, written by Herself (1801)*.

Sedgwick, Thomas (d. 1803), 2d Spahi in *Blue-Beard*, actor and singer, was an ironmonger until he was discovered to be a fine singer; he debuted at Drury Lane on 25 October 1787 where he would play for the rest of his career, except during the short life of the Royalty where he joined "Plausible Jack" Palmer.

Smith, Miss Sarah, later Mrs. Sarah Bartley, also Miss Williamson and Miss O'Shaughnessy (1783/5–1850), Teresa in *Remorse*, was in the brief period between the retirement of Mrs. Siddons in 1812 and the arrival in London of Eliza O'Neill in 1814 considered to be the most promising tragic actress on the London stage. Born in 1783 or 1785, she claimed her father was a country actor named Williamson and that her mother was the daughter of General Dillon of Galway. Others claimed that her name was O'Shaughnessy and that her parents were Irish. In any event, she adopted the name of Smith after her mother married a second time in 1793. She probably debuted in Liverpool before joining the company in Edinburgh; she then desired to retire from the stage. However, she joined Tate Wilkinson's company on the York circuit until his death in 1803 when she went to Birmingham and then Bath. Harris engaged her for Covent Garden on 2 October 1805. Covent Garden wanted to end her engagement as she covered the same parts as Mrs. Siddons. After a triumph in Dublin in 1808–9 where she recited a monologue written for her by Thomas Moore, she returned to London and joined Drury Lane. On 23 August 1814 she married George Bartley, a comic actor. In 1818, she and her husband successfully toured America; she returned to England in 1820 but played infrequently thereafter.

Stevens, William, stage name of William Catstevens (d. 1790), Pedro in *A Bold Stroke for a Husband*, is first heard of performing at the Haymarket Theatre on 24 May 1775 as Robin in *Cross Purposes*. He acted mostly minor comedic roles at both Covent Garden and the Haymarket Theatre. Around 1786, Stevens became engaged with the Richmond Theatre, which he managed during the summers until 1788.

Suett, Richard (1758?–1805), Ibrahim in *Blue-Beard*, an actor, singer, and music composer, began his career as "Master Suett," singing in various choirs and at Renelagh Gardens and Marylebone Gardens. He received his first notice for a performance in a musical entertainment at the Grotto Gardens on 22 June 1771. He then joined Tate Wilkinson's York circuit in 1771 and the Drury Lane company in 1780, where he remained for the rest of his career, also being engaged by the Haymarket for the summer sea-

sons. His musical training won him parts in comic operas, the majority of his roles being in low comedy and most frequently that of a clown or drunkard. In 1781, he married Louisa Margarette West, though they later separated. He was known for his extensive collection of wigs and also for his problems with alcohol.

Thompson, James (fl. 1770–1812?), the Porter in *Every One Has His Fault*, was a minor actor, singer, and dancer. Not much is known of Thompson except for the fact that he was on the boards at Covent Garden and that he did not play parts of much consequence: officers, servants, villagers, and parts with no names. He rarely strayed from Covent Garden, though he occasionally took a part at Haymarket.

Treby, Mr., Bermeddin in *Timour the Tartar*, is perhaps **James Treby,** an actor about which little is known. He was at Covent Garden at least during 1815–16; Hazlitt disliked him and criticized him in *The Examiner* (29 October 1815, 21 January 1816).

Trueman, Mr. (fl. 1793–1817), 5th Spahi in *Blue-Beard*, is first mentioned in the chorus of witches and spirits for Kemble's inaugural production of *Macbeth* at Drury Lane on 21 May 1794. He played at the Haymarket in the summers and remained with Drury Lane until Kemble left for Covent Garden in 1803–4. Trueman would later depart for Edinburgh where he acted at least until 1816–1817. He mainly played minor parts, though sometimes filling in larger roles when a regular performer was sick.

Valency, Miss, Columbine in *Harlequin and Humpo*, has not been identified beyond the fact that there is a contemporary portrait of her in the Harvard Theatre Collection.

Wallack, William (c. 1760–1850), Naomi in *Remorse*, began performing at Astley's Amphitheatre in 1785. He was in Edinburgh, at both a circus and the Theatre Royal, in 1792 and then in Dublin during 1795–96. He returned to Astley's in 1796 and moved to the Royal Circus in the early 1800s. Between 1809 and 1818, he was on the paylist at Drury Lane.

Wathen, George (1762–1849), 3rd Spahi in *Blue-Beard*, was an actor, singer, and stage manager whose theatrical career began with amateur performances while in the army and then at Dublin's Crow Street Theatre. He debuted at the Haymarket in 1793 and then Drury Lane in 1795. Wathen was seen on the various London stages, although his career seems to have been marked by heated disagreements with other actors and occasional legal troubles.

Webb, Alexander (d. 1823), 1st Slave in *Blue-Beard*, was discovered by Kemble in Liverpool in 1788. He played at the Haymarket and then had his Drury Lane debut during the 1789–90 season. Known for his dependability, he remained at Drury Lane until 1812, playing more than one hundred minor roles and walk-on parts.

Webb, Mrs. [Richard?], née Child, formerly Mrs. [George?] **Day** (d. 1793), Miss Spinster in *Every One Has His Fault*, made her debut at Norwich on 17 March 1764 and seems to have married Mr. Day by the end of the 1760s. During the 1772–73 season, Mrs. Day was at the Edinburgh Theatre Royal acting comic roles. By 1774, she had become Mrs. Webb and was acting regularly in Edinburgh. She stayed in Edinburgh, adding to her repertoire, until the elder George Colman gave her a summer contract to act at the Haymarket in 1778. By the fall of 1779, she was on Colman's list at Covent Garden where she stayed until the end of her career—spending her summers mainly at the Haymarket, but ultimately performing in most of the theatres of Scotland, Ireland, and England. Mrs. Webb was notoriously large, a fact that Gillray could not help but caricature in his portrait of her as Cowslip. She played tragic roles successfully and also had a reportedly good voice, but her career was predominated by roles that fit her impressive size and her ability to play off her external appearance in comic and farcical pieces. She died of a stroke at the age of 56.

West, Mr., Humpo in *Harlequin and Humpo*, is perhaps **William West** (1796?–1888), a comedian and musical composer born to a father with Drury Lane connections. After studying music, West appeared at the Haymarket as Tom Thumb in 1805. He played various small parts after that at Drury Lane. He moved to Edinburgh in 1814 with Miss Cooke (who played in *The Students of Salamanca* opposite *Remorse* and *Harlequin and Humpo*), whom he married in 1815. He also played in Bath and Bristol before returning to London where his wife joined the company at Drury Lane in 1818 as a major tragic actress of the day. His songs were quite popular.

Whitfield, John (1752–1814), Don Garcia in *A Bold Stroke for a Husband*, was possibly the son of Covent Garden tailor and wardrobe keeper Robert Whitfield. There is much speculation surrounding just how John Whitfield came to be an actor. Although it seems likely that he acted prior to the occasion, the 26 September 1774 Covent Garden playbill listing "Mr. Whitefield" as Trueman in *George Barnwell* is Whitfield's earliest recorded performance. While he was never considered a top actor, he played in over 200 parts at both Drury Lane and Covent Garden and became known for his comedic abilities.

Whitfield, Mrs. John, Mary, née Lane (d. 1795), Laura in *A Bold Stroke for a Husband*, may have been an actress before becoming the wife of actor John Whitfield, but records of her acting exist only following her marriage. She acted in Leicester and Norwich before arriving in London in 1774 to begin her career at Covent Garden, Drury Lane, and Haymarket. Although she mostly acted in comedic roles, Mrs. Whitfield's repertoire was diverse, including roles in tragedy and Shakespeare as well as parts as young heroines of sentimental comedy and coquettish chambermaids.

Wilson, Richard (1744–1796), Gasper in *A Bold Stroke for a Husband*, was first a minor actor in small companies in Scotland and the North of England who began acting professionally around 1770. We know little of his roles before 23 November 1772 when he played King Lear at the Theatre Royal, Edinburgh. After becoming favored in Edinburgh for his ability to act low comedy, Wilson joined Covent Garden, debuting as Grub in *Cross Purposes* on 9 October 1775. From that time on, he worked at the Covent Garden Theatre and the Haymarket Theatre, becoming renowned for his ability to play old men in comedy. Wilson's career was cut short, however, when his debts caught up with him and he was subsequently imprisoned at King's Bench around 1795.

Wilson, Mrs. Richard the Second, Sarah Maria, née Adcock, formerly Mrs. Weston (1752–1786), Minette in *A Bold Stroke for a Husband*, was the supposed daughter of Drury Lane actor William Adcock who began her career as a child at fairs and in small towns giving her "Lecture of Hearts." Premiering at age twelve at the Theatre Royal, Dublin, she continued traveling as an actor with her parents until 1773 when she was married. After acting at Edinburgh in a number of roles and after leaving her husband in 1775, Sarah joined with the actor Richard Wilson and began her career at the Haymarket and Covent Garden, a career that ended in 1785. Known as a satisfactory actress with a great deal of possibility, it was felt she never polished her art.

Wroughton, Richard (1748–1822), Don Carlos in *A Bold Stroke for a Husband*, made his debut on 24 October 1768 at the Covent Garden Theatre as Zaphna in *Mahomet*. After continuing as an actor at Covent Garden for 15 seasons, he was dismissed after striking the manager of the theater, William Thomas Lewis, during a quarrel. While an actor with Covent Garden and during his subsequent employment with the Drury Lane Theatre, Wroughton managed Sadler's Wells and worked to establish a third patent theater in London, a patent that was never granted. In his 37 years on the London stage, Wroughton acted in over 200 major roles, many of them as rakes and beaux in sentimental comedy. He was more a favorite of audiences than of critics.

Suggested Readings

Backscheider, Paula R. Introduction. *The Plays of Elizabeth Inchbald*. New York: Garland, 1980.

——. "Reflections on the Importance of Romantic Drama." *Texas Studies in Literature and Language* 41.4 (1999): 311–29.

——. *Spectacular Politics: Theatrical Power and Mass Culture in Early Modern England*. Baltimore: Johns Hopkins University Press, 1993.

Baer, Marc. *Theatre and Disorder in Late Georgian London*. Oxford: Clarendon Press, 1992.

Baines, Paul, and Edward Burns, eds. *Five Romantic Plays, 1768–1821*. Oxford and New York: Oxford University Press, 2000.

Bate, Jonathan. *Shakespeare and the English Romantic Imagination*. Oxford: Clarendon Press; New York: Oxford University Press, 1986.

——. *Shakespearean Constitutions: Politics, Theatre, Criticism 1730–1830*. Oxford: Clarendon Press; New York: Oxford University Press, 1989.

Booth, Michael. *English Melodrama*. London: Jenkins, 1965.

Brooks, Peter. *The Melodramatic Imagination*. New Haven: Yale University Press, 1976.

Bugajski, Ken A. "Joanna Baillie: An Annotated Bibliography." *Romanticism On the Net* 12 (November 1998). <http://users.ox.ac.uk/~scat0385/bwpbaillie.html>.

Burroughs, Catherine B. *Closet Stages: Joanna Baillie and the Theater Theory of British Romantic Women Writers*. Philadelphia: University of Pennsylvania Press, 1997.

——. "Teaching the Theory and Practice of Women's Dramaturgy." *Romanticism On the Net* 12 (November 1998). <http://users.ox.ac.uk/~scat0385/bwpteaching.html>.

——, ed. *Women in British Romantic Theatre: Drama, Performance, and Society, 1790–1840*. Cambridge: Cambridge University Press, 2000.

Burwick, Frederick. *Illusion and the Drama: Critical Theory of the Enlightenment and Romantic Era*. University Park: Pennsylvania State University Press, 1991.

Carhart, Margaret. *The Life and Work of Joanna Baillie*. New Haven: Yale University Press, 1923; rpt. Archon, 1970.

Carlson, Julie A. "Coming After: Shelley's Proserpine." *Texas Studies in Literature and Language* 41.4 (1999): 351–72.

——. "Forever Young: Master Betty and the Queer Stage of Youth in English Romanticism." *SAQ* 95.3 (Summer 1996): 575–602.

——. *In the Theater of Romanticism: Coleridge, Nationalism, Women*. Cambridge: Cambridge University Press, 1994.

——. "Trying Sheridan's *Pizarro*." *Texas Studies in Literature and Language* 38.3–4 (1996): 359–78.

Carney, Sean. "The Passion of Joanna Baillie: Playwright as Martyr." *Theatre Journal* 52 (2000): 227–52.

Cave, Richard, ed. *The Romantic Theatre: An International Symposium*. Gerrards Cross, Buckinghamshire: Collin Smythe, 1986.

Conolly, Leonard W. *The Censorship of the English Drama 1737–1824*. San Marino: Huntington Library, 1976.

Cox, Jeffrey N. "The French Revolution in the English Theatre." *History & Myth: Essays on English Romantic Literature*. Ed. Stephen C. Behrendt. Detroit: Wayne State University Press, 1990. 33–52.

——. "Genre and Ideology in the Anti-Revolutionary Drama of the 1790s." *ELH* 58 (1991): 579–610.

——. "The Ideological Tack of Nautical Melodrama." *Melodrama: The Cultural Emergence of a Genre*. Ed. Michael Hays and Anastasia Nikolopoulou (New York: St. Martin's Press, 1996). 167–89.

——. *In the Shadows of Romance: Romantic Tragic Drama in Germany, England, and France*. Athens: Ohio University Press, 1987.

——, ed. *Seven Gothic Dramas 1789–1825*. Athens: Ohio University Press, 1994.

——, ed. *Slavery, Abolition, and Emancipation in the British Romantic Period*. Volume 5: *The Drama*. London: Pickering & Chatto, 1999.

——. "Spots of Time: The Structure of the Dramatic Evening in the Theater of Romanticism." *Texas Studies in Literature and Language* 41.4 (1999): 403–25.

——. "Staging Hope: Genre, Myth, and Ideology in the Dramas of the Hunt Circle." *Texas Studies in Literature and Language* 38.3–4 (1996): 245–64.

Crochunis, Thomas C. "Electronic Editing of Women's Theater Materials: Purposes, Contexts, and Questions." *British Women Playwrights around 1800.* <http://www-sul.stanford.edu/mirrors/romnet/wp1800/cro1.html>.

——. "The Function of the Dramatic Closet at the Present Time." *Romanticism On the Net* 12 (November 1998). <http://users.ox.ac.uk/~scat0385/bwpcro.html>.

——, ed. *Joanna Baillie, Romantic Dramatist: Critical Essays.* Routledge, forthcoming.

——. "The Smell of the Greasepaint, the Roar of the Crowd, the Crinkle of the Archive's Paper." *British Women Playwrights around 1800.* <http://www-sul.stanford.edu/mirrors/romnet/wp1800/newey2.html>.

——. "The Theatre of Britain, 1789–1832: Recent Scholarship on Post-Revolutionary Performance and Politics." *Nineteenth-Century Theatre* 24.1 (1996): 42–55.

——, and Michael Eberle-Sinatra. "Editing Electronically Women Playwrights of the Romantic Period." *British Women Playwrights around 1800.* <http://www-sul.stanford.edu/mirrors/romnet/wp1800/nassr99.html>.

Cross, Gilbert. *New Week — East Lynne.* Lewisburg: Bucknell University Press, 1997.

Curran, Stuart. *Shelley's "The Cenci": Scorpions Ringed with Fire.* Princeton: Princeton University Press, 1970.

Davis, Tracy C. *Actresses as Working Women: Their Social Identity in Victorian Culture.* London: Routledge, 1991.

——. *The Economics of the British Stage, 1800–1914.* Cambridge: Cambridge University Press, 2000.

——. "'Reading Shakespeare by Flashes of Lightning': Challenging the Foundations of Romantic Acting Theory." *ELH* 62.4 (1995 Winter): 933–54.

——. "The Sociable Playwright and Representative Citizen." *Romanticism On the Net* 12 (November 1998). <http://users.ox.ac.uk/~scat0385/bwpcitizen.html>.

——, and Ellen Donkin, eds. *Women and Playwriting in Nineteenth-Century Britain.* Cambridge: Cambridge University Press, 1999.

Donkin, Ellen. *Getting into the Act: Women Playwrights in London 1776–1829.* London: Routledge, 1995.

Donohue, Joseph W., Jr. *Dramatic Character in the English Romantic Age.* Princeton: Princeton University Press, 1970.

——. *Theatre in the Age of Kean.* Totowa, NJ: Rowman and Littlefield, 1975.

Dowd, Maureen A. "'By the Delicate Hand of a Female': Melodramatic Mania and Joanna Baillie's Spectacular Tragedies." *European Romantic Review* 9.4 (1998 Fall): 469–500.

Evans, Bertrand. *Gothic Drama from Walpole to Shelley.* Berkeley and Los Angeles: University of California Press, 1947.

Finberg, Melinda C. Introduction. *Eighteenth-Century Women Dramatists.* Oxford and New York: Oxford University Press, 2001.

Finkel, Alicia. *Romantic Stages: Set and Costume Design in Victorian England.* London: McFarland, 1996.

Fletcher, Richard M. *English Romantic Drama 1795–1843: A Critical History.* New York: Exposition, 1966.

Forry, Steven Earl. *Hideous Progenies: Dramatizations of "Frankenstein" from Mary Shelley to the Present.* Philadelphia: University of Pennsylvania Press, 1990.

Franceschina, John, ed. *Sisters of Gore: Seven Gothic Melodramas by British Women, 1790–1843.* New York: Garland, 1997.

Friedman-Romell, Beth H. "Duelling Citizenships: Scottish Patriotism v. British Nationalism in Joanna Baillie's *The Family Legend.*" *Nineteenth-Century Theatre* 26 (1998): 25–49.

Gamer, Michael. "Authors in Effect: Lewis, Scott, and the Gothic Drama." *ELH* 66.4 (1999 Winter): 831–61.

——. "National Supernaturalism: Joanna Baillie, Germany, and the Gothic Drama." *Theatre Survey* 38.2 (1997): 49–88.

——. *Romanticism and the Gothic: Genre, Reception, and Canon Formation.* Cambridge: Cambridge University Press, 2000.

Gaull, Marilyn. "Romantic Theatre." *The Wordsworth Circle* 14 (1983): 255–63.

Gillespie, Gerald, ed. *Romantic Drama*. Amsterdam: Benjamins, 1994.

Gleckner, Robert, and Bernard Beatty. *The Plays of Lord Byron: Critical Essays*. Liverpool: Liverpool University Press, 1997.

Hadley, Elaine. "Home as Abroad: Orientalism and Occidentalism in Early English Stage Melodrama." *Texas Studies in Literature and Language* 41.4 (1999): 330–50.

——. *Melodramatic Tactics: Theatricalized Dissent in the English Marketplace, 1800–1885*. Stanford: Stanford University Press, 1995.

Hanley, Keith, and Amanda Gilroy. Introduction. *Joanna Baillie: A Selection of Plays and Poems*. London and Brookfield, VT: Pickering & Chatto, 1997.

Heller, Janet Ruth. *Coleridge, Lamb, Hazlitt, and the Reader of Drama*. Columbia: University of Missouri Press, 1990.

Henderson, Andrea. "Passion and Fashion in Joanna Baillie's 'Introductory Discourse'." *PMLA* 112.2 (1997): 198–213.

Highfill, Philip H., Jr., Kalman A. Burnim, and Edward A. Langhans. *A Biographical Dictionary of Actors, Actresses, Musicians, Dancers, Managers & Other Stage Personnel in London, 1660–1800*. 16 vols. Carbondale: Southern Illinois University Press, 1975.

Hoagwood, Terence Allan, and Daniel P. Watkins, eds. *British Romantic Drama: Historical and Critical Essays*. London: Associated University Presses, 1998.

Hume, Robert D., ed. *The London Theatre World, 1660–1800*. Carbondale: Southern Illinois University Press, 1980.

——. *The Rakish Stage: Studies in English Drama 1660–1800*. Carbondale: Southern Illinois University Press, 1983.

Jewett, William. *Fatal Autonomy: Romantic Drama and the Rhetoric of Agency*. Ithaca: Cornell University Press, 1997.

Kucich, Greg. "Staging History: Teaching Romantic Intersections of Drama, History, and Gender." *Approaches to Teaching British Women Poets of the Romantic Period*. Ed. Stephen C. Behrendt and Harriet Kramer Linkin. New York: Modern Language Association of America. 89–96.

Lansdown, Richard. *Byron's Historical Dramas*. Oxford: Clarendon Press; New York: Oxford University Press, 1992.

Leacroft, Richard. *The Development of the English Playhouse*. London: Methuen, 1988.

Link, Frederick M. Introduction. *The Plays of Hannah Cowley*. New York: Garland, 1979.

Macdonald, D. L. *Monk Lewis: A Critical Biography*. Toronto: University of Toronto Press, 2000.

MacMillan, Douglas. *Catalogue of the Larpent Plays in the Huntington Library*. San Marino, CA: Huntington Library, 1939.

Mann, David, Susan Garland Mann, and Camille Garnier, eds. *Women Playwrights in England, Ireland, and Scotland, 1660–1823*. Bloomington: Indiana University Press, 1996.

Manvell, Roger. *Elizabeth Inchbald: England's Principal Woman Dramatist and Independent Woman of Letters in 18th Century London*. New York: Lanham, 1987.

Mayer, David. *Harlequin in His Element: The English Pantomime, 1806–1836*. Cambridge, MA: Harvard University Press, 1969.

Moody, Jane. "'Fine Word, Legitimate': Toward a Theatrical History of Romanticism." *Texas Studies in Literature and Language* 38.3–4 (1996): 223–44.

——. *Illegitimate Theatre in London, 1770–1840*. Cambridge: Cambridge University Press, 2000.

——. "The Silence of New Historicism: A Mutinous Echo from 1830." *Nineteenth Century Theatre* 24.2 (1996): 61–89.

Morse, John David. "Coleridge and the 'Modern Jacobinical Drama': *Osorio*, *Remorse*, and the Development of Coleridge's Critique of the Stage, 1797–1816." *Bulletin of Research in the Humanities* 82 (1979): 236–48.

Nicoll, Allardyce. *A History of English Drama, 1660–1900*. 6 vols. Cambridge: Cambridge University Press, 1952–59.

O'Quinn, Daniel J. "Inchbald's Indies: Domestic and Dramatic Re-Orientations." *European Romantic Review* 9.2 (1998): 217–30.

——. "Scissors and Needles: Inchbald's *Wives as They Were, Maids as They Are* and the Governance of Sexual Exchange." *Theatre Journal* 51 (1999): 105–25.

Otten, Terry. *The Deserted Stage: The Search for Dramatic Form in Nineteenth-Century England*. Athens: Ohio University Press, 1972.

Parker, Reeve. "Osorio's Dark Employments: Tricking out Coleridgean Tragedy?" *Studies in Romanticism* 33 (Spring 1994): 119–60.

——. "Reading Wordsworth's Power: Narrative and Usurpation in *The Borderers*." *ELH* 54.2 (1987): 299–331.

Pascoe, Judith. *Romantic Theatricality: Gender, Poetry, and Spectatorship*. Ithaca: Cornell University Press, 1997.

Peck, Louis F. *A Life of Matthew G. Lewis*. Cambridge, MA: Harvard University Press, 1961.

Purinton, Marjean D. *Romantic Ideology Unmasked: The Mentally Constructed Tyrannies in Dramas of William Wordsworth, Lord Byron, Percy Shelley, and Joanna Baillie*. Newark: University of Delaware Press, 1994.

Ranger, Paul. *"Terror and Piety Reigned in Every Breast": Gothic Drama in the London Patent Theatres, 1750–1820*. London: Society for Theatre Research, 1991.

Rees, Terence, and David Wilmore, eds. *British Theatrical Patents, 1801–1900*. London: Society for Theatre Research, 1996.

Reno, Robert P. "James Boaden's *Fontainville Forest* and Matthew Lewis's *The Castle Spectre*: Challenges of the Supernatural Ghost on the Late Eighteenth-Century Stage." *Eighteenth-Century Life* 9 (1984): 95–106.

Richardson, Alan. *A Mental Theatre: Poetic Drama and Consciousness in the Romantic Age*. University Park: Pennsylvania State University Press, 1988.

Rosenfeld, Sybil. *A Short History of Scene Design in Great Britain*. Oxford: Blackwell, 1973.

——. *Temples of Thespis: Some Private Theatres and Theatricals in England and Wales, 1700–1820*. London: Society for Theatre Research, 1978.

Rubik, Margaret. *Early Women Dramatists 1550–1800*. Basingstoke: Macmillan; New York: St. Martin's Press, 1998.

Russell, Gillian. *The Theatres of War: Performance, Politics, and Society, 1793–1815*. Oxford: Clarendon Press, 1995.

Rzepka, Charles J. "*Bang Up!* Theatricality and the 'Diphrelatic Art' in De Quincey's *English Mail Coach*." *Nineteenth-Century Prose* 28 (2001): 75–101.

Schofield, Mary Anne, and Cecilia Macheski, eds. *Curtain Calls: British and American Women and the Theatre 1660–1820*. Athens: Ohio University Press, 1991.

Scullion, Adrienne, ed. *Female Playwrights of the Nineteenth Century*. London: J.M. Dent, 1996.

Simpson, Michael. *Closet Performances: Political Exhibition and Prohibition in the Dramas of Byron and Shelley*. Stanford: Stanford University Press, 1998.

——. "Re-OPening After the Old Price Riots: War and Peace at Drury Lane." *Texas Studies in Literature and Language* 41.4 (1999): 378–402.

Slagle, Judith Bailey. *Joanna Baillie: A Literary Life*. Madison, NJ: Fairleigh Dickinson University Press, 2002.

Stephens, John Russell. *The Profession of the Playwright: British Theatre 1800–1900*. Cambridge: Cambridge University Press, 1992.

Straub, Kristina. *Sexual Suspects: Eighteenth-Century Players and Sexual Identity*. Princeton: Princeton University Press, 1992.

Sutcliffe, Barry. Introduction. *Plays by George Colman the Younger and Thomas Morton*. Cambridge: Cambridge University Press, 1983.

Tasch, Peter. Introduction. *The Plays of George Colman the Younger*. New York: Garland, 1981.

Van Lennep, W., E. L. Avery, A. H. Scouten, G. W. Stone, and C. B. Hogan, eds. *The London Stage, 1660–1800; A Calendar of Plays, Entertainments and Afterpieces, Together with Casts, Box-Receipts, and Contemporary Comment*. 5 vols. in 11. Carbondale: Southern Illinois University Press, 1968.

Watkins, Daniel P. *A Materialist Critique of English Romantic Drama*. Gainesville: University Press of Florida, 1993.

Watson, Ernest Bradlee. *Sheridan to Robertson: A Study of the Nineteenth-Century Stage*. New York: Benjamin Blom, 1926.